The
Child Protection Handbook

5

The
Child Protection Handbook

edited by

Kate Wilson
BA(Oxon), DipSW, Dip Couns
Senior Lecturer in Social Work
University of York
York, UK

and

Adrian James
BA, MA, GDSA, DASS
Senior Lecturer in Applied Social Studies
University of Hull
Hull, UK

Baillière Tindall
London Philadelphia Toronto Sydney Tokyo

Baillière Tindall   24–28 Oval Road
                           London NW1 7DX

                           The Curtis Center
                           Independence Square West
                           Philadelphia, PA 19106–3399, USA

                           Harcourt Brace & Company
                           55 Horner Avenue
                           Toronto, Ontario, M8Z 4X6, Canada

                           Harcourt Brace & Company, Australia
                           30–52 Smidmore Street
                           Marrickville
                           NSW 2204, Australia

                           Harcourt Brace & Company, Japan
                           Ichibancho Central Building
                           22-1 Ichibancho
                           Chiyoda-ku, Tokyo 102, Japan

A catalogue record for this book is available from the British Library

ISBN 0-7020-1743-4

Typeset by WestKey Ltd, Falmouth, Cornwall
Printed and bound in Great Britain by WBC Book Manufacturers, Bridgend, Mid Glamorgan

Contents

Section III: Intervention

Section IV: Training and New Directions for Research and Practice

List of Contributors

Margaret Adcock, BA(Hons) is a Social Work Consultant and has worked in Family Placement in the Local Authority as an Assistant Director at British Agencies for Fostering and Adoption and as a Guardian *ad litem*.

Anne Bannister, CQSW, R.Dth, Ad.Dip.Psych, is Team Manager, NSPCC, Child Sexual Abuse Consultancy, Swinton, Manchester, UK.

Liza Bingley Miller, BA(Hons) Social Administration, MSc Social Work Studies, CQSW, is a Lecturer in Social Work, Department of Social Policy and Social Work, University of York, York, UK.

Kevin Browne, BSc, MSc, PhD, C.Biol, C.Psychol, is a Senior Lecturer in Clinical Criminology, School of Psychology at the University of Birmingham, UK.

Katy Cigno, MA, MA, CQSW, Member of BASPCAH, BABCP, BSWG is Lecturer in Social Work at the University of Hull and Specialist Practice Teacher at Wakefield Community and Social Services Department, Wakefield.

Brian Corby, BA, DSA, DASS, CQSW is a Senior Lecturer in Applied Social Studies, Department of Sociology, Social Policy and Social Work Studies, University of Liverpool, Liverpool, UK.

Susan Creighton, BSc, MSc, is a Senior Research Officer, NSPCC National Centre, London, UK.

Margaret Crompton, BA, CQSW (Diploma in Social Studies; Cert in Applied Social Work Studies) is Writer and Lecturer, Lincoln, UK.

Stephen Frosh, BA, M.Phil, PhD is a Senior Lecturer in Psychology at Birkbeck College University of London and Consultant Clinical Psychologist, Tavistock Clinic, London, UK.

Tilman H Furniss, MD, M.Phil, MRCPsych is Professor of Child and Adolescent Psychiatry at Universitatskliniken, Munster, Germany.

Eileen Gallagher, C.Q.S.W, Training Group Analyst, is Deputy Manager, Child Sexual Abuse Consultant at the NSPCC, Child Sexual Abuse Consultancy, Manchester, UK.

Liz Hall, BA Hons Psychology, Diploma in Clinical Psychology, Diploma in Psychotherapy, is a Consultant Clinical Psychologist at the Royal Cornhill Hospital, Aberdeen, Scotland, UK.

x The Child Protection Handbook

Christine Hallett, MA, PhD is Professor of Social Policy and Head of Department of Applied Social Science at the University of Stirling, Stirling, Scotland, UK.

Helga G I Hanks, BSc, MSc, Dip.Psych., AFBPsS (Chartered) is an Honorary Lecturer at Leeds University and Consultant Clinical Psychologist at St James' and Seacroft University Hospitals, Leeds, UK.

Robert Harris, BA, MA, Dip A.S. (Soc. Admin), DSW, is Pro-Vice Chancellor & Professor of Social Work at the University of Hull, Hull, UK.

Ann Head, BA(Hons), Diploma in Social Work, is Chairperson, Thames Association of Guardians and a Guardian *ad litem*, Oxon, UK.

Jocelyn Jones, BA, MA, CQSW is Course Director in Diploma/MA in Child Protection Studies at the School of Social Work at Leicester University, Leicester, UK.

Margaret Kennedy, SEN.PSA(Oxon), CQSW, Advanced Certificate Child Abuse Studies is Freelance Trainer/Consultant on Disability and Child Protection. Former National Co-ordinator of the Keep Deaf Children Safe Project at the National Deaf Children Society, London, UK.

Mary Lane, BA(Hons) Psychology & Sociology, LLB, MSW is a Solicitor at Oldham Metropolitan Borough Council, Legal Services, Oldham, Lancs, UK.

Siobhan Lloyd, BA(Hons), MSc, is Head of Counselling Service and a Lecturer in Sociology at University of Aberdeen, Aberdeen, UK.

Christina M Lyon, LLB, Solicitor of the Supreme Court, FRSA, is Professor of Common Law, Director of the Centre for the Study of the Child, the Family and the Law, at the Faculty of Law, University of Liverpool, Liverpool, UK.

Anne Peake, B.Ed(Hons), MSc, MPhil, Dip. Child Protection, C.Psychol, is Principal Psychologist, Oxfordshire Social Services, Yarnton, Oxon, UK.

Stephanie Petrie, BA(Hons), DASS/CQSW, MSoc.Sc is a Lecturer at University of Bradford, West Yorkshire and was formerly Principal Officer, Save the Children.

Melanie Phillips, BA(Hons), CQSW, Postgraduate Diploma in Applied Social Science is a Freelance Trainer and Consultant, London, UK.

Virginia Ryan, PhD, C Psychol is a Child Psychologist and a freelance play therapist.

John Simmonds, PhD, BSc(Econ), is Director of Studies (Social Work) at the Department of Community Studies, University of London, London, UK.

Olive Stevenson, D.Litt, MA(Oxon) is Professor of Social Work Studies at the School of Social Studies, University of Nottingham, Nottingham, UK.

Peter Stratton, BSc, PhD, Dip. Psychotherapy, FBPsS is a Senior Lecturer & Director, Leeds Family Therapy and Research Centre, University of Leeds, Leeds, UK.

June Thoburn, Litt D, MSW, BA is Professor of Social Work at the School of Social Work, University of East Anglia, Norwich, UK.

Terry Walsh, Solicitor, Recorder, Deputy District Judge is Senior Partner, Chivers Walsh Smith, Bradford.

Corinne Wattam, BA, CQSW, DASS is a NSPCC Research Fellow, Department of Applied Social Science, Cartmel College, Lancaster University, Lancaster, UK.

John Williams, LL.B (Wales), LL.B (Cantab), Barrister at Law, is Dean of the Faculty of Economics and Social Studies and Senior Lecturer in Law at University of Wales, Aberystwyth.

Introduction

At the time of writing the introduction to this *Handbook*, child abuse and the failure of child protection agencies and procedures to ensure that children are protected against abuse are in the papers – once again. 'Social work muddle led to girl's death', read the headlines. 'Child protection arrangements which should have saved a 3-year-old girl from prolonged abuse and eventual murder collapsed in an unco-ordinated muddle, according to a report on Nottinghamshire social services', continues the story (*The Guardian*, 8.2.94).

The seemingly frequent, repeated occurrences of such failures, so long after the sad death of Maria Colwell first brought child abuse to the attention of the British press and public, provides both the context and the rationale for this *Handbook*. It is a phenomenon which stirs deep-seated emotion in all of us, not least because of our apparent failure to 'get it right'. This seems all the more remarkable in view of the by now considerable body of knowledge which welfare professionals of various kinds have about the nature, causes and distribution of child abuse. To this must also be added the substantial body of guidance, gleaned from hard-won experiences in the many cases of child abuse which have come to our attention over the past two decades, about the procedures which ought to be established and followed by agencies involved in the care and protection of children.

Such failures, which all too often result in tragic consequences of the type mentioned above, inevitably attract a great deal of attention and criticism for those most centrally involved – in most cases social workers – and this is often justified. What we do not and cannot know about, however, are the many cases in which this knowledge and these guidelines have been used to good effect and, as a result, have avoided many potential tragedies. Such is the nature of the work of caring professionals, of the news media and of the public conscience.

This realisation also gives us some important clues, however, about the limits of our capabilities for dealing with such issues and about how further progress can be made. It is becoming clear that no matter how much knowledge we accumulate and how many lessons we learn from our previous experience, the nature of human problems and human responses to them is such that tragedies will continue to occur. Unless we are able to accept as a society previously unconsidered levels of intervention in the lives of many families in the name of prevention and to provide the vast resources which would be necessary for such a 'service', child abuse will continue to occur, and occasionally children will die as a consequence. Indeed, even if such levels of intervention were conscionable and could be resourced, it is difficult seriously to entertain the prospect that we should ever be able to eradicate child abuse entirely. If this is, indeed, the case the way forward must lie in another direction.

A major problem for those whose contact with children is such that they can be deemed to be the 'front-line' workers in the field of child protection – social workers, health visitors, teachers, doctors or members of related professions – is that, by and large, they are very busy. Indeed, they are so busy that they have little or no time to keep fully abreast of the latest research, the latest thinking and the latest guidance relating to child abuse and protection. There are therefore often gaps in their knowledge, or it is out of date and consists of what (in some cases all-too-little) training they received whilst working for their professional qualifications, which may have been some years ago.

Furthermore, different professions have different responsibilities and priorities, and therefore place a different emphasis on child protection, not only in pre-qualifying training but also in post-qualifying training and day-to-day practice. Those such as social workers specialising in child protection and guardians *ad litem* might therefore reasonably be expected to be better informed than teachers, even though the latter may have substantially more face-to-face contact with much larger numbers of children. All, however, are hard-pressed public servants, most of whom work in an organisational context in which the principal means of achieving the objective of providing value for public money in service delivery is frequently that of reducing unit costs.

In such circumstances, training is often one of the first areas of activity to be cut back. Such a context is not conducive to keeping abreast of theoretical and practical developments in child abuse and protection, important though this is universally recognised to be. This same imperative, and the difficulty of complying with it, can also serve to increase the anxiety levels of those in the 'front line', where the pressures, uncertainties and responsibilities of practice are already a heavy burden. The fact that agencies may be less able to resource the necessary training does not necessarily remove from practitioners the feeling of personal and professional responsibility for keeping abreast of such developments, however. Their problem is how best to accomplish this.

An additional difficulty mirrors one of the continuing problems of practice – that of how to communicate effectively about theoretical, research and practice knowledge across professional and disciplinary boundaries. This has been a central issue in many child abuse inquiries and is one which is embedded in the way in which training is traditionally organised (for individual groups of professionals, often entirely in isolation from other professionals working, at least in part, in the same or overlapping areas) and knowledge is most often disseminated (through profession-specific rather than multi-disciplinary channels). Thus, for example, the medical discourse about child abuse and the social work discourse have proceeded with a much higher level of separation than is desirable, communicating largely through their own professional journals and their own professionally orientated conference networks. Neither has made consistent or effective attempts to break out of their respective frameworks to engage with each other, let alone with other professionals, such as teachers. There is therefore also a problem about how best to accomplish this.

This is the rationale for this *Handbook*. In producing it, our three main objectives were:

• to produce a reader and a sourcebook which brings together a series of reviews, by nationally and internationally recognised experts in various fields related to the emotional, physical and sexual abuse of children, providing succinct accounts of issues of both policy and practice, as well as an up-to-date review of research and other relevant literature;

• to produce a reader which, by virtue of its coverage and presentation, makes key information about child abuse accessible, comprehensible and helpful to a wide range of professionals, at both qualifying and post-qualifying levels, who have an interest in and need to know about child abuse; and

• to produce a reader which is coherent enough to be read as a whole but in which the contributions are of sufficient substance and relevance to be read or referred to independently.

These are, perhaps, ambitious objectives and it is inevitable that in covering such a wide range of issues there will be some variations. These are reflected not only in different writing styles, but in the balance between theoretical and practical issues, between a macro analysis of concepts and theories and a micro analysis of skills and behaviours. Such variations are not a weakness but a strength, an inevitable consequence of producing such a book. They reflect the complex nature of child abuse itself, the debate surrounding it and the many different levels of knowledge and skills which are integral to an understanding of child abuse and to high standards of professional practice in providing services for the protection of children.

Having said this, it is also inevitable that the individual chapters reflect both current concerns and preoccupations, and also the level of knowledge available about certain aspects of child maltreatment. One result of this is that in a number of chapters, issues concerning child sexual abuse are addressed virtually to the exclusion of other forms of abuse. Sometimes this reflects the way in which a service has grown from the identification of a particular need. Services for adult victims of sexual abuse, for example (discussed in the chapter by Liz Hall and Siobhan Lloyd, Section III), were substantially developed as a result of the early help given to women through women's support networks, and little work has been done with victims of physical or emotional abuse who on the whole have not come together as an identifiable group. In other areas such as family therapy, practice with families involving incestuous abuse arose out of earlier work with physical abuse, and the emphasis on the former in Tilman Furniss and Liza Bingley Miller's chapter (Section III) reflects a current concern to develop practice with what are seen to be problems of particular complexity.

The amount and quality of the research cited in different chapters also reflects wider policy issues. The range of the research cited in the chapters on the early stages of the protective process (for example, the chapters on investigation and case conferences in Section II) contrasts with the paucity of research material which can be drawn on to support the discussion on children with disabilities who have been abused. June Thoburn's discussion of research findings concerning out-of-home care for children highlights the absence of any similar detailed work on therapeutic services for children, a point we explore further in the introductory chapter to Section III. This imbalance reflects large differences in resources allocated to different aspects of the protective process. To some extent, any book that tries to provide a 'state of the art' picture of child protection will reflect this imbalance, although it will also try, as we do here and other writers do throughout, to highlight deficiencies in the current state of knowledge and practice. Christine Hallett returns to this theme in the final chapter.

As far as possible, however, given the diverse nature of the topics covered, each chapter provides: an introduction to the general issues to be addressed; a review of recent literature and research; an analysis of policy issues where this is appropriate; discussion of the implications for practice of the issues raised; a summary of the key issues followed by a conclusion; a bibliography and, finally, recommendations for further reading which have been annotated to give guidance to those wishing to pursue particular issues further. We have sought throughout to ensure that the emphasis is on communicating as clearly and simply as possible, avoiding jargon wherever possible.

In order to facilitate further ease of use, we have organised the book in sections which bring together contributions dealing with broadly comparable issues. Section I is concerned with our understanding of child abuse, not only in terms of what we 'know' about it – what 'it is', how often it 'occurs', who 'does' it and what 'causes' it – but also the social processes which define our knowledge and understanding of these key areas of 'knowledge' about child abuse.

Section II contains those chapters which contribute primarily to the analysis of the frameworks (such as that provided by the law), structures (such as case conferences and courts of law) and processes (such as assessment, monitoring and inter-professional co-operation) which have been developed for and are integral to the process of managing the process of child protection.

Section III includes chapters which focus on both the context and the main methods which can be employed when working with families where abuse has occurred, and with those adults and children who have experienced abuse. The final section addresses training issues, both at the level of general trends and specific issues in terms of content, and concludes with an overview and summary of the main issues to have emerged from all the contributions.

In all probability, few will have either the time or the inclination to read this book from cover to cover, and it was not our expectation that it should be used in this way. Rather, we envisaged a book which would find a place on the reading lists for courses for every profession involved in working with child abuse and providing child protection services. We also envisaged a book which would be a useful source of reference on the bookshelves or desks of busy practitioners in different professions everywhere.

We are grateful to a number of colleagues and friends for their advice and encouragement during the development of this book; to the anonymous assessors for their comments; and to Hilary Woodward for her particular help.

Kate Wilson
Adrian L. James

I

Understanding Child Abuse

The question 'What is child abuse?' is of central importance to an understanding of the topic, and that understanding is, of course, of central importance to all those who are concerned with child abuse and child protection, be they researchers, lawyers, social workers, health visitors, teachers or police officers. Until we know what constitutes child abuse, we cannot begin to ask questions about incidence and distribution (how frequently does it occur? Where does it occur most, either geographically or demographically?). Nor can we ask questions about who is responsible for abuse or what are its causes. And until we can provide some answers to these questions, we cannot even begin to answer the crucial question 'what remedies might there be?'

The analysis of other important issues depends on the answer to this pivotal question. Thus, until we can define child abuse, we cannot begin to determine or understand what is *not* child abuse, a matter which is clearly of equal importance. We understand *why* some closely related behaviours are defined as abusive and others are not, but we cannot identify what social and political dynamics underpin the process by which such 'knowledge' is defined. And we cannot address the question of why such definitions are historically specific: why, for example, what was reasonable physical chastisement of a child 100 years ago would today, in all probability, be considered abuse.

Section I addresses these and related issues. In Chapter 1, Susan Creighton addresses the question of the incidence of child abuse, to discuss some of the research issues that need to be addressed when studying child abuse, and to clarify the factors which practitioners need to bear in mind when making use of data about the incidence and prevalence of child abuse to inform their work. Such issues are of particular importance in enabling those working with children to have an informed awareness of the probability of there being abused children amongst those with whom they come into contact, some of the likely characteristics of those children, and the likely levels of incidence of such cases. In concluding, she draws attention to the impact of increased reporting of child abuse in recent years combined with cutbacks in local authority resources. This, she argues, has led to priority being given to child protection at the expense of child care, thus drawing a distinction developed in the following chapter.

In Chapter 2, Robert Harris tackles the important but complex issues raised by a consideration of the way in which child abuse is socially constructed by exploring what distinctions, if any, can be drawn between child protection and child care in the context of a broader consideration of child welfare. In the process, he considers in some detail the relationship between the child, the family and the State, and how this is mediated through the activities of welfare professionals. His conclusions – which are important but do not offer much comfort for practitioners – are that certain ambiguities and tensions inhere in the role of child welfare professionals. As a consequence, although there are areas in which practice can be improved and some problems to which answers can be found, there are also problems for which there are no solutions and in relation to which welfare professionals must bear their share of the resulting burden of discomfort, uncertainty and even opprobrium.

In Chapter 3, Kevin Browne delineates some of the issues and problems inherent in defining child abuse and considers some of the different theories of causation which have emerged.

Some of these issues are developed further by Stephen Frosh who, in Chapter 4, discusses the characteristics of child abusers and, in particular, those who abuse sexually. In doing so, he distinguishes between child sexual abuse and sexual offending more generally by considering the relationship between non-sexual and sexual abuse, and the extent to which the latter is concerned with sexual gratification as distinct from the use of power. He also usefully considers the reliability and limitations of the empirical evidence which is currently available, and the implications of this for the choice of treatment method.

In Chapter 5, Helga Hanks and Peter Stratton consider the effects of abuse on children, distinguishing between the effects of physical, emotional and sexual abuse, and the effects of neglect. Throughout their discussion, they develop an interactive model. In this, they consider children as active and self-conscious actors rather than as passive recipients of abuse, exploring how they react to and attempt to moderate the consequences of abuse and the role that the personality and characteristics of the abuser can play in shaping a child's adaptations. The chapter outlines both the direct physical and behavioural consequences of abuse, and the psychological and secondary consequences on other aspects of a child's life. They conclude by considering the longer-term consequences of abuse in terms of later childhood, adolescence, adulthood and the victim as parent, exploring in the process the possibility of a cycle of abuse.

The study of relatively new areas of interest rarely, and perhaps inevitably, proceeds in a uniform way. As a consequence of more immediate and mainstream concerns which follow the 'discovery' of a phenomenon like child abuse, such as the need to delineate its prevalence and understand its causes, minority issues such as those relating to ethnicity and culture, or to disability, tend initially to be marginalised. Chapters 6 and 7 draw attention to this process of marginalisation and seek to rectify it. Melanie Phillips highlights the persistent failure of policy-makers and practitioners to address the needs of black families and calls for a thorough rethinking of practice. She questions the relevance of the theoretical models commonly used in child protection and asks whether they are universally applicable, or whether they simply reinforce stereotypical views of black families. The solution, she argues, lies in developing an approach to working with families from black cultures in a way which challenges racist myths and assumptions through more open discussion with the families themselves.

In the final chapter, Margaret Kennedy also explores the myths that relate to abuse and the disabled child, and points to the almost complete lack of research in the UK into the prevalence or incidence of abuse of disabled children. In the process, she also contributes to the debate outlined in previous chapters about definitions of abuse, identifying some forms of abuse unique to children with disabilities. She also identifies the greater resistance of adults to disclosures of abuse by children with disabilities and some of the problems of identifying abuse using behavioural indicators and of communication, both in the context of identification and any subsequent therapy. Echoing Melanie Phillips, she questions the suitability of current child protection services for coping with the needs of children with disabilities and calls for the development of a new and more sensitive approach which challenges stereotypes and which acknowledges the unique needs of disabled children.

1

Patterns and Outcomes

Susan J. Creighton

Introduction

How many children in the UK have been abused? What are the chances of a baby born this year being abused by the time she or he is 18 years old? In the average classroom how many children are recovering, or not, from past abuse and how many are still suffering, or not, from continuing abuse? Is abuse sexual abuse, or does it include other forms of abuse as well? Are particular children more, or less, at risk of abuse?

Professionals working with children need to know the answers to these and other similar questions. They need to know so they can respond sensitively to individual children potentially in need, and confidently institute their local child protection procedures for those children they identify as in need of protection.

Estimates of abuse range from 'one in two girls and one in four boys will experience some form of sexual abuse before their 18th birthday' (Kelly *et al.*, 1991) to 3800 sexually abused children, a rate of 0.34 per 1000 population under the age of 18 years in 1991–2 (Department of Health, 1993). The discrepancy between these two estimates creates confusion in the minds of the general public and professionals alike. This chapter attempts to outline the reasons behind such a discrepancy. It aims to clarify the factors that practitioners need to consider when using incidence or prevalence figures for abuse and how these impinge on their work with children.

Review of Frequency Literature

Estimates of the frequency of child abuse are usually derived from either incidence or prevalence studies. Incidence refers to the number of new cases occurring in a defined population over a specified period of time – usually a year. Prevalence refers to the proportion of a defined population affected by child abuse during a specified time period – usually childhood.

There are five levels of professional recognition or public awareness of child abuse and neglect:

Level 1. Those children who are reported to protective agencies such as social services, the police or the National Society for the Prevention of Cruelty to Children (NSPCC) as having been abused or neglected, regardless of whether they are subsequently registered or not.

Level 2. Those children who are 'officially known' to a variety of investigatory agencies, such as social services, health services and the police for reasons other than abuse or neglect. These could include matrimonial disputes, delinquency, 'children in need of control', truancy, nutritional and hygiene problems. These children are not regarded by the community as abused or neglected in the same sense as Level 1 children are, and they are unlikely to receive assistance which specifically targets abuse and neglect.

Level 3. Abused and neglected children who are known, and of concern, to other professionals such as schools, hospitals, GPs, day care facilities and mental health agencies but are not reported as abused or neglected. These children may be thought of as 'children in need' (Children Act, 1989) but not as children in need of protection. Alternatively, some professions may feel that they are better able to help these children and their families outside the child protection system, or they may not trust the child protection system to handle the problem effectively, or they may not wish to become involved in the investigative process (NB see Implications for Practice below for a discussion of mandatory reporting).

Level 4. Abused and neglected children recognised as such by neighbours, relatives or by one or both of the involved parties – the perpetrator and the child. None of these individuals, however, have reported it to a professional agency.

Level 5. Children who have not been recognised as abused or neglected by anyone. These are cases where the individuals involved do not regard their behaviours or experiences as child maltreatment and/or where the situations have not yet come to the attention of outside observers who would recognise them as such.

It is helpful to bear these five levels of awareness and/or discovery in mind when looking at the cases which are most likely to be included in incidence and prevalence studies.

Incidence studies are mainly concerned with reported and recorded cases of abuse to children – Level 1 children. Many cases of child abuse do not come to the notice of potential reporting authorities. Prevalence studies attempt to find out these hidden cases by asking a sample of adults if they were abused during their childhood, regardless of whether or not that abuse came to light and was reported.

In the UK, the best known incidence studies of child abuse are drawn from children placed on child protection (previously child abuse) registers (Creighton, 1992a; Department of Health, 1993). The best known prevalence studies are the MORI (Baker and Duncan, 1985) and Childwatch (BBC, 1987) surveys of child sexual abuse. The Childwatch survey included questions on child abuse other than sexual abuse, but it concentrated on the sexual abuse cases when presenting its findings. This is interesting in view of the fact that more people reported having been emotionally or physically abused as children than sexually abused. More children are also registered annually as having been physically abused than as having been sexually abused (Creighton, 1992a). Yet, apart from the Childwatch survey, all the child abuse prevalence studies conducted in the UK, and the majority in the USA, have been on sexual abuse. This may be because of the different age distributions of the different types of abuse. The youngest age group, the 0–1-year-olds, are more vulnerable to physical abuse and neglect (Creighton, 1992a), whereas the average age of the children registered for sexual abuse was 9 years 7 months. Adults' recall of childhood experiences is very limited for the first 3 to 4 years of their lives, so if the physical abuse or neglect ceased before they were 4, they may well have no memory of it. The preponderance of child sexual abuse prevalence studies in the literature and the media has led to a sizeable proportion of the general public equating child abuse with child sexual abuse. Children have been murdered (e.g. in 1991 Claire McIntyre, Karin Griffin, Angela Flaherty and Sarah Furness were all killed) following sexual abuse, but usually by strangers or acquaintances, not family members. Many more children die following physical abuse or neglect (Creighton, 1992b), mostly at the hands of their immediate caretakers. Abuse within the family has, up to now, been the major concern of professionals working in child protection.

Incidence studies

In 1991, seven people were found guilty of or were cautioned for the offence of 'infanticide', 343 for 'cruelty to or neglect of children' and 18 for 'abandoning a child aged under 2 years'. A further 168 were found guilty of or were cautioned for the offence of 'unlawful sexual intercourse with a girl under 13 years', 1073 for 'unlawful sexual intercourse with a girl under 16', 157 for 'incest' and 300 for 'gross indecency with a child' (Home Office, 1993). Criminal statistics represent the most extreme end of the child abuse recognition continuum, where it is not sufficient for children to be recognised and reported as abused. The perpetrators of abuse also have to be recognised and reported, and sufficient evidence gathered to mount a successful prosecution.

The next level of public recognition are those cases which are officially recorded as child abuse. In the UK, these are the children who are placed on child protection registers. In the Netherlands they are those reported to the 'confidential doctor' system, and in the USA they are those reported officially to the Child Protection Services in each state under the Child Abuse and Neglect Prevention and Treatment Act (1974). Not all children who are reported as abused or neglected will be officially recorded as such. In England and Wales, various studies (Association of Directors of Social Work (ADSS), 1987; Giller et al., 1992; Gibbons, 1993) have shown that for every ten children referred for child protection only two will be registered. The remaining eight will be filtered out during the course of investigation and case conferencing. In the USA, approximately 40% of reports of maltreatment are substantiated (McCurdy and Daro, 1993). In the Netherlands, every report to the confidential doctors is verified by the Office (Pieterse and Van Urk, 1989). Many reports are incomplete, too short or sometimes unreliable, and further enquiry is necessary. Only the verified cases are accepted.

Table 1.1 shows the officially recorded cases of child maltreatment in various countries.

The wide variations in rates per 1000 children and the breakdown in cases reflect a number of factors. These include the length of time the reporting system has been operating, the general level of public awareness and willingness to report, and the criteria for recording, in addition to the underlying levels of abuse and neglect in the

Table 1.1 *Official records of child maltreatment.*

Country	Year	Number of cases	Rate per 1000	Breakdown of cases	(%)	Source
USA	1992	1 160 400	17.8	physical abuse sexual abuse neglect emotional maltreatment other	24 19 43 10 11	National Center on Child Abuse research (McCurdy and Daro, 1993)
Netherlands	1983	2619	0.71	*physical abuse medical – physical neglect emotional abuse/neglect sexual abuse not specified	39 28 80 7 4	Pieterse and Van Urk (1989)
Scotland	1987	2316	2.01	physical abuse neglect emotional abuse sexual abuse non-specific risk	32 12 9 15 33	Association of Directors of Social Work. *Scottish Child Abuse Statistics* (1987)
Wales	1991–2	1428	2.15	physical abuse neglect sexual abuse emotional abuse multiple abuse grave concern	23 13 11 5 3 45	*Child Protection Register Statistics for Wales* 1992 (Welsh Office, 1993)
England	1991–2	24 700	2.25	physical injury neglect sexual abuse emotional abuse mixed abuse grave concern	25 12 15 7 3 36	*Children and Young People on Child Protection Registers*, year ending 31 March 1992, England (Department of Health, 1993)

* Multiple types of abuse exist for some victims.

country. Mandatory reporting was established in the USA in 1974 with the passage of the Child Abuse Prevention and Treatment Act. Non-mandatory guidance on the management of cases of non-accidental injury to children, including the establishment of registers, was issued by the Department of Health in late 1974 (Department of Health and Social Security (DHSS), 1974). Similar guidance was offered in Wales. Four 'confidential doctors' were introduced in the Netherlands as an experiment on 1 January 1972 for 2 years. After this, a governmental institute for the prevention of child abuse and neglect was established. Official reporting appears to have started at similar times in the Netherlands, the USA and the UK. The resources made available and the public and professional awareness campaigns in the different countries varied enormously.

Officially recorded cases of child abuse and neglect are at Level 1 of the professional recognition continuum. There have been two incidence studies which attempted to ascertain cases from all professionals, i.e. Levels 1 through 3, one in the USA and one in Northern Ireland. The US Department of Health and Human Services commissioned research into the national incidence of child abuse and neglect in both 1980 and 1986. The 1986 survey (US Department of Health and Human Services, 1988) looked at all the cases reported to the Child Protective Services staff, as well as cases reported by a variety of professionals in other agencies who served as 'sentinels'. They were asked to be on the lookout during the study period for cases meeting the study's definitions of child maltreatment. These definitions were designed to be clear, objective and to involve demonstrable harm to the child. The research found that, in 1986, just under 1 000 000 children, an estimated 14.8 children per 1000 nationwide, experienced abuse or neglect as defined by the study. Only 44% of these children were known to the Child Protective Services through official reports. Non-investigatory agencies (which included schools, hospitals, social services and mental health agencies) recognised more than five times the number of child victims than did investigatory agencies (police/probation service/courts and public health agencies). The most frequent type of abuse was physical, followed by emotional and then sexual abuse. The relative incidence rates for these were 4.3 for physical, 2.5 for emotional and 1.9 for sexual abuse per 1000 children. The overall incidence rate for abuse was 8.1 per 1000 children. Educational neglect (i.e. permitted chronic truancy or inattention to special educational needs by parents) was by far the most frequent form of neglect, with an incidence rate of 4.5 per 1000 children. This was followed by physical neglect, at a rate of 2.7, and then emotional neglect with an incidence rate of 0.8 per 1000 children. The overall incidence rate for neglect was 7.5 per 1000 children. These were calculated using the stringent criterion that the child had to have already experienced demonstrable harm as a result of maltreatment in order to be included.

The other study was conducted in Northern Ireland by the Research Team from the Departments of Child Psychiatry, Royal Belfast Hospital for Sick Children, and Epidemiology and Public Health at Queen's University, Belfast (1990). This was a research study of the annual incidence of child sexual abuse in Northern Ireland during a 1-year period, 1 January 1987–31 December 1987. It was a multi-source notification study whereby all professional staff from all agencies concerned with children completed a specially designed notification form when they came across a case of sexual abuse which fulfilled the study definition. These staff were interviewed later by one of the researchers and the information recorded on a standard questionnaire. In the year prior to data collection, 1986, the researchers contacted all the possible agencies likely to come across cases of child sexual abuse, explained the study to them and gained their co-operation. Information was sought for cases which were:

1. Suspected – when the reporter has been given any reason at all to believe that an incident of child sexual abuse may have occurred.
2. Alleged – where someone communicates to the reporter that an incident of sexual abuse has occurred.
3. Established – where the reporter and others are satisfied that an incident of child sexual abuse has occurred.

The incidence rate for established cases of child sexual abuse in Northern Ireland discovered by the study was 1.2 per 1000 children under 17 years. This contrasts with the sexual abuse registration rate over a similar period in England of 0.36 (Department of Health, 1989). It may be that the underlying rate of child sexual abuse is higher in Northern Ireland than in England, but it seems more likely that the methods employed in this study pick up cases that would not normally be reported.

Incidence studies which attempted to ascertain cases at Level 4, where no professional agency is involved, are those conducted in 1975 and 1985 by the Family Violence Research Program at the University of New Hampshire (Straus, 1979; Straus and Gelles, 1986). These studies were of a nationally representative selection of American families with at least one child aged between 3 and 17 years living at home. One of the parents was interviewed and the studies attempted to determine whether physical abuse had occurred and at what levels of severity. Abusive violence was ascertained when the parent acknowledged that they, or their spouse, had 'punched, kicked, bitten, hit with an object, beaten up or used a knife or gun' on their child in the last year. The 1986 study obtained a rate of one in every ten American children aged between 3 and 17 years subjected to severe physical violence each year. Compared to the rate of officially reported cases of physical abuse (Schene, 1987), 'only one child in seven who is physically injured is reported'. Both these studies only included children aged between 3 and 17 years, whereas the youngest age groups, the 0–1-year-olds and the 2–3-year-olds, are the most vulnerable to physical abuse (Department of Health, 1993). Hence, the rates the authors obtained for the older age groups are likely to be underestimates of the incidence of physical abuse to all children in America.

Prevalence studies

Table 1.2 summarises the four main prevalence studies of child sexual abuse conducted in the last 10 years in Canada and the USA. The percentage of adults affected varies from 6.8–54% of women and 3.8–25% of men.

The earliest prevalence studies (e.g. Finkelhor, 1979) were usually conducted on samples of college students on social science courses. Social science students have the advantage of providing a captive sample but are probably not representative of the population as a whole. The studies included in this Table concentrate on samples drawn from the entire population. The wide variations between them probably reflects the differences in the methods used rather than significant geographical variation. These include items such as definitions used, how the sample was chosen and approached, the methods used to get the information from the respondents and how many refused to participate. The methodological issues involved in these studies will

Table 1.2 *Prevalence studies of child sexual abuse in the USA and Canada.*

Country	Authors	Sample	Method	Response rate (%)		Prevalence
USA	Russell (1983)	930 women 18 +, random sample, San Francisco	face-to-face interviews	50	<18	38% involving contact 54% including non-contact
					<14	28% involving contact 48% including non-contact
Canada	Badgley *et al.* (1984)	representative population study 18 +, over 2000 men and women	hand-delivered questionnaires	94		42% women⎤ 25% men ⎦ including non-contact
					<14	10% girls involving contact
USA	Siegal *et al.* (1987)	two-stage probability sample of 3132 adults (male and female), Los Angeles	mental health survey; face-to-face interviews	68		6.8% women⎤ 3.8% men ⎦ involving contact
USA (1990)	Finkelhor *et al.*	sample of 2626 adults (male and female)	telephone interviews	76		27% women⎤ largely involving contact 16% men ⎦

be discussed later in this chapter but brief details are included in Table 1.2. The factor which has the greatest effect on the prevalence figures is whether or not the definition of child sexual abuse used includes non-contact experiences such as exposure, in addition to contact experiences. Table 1.2 shows whether or not the definition included contact and non-contact experiences in the prevalence figures.

In the UK, there have been only two prevalence studies which have attempted to use a nationally representative sample; the MORI poll reported by Baker and Duncan (1985) and the BBC Childwatch Survey (1987), the full results of which were never published. Table 1.3 summarises the main prevalence studies conducted in the UK with brief details of the methods employed. The 90% prevalence produced by the BBC Childwatch Survey (1986) is what you might expect from a self-selected sample. If you produce a high-profile TV programme on a particular social problem and then invite viewers who have experienced this problem to write in and complete a questionnaire on it, you might expect a 100% prevalence of the problem among the returned questionnaires. This survey really highlights the relevance of the methods employed in these studies.

Methodological factors

The factors which need to be taken into account when planning or assessing studies of the frequency of childhood maltreatment include:

- Definitions;
- Method of sampling;
- Case ascertainment;
- Measurement tools;
- Bias;
- Generalisability;
- Comparability.

Definitions. The definition of childhood sexual abuse used in the MORI survey (Baker and Duncan, 1985) was:

> 'A child (anyone under 16 years) is sexually abused when another person, who is sexually mature, involves the child in any activity which the other person expects to lead to their sexual arousal. This might involve intercourse, touching, exposure of the sexual organs, showing pornographic material or talking about sexual things in an erotic way.'

Ten percent of their respondents (12% female, 8% male) reported that this had occurred to them. The definition employed by Siegal *et al.* (1987) in their mental health survey took the form of the question:

> 'In your lifetime, has anyone ever tried to pressure or force you to have sexual contact? By sexual contact I mean their touching your sexual parts, or sexual intercourse?'

Respondents who answered affirmatively were asked if they had ever been forced or pressured for sexual contact before the age of 16 years (childhood sexual assault). These specific questions, which focus on the nature of the behaviour – contact and pressured – plus the age when it happened (under 16 years), led to a prevalence figure of 5.3% (6.8% women, 3.8% men). This is the smallest figure for the studies but is very similar to that for the 'contact' cases in the Baker and Duncan study (derived from their

Table 1.3. *Prevalence studies of child sexual abuse in the United Kingdom.*

Authors	Sample	Method	Response rate (%)	Prevalence
Nash and West (1985)	223 female GP patients aged 20–39 years	questionnaires and face-to-face interviews	53	42% including non-contact 22% involving contact
BBC Childwatch (1986)	almost 3000 self-selected viewers, male and female	viewers wrote in for and completed questionnaires	75	90%
Baker and Duncan (1985)	nationally representative sample of adults aged 15 + in Great Britain, 2019 men and women	face-to-face interviews in homes	87	12% female } 8% male } including non-contact 5% female } 4% male } involving contact
BBC Childwatch national interview survey (1987)	probability sample of 2041 adults aged 16 + in UK	interviews (full results not published)	not known	3% of } sample } involving contact
Kelly *et al.* (1991)	1244 polytechnic students aged 16–25 years	questionnaires in class	97	59% women } 27% men } including non-contact 27% women } 11% men } involving contact

Table 3, page 461). Kelly *et al.* (1991) provide a detailed breakdown of the influence of definitions on prevalence findings in their study (see their Appendix C, page 20). As the definitions get more 'serious' (in the sense of more intrusive and unwanted contact), so the numbers affected drop from 59% for the widest definition to 5% for the strictest.

Method of sampling.   The four most commonly used methods in maltreatment studies have been: volunteer (e.g. BBC Childwatch, 1986), quota (e.g. Baker and Duncan. 1985; BBC Childwatch, 1987), random (e.g. Russell, 1983) and national random (e.g. Badgley *et al.*, 1984). Volunteer samples are obviously going to be biased towards those with something to report. Quota samples – in which people or households are approached until the required quota of subjects is obtained – run the same risk: that those choosing to participate will not be typical of the general population. Random samples, where each person in a population has an equal probability of being included in the sample, are preferred. Ideally, it should be a national random sample. A random sample in only one area might give the prevalence for that area but not be suitable for generalisation to other areas.

Case ascertainment.   Even if a random sample of the population has been approached, the actual cases ascertained can be biased due to factors relating to: the subject, the interviewer and the measurement tool (the questionnaire). In such an emotive area as child maltreatment, subjects can either fail to recognise themselves as abused (Berger *et al.*, 1988) or repress memories of parental abuse and fail either to recall or report them. The gender, age and ethnicity of the interviewer in relation to the subject have all been shown to affect the likelihood and accuracy of the responses. Both men and women prefer to be interviewed about sexual topics by a woman, even adolescent males who have been abused by a woman (Kaplan *et al.*, 1991).

The way the survey questionnaire is introduced can affect the likelihood of getting any answers. A survey presented as one on child sexual abuse is more likely to encounter a refusal than one on general health or attitudes.

Measurement tools.   The wording of the questions or their position in the questionnaire (or interview) can have an impact on subject response. Questions need to be clear, simple and unambiguous. Sensitive questions which at the beginning of an interview may inhibit responses may, if placed at the end, be answered. Respondents are more likely to be engaged in the survey by a personalised approach but they may be embarrassed to answer personal questions. Surveys such as Badgley *et al.'s* (1984) study, which employed a personal approach coupled with a self-completed questionnaire, were very successful.

It is very important to get a high response rate to the survey. Those people who refuse to answer questions are unlikely to be like those who agree, particularly in relation to child maltreatment. If only half the people you approach agree to answer the questions, then a high rate among them is misleading. The other half who refused may have done so because they were not affected. This effectively halves the prevalence estimate reported. A low response rate has the effect of turning a random sample into more of a volunteer sample. Although there is no simple acceptable response rate, rates lower than 80% are considered undesirable (Markowe, 1991).

Missing data pose a similar problem. If a particular question is not answered by the majority of the respondents, the answers gained cannot be considered representative of the sample as a whole. It is important to pre-test and pilot the questionnaire or survey instrument to avoid including questions which will not be answered.

Bias. Bias is any trend in the collection, analysis, interpretation, publication or review of data that can lead to conclusions that are systematically different from the truth. Bias can be introduced in the ascertainment of cases, the design of a survey and the sample method employed. In child abuse reporting, it has been shown that the children of the middle and upper classes are less likely to come to the attention of the child protection agencies than those of the poor and disadvantaged. The perceived social status of the parents also affects the level of suspicion of experienced professionals about the possible non-accidental nature of an injury (O'Toole *et al.*, 1983). Higher social class parents were less likely to be judged as abusive than lower class parents. Nurses and more experienced professionals were not affected by this social class bias. There are also likely to be reporting and substantiation biases in cases involving ethnic minorities, disabled children or children in out-of-home care. Hong and Hong (1991), using a sample of Californian students, found that the Chinese were more tolerant of parental conduct than the Hispanics and Whites, and were less likely to ask for investigation by protective agencies in potential cases of child abuse and neglect. Nunno (1992) reported a survey of complaints of maltreatment of children in out-of-home care in the USA in 1989. Only 27% of these complaints were substantiated by child protection workers compared to 53% for familial maltreatment reports.

In addition to the characteristics of the child, the characteristics of the reporter – professional or other – has an effect on the process. In the USA, cases of child abuse reported by non-mandated sources, e.g. neighbours and schools, are less likely to be substantiated than cases reported by mandated sources, e.g. child protection services (Eckenrode *et al.*, 1988). Similarly, in the UK Stevenson (1989) has described the relative status and perceived powers of the different agencies involved in child protection. These are all factors which can lead to bias in the recognition, reporting and registering of cases of child abuse.

Generalisability. If a prevalence or incidence study is thought to be methodologically sound, the next step is to assess how far it can be generalised. Are students in further education colleges, as in Kelly *et al.*'s 1991 sample, or students on social science courses (Finkelhor, 1979) representative of all students? Are students representative of all young adults? Follow-up studies of abused children (Zimrin, 1986; Finkelhor, 1988; Wind and Silvern, 1992) would seem to indicate that the loss of self-esteem, the development of behavioural problems and the inability to concentrate often found in abused children would make them less likely to go into further education than other young adults. Although the problem of generalisability is not easily satisfied it should always be considered.

Comparability. Can we compare child abuse or maltreatment in the USA or Canada with that in the UK – or that reported in London with that in Newcastle? Can the results of one study be directly compared with that of another? These are likely to be subjective judgements to some extent, but comparison of the methodological factors discussed in this section should help to provide a more objective basis for such a judgement.

Time trends

One of the most interesting areas of comparability in child maltreatment is between different times. Has child maltreatment increased or decreased over the years, or have individual types of abuse changed? Do increases or decreases in reported rates reflect actual changes in maltreatment levels or changes in professional and public awareness and willingness to report? There have been a number of studies which have looked at changes in officially reported cases and in the incidence and prevalence rates of child maltreatment over time.

Reported cases

In the Netherlands, Pieterse and Van Urk (1989) compared the data on reports received by the 'confidential doctor' system in its first official year, 1974, with that of 1983. They found a threefold increase in the number of verified cases over the 10 years, for both boys and girls. The incidence (number of cases per 1000 children) increased fourfold from 0.19 per 1000 children in 1974 to 0.71 in 1983. The types of abuse reported and verified had changed, from a preponderance of physical abuse cases in 1974 (64% of cases) to a preponderance of emotional abuse/neglect in 1983 (50% of cases). There were only seven cases of sexual abuse reported in 1973 compared to 189 (7% of all cases) in 1983. The increases in all types of abuse were mostly in the older age group, the 12–17-year-olds, for both boys and girls. There was an increase in the detection of child fatalities but a decrease in the severity of physical abuse. No change was found in the identity of the suspected perpetrators – primarily fathers and/or mothers – or in the social conditions of the families. There was a decrease in the percentage of married parents and a corresponding increase in single mothers. There was an encouraging increase in the numbers of victims residing at home rather than in children's homes which the authors attributed to the improvement in aftercare for these children.

In the USA, the rate of children reported for child abuse and neglect between 1985 and 1992 increased 50% from 30 per 1000 children in 1985 to 45 per 1000 in 1992 (McCurdy and Daro, 1993). Between 1980 and 1985, there had been an average 11.4% annual increase in reports (Daro and Mitchel, 1990). The rapid increase in reported cases during the last 8 years was attributed to the increased economic stress caused by the recession, an increase in substance abuse and increased public awareness leading to greater reporting.

The different types of abuse reported in the USA did not show the changes that the Netherlands data did. In the USA, cases of neglect were most likely to be reported (45% in 1992), followed by physical abuse (27%), sexual abuse (17%), emotional maltreatment (7%) and other (8%). As in the Netherlands between 1974 and 1983, the rate of confirmed child maltreatment fatalities in the USA has risen steadily between 1985 and 1992 from 1.3 per 100 000 children in 1985 to 1.94 per 100 000 in 1992. As McCurdy and Daro (1993) report: 'This means that more than three children die each day in the US as a result of maltreatment.' (page 13.)

By contrast, in the UK three children die each week following abuse or neglect (Creighton, 1992b). As with deaths, the reporting or registration rates for child maltreatment are much lower in the UK than in the USA, although they have also shown increases over the years. The registration rate has trebled over the 7 years from 1.16 per 1000 children in 1984 to 3.40 per 1000 children in 1990 (Creighton, 1992a). This was largely due to the change from Child Abuse Registers to Child Protection Registers in 1988 following the DHSS guidance *Working Together* (DHSS, 1988). This led to a massive increase in registrations in the 'grave concern' category, i.e. children who had not been abused but were thought to be at significant risk of abuse. In the UK, registers were initially 'Non-Accidental Injury Registers' between 1975, when most were established, and 1980 when they became Child Abuse Registers. Cases of phys-ical abuse are the only type of abuse to have been reported since 1975. Between 1976 and 1979, the registration rate for cases of physical abuse remained steady but in-creased gradually from 1979 to 1984. There was a marked increase between 1984 and 1985, and between 1985 and 1990 the rate has fluctuated from year to year. The physical abuse rate has ranged from 0.44 in 1976 to 1.02 per 1000 children under 15 years in 1989 (Creighton, 1992a).

Among the abused children placed on UK registers cases of physical abuse have always predominated, followed by sexual abuse, neglect and emotional abuse. The rate of registrations for sexual abuse increased most between 1985 and 1986, reaching a peak of 0.65 per 1000 children under 17 years in 1987 (Creighton and Noyes, 1989), after which it has declined. The sudden increase in reported cases of sexual abuse in Cleveland (Butler-Sloss, 1988) was in 1987. Whether the decline in registered cases of sexual abuse following 1987 was due to fewer cases being recognised, or greater caution in reporting and registering them, could not be determined. The register data (Creighton, 1992a) showed evidence of increased caution in cases of sexual abuse with regard to assessing severity and the suspected perpetrator. It failed to show any evidence of workers assigning cases they would have registered as sexual abuse in the past to the grave concern category instead. There was also a slight increase between 1988 and 1989 before declining again in 1990. It is unfortunate that the changes in registration criteria introduced by the new guidance *Working Together under the Chil-dren Act, 1989* (Home Office *et al.*, 1991) mean that the registrations for sexual abuse from 1991 are not comparable with those from 1988 to 1990. The 1991 guidance excluded the grave concern category as a separate reason for registration. Children who were thought likely to be physically, sexually or emotionally abused or neglected were to be registered in the appropriate category. This means that the registrations for sexual abuse from 1991 will include both children who have been sexually abused and children thought likely to be sexually abused. It will not be possible to see if the decline in registrations for actual child sexual abuse between 1987 and 1990 has continued or reversed.

As in the Netherlands, there was a decline in the rate of serious and fatal injuries in the early years (1975–1976) of the registers (Creighton, 1992a). From 1976 to 1984 the rate remained fairly stable but there was a marked increase between 1984 and 1985. Since then, the rate of serious and fatal injuries has fluctuated but at a higher rate than that between 1976 and 1984.

As registers have become established, more older children have been placed on them, particularly for sexual abuse but also for physical injury. The Netherlands data showed an increase in older children being reported to the confidential doctors between 1974 and 1983. In the UK, the average age of the children registered for physical abuse increased from 3 years 8 months in 1975 to 7 years 1 month in 1990 (Creighton, 1992a). Boys have been consistently over-represented amongst the chil-dren registered for physical abuse, whilst the overwhelming majority of children registered for sexual abuse have been girls. More boys than girls have been registered for neglect.

The family situation of the registered children changed over the years from 1975 to 1990, with fewer children living with both their natural parents and more living with their natural mother alone and with their natural mother and a father substitute. The Netherlands data showed a similar decrease over the years in children living with both their natural parents and an increase in mothers alone, but they do not include information on father substitutes. In the UK generally, there have been major demographic changes over the period of the register research (Central Statistical Office (CSO), 1993), with increases in divorces and the numbers of single mothers. In spite of these changes, and some of the more lurid headlines in the tabloid press, the majority of UK children continue to live with both their natural parents. This is not the case for the children placed on Child Protection Registers in England. By 1990, just over a third of the registered children were living with both their natural parents (Creighton, 1992a). The registered children were eight times more likely to be living with a father substitute than children nationally from similar social classes.

The three studies on the officially reported cases of child maltreatment in the three countries, the Netherlands, the USA and the UK, show some differences but more similarities. Over the different time periods covered by each they all show increases in the numbers of children officially reported as having been maltreated.

Incidence and prevalence changes

There have been two major studies looking at incidence rates of child maltreatment at different times, both conducted in the USA. The first, the two National Incidence Studies (NIS-1 and NIS-2) (US Department of Health and Human Services, 1988; Sedlak, 1990) were conducted in 1980 and 1986. They collected all cases of child maltreatment recognised and reported to the study by 'community professionals' in a national probability sample of 29 counties throughout the United States where the child had experienced demonstrable harm as a result of the maltreatment. The data included all the cases reported to the Child Protection Services (CPS) staff during the study period, plus cases coming to the notice of other non-CPS agencies (such as hospitals and schools, etc.) who were acting as 'sentinels' on the look out for such cases during the study. The data coming to light here would cover Levels 1 through 3 of public awareness outlined at the beginning of this chapter. The second study from the Family Violence Research Program (Straus, 1979; Gelles and Straus, 1987) attempted to assess the physical abuse conducted at public awareness Level 4 by asking a nationally representative sample of parents with a child aged 3 through 17 years at home about their behaviour towards a randomly selected child in the last year. They conducted national surveys in 1975 and 1985. The two sets of studies produced very different findings.

The two National Incidence Studies (NIS-1 and NIS-2) found a significant increase (51%) in the incidence of maltreatment cases coming to the attention of their survey respondents in 1986 compared to 1980. This was largely due to cases of abuse (53% increase), as no form of neglect showed reliable changes in incidence rate since the earlier study. Emotional abuse also showed no change in incidence rate in 1986 compared to 1980. The significant rises in incidence rates were in cases of sexual abuse, where the rate tripled between 1980 and 1986, and physical abuse where it increased by 39%.

By contrast, the two national surveys conducted by the Family Violence Research Program in 1975 and 1985 showed a 47% decrease in the rate of child physical abuse between 1975 and 1985. The disparity between these two sets of findings for the physical abuse of children can be explained if we look at the definitions employed and the actual rates in the two studies.

The National Incidence Studies used a definition of physical abuse which specified that the child must be live-born and under 18 years of age at the time of the abuse, the abusive behaviour must have been non-accidental and avoidable, the perpetrator had to be either a parent or adult caretaker (over 18) and the child must have suffered demonstrable harm. The incidence rates they discovered were 3.1 per 1000 children in the population in 1980 and 4.3 per 1000 in 1986.

The Family Violence Research Program surveys used a definition of physical child abuse which included acts of behaviour by a parent to a child between the ages of 3 and 17 years which had a relatively high probability of causing an injury. These included: kicking, biting, punching, hitting with an object, beating up and threatening or using a knife or gun on the child. The incidence rates they found for these types of behaviour were 140 per 1000 children in 1975 and 107 per 1000 in 1985. Although this 1985 figure represents a considerable decrease compared with the 1975 figure, it is still nearly 25 times greater than the 1986 incidence figure found in the National Incidence Study.

The severe violence inflicted on children uncovered by the Family Violence Research Program surveys may not have caused any noticeable injuries or demonstrable harm. Very few of the children so affected would have been reported, or recognised, as abused to either child protection or other agencies. Schene (1987) estimated, on the basis of the 1985 national survey incidence rate and the official reported rate for that year, that only one physically abused child in seven was reported.

Changes in childhood sexual abuse prevalence rates over the years have been assessed by comparing a number of studies conducted in the 1970s and 1980s with that of Kinsey and his co-workers in the 1940s (Kinsey et al., 1953). Feldman et al. (1991) reviewed the Kinsey report and 19 prevalence studies reported since 1979 using predetermined criteria for quality of information, commonality of definitions of childhood sexual abuse and research design. They found that the more recent studies, with the strongest methodology and where definitions of childhood sexual abuse were similar, reported prevalence figures similar to those of Kinsey in the 1940s, in spite of differences in study designs and populations surveyed. Using a definition close to Kinsey's, i.e. girls younger than 14 years of age having sexual contact with an adult male at least 5 years older, and the studies with the best research design gave three studies, including Kinsey's. The other two were reported in 1984 (Badgley et al.) and 1987 (Siegal et al.), and all three produced prevalence figures of between 10 and 12% for girls younger than 14 years of age. Feldman et al. concluded that the increased number of reports of child sexual abuse was not due to a true increase in prevalence but to changes in legislation and public awareness. They stressed that this should not deter child protection professionals from continuing to provide treatment and preventative services to sexually abused children.

Implications for Practice

There are a number of implications for practitioners to be drawn from the review of the literature in the previous section. The most important of these is probably the fact that in spite of the varying estimates produced by the different studies, there can be no doubt that there is a large base group of children who have been, or are being, maltreated. What is also clear is that only a fraction of them are being reported to child protection practitioners. Before feeling overwhelmed by the size of the problem confronting them, practitioners should also bear in mind that the majority of children are not abused or maltreated. The importance of incidence and prevalence studies on child maltreatment is in giving practitioners a sense of the base underlying rate of the problem and the characteristics of that population. It is against that background of knowledge that they can look at the individual cases referred to them and assess the likelihood that they are cases of maltreatment.

The finding that, even with vastly increased reporting rates, only one American child in seven who is physically injured is reported (Schene, 1987, commenting on the Gelles and Straus survey) has implications for intervention. Are practitioners concerned only about the cases which come to light or the abusive behaviour *per se?* Gelles and Straus (1987) quote Erikson's theory that 'the number of acts of deviance that come to community attention is a function of the size and complexity of the community's social control apparatus – in this case, the child protection system'. There is increasing concern (Dingwall, 1989; Parton and Parton, 1989) that social control is taking over from social support in the child welfare services. Child protection is taking increasing priority over child care. As more and more resources are put into increasing the size and complexity of the child protection system, and hence identifying more 'cases', there seem to be fewer resources available for the treatment and monitoring of these identified cases. There is a worrying dearth of research and evaluation studies into the effectiveness of the various forms of intervention in child abuse and neglect cases both in the UK and the USA. As Starr (1990) argues, 'Without such studies we cannot determine the effectiveness of treatment and prevention efforts that, while well intended, may have no effects on the participating parents and children, or, worse still, may have unintended negative consequences.'

Child protection practitioners are compelled to intervene in identified cases of child abuse and neglect for largely negative reasons. These include the social control system within which they work, the fear that if they do not intervene the child will die or be seriously damaged, and the longer term adverse effects on the abused child deprived of treatment.

These are powerful motivators for action, though contrary to the general ethos of help and support that brought many practitioners into the child welfare services. The available evidence from the prevalence, incidence and other studies is not encouraging. It implies that the more the child protection system is expanded, the more cases of child abuse and neglect will come to official recognition. Intervention, tragically (e.g. Jasmine Beckford, Tyra Henry), does not always save a child's life. The findings on the long-term effects of child abuse and neglect are equivocal. Prevalence studies on general populations reveal large numbers of adults, abused as children, who appear not to have suffered long-term adverse consequences. Similarly, follow-up studies of abused children (Toro, 1982; Finkelhor, 1988) have found that about a third of the victims show no symptoms of abuse in the short term, and larger numbers none in the longer term. Socio-economic status and related factors may be more important than abuse in determining the course of child development. More research needs to be conducted into those factors which protect individual children, and which are the cases of abused and neglected children and their families where practitioners can most usefully intervene. Practitioners should also be lobbying for a radical re-appraisal of the child protection system, to assess whether it provides the most effective use of human and financial resources. Gelles and Straus (1987), speculating about the reasons behind the decrease in incidence rates over the 10 years 1975 to 1985, suggest that changes in attitudes and cultural norms regarding the social acceptability of family violence may have led to changes in overt behaviour. Public education campaigns play a vital role in attempting to change such attitudes.

The wide differences between the reported rates and types of abuse in the different countries also have implications for practitioners. Is the USA intrinsically more abusive to its children than such European countries as the UK and the Netherlands, as the relative reporting rates would suggest? Or does mandatory reporting, a massive public education programme and nationally available treatment programmes lead to a narrowing of the gap between actual and reported incidence? There have been no incidence studies similar to those of Gelles and Straus conducted in the UK which could throw light on underlying incidence rates here. Pieterse and Van Urk (1989) advocated mandatory reporting in the Netherlands in an attempt to reduce the discrepancy between the two countries' reported rates. Would mandatory reporting in the UK lead to more reports than the present non-mandatory inter-agency collaboration? Although UK professionals are not statutorily required to report cases of child abuse, most of them have some reporting duty written into their codes of ethics. Not to report a case would be an exception in the UK. In the USA, with mandatory reporting, the National Committee for Prevention of Child Abuse found a 40% substantiation rate for reports in 1992 (McCurdy and Daro, 1993). In the UK, with a non-statutory system of referring, only 15% of child protection referrals in eight local authority social services departments in 1991 were subsequently registered (Gibbons, 1993). A non-statutory system does not seem to lead to a decrease in initial referrals in relation to final registration.

The UK differs from the USA in registering so few cases of neglect, and from the Netherlands in the small number of cases of emotional abuse registered. The fact that Child Protection Registers were initially Non-Accidental Injury Registers until 1980 may have led to a professional bias towards physical abuse in the UK at the expense of other forms of abuse. Gibbons (1993) found that only 7% of the cases initially referred for neglect reached the register and most were screened out of the system at an early stage, usually without the offer of other services. Very few cases of emotional abuse were referred initially. The child protection system in the UK is a very reactive one, designed to rescue children in immediate danger, and, as such, unsuited to the more insidious effects of neglect or emotional abuse. Neglected and emotionally abused children may not be in immediate need of protection but they are nevertheless 'in need'. Practitioners should be aware of, and be responsive to, those needs.

Finally, practitioners need to be aware of the methodological factors underlying the various published studies of child abuse and neglect incidence and prevalence. In child protection, practitioners walk a tightrope between either too much (e.g. Cleveland) or too little (e.g. Kimberley Carlile) intervention in the public's mind. In choosing either to intervene or not to intervene in a particular case, they need to be able to speak authoritatively about the population base they are drawing from. How rare is this particular type and severity of abuse in the general population? Does this case share any of the characteristics of cases identified in the most rigorous studies? Might various biases be operating in the reporting or ascertainment of this case? The more aware practitioners are of these factors, the more likely they are to make a convincing case for either intervention or non-intervention.

Summary

This chapter has looked at the five levels of public and professional awareness of child abuse and neglect on which any estimate of the frequency of the problem will be based. The UK is at the first levels of official reporting of cases of child abuse and neglect in its incidence figures.

The incidence and prevalence studies reviewed have shown wide variations, between and within countries, in the rates of child maltreatment reported and the different types of child abuse. A large part of these differences may be due to the methods employed in the studies, in particular the definitions used and possible sources of bias. A broad definition of abuse, say sexual abuse not involving contact, will ascertain many more cases than one involving only contact or penetrative acts. With any socially deviant act, particularly one that attracts the moral opprobrium that child abuse and neglect does, the possible sources of bias increase. Social class, ethnicity, perceived status, experience and the characteristics of the children themselves are all factors which can lead to bias in the recognition, reporting and registering, or substantiation, of cases of child abuse and neglect.

The methodological factors of generalisability and comparability of prevalence and incidence studies are particularly important for practitioners. It is against these that they have to weigh up their own individual referrals and decide whether, or to what extent, they should intervene.

Examination of the changes in incidence and prevalence rates of child maltreatment over time have shown increases in reported cases, decreases in the incidence of physical abuse and no change in the prevalence of child sexual abuse. Possible reasons for the discrepancies between these findings are discussed. The role of public education and a change in public attitudes towards violence within families, and their effect in reducing the incidence of physical abuse of children, is stressed.

The gap between actual and reported cases has important implications for practitioners, as has the somewhat negative controlling ethos of current child protection practices. Practitioners can feel helpless in the face of an ever increasing number of child maltreatment referrals and the possible consequences of not intervening. Incidence and prevalence studies provide a picture of the underlying base rate of maltreatment and the characteristics of the abused population. Research is needed into identifying those children and families where intervention is vital and those which can be diverted into less controlling and more supportive systems.

Conclusions

In the UK, the television companies – the BBC's Childwatch and Channel 4's MORI poll – have been the agencies most concerned with finding out the underlying frequency of child abuse. They are the only studies to have attempted to discover how many children nationally have been abused (the prevalence rate). The prevalence they were concerned with was that of child sexual abuse. Other prevalence studies, also of child sexual abuse, have been on nationally unrepresentative samples such as GP patients or college students. Incidence studies in the UK have been drawn entirely from cases of child abuse and neglect reported each year. The evidence from studies in the USA and Canada indicates that actual rates of abuse are much higher. Research should be conducted in the UK to ascertain what is the gap between actual and reported cases of abuse. The Department of Health has commissioned a feasibility study on carrying out a nationally representative prevalence study of child sexual abuse (Ghate and Spencer, 1995). An incidence study of physically abusive parental behaviour, similar to that of the Family Violence Research Program in the USA, should also be conducted in the UK.

The increases in reported incidence rates over the years, accompanied in recent years by the recession and cutbacks in local authority resources, have led to child protection taking increasing priority over child care. It is to be hoped that the Children Act (1989), with its emphasis on providing services for all children in need, will help to reverse this trend. Neglected and emotionally abused children, who are as equally needy as physically and sexually abused children, tend to get disproportionately filtered out of the child protection system in the UK but with no compensating services. A revised system, focusing on children in need and not just on those in need of immediate protection, is more likely to tackle the adverse effects of child abuse and neglect.

Annotated Reading List

Creighton, S.J. (1992). *Child Abuse Trends in England and Wales 1988–1990 and an Overview from 1973–1990.* London: NSPCC.
Provides an overview of the trends in registered cases of child abuse and neglect in the UK over the last 18 years. It also examines the characteristics of the different types of abuse, the children, their parents, suspected perpetrators and families in addition to the management of the cases.

Kelly, L., Regan, L. & Burton, S. (1991). *An Exploratory Study of the Prevalence of Sexual Abuse in a Sample of 16–21 Year Olds.* Child Abuse Studies Unit London: PNL.
Provides an extremely useful breakdown of prevalence rates by different definitions of sexual abuse.

Markowe, H. (1988). The frequency of child sexual abuse in the UK. *Health Trends 20(1):* 2–6. London: HMSO.
Provides a concise survey of UK sexual abuse frequency studies and detailed consideration of their methodological weaknesses.

The Research Team. (1990). *Child Sexual Abuse in Northern Ireland.* Antrim: Greystoke Books.
Provides a detailed report on the methodology of mounting a national incidence study and details of the cases ascertained.

References

Association of Directors of Social Services. (1987). *Child Abuse: Incidence of Registrations for Child Abuse Between 1985 and 1986.* Press Release. Berkshire Social Services Department.

Association of Directors of Social Work. (1988). *Scottish Child Abuse Statistics 1987.* Scotland: ADSS and SSRG Glasgow: Association of Directors of Social Work and Social Services Research Group, June 1988.

Badgley, R.F., Allard, H.A., McCormick, N. *et al.* (1984). *Sexual Offences Against Children*. Volume 1. Report of the Committee on Sexual Offences Against Children and Youths. Ottawa, Canada: Minister of Supply and Services.

Baker, A.W. & Duncan, S.P. (1985). Child sexual abuse: a study of prevalence in Great Britain. *Child Abuse and Neglect 9:* 453–467.

BBC. (1986). *Childwatch – Overview of Results from 2530 Self-completion Questionnaires.* BBC Broadcasting Research (unpublished).

BBC. (1987). *Childwatch – National Survey on Child Abuse.* BBC Press Briefing, 9 July.

Berger, A.M. Knutsen, J.F,. Mehm, J.G. & Perkins, K.A. (1988). The self-report of punitive childhood experiences of young adults and adolescents. *Child Abuse and Neglect 12(2):* 251–262.

Butler-Sloss, E. (1988). *The Report of the Inquiry into Child Abuse in Cleveland 1987.* London: HMSO.

Central Statistical Office. (1993). *Social Trends 23,* 1993 Edition. London: HMSO.

Children Act (1989). London: HMSO.

Creighton, S.J. (1992*a*). *Child Abuse Trends in England and Wales 1988–1990 and an Overview from 1973–1990.* London: NSPCC.

Creighton, S.J. (1992*b*). *Child Abuse Deaths.* Information Briefing No. 5. London: NSPCC.

Creighton, S.J. and Noyes, P. (1989). *Child Abuse Trends in England and Wales 1983–1987.* London: NSPCC.

Daro, D. and Mitchel, L. (1990). *Current Trends in Child Abuse Reporting and Fatalities: The Results of the 1989 Annual Fifty State Survey.* Working Paper No. 808. Chicago: National Center on Child Abuse Prevention Research.

Department of Health and Social Security and the Welsh Office (1988). *Working Together. A guide to arrangements for inter-agency co-operation for the protection of children from abuse.* London: HMSO.

Department of Health. (1989). *Survey of Children and Young Persons on Child Protection Registers.* Year Ending 31 March 1988 – England. London: Government Statistical Service.

Department of Health. (1993). *Children and Young People on Child Protection Registers.* Year Ending 31 March 1992 – England. Provisional Feedback. Personal Social Services Local Authority Statistics. London: Government Statistical Service.

Department of Health and Social Security (1974). *Non-accidental injury to children.* Local Authority Social Services Letter/74.

Dingwall, R. (1989). Some problems about predicting child abuse and neglect. Ch. 2 in: O. Stevenson (ed.) *Child Abuse: Professional Practice and Public Policy.* Herts: Harvester Wheatsheaf.

Eckenrode, J., Munsch, J., Powers, J. & Doris, J. (1988). The nature and substantiation of official sexual abuse reports. *Child Abuse and Neglect 12(3):* 311–319.

Feldman, W., Feldman, E., Goodman, J.T., McGrath, P.J., Pless, R.P., Corsini, L. & Bennett, S. (1991). Is childhood sexual abuse really increasing in prevalence? An analysis of the evidence. *Pediatrics 88(1):* 29–33.

Finkelhor, D. (1979). *Sexually Victimized Children.* New York: Free Press.

Finkelhor, D. (1988). *Initial and Long Term Effects of Child Sexual Abuse.* Paper at SRIP conference, Leeds.

Finkelhor, D., Hotaling, G., Lewis, I.A. & Smith, C. (1990). Sexual abuse in a national survey of adult men and women: prevalence, characteristics and risk factors. *Child Abuse and Neglect 14(1):* 19–28.

Gelles, R.J. & Straus, M.A. (1987). Is violence toward children increasing? A comparison of 1975 and 1985 national survey rates. *Journal of Interpersonal Violence 2:* 212–222.

Ghate, D. and Spencer, L. (1995) *The prevalence of child sexual abuse in Britain. A feasibility study for a large scale national survey of the general population.* London: HMSO.

Gibbons, J. (1993). *Operation of Child Protection Registers.* Summary report of a research project commissioned by the Department of Health. University of East Anglia: Social Work Development Unit.

Giller, H., Gormley, C. & Williams, P. (1992). *The Effectiveness of Child Protection Procedures. An Evaluation of Child Protection Procedures in Four ACPC Areas.* Social Information Systems Ltd.

Home Office. (1993). *Criminal Statistics: England and Wales 1991.* Cm 2134. London: HMSO.

Home Office, Department of Health, Department of Education and Science, Welsh Office. (1991). *Working Together under the Children Act, 1989.* London: HMSO.

Hong, G.K. & Hong, L.K. (1991). Comparative perspectives on child abuse and neglect: Chinese vs. Hispanics and Whites. *Child Welfare 70(4):* 463–475.

Kaplan, M.J., Becker, J.V. & Tenke, C.E. (1991). Influence of abuse history on male adolescent self-reported comfort with interviewer gender. *Journal of Interpersonal Violence 6(1):* 3–11.

Kelly, L., Regan, L. & Burton, S. (1991). *An Exploratory Study of the Prevalence of Sexual Abuse in a Sample of 16–21 Year Olds.* Child Abuse Studies Unit. London: PNL.

Kinsey, A.C., Pomeroy, W.B., Martin, C.E. & Gebhard, P.H. (1953). *Sexual Behaviour in the Human Female.* Philadelphia, Pennsylvania: W.B. Saunders.

Markowe, H.L.J. (1988). The frequency of child sexual abuse in the UK. *Health Trends 20(1):* 2–6. London: HMSO.

Markowe, H.L.J. (1991). *Epidemiological Assessment of Studies of Child Abuse.* Paper given at BASPCAN conference 'Turning Research into Practice'. Leicester.

McCurdy, K. & Daro, D. (1993). *Current Trends in Child Abuse Reporting and Fatalities: The Results of the 1992 Annual Fifty State Survey.* National Center on Child Abuse Research, Working Paper No. 808. Chicago: NCPCA.

Nash, C.L. & West, D.J. (1985). Sexual molestation of young girls. In D.J. West (ed.): *Sexual Victimisation.* Aldershot: Gower.

Nunno, M. (1992). *The Abuse of Children in Out of Home Care.* Paper given at Conference on Institutional Abuse. London: NSPCC.

O'Toole, R., Turbett, P. & Nalepka, C. (1983). Theories, professional knowledge and diagnosis of child abuse. Ch. 22 in: *The Dark Side of Families.* Beverly Hills: Sage.

Parton, C. & Parton, N. (1989). Child protection: the law and dangerousness. Ch. 3 in O. Stevenson (ed.): *Child Abuse: Professional Practice and Public Policy.* Herts: Harvester Wheatsheaf.

Pieterse, J.J. & Van Urk, H. (1989). Maltreatment of children in the Netherlands: an update after ten years. *Child Abuse and Neglect 13:* 263–269.

Research Team, The. (1990). *Child Sexual Abuse in Northern Ireland.* Antrim: Greystoke Books.

Russell, D.E. (1983). The incidence and prevalence of intrafamilial and extrafamilial sexual abuse of female children. *Child Abuse and Neglect 7:* 133–146.

Schene, P. (1987). Is child abuse decreasing? Commentary on Gelles and Straus paper. *Journal of Interpersonal Violence 2:* 225–227.

Sedlak, A.J. (1990). *Technical Amendment to the Study Findings: National Incidence and Prevalence of Child Abuse and Neglect: 1988.* Westat, Inc.

Siegal, J.M., Sorenson, S.B., Golding, J.M., Burnam, M.A. & Stein, J.A. (1987). The prevalence of childhood sexual assault: the Los Angeles epidemiologic catchment area project. *American Journal of Epidemiology 126:* 1141–1153.

Starr, R.H. (1990). The need for child maltreatment research and program evaluation. *Journal of Family Violence 5(4):* 311–319.

Stevenson, O. (1989). Multi-disciplinary work in child protection. Ch. 8 in O. Stevenson (ed.): *Child Abuse: Professional Practice and Public Policy*. Herts: Harvester Wheatsheaf.

Straus, M.A. (1979). Family patterns and child abuse in a nationally representative American sample. *Child Abuse and Neglect 3(1)*: 213–225.

Straus, M.A. & Gelles, R.J. (1986). Societal change and change in family violence from 1975 to 1985 as revealed by two national surveys. *Journal of Marriage and the Family 48*: 465–479.

Toro, P.A. (1982). Developmental effects of child abuse: a review. *Child Abuse and Neglect 6*: 423–431.

US Department of Health and Human Services. (1988). *Study Findings. Study of National Incidence and Prevalence of Child Abuse and Neglect*. Washington DC: National Center on Child Abuse and Neglect.

Welsh Office. (1993). *Child Protection Register: Statistics for Wales, 1992*. Cardiff: Government Statistical Service.

Wind, T.W. & Silvern, L. (1992). Type and extent of child abuse as predictors of adult functioning. *Journal of Family Violence 7(4)*: 261–281.

Zimrin, H. (1986). A profile of survival. *Child Abuse and Neglect 10(3)*: 339–349.

2

Child Protection, Child Care and Child Welfare

Robert Harris

Introduction

So overwhelming, both in terms of media coverage and psychological intensity, has the issue of child protection become that it is all too easy to decontextualise it from the broader issues of social philosophy, policy and action of which it is a part.

The main question to be addressed in this chapter is whether child protection should be considered as distinct from child care. This is a surprisingly complicated question. To answer it, we must be clear whether the distinction we have in mind is strategic or conceptual. *Strategically* much is to be gained from developing a specialist literature for practitioners of the kind represented in the second and third sections of this book. It is important, however, not to confuse the part with the whole, and we aim to discourage this heresy by placing strategic intervention in a broader theoretical framework. Although this chapter may therefore disturb more than it reassures, complicate more than it simplifies and offer less practical advice than later ones, it does so to provide a foundation for what follows and a firmer basis for practical action.

Our present concern is with the *conceptual* dimensions of child protection. At this level, designating as 'child protection' only those actions designed to prevent what we normally term 'child abuse' is merely an example of a contemporary tendency towards partialisation and fragmentation. Indeed, because child care itself, as normally understood, actually means child-rearing, it, too, is a restricted notion. We seldom consider, say, road safety training, environmental legislation, subsidised cycle helmets, antenatal care, anti-bullying strategies, school meals, free prescriptions or restrictions on alcohol and cigarette sales as dimensions of child care *or* child protection. And it is especially curious that the child protection literature is so distinct from that of the *genus* of which it is a part, crime prevention.

Yet since all these policies are designed to 'care' for children and 'protect' them from harm, it is against these objectives that their effectiveness must at least in part be judged. And it should surely be judged as firmly as the effectiveness with which those care and protection duties which fall to the social worker are discharged. The proverbial visitor from outer space might accordingly struggle to grasp why our view of both child protection and child care is so restricted.

Child Welfare Enhancement: Some Considerations

Why, first, *should* we protect children? While to ask this question may appear merely pedantic, the general belief that there is a responsibility to care for children is ill-defined and the issue is important and complex. For example, what do our answers to these questions tell us about our 'responsibility' towards children?

- Is our responsibility to abused children in our own society greater than, equal to or less than that to the (immeasurably worse off) children of the developing world?
- In our own society, is our responsibility to abused 'stranger children' greater than, equal to or less than that to our own (immeasurably better off) children?

Unless we are statistically deviant, our attitudes will not favour a wholesale transfer of resources to the developing world; our voting behaviour will not support any political party which stands for a massive wealth and income redistribution of this kind; and our personal behaviour, although it may, as did that of the Victorian philanthropists, involve writing occasional cheques for charitable purposes, will not entail giving more than we can comfortably afford towards the relief of suffering. Our attitude to starving children in Somalia, infant war victims in Bosnia, child refugees from Vietnam or pre-pubescent prostitutes in Thailand is somewhat akin to that of our 19th century forebears to starving or exploited children in England. That is to say, we experience genuine, albeit fleeting, personal distress when their plight is forced on our attention, but they simply do not fall within our perceived ambit of responsibility because they are, as it were, of another world.

This point was fully recognised by the Victorian reformers, for whom the evangelistic ambitions of imperial missions stood in stark contrast to harsh domestic policies rooted in a *laissez-faire* approach. Not for nothing was General William Booth's catalogue of human misery, in a direct parody of Stanley's *Darkest Africa* published the same year, called *In Darkest England and the Way Out* (Booth, 1890), not for nothing did G.R. Sims, the previous year, enquire:

> Is it too much to ask that in the intervals of civilising the Zulu and improving the conditions of the Egyptian fellah the Government should turn its attention to the poor of London and see if it cannot remedy this terrible state of things? (Cited in Bruce, 1961, page 155.)

and not for nothing does legend have it that a party of Ojibway Indians visiting London half a century earlier observed:

> We see hundreds of little children with their naked feet in the snow, and we pity them, for we know they are hungry. . . . You talk about sending blackcoats [missionaries] among the Indians; now we have no such poor children among us . . . we think it would be better for your teachers all to stay at home, and go to work right here in your own streets. (Cited in Tobias, 1972, page 96.)

Clearly, an unwillingness to suffer economic hardship in the interests of starving children or to support a political party which promises to give away such sums of money as would noticeably disturb our comfort cannot be sustained alongside any argument that it is somehow 'natural' to respond to need and distress. Perhaps a century hence, our own *laissez-faire* attitude to developing world children will cause as much surprise as we experience today when we read of the attitudes prevalent a century ago towards the plight of the children of what has been termed 'Outcast London' (Stedman-Jones, 1971).

We can therefore reject the view that the issue of 'responsibility' towards children is somehow simple. On the contrary, it is very problematic. We can equally disabuse ourselves of any belief that social change is the product of a collective increase in humanitarian impulses or an advance in civilisation. Responsibility derives not from moral or religious beliefs but rather from political notions of rights and duties. And this is so notwithstanding the fact that some individuals may choose to make commitments on the basis of such beliefs. To make this point is not to denigrate charity or altruism, which are intrinsically good and hence morally laudable. Our purpose is the more restricted one of distinguishing between charity and responsibility. The former is optional, whereas the latter derives from a contractual relation between donor and recipient which specifies reciprocal rights and duties.

Today our relations with children of the developing world are based primarily on charity, supplemented by the minute proportion of taxes earmarked for overseas aid, and by supranational declarations and charters. These declarations and charters, however, lack the force of national law and themselves reflect the political and economic calculations which drive foreign and overseas aid policy. Developing world children have no right to demand protection from us because we have no corresponding duty to protect them. Yet if child protection were indeed based on considerations other than law and policy – on a hierarchy of need or suffering, for example – it is inconceivable that we should be so exercised by the murder of a single Maria Colwell or Jasmine Beckford yet be so acquiescent in the systematic destruction of young lives in more distant parts of the globe.

If we lack responsibility towards developing world children, in our own country our responsibility towards stranger children is manifestly less than that towards our own children. Hence, we may pass by with impunity while a stranger child is being beaten or even abducted, since no laws determine our actions in relation to such children. The force of legislation defining our responsibilities towards our own children is, however, potentially extensive. This of course merely reflects the centrality of the family in contemporary social arrangements. And as we define the child increasingly as a citizen and decreasingly as family property, both these responsibilities and the manner in which they are discharged must logically extend still further. We shall return to this point later.

Responsibility, then, is a product not of private morality, theology or psychology, but of law and policy. We term this approach the 'Cordelia principle', from Cordelia's view that her love for Lear was a product of filial duty and not boundless love. There is nothing wrong with this. If the law constitutes a recognisable, albeit rather rough and ready, expression of popular will (Oakeshott, 1962) a rights-based security is preferable to a retractable promise based on volatile emotion or an optional and contested theology. Child protection, therefore, turns on a formulation in welfare law which specifies minimum rights for the child, visits minimum responsibilities on the family, and allocates powers and duties to the state to be exercised in the event of family failure. It is this network of rights, duties and powers which both creates and reflects the relations between child, family and state.

It follows that, whereas the practical act of applying skill and knowledge in child protection may well be a distinctive activity, theoretically and conceptually child protection is a product of broader sets of social relations. It is the unsettled nature of these relations which explains the ambivalence with which the actions of professionals tend to be viewed. Hence, social workers in particular frequently complain that when they are not being perceived as passively colluding with the oppression of the child, they are seen as interfering state agents invading the privacy of the home. To this, we can only reply: precisely so.

To argue thus is not, however, to diminish the significance of individual actions taken by agencies involved in child protection. Such actions are, on the contrary, the handmaidens of law and policy. Formal powers, rights and duties derive their social meaning from the defining behaviour of significant actors. Hence police, crown prosecutors, judges and social workers are central players, their interpretations of cases socially constructing, deconstructing and reconstructing a myriad of individual actions as abuse or non-abuse. And they do this in a process of perpetual motion and – because their interpretations are by no means always in accord with each other – a certain unpredictability.

Every protective act is therefore at once unique *and* constitutive of a set of broader political relations. It is an individual, unrepeatable phenomenon which may be good or bad, competent or incompetent. Because, however, it has no 'essential nature' distinct from its legal purpose and social meaning, it is also a social construction. This mode of analysis opens the door to a scrutiny not of the act as a hermetically sealed phenomenon but of the social arrangements which 'created' the act itself. Hence Donzelot's observation:

> We must cease asking, What is social work? Is it a blow to the brutality of centralized judicial sanctions . . . or is it rather the unchecked apparatus of the state, which, under the guise of prevention, is extending its grip on citizens to include their private lives, marking minors who have not committed the least offense with a stigmatizing brand? Instead, we should question social work regarding what it actually does, study the system of its transformations in relation to the designation of its effective targets. (Donzelot, 1980, pages 98–9.)

While the old and weary question of whether the incidence of those forms of conduct we currently term 'child abuse' has increased over time is empirically un-answerable (see Creighton, this section, Chapter 1), what *has* taken place is a shift in the 'meaning' of childhood and children's rights, family responsibility and state power. This shift has led both to a redefinition of child abuse (some acts which were once 'non-abuse' are now 'abuse') and to an increasingly intensive and extensive encroachment of the public sphere into hitherto private domains.

This penetration has in part been achieved by designating child abuse as something more than an illegal act, detectable and punishable by conventional policing methods. Child abuse has gradually but decisively been transformed into a process. Although variously defined, it is normally perceived as containing elements of a voluntarism justifying punishment but also having discernible 'causes' (of which having oneself been abused is high on the list) (see Browne, this section, Chapter 3) demanding therapy. As defined elsewhere, however, the two strands are conflicting but not contradictory:

> Contradiction signifies a situation in which the pursuit of a given objective renders the pursuit of a given other objective a logical impossibility; conflict is one in which the pursuit

of two objectives, though technically difficult, is not impossible. So walking towards and away from a stationary object at the same time would be a contradiction; simultaneously knitting and watching television would not. (Harris and Timms, 1993, page 35.)

They co-exist as aspects of a discourse which is overridingly medical from both victim and perpetrator perspectives (see also Parton, 1979, 1985, 1991).

For the victim, this medicalisation lies in the seeming inevitability of deleterious long-term consequences. For the perpetrator, it lies above all in the seeming compulsiveness of the activity. Accordingly, the perpetrator becomes both actor and acted upon, a criminal liable to deny guilt for both tactical and psychological reasons yet himself simultaneously a victim, a 'type of person'. This transformation is akin to that which, influenced by 19th century positivism, transmogrified the act of sodomy into the state of homosexuality:

> As defined by the ancient civil or canonical codes, sodomy was a category of forbidden acts; their perpetrator was nothing more than the juridical subject of them . . . the psychological, psychiatric, medical category of homosexuality was constituted from the moment it was characterized . . . less by a type of sexual relations than by a certain quality of sexual sensibility, a certain way of inverting the masculine and feminine in oneself. . . . The sodomite had been a temporary aberration; the homosexual was now a species. (Foucault, 1981, page 43.)

More than a century later, child abuse too has become the legitimate domain of both social workers and police (and there could be no better symbol of this than their shared training for that truly remarkable activity the 'joint investigation'). Indeed, the extent to which child protection has transformed the relations between social workers and police can hardly be exaggerated. Little more than a decade ago these agencies were in structural (and often intensely personal) conflict on matters of civil liberties. Today, in spite of periodic local difficulties, they work hand in glove as fellow social professionals in pursuit of the same desirable end. Child abuse, as a seemingly neutral common denominator, has served as a catalyst for co-operation between professionals whose assumptive worlds were hitherto quite different. At the very least, the collaborative endeavours of police and social workers have 'produced' a mode of activity which, by reducing the opportunity for one to be set against the other, has thinned the mesh of the net of control (Cohen, 1985). More fundamentally, they have contributed to the redefinition of privacy itself.

In spite of Government's determined attempt to reduce professional autonomy by ever closer monitoring and accountability (Henkel, 1991; Harris, 1993a), it is through professionals that the state most intensively penetrates the domain of the private. In the case of child protection in particular, it does so on the basis of more tenuous evidence than is required for investigating other alleged crimes. Accordingly, it is strategically necessary for the professionals, if they are to be tolerated in an advanced liberal democracy such as ours, to have curative and supportive as well as investigative functions (Harris, 1990).

This becomes possible precisely as a consequence of the positivism which continues to influence many contemporary 'explanations' of child abuse. Whilst, therefore, it is rare for persistent house burglars to be termed compulsive rather than recidivist and to be offered therapeutic assistance to liberate them from their antisocial addiction in the case of child abuse professionals bend over backwards to give families opportunities to improve (Dingwall et al., 1983; Dingwall and Eekelaar, 1984). It might be thought that 'partnership', which the Children Act defines as a guiding principle for child protection work, would be consistent with such an approach, but the guidelines and procedures which now inform professional intervention also stress the importance of exchanging information with other professionals and creating ever more reliable means of monitoring families under suspicion.

It need scarcely be stressed that to detect a broader political ambition (that of maintaining private order) in a benign and legitimate concern to protect children is to analyse a political process. This is not to imply that protecting children is oppressive, centralist or, above all, undesirable, although in France, where social theory and micropolitical practice have historically sought to mark out and defend the domain of the private, some commentators have come close to saying just that (see, for example, Donzelot 1980, 1984; Meyer, 1983; Thèry, 1989).

In Britain, however, the discourse has focused only secondarily on maintaining privacy (although Harris, 1990, qualifies this point in the wake of the Cleveland problem). Certainly, it has been argued that 'creating' child abuse conceals the central-ity of social injustice by constructing the family itself as first cause of oppressive familial relations (Parton, 1985). It has also been argued that defining child care problems as the product of parental skill deficits ideologically repudiates the aetio-logical status of structural inequality (Wilson and Herbert, 1978). The predominant British concern, however, has been to protect the vulnerable against the abuse of adult, particularly paternal, power.

Power, however, is more easily displaced than removed, and the inhibition of paternal power has had the main effect of relocating it elsewhere. This relocation is simultaneously centrifugal and centripetal (Harris and Timms, 1993), involving both a dispersal and a concentration. Accordingly, at one level the protective intervention of the trained and sanctioned professional is aimed (genuinely and without dissimu-lation) at the liberation of the oppressed child, a child with citizenship rights but lacking adequate powers of enforcement. Yet embedded in this liberating act is another act, this time of constraint, which further undermines the autonomy of the family by active monitoring and verification. Because we cannot protect the child without investigating the supposedly oppressive conduct of the parent, these simultaneous strands of liberation and constraint are fundamental to professions operating in that domain between the public and the private (termed *le social* by Donzelot, 1984; see also Harris, 1989, 1993*b*).

These contrary pulls are unavoidable and inexorable strands of a process neither simple nor unilinear. Nor, to make an obvious point, can the professionals divest themselves of this duality by skill, value or personality. Whatever their genuineness, empathy or charm, their power is analytically separate from such personal attributes or learned skills. Indeed, one of the main effects of the adroit deployment of such modes of professional conduct is likely to be the concealment of the sociopolitical character of the intervention itself.

Child Protection and Citizenship Rights

Child protection, then, is not a recognisable 'thing' like a leg, a tree or a jug, deter-minable over time and place and, though varied in style, identical in nature and usage. Hence, as the idea of what a child or a family 'is' changes over time, or as the state shifts the boundaries of its activities, their interrelationships mutate too. These changes are too numerous to itemise here, but one, citizenship, is crucial.

The nature of a child's citizenship rights has varied as dramatically over time as it currently does over place. To assert that the child was historically the property of the father is now a truism (though for a *caveat* see Harris and Timms, 1993, chapter 2), and the increase in the child's citizenship rights in the present century has led to funda-mental changes in the triangular relation of child, family and state. Prior to the Industrial Revolution, although a direct line of contact between state and child existed in theory, in practice it was exercised almost exclusively through Wardship in Chan-cery in connection with heirs to property (Pinchbeck and Hewitt, 1973, page 363). So while the notion that it was the state's business to protect the child existed as an embodiment of the monarchical function of *parens patriae*, the exclusivity of its appli-cation to the child of property suggests that the child him or herself was an incidental *accoutrement*, the property and not the child being the object of direct concern.

Social legislation, and in particular successive Factory and Education Acts, signalled the more direct intervention of the state in the lives of children and families. This included an increasing concern with child welfare. Although child welfare is distinct from citizenship – after all, laws exist to promote animal welfare but the idea of animals as citizens is nonsensical – to address it is to take a step in the direction of citizenship because to do so severs the exclusive power over the child hitherto exercised by the family. So when by the middle of the century John Stuart Mill was writing of the state's 'absolute authority' over the child (Harris and Webb, 1987, chapters 1–2), the child was on the way to becoming legally and conceptually detachable from the family.

As we have seen, however, it would be an error to attribute this social change primarily to a spread of humanitarianism. For example, much of the social legislation of the reforming Liberal administrations of 1905–14 was targeted at children. This was not because some reified construct called 'society' inexplicably started to care more for them but because powerful sociopolitical discoveries placed concern for children high on the Government agenda. It was factors which included the rise of the Labour movement and the election of the first group of Labour MPs in 1906, the uncovering of public health problems by the Boer War recruitment process and the public recep-tion of Seebohm Rowntree's first social survey of York (Rowntree, 1901) that were decisive. And while the Children Act 1908 certainly sought to protect more children from harm it did so, in a process which will by now be familiar, by extending further the categories of non-delinquent 'at-risk' children detainable for training in an Indus-trial School (Harris and Webb, 1987).

In similar vein, the Children and Young Persons Act 1933 charged juvenile courts with the duty to 'have regard for the welfare of the child or young person' (section 44) but also extended yet further the courts' powers over those same children. Indeed, the comfortable co-existence of welfare enhancement and increasingly intensive state intervention was maintained until the late 1970s. By this time, unprecedented numbers of children were being held in welfare institutions, albeit for less reason than hitherto (Millham *et al.*, 1978, pages 46–7) and often for quite lengthy periods of time. (This literature is helpfully reviewed in Thoburn *et al.*, 1986.)

The end of the 1970s, however, saw a radical shift in political thought. First, the economic crisis of 1976 had caused the Treasury to stress to all spending departments the cost of their policies, so making the continued expansion of institutional care improbable. Secondly, in the wake of the United Nations Year of the Child (1979) the idea of children's 'rights' was beginning to be politically significant. And thirdly, the 1979 Thatcher administration proved surprisingly hostile to the idea of professional discretion. Indeed the view emerged, professionally as well as politically, that children's nascent rights were actually threatened by those arms of the state charged with responsibility for public child care.

The definitive history of the various children's rights movements has still to be written (but see Freeman, 1983; Franklin, 1986; and for a useful review, albeit set in an analysis which has been strongly criticised [Harris and Timms, 1993, pages 33–8], Harding, 1991). It is, however, possible to discern a number of strands:

- the ideological repudiation of the 'treatment' philosophy and the concomitant (if short-lived) renaissance of the justice movement in the early 1980s (see Harris, 1985);
- the growing impact of the European Convention on Human Rights on Government thinking (Harris and Timms, 1993);
- the institution of the Children's Legal Centre and, in an increasingly consumerist environment, groups such as Who Cares? (Page and Clark, 1977), the Voice of the Child in Care and the National Association of Young People in Care;
- increasing media interest in the creation of independent 'helplines' (of which Childline is the best established) which gave children the opportunity to bypass parents and achieve direct access to extra-familial adults;
- increasing attacks on family patriarchy from the women's movement which were influential in raising the profile of sexual abuse. Feminist writers and sympathisers successfully redefined 'consensual' adult–child sexual activity as an abuse of male power (Dominelli, 1989; Droisen and Driver, 1989; Okin, 1989; Parton, 1991) with long-lasting damaging consequences for the child (Finkelhor, 1986; Wyatt and Powell, 1988; Gomes-Schwartz et al., 1990; Walker, 1992). This redefinition combined with a media campaign against the politically unsophisticated Paedophile Information Exchange. The effect of this was to buttress further an attack on the earlier libertarian position that child sexual activity was a blow for individual freedom against the oppressive and repressive structures of bourgeois capitalism.

Out of these developments a contradiction has emerged, doubtless indicative of a more fundamental lack of agreement concerning the 'basic nature' (if such there be) of childhood. A perspective which views children as rational beings is evident in the stipulation of the Children Act 1989 that in defined circumstances in private proceedings (see s.1(3)) the child's views must be taken fully into account, and that in local authority proceedings the child shall be entitled to separate representation. Yet this perspective co-exists with an a priori assumption, in relation to sexuality in particular, that a child cannot, through age and powerlessness, give 'informed consent' to sexual relations with an adult. This view (for a critique of which in relation to man–boy sex see Leahy, 1992) appears to stand almost irrespective of what the child actually says.

In spite of this seeming contradiction, however, these developments have together legitimated the notion of child-as-vulnerable-citizen – and vulnerable on the grounds not only of physical weakness, immaturity and powerlessness but of the dangers now increasingly regarded as characteristic of much family life.

The significance of this relocation of welfarism in relation to children's rights is considerable. Whereas the 1960s–70s witnessed the emergence of a radicalism within a number of what have been termed psy-professions, the politics of the 1980s marginalised any radical tendencies, creating instead unifying symbols and common denominators among different interest groups, of which reducing the prison population was one (Harris, 1992) and child protection another.

Once a child is defined as citizen-with-unenforceable-rights, enforcement is a proper political objective. For a number of reasons, however, the family is an especially sensitive unit in contemporary politics. First, it is empirically a flawed construction, the fragmentation of the traditional family unit having led to a redefinition of the term which is so broad that it can incorporate almost any kind of domestic living arrangement. Secondly, it is now acknowledged to be an unpredictable and sometimes dangerous *locus* for child-rearing. Thirdly, however, notwithstanding these considerations, it remains a cornerstone of contemporary social policy, a function consistently and increasingly stressed in contemporary politics.

If one of the ideological functions of the family in the 1980s was the altruisation of self-seekingness (Harris, 1990) – the man doing his best for his family being a necessary legitimation of competitive individualism – it was necessary in contemporary *Realpolitik* for the family, as a necessary but empirically flawed structure, to be both supported and monitored. Here, child protection was a hard case. The child had new and evolving citizenship rights but lacked enforcement capacity.

At the same time the family was, in a more general sense and for political and economic reasons, required to reassume some aspects of its pre-industrial centrality. While the state withdrew from selected actions which might undermine family autonomy, particularly those of a financially supportive nature, in the case of child abuse the defectiveness of the family as a cornerstone of policy was poignantly and embarrassingly exposed. Here difficulties, which in relation to homelessness, income support or unemployment might be just politically containable, took on the status of a contradiction.

The unstable accommodation of these pulls and pushes constituted the warp and woof of child protection policy in the 1980s and made the endeavour of the Children Act 1989 to redefine the relations of state, family and child so politically necessary. As will be apparent from the argument so far, however, such a 'balance' cannot be struck in a settled way. This is partly because applying the generalised principles of statute to a myriad of specific cases can only be done on the basis of a set of interpretations which are controversial and will mutate over time and place. It is also partly because the character of these relations is itself unsettled, possibly indeed beyond settlement.

If concrete examples of the problem are required, two may suffice. First, it is an enduring irony that, in the midst of so much concern about child abuse, the Children Act 1989 apparently permits those imbued with parental responsibility to impose forms of physical punishment on their children which would in almost any other circumstances be deemed criminal assaults, and hence themselves a legitimate ground for state intervention.

Secondly, although law and policy consistently demand that the child's interests come first, their practical application does not prevent families from providing for their children a physical and emotional environment of strikingly poor quality. That the state does not necessarily step in to remonstrate or place the child somewhere better but characteristically endeavours to sustain and support such families (Dingwall *et al.*, 1983; Dingwall and Eekelaar, 1984) is a precise reflection of this lack of settlement. It entails equivocation in determining the point at which what is agreed to be undesirable becomes unacceptable. It also entails uncertainty as to which of two approaches should have precedence: supporting existing ties with a barely adequate blood family or pursuing an emotionally and physically superior adoptive home.

If the weight of research alone were to carry the day (see, for example, Tizard, 1977; Barth and Berry, 1988), there would be rather less professional *Angst* about decisive removal and relocation. That such *Angst* does exist, however, is a striking reminder that behind the rhetoric of child care lies a political complexity frequently determinant of professional action.

Some Issues for Practitioners

If we are weaned on dependency, security and consistency, it is not surprising we fail to reach our full potential as adults. (Thompson, 1992, page 120.)

It would be perverse in a book for practitioners to omit a section on practical application. Nevertheless, in a chapter like this such a section is difficult to write except at a rather banal level. After all, this is not a chapter which offers practice prescriptions. On the contrary, its focus is on those parts of the child protective activity where prescription is impossible, rules are insufficient and where the world seems especially messy and unpredictable. For child welfare is a rule-driven activity only at the levels of law and policy. The application of law and policy to the individual case is inextricably linked with the moral, practical, strategic and intellectual position and astuteness of the practitioner.

The issue here is not merely one of eliminating grotesque error, vital though that is. Rather, it is the establishment and maintenance of a form of practice which, while working consistently within the framework of law and policy, nevertheless transcends that framework in its individual interventions. The section's epigraph makes the point. It may well be true that every school of psychology and social belief system in the world believes 'security', however defined or implemented, to be constitutive of good child care (Doyal and Gough, 1991, page 204). Even such an uncontroversial good can, however, if taken to an extreme or if misapplied, cease to be the platform for the emergence of a mature and confident adult, and may instead stifle creativity, initiative and independence.

But if the golden mean of moderation in all things is to be the proper objective of intervention, how are we to conceive of, never mind express, such a goal in a culture as conceptually and linguistically dualistic as that of the contemporary West? The idea that any good pushed to its obsessional extreme becomes bad is especially difficult to handle tactically in child care if we are not to run into the problem of the 'double-bind', regarded by the anti-psychiatrists of a quarter of a century ago (Laing, 1965) as a basis of some of the schizophrenias. In common parlance it is good to be good but bad to be goody-goody. For the professional, therefore, to acquire a mature sense of paradox and contradiction, to eschew the blind pursuit of one goal at the expense of others and to maintain a sense of balance are underpinning prerequisites for work which is 'sensible' as well as competent.

Unless the point is grasped that the relations between the public and the private spheres are structurally and psychologically unsettled – after all, people may demand both that children be protected from harm and that their own family be entitled to live free of state inspection – professionals may take too personally any criticisms which come their way. This is not to excuse bad work but to etch the need to distinguish between those aspects of the work which can be addressed by improvements in practice and those which necessitate bearing discomfort, even opprobrium. It is of the first importance for professionals to distinguish within their own spheres of activity between *problems to be solved* and *states to be endured*. The notion of a problem without a solution, though essential for social workers, health visitors, teachers, police, doctors and others engaged in the professional pursuit of the intermittently unattainable, is, however, alien to much western intellectual thought and political behaviour.

There is accordingly no 'answer' to at least some of the awkwardnesses raised in this chapter. Although it hardly need be stressed that a practical sensitivity towards them is necessary, even the most exemplary conduct will not make social workers popular or successful overnight. But to members of a profession of which 88% of a sample have admitted to feeling undervalued and 38% to concealing their profession at social events (Davies and Brandon, 1988) it is worth saying that the burden should not be theirs alone.

Summary and Conclusion

This chapter has addressed the question of whether child protection is distinct from child care. It was argued that conceptually child protection must be perceived as a product of the relations between state, family and child at a specific historical moment. Accordingly, it draws its logic and purpose not from private acts of altruism or morality but from the status of the family and the citizenship status of the child as defined in law and policy. Child protection guarantees rights for the child and places duties on family and state as protectors, a mode of responsibility which, because it is contractual in nature, we termed the 'Cordelia principle'.

Nevertheless, notwithstanding the centrality of law and policy in child protection, the words of statute have only limited meaning outside the defining behaviour of significant actors such as police, magistrates and social workers. Because definitions are unsettled and sometimes controversial, however, child protection is constructed, deconstructed and reconstructed in ways which may be uncertain and unpredictable. This may lead to controversies in particular 'cases', often based on complaints of over- or under-intervention, albeit that each is dealt with under the identical framework of law and policy.

In the case of child protection the state may intervene in the family domain on the basis of tenuous evidence, with the aid of professionals with a dual mandate to help and monitor, liberate and constrain at their discretion. As this activity is interprofessional, child protection has effected a shift in relations among the professionals themselves, particularly between police and social workers, who are now joined in a common cause and aspire to the same objective. This objective, while seemingly politically neutral, has led to a redefinition of the character and boundaries of public and private spheres. Because it is impossible to protect a child and not control a family, as child protection has developed so have new dimensions of social control emerged.

This point was demonstrated by a brief historical *excursus* which illustrated the increasing encroachment of the state into the lives of families and children, the attenuation of the link between child and family, and the strengthening of the link between child and state. These great but often imperceptible changes emerged alongside the increasing assumption of citizenship rights by children whose enforcement capacity was limited.

Contemporary child protection must be viewed against the backdrop of the politics of the 1970s and 1980s: an economic crisis, the delegitimation of professional autonomy and the social construction of the family as an autonomously functioning unit. The contradictions in this latter policy in particular illuminated some of the dilemmas of child protection. The ideological necessity of idealising the family has rested uneasily with the seeming empirical reality of family disintegration (or diversification *ad absurdum*) and behavioural corruption. Hence, this cornerstone of 1980s social policy proved insufficiently robust to bear the strain, and while this reality was politically containable in other spheres it was not in the case of child protection.

Thus, the manner in which the state treats children is indicative of broader strands of social and political philosophy. Because of the ambiguities and contradictions with which it is surrounded, it also exposes as wanting many strands of conventional western philosophical discourse (Harris and Timms, 1993, chapter 2). Since child welfare is a product not of altruism, psychology or theology but of citizenship rights, its day-to-day implementation teaches us much about the contemporary meaning of citizenship.

Citizenship visits enforcement obligations on the state, however, which are normally exercised in the child's own home and against those whom the child frequently professes to love. The means by which the state enforces those rights on behalf of the vulnerable child are eloquent in their practical account of the meaning of concepts such as family, privacy, childhood, needs, rights and interests. The abused child may well say, as did 14-year-old Emily whose telephone call to Childline led to her father's imprisonment, 'I wish I had never told' (Howarth, 1991, page 10), but her father was punished nevertheless. In such a case, was the concern to protect Emily, to protect others like Emily, or to exact retribution from Emily's father? And if the consequence of punishing Emily's father was to cause more distress to Emily, to make her feel responsible, a traitor even, was that simply a misperception on her part to be dealt with therapeutically (a comfortable if paternalistic perception), or was it a necessary price to pay for the imprisonment of a sex offender? In such a situation, for whose protection is child protection *actually* intended?

Questions such as these are hard for intelligent adults, never mind small children, to answer. Child welfare, however, once it is regarded other than simplistically, raises these kind of questions. Nevertheless, it seems intrinsically desirable not to shield practitioners from such issues. Rather, those who operate at, and therefore help define, the very boundaries of the public and the private spheres, should challenge them as part of their own professional responsibilities. They should engage with these complexities, think and talk about them, and move towards a position, if not of perfect settlement – for such may be impossible – then of mature accommodation. Accommodating conflicting goods in a world where clarity and purposiveness of action are all too seldom possible is a necessary, honourable and attainable professional objective.

Further Reading

Our themes in this chapter included social change, and citizenship, care and responsibility.

For a useful overview of sociological theories of social change generally, see Strasser and Randall (1981). Our own interest, however, was more specifically in the nature and character of 'progress'. Here two seminal articles, written from a phenomenological perspective rather than in the tradition of historical materialism normally associated with the revisionist approach (Carrier and Kendall, 1973, 1977) challenge, in a manner relevant to students of social policy, the simplistic positivism which suggests that we simply get 'more humane' or 'advanced' with time.

Many readers will recognise the influence of Michel Foucault at work in this chapter. The critical consideration of history is fundamental to almost all of Foucault's work, but for a professional readership his most accessible attack on conventional approaches is probably in *Discipline and Punish* (Foucault, 1977). Readers who wish for a more general guided introduction to Foucault's *opus* can do no better than consult Rabinow (1986), the Introduction to which (pages 3–29) is especially helpful in this area. Some of the best discussions of Foucault's theory of history are to be found in Dreyfus and Rabinow (1982) and Boyne (1990), but neither of these texts is for the intellectually timorous. Harris and Webb (1987) consider aspects of Foucault's work in relation to juvenile justice in England and Wales.

In relation to citizenship, care and responsibility it will be unhelpful to provide detailed references on the numerous conflicting theories of citizenship, although many readers will know Marshall's classic text (Marshall, 1950). This, however, is very much a product of its time. A helpful and accessible introduction to contemporary theories of citizenship in relation to the politics of the 1980s is to be found in Plant and Barry (1990), a pamphlet with the dual benefits of brevity (it is 77 pages long) and – because it contains essays from both socialist and liberal capitalist perspectives – balance. It will also steer the enthusiast towards more developed analyses.

A possible objection to one argument advanced in this chapter may come from professional readers concerned with the seeming relegation of care to 'duty' implied by the 'Cordelia principle'. I should not wish the text to be read thus, however, and it is important to be clear that the intellectual tradition in which this chapter is written is separate from and does not contradict that on moral values and professional ethics. Social workers in particular have not always been well served by their 'values' literature, but by far the most lucid and serious discussion is to be found in Timms (1983), although this is not a book to be skimmed through. Readers interested in pursuing moral issues surrounding 'care' may usefully go back to Ragg (1977), Downie and Telfer (1980) and Watson (1980), texts which will complement the arguments contained in this chapter in a manner which sceptical practitioners may find useful.

References

Barth, R. & Berry, M. (1988). *Adoption and Disruption: Rates, Risks and Responses*. New York: Aldine de Gruyter.

Booth, General W. (1890). *In Darkest England and the Way Out*. London: International Headquarters of the Salvation Army.

Boyne, R. (1990). *Foucault and Derrida: the Other Side of Reason*. London: Unwin Hyman.

Bruce, M. (1961). *The Coming of the Welfare State*. London: Batsford.

Carrier, J. & Kendall, I. (1973). Social policy and social change – explanations of the development of social policy. *Journal of Social Policy* 2: 209–224.

Carrier, J. & Kendall, I. (1977). The development of welfare states: the production of plausible accounts. *Journal of Social Policy* 6: 271–289.

Cohen, S. (1985). *Visions of Social Control: Crime, Punishment and Classification*. Cambridge: Polity Press.

Davies, M. & Brandon, M. (1988). The summer of '88. *Community Care, 733:* 16–18.

Dingwall, R. & Eekelaar, J. (1984). Rethinking child protection. In: M. Freeman (ed.) *The State, the Law, and the Family: Critical Perspectives*. London: Tavistock Publications in association with Sweet and Maxwell.

Dingwall, R., Eekelaar, J. & Murray, T. (1983). *The Protection of Children: State Intervention and Family Life*. Oxford: Basil Blackwell.

Dominelli, L. (1989) Betrayal of trust: a feminist analysis of power relationships in incest abuse and its relevance for social work practice. *British Journal of Social Work 19:* 291–307.

Donzelot, J. (1980). *The Policing of Families: Welfare Versus the State*. London: Hutchinson.

Donzelot, J. (1984). *L'Invention du Social*. Paris: Fayard.

Downie, R.S. & Telfer, E. (1980). *Caring and Curing: A Philosophy of Medicine and Social Work*. London: Methuen.

Doyal, L. & Gough, I. (1991). *A Theory of Human Need*. London: Macmillan.

Dreyfus, H. & Rabinow, P. (1982). *Michel Foucault: Beyond Structuralism and Hermeneutics*. Chicago: University of Chicago Press.

Droisen, A. & Driver, E. (eds) (1989). *Child Sexual Abuse: Feminist Perspectives*. London: Macmillan.

Finkelhor, D. (ed.) (1986). *A Sourcebook on Child Sexual Abuse*. Beverly Hills, California: Sage Publications.

Foucault, M. (1977). *Discipline and Punish: The Birth of the Prison*. Harmondsworth: Allen Lane.

Foucault, M. (1981). *The History of Sexuality, Vol. I, An Introduction*. Harmondsworth: Penguin Books.

Franklin, B. (ed.) (1986). *The Rights of Children*. Oxford: Basil Blackwell.

Freeman, M. (1983). *The Rights and Wrongs of Children*. London: Frances Pinter.

Gomes-Schwartz, B., Horowitz, J. & Cardarelli, A. (1990). *Child Sexual Abuse: The Initial Effects*. Beverly Hills, California: Sage Publications.

Harding, L. (1991). *Perspectives in Child Care Policy*. London: Longman.

Harris, R. (1985). Towards just welfare: a consideration of a current controversy in the theory of juvenile justice. *British Journal of Criminology 25:* 31–45.

Harris, R. (1989). Social work in society or punishment in the community? In: R. Shaw & K. Haines (eds).

Harris, R. (1990). A matter of balance: power and resistance in child protection policy. *Journal of Social Welfare Law 5:* 332–340.

Harris, R. (1992). *Crime, Criminal Justice and the Probation Service*. London: Routledge.

Harris, R. (1993a). Probation in the United Kingdom today. *International Journal of Offender Therapy and Comparative Criminology*.

Harris, R. (1993b). The state, the family and the child: a UK perspective. In: G. Bradley & K. Wilson (eds). *The Family, the State and the Child*. Papers from the Four Nation Conference, September 1992. Hull: University of Hull, Department of Social Policy and Professional Studies.

Harris, R. & Timms, N. (1993). *Secure Accommodation in Child Care: Between Hospital and Prison or Thereabouts*. London: Routledge.

Harris, R. (1994) Continuity and change: Probation and politics in contemporary Britain. *International Journal of Offender Therapy and Comparative Criminology.* 38: 33–45.

Harris, R. & Webb, D. (1987). *Welfare, Power and Juvenile Justice: the Social Control of Delinquent Youth*. London: Tavistock Publications.

Henkel, M. (1991). *Government, Evaluation and Change*. London: Jessica Kingsley.

Howarth, V. (1991). The child's view of the process. In: K. Wilson (ed.).

Laing, R.D. (1965). *The Divided Self*. Harmondsworth: Penguin Books.

Leahy, T. (1992). Positively experienced man/boy sex: the discourse of seduction and the social construction of masculinity. *Australian and New Zealand Journal of Sociology* 28: 71–88.

Marshall, T.H. (1950). *Citizenship and Social Class*. Cambridge: Cambridge University Press.

Meyer, P. (1983). *The Child and the State: The Intervention of the State in Family Life*. (Translated by J. Ennew & J. Lloyd). Cambridge and Paris: Cambridge University Press and *Editions de la Maison des Sciences de l'Homme*.

Millham, S., Bullock, R. & Hosie, K. (1978). *Locking Up Children: Secure Provision Within the Child Care System*. Farnborough: Saxon House.

Oakeshott, M. (1962). *Rationalism and Politics*. London: Methuen.

Okin, S. (1989). *Justice, Gender and the Family*. New York: Basic Books.

Page, R. & Clark, G. (eds) (1977). *Who Cares? Young People in Care Speak Out*. London: National Children's Bureau.

Parton, N. (1979). The natural history of child abuse: a study in social problem definition. *British Journal of Social Work 9*: 431–451.

Parton, N. (1985). *The Politics of Child Abuse*. London: Macmillan Education.

Parton, N. (1991). *Governing the Family: Child Care, Child Protection and the State*. London: Macmillan Education.

Pinchbeck, I. & Hewitt, M. (1973). *Children in English Society, vol. II, From the Eighteenth Century to the Children Act 1948*. London: Routledge and Kegan Paul.

Plant, R. & Barry, N. (1990). *Citizenship and Rights in Thatcher's Britain: Two Views*. London: Institute of Economic Affairs Health and Welfare Unit.

Rabinow, P. (ed.) (1986). *The Foucault Reader*. Harmondsworth: Penguin Books.

Ragg, N. (1977). *People Not Cases: A Philosophical Approach to Social Work*. London: Routledge and Kegan Paul.

Rowntree, B.S. (1901). *Poverty: A Study of Town Life*. London: Macmillan.

Shaw, R. & Haines, K. (eds) (1989). *The Criminal Justice System: A Central Role for the Probation Service*. Cambridge: University of Cambridge Institute of Criminology.

Smart, C. & Sevenhuijsen, S. (eds) (1989). *Child Custody and the Politics of Gender*. London: Routledge.

Stedman-Jones, G. (1971). *Outcast London*. Oxford: The Clarendon Press.

Strasser, H. & Randall, S. (1981). *An Introduction to Theories of Social Change*. London: Routledge and Kegan Paul.

Thèry, I. (1989). 'The interest of the child' and the regulation of the post-divorce family. In: C. Smart & S. Sevenhuijsen (eds).

Thoburn, J., Murdoch, A. & O'Brien, A. (1986). *Permanence in Child Care*. Oxford: Basil Blackwell.

Thompson, N. (1992). *Existentialism and Social Work*. Aldershot: Avebury.

Timms, N. (1983). *Social Work Values: An Enquiry*. London: Routledge and Kegan Paul.

Tizard, B. (1977). *Adoption; A Second Chance*. London: Open Books.

Tobias, J. (1972). *Crime and Industrial Society in the Nineteenth Century*. Harmondsworth: Penguin Books.

Walker, M. (1992). *Surviving Secrets: The Experience of Abuse for the Child, the Adult and the Helper*. Milton Keynes: Open University Press.

Watson, D. (1980). *Caring for Strangers: An Introduction to Practical Philosophy for Students of Social Administration*. London: Routledge and Kegan Paul.

Wilson, H. & Herbert, G. (1978). *Parents and Children in the Inner City*. London: Routledge and Kegan Paul.

Wilson, K. (ed.) (1991). *Child Protection: Helping or Harming?* A Report of the Conference held on 23 March 1991. Hull: University of Hull Department of Social Policy and Professional Studies.

Wyatt, G.E. & Powell, G.J. (eds) (1988). *Lasting Effects of Child Sexual Abuse*. Beverly Hills, California: Sage Publications.

3

Child Abuse: Defining, Understanding and Intervening

Kevin Browne

Introduction

Child abuse and neglect is one of the most common causes of death in young children in the United Kingdom today. It has been claimed that up to four children under 16 years die of non-accidental injury every week (National Society for Prevention of Cruelty to Children, 1985) Indeed, child homicide figures for 1992 support this claim, showing that parents and relatives were responsible for three-quarters of the deaths (Central Statistical Office, 1994). These grim statistics highlight the fact that not enough is being done to protect children in our society, as exemplified by the increasing number of families maltreating children without social work support (Social Services Inspectorate, 1990; Browne and Lynch, 1994). As a result, many children are growing up physically and emotionally scarred for life.

The Extent and Definition of Child Abuse

In the book *Early Prediction and Prevention of Child Abuse* (Browne *et al.*, 1988), three major forms of child maltreatment are identified; physical, sexual and psychological or emotional abuse. Each type of maltreatment is characterized into 'active' and 'passive' forms (Table 3.1). Active abuse involves violent acts that represent the exercise of physical force so as to cause injury or forcibly interfere with personal freedom. Passive abuse refers to neglect, which can only be considered violent in the metaphorical sense, as it does not involve physical force. Nevertheless, it can cause both physical and emotional injury, such as non-organic failure to thrive in young children (Browne, 1993). However, victims of child maltreatment are unlikely to be subjected to only one type of abuse. For example, sexual abuse and physical abuse are always accompanied by emotional abuse, which includes verbal assault, threats

Table 3.1 *Two-way classification of abuse with examples of major forms.*

	Physical	Psychological	Sexual
Active	non-accidental injury poisoning	emotional abuse denigration and humiliation	incest assault and rape
Passive	non-organic failure to thrive, poor health care and physical neglect	emotional neglect lack of affection	failure to protect prostitution

(Adapted from Browne *et al.*, 1988, page 293.)

of sexual or physical abuse, close confinement (such as locking a child in a room), withholding food and other aversive treatment (Browne and Herbert, 1995). Within each type of abuse there is a continuum of severity ranging from mild to life-threatening.

Since 1990, the Department of Health (DOH) has accurately assessed each year the number of children and young persons on Child Protection Registers in England. The estimates are based on annual statistical returns from Local Government Authorities. Figure 3.1 shows the rate per 10 000 children for those currently on the register at 31 March 1993 and the number of children registered during the past year, by various age groups (Department of Health, 1994). The overall rate was three children per 1000 under 18 years of age. The highest rates were found in very young children under 5 years (four to five per 1000). The likelihood of being on the registers then decreases with age. Therefore, 68% of children on registers are aged under 10 years, with boys and girls equally represented in that age group. In the 10 and over age group, girls account for 59% of registrations. This is due mainly to registrations for sexual abuse in adolescent girls. Overall, girls account for 63% of those registered for 'sexual abuse'. Thus, boys on the register are younger and represent 54% of those registered for 'physical injury'. Indeed, NSPCC figures show that over 80% of the physical abuse most likely to cause death or handicap (i.e. head injury) occurs to children aged less than 5 with an over-representation of boys. Over half of all head injuries occur to infants aged less than 1 year (Creighton and Noyes, 1989; Creighton, 1992).

The definitions of child abuse recommended as criteria for registration throughout England and Wales by the Departments of Health, Education and Science, the Home Office and Welsh Office (1991) in their joint document *Working Together under the Children Act, 1989* (pages 48–9) are as follows.

Neglect. The persistent or severe neglect of a child or the failure to protect a child from exposure to any kind of danger, including cold and starvation or extreme failure to carry out important aspects of care, resulting in the significant impairment of the child's health or development, including non-organic failure to thrive.

Physical injury. Actual or likely physical injury to a child, or failure to prevent physical injury (or suffering) to a child, including deliberate poisoning, suffocation and Munchausen's syndrome by proxy.

Sexual abuse. Actual or likely sexual exploitation of a child or adolescent. The child may be dependent and/or developmentally immature.*

* Sexual exploitation represents the involvement of dependent, developmentally immature children and adolescents in sexual activities they do not truly comprehend, to which they are unable to give informed consent or that violate social taboos of family roles (Kempe and Kempe, 1978).

Emotional abuse. Actual or likely severe adverse effect on the emotional and behavioural development of a child caused by persistent or severe emotional ill-treatment or rejection. All abuse involves some emotional ill-treatment. This category is used where it is the main or sole form of abuse.

All the above categories are used for both intrafamilial and extrafamilial abuse and neglect, perpetuated by someone inside or outside the child's home. Mixed categories are also recorded, which register more than one type of abuse and/or neglect occurring to a child. This is especially important when considering 'organised abuse', which is defined in the same document (op. cit., page 38) as: 'Abuse which may involve a number of abusers, a number of abused children and young people and often encompass different forms of abuse. It involves, to a greater or lesser extent an element of organisation'. For further discussion on the definition of 'organised abuse', see La Fontaine (1993).

Previous recommendations (DHSS, 1986) also included a 'grave concern' category. This category, which accounted for approximately half the children on the register, was withdrawn as a category for registration in 1991. Children already registered under the 'grave concern' category were reallocated at the next review (if the child was

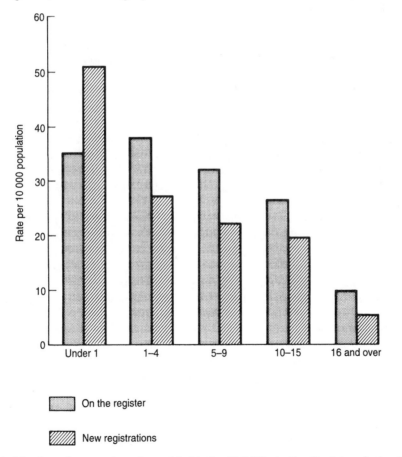

Figure 3.1 Number of new registrations added to the Child Protection Registers during the year ended 31 March 1993, including numbers on the register at that date by age. (From Department of Health, 1994, page 7.) Reproduced with permission from the DoH.

Table 3.2 *Number, percentages and rates of registrations by categories of child abuse under which they were recorded for the year ending 31 March 1993.*

	Number of children under 18	Percent %	Rate per 10 000
Neglect, physical injury and sexual abuse	200	1	<1
Neglect and physical injury	700	3	1
Neglect and sexual abuse	200	1	<1
Physical injury and sexual abuse	400	2	<1
Neglect (alone)	4800	20	4
Physical injury (alone)	8400	34	8
Sexual abuse (alone)	5600	22	5
Emotional abuse (alone)	2500	10	2
Grave concern (alone)	1800	7	2
Total	24 700	100	23

(Adapted from Department of Health, 1994.)

to remain on the register). A small number of children are still registered under this category which is defined as:

Grave concern. Children whose situations do not currently fit the above categories, but where social and medical assessments indicate that they are at a significant risk of abuse. This includes situations where another child in the household has been harmed or the household contains a known abuser.

Local authorities in England record each child on their Protection Register in only one of the nine categories presented in Table 3.2, choosing the one which provides the most accurate picture of the situation.

Overall, 16 400 girls and 16 000 boys in England were considered to require protection from maltreatment on the 31 March 1993 (31 and 28 in 10 000 children, respectively), and one in five (21%) of them were 'looked after' by local authorities (in care). Of the 6700 children in care on 31 March 1993, 4100 were placed with foster parents and 1000 were living in residential homes or hostels (DOH, 1994).

Similar registration rates for child abuse and neglect (30 in 10 000) children were reported previously by the NSPCC (Creighton and Noyes, 1989; Creighton, 1992). Furthermore, the NSPCC claim that their figures for reported physical and sexual abuse were not increasing (Creighton, 1992), although the Department of Health admit to a 6% decrease in the number of deregistrations from 1992 to 1993 (DOH, 1994). During the year, 15% of registrations involved children who had been previously registered and perhaps taken off the register prematurely.

Thus, it is not surprising that a report of a particularly nasty incident of sexual abuse or cruelty to an infant or a child murder often makes its way onto the front pages of our daily newspapers, then to a special inquiry and back again to the media. After much painful analysis and discussion, an attempt is made to discover where 'procedures' for managing cases have broken down.

There is a need to recognise the fact that it is not the 'procedures' but parents' social circumstances, attitudes and behaviour that need to be changed in order to prevent children being impetuously attacked. If these facts were faced honestly, education and training could be offered to parents who are unable to cope. This might actually prevent the recurrence, if not occurrence, of child maltreatment. Studies have shown (for example, Hyman, 1978) that 40% of cases of child abuse coming up for case conference are already known to the relevant authorities either on account of previous injury to the child under review or to one of his or her siblings. Repeat victimisation is a common finding throughout the child abuse literature, yet it is one apparently little appreciated by those who intervene in child abusing families. Nevertheless, the prevention of child maltreatment must be based on a comprehensive understanding of the causes of child abuse and neglect.

Causes of Child Abuse and Neglect

In seeking to understand the many causal factors involved in child abuse and neglect, several theoretical models have been proposed. However, some researchers distinguish between acts of physical violence and other forms of abuse because the causes and their potential solutions are different (see Frude, 1989, 1991). While all harmful acts have some causes in common, other factors are unique to physical abuse and neglect. It may be suggested that the following outline is related more to physical maltreatment. However, poverty, social isolation, family breakdown and poor parent–child relationships are associated with all forms of child abuse and neglect and have been cited as risk factors for child sexual abuse (Finkelhor, 1980; Bergner et al., 1994). Furthermore, a third of sexually abused children have been previously physically abused (Finkelhor and Baron, 1986), indicating that a number of common factors are involved.

Social and environmental focused models

Social stress perspective. Studies of abusing families (e.g. Garbarino, 1977; Krugman, 1986; Browne and Saqi, 1988a) have shown that factors such as low wages, unemployment, poor housing, overcrowding, isolation and alienating work conditions are associated with child maltreatment. Such factors are seen by Gelles (1987) and Gelles and Cornell (1990) as causing frustration and stress at the individual level, which in turn may lead to violence in the home. Gelles concluded from his research that 'violence is an adaptation or response to structural stress'. However, since physical abuse of children is not confined to families in the lower socio-economic groups but is spread across the entire class spectrum, this interpretation may be questioned. Nevertheless, it is suggested that social and environmental stress factors may have a greater influence on child maltreatment in lower class families than in middle-class families. Higher socio-economic groups may be more susceptible to individual factors which influence child abuse and neglect, such as psychological disturbance, alcohol and drug abuse. For all social classes, Gelles' (1983) 'exchange theory' proposes that the private nature of the family home reduces the 'costs' of behaving aggressively, in terms of official sanction. This results in a higher probability of violence in the home, where there are fewer social constraints on aggressive emotional expression. Thus, family 'privacy' makes child abuse less detectable and easier to commit, (Browne, 1988; Straus et al., 1988).

Environmental and cultural perspective. An alternative approach, but one which is also couched in terms of the social position of the people involved, can be referred to as the micropolitical view. This holds that individual violence is a microcosm of the power relations in the wider society. For example, a common feminist explanation of violence towards women and children is to view it as a function of their generally oppressed position in society. Within this framework, the purpose of male violence is seen as to control other family members (Gilbert, 1994).

The broadest sociological perspective (Gil, 1970, 1978; Straus, 1980; Goldstein, 1986; Levine, 1986) holds that cultural values, the availability of weapons and the exposure to unpunished models of aggression affect personal attitudes towards violent behaviour. These, in turn, influence an individual's acceptance and tolerance of aggression as a form of emotional expression and as a method of control over others. Within British and American societies, it would appear that violence in the family home is considered to be less reprehensible than violence outside it. There is a general acceptance of physical punishment as an appropriate method of child control, with nine out of ten children being disciplined in this way (Gelles and Cornell, 1990).

Individually focused models

This perspective concentrates on individual personality characteristics, often of a psychopathological or deviant nature. This research tradition is characterised by the use of rating scales to measure aggressiveness and hostility (e.g. Buss and Durkee, 1957; Novaco, 1978; Edmunds and Kendrick, 1980) and the study of biological variables which underlie a tendency to be violent.

Other authors have attempted to establish a causal connection between testosterone levels and violence (Persky *et al.*, 1971) and the identification of specific pathological conditions, such as alcoholism, which are likely to be predisposing or determining factors in violent behaviour (Gerson, 1978; Steinglass, 1987).

The psychopathic perspective. This focuses on the abnormal characteristics and psychological dysfunctions of abusing adults. Based on the theories of Freud (1964), Dollard *et al.* (1939) and Lorenz (1966) to explain aggression, the emphasis of psychiatry is on a psychodynamic approach to the abuser's 'abnormal death instinct' or 'excessive drive' for aggressive behaviour. This is seen as the result of genetic make-up and adverse socialisation experiences that produce a 'psychopathic' character with a predisposition to behave violently, especially when 'frustrated'.

One form of this predisposition is referred to as 'transference psychosis' (Galdston, 1965). This involves transference from parent to child. For example: the parent often interprets the child as if he/she were an adult and perceives the child as hostile and persecuting, projecting that part of their own personality they wish to destroy (Steele and Pollock, 1968). Thus, the child is seen as the cause of the parent's troubles and becomes a scapegoat towards which all anger is directed (Wasserman *et al.*, 1983). However, Kempe and Kempe (1978) suggested that only 10% of child abusers can accurately be labelled as mentally ill. Nevertheless, this model has been useful in recognising certain predispositions of abusive individuals. These include a tendency to have distorted perceptions of their children (Rosenberg and Reppucci, 1983), difficulty dealing with aggressive impulses as a result of being impulsively immature, self-centred, often depressed, and possibly having a history of having been abused, neglected or witnessing violence as children (Wolfe, 1991).

The social learning perspective. This provides an alternative form of individual explanation to biological or psychodynamic determinism. More than 30 years ago, Schultz (1960) claimed that the source of violence in a family context lies in unfulfilled childhood experiences. Gayford (1975) later carried out research in conjunction with

Chiswick Women's Aid and attempted to show the learned character of domestic violence within the family of origin.

This approach is based on the assumption that people learn violent behaviour from observing aggressive role models (Bandura, 1973). In support of this argument, Roy (1982) has stated that four out of five abusive men ($n = 4000$) were reported by their partners as either observing their fathers abusing their mothers and/or being a victim of child abuse themselves. In comparison, only a third of the abused partners had witnessed or had been victims of parental violence as a child. Findings from many other studies have supported this observation of the intergenerational transmission of violent behaviour (Browne, 1993, 1994).

There is evidence that violence between parents affects the children in a family (Jaffe et al., 1990; Carroll, 1994). The behaviour and psychiatric problems discovered in children of violent marriages include truancy, aggressive behaviour at home and school, and anxiety disorders (Hughes and Barad, 1983; Jaffe et al., 1986; Davis and Carlson, 1987). It is suggested that such children learn aversive behaviour as a general style for controlling their social and physical environments, and this style continues into adulthood (Gully and Dengerink, 1983; Browne and Saqi, 1987).

The special victim perspective. In direct contrast with the viewpoints considered so far are suggestions that the victims themselves may be instrumental in some way in eliciting attack or neglect. Friedrich and Boroskin (1976) review the complex reasons why a child may not fulfill the parent's expectations or demands. The child may in some way be regarded as 'special'. For example, studies have found prematurity, low birth weight, illness and handicap to be associated with child abuse (Elmer and Gregg, 1967; Lynch and Roberts, 1977; Starr, 1988). Indeed, it has been pointed out that the physical unattractiveness of these children may be an important factor for child abuse (Berkowitz, 1989).

A link between the social learning and special victim perspectives has been suggested by Lewis (1987), who claims that some women learn to accept violent behaviour towards themselves as a result of childhood experiences.

Interaction focused models.

Some researchers have advocated a more interactive approach that includes the social relationships of the participants and their environmental setting, rather than seeking to isolate the person or situation. This entails a move from the individual psychological level to a study of social interactions between members of the family.

The interpersonal interactive perspective. Toch (1969), for example, in his study entitled *Violent Men* looked not only at the characteristics of these men but also at the context of their violence and the characteristics of their victims. He concluded that aggressive behaviour was associated with 'machismo' and the maintenance of a particular personal identity in relation to others.

The person–environment interactive perspective. Frude (1980) puts forward the notion of a causal chain leading to 'critical incidence' of child abuse. This is a function of complex interactions between the individual and their social and physical environments. The 'critical incidence model' of child abuse is presented in Figure 3.2 and can be described as follows.

1. Environmental stress situations which are usually long term, such as poverty,

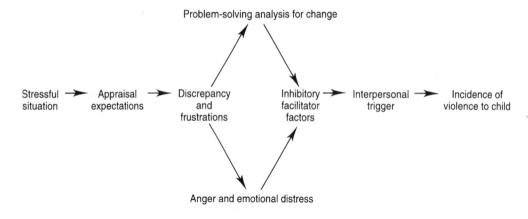

Figure 3.2   The critical incidence model of child abuse (adapted and modified from Frude, 1980.)

influence domestic abusers to assess their personal situations differently from non-abusing family members (i.e. as threatening).

2. They perceive a discrepancy between their expectations for life and social interactions and what they actually see happening. This often results in feelings of frustration for the person.

3. Anger and emotional distress are likely as a response to these situations rather than problem-solving strategies for change.

4. Lack of inhibitions with regard to violent expression, together with a lower threshold of tolerance, increases the possibility for violence. This is of course enhanced by disinhibitors such as alcohol or drugs.

5. Under the above conditions, even a facial expression (perceived as a dirty look) can lead to, or trigger, an incidence of violence.

These causal links result in the caregiver being more easily provoked to take violent action. Frude (1991) challenges the assumption that 'abusers' differ from 'non-abusers' and suggested that they might be more usefully considered as points on a continuum. For this reason, he argued that studies of interactions in the family may have much to contribute towards our understanding of domestic violence and child abuse and neglect. Frude's causal chain model demonstrates the need to assess a violent person's understanding of the environment. Their perceptions, attitudes and attributions will all influence the possibility of overt aggressive behaviour. In relation to violent behaviour, Howells (1989) has developed the work of Novaco (1978) on anger arousal. This work emphasises the role played by cognitive processes, such as appraisal and expectations of external events, in evoking an aggressive response.

Recently, there has been a move away from accounting for violence in the family purely in terms of individual psychopathology towards models that attempt to integrate the characteristics of abusing parents, their children and the situation in which they live. Child abuse and neglect cannot be explained by a single factor, it is a consequence of complex interactions between individual, social and environmental influences (see Belsky, 1988; Browne, 1989*a*).

Integrated models

The different explanations for the causes of violence towards children and other family members have been useful in that together they have served to emphasise the diverse nature of the variables involved in child abuse and neglect. Simple explanations make the solution to this pervasive problem appear easy. For example, the 'demon rum' exploration of physical and sexual violence towards women and children is an old and popular one (Gelles and Cornell, 1990). It is true that alcohol appears to exacerbate pre-existing impulse control and emotional problems, thus increasing the likelihood of serious injuries (Coleman, 1980). This seems to be especially the case in the evening, at weekends and on holiday, when children and couples are alone with their problems and are relaxing with drink (Frude, 1991).

However, the majority of alcohol abusing individuals who are violent to members of their family when drinking heavily also admit that they have been violent while not under the influence of alcohol (Sonkin *et al.*, 1985). Therefore, alcohol abuse is neither a necessary nor sufficient condition for violent behaviour.

Heavy drinking and drunkenness is not the cause of child abuse and neglect, but rather a condition that co-exists with it, like many other factors. Nevertheless, it is often used as an excuse for violent behaviour personally, socially and legally (Pahl, 1985).

Psychosocial perspective.   The inadequacies of single factor explanations has led to a psychosocial approach which integrates sociological and psychological explanations for family violence and child abuse. Originally proposed by American researchers (for example, Gelles, 1973), this perspective suggests that certain stress factors and adverse background influences may serve to predispose individuals to violence. As Frude (1980, 1989, 1991) suggested, violence will occur in the presence of precipitating factors, such as a child misbehaving.

It has been claimed that 'predisposing' factors may form a basis for identification of families 'at risk' of violence (e.g. Browne and Saqi, 1988*a*; Browne, 1989*b*, 1995*a*, *b*). However, a more pertinent question is why the majority of families under stress do not abuse their children. It may be that stress will only lead to violence when adverse family interactions exist. Belsky (1988) and Browne (1989*a*) have taken this approach to child abuse. They conceptualise child maltreatment as a social–psychological phe-nomenon that is 'multiply determined by forces at work in the individual, the family, as well as in the community and the culture in which both the individual and the family are embedded' (Belsky, 1980). Given a particular combination of factors, an interac-tional style develops within the family, and it is in the context of this interaction that child abuse occurs. This approach may be equally adopted to explain other forms of family violence.

Multifactor perspective.   The study of social interactions and relationships can be seen as occupying a central and potentially integrating place in explaining the causes of aggression in the family. In relation to child abuse and neglect, Browne (1988, 1989*a*) presents a multifactor model which suggests that stress factors and background influences are mediated through the interpersonal relationships within the family (see Figure 3.3).

The model assumes that the 'situational stressors' are made up of the following four components:

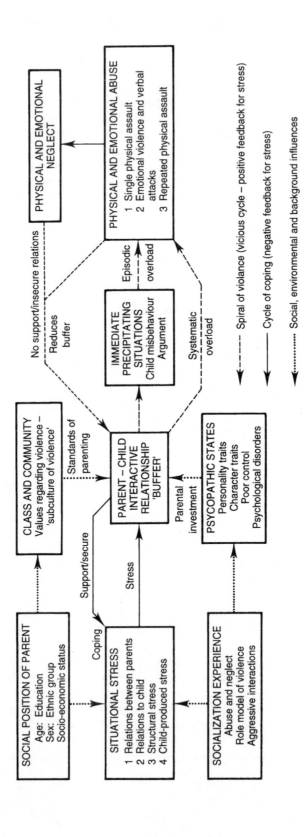

Figure 3.3 The causes of child abuse and neglect. [From Browne, K. (1988). 'The nature of child abuse and neglect: An overview', Chapter 2 *In* K. Browne, C. Davies and P. Stratton (Eds.) *Early Prediction and Prevention of Child Abuse*, Chichester: Wiley. p23. (Figure 1). With kind permission from J. Wiley & Sons]

1. Relations between care givers – inter-marriage, marital disputes, step-parent/cohabitee or separated/single parent.
2. Relations to children – such as spacing between births, size of family, care givers' attachments to expectations of their dependents.
3. Structural stress – poor housing, unemployment, social isolation, threats to the care giver's authority, values and self-esteem.
4. Stress generated by the child – for example, an unwanted child; one who is incontinent, difficult to discipline, often ill, physically or mentally disabled; one who is temperamental, frequently emotional or very demanding.

The chances of these situational stressors resulting in abuse and neglect are mediated by and depend on the interactive relationships within the family. A secure relationship between family members will 'buffer' any effects of stress and facilitate coping strategies on behalf of the family (Browne, 1988, 1989a). By contrast, insecure or anxious relationships will not 'buffer' the family under stress and 'episodic overload', such as an argument or a child misbehaving, may result in a physical or emotional attack. Browne (1988, 1989a) suggests that overall this will have a negative effect on the existing interpersonal relationships and reduce any 'buffering' effects still further, making it easier for stressors to overload the system once again. Hence, a positive feedback ('vicious cycle') is set up which eventually leads to 'systematic overload', where constant stress results in repeated physical and emotional assaults. This situation becomes progressively worse without intervention and could be termed 'the spiral of violence'.

In some cases, violent parents will cope with their aggressive feelings towards their child by physical or emotional neglect, to avoid causing a deliberate injury.

As indicated earlier, culture and community values may also affect attitudes and styles of interaction in family relationships which, in turn, will be influenced by the social position of individuals in terms of their age, sex, education, socio-economic status, ethnic group and social class background.

According to Rutter (1985), aggression is a social behaviour within everyone's repertoire, and he suggests that it is under control when the individual has high self-esteem, good relationships and stress is appropriately managed. However, the quality of relationships and responses to stress in the family will depend on the participant's personality and character traits and their pathology, such as low self-esteem, poor temperament control and psychological disorders. These may be a result of early social experiences, which may indirectly affect behavioural investment in the family.

Two main features of violent families are a lack of skill in handling conflict and discipline and high rates of aversive behaviour. These coercive family interactions have been previously described by Patterson (1982) and are seen as the primary focus for intervention.

In conclusion, it is suggested that stress factors and background influences are mediated through the interpersonal relationships within the family. Indeed, it is these relationships that should be the focus of work on prevention, treatment and management of family violence and child maltreatment. It is at this level that health and social service professionals can make a significant contribution.

Intervention Strategies

Effective intervention strategies to control and prevent family violence have recently been reviewed (Willis *et al.*, 1992; Gough, 1994). The majority of current intervention techniques operate at the third level of treatment, i.e. after violence to the child has occurred. This is despite the fact that there are three levels of prevention (Browne, 1988).

Primary prevention: fundamental changes in society and family life

Techniques of intervention which attempt to prevent the problem before it starts are termed 'primary preventions'. These usually operate at the societal level through public awareness campaigns and advocacy groups, and then are realised by social, legal and educational processes of change. Gelles and Cornell (1990) suggest the following actions for the primary prevention of violence in the family:

1. Eliminate the norms that legitimate and glorify violence in the society and the family, such as the use of violence as a form of media entertainment.
2. Reduce violence-provoking stress created by society, such as poverty and inequality.
3. Incorporate families into a network of kin and community and reduce social isolation.
4. Change the sexist character of society by educational development.
5. Break the cycle of violence in the family by teaching alternatives to violence as a way of controlling children.

The above proposals call for fundamental changes in family life and society as a whole. If they are not unrealistic, they are at least long-term solutions.

Secondary preventions: early prediction and identification

In the short term, intervention techniques aimed at the early identification of potential or actual violence are more realistic. This is considered to be secondary prevention and includes professionals involved in counselling, telephone helplines, home visits, and clinic, health centre or hospital care. Such professionals can be instructed to screen routinely all families who come into contact with the service they are providing and identify predictive characteristics.

It is difficult to predict the chances of child abuse and neglect in the family, as some people resort to violence inconsistently while others may do so only under extreme stress. However, studies on the causes of child abuse and neglect have identified factors that are usually present when parents maltreat their children (Browne and Saqi, 1988*a*; Browne, 1995*a*).

Men and women are often reluctant to admit relationship problems and may feel ashamed of their own violent interactions and their abuse and neglect of their children. Predictive characteristics are helpful, therefore, in identifying the possibility of violence for both the family and the health professional. Where there is undue concern about the possibility of violence, the problem should be referred to a more appropriate agency who may fully assess the coercive relationships and adverse factors affecting the family (see Browne, 1995*b*).

Tertiary prevention: intervention, treatment and control of the problem

At the tertiary level of prevention, techniques are employed when child maltreatment has actually been determined. Without secondary prevention, this will only be after many repeated episodes of maltreatment have occurred and have become established in the family system. Section III of this book puts forward ideas for intervention in families where a high risk of child maltreatment has been identified, the aim being to ameliorate the adverse effects and to reduce the risk of it recurring. Even for individuals who were maltreated as children, the prognosis may be good with effective intervention (see Hall and Lloyd, Section III, chapter 23).

Implications for assessment and intervention

The causal factors of child abuse and neglect must be considered within the context of the family's interpersonal network. Affectionate familial relationships act as a buffer against internal and external stress (Browne and Saqi, 1987; Browne, 1988, 1989a). An awareness and concern for other family members characterises affectionate relationships (Browne, 1986). It is important to consider maltreatment in the light of these family dynamics. Hence, intervention needs to be aimed at any negative interaction or lack of interaction between a child and his or her care giver which results in harm to the child's physical and psychological development (Patterson, 1982).

For all forms of child maltreatment, physical, sexual, emotional abuse and neglect, views range from the necessity of working with a family together from the earliest point of diagnosis (e.g. Bentovim, 1991) to the view that work has to be focused on members of the family separately. For example, Berliner and Wheeler (1987) suggest that the sexually abused victim should be separated from the offender in the family (and the two treated independently), together with the non-abusing family members. Conjoint family work is seen only as a final step in suitable families. Issues concerning the need to offer individuals therapeutic work as well as working with the whole family are explained more fully by Furniss and Millar (Section III, chapter 21).

There is a growing body of therapeutic experience, practice and conceptual models to help the clinician, but little empirical data on the time when it is safe and appropriate to return the child to the home of an abusing family. The assessment of families in terms of the danger of repeated physical and sexual assault to the child will be outlined and discussed.

Assessing Violent Families: How safe is the child?

There are five important aspects to consider when assessing violent parent–child relationships (Browne, 1995a):

1. Caretaker's knowledge and attitudes towards child rearing.
2. Parental perceptions of the child's behaviour.
3. Parental emotions and responses to stress.
4. Parent–child interaction and behaviour.
5. Quality of child and parent attachment.

Knowledge and attitudes towards child rearing

Research suggests that abusing and non-abusing families have different attitudes about child development. Martin and Rodeheffer (1976) commented that abusers have unrealistic and distorted expectations about their children's abilities. They are said to have much higher expectations of their children and this influences discipline and punishment. Therefore, a significant proportion of sexual and physical abusive incidents involve senseless attempts by parents to force a child to behave in a manner that is beyond the child's developmental limitations.

Research also suggests that these deficits in parental knowledge or understanding were due to low adult intelligence (Smith, 1975), but this has been refuted. The parents know what to expect and do with young children but do not apply this knowledge to their own children. Starr (1982) found that one of the differences between abusing and non-abusing parents is that the abusing group see child rearing as a simple rather than a complex task. Many of them show a lack of awareness of their child's abilities and needs (Hyman and Mitchell, 1975).

Parental perceptions of child behaviour

It has been shown that abusing parents have more negative conceptions of their children's behaviour than non-abusing parents. They perceive their children to be more irritable and demanding (Browne and Saqi, 1987). This may be related to the fact that abused children are more likely to have health problems, eating or sleeping disturbances. Alternatively, it may be a direct result of the unrealistic expectations often reported for abusing parents (Rosenberg and Reppucci, 1983).

It has previously been suggested that the child contributes to its own abuse (Kadushin and Martin, 1981). Browne and Saqi (1987) do not support this notion, for example, they found no significant differences in children's health records. The abuse may be attributed to the fact that the parents have unrealistic expectations of their children. They interpret certain age-appropriate behaviours as deliberate or intentional non-compliance, concluding that this behaviour is an indication of the child's inherent 'bad' disposition. Thus, abusive parents may see their child's behaviour as a threat to their own self-esteem, which then elicits a punitive attitude and an insensitive approach to parenting.

Parental emotions and responses to stress

A factor common to many child abusers is a heightened rate of arousal in stressful situations. In a study conducted by Wolfe and colleagues (1983), abusive and non-abusive parents were presented with scenes of videotaped parent–child interaction, some of which were highly stressful (such as children screaming and refusing to comply with their parents) and some of which were non-stressful (for example, a child watching television quietly). The abusive parents responded with greater negative psychophysiological arousal than did the non-abusive comparison group. Thus, it may be suggested that poor responses to stress and emotional arousal play a crucial role in the manifestation of child abuse and neglect.

The majority of incidents of physical abuse which come to the notice of the authorities arise from situations where parents are attempting to control or discipline their children. Abusive parents are significantly more harsh to their children on a day-to-day basis and are less appropriate in their choice of disciplinary methods compared to non-abusive parents. It is the ineffectiveness of the abusive parent's child-management styles which contributes to the abuse. If the parent's initial command is ineffective and is ignored by the child, the situation will escalate and become more and more stressful until the only way the abusive parent feels they can regain control is by resorting to violence.

Patterson (1986) described rejecting parents as very unclear on how to discipline their children. They punish for significant transgressions, whereas serious transgressions such as stealing go unpunished. Where threats are given, they are carried through unpredictably. Neglectful parents show very low rates of positive physical contact, touching and hugging and high levels of coercive, aversive interactions.

In contrast, effective parenting is characterised by a flexible attitude, with parents responding to the needs of the child and the situation. House rules are enforced in a consistent and firm manner, using commands or sanctions where necessary. In most situations, the child will comply to the wishes of the parent and conflict will not arise.

Parent–child interaction and behaviour

Interaction assessments demonstrate that abused infants and their mothers have interactions that are less reciprocal and fewer in number than their matched controls, whether in the presence or absence of a stranger (Hyman *et al.*, 1979; Browne, 1986; Browne and Saqi, 1987, 1988*b*).

Observational studies provide evidence that social behaviours and interaction patterns within abusing and non-abusing families are different. Abusing parents have been described as being aversive, negative and controlling, with less pro-social behaviour (Wolfe, 1985). They also show less interactive behaviour, both in terms of sensitivity and responsiveness towards their children. This may result in infants developing an insecure attachment to their abusive caretakers, which in turn produces marked changes in the abused children's socio-emotional behaviour, in accordance with the predictions of attachment theory (Browne and Saqi, 1988*b*). Nevertheless, the consequences of maltreatment are not the same for all children. Findings suggest there are more behaviour problems in children who are both abused and neglected (Crittenden, 1985, 1988). Abusing and neglectful parents, together with their children, suffer from pervasive confusion and ambivalence in their relations with each other. This is not the same as simple parental rejection. It reflects rather an uncertainty in the relationship which leaves the child vulnerable and perplexed as to what is expected.

Quality of child and parent attachment

The view that children are predisposed to form attachments during infancy (Bowlby, 1969) has considerable importance for the study of child abuse. The literature contains numerous reports regarding the high number of abusive parents who were themselves victims of abuse as children (e.g. Egeland, 1988). It has been suggested that, in some cases, the link between experiences of abuse as a child and abusing as a parent is likely to be the result of an unsatisfactory early relationship with the principal caretaker and a failure to form a secure attachment (Browne and Parr, 1980; DeLozier, 1982; Bowlby, 1984).

Ainsworth *et al.* (1978) have examined the relationship between the infant's attachment (as measured by the infant's responses to separation and reunion) and the behaviour of the mother in the home environment. Their findings suggest that maternal sensitivity is most influential in affecting the child's reactions. In the homes of the securely attached infants, the mother was sensitive to the infant's behaviour and interactions. While insecurely attached, avoidant infants were found to be rejected by the mothers in terms of interaction, and it was suggested that the enhanced exploratory behaviours shown by these infants were an attempt to block attachment behaviours which had been rejected in the past. In the home environments of the insecurely attached, ambivalent infants, a disharmonious mother–infant relationship was evident, and the ambivalent behaviours shown were seen as a result of inconsistent parenting.

Maccoby (1980) concludes from the above findings that the parents' contribution to attachment can be identified within the four following dimensions of caretaking style.

Sensitivity/insensitivity. The sensitive parent 'meshes' her responses to the infant's signals and communications to form a cyclic turn-taking pattern of interaction. In contrast, the insensitive parent intervenes arbitrarily, and these intrusions reflect her own wishes and mood.

Acceptance/rejection. The accepting parent accepts in general the responsibility of child care. He/she shows few signs of irritation with the child. However, the rejecting parent has feelings of anger and resentment that eclipse her affection for the child. He/she often finds the child irritating and resorts to punitive control.

Co-operation/interference. The co-operative parent respects the child's autonomy and rarely exerts direct control. The interfering parent imposes his/her wishes on the child with little concern for the child's current mood or activity.

Accessibility/ignoring. The accessible parent is familiar with his/her child's communications and notices them at some distance, and hence is easily distracted by the child. The ignoring parent is preoccupied with his/her own activities and thoughts, and often fails to notice the child's communications unless they are obvious through intensification. He/she may even forget about the child outside the scheduled times for caretaking.

The four dimensions above are heavily influenced by parental attitudes, emotions and perceptions of the child, as discussed earlier. The dimensions are inter-related and together they determine how 'warm' the parent is towards the child. Indeed, Rohner (1986) has developed a description of parental warmth and rejection which he terms the warmth dimension. This can be considered as the overall picture when Maccoby's four dimensions are integrated together. A summary of Rohner's warmth dimension is given in Figure 3.4.

It has been suggested that helping to promote secure mother–child attachments may also prevent sexual abuse of the child by another family member(s), but many mothers are also maltreated by the child sex offender (Goddard and Hiller, 1993), so this notion has been brought into question. Nevertheless, many sexually abused children (approximately one-third) have been physically abused (Finkelhor and Baron, 1986). Therefore, comprehensive approaches to assessment and intervention for emotional/physical abuse and neglect early in the child's life may also help to prevent sexual abuse.

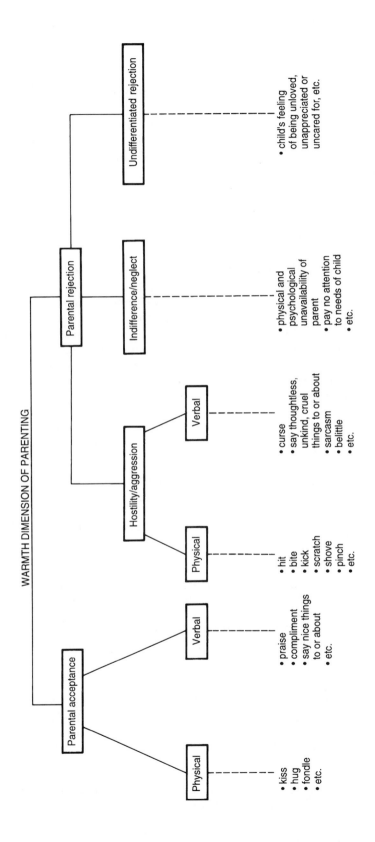

Figure 3.4 Conceptual Framework of Principal Parenting Concepts in Parental Acceptance–Rejection Theory [From R.P. Rohner, (1986). The Warmth Dimension: Foundations of Parental Acceptance–Rejection theory Beverley Hills: Sage. p. 20 (Figure 1). With kind permission of Sage publications].

Conclusion

Intervention with potential or actual child abusing families

The inability of child abusing parents to interact adaptively with their children is seen by many researchers as being representative of their general lack of interpersonal skills. Abusive parents share a common pattern of social isolation, poor work history and few friendships with others outside the home. This isolation means that child-abusing parents are not willing or able to seek help from outside agencies who could provide assistance or emotional support. If they do interact with other people, abusive parents are most likely to choose people in similar situations to themselves, so they gain no experience of alternative parental styles or coping strategies and continue to be ineffective in controlling their children.

It follows that it is the parent–child relationship that should be the focus of work on the prevention, treatment and management of child abuse and neglect and that interventions to achieve these goals are most effectively carried out in the homes of abusing families (Olds *et al.*, 1986; Wolfe, 1993). Therefore, those involved in the treatment of abusive families should be concerned with the development of a 'secure' relationship between parent and child. It is not sufficient to evaluate treatment programmes on the basis of the occurrence or non-occurrence of subsequent abuse. Helping parents to inhibit violence towards their children may still leave the harmful context in which the initial abuse occurred quite unchanged.

References

Ainsworth, M.D.S., Blehar, M.C. Waters, E. & Wall, S. (1978). *Patterns of Attachment: A Psychological Study of the Strange Situation.* New Jersey: Lawrence, Erlbaum Associates.

Bandura, A. (1973). *Aggression: A Social Learning Analysis,* Englewood Cliffs, New Jersey: Prentice-Hall.

Belsky, J. (1980). Child maltreatment: an ecological integration. *American Psychologist* 35: 320–335.

Belsky, J. (1988). Child maltreatment and the emergent family system. Chapter 17 in K. Browne, C. Davies & P. Stratton (eds): *Early Prediction and Prevention of Child Abuse,* pp. 267–287. Chichester: Wiley.

Bentovim, A. (1991). Clinical work with families in which sexual abuse has occurred. In C.R. Hollin & K. Howells (eds): *Clinical Approaches to Sex Offenders and their Victims,* pages 179–208. Chichester: Wiley.

Bergner, R.M., Delgado, L.K. & Graybill, D. (1994). Finkelhor's risk factor checklist: a cross validation study. *Child Abuse and Neglect 18(4):* 331–340.

Berkowitz, L. (1989). Laboratory experiments in the study of aggression. In J. Archer & K. Browne (eds): *Human Aggression: Naturalistic Approaches,* page 42–61. London: Routledge.

Berliner, L. & Wheeler, J.R. (1987). Treating the effects of sexual abuse on children. *Journal of Interpersonal Violence 2:* 415–434.

Bowlby, J. (1969). *Attachment and Loss, vol. 1, Attachment.* London: Hogarth.

Bowlby, J. (1984). Violence in the family as a disorder of attachment and caregiving systems. *American Journal of Psychoanalysis 44(1):* 9–31.

Browne, K.D. (1986). Methods and approaches to the study of parenting. Chapter 12 in W. Sluckin & M. Herbert (eds): *Parental Behaviour*, pages 344–373. Oxford: Blackwell.

Browne, K.D. (1988) The nature of child abuse and neglect: an overview. Chapter 2 in K.D. Browne, C. Davies & P. Stratton (Eds). *Early Prediction and Prevention of Child Abuse*, pages 15–30. Chichester: Wiley.

Browne, K.D. (1989*a*). The naturalistic context of family violence and child abuse. Chapter 8 in J. Archer & K. Browne (eds): *Human Aggression: Naturalistic Approaches*, pages 182–216. London: Routledge.

Browne, K.D. (1989*b*) The health visitor's role in screening for child abuse. *Health Visitor* 62: 275–277.

Browne, K.D. (1993). Violence in the family and its links to child abuse. *Bailliere's Clinical Paediatrics 1(1):* 149–164.

Browne, K.D. (1994). Child sexual abuse. In J. Archer (ed.): *Male Violence*, pages 210–230. London: Routledge.

Browne, K.D. (1995*a*). The prediction of child maltreatment. In P. Reder (ed.): *The Assessment of Parenting*, pages 118–135. London: Routledge.

Browne, K.D. (1995*b*). Preventing child maltreatment through community nursing. *Journal of Advanced Nursing* 21: 57–63.

Browne, K.D. & Herbert, M. (1995). *Preventing Family Violence*. Chichester: Wiley. In press.

Browne, K.D. & Lynch, M.A. (1994). Prevention: actions speak louder than words. *Child Abuse Review 3(4):* 240–243.

Browne, K.D. & Parr, R. (1980). Contributions of an ethological approach to the study of abuse. Chapter 6 in N. Frude (ed.): *Psychological Approaches to Child Abuse*, pages 83–99. London: Batsford Press.

Browne, K.D. & Saqi, S. (1987). Parent–child interaction in abusing families: possible causes and consequences. In P. Maher (ed.): *Child Abuse: An Educational Perspective*, pages 77–104. Oxford: Blackwell.

Browne, K.D. & Saqi, S. (1988*a*). Approaches to screening families at high risk for child abuse. Chapter 5 in K.D. Browne, C. Davies & P. Stratton (eds): *Early Prediction and Prevention of Child Abuse*, pages 57–85. Chichester: Wiley.

Browne, K.D. & Saqi, S. (1988*b*). Mother–infant interactions and attachment in physically abusing families. *Journal of Reproductive and Infant Psychology 6(3):* 163–282.

Browne, K.D., Davies, C. & Stratton, P. (1988). *Early Prediction and Prevention of Child Abuse*. Chichester: Wiley.

Buss, A.H. & Derkee, A. (1957). An inventory for assessing different types of hostility. *Journal of Consulting Psychology* 21: 343–349.

Carroll, J. (1994). The protection of children exposed to marital violence. *Child Abuse Review, 3(1):* 6–14.

Central Statistical Office (1994). *Social Focus on Children '94*. London: HMSO.

Coleman, K.H. (1980). Conjugal violence: what 33 men report. *Journal of Marriage and the Family 6:* 207–313.

Creighton, S.J. (1992). *Child Abuse Trends in England and Wales 1988–1990*, 80 pages London: NSPCC.

Creighton, S.J. & Noyes, P. (1989). *Child Abuse Trends in England and Wales 1983–1987*. London: NSPCC.

Crittenden, P.M. (1985). Maltreated infants: vulnerability and resilience. *Journal of Child Psychology and Psychiatry 26(1):* 85–96.

Crittenden, P.M. (1988). Family and dyadic patterns of functioning in maltreating families. Chapter 11 in K.D. Browne, C. Davies & P. Stratton (eds): *Early Prediction and Prevention of Child Abuse*, pages 161–189. Chichester: Wiley.

Davis, L.V. & Carlson, B.E. (1987). Observation of spouse abuse: what happens to the children? *Journal of Interpersonal Violence 2(3):* 320–345.

DeLozier, P. (1982). Attachment theory and child abuse. In C.M. Parkes & J. Stevenson-Hinde (eds): *The Place of Attachment in Human Behaviour*. London: Tavistock.

Departments of Health, Education and Science, Home Office and Welsh Office (1991). *Working Together under the Children Act 1989*. London: HMSO.

Department of Health (1994). *Children and Young Persons on Child Protection Registers Year Ending 31st March 1993, England*. Department of Health Personal Social Services Local Authority Statistics. London: HMSO.

Department of Health and Social Security (1986). *Working Together*. London: HMSO.

Dollard, J., Doob, L.W., Miller, N.E., Mowrer, O.H. & Sears, R.R. (1939). *Frustration and Aggression*. New Haven: Yale University Press.

Edmunds, G. & Kendrick, D.C. (1980). *The Measurement of Human Aggressiveness*. Chichester: Ellis Horwood (Wiley).

Egeland, B. (1988). Breaking the cycle of abuse: implications for prediction and intervention. Chapter 6 in K.D. Browne, C. Davies & P. Stratton (eds): *Early Prediction and Prevention of Child Abuse*, pages 87–102. Chichester: Wiley.

Elmer, E. & Gregg, G. (1967). Developmental characteristics of abused children, *Pediatrics 40:* 596–602.

Finkelhor, D. (1980). Risk factors in the sexual victimization of children. *Child Abuse and Neglect 4:* 265–273.

Finkelhor, D. & Baron, L. (1986). Risk factors for child sexual abuse. *Journal of Interpersonal Violence 1(1):* 43–71.

Freud, S. (1964). New Introductory Lectures on Psychoanalysis (1932–36). London: Hogarth Press.

Friedrich, W.N. & Boroskin, J.A. (1976). The role of the child in abuse: a review of the literature. *American Journal of Orthopsychiatry 46(4):*, 580–590.

Frude, N. (1980). Child abuse as aggression. In N. Frude (ed.): *Psychological Approaches to Child Abuse*, pages 136–150. London: Batsford.

Frude, N. (1989). The physical abuse of children. Chapter 7 in K. Howells & C. Hollin (eds): *Clinical Approaches to Violence*, pages 155–181. Chichester: Wiley.

Frude, N. (1991). *Understanding Family Problems: A Psychological Approach*. Chichester: Wiley.

Galdston, R. (1965). Observations of children who have been physically abused by their parents. *American Journal of Psychiatry 122(4):* 440–443.

Garbarino, J. (1977). The human ecology of child maltreatment. *Journal of Marriage and the Family 39(4):* 721–735.

Gayford, J.J. (1975). Wife battering: a preliminary survey of 100 cases. *British Medical Journal 25(1):* 94–97.

Gelles, R.J. (1973). Child abuse as psychopathology: a sociological critique and reformulation. *American Journal of Orthopsychiatry 43:* 611–621.

Gelles, R.J. (1983). An exchange/social control theory. In D. Finkelhor, R. Gelles, M. Straus & G. Hotaling (eds): *The Dark Side of the Family: Current Family Violence Research*, pages 151–165. Beverly Hills, California: Sage.

Gelles, R.J. (1987). *Family Violence*, 2nd edn, Library of Social Research No. 84. Beverly Hills, California: Sage.

Gelles, R.J. & Cornell, C.P. (1990). *Intimate Violence in Families*, 2nd edn. Beverly Hills, California: Sage.

Gerson, L.W. (1978). Alcohol-related acts of violence. *Journal of Studies on Alcohol 39:* 1294–1296.

Gil, D. (1970). *Violence Against Children.* Cambridge, Massachusetts: Harvard University Press.

Gil, D. (1978). Societal violence in families. In J.M. Eekelaar & S.N. Katz (eds): *Family Violence,* pages 14–33. Toronto: Butterworths.

Gilbert, P. (1994). Male violence: towards an integration. In J. Archer (ed.): *Male Violence,* pages 352–389. London: Routledge.

Goddard, C. and Hiller, P. (1993) Child sexual abuse: Assault in a violent context. *Australian Journal of Social Issues. 28(1):* 20–33.

Goldstein, J.H. (1986). *Aggression and Crimes of Violence,* 2nd edn. Oxford: Oxford University Press.

Gough, D. (1994). *Child Abuse Interventions.* London: HMSO.

Gully, K.J. & Dengerink, H.A. (1983). The dyadic interaction of persons with violent and non-violent histories. *Aggressive Behaviour 9(1):* 13–20.

Howells, K. (1989). Anger management methods in relation to the prevention of violent behaviour. Chapter 7 in J. Archer & K. Browne (eds): *Human Aggression: Naturalistic Approaches,* pages 153–181. London: Routledge.

Hughes, H.M. & Barad, J. (1983). Psychology functioning of children in a battered women's shelter: a preliminary investigation. *American Journal of Orthopsychiatry 53(3):* 525–531.

Hyman, C.A. (1978). Non-accidental injury. A report to the Surrey County Area Review Committee on child abuse. *Health Visitor 51:* 168–174.

Hyman, C.A. & Mitchell, R. (1975). A psychological study of child battering. *Health Visitor 48:* 294–296.

Hyman, C.A., Parr, R. & Browne, K.D. (1979). An observation study of mother–infant interaction in abusing families. *Child Abuse and Neglect 3:* 241–246.

Jaffe, P., Wolfe, D., Wilson, S. & Zak, L. (1986). Similarities in behaviour and social maladjustment among child victims and witnesses to family violence. *American Journal of Orthopsychiatry 56:* 142–146.

Jaffe, P.G., Wolfe, D.A. & Wilson, S.K. (1990). *Children of Battered Women,* 132 pages Beverley Hills, California: Sage.

Kadushin, A. & Martin, J. (1981). *Child Abuse: An Interactional Event.* New York: Columbia University Press.

Kempe, T.S. & Kempe, C.H. (1978). *Child Abuse.* London: Fontana/Open Books.

Krugman, R.D. (1986). The relationship between unemployment and physical abuse of children. *Child Abuse and Neglect 10(3):* 415–418.

La Fontaine, J.S. (1993). Defining organised sexual abuse. In K.D. Browne & M.A. Lynch (eds): Special issue on organised abuse. *Child Abuse Review 2(4):* 223–231.

Levine, E.M. (1986). Sociocultural causes of family violence: a theoretical comment. *Journal of Family Violence 1(1):* 3–12.

Lewis, B.Y. (1987). Psychosocial factors related to wife abuse. *Journal of Family Violence 2(1):* 1–10.

Lorenz, K. (1966). *On Aggression.* New York: Harcourt, Brace and World.

Lynch, M. & Roberts, J. (1977). Predicting child abuse. *Child Abuse and Neglect 1:* 491–492.

Maccoby, E.E. (1980). *Social Development: Psychology Growth and the Parent–Child Relationship.* New York: Harcourt Brace Jovanovich.

Martin, H.P. & Rodeheffer, M. (1976). Learning and intelligence. In H.P. Martin (ed.): *The Abused Child: A Multi-disciplinary Approach to Developmental Issues and Treatment.* Cambridge, Massachusetts: Ballinger.

National Society for the Prevention of Cruelty to Children (1985). Child abuse deaths. *Information Briefing No. 5*. London: NSPCC.

Novaco, R.W. (1978). Anger and coping with stress. In J.P. Foreyt, D.P. Rathjen & D.P. Rathjen (eds): *Cognitive Behaviour Therapy*. New York: Plenum.

Olds, D., Henderson, C., Chamberlin, R. & Tatelbaum, R. (1986). Preventing child abuse and neglect: randomized trial of nurse home visiting. *Pediatrics 78*: 65–78.

Pahl, J. (1985). Violent husbands and abused wives: a longitudinal study. In J. Pahl (ed.): *Private Violence and Public Policy*, pages 23–94. London: Routledge and Kegan Paul.

Patterson, G.R. (1982). *Coercive Family Process*, Oregon: Castalia Publications.

Patterson, G.R. (1986). Maternal rejection. Determinant or product for deviant child behaviour. In W.W. Hartup & Z. Rubin (eds): *Relationships and Development*. Hillsdale, New Jersey: Lawrence Erlbaum Associates.

Persky, H., Smith, K.D. & Basu, G.K. (1971). Relation of psychological measures of aggression and hostility to testosterone production in man. *Psychosomatic Medicine 33*: 265–277.

Rohner, R.P. (1986). *The Warmth Dimension: Foundations of Parental Acceptance–Rejection Theory*. Beverley Hills, California: Sage.

Rosenberg, M.S. & Repucci, N.D. (1983). Abusive mothers: perceptions of their own and their children's behaviour. *Journal of Consulting and Clinical Psychology 51(5)*: 674–682.

Roy, M. (1982). *The Abusive Partner*. New York: Van Nostrand Reinhold.

Rutter, M. (1985). Aggression and the Family. *Acta Paedopsychiatrica 6*: 11–25.

Schultz, L.G. (1960). The wife assaulter. *Journal of Social Therapy: 6*: 103–112.

Smith, S. (1975). *The Battered Child Syndrome*. London: Butterworths.

Social Services Inspectorate (1990). *Child Protection in London: Aspects of Management Arrangements in Social Service Departments*, September 1990. London: DHSS.

Sonkin, D., Martin, D. & Walker, L. (1985). *The Male Batterer: A treatment approach*. New York: Springer.

Starr, R.H. (1982). *Child Abuse and Prediction: Policy Implications*. Cambridge, Massachusetts: Ballinger.

Starr, R.H. (1988). Pre and perinatal risk and physical abuse. *Journal of Reproductive and Infant Psychology 6(3)*: 125–138.

Steele, B.F. & Pollock, C.B. (1968). A psychiatric study of parents who abuse infants and small children. In R.E. Helfer & C.H. Kempe (eds): *The Battered Child*, pages 103–147. Chicago: University of Chicago Press.

Steinglass, P. (1987). *The Alcoholic Family*. London: Hutchinson.

Straus, M.A. (1980). A sociological perspective on causes of family violence. In R. Green (ed.): *Violence and the Family*, pages 7–13. New York: Bould & Westview.

Straus, M.A., Gelles, R.J. & Steinmetz, S.K. (1988). *Behind Closed Doors: Violence in the American Family*, 2nd edn. Beverley Hills, California: Sage.

Toch, H. (1969). *Violent Men*. Chicago: Aldine.

Wasserman, G.A., Green, A. & Allen, R. (1983). Going beyond abuse: maladaptive patterns of interaction in abusing mother–infant pairs. *Journal of American Academy of Child Psychiatry 22(3)*: 245–252.

Willis, D.J., Holden, E.W. & Rosenberg, M. (1992). *Prevention of Child Maltreatment*. New York: Wiley.

Wolfe, D.A. (1985). Child abuse parents. An empirical review and analysis. *Psychological Bulletin 97*: 461–482.

Wolfe, D.A. (1991). *Preventing Physical and Emotional Abuse of Children*. New York: Guildford.

Wolfe, D.A. (1993). Child abuse prevention: blending research and practice. *Child Abuse Review 2:* 153–165.

Wolfe, D.A., Fairbank, J., Kelly, J.A. & Bradlyn, A.S. (1983). Child abusive parents and physiological responses to stressful and nonstressful behaviour in children. *Behavioural Assessment 5:* 363–371.

4

Characteristics of Sexual Abusers

Stephen Frosh

Introduction

This chapter focuses on a specific subgroup of child abusers, those who abuse sexually*. To a considerable degree, there may be overlaps between sexual and non-sexual abusers of children. For example, at least some sexual abuse is associated with physical abuse, and sometimes with extreme abuse such as torture. There may be similarities in attitudes towards children, degree of psychopathology, personal history, social isolation, level of intergenerational continuity and other characteristics (see Kaufman and Zigler, 1989; Feshbach's (1989) account of lack of 'empathy' in physical child abuse is also reminiscent of many clinical descriptions of sexually abusive behaviour). Browne (1993) notes similarities between those 'who physically and sexually abuse their children, those who abuse their wives, and those who abuse their aged relatives' as including:

> 'a misperception of the victim, low self-esteem, sense of incompetence, social isolation, a lack of support and help, lack of empathy, marital difficulties, depression, poor self-control, and a history of abuse and neglect as a child.' (Browne, 1993, page 152.)

More generally, the ambivalent social attitudes and values surrounding children – for example, that they are the property of adults but that they are also entitled to protection, or that they are individuals but must also do what adults demand of them – may be contributory factors to all forms of abuse, seen as a destructive manifestation of adults' power over children.

On the other hand, there are ways in which sexual abusers may be different from those who abuse children physically, or who neglect them. In particular, only some sexual abuse involves overt acts of violence towards the child (see Glaser and Frosh, 1993). The seductive behaviour and degree of planning employed by some paedophiles may also mark them out as different from non-sexual abusers, whose

* I would like to acknowledge the influence on this chapter of a presentation of 'Sexual offenders against children' made by Dr Eileen Vizard at the Tavistock Clinic in the autumn of 1992.

behaviour is characterised more by an inability to respond appropriately to their children's cues or to deal with relatively minor difficulties before they escalate (see Rutter, 1989). There may also be meaningful differentiations to be made regarding the identity of the abuser. Whereas in the field of physical abuse, the roles of abuser and care giver are very likely to be (but are not invariably) fused, a far greater proportion of sexual abusers of children are not their primary care givers (see Glaser, 1993).

From the point of view of understanding the characteristics of abusers, a crucial question concerning the relationship between sexual and non-sexual forms of child abuse is that of the degree to which sexual abuse is actually *sexual*, that is, concerned with the sexual gratification of the adult over and above the use of power to assert the adult's will over the child. It will be argued below that this is indeed a component of sexual abuse – that the sexual element is no accident or irrelevance – and that degree of sexual arousal in response to children is one of the few features which can reasonably reliably be shown to discriminate between sexual abusers and non-abusers. Furniss (1991) goes so far as to suggest that the main difference between physical and sexual abuse is that the 'addictive egosyntonic' aspect of sexual abuse – the 'kick' the abuser gets from it – is generally absent in all but the most severe forms of physical abuse. According to Furniss, this is specifically due to the sexual aspect of sexual abuse – the pattern of arousal and release that creates both dependence and a denial of dependence in the perpetrator.

There are other characteristics which differentiate sexual and non-sexual abusers, the most important of which is gender. The high preponderance of male sexual abusers differs from the pattern amongst non-sexual abusers of children (Meier, 1985). As will be seen, recognition of this gender imbalance and its possible connection with sexual socialisation fuels some of the currently existent theories about sexually abusive behaviour. Nevertheless, the overlaps mentioned above should not be lost sight of. All forms of child abuse involve an assertion of adult power over children, a betrayal of trust and dependence, and a disavowal of the protective and nurturing elements in adult psychology upon which children rely for the creation of a stable and supportive developmental context.

Methodological Issues

Research in the area of child sexual abuse has always been fraught with methodological difficulties, ranging from divergences in definition resulting in non-comparable studies, to the ethical issues involved in comparing the effectiveness of various forms of therapy or no-treatment for children who have been sexually abused (Haugaard and Emery, 1989; Glaser and Frosh, 1993). Sample selection has also been a problem, with children identified through social services or mental health facilities probably being a select group of the wider population of abused children, as the differences in incidence and gender distribution suggest (Haugaard and Reppucci, 1988). All these factors also apply in research on sexual abusers. There are variations in definitions and in the usage of terms such as 'abuser', 'offender' and 'paedophile'. There is confusion as to the extent to which findings about incestuous abusers can be generalised to cover non-incestuous abusers and vice versa. There are problems connected with the reliance of research on incarcerated offenders, as most abusive acts probably remain undetected and certainly go unpunished. And there is the possibility that certain types of abusers, e.g. middle-class abusers, may be systematically less likely to be discovered and prosecuted (Bentovim *et al.*, 1988). In addition, the criminal justice system in Britain and in the United States does not encourage abusers to admit their guilt and responsibility for their actions, something which has deleterious effects both on research and on the well-being of victims.

Araji and Finkelhor (1986) propose that it might be possible to differentiate between the various terms employed to describe abusers in the literature on logical grounds, with 'sexual abuse' and 'child molesting' referring to behaviours which can also be regarded as indicators of the existence of the underlying state of 'paedophilia'. With regard to the latter term, they write:

> 'We define paedophilia as occurring when an adult has a conscious sexual interest in prepubertal children. We infer that sexual interest from one of two behaviours: (1) the adult has had some sexual contact with a child (meaning that he or she touched the child or had the child touch him or her with the purpose of becoming sexually aroused), or (2) the adult has masturbated to sexual fantasies involving children. Thus we are defining paedophilia to be a little broader than sexual abuse or child molesting. It includes the conscious fantasising about such behaviour, too.' (Araji and Finkelhor, 1986, pages 90–1.)

They also note that paedophilia 'can be a state and not necessarily a trait' (ibid.), thus producing a very broad category of which convicted offenders, who represent the standard research sample, are only a very small subsection. While one can appreciate the rationale behind the distinction between sexually abusive behaviours and the hypothesised or actual underlying state from which they arise, creating a category of paedophilia which includes fantasy with no attached activity as well as overt sexual abusiveness towards children is highly problematic. Using the terms associated with Finkelhor's own model of sexual abusiveness (see below), this obscures the important dynamic of inhibition – the barrier between impulse or desire, and action. If there are systematic connections between, for example, masculine sexual socialisation in general and sexual abusiveness, the question of why only some men translate their desires into actions is an important one, and one which does not seem to be totally answered by stating that only some men have the requisite opportunity.

Given the inchoate state of research into sexually abusive behaviour towards children, it is probably better to follow the advice given by Haugaard and Reppucci (1988) in regard to classifying sexually abused children. They advocate providing as clear and exact as possible an account of the actual behaviour in question, leaving issues of differentiation and classification to be worked out empirically. Hence, 'incestuous' or intrafamilial abusers should be identified separately from abusers who focus on children outside their own family. Those who abuse in the context of a relationship should be categorised differently from those who abduct children they do not know. Those who only have sexual relations with children should be considered independently from those whose sexuality is more promiscuous and undifferentiated. And so on. In particular, given what has taken place in the research literature, generalisations from sexual *offenders* to sexual abusers of all kinds should be treated with the utmost caution – there are all sorts of reasons why some abusers pass through the criminal justice system and others do not. The question of which, if any, of these or other possible groups is genuinely 'paedophiliac' is not at present an issue of primary significance.

These guidelines are easier to make than to adhere to, given the confusion which prevails in the literature. In what follows, the available data on the characteristics of sexual abusers are outlined, and some theoretical points are made as to how to understand and explain the psychology of sexual abusiveness. However, it should be noted that there is a high level of methodological uncertainty in all the reported studies, described repeatedly in reviews in the area, so all integrative and theoretical efforts are more speculative than might be desirable. There is insufficient space here for a full methodological critique of the material employed, even if this would have been helpful, but where possible the strength or weakness of the research evidence is indicated. Unless otherwise noted, however, all quoted research findings in the area should be handled with care, and grandiose claims should be automatically discounted.

Research on Abuser Characteristics

One of the most notable features of the literature on child sexual abuse is the extent of agreement over the gender distribution of abusers. It is men and adolescent boys who make up the vast majority of abusers. All the studies which have investigated the question have uncovered only a very small proportion of female abusers, at most 4% where the victims are girls (Russell, 1983) and 20% where the victims are boys (Finkelhor, 1984). Finkelhor comments that:

> 'Especially since contacts with female children occur with at least twice or three times the frequency as [those with] male children, the presumption that sexual abusers are primarily men seems clearly supported.' (Finkelhor, 1984, page 177.)

In arriving at these conclusions, Finkelhor suggests that the reasons for a preponderance of male abusers is unlikely to be due simply to abuse by women going undetected, because the findings apply to retrospective non-clinical surveys, and also because they remain constant even when only sexual 'contacts' rather than 'abuses' are asked about.

Nevertheless, there is some more recent evidence that the numbers of female abusers may have been systematically underestimated in the past. For example, Lawson (1993) points out that the majority of documented cases of mother–son abuse are found in the clinical rather than in the survey literature. 'These reports indicate that cases of mother–son sexual abuse are more likely to be disclosed in long term therapeutic treatment, are rarely reported to child abuse authorities (or rarely treated seriously), and are not included in public statistics.' (Lawson, 1993, page 261.) Wakefield and Underwager (1991) note the existence of a great range in the estimated frequency of child sexual abuse by females in different studies. According to these researchers, there are widely differing circumstances under which women abuse children, and these may in turn be different from those circumstances under which men abuse. Many studies depict female abusers as socially isolated, alienated, coming from abusive backgrounds and having emotional problems, although most are not psychotic. This seems to suggest a more homogeneous group than is the case for male abusers, but the research is still much too unclear to establish this with any degree of confidence.

Despite recognition of the way the numbers of female abusers may have been underestimated in the past, there remains little doubt that the great majority of abusive acts are perpetrated by men, and it is the characteristics of such men with which the research literature is primarily concerned. Given how much of this literature focuses on incest, it is worth noting first that the stereotypical notion that most abuse is incestuous abuse by fathers or step-fathers is not completely accurate. Just as much abuse is perpetrated by other relatives, family friends (who may concurrently incestuously abuse their own children) or other adults in positions of power over the children concerned. In Baker and Duncan's (1985) study, 49% of abusers were known to their victims and 14% of all reported abuse took place within the family. Girls were more likely to have been abused by parents, grandparents or siblings, while boys were more at risk from people outside the family but known to them. Russell (1983) found that abusers were usually not relatives, but also were not likely to be strangers. Only 11% were total strangers, 29% were relatives and 60% were known to the victims but were not related to them. Within the extrafamilial abuse group, 40% of abusers were classified as 'authority figures'.

It is quite clear from the literature that sexual abuse of children is often a repetitive act and that it may have 'addictive' components. However, despite the claim by Furniss (1991) reported above, it is uncertain to what extent this is due to the specifically sexual element of the abuse or to other elements such as the exploitation of power. For example, Herman (1981) suggests that some incestuous fathers enjoy the unhappiness of their victim, implying that the power–denigration dynamic is operating. On the other hand, as others such as Finkelhor (1984) have pointed out, this does not mean that the sexual component of sexual abuse is not also bound up with this same dynamic. Whatever the cause, there is good evidence that amongst convicted abusers there are very few 'one-off' offences. Although one cannot be sure that this picture extends to non-convicted abusers, it seems unlikely that an unpunished addictive act should be repeated less frequently than a punished one, even if it is the case that the convicted group are caught partly because of their repetitive behaviour. In the most quoted study in this area, Abel et al. (1987) found that the total number of sexual acts against children committed by 561 sexual offenders in their outpatient treatment programme was 291 737. The subgroup of offenders with the largest number of victims were the 155 non-incestuous paedophiles targeting male children – they admitted to a total of 29 981 victims between them. The incestuous paedophiles had a much smaller number of victims (an average of under two each), but as one would expect they tended to commit more sexual acts per victim. In a similar study of 129 outpatient child molesters by Murphy's group, quoted by Murphy et al. (1991), the offenders against males averaged 376 victims, the offenders against females outside the home five victims, and the incest cases one victim. Reviewing material of this kind, Conte (1991) comments that the findings 'raise questions about the validity of the assumption that the initial referral diagnosis (e.g. father or step-father incest) has any significance in understanding the nature of the incest father or step-father's problem.' (Conte, 1991, page 26.)

On the face of it, the data do suggest a potentially useful distinction between the abuse which occurs within the context of a relationship (such as incest) and other kinds of abuse. However, this distinction is called into question by other data demonstrating at least some overlap between these different groups of abusers. For example, in a further study by Abel et al. (1988), 49% of the incestuous fathers and step-fathers referred for outpatient treatment at their clinics abused children outside the family during the same time period when they were abusing their own children. Eighteen percent of these men were raping adult women at the same time as they were sexually abusing their own child.

In a similar vein to the evidence concerning the widespread nature of abusers' sexual acts, it also appears that a more formal psychiatric evaluation of their sexuality calls into question any claim that paedophilia or incest is a specific and circumscribed disorder. Again, working with an offender group, Abel et al. (1988) found that the average number of sexual disorder diagnoses (paraphilias) elicited from sexual offenders in treatment was 2.02. On the other hand, the number of paraphilias is not unlimited. Marshall et al. (1991) interviewed 129 outpatient child molesters (91 non-familial, 38 father–daughter). Fourteen percent of the non-familial offenders against boys, 11.8% of the non-familial offenders against girls and 7.9% of the incest offenders had one or more paraphilias in addition to their index offence. However, only three individuals in the total sample had more than two additional paraphilias.

Given the frequency with which at least convicted offenders abuse children, and the extent to which their sexual disturbance seems to spread, it is perhaps not surprising to discover that there is a considerable amount of pessimism concerning recidivism. Finkelhor (1986) reviewed the literature available up to the mid-1980s, finding recidivism rates between 6% and 35% for sexual offences, with general agreement that abusers of boys and exhibitionists are most likely to repeat their offences. However, he points out serious problems with most of the studies, undermining the certainty of any conclusions. For example, recidivism is often measured in terms of new convictions, and the studies themselves only apply to convicted offenders, who are a selected group. The finding of lower rates for incest offenders may also be unreliable, as they might need very long follow-ups to control for the possibility of intergenerational (e.g. grandfather–grandchild) abuse. In a slightly more recent review, Furby et al. (1989; page 27) comment that, 'The vast majority of existing studies either do not give a breakdown of their sample in terms of offender type or do not present recidivism results separately for each type'. In those that do, recidivism for paedophiles tends to be lower than that for exhibitionists and rapists, and there may also be lower rates for homosexual versus heterosexual paedophiles. The actual recidivism figures in the studies are between 7% and 35%, but variations in samples and follow-up times, as well as in type of treatment received, make these difficult to interpret.

A considerable amount of laboratory-based research has been carried out on the sexual responsiveness of sexual abusers, again focusing primarily on convicted offenders. In their 1986 review (page 101), Araji and Finkelhor comment, 'There is a fairly impressive body of experimental evidence suggesting that [child molesters] are indeed unusually sexually responsive to children.' However, it was not clear to them whether all molesters are sexually responsive to children under laboratory conditions, with incest offenders being the most likely exceptions. On the whole, amongst contradictory data, it seems likely that whereas non-abusive males seem to show a substantial increase in arousal to children 14 years and older, offenders may be more aroused by younger children. For example, Marshall et al. (1986), using the favoured penile plesythmographic method, found child molesters to be maximally aroused by 9-year-old children, although they were also aroused by adults. Conte (1991), reviewing the area notes as follows.

'Some studies have found that physiological sexual arousal measures can discriminate between violent and less violent offenders. . . In addition, child molesters respond differentially to adult and child stimuli, with more arousal to child stimuli (both male and female children), however a sample of normals selected from the community and non-sexual offenders responded only to adult, consenting stimuli.' (Conte, 1991, page 28.)

Quinsey and Chaplin (1988), on whose work Conte bases part of his conclusion, also showed that arousal to children and women may involve both sexual and sadistic images of victims, and that physically violent child molesters are more sexually responsive to scenarios involving gratuitous violence (sadism) towards victims than are non-violent offenders.

Some caution needs to be exercised in interpreting these findings, however, as there are also contradictory data obscuring any neat divisions between offenders and 'normals'. For instance, Hall *et al.* (1988) suggest that up to 80% of sexual offenders do not respond to supposedly sexually arousing stimuli under laboratory conditions, while Freund *et al.* (1972) found that a group of non-paedophiliac community volunteers showed significant penile tumescence to female children as young as 6 years of age. Frenzel and Lang (1989) showed erotic and sexually neutral movie clips of males and females aged between 6 and 25 years to 62 heterosexual intrafamilial abusers, 57 heterosexual and 25 homosexual extrafamilial abusers, and 47 community controls. Penile volume changes were recorded during the 30-second presentations. Homosexuals in the sample reacted most to pictures of 13–15-year-old boys. This discriminated them from other groups. Intrafamilial abusers overlapped considerably with controls, and only 10% showed a pattern of responses expected for the 'classical paedophile' (i.e. largest responses to female children). This implies that abusers are more heterogeneous in their sexual preference profiles than has previously been suggested in the literature. Murphy *et al.* (1991) argue on the basis of this and similar evidence that penile plethysmography or phallometry measuring erection responses to deviant stimuli does not give a specific response profile for all sex offenders, or for certain types of offender. Its utility for legal and model-building purposes is therefore limited. Overall, it is likely that the laboratory studies have exaggerated the difference between abusers and non-abusers. This suggestion is supported by other forms of evidence. For example, Briere and Runtz (1989), in a study of male university students, found that 21% reported sexual attraction to some small children, 9% described sexual fantasies involving children, 5% admitted to having masturbated to such fantasies, and 7% indicated 'some likelihood' of having sex with a child if they could avoid detection and punishment. These are higher rates than would be expected from the number of university students who actually are known to abuse children.

Other suggestions concerning the possible personality characteristics of abusers also receive only mixed support from the empirical literature. Araji and Finkelhor (1986) comment,

> 'there seem to be a number of investigators who are in general agreement that child molesters are immature or inadequate. . . . However, these investigators have often made broad and unwarranted inferences from test data and we believe that the hypothesis is not much advanced beyond the state of a clinical inference.' (Page 99.)

From clinical accounts, it seems that many sex abusers may have problems relating to women and 'possibly poor social skills and sexual anxiety contribute to this.' (Araji and Finkelhor, 1986, page 110.) However, when explored empirically it appears that heterosexual and bisexual paedophiles (but not, for obvious reasons, homosexual paedophiles) have average levels of sexual contact with adult females (e.g. Langevin *et al.*, 1985). This makes it less likely that paedophiles suffer greatly from what is sometimes tendentiously referred to as 'reduced outlets' for adult sexual gratification.

In addition, the meek and unassertive stereotype attached at least to paedophile abusers is undermined by research suggesting that violence may be a more common and integral part of the lives and sexual behaviour of some paedophiles and incest offenders than was previously believed (Langevin, 1985; Lang et al., 1988). For example, Langevin et al. (1985) quote data from the late 1970s suggesting that a half to two-thirds of sexual offenders of all types employ violence or serious threats of violence as part of their abusive behaviour. Again, it is uncertain to what extent this finding can be generalised to include non-incarcerated abusers.

The notion that alcohol abuse may be linked to sexual abuse, at least as a disinhibiting influence, is better supported in the literature (Langevin et al., 1985; Araji and Finkelhor, 1986). Many studies do support another common contention that a high proportion of convicted child molesters were themselves abused in childhood. However, the majority of these studies report rates well below 50%, making it apparent that this can by no means be seen as a full explanation of sexual abusiveness (Araji and Finkelhor, 1986). Usually, rates of under one-third are found. For example, Groth and Burgess (1979) report childhood sexual abuse in 32% of their sample, and Abel et al. (1984) similarly document rates of 24% (amongst abusers of girls) and 40% (amongst abusers of boys) for a past history of sexual abuse. Hanson and Slater (1988), reviewing the literature, suggest that 28% of sexual abusers of children were themselves sexually victimised in childhood – a rate similar to those found in other sexual or non-sexual offender populations. On the other hand, over 50% of Lang and Langevin's (1991) sample of paedophile and incest offenders had themselves been sexually victimised as children, and nearly as many had been physically abused. In general, then, it is likely that there is a raised incidence of sexual victimisation in the histories of sexual offenders against children, but it is less clear that this is different from other sexual offenders, and indeed it may be that all 'disturbed' populations show an increase in previous sexual abuse. In addition, the finding is mostly based on studies of incarcerated child molesters, and it is unclear how far it applies to a more representative group (Finkelhor, 1986) or how well it differentiates child sexual abusers from other sexual or non-sexual offender groups. Once again, the absence of studies of non-incarcerated abusers increases the tentativeness of any conclusions.

It should be clear from everything reported here so far that there is unlikely to be any simple typological system which can be used to classify child sexual abusers. Even setting aside the restriction that most of the evidence derives from work with convicted sexual offenders, there is an enormous amount of uncertainty and heterogeneity amongst the abuser population, and often what appear to be relatively strong findings (such as that available from the sexual preference research) melt away when one looks at them closely. The utility of theoretical systems will be returned to towards the end of this chapter, but the evidence thus far does seem to call into question conventional typologies such as that of Weinberg (1955), who proposed a division between abusers on the basis of whether they are 'endogamic', 'psychopathic' or 'paedophilic'. The more popular distinction between 'fixated' and 'regressed' abusers advanced by Groth et al. (1982) also looks rather shaky. Fixated abusers are supposed to have a primary sexual orientation to children, beginning in adolescence with no precipitating events and with males as the main targets. Regressed abusers reportedly have a primary sexual orientation to age-mates, so that sexual involvement with a child is a clear change in interest and behaviour, occurring usually at times of stress and primarily with female victims. But there is no empirical evidence to support the validity of this distinction, which was made using a prison sample, and there is some evidence against it. For example, Simon *et al.* (1992) studied 136 consecutive cases of convicted child molesters who had personality data available for inspection, finding a continuum rather than a dichotomy on the regression–fixation dimension. More generally, Murphy and Peters (1992) have argued that there is no research evidence to suggest that clinicians – using all the tools available – can profile sexual offenders with sufficient validity and reliability for use in criminal trials, and Conte (1991; page 25) comments that, 'reviews of the existing empirical literature have failed to identify a consistent psychological profile or set of characteristics which discriminates between sexual offenders and others.'

If it is unlikely that there is a psychological profile of the 'sexual abuser', it may be that what has to be examined is the extent to which contingent factors such as access to vulnerable children and absence of inhibiting forces are the crucial determinants of the likelihood of abuse. This unpalatable idea will be returned to below, but it is worth noting here that at least some offenders would support that view. Conte (1991), for instance, reports earlier research by his group in which a sample of sexual offenders treated in the community were interviewed about the victimisation process. These offenders claimed to have the ability to identify and use vulnerabilities in a potential child victim in order to gain sexual access to and maintain control over the child. Such vulnerabilities were defined in terms of 'status conditions' (e.g. living in a single-parent family), 'emotional characteristics' (e.g. a child who was needy, unhappy or shy) and 'situational factors' (e.g. the child was alone and unprotected). Such findings do not, of course, demonstrate that *any* man would abuse children given these circumstances, but they do indicate that the determinants of abusive behaviour consist of far more than just the personality characteristics of the abusers themselves. On the other hand, it also appears to be true that at least some paedophiles are extremely skilled at, and invest a great deal of energy and planning in, the task of obtaining access to vulnerable children; for example, by becoming responsible for children's homes and other institutions to which needy children might be sent. The extent to which the paedophilia predates the acquisition of a position of power, as opposed to its being constructed in the context of access to vulnerable children, is an open and currently unanswerable question.

Adolescent Abusers

Before discussing theoretical models of abuse, it is important to deal with a topic which has come to be of great interest recently – the large proportion of sexual abuses which seem to be perpetrated by adolescents. Kelly *et al.* (1991) found that 27% of their sample of abused 16–21-year-olds had been abused by adolescents. In the UK, 34% of males convicted for rape in 1985 were under 21 years of age (Lloyd and Walmsley, 1989, quoted in Bentovim, 1991). Davis and Leitenberg (1987; page 417), reviewing the literature on adolescent sex offenders, state that,

'Arrest statistics and victim surveys . . . indicate that about 20% of all rapes and about 30% to 50% of all cases of child sexual abuse can be attributed to adolescent offenders (. . .). In addition, approximately 50% of adult sexual offenders report that their first sexual offence occurred during adolescence.'

These arrest rates are probably substantial underestimates of the actual proportion of abusive acts carried out by adolescents, as a number of factors inhibiting legal action operate more strongly with adolescents than with adults (e.g. not perceiving the seriousness of abusive acts). Nevertheless, the arrest rates do give an indication of the scale of the problem, and it is of importance that the largest proportion of victims of adolescent male sexual offenders are younger children. For example, in a study by Feherenbach et al. (1986), 62% of victims were under 12 years and 44% were 6 years old or younger. Most of these boys' victims were female, but the proportion of male victims seems higher than in samples of adult abusers.

The seriousness of adolescent abusive acts is considerable. In a study of substantiated physical and sexual abuse carried out by care givers and resulting in entry of the child on the Iowa Child Abuse Registry for 1985–6, Margolin and Craft (1990; page 369) found that adolescents were the most severely sexually abusive care givers and represented a significantly higher proportion of those who committed sexual abuse than of those who committed physical abuse. 'Not only did adolescents account for 44% of all cases of child sexual abuse among non-parental care givers, a proportion which was more than twice that of any other care giver cohort, but . . . the sexual abuse they committed was more likely to involve threats, physical injury and intercourse than was true of older care givers.'

There is little empirical data bearing on the comparative attributes of adolescents who do or do not sexually abuse children. Davis and Leitenberg (1987; page 421) list the following clinical suggestions on possible aetiological factors: 'feelings of male inadequacy; low self-esteem; fear of rejection and anger towards women; atypical erotic fantasies; poor social skills; having been sexually abused; and exposure to adult models of aggression, dominance and intimidation.' Of these suggestions, a history of having been abused oneself seems to be the best supported in the general adolescent sexual offender group, although it is not clear how well these findings apply to those adolescents who abuse children (a subgroup of the whole). For example, Van Ness (1984) found that 41% of adolescent sex offenders reported histories of physical abuse or neglect, compared with 15% of a matched group of delinquents. Awad and Saunders (1991) conducted clinical assessments of 49 male adolescent sex offenders, revealing that most of them were recidivists, had a history of antisocial behaviour predating and coinciding with their sexual offences, and came from a disturbed family background. One-third of the sample had a history of physical abuse in childhood, but the authors state that sexual abuse could be confirmed in only two cases.

Bentovim (1991), noting the high proportion of adolescent abusers who appear to have been abused themselves, distinguishes between the situation with female abusers – of whom almost all seem to have been previously abused – and male abusers, for whom rates of about 50% are more characteristic. More generally, it is clear that many juvenile offenders of various kinds have a past history of physical and sexual abuse (e.g. Brannon et al., 1989), so it is unlikely that a specific causal mechanism operates to link abusive experiences with becoming a sexual abuser in adolescence oneself. As Bentovim (1991) suggests, a more subtle and yet broad set of factors must be operating, possibly connected with what he calls 'the notion that if during development a child is treated as a thing instead of a person, then he or she will treat the other as a thing'. Again, how closely this refers to specifically sexual forms of abuse is a moot point.

Towards a Theory of Sexual Abusiveness

The material presented in this chapter so far is deeply unsatisfying with regard to its coherence and implications for theory and practice. On balance, the research on male sexual abusers has found little to distinguish them from other offenders, and perhaps little to distinguish them from men in general, other than the possibility of an increased rate of prior history of sexual victimisation and some suggestion of unusually marked specific sexual interest in children. Part of the difficulty derives from the absence of studies of non-institutionalised abusers, which means that generalisations concerning the characteristics of most abusers (who do not get imprisoned) cannot be made. But it may also be true that the differences between abusers and non-abusers are rather subtle, residing more in a set of contingencies such as access to vulnerable children and an absence of other inhibiting factors, rather than being due to the psychological characteristics of the abusers alone. It is on the assumption that this is true that the most influential theoretical model of sexual abusiveness, that of Finkelhor (1984), is based (described and discussed below). The model suggests that there is some systematic component in male sexual socialisation particularly that contributes to the abusiveness of so many men – that is, there is something in most or all men which can trigger abusive acts given the appropriate circumstances. The next part of this section discusses one possible psychoanalytical and feminist-influenced reading of what these socialisation influences might be.

A major attraction of Finkelhor's 'four factor model' of child sexual abuse is precisely that it does not claim that abusiveness is the determinate product of any one elemental cause. The mixed and confusing evidence about the characteristics of abusers described earlier provides one argument why such a multifactorial model is required. More generally, the enormous range of behaviours which might be termed 'abusive' makes it unlikely that any one simple descriptive, let alone causal, framework will encompass all the relevant phenomena. An additional attraction of the model is that, even given the poor state of most of the research, the empirical evidence which exists can be incorporated into its claims.

Araji and Finkelhor (1986) describe the model as arising out of a review of the theories of sexual abusiveness, suggesting (page 92) that most of these theories,

> 'could be categorised as trying to explain one of four factors: (1) why a person would find relating sexually to a child to be emotionally gratifying and congruent (in the sense of the child fitting the adult's needs), (2) why a person would be capable of being sexually aroused by a child, (3) why a person would be frustrated or blocked in efforts to obtain sexual and emotional gratification from more normatively approved sources, and (4) why a person would not be deterred by the conventional social restraints and inhibitions against having sexual relations with a child.'

These four factors are then collected in the model to form a series of interconnections which may have sexual abuse as their outcome. For some of these connections there is empirical support. For most there is only speculation or logic, but they still offer the best available framework for conceptualising the complex pathways that may result in abusive acts. In summary, the suggested elements in each factor are as follows (adapted from Araji and Finkelhor, 1986, pages 93–4).

Factor 1: emotional congruence. Children attractive because of lack of dominance; arrested development/immaturity; low self-esteem; mastery of trauma through repetition; identification with aggression; narcissism; male socialisation to dominance.

Factor 2: sexual arousal. Heightened arousal to children; conditioning from early childhood experience; modelling from earlier childhood experiences; hormonal abnormalities; misattribution of arousal; socialisation through child pornography or advertising.

Factor 3: blockage. Difficulty relating to adult females; inadequate social skills; sexual anxiety; unresolved Oedipal dynamics; disturbances in adult sexual romantic relationships; repressive norms about sexual behaviour.

Factor 4: disinhibition. Impulse disorder; senility; mental retardation; alcohol; failure of incest avoidance mechanism; situational stress; cultural toleration; patriarchal norms.

From the overview of research evidence presented above, it will be apparent that many of the subsidiary elements in each factor are not supported by evidence, and that in some instances there is little apart from clinical reports to prop up an entire hypothetical factor. For example, few studies offer anything positive on Factor 3 (Blockage), and Factor 4 only really has supportive evidence from recordings of alcohol as a disinhibitor. Factor 2 also has equivocal support from the laboratory studies of sexual arousal, while Factor 1, while seeming very plausible, is again reliant on clinical reports and speculation for support. Once again, it has to be noted that research in this area is very insubstantial, and even the best and most cautious of models relies mainly on face validity and clinical appropriateness for its influence. But Finkelhor's approach does offer very specific suggestions for research, and is potentially falsifiable and improvable – hallmarks of a move towards something a little less speculative for the future.

As mentioned above, one of the implications of the multifactorial approach is that, given certain circumstances, many men could be abusers. Upon inspection of the model, it is interesting how many of the suggestions in each factor are couched at a fairly general social level, concerned with masculine dominance, repressive sexual norms, the influence of pornography, and so on. This reflects a painful question facing all men working in the area of sexual abuse: to what extent must abusiveness be seen as an element of masculinity, as opposed to an attribute only of some (pathological) men? The difficulty of establishing clear differences between abusers and others suggests that the shared abusive potential of men might be more general than one might wish. These questions, along with the influence of feminist thinking on sexual violence in general, have led to some attempts to piece together a model of masculine sexual socialisation that might have some explanatory power and also suggest ways forward for therapy, prevention and even – over-optimistically perhaps – social change. One such theoretical perspective worthy of consideration arises from recent psychoanalytic thinking, coupled with a general project to try to analyse the components of contemporary masculinity. Here, I shall present the version of this approach given in Glaser and Frosh (1993). Interested readers are referred to Frosh (1994) for a fuller account, and to Jukes (1993) for a related description arising out of engagement in therapeutic work with violent men.

In recent years, feminist-influenced analyses of the characteristics of masculine sexuality have converged on the notion that at the core of the problematic elements is a combination of power and fear. Seidler (1985; page 169) comments,

> 'Masculine sexual identity is established through feeling superior to women we are close to and through establishing our sense of identity in a masculine competitive world. It is as if we only know how to feel good ourselves if we put others down.'

Traditional 'masculinity' focuses on dominance and independence, an orientation to the world which is active and assertive, valorising competitiveness and turning away from intimacy. The fear at the heart of this image is of emotion – that which makes us vulnerable and 'womanly'. Emotion is dangerous not only because it implies dependence, but also because (with the important exception of anger) it is alien, a representation of the maternal dimension with which masculinity is contrasted. This fear of emotion in turn makes men both over- and under-invest in sex. Sex is one of the few socially acceptable ways in which men can aspire to closeness with others, and as such it becomes the carrier of the unexpressed desires which men's emotional illiteracy produces. However, this same power of sex to produce emotionality makes it dangerous to men, whose identity is built upon the rejection of emotion. Sex then becomes split off, limited to the activity of the penis, an act rather than an encounter. It is also a means of taking up a particular place in the world of men: sexual 'conquest' as a symbol of male prowess. The link between such a form of masculinity and sexual abuse is inherent in the rejection of intimacy, producing the possibility of a slide from sex as achievement to sex as degradation of the other.

There are numerous different accounts of the processes that might construct masculinity along these lines, ranging from the sociobiological 'male sexual drive' discourse to radical feminist readings of masculine psychology as little more than an organisation of force relations to oppress women. The approach deriving from feminist psychoanalytic writers such as Chodorow (1978) and Benjamin (1988) has been particularly influential in its emphasis on the negative impact of gender-differentiated child care on the ability of boys to experience themselves as dependent and emotionally connected to others. In outline, such accounts of masculine development run something like this. At first, there is a tremendously powerful bond between infant and mother, an absorption of the one in the other which is bodily, relatively unmediated, perhaps already infused with anxieties and a horror of separation. Girls may have problems arising from this, problems of differentiation, of constructing a feminine self which is both bodily and autonomous, of entering the world of symbols and culture, and of becoming true 'subjects'. For boys, attaining masculinity involves striving towards something unknown and unknowable: a state of difference from the mother, yet grounded in her. The trend of early experience is to suck the boy in, to make him fused with the mother. But if fused he cannot become independent of her, nor take on the vague but intensely felt promise of masculine mastery. Consequently, his temptation is to repudiate the mother, a repudiation aided by her own fantasy of him as 'other', different from her, and also by the cultural fantasy that the masculine dominates the feminine.

The boy's sense of mastery, however, is far from secure. He knows that he is really dependent, that he cannot survive without help. Consequently, as a defensive manoeuvre against his own emotional needs, and reinforced by the cultural derogation of womanhood and the opposition between 'feminine' and 'masculine' qualities, the boy's ability to form intimate relationships is suppressed while his assertive, aggressive and spoiling elements are encouraged: 'the devaluation of the need for the other becomes a touchstone of masculine development.' (Benjamin, 1988, page 171.) Hence, 'successful' masculine socialisation involves effective action in the world at the expense of a fragile and underdeveloped emotional capacity, which fuels both an urgent demand for more closeness with the mother and a destructive rejection of her. Sexually, the boy learns to fear his desire, because it brings back the loss of mastery. Hence, its conversion into conquest and performance.

'The common product of this developmental process is an adult male whose capacity to nurture is severely impaired, whose ability to form affectionate relationships is restricted, and whose masculine identity, since it rests upon a repudiation of his identification with the person who first cared for him, is forever in doubt.' (Herman, 1981, page 56.)

There are several difficulties with this simplified and partial version of the psychoanalytic theory of masculine development. For instance, it is not clear how some people come to rebel against their traditional gender role, and it concentrates too strongly on the mother–child bond, neglecting a consideration of wider social processes (see Frosh, 1987). It does one important thing, however, and that is to move the discussion of the sources of sexual abuse away from specific traumatic events that occur almost accidentally to particular men towards those normative processes in socialisation that make sexual abuse possible. This is not to say that there may not be particular causes that create an abuser out of a particular man. Finkelhor's model supplies examples of just such possible causes, the experience of being abused oneself being a powerful one. Rather, the point here is that there may be systematic features of masculine sexuality that contribute to sexual abuse. Of course, this does not mean that all men abuse children, and the differences between those who do and those who do not are crucial for theory and for therapeutic practice. These differences may in principle arise from a number of sources: for example, the quality of early relationships as well as those formed during adulthood; challenges to emotional distancing faced during development; differences in patterns of gender socialisation; and specific experiences of trauma or reparation. But amongst all the vague and contradictory empirical data, the finding that most abusers are men seems a secure one, requiring explanation. The suggestion in this theoretical material is that the systematic links between masculinity and abuse are not given through biology, nor are they caused only by the organisation of society on patriarchal lines. Rather, they are constructed in the specific patterns of relationship and desire which are characteristic of masculine sexual socialisation. The painful mixture of impulse and over-control, of separation and intimacy, of fear and desire: this mixture so common in men is also something that infiltrates men's relationships with children, sometimes leading to abuse.

Implications for Practice

If the empirical and theoretical material described in this chapter offers reasonably strong evidence of anything, it is that sexual abusers are an extremely heterogeneous group; that they are a dangerous group because they are prone to abuse in multiple and repetitive ways and, when prosecuted and punished, their recidivism rate is not particularly low; that most abusers are male, although more women abuse than was previously thought; that many abusers are very young themselves, with abusing careers often beginning in adolescence; and that the sources of abusive behaviour lie in a mixture of individual history and shared socialisation processes.

Given all this, it is perhaps not surprising that attempts to draw up characterological profiles of abusers are unsatisfactory, and even that the work on sexual arousal patterns now looks less powerful than was once thought. Sexually abusive behaviour arises out of a particular cultural milieu in which sex is something done *to* another, and in which children are available for exploitation. It is linked with, but not specific to, the experiences of abuse suffered by some who go on to abuse others, and it may be closely connected with dynamics of power and powerlessness, and fears of inti-macy and dependence. Its repetitive nature suggests that it might have addictive components and thus may need to be managed cognitively and behaviourally. How-ever, an approach that does not separate 'sex' from sexuality and personality is needed for a fuller account of the meaning and potency of abusiveness. For this reason, and despite the lack of supportive empirical data, it is important that focused psychotherapeutic work with abusers continues alongside more cognitive–behavioural approaches. Currently, there is little evidence to support any one way of working over another – nothing seems to offer particularly good omens of success. But it may be that intensive therapeutic work across a range of theoretical orientations can lead to a better understanding of the nature and vicissitudes of abusive behaviour towards children.

A final point returns us to the problem of working only with incarcerated offenders. It is still extremely difficult to persuade abusers to enter into treatment programmes, because if they do so they are in effect admitting their responsibility or guilt for acts of sexual abuse, and they thus may incriminate themselves and receive substantial pun-ishment when they would otherwise not be prosecuted. Unfair though it may seem to some or even many victims of abuse, if any substantial impact is ever to be made on abusers it is going to be necessary to establish legal practices resulting in non-custodial, treatment-oriented interventions. This does not mean that such treatments will neces-sarily be effective. However, prison sentences do not work particularly well either, and therapeutic efficacy cannot develop unless it has a chance.

Conclusion

This chapter contains a presentation of some empirical and theoretical work on the characteristics of sexual abusers of children. It will be clear to the reader that the empirical situation is very unsatisfactory, partly for good reason given the endemic difficulties of researching an area in which secrecy, shame, dissimulation and obscurity are the norm. Most of the research is little more than clinical speculation, and where empirical studies have been carried out the sample populations concerned have usually been varieties of incarcerated sexual offenders, making generalisations to the wider population of non-convicted abusers problematic. It is important that future efforts both in research and in therapy move beyond this narrowly defined group, but it must be acknowledged that, given current legislation, this is going to be difficult to achieve. In particular, more focused studies of, and intervention programmes with, adolescent abusers are needed. It may be that such studies and programmes will also provide clearer documentation of the way in which social mores – especially those relating to the sexual socialisation of males – are linked to the production and perpetuation of sexually abusive behaviour.

References

Abel, G., Becker, J., Cunningham-Rathner, J., Rouleau, J., Kaplan, M. & Reich, J. (1984). *The Treatment of Child Molesters*. Unpublished manuscript, quoted in Conte (1991).
Abel, G., Becker, J., Mittleman, M., Cunningham-Rathner, J., Rouleau, J. & Murphy,

W. (1987). Self-reported sex crimes of non-incarcerated paraphiliacs. In R. Stuart (ed.): *Violent Behavior*. New York: Brunner/Mazel.

Abel, G., Becker, J., Cunningham-Rathner, J., Mittleman, M. & Rouleau, J. (1988). Multiple paraphiliac diagnoses among sex offenders. *Bulletin of the American Academy of Psychiatry and the Law 16:* 153–168.

Araji, S. & Finkelhor, D. (1986). Abusers: a review of the research. In D. Finkelhor (ed.): *A Sourcebook on Child Sexual Abuse*. London: Sage.

Awad, G. & Saunders, E. (1991). Male adolescent sexual assaulters: clinical observations. *Journal of Interpersonal Violence 6:* 446–460.

Baker, A. & Duncan, S. (1985). Child sexual abuse: a study of prevalence in Great Britain. *Child Abuse and Neglect 9:* 457–467.

Benjamin, J. (1988). *The Bonds of Love*. London: Virago, 1990 (Virago Edition).

Bentovim, A. (1991). Children and young people as abusers. In A. Hollows & H. Armstrong (eds): *Children and Young People as Abusers*. London: National Children's Bureau.

Bentovim, A., Elton, A., Hildebrand, J., Tranter, M. & Vizard, E. (1988). *Child Sexual Abuse Within the Family*. London: Wright.

Brannon, J., Larsen, B. & Doggett, M. (1989). The extent and origin of sexual molestation and abuse among incarcerated adolescent males. *International Journal of Offender Therapy and Comparative Criminology 33:* 161–172.

Briere, J. & Runtz, M. (1989). Post sexual abuse trauma. In G. Wyatt & G. Powell (eds): *Lasting Effects of Child Sexual Abuse*. London: Sage.

Browne, K. (1993). Violence in the family and its links to child abuse. In C. Hobbs & J. Wynne (eds): *Baillière's Clinical Paediatrics: Child Abuse*. London: Baillière Tindall.

Chodorow, N. (1978). *The Reproduction of Mothering*. Berkeley: University of California Press.

Conte, J. (1991). The nature of sexual offences against children. In C. Hollin & K. Howells (eds): *Clinical Approaches to Sexual Offenders and their Victims*. Chichester: Wiley.

Davis, G. & Leitenberg, H. (1987). Adolescent sex offenders. *Psychological Bulletin 101:* 417–427.

Feherenbach, P., Smith, W., Monastersky, C. & Deisher, R. (1986). Adolescent sexual offenders: offender and offense characteristics. *American Journal of Orthopsychiatry 56:* 225–233.

Feshbach, N. (1989). The construct of empathy and the phenomenon of physical maltreatment of children. In D. Cicchetti & V. Carlson (eds): *Child Maltreatment*. Cambridge: Cambridge University Press.

Finkelhor, D. (1984). *Child Sexual Abuse*. New York: Free Press.

Finkelhor, D. (1986). Abusers: special topics. In D. Finkelhor (ed.): *A Sourcebook on Child Sexual Abuse*. London: Sage.

Frenzel, R. & Lang, R. (1989). Identifying sexual preferences in intrafamilial and extrafamilial child sexual abusers. *Annals of Sex Research 2:* 255–275.

Freund, K., McKnight, C., Langevin, R. & Cibiri, S. (1972). The female child as a surrogate object. *Archives of Sexual Behavior 2:* 119–133.

Frosh, S. (1987). *The Politics of Psychoanalysis*. London: Macmillan.

Frosh, S. (1994). *Sexual Difference: Masculinity and Psychoanalysis*. London: Routledge.

Furby, L., Weinrott, M. & Blackshaw, L. (1989). Sex offender recidivism: a review. *Psychological Bulletin 105:* 3–30.

Furniss, T. (1991). *The Multiprofessional Handbook of Child Sexual Abuse*. London: Routledge.

Glaser, D. (1993). Emotional abuse. In C. Hobbs & J. Wynne (eds): *Baillière's Clinical Paediatrics: Child Abuse*. London: Baillière Tindall.

Glaser, D. & Frosh, S. (1993). *Child Sexual Abuse*. London: Macmillan.

Groth, A. & Burgess, A. (1979). Sexual trauma in the life histories of rapists and child molesters. *Victimology 4:* 10–16.

Groth, A., Hobson, W. & Gary, T. (1982). The child molester: clinical observations. *Social Work and Human Sexuality 1:* 129–144.

Hall, G., Proctor, W. & Nelson, G. (1988). Validity of physiological measures of pedophilic sexual arousal in a sexual offender population. *Journal of Consulting and Clinical Psychology 56:* 118–122.

Hanson, R. & Slater, S. (1988). Sexual victimisation in the history of sexual abusers. *Annals of Sex Research 1:* 485–499.

Haugaard, J. & Emery, R. (1989). Methodological issues in child sexual abuse research. *Child Abuse and Neglect 13:* 89–100.

Haugaard, J. & Reppucci, N. (1988). *The Sexual Abuse of Children*. London: Jossey-Bass.

Herman, J. (1981). *Father–Daughter Incest*. Cambridge, Massachusetts: Harvard University Press.

Jukes, A. (1993). *Why Men Hate Women*. London: Free Association Books.

Kaufman, J. & Zigler, E. (1989). The intergenerational transmission of child abuse. In D. Cicchetti & V. Carlson (eds): *Child Maltreatment*. Cambridge: Cambridge University Press.

Kelly, L., Regan, L. & Burton, S. (1991). *An Exploratory Study of the Prevalence of Sexual Abuse in a Sample of 16–21 Year Olds*. London: Polytechnic of North London.

Lang, R. & Langevin, R. (1991). Parent–child relations in offenders who commit violent crimes against children. *Behavioral Sciences and the Law 9:* 61–71.

Lang, R., Black, E., Frenzel, R. & Checkley, K. (1988). Aggression and erotic attraction towards children in incestuous and pedophilic men. *Annals of Sex Research 1:* 417–441.

Langevin, R. (1985). Pedophilia and incest. In R. Langevin (ed.): *Erotic Preference, Gender Identity and Aggression in Men*. New Jersey: Lawrence Erlbaum Associates.

Langevin, R., Hucker, S., Handy, L., Hook, H., Purins, J. & Russon, A. (1985). Erotic preference and aggression in pedophilia. In R. Langevin (ed.): *Erotic Preference, Gender Identity and Aggression in Men*. New Jersey: Lawrence Erlbaum Associates.

Lawson, C. (1993). Mother–son sexual abuse: rare or under reported? *Child Abuse and Neglect 17:* 261–269.

Margolin, L. & Craft, J. (1990). Child abuse by adolescent care givers. *Child Abuse and Neglect 14:* 365–373.

Marshall, W., Barbaree, H. & Christophe, D. (1986). Sexual offenders against children: sexual preference for age of victims and type of behavior. *Canadian Journal of Behavioral Science 18:* 424–439.

Marshall, W., Barbaree, H. & Eccles, A. (1991). Early onset and deviant sexuality in child molesters. *Journal of Interpersonal Violence 6:* 323–335.

Meier, J. (1985). Definition, dynamics and prevalence of assault against children. In J. Meier (ed.): *Assault Against Children*. London: Taylor & Francis.

Murphy, W. & Peters, J. (1992). Profiling child sexual abusers: psychological considerations. *Criminal Justice and Behavior 19:* 24–37.

Murphy, W., Haynes, M. & Worley, P. (1991). Assessment of adult sexual interest. In C. Hollin & K. Howells (eds): *Clinical Approaches to Sexual Offenders and their Victims*. Chichester: Wiley.

Quinsey, V. & Chaplin, T. (1988). Penile responses of child molesters and normals to descriptions of encounters with children involving sex and violence. *Journal of Interpersonal Violence 3:* 259–274.

Russell, D. (1983). The incidence and prevalence of intrafamilial and extrafamilial sexual abuse of female children. *Child Abuse and Neglect 7:* 133–146.

Rutter, M. (1989). Intergenerational continuities and discontinuities in serious parenting difficulties. In D. Cicchetti & V. Carlson (eds): *Child Maltreatment*. Cambridge: Cambridge University Press.

Seidler, V. (1985). Fear and intimacy. In A. Metcalfe & M. Humphries (eds): *The Sexuality of Men*. London: Pluto.

Simon, L., Sales, B., Kaszniak, A. & Kahn, M. (1992). Characteristics of child molesters: implications for the fixated–regression dichotomy. *Journal of Interpersonal Violence* 7: 211–255.

Van Ness, S. (1984). Rape as instrumental violence: a study of youth offenders. *Journal of Offender Counselling, Services and Rehabilitation 9:* 161–170.

Wakefield, H. & Underwager, R. (1991). Female child sexual abusers: a critical review of the literature. *American Journal of Forensic Psychology 9:* 43–69.

Weinberg, S. (1955). *Incest Behavior*. New Jersey: Citadel Press, 1976.

The Effects of Child Abuse: Signs and Symptoms

Helga Hanks and Peter Stratton

Introduction

An accurate evaluation of the effects of child abuse is fundamental in the protection of children from maltreatment. It is essential in specific cases to know what level of risk the child is exposed to by being left in the abusive family; what aspects of abuse are most damaging and therefore are the most urgent targets for protection; and what consequences, both short and long term, the child may need professional help to overcome. Also, much diagnosis and detection depends on working back from signs, physical and behavioural, in the child to forms of abuse known to produce these signs. At a service level, an estimate of the effects of abuse is needed to plan services, and to specify the training needed by workers. Nationally and internationally, a realistic understanding of the widespread and serious consequences of abuse would indicate the scale of need, the urgency of the problem, and the resources needed to tackle it.

At present there are many factors which work against being able to make even an approximate evaluation of the effects of abuse. This is true both for individual cases, and in the general context. The history of child abuse has been one in which clear medical evidence has been the first, and necessary, indicator before the problem was accepted. Even in physical abuse more than 30 years after Kempe's seminal article (1962) medical consequences of abuse are still regarded as more tangible evidence, and are better understood, than the psychological consequences. But the resistance to recognising the full range and severity of the effects of abuse goes much deeper. Abuse is a painful reality and everybody, given the chance, would prefer to avoid the pain of recognising it. Maybe our own relative terrors as children, or our inadequacies as parents are brought closer to awareness as we encounter obvious examples of abuse. And of course, many professionals who work in this field, have been victims of earlier maltreatment in their own lives. Finally, by confronting maltreatment we risk becoming aware of our own capacity to abuse and we risk being overwhelmed by the scale and horror of the problem.

Because of the variety of factors working against a clear recognition of the effects of maltreatment, we start this chapter with a consideration of two sources of difficulty: myths about children, and the power of denial. Next we provide a framework for understanding the consequences of maltreatment which is designed to give full weight to psychological as well as physical effects. The core of the chapter uses representative examples from the great volume of research and clinical experience to map out the major consequences in different areas of child maltreatment.

Perceptions of Children, or the 'Spoilt Child' – can we put the record straight

During the last century Western society has given considerable thought and discussion on the issue of how children should be brought up. We entered the so-called 'child centred' era. With hindsight we can easily detect deficiencies in earlier views, and with insight we may even criticise our current beliefs. Two themes that apply both to the past and the present relate to the idea that if children get their way they will become too powerful and the rather contradictory image of the child as a helpless recipient of influence.

For instance, Western societies put great emphasis on sameness, uniformity and despite what they often say, obedience, compliance and competition at the same time. The competitive struggle was proposed by politicians as an economic one (making money) but has become firmly established in the interpersonal and family sphere with at times destructive consequences. Partly because of this, the accepted way to bring up children is to mind that they are not made too comfortable, don't get their way even when it might be quite sensible, but for the parents always to win. The four hour feeding schedule is an example of compliance, sameness and teaching obedience. The child that cries at night must not be picked up and comforted; the child which has not eaten his/her dinner must not have a pudding; there must be no talking during mealtimes etc. These are just a few examples of what people generally think might spoil a child.

What word do we have for a child who is being treated really nicely, listened to etc.? The only word you will hear is that the child is being spoilt. Mothers are advised not to feed their baby whenever it shows signs of wanting food in case it becomes too powerful, learns how to exploit you, and is spoilt. Though it is not an original idea we would like to draw attention to what we consider to be the true meaning of a 'spoilt' child. Something being spoilt is defined in the dictionary as being damaged or injured, something made useless, valueless . . . destroyed. The abused, maltreated children are the children that are spoilt. The paradoxical juxtaposition of the meaning of 'the spoilt child' in the English language alerts us to a fundamental ambivalence about the rights of children. When attempting to help maltreated children professionals and parents alike have to take into consideration that these are the children that someone has tried to spoil in the 'real' (dictionary) sense.

This issue is important for another reason too. Many children, adolescents and adults who have been maltreated have over the years described how they feel. The cry from those who have been maltreated that they feel and are treated as 'damaged goods' is a stark reminder of what being spoilt really means.

The other myth, which can damage professional attempts to care for maltreated children, is of the child as passive recipient of influence. Our whole approach to child rearing, and to education reflects this assumption. We are very ready to talk of the effects of education, of child care practices, and of maltreatment on the child. It is much more difficult to recognise that children are active participants in creating their worlds. Perhaps we are afraid of blaming the victim; perhaps it is just easier to see things from an adult's point of view. But damage is not primarily something that can be put into a child to be carried around invisible inside them. Damaging environments are places in which children function and grow. The ways they function and the form of their growth will be affected and that is what we need to understand. It may be helpful to think in terms of the child adapting to the environment. The important effects of abuse are at least as likely to be in the kinds of adaptations the child comes to make as in simple direct consequences. This is an idea we return to after considering the second issue which obstructs the clear recognition of the effects of abuse.

Denial

'In every eye there is a spot that is incapable of sight. The optic disc exists as a black hole right next to the central point of clearest vision. Yet anyone who has not learned the trick of finding it would swear that there is no such void.' (Summit, 1988; page 51)

Kempe & Kempe (1978) pointed to the stages that society needs to go through in its progressive recognition of the reality of child abuse. These stages are progressive defences of denial to keep out a recognition of something that is unacceptable and at odds with the view we want to have of ourselves and our society. Equally we know very well that abused children may take refuge in denial to avoid the destructive effects of recognising what is being done to them. But in our experience, even committed professionals still have to use denial in self-protection (Summit, 1988).

Denial and the effects of abuse are intricately linked. The reader is referred particularly to Summit (1988) and Furniss (1991). The material that follows about the forms, function and areas of denial of Child Sexual Abuse (CSA) has been taken from Furniss (1991). *Forms of denial.* These can be seen in the context of the abuse being denied by the abuser, the non-abusing caretaker the child or other family members. Each of them might deny different aspects of the abuse. It may be total denial that any abuse has taken place or it can be partial denial:

- of the abusive circumstances;
- of the damaging effects;
- of the addictive and repetitive nature of CSA;
- and of the abuser's responsibility.

The function of denial. This can relate to anxieties about:

- the legal consequences;
- consequences for family and relatives;
- psychological consequences;
- social consequences;
- financial/work/career consequences.

Areas of denial to disclaim responsibility for abuse:

- primary denial of any abuse;
- denial of severity of acts;

- denial of knowledge of abuse (perpetrators may say they were drunk, asleep, depressed, tired, etc.);
- denial that the maltreatment was abusive. This may involve pretending that the abuse was a normal/educational activity;
- denial of the harmful effects of the abuse. The abusive act is said not to have harmed the child;
- denial of responsibility. The perpetrator makes the child responsible for the abuse, saying that the child triggered the abuse by his or her behaviour.

Child maltreatment is linked to denial because the pain, helplessness, worthlessness and rejection that children feel when they are maltreated has to be hidden in some way. We have many examples in Western Society which indicate that child abuse is much easier to blame on professionals who identify the children and the problem, than on an acknowledgement that all is not well in society and particularly in the family where unfortunately but undeniably most abuse takes place.
Case:

> Keely, who is 9 years old was in therapy because she had been severely maltreated all her life. She had been in care in a stable foster home for a number of months and recently began not only to disclose further specific incidences of her abuse but also to behave in a way that made it difficult to contain and look after her. She began hitting adults and children alike, ran away (the foster parents thought she was with older youngsters and experiencing sex), lied, stole and then felt terribly sorry, sobbing and pleading with the foster parents not to send her away. The discussions between the professionals and foster parents centred on the fact that Keely was going through a very difficult time. One way of explaining what is happening is as follows.

When children are maltreated consistently and severely (though what children can take varies from one to another), they have to build up some defences in order to bear what is happening to them. When there is no help to deal with the psychic pain, the pain becomes encapsulated, as if put into a sealed space. This idea comes from psychoanalytic literature and there is called encapsulation (Ferenczy 1949). The sealed space might be thought of as a nut with a shell that has become harder over time and all the painful, angry, desperate, etc., feelings are contained in this nut.

However, when children like Keely have the chance to 'open up' so to speak, feel secure to let the feelings come out through a crack in the nut's shell, what has been described above might occur.

When Keely talked in her therapy session about what had been happening in the last few weeks the therapist told her the story of the nut and said: 'it feels as if nobody knows the strength of the feelings that are in this nut. It is such a surprise to you to discover some of the terrible feelings of revenge and anger you might have inside that nut. So much so that you feel that you could kill someone (Keely had taken a broom and tried to hit her foster mother with it during the last week. She had also said afterwards that it was a terrible feeling because at that moment she could have killed her). The feelings are so strong that at that moment of discovery they are difficult to control'. Keely who had been sitting very still and listening burst into tears and wept bitterly.

Becoming very sad is one aspect of therapy that needs to happen when there has been abuse, and being angry is another. But these children with their strong feelings also need some very practical input. The therapist had a meeting with the child, the mother and the social worker and discussed with them the fact that Keely needed some help to manage her angry feelings. The issues about setting boundaries, what could be done and what could not be done by Keely were discussed particularly in relation to feeling and being out of control. It was suggested that she should try not to hurt either herself or others. The foster parents were asked to see Keely through these difficult times and not be afraid to call for help if they needed it from the social worker.

Once it is possible to recognise the range of factors which might make one underestimate the effects of abuse, we are better able to confront the huge amount of evidence on particular aspects of these effects. In order not to be overwhelmed by the complexity, we offer three sets of concepts to help co-ordinate the material: abuse as trauma; the child's adaptation to abuse; and the central issue of attachment.

Fundamental Concepts in Abuse

Trauma

Recent research on victims (often adult) of a variety of catastrophes has given us an understanding of the effects of trauma which is also very helpful in making sense of events surrounding abuse.

Bentovim (1992; page 24) points out that: 'Trauma comes from the Greek word meaning to "pierce". In the context of physical injury it implies that "skin is broken", that something intact has been breached. It implies a certain intensity of violence, with long-standing consequences for the organism. From the physical notion of trauma to the notion of psychological trauma arises: an event that in a similar intense or violent way ruptures the protective layers surrounding the mind with equally long-lasting consequences for psychic well-being. Helplessness overwhelms, mastery is undermined, defences fail, there is a sense of failure of protection, disintegration, acute mental pain as the memory of the event intrudes and replays itself repeatedly.' The traumatic stress response thus imperceptibly becomes the 'post-traumatic stress disorder'. This notion of trauma applies to any victim of a traumatic event. A car accident, floods, fires, earthquakes and more personal tragedies will all be included.

The physical pain is closely linked to the psychological experience and pain of the individual. There is a difference between adults experiencing trauma and when this happens to children. Something additional happens to children because they, by virtue of their age, are in a developmental stage in which they lack the perspectives by which adults can distinguish and make sense of the traumatic event in which they have been involved. Because trauma, and what it means to human beings, is a complex issue it is important to think about two major issues when considering the consequences of such an event:

- Short-term consequences;
- Long-term consequences.

It also has to be recognised that the effects of child abuse are dynamic and interact with each other; that the experiences and adaptations interweave and become part of the child's developmental process, shaping their view of the world and most importantly themselves.

So childhood trauma is likely to affect the child immediately – during and after the abuse – and this can cause post-traumatic stress, result in painful (physical and emotional) effects, and contribute to cognitive distortions (see Bowlby 1980) of all kinds. It will often influence the developmental stage the child is in at the moment of the abuse, and show itself in arresting development or slowing it down with the child's resources having to go into coping with the abusive situation.

Many children, sometimes after a brief period of protest, start developing ways of 'coping', as one might describe it, and keeping as safe as possible. Summit (1983) called this 'accommodation', others also described an important developmental process called 'adaptation' (see below). Both these processes are like psychological survival mechanisms and help the child and adult to cope with the continuing maltreatment. They may take the form of any behaviour the child thinks may keep them safe or lessen the immediate physical and emotional pain. It is well to note here that children who have been abused by a stranger once and then made safe will not have to engage in this accommodation of the abusive situation.

Trauma will also affect the child and adult in the long term. The long term consequences which will encompass the above two notions set adaptation and accommodation firmly into a defensive pattern from which some victims never return. These patterns become a more intrinsic part of the individual's functioning and are likely to generalise to other aspects of their psychological development throughout life.

> Zake, a 5 year old boy, had witnessed the brutal murder of his father, and had developed a way of existing in the world by abandoning speech and only humming tunes. He said later that he thought that if he only hummed tunes he could stop thinking of what he witnessed around his father's death, and if he could stop thinking about it then he would not feel so terrible.

Thinking of the unthinkable, experiencing and then re-experiencing painful and humiliating episodes is what the children attempt to avoid both in the short term and in the long term. But such psychological manoeuvres are not accomplished without a price. In order to repress such events considerable psychic energy has to be expended.

The developmental stage might be influenced in such a way that the child is arrested in his/her development at the time of the abuse. For instance many small children, though not all, who have been maltreated have very little language. Also cognitive distortions as a consequence of trauma: misunderstandings, memory loss, blocking and dissociation may occur.

Adaptations

It is often useful to take behaviour that we might describe as 'symptomatic', and instead see it as an adaptation the person has made. With adults, if we think of, say, depression as a symptom, there is a certain range of things we can think of doing to cure it. If we think of it as the best adaptation that a person could manage to the circumstances they are in, we can have different ideas about how it helps them; for instance whether they could achieve the same with some alternative adaptation; whether they could change the demands they have felt obliged to meet. The shift is not towards blaming them but to see them as having made the best response they could manage at the time, while opening up the possibility of helping them to make a more useful response from now on. Adaptation is a broader version of the ideas contained in the concept of accommodation.

To a large extent the emotional and behavioural effects that we see are attempts of the maltreated children to adapt to the environment surrounding them including their caretakers. From this point of view the behaviour of the child is not a 'symptom' but the best response they could make for their own protection. Think of a child who flinches every time someone moves suddenly anywhere near them. Classifying this as a symptom of twitchiness, or as a neurotic behaviour, is not only unhelpful; it is disparaging the child. Seeing it as an adaptive response to an environment in which you might be suddenly assaulted without warning makes more sense and also opens up ideas of what might be done about it.

A child's withdrawal and isolation from peers for instance may be the result of parental rules that wish for a quiet and unassuming child. Other parents may be irritated by a timid withdrawn child and respond angrily to the child who may adapt by putting on displays of aggressive behaviour. Some children find mealtimes traumatic because of emotional tension surrounding eating or at a more extreme level because they have had burning hot food forced into their mouths. They may adapt by using every way possible to avoid meals (and become labelled as 'poor feeders' as a result). Children who have been sexually exploited may adapt by using the sexual behaviour they have been 'taught' in order to obtain much needed cuddles from adults. Or they may provide the sexual behaviour to avoid punishment. Either way they may be further maltreated by having their adaptation labelled as a symptom of sexual promiscuity.

The ways that cycles of adaptation to abuse build up, and the implications of these cycles for treatment have been described in detail by Stratton and Hanks (1992). For the purposes of this chapter we would ask the reader to keep in mind that *all* of the consequences of abuse that have been identified should be thought of as adaptations by the child. The outcome of abuse can then be more clearly seen as following from the adaptation the child is forced into, and not just as a direct effect of the abuse itself.

Attachment relationships of maltreated children

Attachment is a specific relationship and human beings are quite unable to exist without it. For the infant and child it provides a base from which to explore the world and works in a way to ensure that the child's needs are met (Bowlby, 1988).

This exploration of the world is recognised as being vital for the infant's development and shows optimal effects when a parent figure is available to provide a secure base. A baby can attach to about 5 people who are close to the infant and develops the first most important steps of attachment during its first year of life. The role of the attachment figure(s) is to reduce anxiety in stressful situations and provide the infant and child with the confidence to explore and experience unknown and new situations. Attachment to significant adults in infancy is also the foundation for lasting relationships throughout life. So for instance, anxious attachment is often the consequence when a child has to take responsibility for keeping close to an attachment figure (most often the mother).

Infants and young children attach to figures who are their caretakers even when these caretakers are reluctant, neglectful and maltreating towards the child. What it encourages the child to do is to try harder, and stay closer, in their effort to make the situation more tolerable. It seems also that the children often believe that if only they behaved in a different way, or engaged in more of the same behaviours the adults would stop being maltreating. This issue of the children thinking and believing that somehow this abusive relationship is their fault feeds into the adaptational cycle of trapped attachments. Adults who have been maltreated as children, in later life often puzzle over why and how it was that they would run towards the caretaker or close adult and greet them warmly even though they were fully aware of the painful relationship and afraid of it.

Poor relationships may also occur because of the loss of a primary figure especially if this happens while the infant is between 6 month and 3 years. Also, multiple breaks and separations can have considerable consequences and cause more long term distress to the child. It needs to be acknowledged that some separations are inevitable and will not harm the child. In a 'good enough' environment, separations can in fact give a child the experience that they are safe even when, say, mother is not there, and also that she will return. However, longer term separations repeated over this sensitive period between 6 month and 3 years can lead to the child becoming very withdrawn and uncommunicative, agitated and anxious. Or the child may show in their behaviour that they cannot discriminate and are therefore inappropriately friendly and/or overfriendly to any adult, even someone strange to the child. For professionals this may become quickly obvious when a child on a first visit to a clinic for instance offers kisses and demands cuddles from people s/he has never met before.

The early attachment patterns are the foundation for future development. The pattern is a dynamic one and changes over time throughout the child's growth and development and depends on the experiences the child has. It is a powerful process and has strong links to the development of how the child and later adult perceive themselves. Children model their significant caretakers and will react to many situations with the model in their minds. This is particularly relevant when it comes to the maltreated child as a grown-up in a parenting position, when their experience becomes a model for their own parenting. Early attachment patterns influence the adult's way of behaving and form part of a cyclic pattern which has intergenerational consequences.

Physical Maltreatment and its Consequences

Physical abuse like all other forms of abuse has a strong emotional component, and disentangling the specific consequences of the physical and emotional aspect is not as yet possible. Physical abuse can vary from moderate to severe and in a considerable number of cases it can be fatal (Hobbs *et al.*, 1993). The review of the child abuse inquiries presented by Reder *et al.*, (1993) describes the devastating end of the continuum of all forms of child abuse and affords us some insight into the seriousness of the maltreatment of children.

Figures released by the NSPCC in their annual report (Creighton & Noyes, 1989) showed that over 8000 cases of physical abuse were placed on the register for England and Wales during 1987. These statistics also highlighted the fact that the natural parents inflicted over 90% of the injuries. Speight (1989) pointed out that diagnosing physical abuse or non-accidental injury is important not least because the maltreatment can be so severe that the child dies, or that brain damage persists and handicap is the consequence.

Wissow (1990; page 172) states that:

> 'homicide is among the leading causes of death for American children ages 1–14. . . Most of the deaths among children under the age of 3 represent fatal child abuse . . . A consequence so grave . . . our actions if there were any were too late, thoughts about prevention were either not there or so hesitantly formed they came too late and there is nothing we can make good about it'

Detailed descriptions of the issues can be found in Hobbs *et al*, (1993) and Wissow (1990), who address the medical issues and link them to psychological and emotional factors.

> 'Bruises are the most commonly encountered injury, followed by fractures and brain injury.' (Hobbs *et al.*, 1993.)

These authors pointed out (page 57) that 'abusive fractures usually result from the more extreme forms of violence and represent serious injury. They may co-exist with other signs of trauma: external, (e.g. bruises, scratches) or internal injuries. The internal injuries may result in subdural haematoma, retinal haemorrhage or internal injuries to the abdomen.'

Physical abuse results in the physical injuries which leave wounds to heal and scars visible. Such scars can occur from bruises, cuts, bites, kicks, marks from beatings with objects, burns, scalds. The invisible/internal injuries as in bone fractures, breaks, and other internal injuries can also be present. Powerful as these images of physical damage are, it is essential also to consider our three concepts: the trauma for the children in experiencing such assaults; the kinds of adaptations they will have had to make simply to try to survive; and the effects on attachment processes when their parents have maltreated them or failed to protect them. Psychological interventions need to go alongside the physical treatment for any of these injuries.

All professionals have to be vigilant in order to detect the physical injuries children present with, either in hospital and medical centres or in social services offices. Denial can occur when children are brought with obvious physical injuries just as much as with less visible or detectable signs in emotional abuse, sexual abuse or forms of neglect.

The effects of physical abuse are influenced by several factors that can either stand alone or arise in combinations. These factors are:

- the relationship of abuser to child;
- the nature of the abuse;
- the child's age;
- the child's development;
- how long the traumatic event lasted;
- how often the traumatic event was repeated.

For instance the more often the abusive situations are repeated, the more likely will it become that successive stages of development are affected. The effects are either disruptive to the developmental process of the child or halt it in a certain phase. This is often called being 'stuck', or fixated in a certain developmental stage.
Case:

> One of the children presenting for a medical absolutely and resolutely refused to take off his t-shirt to have his chest listened to. The doctor tried to persuade the child and eventually became firm, telling the child that he would not be hurt but that they had at

least to lift his shirt and put the stethoscope to his chest. When they lifted the garment the child let out a piercing yell as if he was very badly hurt. What the doctor saw was a chest full of scars from a burn which had occurred 2 years previously. The child became inconsolable and wept for a long time, kicking anyone who tried to come near him. A little later he told his mother that when the doctor lifted his shirt he felt as if he was back in the time and place when he was burnt 2 years ago. He said this happened every time he had to take his shirt off and that he had learned to keep it on. If he could keep a shirt on always, day and night he said, he would not see the scars, not be reminded of what had happened, and therefore not feel the pain over and over again. We know of course that this phenomenon is called 'flashback'.

'Flashbacks' are not only caused by such visible stimuli, but for children with physical injuries such as burns or badly healed breaks the injury is a constant reminder of what happened. As Bentovim (1992; page 25) pointed out when any human being has to 'cope with the uncopeable' the individual devises strategies, often quite unique and individual to avoid the stress which is caused. Bentovim said:

'The basic response is the replaying and re-enactment of the event thrust into experience, e.g. through flashbacks triggered by reminders, spontaneously, or during play, through dreams or nightmares. There are struggles to overcome these experiences by "avoidance" or attempts to delete reminders, avoiding places, people, situations that trigger memories; or through dissociation – a form of self hypnotism which blanks the experience out, creating a hole in the mind. Finally the overwhelming traumatic experience can induce a state of arousal and irritability, and can affect sleep and the ability to relax.'

Links between physical and psychological pain

Making links between the physical pain and emotional pain is an important step. It is also realistic to recognise that some children are more resilient than others and that the consequences of physical abuse do not in all cases lead to the same effects. What has to be acknowledged is that some effects are inevitable and that the length of time during which a child has been subjected to abuse as well as the severity of the injury are contributing factors in terms of effects.

Children who have been subjected to deliberate, and sometimes planned, harm have a very different experience of their treatment from those in whose care they grow up than children who may have been smacked or even hit hard by their caretakers but have been given explanations, ways of changing the cause which lead them to be chastised and possibly even an apology.

The well known facial expression of frozen watchfulness which can be seen in many maltreated children is there for a very long time if not for life. It relates to the mistrust of others, of feelings about being unsafe in an unpredictable position and the likelihood of being harmed at any time. Threats to the child's basic sense of security can trigger adaptations in the form of emotional responses ranging from anxiety and withdrawnness to angry and uncontrollable acting-out behaviour.

Major signs of physical maltreatment

- Stress related symptoms (tension, headaches, psychosomatic symptoms);
- being very alert and aroused as if in a constant state of readiness of an attack, sudden fear of being injured;

- intrusive thoughts appearing as if from nowhere;
- sudden intrusive thoughts and consequent action of being violent often perceived by others as uncontrollable aggressive impulses (see Keely's case);
- flinching as if for no specific reason;
- avoiding any thought or talk of the abusive event(s);
- dreams and nightmares of the traumatic abusive events.

Simultaneously, delays can include:

- developmental delays;
- delayed fine or gross motor development (gross: walking, jumping, climbing; fine: holding a pencil, picking things up, holding feeding implements etc.).

As the children get older the consequences can manifest themselves in:

- angry behaviour;
- depression;
- anxiety;
- dissociation which includes detachment and numbing effects;
- repression (developing a way of not consciously remembering the abusive event).

Unpredictableness of maltreatment and its consequences

The unpredictable nature of maltreatment is often an added strain on the child and later adult, which precludes having the time or energy to concentrate, learn, play, and form relationships. Instead it leaves the child with a need to be watchful, careful, predict when an attack might occur, pretend that nothing is worrying the child, etc. This pattern of alertness can be seen in adults who have been maltreated as children, and as in childhood it still prevents the adult from concentrating learning, and forming relationships.

There is also the issue of parental models. Children who have been maltreated often say as adults that hitting and punishing is the right way to bring up children, as if there is no other way.

Emotional Abuse and its Consequences

'Rather than casting psychological maltreatment as an ancillary issue, subordinate to other forms of abuse and neglect, we should place it as the centrepiece of efforts to understand family functioning and to protect children'. (Garbarino et al., 1988, page 7.)

Society's response to this form of maltreatment has been slow and lags behind. Wissow (1990) quite rightly reminds us that though it is now much more accepted that parents should pay more attention to their children in every respect, how they should relate to their children remains a controversial issue. He said (p158) that; 'while a warm and loving parent–child relationship is widely advocated as essential, significant minorities still feel that strict discipline and a certain detachment (especially from fathers) are important elements of child-rearing.'

It is not fully understood why children react differently in the face of maltreatment and why some show more severe consequences than others when they have had abusive experiences. Kagan et al. (1978) showed that how children perceive themselves, and how their inner self develops is of crucial importance. The self is influenced by both adults and peers and if a child receives persistently negative feedback then the child's view of him or herself will be affected.

There is no such thing as a perfect parent or a perfect child. Every parent will at some time or other behave towards the child in such a way that the child will be upset, may be frightened or feel rejected and suffer a loss of self-esteem, etc. What happens after this event of commission (an active or cruel behaviour towards the child) or omission (behaviour which neglects or ignores the child even when they are in unsafe or dangerous situations) in the adult's behaviour towards the child is what matters. The parents may manage to acknowledge and 'make good' the situation, giving the child appropriate alternative options for behaving. If reparation is made, the child learns that people/parents/caretakers can make mistakes but that they can recognise them as such. However, even 'the making good' of a poor/hurtful situation to the child is not going to be helpful if the situation occurs repeatedly. When the caretaking is constantly changing (doing hurtful things then making good), it becomes inconsistent and potentially damaging.

Garbarino *et al.* (1988) provided us with a helpful model which distinguishes between the different forms of emotional maltreatment:

- rejecting;
- isolating;
- terrorising;
- ignoring;
- corrupting.

These are the categories essential in order to recognise children who are maltreated emotionally. Childhood inevitably includes experiencing some of these patterns at sometime or other, but our capacity to cope with such treatment in an environment where it is repeated over and over again is fairly limited. Such behaviour delivered consistently towards a child is damaging.

Egeland *et al.* (1983) claim from their longitudinal study that emotional abuse has the most serious consequences for a child's social and intellectual development. These researchers showed for instance that verbal abuse and psychological unavailability as well as physical abuse and neglect produced children who presented with anxious rather than secure attachments and that they showed frustration, hostility and anger. Developmental skills also declined for the group of children having to live with verbal abuse and the unavailability of their parents. The children in this group were quickly frustrated when attempting tasks and approached new tasks feeling negative towards them and anxious. From this study, it seemed that children who were emotionally maltreated suffered more severe setbacks in their performance skills than those children who were physically abused or neglected. This is particularly important to recognise and gives an insight into the possibility that emotional abuse can be more damaging than physical abuse. The research indicated that this may be because the children who are physically harmed may receive this treatment more sporadically than those children who are emotionally abused whose maltreatment is much more likely to be a constant feature in their and their parents' lives.

Glaser (1993) developed a model that has enhanced our understanding further. She suggested that there are certain dimensions of emotional abusive or inappropriate relationships.

They consist of:

- persistent negative attitudes (negative attributions and attitudes, harsh discipline and over-control);
- promoting of insecure attachments (through conditional parenting);
- inappropriate developmental expectations and considerations;
- emotional unavailability;
- failure to recognise a child's individuality and psychological boundaries;
- cognitive distortions and inconsistencies.

Crittenden (1988) described different family patterns in maltreating families. For instance, the neglecting families had a pattern of ignoring the children, and these children – who were practically invisible to their caretakers – were passive and cognitively delayed before they reached year 1. As they grew older, their behaviours altered and they became 'uncontrolled and seekers of novel experiences'. At that stage, these children need a great deal of looking after and fall into the category of being abused by 'omission' as much as by 'commission'. Claussen and Crittenden (1991) showed that much psychological abuse intercorrelates with physical abuse and other forms of abuse of children and that when this happens the developmental risks increase accordingly. Both Wissow (1990) and Hobbs *et al.* (1993) would endorse these findings.

Non-organic Failure to Thrive (FTT) and its Consequences

Taylor (1976) stated what is in essence still echoed today when he said:

'The period between the start of weaning and the fifth birthday is nutritionally the most vulnerable segment of the human life cycle. Rapid growth, loss of passive immunity and as yet undeveloped acquired immunity against infection produce dietary needs more specific and inflexible than at later periods' (Page 820.)

We would add that special attention is necessary to the infant's needs in the feeding situation from birth onwards. It is recognised that many children, for example, 5% of an inner city population fail before the weaning period (Skuse, 1985; Hobbs *et al.*, 1993).

The consequences for children who fail to thrive for non-organic reasons are better understood now, and discussions about this can be found in Frank and Zeisel (1988), Boddy and Skuse (1994), Hanks and Hobbs (1993) and Hobbs *et al.* (1993). The overall

Table 5.1 The physical consequences of failure to thrive. (After Hobbs *et al.* 1993a, Hanks and Hobbs 1993)

Overall body shape:	thin and wasted, little fat.
Feet and hands:	may be swollen, red and cold.
Arms:	thin and when mid-upper arm circumference is measured it is low (Hobbs *et al.* 1993).
Stomach:	large and swollen.
Hair:	no shine, looks wispy, thin, is falling out
Brain:	can be retarded particularly in early months (Illingworth 1983, Frank and Zeisel 1988).
Physical growth:	can be permanently damaged including a poor posture.

Table 5.2 Developmental consequences of non-organic Failure To Thrive.

- Developmental delay
- Delayed motor development
- Delayed language development
- Delayed intellectual development
- Delayed social development
- Delayed behavioural development

consequences of FTT relate to developmental retardation and include motor, language, intellectual, social and behavioural components.

A definition needs to encompass the range – from the child not growing fully to his or her potential at one end and at the other end of the continuum, the situation being life threatening for the child (Table 5.1). Psychological aspects of development can be delayed, sometimes irreversibly, with emotional and cognitive deficits (Table 5.2).

It is interesting to note where different definitions put their emphasis. Is it something that the child is to be responsible for? 'The feeding interaction in FTT appears to be unsuccessful, because the child does not achieve an adequate nutritional intake.' (Boddy and Skuse, 1994; page 407); is it that 'the child refuses to gain weight in an appropriate manner' (Illingworth 1983); or is it that FTT results from feeding an infant inadequate calories – not enough food or an inappropriate diet? It is important for the practitioners to look at this and decide where to put their energies in terms of interventions. Failure to thrive in small children is a potentially life threatening situation and needs clear thinking which will not be helped by concentrating on deciding who is to blame.

Both parents and professionals alike find it difficult and emotionally taxing to recognise and acknowledge when a child fails to thrive, let alone realise that if nothing is done to remedy this state of affairs the consequences can be severe and at times lead to death. Iwaniec *et al.* (1985; page 251) pointed out that children who fail to thrive can show consequences which can lead to the child having a 'pattern of unmalleable behaviour, resistance to new routines' and that their 'general volatility of mood and behaviour, appeared to make them difficult to rear from early life. Feeding routines, and other training tasks, were made into fraught enterprises for many parents'.

This leads to a further complication in intergenerational terms and warrants detailed research. Hanks *et al.* (1995, in preparation) have shown that mothers' attributions and belief systems are powerful aspects in a situation where a child is failing to thrive. Understanding how they perceive the causes is crucial to any intervention in this relationship and to aiding the ultimate growth of the child. FTT is one situation in which the child's adaptation to mistreatment or mishandling may easily be misconstrued by a parent. The child's avoidance of the (possibly traumatic) mealtime may be interpreted as the child's wilfulness, or just lack of interest in food on the child's part, and so the underfeeding continues.

McCann *et al.* (1994) researched into the eating habits and attitudes concerning body shape and weight of 26 mothers who had children who were failing to thrive non-organically. These mothers, none of whom were either bulimic or anorexic, restrained their FTT children from eating, for instance, 'sweet' foods. Thirty percent of these mothers restricted their children in the consumption of foods which they considered fattening or not healthy. Despite the objective measurements of weight and height which were low in the FTT children, fifty percent of these mothers believed that their FTT children had 'normal' weights and thirty eight percent were convinced that their children's shape was the same as that of other ordinary children who did not fail to thrive. They did not seem to be able, for whatever reason, to perceive their children's position. This coincides with our clinical experience (Hobbs *et al.*, 1993).

Parents, grandparents and professionals have made the following comments when working with children who are severely failing to thrive and are well below the third centile in weight, look thin, and who are visibly much smaller than children of the same age:

- 'Not to worry we are all small in our family'.
- 'He runs around too much to put on weight, that is why he is thin and little'.
- 'His dad says he will catch up when he's older'.
- Grandmother said in the clinic; 'all my children were small when they were young, he will catch up, just leave him alone'.
- 'I will not have you think I don't feed him, he is to blame he won't eat'.
- 'I think you (Doctor, psychologist) are fussy, there are much thinner children on the estate where I work, you should see them and not worry his mother'.

Such statements indicate the difficulties caregivers can have while trying to protect themselves from the psychological distress of a child who does not eat. However this has considerable consequences for the child particularly when the lack of food intake continues because of such beliefs and makes it difficult to achieve change.

Observations of children eating

In an attempt to understand the mutual adaptations of parent and FTT child, we have been observing or if possible filming children during a main mealtime. Their eating behaviour and the families' rules about eating have often provided us with the information we needed in order to come up with adequate interventions.

The video recordings have also enabled us to detect some of the interactions that have become established in the pattern of poor feeding and how this has made itself felt in the child's behaviour and development.

Children can become frightened and stop eating when:

- the food is too hot and the child mouth is burnt during feeding;
- the pieces of food are too large and the child cannot chew them adequately;
- they are fed roughly and injured during feeding;
- they are left alone to eat the food and have no social contact.

Recognising the emotional consequences in FTT

The emotional consequences of FTT need to be assessed for each individual child. We have recognised that a checklist is helpful in determining how the child is emotionally behaving and what the carer's experience is in looking after the child.

Hobbs *et al.* (1993) compiled such a checklist which includes the child presenting as:

- still
- expressionless
- unresponsive

confused
insecure
anxious

- sad
- depressed
- not inquisitive
- minimal or no smiling
- little vocalisation
- detached

demanding
frustrated
frantically searching
tearful
angry
rejecting

This checklist is a guideline only. It is not a diagnostic tool but may help the professional and parent to recognise that behaviours like the ones listed above are often present in children who fail to thrive. Further it may help those involved to be more able to help the child in these areas rather than to ignore them.

Neglect and its Consequences

Neglect of children is one of the most obvious aspects of maltreatment where not only the caretakers of the children are responsible, but where the issue has to be widened to include society as a whole and a global view has to be adopted. As an example: the neglect of children in the Third World is the responsibility of the individual country, but also that of the industrialised nations who may exploit a Third World country's natural resources. Poor health care, poor education, drug addiction, crime and starvation are often the consequences on one level in society.

Helfer (1990) stated that it is within all our grasps to understand the consequences of a neglected childhood and how this permeates from one generation to the next. Hobbs *et al.* (1993; page 89) take this further and point out that 'Childhood is a vulnerable time and needs which are not met during the child's period of growth and development may have irreversible consequences'.

Neglect is defined in 'Working Together' (1991) as: 'The persistent or severe neglect of a child, or the failure to protect a child from exposure to any kind of danger, including cold or starvation, or extreme failure to carry out important aspects of care, resulting in the significant impairment of the child's health or development, including non-organic failure to thrive.'

Kempe and Goldbloom (1987) defined neglect as 'a very insidious form of maltreatment. It implies failure of the parents to act properly in safeguarding the health, safety and well-being of the child.'

The consequences of neglect, as in physical abuse, can range from death of a child through neglect (death from cold, starvation, lack of medical and daily care) to children who are dirty and unkempt, not stimulated to learn and left to their own devices, etc.

Hobbs *et al.* (1993) described the various patterns of neglect, including lack of car seat belts, helmets when cycling, lack of medical care, lack of hygiene in the home, clean food, drink and water, physical and emotional care and adequate supervision appropriate to the developmental stage of the child and teenager.

As with failure to thrive, there are cases in which the needs of the child are clearly not being met, but which it would not necessarily be appropriate to label as abuse. For example, if the parents fail to provide the kinds of interaction needed for the child to form attachments. We have suggested that the important task is to decide upon the child's requirements for healthy growth, and not be so concerned about apportioning blame (Stratton & Hanks, 1992). To some extent the decision will vary between cultures, and the decision about whose responsibility it is to provide these requirements will also vary. It is appropriate that we should have a progressive debate, and a progressive raising of the level of what we regard as essential requirements. In 1995 we would, for example, claim that there is clear evidence about the negative consequences for a child of having inadequate models of attachment relationships. The disruption to both the childhood and the long-term development seem to be serious enough to justify a claim that the child who is not given the basics of social development is suffering neglect.

Neglect is closely linked to emotional abuse in that, as a result of their neglect, the children often:

- are very passive in infancy;
- are sometimes very active, but totally unfocused when older;
- have a limited ability to attend to the behaviour of others;
- show significant developmental delay;
- have poor speech and learning ability;
- have poor ability to interact socially;
- are accident prone because they are not properly protected;
- may have stunted growth.

Sexual Abuse and its Consequences

Sexual maltreatment of children is the subject most written about during the last 15 years. It is in this area that more distinct categories of effects can be recognised. There is now considerable evidence (Kempe and Mrazek, 1981; MacFarlane and Waterman, 1986; Finkelhor, 1986; Wyatt and Powell, 1988; Furniss, 1991; Bentovim et al., 1988; Glaser and Frosh, 1988; Briere, 1992) to mention just some of the most influential texts on the matter of child sexual abuse, that CSA is an aversive and damaging experience to children, with often harmful effects in the long term.

Physical consequences.   Paediatricians, starting with Henry Kemp, have taken a lead in working in the area of abuse and sexual maltreatment. We recommend that the reader makes himself/herself familiar with the physical aspects of this form of abuse so that he/she can co-operate with medical staff in such situations. Texts to consult include Wissow, 1991; Hobbs and Wynne, 1993; Hobbs et al., 1993; Meadow, 1993. What is striking in CSA is that the physical injuries exist along a continuum from severe injury and death to no physical injuries at all.

Psychological consequences.   Effects of CSA may be short-term and long-term, and usually the child experiences both forms. Further division may be useful: 1) emotional and behavioural effects; 2) educational and learning; and 3) all forms of interpersonal relationships. The short-term effects of CSA can show in terms of: fear, anxiety, aggressive behaviours, angry outbursts, hostility and feeling got at (persecuted), and developmentally inappropriate sexual behaviour.

The long-term effects of CSA have been found in terms of: anxiety, depression, feeling isolated, lack of trust, poor self-esteem, self-harming behaviours (including eating disorders), dissociation, the range of traumatic and post-traumatic effects. Guilt and shame are invariably present.

It is sobering to reflect on the fact that potentially the list of effects on the child both short and long term can be overwhelming. We give some indication of the consequences below, dividing the most salient effects into three age groups. These effects may stand singly or present in clusters of behaviours, depending on each child's environment and specific situation.

For the pre-school child, the effects may show in:

- sexually explicit play and behaviour;
- wetting and soiling;
- delayed language and development;
- eating and sleeping problems;
- dysfunctional attachment behaviour;
- withdrawn or over-active states;
- aggressive behaviours (to self and others);
- clinging behaviour and becoming mute.

For the children between the ages of 6 and 12 years, the above effects may be recognisable with further elaborations:

- poor learning and concentration;
- heightened sexual behaviour and arousal;
- truanting and self neglecting;
- depression and anxiety;
- psychosomatic illnesses;
- physical risk taking;
- poor social skills;
- as if out of control at times;
- avoidance of men or women (depending on gender of abuser).

For the older child, the effects include any of the above-mentioned patterns with further escalations:

- sexually precocious behaviour and prostitution;
- solvent/alcohol/drug abuse;
- self harming and suicide attempts;
- anorexia and bulimia;
- changes in school performance;
- isolation from peers;
- starting to sexually abuse other children.

Overall, one may view the child's position in the following way. The difficulties of sexually abused children are:

- lack of individuation;
- poor interpersonal relationships;
- communication problems;
- inappropriate sexual behaviour and confusion about it;
- low self esteem, feelings of depression and anxiety;
- feelings of shame, guilt and powerlessness;
- feelings of dissociation;
- experiencing something akin to the 'damaged goods syndrome';
- trauma and post-traumatic stress syndrome.

The behaviours can have both a delayed and immediate impact on a child. What we have witnessed is that it can take a long time before certain behaviours emerge. Some consequences can emerge quickly, some emerge over time and then fade, yet others can be triggered by events such as having a baby, the death of the perpetrator, the death of a non-abusing parent, etc.

Vizard (1993) highlighted another dimension when she stated that:

'sexually abused children often behave in a confusing way in relation to the abuse experience. This may be because their experience of sexual abuse was itself confusing.'

She proposes three levels of experience:

1. the bodily experience;
2. the external world experience;
3. the inner world experience.

She also postulates that many children who have been subjected to CSA experience physiological arousal at the time of abuse and this results in a body memory. The memory is then lodged both as a thought and as a feeling, sexual and exciting in nature, which can give rise to a memory of sounds or visual images connected to the abusive situation. This feeling memory, so to speak, stands instead of the psychic memory of the actual event. So the intense experience of the act of CSA may have switched off the mind memory but activated the body memory. In children who have been chronically sexually abused this body memory can function quite independently. It also includes passive and active modes. The active body memory can present in physical arousal. The passive body memory may appear like a psychosomatic conversion (headaches, stomach aches, wetting and soiling, being mute). The stress factors related to this dimension are further discussed below.

Most professionals working in this area recognise that CSA has consequences which are difficult to overcome and usually leave the person with lifelong problems. The degree to which these problems rule a person's life can, as with all forms of maltreatment, vary. We have begun to talk to a very small group of people who experienced CSA as children but who feel they are leading a life which is not dominated by the consequences of this experience. What has made it possible for these people to be different is not quite clear. One of the recognisable factors is that they have been able to tell a trusted adult and that they have been believed and protected from that moment on. Another important factor seems to be that they have not been blamed for the event.

There is considerable evidence that CSA is an aversive experience for children. It has also been recognised that very young children often go through periods when they are not aware that the sexual contact imposed on them is abusive. As the children get older, they do become aware of the fact that they are involved in a relationship(s) which is wrong or disapproved of. Often, this awareness comes about when the child has been given an injunction to secrecy. The issue of secrecy in itself leads to considerable difficulties both for the children and those around them. Should the children attempt to disclose, they often enter into a world of denial, described above, and then into internal confusion.

Even if they have not been warned by the perpetrator, the children are often painfully aware of the consequences of releasing their secret. Not only will they be disapproved of in many cases, but also the turmoil created within their family or institution will be extremely painful to them and often result in they themselves being blamed. This recognition is often built in to the perpetrator repertoire of both 'grooming' the child and maintaining the abusive situation. The use of threats to silence children in intrafamilial CSA is common and includes the threat of loss of love, separation or physical harm.

Another important distinction has to be drawn between children who have been sexually abused within the family, and thus experienced incest, and those children who have been abused by someone outside the immediate family.

Incest at any age seems to leave considerable consequences, particularly in the areas of relationships, trust, closeness and dependency. If the incest started early in life and continued over time, the child is shaped into sexualised behaviours which are observable but difficult to overcome. Summit's (1983) 'Accommodation Syndrome' describes the position of the child and leaves no doubt about the consequences of incest and the breaking of the incest taboo. In respect of the sexualised behaviour so often witnessed when children have been abused over a considerable time, Kempe and Kempe (1984; page 190) pointed out that these children are 'trained to be a sexual object'. They also highlighted how in such circumstances, the children 'try to make each contact with any adult male an overt sexual event'. It is interesting that in 1985 sexual abuse by women was not discussed in public at least. However, it can now be said that women do abuse children sexually, and the same behaviour occurs for boys and girls abused by men and women (Hanks and Saradjian, 1991; Elliott, 1993; Mathews et al., 1989).

The effects of post-traumatic stress are described in (Finkelhor, 1988; Wyatt and Powell, 1988; Briere, 1993; Bentovim, 1993). Children and adults who experience traumatic responses to their abuse are often in the grip of that experience in a manner which is well outside their control. They may re-enact the events, engage in inappropriate sexual behaviours (hence the often witnessed sexualised behaviour), have visualisations of the event(s), have actual flashbacks, and triggering memories which obscure any concentration on ordinary aspects of their lives. It leads to avoiding places, things and people which may trigger memories of the event, and it can also lead to dissociation and sometimes multiple personality, deletion of memories, which further leads to irritability or distractedness.

For the adult the long-term difficulties can include problems in sexual adjustment or aversion to appropriate sexual contact. Equally, consequences can occur when the abused child grows up and has his or her own child. As parents, they may become overprotective (thinking I will never leave my child with any person because they may be abused), or they may be neglectful, not having had any experience themselves of being adequately cared for. Boundaries may be blurred and crossed, and closeness may be difficult to achieve. Once again, our increasing understanding of attachment is relevant here, but in sexual abuse in particular we think it is essential to think in terms of adaptation rather than deprivation. The child who experiences sexual abuse will have to adapt in ways that preserve their psychological and physical integrity as much as possible. Most adaptations will be in a form that leaves them resistant to forming trusting emotionally close relationships. Such adaptations, however sad, are entirely understandable. The challenge to the professional, and to society more generally, is to provide contexts in which the child can begin to explore alternative adaptations and so start to undo some of the harm that has been done to them.

Conclusion

One point we wish to make is that there is an important distinction relating to the intergenerational patterns of abuse. What we know about the repeating cycle of abuse is that many of the adults who sexually abuse have been abused sexually as children themselves. This connection is sometimes taken to mean that a sexually abused person automatically abuses sexually when they grow up. Many adult survivors voice this concern and feel as if they are doomed to repeat the pattern. What has to be added to the equation is that not every adult who has been sexually abused will become a perpetrator of abuse. Furthermore, we know of specific factors which can be protective, as discussed above and by Egeland (1988). What we can say is that when the history of those abusing children and adults is examined, it almost always shows that they have been abused as children themselves.

It is the issue of protective factors on which we wish to conclude. Much of the value of knowing about the consequences of abuse is that the knowledge is a first step towards effective protection of children. Knowing the common consequences alerts us to the possibility that abuse has occurred when we see children showing these signs. It indicates the tasks that treatment must undertake. And it enables us to identify maltreated individuals who have managed to avoid these consequences, and to discover what has been protective, or ameliorative for them. Recognising the full extent of the consequences of abuse may look like a dispiriting exercise. But when the positive potential of this knowledge is recognised, there is every good reason to continue to try to understand the significance of the harm that abuse does to children.

Acknowledgements:

To our patients – all the people who have entrusted us with their difficulties. The cases quoted in this chapter are composite cases so as not to break confidentiality of any specific individual and to respect peoples' trust. We would also like to thank Dr Chris Hobbs and Dr Jane Wynne for their support.

Annotated Books

Adcock, M., White R. & Hollows A. eds. (1991). *Significant Harm*. Croydon: Significant Publications.
This book centres on the 1989 Children Act which has had a profound influence on everyone's practice. It covers all forms of abuse. A must for every practitioner.

Bentovim, A. (1992). *Trauma Organised Systems*. London: Karnac Books.
Another important book by Bentovim discussing all forms of abuse and relating it to trauma organised systems and what that might entail for the child, family and professional involved.

Briere, J.N. (1992) *Child Abuse Trauma*. Newbury Park: Sage Publications.
This book describes the theory and treatment of the lasting effects of child abuse examining the interrelationship between the different forms of abuse and neglect with an emphasis on the trauma such experiences have on the victim of abuse.

Hobbs, C.J., Hanks, H.G.I. & Wynne J.M. (1993). *Child Abuse and Neglect – A Clinician's Handbook*. Edinburgh: Churchill Livingstone.
A textbook written with both the medical and therapeutic practitioner in mind. It has been described by reviewers as 'a landmark textbook in the field of child abuse and neglect'. The many tables, diagrams, drawings and the photography make the material accessible to the reader in a way that is quite unique.

Hobbs, C.J. & Wynne, J.M. (Eds). (1993). *Child Abuse. Balliere's Clinical Paediatrics*, Vol. 1, No.1, February 1993. London: Baillière Tindall.
This is an important collection by some of the most experienced writers in the field. It covers aspects of ritual abuse, the handicapped child and maltreatment, recent advances in radiology with reference to child abuse as well as interviewing children, emotional abuse, the cycle of abuse in adolescents as well as other contributions, 14 chapters in all. All very well written and relevant to the practitioner.

Wissow, L.S., (1990). *Child Advocacy for the Clinician – an approach to child abuse and neglect*. Baltimore: Williams & Wilkins.
Another important textbook combining physical issues of child maltreatment and psychological issues. A powerful and thorough piece of work combining the medical and psychological.

Wyatt, G.E. & Powell G.J., (1988). *Lasting Effects of Child Sexual Abuse*. Newbury Park: Sage Publications.
Outstanding contributions focusing on the effects of child sexual abuse.

References

Bentovim, A. (1992). *Trauma Organised Systems – Physical and Sexual Abuse in Families*. London: Karnac Books.
Bentovim, A., Elton, A., Hildebrand, J., Tranter, M. & Vizard, E. (1992). *Child Sexual Abuse within the Family*. London: Wright.
Boddy, J. & Skuse, D. (1994). Annotation: the process of parenting in failure to thrive. *Journal of Child Psychology and Psychiatry. 35(3): 401–424.*
Bowlby, J. (1988). *A Secure Base*. London: Routledge.
Briere, J.N. (1992). *Child Abuse Trauma*. Newbury Park: Sage Publications.
Creighton, S. & Noyes, P. (1989). *Child Abuse Trends in England and Wales 1983–87*. London: NSPCC.
Claussen, A. & Crittenden, P. (1991). Physical and psychological maltreatment: relations among types of maltreatment. *Child Abuse and Neglect 15: 5–18.*
Crittenden, P. (1988). Family and dyadic patterns of functioning in maltreating families. In K. Browne, C. Davies & P. Stratton (eds): *Early Prediction and Prevention of Child Abuse*. Chichester: Wiley & Sons.
Crittenden, P. & Claussen, A. (1993). Severity of maltreatment: assessment and policy. In C. Hobbs & J. Wynne (eds): *Baillière's Clinical Paediatrics – Child Abuse 1(1): 87–100.*
Egeland, B. (1988). Breaking the cycle of abuse. In K. Browne, C. Davies & P. Stratton (eds): *Early Prediction and Prevention of Child Abuse*. Chichester: Wiley & Sons.
Elliott, M. (ed.) (1993). *Female Sexual Abuse of Children*. Harlow: Longman Group UK.
Ferenczy, S. (1949). Confusion of tongues between the adult and the child. *International Journal of Psycho-Analysis 30: 225–230.*
Finkelhor, D. (1986). *A Sourcebook on Child Sexual Abuse*. Beverley Hills: Sage Publications.

Frank, D. & Zeisel, S. (1988). Failure to thrive. *Paediatric Clinics of North America 35:* 1187–1206.

Freud, S. (1914). Remembering, repeating and working through. In: *The Standard Edition of the Complete Psychological Works of Sigmund Freud 1950–1974.* London: Hogarth Press.

Furniss, T. (1991). *The Multiprofessional Handbook of Child Sexual Abuse.* London: Routledge.

Garbarino, J., Guttman, E. & Wilson Seely, J. (1986). *The Psychologically Battered Child.* San Francisco: Jossey-Bass Publishers.

Glaser, D. (1993). Emotional abuse. In C. Hobbs & J. Wynne (eds): *Baillière's Clinical Paediatrics.* London: Baillière Tindall.

Glaser, D. & Frosh, S. (1988). *Child Sexual Abuse.* London: Macmillan.

Hanks, H. & Hobbs, C. (1993). Failure to thrive: a model for treatment. In C. Hobbs & J. Wynne (eds): *Baillière's Clinical Paediatrics.* London: Baillière Tindall.

Hanks, H. & Saradjian, J. (1991). Women who abuse children sexually. *Human Systems Journal of Systemic Consultation and Management 2:* 247–262.

Hanks, H., Stratton, P., Bayliss, K. & Hobbs, C. (1994). Beliefs and actions around food when children are failing to thrive. In preparation.

Helfer, R. (1990). The neglect of our children in child abuse. *Paediatric Clinics of North America 37(4):.*

Hobbs, C.J. & Wynne, J.M. (1993). The evaluation of child sexual abuse. In: *Baillière's Clinical Paediatrics.* London: Baillière Tindall.

Hobbs, C.J., Hanks, H.G.I. & Wynne, J.M. (1993). *Child Abuse and Neglect – A Clinician's Handbook.* Edinburgh: Churchill Livingstone.

Illingworth, R.S. (1983). Weight and height. In: *The Normal Child, Some Problems of the Early Years and their Treatment.* Edinburgh: Churchill Livingstone.

Iwaniec, D., Herbert, M. & McNeish, A. (1985). Social work with failure to thrive children and their families. *British Journal of Social Work 15:* 243–259.

Kagan, J., Kearsley, R.B. & Zelazo, P.R. (1978). *Infancy: Its Place in Human Development.* Cambridge, Massachusetts: Harvard University Press.

Kempe, R. & Goldbloom, B. (1987). Malnutrition and growth retardation in the context of child abuse and neglect. In R. Helfer & R. Kempe (eds): *The Battered Child.* Chicago: University of Chicago Press.

Kempe, S. & Kempe, C. (1984). *Sexual Abuse of Children and Adolescents.* New York: W.H. Freeman & Co.

Kempe, C. *et al.* (1962). The battered child syndrome. *Journal of the American Medical Association 181:* 17.

Mathews, R., Matthews, J. & Speltz, K. (1989). *Female Sexual Offenders.* Orwell: The Safer Society Press.

MacFarlane, K. & Waterman, J. (1986). *Sexual Abuse of Young Children.* London: Holt, Rinehart & Winston.

McCann, J., Stein, A., Fairburn, C. & Dunger, D. (1994). Eating habits and attitudes of mothers of children with non-organic failure to thrive. *Archives of Diseases in Childhood 70:* 234–236.

Meadow, S. (1989). *ABC of Child Abuse.* London: BMA Publications.

Mrazek, P. & Kempe, C. (1981). *Sexually Abused Children and their Families.* Oxford: Pergamon Press.

Reder, P., Duncan, S. & Gray, M. (1993). *Beyond Blame – Child Abuse Tragedies Revisited.* London: Routledge.

Skuse, D. (1985) Failure to thrive: failure to feed. *Community Paediatric Group Newsletter.* (British Paediatric Association) August, pp. 6–7.

Speight, N. (1989). Non-accidental injury. In R. Meadow (ed.): *ABC of Child Abuse.* London: British Medical Journal.

Stratton, P. & Hanks, H. (1991). Incorporating circularity in defining and classifying child maltreatment. *Human Systems 2:* 181–200.

Summit, R. (1988). Hidden victims, hidden pain: societal avoidance of child sexual abuse. In G. Wyatt & G. Powell (eds): *Lasting Effects in Child Sexual Abuse.* Newbury Park; Sage Publications.

Taylor, C. & Taylor, E. (1976). Multifactorial causation of malnutrition. In D. McClaren (ed.): *Nutrition in the Community.* Chichester: Wiley & Sons.

Vizard, E. (1993) Interviewing sexually abused children. In C. Hobbs & J. Wynne (eds.) *Baillière's Clinical Paediatrics* London: Baillière Tindall.

Wissow, L.S. (1990). *Child Advocacy for the Clinician.* Baltimore: Williams & Wilkins.

Wyatt, G. & Powell, G. (1988). *Lasting Effects of Child Sexual Abuse.* Newbury Park: Sage Publications.

6

Issues of Ethnicity and Culture

Melanie Phillips

Introduction

Is it a social service to steal our culture
Is it a social service to take the fruit from the trees
Which our families grew
      Our ancestors knew
      That the fruit from the trees
      Which our families grew
      Is being stolen, social worker,
      By you.
(Sissay, 1988)

These are the powerful words of Lemn Sissay, a black poet and writer who grew up in care. They describe the anger and bitterness of many black children who experience the care system at first hand, and they are a powerful lesson to all professionals who work in child protection because they pose the uncomfortable question: what are we protecting children from?

The child abuse debate often centres on better ways of protecting children who are suffering or likely to suffer significant harm as a consequence of the care that they are receiving from their parents. In fact, the legal preconditions for statutory intervention to protect children from abuse in the Children Act 1989 is based on this concept of harm.

There is no doubt that there needs to be a system of state protection which exists to safeguard the welfare of children. However, 'harm' also has a wider meaning in a broader social context, as discrimination and social inequality are in themselves harmful to the welfare of children and their families.

For black families (for the purposes of this chapter, black refers to peoples of Asian, African or African Caribbean origin) this social reality has tangible consequences, since there is clear evidence that in this country the colour of your skin is a determining factor in your access to resources and life opportunities:

'Children's skin colour is a strong determinant of their life chances and so black children fare worse on the whole range of social and economic indicators in comparison to whites.' (Popple, 1986.)

Discriminatory treatment on the basis of skin colour is a component of racism, and it is racism which institutionalises the power imbalance between black and white communities to produce socially reinforced inequality.

'Racism refers to the construction and institutionalisation of social relationships based on the assumption of the inferiority of ethnic minority groups, their customs, lifestyles and beliefs. As a result they experience marginalisation in the economic and social spheres. Prejudice and crude racial stereotypes reinforce and legitimate such divisions. While there is a range of ethnic minority groups, the major division is in terms of black and white.' (Channer and Parton, 1990.)

An understanding of the impact of racism on the lives of black communities is a vital adjunct to any discussion of culture and ethnicity in child protection services because it is impossible to adequately respond to the needs of black children without taking into account the social consequences that this power differential has on the lives of black families.

As definitions of abuse have become increasingly 'professionalised' in legislation and professional guidance to welfare agencies, the impact of racial inequality and racial injustice has been largely ignored. Abuse and protection are not so much discussed within a social and economic context as within an individual and pathological framework, which sees the child's family and carers as the targets for intervention.

In looking at the effect of local authorities' intervention on black children and their families, it is evident that they have not only failed to promote equality but their own practices and procedures have discriminated against black families.

'Experience sustained by members of black communities suggests that there is a deep and ingrained racism that perceives them as more threatening than whites, and, accordingly, metes out harsher measures to them. It seems that the strengths of black families and communities are not recognised.' (Channer and Parton, 1990.)

The report of the Black and In Care Group to the NSPCC (1992) summarises the views of large numbers of black families:

'While black children, like white children, need to be protected from harm and helped to overcome the effects of abuse, the way in which both the social Services and the NSPCC have professionalised the issues has left many people feeling powerless and victimised.' (Black and In Care Group, 1992.)

As demonstrated later in this chapter, this view is not just impressionistic since evidence suggests that black children enter care far more quickly than white children, and that black children of all age groups are over-represented in care (Barn, 1990). The message from the black communities is clear: state intervention in family life can in itself leave children vulnerable to other forms of abuse, some of which are as a direct consequence of the intervention itself.

This does not mean that welfare agencies cannot and should not intervene to protect children from harm. It means that welfare agencies in general, and social services in particular, need a wider perspective when looking at child abuse rather than diagnosing individual or family pathology. They need to keep in mind the personal and social consequences of racism, and adopt models of assessing families that are inclusive of these factors rather than exclusive of them.

Culture, ethnicity and social policy

In social work in general, and child protection in particular, race, culture and ethnicity have appeared only comparatively recently on the professional agenda in this country. This reflects the developing political climate of race relations which has shaped social policy in this country over the last 40 years.

For the purposes of this chapter, race refers to the social categorisation of people defined by skin colour and physical characteristics. Culture represents the shared behaviours, attitudes and traditions of a group of people which are characterised by similar language, symbols, food, dress, history, etc. Ethnicity describes geographic origin and heritage which is acquired by birth.

Following the arrival of black migrants to this country in the 1950s there was increasing concern about potential racial conflict. Many white communities expressed open hostility towards black immigrants, and black people were organising resistance to the racism that they were experiencing.

In this uneasy racial climate, it was politically important that the impact of black communities in British society was underplayed as much as possible. It is not a coincidence, therefore, that from the 1960s to the 1980s the notion of 'assimilation' or 'integration' underpinned most political debate about race relations at a national and local level.

Assimilation was a useful term for the public and politicians alike, portraying a more comfortable concept of future relationships between the races in which black migrants adapted to the requirements of British society by assimilating into the British way of life. It contained none of the perceived threats of separateness or difference.

The policies of the personal social services during this period are a reflection of this. Up until the 1980s, the general practice of social services and other child welfare agencies was to adopt a 'colour blind' approach to the organisation of services for families in which a 'same for all' policy operated. This was represented as the fairest way of providing services, since it meant that there was no special treatment for any particular family or community. Child welfare legislation, central government and local departmental guidance all presented this view. Race and culture were not mentioned, and the illusion was created that black families were being treated equally within the systems of welfare provision.

However, the reality was very different. From 1970 onwards, there was an ever-increasing body of evidence revealing a widespread pattern of discrimination on the basis of colour. It was clear that local government institutions were no less guilty than any other social institution, since they were not only treating black people differently from whites but their policies and procedures were in themselves discriminatory. In 1973, the Race Relations Board highlighted this point by arguing that, 'racial discrimination was less a matter of "active discrimination against individuals" than the reproduction of "situations in which equality of opportunity is consciously or unconsciously denied" ' (Solomos, 1989.)

In 1976, the government responded by passing the third Race Relations Act. Unlike the two previous Race Relations Acts in 1965 and 1968, the 1976 Act was a public recognition that racism was not only about hostile and individual acts of discrimination, but that it was also institutionalised in employment and the provision of services to black communities.

Section 17 of this Act places a specific duty on local authorities to tackle the effects of racism:

> 'It shall be the duty of every local authority to make appropriate arrangements with a view to securing that their functions are carried out with regard to the need;
>
> a) To eliminate unlawful racial discrimination; and
> b) To promote equality of opportunity and good relations, between persons of different racial groups.' (Race Relations Act, 1976.)

Enshrined in the Act was the concept that local authorities were the key agents of change, and that it was through their intervention that discrimination and disadvantage could be tackled.

However, the response from local authorities was poor. A study conducted by Jones in 1977 (*Immigration and Social Policy in Britain*) reported that most Social Services departments had not responded to the needs of black clients, either in service provision or in staff training and ethnic record keeping. According to the Community Relations Commission Report of 1977, 'It was very rare for Social Services Committees to have even discussed the needs of minorities.' (Husband, 1989.)

It was evident that the Race Relations Act was making little difference to service provision, and that local authorities were largely reneging on their responsibilities. Services continued to be offered on the same basis as before, with scant attention being paid to the needs of the varied communities in their localities. The 1980s sparked a shift in policy, however, as a consequence of the urban resistance of 1981. The demands of the black communities could no longer be ignored and even the Scarman report (Scarman, 1981) had highlighted a desperate need for change.

During this period, two influential schools of thought began to emerge about the best way of tackling racial inequality. They both had their origins in education, but they rapidly gained popularity in social services. The first of these was multiculturalism. In the late 1970s and early 1980s a number of articles began to appear in Social Work Journals about the importance of culture and language in service provision to families who were not a part of the majority culture (Powell, 1978; Reynolds, 1978; Roskill, 1979).

> 'Multi-culturalism, as outlined in the 1985 Swann Report "Education for All" was essentially a recognition that assimilationist and colour blind approaches to service provision were grossly inappropriate ways of responding to the needs of black communities, whose cultures and lifestyles were different to white cultures.' (Rattansi, 1992.)

At the heart of the multi-cultural perspective was the concept that racism was based on ignorance and prejudiced beliefs about cultural practices. Recognition of, and respect for, cultural difference was an important step in tackling racism and disadvantage, as it allowed cultural diversity to be seen positively as an asset rather than negatively as a threat. It essentially challenged the assimilationist position:

> 'The expectation that the Afro-Caribbean and Asian minorities would simply blend into a homogeneous British or even English stew, perhaps adding some harmless spice, was revealed as not only hopelessly unrealistic but symptomatic of a form of racism which regarded "Britishness" and "Westernness" as the only touchstones of cultural value.' (Rattansi, 1992.)

At the same time, the second school of thought, anti-racism, was also gaining ground as the solution to racial disadvantage: 'The 1980s was . . . an important decade with a move away from multi-culturalism and towards the more strategic approach of anti-racism and equal opportunity.' (Phillips, 1992)

Like multi-culturalism, anti-racism emerged in the wake of the civil unrest of the early 1980s. Its precise roots are hard to trace, but its origins represent the collective impact of black youth, black communities, black professionals and supportive white radicals. It manifested itself in different forms, ranging from youth protest and community action to political and professional debate, but it was essentially a political, intellectual and social opposition to racism. Anti-racists saw race, and not culture, as the central issue in tackling racial disadvantage. Racism was about unequal access to jobs, housing and education. It was based on social and institutional discrimination on the basis of colour, and not just on prejudiced views about lifestyles and traditions.

As these two approaches identified different causes for racism and racial disadvantage, they both offered differing solutions for the problem. Multi-culturalists essentially saw education and cultural sensitivity as the solution, whereas anti-racists saw the need for a more fundamental political change that tackled disadvantage through the policies and practices of state and government institutions rather than focusing on attitudinal change.

Whilst multi-culturalism was often seen to represent a tokenistic approach to tackling inequality which left the roots of the problem untouched, anti-racism gained popularity with black and white radicals alike. It provided an opportunity for a political unity between black and white professionals to launch a collective assault on the racist practices of state institutions.

> 'During the early 1980s, at the height of local authority intervention in the area of racial equality, much hope was placed in the role of local authorities, as an agent of change, particularly in the context of the neglect of racial equality by the Thatcher administrations.' (Solomos, 1989.)

Change, however, was short-lived. In the face of a media 'backlash' about the 'loony left' policies of local authorities such as Hackney, Lambeth and Haringay, many local authorities saw race as a political hot potato to be avoided at all costs. Anti-racism was a vote loser, and local authorities backtracked on their earlier promises in the hope that they would avoid the glare of media attention: 'During the late 1980s there have been signs that even previously radical local authorities are now adopting a lower profile on issues concerned with racial equality.' (Solomos, 1989.)

In the face of inaction and backtracking on the part of local authorities, many black professionals became increasingly disillusioned. The promises of the early 1980s had proved to be hollow, and change was seen to be slow and tokenistic. For many, being a cog in the anti-racist wheel was unsatisfactory and exploitative. They wanted the opportunity to define their own models of practice. They wanted a black perspective.

From the mid 1980s onwards, there has been an increasing body of social work literature written from a black perspective. This was not a new phenomenon, for black professionals had been active in writing about their experiences and demanding change from the time of their entrance into the profession. It was only that the concept of a black perspective gave these collective experiences a name and an identity that represented a sense of solidarity and of achievement.

'The factors that prescribe a black perspective have a long history of subjugation and subordination. The circumstances that shape a black perspective stem from the experience of racism and powerlessness, both past and present. The motivation that energises a black perspective is rooted in the principle of racial equality and justice.' (Ahmad, 1990.)

Whilst black perspectives in social work have often been marginalised within mainstream social work theory, policy and practice, the assimilationist, multi-cultural and even the anti-racist approaches have had varying degrees of impact on social work education and training. In the field of child protection in particular, however, it is evident from research that the perspective has not had a significant impact on practice with black families.

Review of Literature and Research

Race ethnicity and culture in research

Despite attempts to make social work practice with black children and families more sensitive and relevant, statistics show that over the last 30 years there has been a consistent over-representation of black children within the care population. The first study conducted in the 1960s found that children of 'mixed origin' were eight and a half times more likely to come into care than 'white indigenous' and 'Afro-Caribbean and Asian' children. (Barn, 1990.)

In 1975, a similar study conducted by Batta *et al.* showed a similar pattern, indicating that, 'the number of Afro-Caribbean and Asian children coming into care had increased much faster than the other two groups since the study was done.' (Barn, 1990.)

'The Soul Kids Campaign' in 1977 was a response to growing concern about this issue: 'the picture that gave rise to the steering group's concern (was) a large number of black children coming into and remaining in care, usually growing up in a predominantly white, institutional environment.' (Soul Kids Campaign, 1977.)

Two studies in the 1980s also reflected the high proportion of black children in the care of local authorities: 'The Lambeth study (Adams, 1981) selected a random sample of children in care and found that 49 of the 90 children were black (54%). The Tower Hamlets study stated that over 50% of the children in their care were black (Wilkinson, 1982).' (Barn, 1990.) In their 1989 study, Rowe *et al.* also state that: 'Black children were over-represented in admissions to care of all six project authorities, although the extent to which this was happening varied considerably.' (Rowe *et al.*, 1989.)

Whilst it does not automatically follow that black children are more likely than white children to be admitted into care, the consistently high proportion of black children in the care system is clear evidence that skin colour is a significant factor in admission rates into the care system, a conclusion that is borne out by later research. (Barn, 1990).

Some of the studies do not distinguish between the ethnic and cultural groups that make up their samples of black children. From the statistics available, however, the indications are that mixed parentage children (particularly where one parent is African Caribbean and one is white European) are over-represented in the care population. Batta *et al.* (1975) also found that children of mixed parentage came into care at an earlier age and tended to stay in care for longer periods. Rowe *et al.* (1989) found the same to be true in her study of 6 London authorities, and also found that children of mixed parentage were the most likely to have multiple admissions.

What these studies do not show us is on what basis children were admitted into care, what the precipitating factors were, and what alternatives were offered to families in order to prevent admission into the care system. The only study which attempts to do this is one conducted by Barn (1990, 1993) in a London authority. This demonstrates that race, culture and ethnicity do not only have an impact on the numbers of children in the care but that they are also significant in terms of the circumstances under which admission took place.

Barn found a link between race and rapidity of admission:

'The "speed" at which black children enter care has been left relatively unexplored in the past. The Wenford research was able to ascertain that black children came into care much more quickly than white children. For example, in the first 4 weeks of referral, 28% of black children were admitted into care compared to 15% of white children.' (Barn, 1990.)

She also found that, 'black children were much more likely than white children to come from higher socio-economic groups. For example, 47% of the black children's mothers were in white collar and skilled manual occupations compared to 22% of white children.' (Barn, 1993.)

Whilst economic and social factors are significant contributory factors in admission rates to care and black families are economically disadvantaged through racism, it is also apparent from this that an explanation of the statistics based purely on economic and social disadvantage is inadequate.

This is supported by Barn's examination of case files and interviews with social workers and natural parents, where 'it became apparent that preventative work was less likely to be done with black families.' She also found that although the majority of black children entered care via the voluntary route, they were as likely as white children to be made subject to compulsory care and that they were much more likely to be made subject to parental rights resolutions than white children.

From this evidence, it is possible to echo Barn's conclusion that black and white children follow different paths in their care careers, and that race and culture are significant variables in determining the decisions that are made at different points in the care history of a black child.

Apart from this specific research, there are also broader indicators that this is the case. Whilst there are no published national statistics about child protection registration and ethnicity, NSPCC research indicates that ethnicity may be a significant determinant in registration of children as well as entry into care: 'it would appear that ethnic minorities are over-represented amongst the parents of the registered children.' (Creighton, 1992.)

Although there is a dearth of British research on the link between ethnicity, culture and child abuse, studies from America have shown that rates of abuse are consistently similar across different ethnic groups, and that black children are at no greater risk of abuse or maltreatment than their white counterparts: 'across the board studies have consistently failed to find any black–white differences in rates of sexual abuse.' (Finkelhor, 1986.) The same is also true of physical and emotional abuse: 'Race stands out due to the similarities between blacks and white.' (Jones and McCurdy, 1992)

This clearly suggests that the incidence of abuse should not be the focus of concern in considering race, ethnicity and culture in child protection, but that it is the professional response to child abuse which is at issue.

Race, ethnicity and culture in child protection literature

Until the late 1970s, social work literature adopted a broadly 'colour blind' approach to explanations of psychosocial problems. Most theoreticians came from the assimilationist school, whereby race and culture were largely seen as irrelevant to the debate. Child protection was no exception to this rule.

In British society, the recognition of child abuse as a social problem is a surprisingly recent phenomenon. In 1961, child abuse was 'discovered' by Henry Kempe in America. He drew on past work by paediatric radiologists in the 1940s who thought that some of the bone fractures that they were seeing in childrens' bones appeared to be linked with parents as possible sources of the injuries. Kempe developed the term 'battered baby syndrome' to explain this form of physical abuse.

In response to this, in 1963, two British orthopaedic surgeons, Griffiths and Moynihan published an article in the *British Medical Journal* entitled 'The battered baby syndrome' (Parton, 1985). Consequently, during the 1960s the recognition of the battered baby syndrome provided a catalyst for change in the state's response to children. The recognition that children can and do suffer physical harm at the hands of their parents came to be seen as a strong justification for state intervention in family life. If parents abused their children, then the state had a duty to protect.

With the 'discovery' of abuse emerged theories about the causes and effects of such abuse (see preceding chapters in this section). Causal theories ranged from the concept of individual family pathology to the concept of society as the abuser, originating from psychological perspectives, on the one hand, to sociological analysis on the other.

One of the core principles of psychological theory to be applied to child protection is that individuals and families are a product of their past experiences. The work of Bowlby in the 1960s had paved the way for this view, his concept of 'maternal deprivation' providing a theoretical link between early childhood experience and psychological development (Bowlby, 1965). Children were seen to be products of their early development, and trauma in their early years would therefore have negative consequences for the developing adult.

If individual and family pathology was identified as the cause of abuse, then it followed that particular families were more likely than others to abuse their children. The task for social workers, therefore, was to identify which families were potentially abusive: 'The proportion of "high risk" cases out of all proved cases of persistent child abuse will be small, and the task of identifying may not be easy. But the attempt to isolate such cases from the majority of child abuse must always be made.' (A Child In Trust, 1985.)

There were a variety of methods suggested to facilitate this, ranging from individual to family assessment, but all shared a common assumption – that there is a normative standard of family functioning against which pathology can be measured. From this the level of risk could be established.

'Good enough parenting' was the key phrase in this type of assessment. It was based on the work of Margaret Adcock and Christine Cooper (Adcock and White, 1985), amongst others, in the mid-1980s. It essentially set out the standards of care which were necessary for a child to grow into a healthy adult. The task of the social work assessment was to establish how far the family were short of the required standards of parenting.

The notion that there are characteristics present in families which predispose them to abuse their children, and which can be detected and acted upon, leads to the concept of 'dangerousness' in families. Checklists for dangerousness have been produced by theorists such as Greenland (Parton and Parton, 1989). Such checklists were based on retrospective studies of families where abuse had taken place – early family history, social and economic status, and family composition were all factors that were given weighting.

Theories about family dynamics also offered explanations for abuse which were linked to the nature of family functioning. There are various schools of family therapy, but they all share the essential belief that the family is a system which is reliant on its component parts for it to work effectively. For family therapists, abusive families are ones in which parts of the family system are dysfunctional, which may be either the cause or the effect of the abuse. The task of the therapist is to restore normal or effective functioning to the family through realigning and strengthening parts of the family system whose weakness has contributed to the dysfunction.

Despite the differences between such theories, all theories of family pathology share certain characteristics. The first is that the family itself is the focus of attention, and that problems inherent in the family have a role to play in creating preconditions for the abuse. The second is that they identify characteristics that are present in the family as dysfunctional or dangerous, and that need to be changed if the child is to be protected. Identifying the deficiencies that exist requires that a benchmark of normative family functioning is applied to an assessment of family behaviour. This enables the level of dangerousness or the level of unhealthy functioning in a given family to be established.

It is here that the drawbacks of these approaches can be identified in relation to working with black families. These models have all the inherent problems of an assimilationist or 'colour blind' approach to child protection. It is not simply that they ignore race, culture and ethnicity, but that they require that families are judged according to a white (and middle class) view of normality. In making such a judgment, black families will not just be seen as different but as negatively different. Factors which are environmentally or socially determined will be pathologised and racist stereotypes perpetuated: 'Many texts simply ignore the existence of black families. Discussion is framed in terms of "families" as if all families are white. There is an assumption that the concepts and methods set out are applicable to all families.' (Gambe et al., 1992.)

The sociological view of child abuse, on the other hand, does include an analysis of social and environmental factors. One of the first sociologists to research this link was Gil, whose study of physically abused children in the 1960s emphasised the social context of abuse: 'by looking at a broad sample of child abuse cases Gil widened the parameters of the subject and pointed to major structural changes in society as the means of tackling child abuse.' (Corby, 1987)

Essentially, the sociological view of child abuse is that it is a social problem, which requires a social and political solution. In terms of the race, ethnicity and culture therefore, the sociological perspective does consider the impact of structural inequality on the lives of families. However, few sociologists have considered the impact of racism and cultural stereotyping in the context of child abuse. Discussions of race within sociological texts have normally confined themselves to discussions of race policy and ethnic relations, rather than child protection practice. Along with psychological theories, sociological theories have often ignored the relevance of race, culture and ethnicity to social work theory, and most theoreticians have taken an essentially assimilationist stance.

One further theoretical perspective that has been influential in child protection practice, and work with child sexual abuse in particular, is feminist theory. It does not fit into a broad psychological or sociological niche because it developed as a critique of theories of child abuse for failing to take into account the relevance of gender to the debate.

Feminists saw child sexual abuse as simply an extreme of the continuum of sexual violence that is a consequence of a patriarchal society: 'In western society there has for 500 years also been an association of sexual domination and racism. . . . This is the ideology that not only makes possible sexual violence of every kind, but also makes it invisible.' (McLeod and Saraga, 1988.) Their position was to challenge the 'orthodoxy' of male theorists and therapists, whom they regarded as blaming women and holding them responsible for abuse perpetrated by male abusers.

Whilst the feminists recognised the oppressiveness of sexist ideology, however, they made only fleeting reference to race and culture because, 'Feminism, like social-ism, is a political construct which provides many opportunities for generating racial disadvantage and exclusion.' (Knowles and Mercer, 1992) In challenging the oppres-sion of women, feminists assimilated black families into a generalised view of the nature of family life. Whilst sexism is a feature of black family life, as it is in white family life, a universal formula based on the experiences of white women only serves to subsume the impact of racism and deny the experiences of black women.

The central problem with many of the theoretical perspectives on child abuse is that they tend to ignore the social and environmental context in which black families live and represent external pressures which affect family functioning, such as racism, economic disadvantage, poor housing and unemployment as if they are inherent deficiencies in that family's ability to cope.

A more effective approach to the assessment of black families is one which recog-nises the inherent strengths that are present in black families, who are struggling to deal with the effects of racism. Rather than using normative models of white, middle class family functioning to assess how far the family is falling short of this goal, the aim of our intervention should be to help the family better to care for their children in the context of the social reality for that family. This approach focuses on strengths, as well as weaknesses, and allows the family to engage in a much more meaningful debate about protection that is based on a realistic plan for change.

Analysis of Policy Issues

The death of Maria Colwell in 1973 provided the impetus to develop local government structures and procedures for dealing with cases of child abuse. Prior to this, there had been no nationally co-ordinated guidelines. In 1974 the Department of Health and Social Security (DHSS) issued circular LASSL (74)(13) (Parton, 1985), which referred to 'Non-accidental injury to children' and set out the procedures that should be followed by professionals in investigating such cases (Lee, 1978).

Subsequent circulars in 1976 and 1980 (DHSS (LASSL (76)(2) and DHSS; Child Abuse: Central Register Systems (LASSL) (80)) set out detailed procedures regarding Area Review Committees and central child abuse registers, and in 1988 the DHSS published the first *Working Together: A Guide to Arrangements for Inter-agency Co-operation for the Protection of Children*. This was updated in 1991 with *Working Together Under the Children Act 1989*.

However, none of this guidance, including the most recent version of *Working Together*, refers in any way to race, culture and ethnicity. In setting out local authority procedures and guidance in child protection, the Department of Health has taken an essentially assimilationist stance, in which 'the same for all' applies. This means that local authorities have been left to their own devices about whether or not they choose to include race, culture and ethnicity in their multi-disciplinary guidelines on child protection.

Judging from past experience, this will mean that race and race equality will continue to be marginalised and that discrimination in practice, as evidenced by the research on black children in the care system, will remain unchallenged: 'Although the last decade has witnessed an increase in the employment of black social workers, emphasis on race awareness training and the introduction of equal opportunities, the overall picture is one of little change.' (Barn, 1993)

In 1988, *Protecting Children* was published by the Department of Health (DOH) in response to a growing level of concern about child protection assessments. It followed a number of inquiry reports in the 1980s into the deaths of children and an inspection by the Social Services Inspectorate (DHSS, 1988), all of which had highlighted the need for a higher standard of child protection assessments.

Protecting Children was one of the first publications produced by the DOH which had not taken a 'colour blind' approach, as it specifically referred to the need for 'cultural sensitivity' in child protection work:

> 'Although no culture sanctions extreme harm to a child, cultural patterns in child-rearing patterns exist. A balanced assessment must incorporate a cultural perspective, but guard against being over-sensitive to cultural issues at the expense of promoting the safety and well-being of the child.' (DOH, 1988.)

The Children Act in 1989 was the first piece of child care legislation which conveyed specific requirements upon local authorities in relation to religion, race, culture and language for children who are 'looked after'. Section 22 5 (c) of the Act states that, 'In making any such decision (in respect for a child who is looked after) a local authority shall give due consideration . . . to the child's religious persuasion, racial origin and cultural and linguistic background.'

In 1992, the *Memorandum of Good Practice on Video Recorded Interviews with Child Witnesses for Criminal Proceedings* was published. This took the same position in relation to the need to be 'culturally sensitive'.

> 'The joint investigating team should consider whether there are any special factors arising from the child's cultural and religious background which are relevant to planning an effective interview. In some cases it will be necessary for the team to seek advice about particular customs or beliefs. Consideration of race, language and also gender may influence the choice of interviewer.' (*Memorandum of Good Practice*, 1992.)

Whilst it is helpful that legislation and guidance have finally acknowledged the relevance of cultural difference to social work practice in protecting children, the 'culturally sensitive' model contains many of the flaws that are present in its multi-cultural origins. Multi-culturalism suffers from an over-simplisitic and often tokenistic view of cultural difference. It also assumes a base line where all cultures, whether black or white, are equally regarded.

However, British society is not a culturally pluralist society. The historical legacy of slavery and colonialism in this country has produced a society in which black cultures are not simply viewed as different, but as negatively different: 'For black children growing up in this country this means that their traditions, languages, lifestyles and social mores may be viewed negatively in comparison with English culture.' (Phillips, 1993.)

Within every society there are sanctions which operate to control the excesses of individuals, there are taboos which operate to protect the integrity of the society, and there are mechanisms which operate to protect the vulnerable. This does not prevent individuals from transgressing these unwritten codes of behaviour, nor does it ensure that all the vulnerable are protected. However, these situations arise in spite of the checks and balances, and not because of them: 'While cultures differ in their definitions of child maltreatment, all have criteria for behaviours that fall outside the range of acceptability, and some individuals in all cultures exceed the boundaries of their society's standards.' (Korbin, 1991.)

It is when these safety mechanisms break down, or do not come into operation, that institutional protection in the form of social services involvement is required. The decision about when and how intervention is required must involve a process of fine judgment, based on assessment of what protective factors exist in the situation relative to the risk factors that are present. Social work is not and cannot be an exact science, however. As it is socially constructed, so is the protective task of the social worker. Child protection assessments cannot be value-free.

What this means in practice is that the judgments about risk factors and protective factors are themselves informed by the worker's own view of what constitutes risk and what represents protection:

'Child abuse now embraces social and emotional as well as physical aspects. It involves not only physical injury, but also neglect, sexual and emotional abuse. Although there would be general agreement about serious acts of abuse at the other end of the continuum there are different views and the boundary between adequate parenting and minor forms of abuse is blurred. Judgment as to what constitutes abuse is therefore a matter of degree, opinion and values.' (*Protecting Children*, DOH, 1988.)

Opinions and values derive from a personal belief system that is socially constructed and culturally defined. They reflect the dominant ideology for the community from which they originate. In this society, since racism is a part of that dominant ideology, racism itself is socially constructed and culturally defined. Thus, 'although child abuse occurs in all races and cultures workers must guard against viewing suspected abuse through the norms and values of their own background. Different cultural/racial groups organise their own traditions, regions, community of origin and history.' (British Association of Social Workers, 1989)

When black families are assessed, these cultural differences provide a backdrop to the views and values held by white professionals about black families and distort the assessment in the process. In practice, this means that widely held assumptions about black families can have a direct impact on assessments of risk that are made by child protection professionals. An examination of these stereotypes and their consequent effect on decision-making can help to unpack the dynamics of racism in professional practice.

Implications for Practice

The stereotypes which exist in this society often present us with conflictual and confusing ideas about black family life:

> 'The Asian family is seen as strong but the very strength of Asian culture is seen to be a source of both actual and potential weakness. The hierarchical family structure is said to produce "stress-ridden relationships"; Asian women are seen to be isolated because of their traditional customs and views of the world.' (Fernando, 1988.)

'Culturally racist' views such as these can have a powerful impact on social work practice with black families.

One example of this is the traditional system of marriage in the Asian community, popularly referred to as 'arranged marriages'. There is a widely held view in white Western society that arranged marriages in Asian families are in themselves abusive because they do not give control and choice to the marriage partners, particularly young women. This view has been reinforced by media 'exposés' of marriages which have involved coercion and abduction and have, on occasions, resulted in suicide.

It is clearly the case that some young Asian people do have bad experiences of marriage. Some young people are abused or abducted, or forced to get married or to have sex under age. But this has nothing to do with the marriage traditions of the Asian community. This is not cultural, any more than child abuse or domestic violence is cultural in English society. It is the result of individual circumstances that have transgressed the usual expectations of behaviour, and which require intervention.

There are, however, numerous examples of social services intervention in families to prevent young Asian women from having arranged marriages. As a social worker, I was myself involved in a number of cases where young women had already been removed from home and placed in residential care at their request, in order to prevent their parents from arranging their marriages. This was seen as a protective measure, by the social workers involved, to allow the young women freedom to choose their own partner. The result was that the young women were cut off from their family and community in an unfamiliar and often unsafe 'care' environment.

In these cases, what was not recognised was that the parents' motivation was actually protective. They wanted their daughters to be safe and cared for as part of a family system. Whilst some of their expectations of their children may have been at odds with those of their daughters, the situation required a process of negotiation about difference, rather than intervention which was based on an inaccurate, and culturally racist, perception of risk.

Although the myths about African Caribbean family life are different, the impact of these assumptions on social work practice is the same:

> 'Afro-Caribbeans in Britain are seen as having suffered "cultural stripping" during slavery leaving them with a "weak" version of European culture . . . Afro-Caribbean family life in contemporary Britain is seen as weak and unstable, with the lack of a sense of parental responsibility towards children (Pryce, 1979), a failure by the family to apply adequate social control over its youth (Cashmore, 1979) and a negative personal self image.' (Fernando, 1988.)

This negative view of African Caribbean culture is sometimes juxtaposed with an over-idealised view about the strength and resilience of African Caribbean women, resulting in an unrealistic and unhelpful approach to working with African Caribbean families.

A clear example of this is the Tyra Henry case, in which Tyra's grandmother Beatrice Henry was seen as capable of providing protection for her granddaughter, Tyra, in the face of concerns about the care she was receiving from her mother and step-father, without adequate back-up being provided from social services to assist her in this task. The *Report of the Public Inquiry into the Death of Tyra Henry* (London Borough of Lambeth, 1987) makes it clear that practice in this case was influenced by cultural stereotypes about black families:

> 'There is a "positive", but nevertheless, false stereotype in white British society of the Afro-Caribbean mother figure as endlessly resourceful . . . essentially unsinkable . . . it may have been an unarticulated and unconscious sense that a woman like Beatrice Henry would find a way to cope no matter what that underlay the neglect of . . . social services to make adequate provision for her taking responsibility for Tyra.' (London Borough of Lambeth, 1985.)

The essential irony of the culturally sensitive approach to child protection work with children and their families is that over-reliance on an inaccurate notion of culture can actually produce a discriminatory rather than a sensitive style of practice. Assessments that are informed by prescriptive and stereotypical views of families will reinforce, rather than challenge, racist practice with black children and their families:

> 'the issue is not simply that some form of "cultural knowledge" can be superimposed upon the working practices of social workers to equip them to deal adequately with black families. It is that those working practices themselves need to be reviewed as to their relevance to the assessment of black families.' (Dutt and Phillips, 1990.)

The role of social services in working with children and families is to provide state protection for children where they are at risk, either through preventative service for their children and their families, or by statutory intervention where a child may be at risk of significant harm. This protective role relies on a basis of partnership and negotiation with children and their families, in order to ensure that actions taken are in the best interests of the children in their locality: 'local authorities must work in partnership with parents, seeking court orders when compulsory action is indicated in the interests of the child but only when this is better for the child than working with the parents under voluntary arrangements.' (*Working Together*, DOH 1991.)

It is only possible to work in partnership with parents to protect children from abuse by having a clear view about what children need to be protected from. If professional views are influenced by a deficit model of family functioning which is the result of negative stereotypes about family life, the result will be over-intervention, by seeking to protect children from harm that is attributed to particular cultural practices or beliefs, as in the example of arranged marriages with Asian families.

If, on the other hand, there is an idealised and over-optimistic view about a family's potential based on stereotypical views, then the result will be under-intervention, and a resulting lack of protection for the child combined with a failure to adequately support the family by providing the practical help which they need, as in the Tyra Henry case.

There is no magic formula or instant solution to better practice with black children and their families. The only way in which more accurate assessments of risk can be made, and appropriate interventions formulated, is by returning to the basic principle of partnership.

Partnership in child protection does not mean that parents make all the decisions about the protection of their children. The only reason that statutory agencies should be involved in the first place is because there are sufficient concerns the children are not being adequately protected. What partnership *does* mean is that workers must be proactive in eliciting the family's own views about how they may best protect their own children, what problems they see as being significant, what solutions they identify for overcoming these, and what support they require from professionals which will help them to achieve their plan (see Petrie and James, Section III, Chapter 17).

This does not mean that families themselves will always have the internal resources to achieve the plan, or that the plan will always be realistic, but it will help the workers involved to identify the strengths, discuss the gaps, and explore the outcomes with the families themselves. Workers are neither required, nor do they need to be experts in child-rearing patterns in all cultures. They do not have to have a detailed knowledge of the religious practices of families from all religions.

However, professionals *do* have to think about culturally racist assumptions that they carry with them about black cultures. Where did they get this information from? How applicable is it? What would be the consequences of making decisions based on this information? Does this information really help their assessment about protection of children in this family?

In most cases, the answers to the above questions will be no. Black families, just like white families, come from all classes and economic backgrounds, and have a variety of social and political values. Just as it is impossible to be prescriptive about normative values in white families, so the same is true of black families.

In short, as professionals we cannot prevent children being abused by other children or adults who are supposed to protect them. We cannot predict which children will be abused, nor by whom. But we can divest ourselves of erroneous and unhelpful notions about black families which cloud our judgment, and which result in discriminatory and racist practice. When we ask ourselves what we are protecting children from, we have to be able to say that we are protecting children from professional racism, as much as from abuse within their own families.

Summary and Conclusion

The irony of the last 30 years is that despite local authority policy changes and political backtracking, the move from an assimilationist stance to a 'culturally sensitive' practice, and the influence of 'anti-racism' on raising awareness about racism in service provision, little has changed for black families. There is still a disproportionate number of black children in care, and child protection practice is still not responding appropriately to the black communities.

The main reason for this is the marginalisation of issues of race, culture and ethnicity within the child protection system. In child protection theory, legislation, guidance and practice, race, ethnicity and culture are still seen as additional, separate or special needs that require attention from professionals alongside the consideration of risk and safety. A child protection service that attempts to 'graft on' a sensitive response to black children without looking at how that service inherently misrepresents the position of black children will not be effective.

What is required is a rethinking of practice. Theoretical models commonly used in child protection have to be critically examined. Are they universally applicable, or do they simply reinforce stereotypical views of black families? Guidance and procedures need to include a black perspective. It is not enough to urge professionals to be 'culturally sensitive' in a climate in which cultural sensitivity often results in cultural racism: 'If practitioners have had no help or preparation in raising their awareness of racism then there are bound to be problems with cultural explanations.' (Ahmed *et al.*, 1986)

Since racism distorts views of black cultures and imbues them with negative characteristics, a sensitive approach to working with families from black cultures is one in which racist myths and assumptions are challenged through open discussions with the families themselves.

The challenge to professional practice is succinctly stated by the Black and in Care Group:

> 'If the changes in agency practice do not result in real benefits for Black people, then there have been no real changes.' (Black and in Care Group, 1992.)

Annotated Suggestions for Further Reading

Ahmad, B. (1989). Protecting black children from abuse. *Social Work Today*, 8 June.
Provides a pertinent comment on the outcome of professional intervention with black families.

Ahmad, B. (1990). *Black Perspectives in Social Work*. Venture Press.
Outlines a positive black critique in relation to social services practice, including child care and child protection, with case study illustrations.

Ahmed, S. *et al.* (1986). *Social Work with Black Children and their Families*. Batsford.
Contains an invaluable critique of cultural racism within social work practice.

Barn, R. (1990). Black children in local authority care: admission patterns. *New Community*, January.

Barn, R. (1993). *Black Children in the Public Care System*. Batsford, in association with BAAF.
Outlines detailed research undertaken in a London authority on black children within the care system, and draws important conclusions in relation to the care paths of black children.

Black and in Care Group (1992). *Saying It As It Is*. Report of the Black and in Care Group to the National Society for the Prevention of Cruelty to Children. NSPCC.
Presents the view of black children and young people, who themselves have been a part of the care system.

Bridge Child Care Consultancy Services. *Sukina – An Evaluation Report of the Circumstances Leading to her Death*.
Includes an analysis and recommendations as to the impact of race and culture on the decisions made in relation to Sukina.

Channer, Y. & Parton, N. (1990). Racism, cultural relativism and child protection. Chapter 6 in: *Taking Child Abuse Seriously*. The Violence against Children Study Group. Unwin Hyman.

Gives a useful perspective on racism within the child protection services, and the impact of cultural relativism on child protection assessments.

Dutt, R. & Phillips, M. (1990). *Towards a Black Perspective in Child Protection*. Race Equality Unit. Personal Social Services.
Looks at the impact of personal views and values on assessments in child protection with black families, and offers some checklists for improving practice with black families.

Fernando, S. (1988). *Race and Culture in Psychiatry*. Routledge.
Although this book focuses on the mental health services, it provides a very useful analysis of the way in which racist stereotypes influence social work assessments with families.

Race Relations Act (1976). London: HMSO.
This needs to be read, as it outlines our responsibilities in promoting equalities in the personal social services.

Rattansi, A. (1992). *'Race', Culture and Difference*. In Donald & Rattansi (eds): Open University Press.
Contains some very thought-provoking essays that challenge the orthodoxy of current approaches to race relations.

Rouf, K. (1989). *Black Girls Speak Out*. The Childrens Society.
A powerful book of poems and writings by black young women who have experienced sexual abuse.

Sissay, L. (1988). *Tender Fingers in a Clenched Fist*. Bogle-Ouverture.
Sissay provides us with a challenging insider view of the experiences of a black young person growing up in care.

Skellington, R. & Morris, P. (1992). *'Race' in Britain Today*. The Open University. Sage Publications
A useful source of annotated statistical information about race and racism in Britain, including information on health, housing, education and social services.

The London Borough of Lambeth (1987). *Whose Child? A Report of the Public Inquiry into the Death of Tyra Henry*.
One of the few inquiry reports on a black child that includes an analysis of the impact of race on the case.

References

A Child in Trust. (1985). *The Report of the Panel of Inquiry into the circumstances surrounding the death of Jasmine Beckford*. London Borough of Brent.

Adams, N. (1981). *Lambeth Directorate of Social Services*. London Borough of Lambeth.

Adcock, M. & White, R. (1985). *"Good enough parenting: a framework for assessment*. British Agencies for Adoption and Fostering.

Ahmad, B. (1990). *Black Perspectives in Social Work*. Venture Press.

Ahmed, S. *et al.* (1986). *Social Work with Black Children and their Families*. Batsford.

Batta, McCulloch & Smith, (1979). Colour as a variable in Childrens' Sections of Local Authority Social Services Departments. *New Community Volume 7* 78–84.

Barn, R. (1990). Black children in local authority care: admission patterns. *New Community*. January

Barn, R. (1993). *Black Children in the Public Care System* Batsford in association with BAAF.

Black and in Care Group (1992). *Saying It As It Is: Report of the Black and in Care Group to the National Society for the Prevention of Cruelty to Children*. NSPCC

Bowlby, J. (1965). *Child care and the Growth of Love* (Second Edition) Harmondsworth: Penguin Books.

British Association of Social Workers. (1989) *A Guide to Policy and Practice in the Management of Child Abuse*. BASW.

Channer, Y. & Parton, N. (1990). Racism, cultural relativism and child protection, Chapter 6. *Taking Child Abuse Seriously*: The Violence against Children Study Group. Unwin Hyman.

Corby, B. (1987). *Working with Child Abuse*. Milton Keynes: Open University Press.

Creighton, S.J. (1992). *Child Abuse Trends in England and Wales 1988–1990*. NSPCC Policy Practice and Research Series

DHSS (1976). (LASSL (76) (2))

DHSS (1980). Child Abuse: Central Register Systems (LASSL) (80)

Department of Health and Social Security (1982). *Child Abuse; A Study of Inquiry Reports 1973–1981*. H.M.S.O.

Department of Health (1988). *Protecting Children: A Guide for Social Workers undertaking a Comprehensive Assessment*. London: HMSO.

Department of Health (1991). *Working Together; A Guide to arrangements for inter-agency co-operation for the protection of children from abuse*. London: HMSO

Dutt, R. & Phillips, M. (1990). *Towards a Black Perspective in Child Protection*. Race Equality Unit. Personal Social Services.

Fernando, S. (1988) *Race and Culture in Psychiatry*. London: Routledge.

Finkelhor, D. (1986) *A Sourcebook on child sexual abuse*. London: Sage

Gambe, D., Gomes, J., Kapor, V., Rangel, M., Stubbs, P. (1992). *Improving Practice with Children and Families: A Training Manual*. Northern Curriculum Development Project Leeds: CCETSW

Home Office Department of Health Department of Education and Science Welsh Office (1991). *Working Together Under the Children Act 1989*: A guide to arrangements for inter-agency co-operation for the protection of children from abuse. London: H.M.S.O.

Home Office in conjunction with Department of Health (1992) *Memorandum of Good Practice* on video recorded interviews with child witnesses for criminal proceedings. London: H.M.S.O.

Husband, C. (1978) *Racism in Social Work*. Community Care 241 39–40.

Husband, C. (1989) *Chapter 1. Racism Prejudice and Social Policy* from Social Policy: a criticical introduction. Ed. Williams F. Cambridge: Polity Press

Jones, C. (1977) *Immigration and Social Policy in Britain* London: Tavistock.

Jones, E. & McCurdy, K. (1992) The links between types of maltreatment and demographic characteristics of children. *Child Abuse and Neglect*. 16.

Kempe, C.H., Silverman, F.N., Steele, B.F., Droegmuller W. & Silver, H.K. (1962). The Battered Child Syndrome. *Journal of the American Medical Association*, *181*, 17–24.

Knowles, C. & Mercer, S. (1992) Feminism and Anti-Racism: an exploration of the political possibilities. In Donald & Rattansi (Eds) *"Race", Culture and Difference*. Milton Keynes: Open University Press.

Korbin, J. (1991). Cross-cultural Perspectives and Research: Directions for the 21st Century, *Child Abuse and Neglect*. 15 Supp.1.

Lee, C.C. (1978) *Child Abuse: A Reader and Sourcebook*. Milton Keynes: Open University Press.

McLeod, M. & Saraga, E. (1988) *Towards a Feminist Theory and Practice*. Feminist Review. Spring.

Parton, N. (1985) *The Politics of Child Abuse* Macmillan.

Parton, C. & Parton, N. (1989) Child Protection: the law and dangerousness. In O. Stevenson (Ed) *Child Abuse; Professional Practice and Public Policy*. Harvester Wheatsheaf.

Phillips, M. (1992) The Abuse of Power. *Social Work Today*. 23, (25) 16–17

Phillips, M. (1993) *Investigative Interviewing: issues of race and culture*. Investigative Interviewing Training Pack Resources Booklet. Milton Keynes: Open University Press.

Popple, (1986) Black childrens' rights' In Franklin, B. (Ed). *The Rights of Children* Oxford: Blackwell.

Powell, D. (1978) The out of step services. *Community Care. 191*, 41–42

Rattansi, A. (1992) *Racism, culture and education*. In Donald & Rattansi (Eds) *"Race", Culture and Difference*. Milton Keynes: Open University Press.

Reynolds (1978) *Leicester: Between two cultures. Community Care. 241*, 27–29

Roskill, C. (1979) A different social work. *Social Work Today 10*, (25) 17–20.

Rowe, J., Hundleby, M. & Garnett, L. (1989) *Child Care Now*. BAAF Research Series 6,

Scarman, Lord. (1981) *The Brixton Disorders 10–12 April 1981: Report of an Inquiry by the Rt. Hon. Lord Scarman OBE*. London: HMSO.

Sissay, L. (1988) *Tender Fingers in a Clenched Fist*. Bogle-Ouverture.

Solomos, J. (1989) *Race and Racism in Contemporary Britain*. Basingstoke: Macmillan.

Soul Kids Campaign (1977) *Report of the Steering Group of the Soul Kids Campaign*. Association of British Fostering and Adoption Agencies.

Whose Child? (1987) *A Report of the Public Inquiry into the death of Tyra Henry*. The London Borough of Lambeth.

Wilkinson, A. (1982) *Children who come into care in Tower Hamlets*. London Borough of Tower Hamlets

7

Perceptions of Abused Disabled Children

Margaret Kennedy

Introduction

As a starting point for this chapter it is important to put the lives of disabled children into context. Theresia Degener, of Germany (disabled herself, and a disability activist and lawyer), says, 'any child born with a disability growing up today has to survive and overcome discrimination and stigmatisation.' (Degener, 1992.) She describes a political process of the oppression of disabled children and adults. When disability is equated with illness or with something or someone being wrong (therefore not right), no concept of oppression or discrimination is or will be entertained. When the condition or impairment becomes the person, and the person becomes the condition, then there is widespread devaluation. The disability movement uses the word 'disabled' not to describe a physical or learning impairment but to *dis*-abling and *de*-valuing by society.

Being different in a way that is negatively valued can trigger a powerful process of rejection, segregation and stigmatisation of which abuse is just one outcome (Wolfensberger, 1987). Garbarino (1987) talks of a 'licence' to abuse disabled children in a society in which they are repeatedly stigmatised. Sullivan *et al.* (1987) contend that 'depersonalisation' is also a contributing factor. 'When disabled children or adults are assumed to be less human because of their disability, then abuse is not that inhumane.' (Sullivan *et al.*, 1987.) For children who have been abused, a similar process emerges. We have pathologised disability, and children thus become objects of the medical profession to be put right, to be made more 'normal'.

We also pathologise the child who is abused. Instead of acknowledging and recognising the discrimination (by virtue of being a child) and the oppression they experience, we now label them sick, disturbed, ill. Professionals 'treat' them and, indeed, in the child protection field phrases such as 'symptoms' and 'treatment' are taken directly from the medical model. When we view the child only in terms of their presenting 'symptoms' and outside the political context of oppression, we again devalue the child's experiences. Pathologising is a weakening process, not an empowering one.

Because disabled children are negatively valued, we neglect to consider their child protection requirements. When I asked a senior policy-maker what she was including in her child protection policies for disabled children (she was writing a new draft), she pondered and then said, 'let me sort out the *normal* child *first.*' (Kennedy and Kelly, 1992.) In another instance, a counsellor said to a mother whose disabled child had been abused, 'well it would have been worse if it had been one of your other (non-disabled) children.' A QC said of a disabled child who had been abused and was applying for criminal injuries compensation, that as the child would obviously(!) not be engaging in sexual relationships in adulthood the harm of the sexual abuse was likely to be less and refused criminal injuries compensation. Such examples of professionals seeing disabled children as 'worthless' are unfortunately not uncommon.

Cumulative Effects of Negative Perception and Myths Concerning Abuse and Disabled Children

Other factors also contribute. Marchant (1991) explores the frequent myths surrounding abuse and the disabled child (see Table 7.1).

Because of the myths that surround these issues, professionals working with disabled children and adults have been reluctant to believe that disabled children are abused at all. Myths about abuse are not particularly unique, but there are unique ones relating to disability and abuse. Empirical evidence clearly shows that every one of these myths is false. All of them are dangerous. They must be challenged.

Some people really do believe abuse of a disabled child doesn't matter. A man with cerebral palsy illustrated for me very eloquently Myth no. 2 (Table 7.1) when he gave as his reason for being abused, 'why bugger up a normal child, when I am defective already?'

It was a personal testimony of a most profound kind, and I meet shades of this reasoning very often. It contributes towards the very dangerous and potent 'backdrop' to the abuse disabled children experience which allows us to ignore child protection issues:

- Discrimination, segregation and oppression.
- Devaluation and depersonalisation.
- Myths about disability and abuse.

Alternatively, disabled children are perceived as rather sad, unfortunate children who *do* require 'over-protection' and 'missionary-like' care and consideration.

Table 7.1 *Myths concerning abuse and children with disabilities.*

Myth	disabled children are not vulnerable to sexual abuse – they simply would not be targeted
Myth	sexual abuse of disabled children is OK, or at least not so harmful as abuse of other children
Myth	it is impossible to prevent abuse of disabled children
Myth	disabled children are even more likely to make false allegations of abuse
Myth	if a disabled child has been abused, it is best to leave well alone once the child is safe

Patronising attitudes are very unhelpful and in fact also lead to disempowerment. In relation to child abuse this disempowerment is positively dangerous. Such attitudes are enshrined in the new Children Act (1989), which places children who are disabled under the category of 'children in need'. This seems to fit in with the popular image of disabled children as recipients of charity (e.g. television appeals). This is an unfortunate development at a time when the disability movement is strenuously discussing the theme of rights, not charity (Kennedy and Cross, 1993).

Far from disability protecting those with a disability, disability rather protects the abusers (Kennedy, 1990). Senn (1988) says, 'in the situation of sexual abuse it does not seem to be the actual disability which creates the vulnerability, but rather the training received and the type of education (or lack thereof) and the environment in which children who are disabled find themselves, that put them at higher risk of sexual abuse.' In other words, society has created a situation in which children who are disabled have been taught to be good 'victims'.

The Missing Research

Very few British/UK studies have been undertaken to determine the prevalence or incidence of abuse of physically disabled children. Most attention (at least in the published literature) appears to have focused on sexual abuse and on victims who have learning disabilities (Westcott, 1993). There are no data on disability contained in the Department of Health (DOH) long-awaited national figures on children on at risk registers (1990), and indeed this information is not a requirement of the at risk registration process. It would nonetheless be invaluable, for we need this information in order to assess:

1. whether abuse may be implicated in the creation of impairment;
2. whether children with impairments may be differentially targeted for abuse. (Kelly, 1992.)

What we know largely comes from America and Canada. The following are some of the studies summarised by Westcott and Cross (1995, in press) covering physical and sexual abuse of disabled children (Tables 7.2, 7.3).

In the main it is not the researchers who have highlighted and informed practice but the activists, advocates and disabled people themselves. When research is undertaken it is worrying to find that the few studies we can look at are not based on direct contact with children/young people/adults who are disabled. This is because research methods fail to accommodate the requirements of these children and young people, by using, for example, questionnaires in Braille, or researchers who can use Sign Language or other augmentative communication systems. The research and what we think we know is based primarily on clinicians', practitioners' and parents' perceptions – the vast majority of whom are not disabled. Nor is there much awareness of the additional factors of oppression due to race, class, gender or sexuality (Kelly, 1992).

Table 7.2 *Physical abuse of disabled children.*

Study	Children	Source of information	Findings
Frisch and Rhoads, 1982 (US)	430 children and young people referred for an evaluation of learning problems during the year 1977–78	assessment records	29 (6.7%) children reported for child abuse and neglect (3.5 times that reported for all children)
Cohen and Warren, 1987 (US)	1. 2771 children under 5 years in pre-school programmes of 42 United Cerebral Palsy (UCP) affiliates. Children having different physical impairments	1. questionnaire survey of UCP staff	1. 94 (3.4% children reported as known physically abused with 209 (7.5%) suspected physically abused/neglected. Of 94 children known abused/neglected, 57 (61%) had been physically abused
	2. 435 children under 5 years in respite care programmes of 14 UCP affiliates. Children having different physical and/or learning impairments	2. questionnaire Survey of UCP staff	2. 4 (0.9%) reported as known physically abused.
Ammerman et al. 1989 (US)	148 children aged 3–19 years, psychiatrically referred and having multiple impairments of varying severity	medical, psychiatric nursing and social work records	1. 39% of children showed evidence of past or current abuse (19% definite, 20% probable/possible) 2. of these 39%, 69% were physically abused 3. increased risk

What is Abuse?

Definitions describing physical, sexual and emotional abuse and neglect are 'standard' until we look at the life of disabled children. In a study undertaken by a British Association for the Study and Prevention of Child Abuse and Neglect (BASPCAN) Working Party, professionals were asked what abuse they had experienced or come across. This revealed a catalogue of 'abuses' which would rarely be considered under statutory provisions, and which included:

- Force feeding – children with cerebral palsy.
- Over-medication – the learning-disabled or hyperactive child.
- Medical photography – children with physical impairments.
- Deprivation of visitors – anorexic children.
- Opening mail – children in residential care.
- Lack of privacy, and personal clothes, toys being used communally – children in residential care.
- Financial abuses – depriving children of rightful access to own money.
- Segregation to special schools (many disabled adults felt this to be abusive).
- Open days where adults would come in and view the children at school.

Table 7.3 *Sexual abuse of disabled children.*

Study	Children	Source of information	Findings
Ammerman et al.1989 (US)	148 children aged 3–19 years, psychiatrically referred and having multiple impairments of varying severity	medical, psychiatric, nursing and social work records	1. 39% of children showed evidence of past or current abuse (19% definite, 20% probable/possible) 2. of these 39%, 36% were sexually abused 3. increased risk
Kennedy, 1992 (UK)	deaf children known to professionals	survey of 156 teachers and social workers for the deaf	1. over 50% 1989 returns reported abuse 2. 70 children were suspected victims of sexual abuse, and 50 children were confirmed sexually abused
Sinason (undated) (UK)	40 children with learning impairments and emotional problems referred to Tavistock clinic 1991–92	psychotherapist seeing children	1. 30 (50%) returns reported abused 2. of 30, 21 (70%) were girls and 9 (30%) were boys
Sullivan et al., 1987 (US)	1. all members of 9th grade at residential school for deaf children 2. 150 pupils at residential school for deaf children 3. 322 students at further education college for hearing-impaired students 4. 100 deaf children attending either residential or mainstream schools	1. questionnaire survey 2. individual interviews 3. questionnaire survey 4. individual interviews	1. 50% children reported sexual abuse 2. 50% children reported sexual abuse 3. 13 students (4%) reported sexual abuse and 24 students (7%) reported both sexual and physical abuse 4. Of 64 children attending residential schools, 40 (63%) were sexually abused at school, 10 (16%) were sexually abused at home, and 15 (23%) were sexually abused at both school and home. Of 35 children in mainstream schools, 21 (60%) were sexually abused at home, 9 (26%) were sexually abused at school, and 5 (14%) were sexually abused at both home and school

- Behaviour modification programmes.
- Physical 'therapy' (some felt that aspects of the Peto and Doman methods of physiotherapy were abusive).

It was disturbing to discover that many disabled children had basic human rights infringed for example, access to their *own* clothes and toys, their *own* mail, their *own* money, and yet we are still powerless to prevent such abuses given the present legislation under which we might take action (BASPCAN Working Party on Disability and Abuse).

It is therefore important to realise again that even *before* we entertain the forms of abuse (as described by Department of Health definitions), children who are disabled have experienced both discrimination *and* the other subtle 'abuses' and infringements of human rights described above. These other forms of 'abuses' or infringements of human rights need to be borne in mind when designing safety and prevention programmes for disabled children. If disabled children are already in an atmosphere/environment which condones even these more subtle abuses, then disabled children may not be able to disclose more extreme forms of physical or sexual abuse.

In child protection, we need to be more proactive, so before I discuss disclosure I will look closely at safety and prevention programmes.

Communication

Large numbers of disabled children use alternative forms of communication and a large range of methods to communicate. Children do feel frustrated when adults cannot communicate with them, and, as I shall discuss in relation to investigative interviews, interpreters or facilitators are required to enable children who wish to disclose abuse to communicate this. The principal systems used are listed below.

Signs

- Makaton (learning-disabled children).
- See and Say.
- Paget Gorman (language-disordered children).
- British Sign Language (BSL) (Deaf children).
- Sign Supported English (SSE) (Deaf children).

Symbols

Augmentive communication systems using communication boards.

- Blissymbolics (children with cerebral palsy).
- Makaton (children with cerebral palsy and/or learning disabled children).
- Sigsymbols.
- Rebus.
- Icons, written words, etc.

Technology aided

- Light writers.
- Liberator/Touch Talkers.
- Possum, etc.

Many child protection workers who cannot sign may provide a pen and paper, thinking that the Deaf child may write down what it is they need to say. Here is what a young girl wrote to me during an initial assessment for counselling. Her signing had been extremely difficult to 'read'. (She had an idiosyncratic signing system and my signing system was Sign Supported English (SSE); hers was a form of British Sign Language (BSL). They are very different.)

> 'My aunt thought me 2 days ill not school but so she still angry with me much go school I'm not want to school'.

This is, in fact, how some profoundly deaf people write English, since it is a second language for signing Deaf children and adults. Asking them to write things down may not necessarily clarify the situation! What it demonstrated to me was that I was not the right person to help in this situation. I was able to refer her to a counsellor with British Sign Language (BSL) signing skills. The communication assessment was vital before undertaking any child protection work, and this will be true of all disabled children who use alternative means of communication. Interpreters may need to be employed who are qualified and skilled in particular language systems.

Safety and Prevention Programmes

Safety and prevention programmes are the main platforms of empowerment for all children.

These were developed following the many concerns connected with the sexual abuse of children. They are helpful provided we aim to 'give children enough information to be able to respond to a sexual abuse situation before it becomes serious, *not to make them responsible for protecting themselves.*' (Mayes *et al.*, 1986.)

What of the disabled child? Senn (1988) suggests that such children lack the effective education necessary to empower them, since many teachers are reluctant to implement any programme even vaguely connected to sexual assault or incest in schools.

In addition, since choosing and decision-making is a fundamental element of any safety programme, and since for many disabled children this has never been an aspect of their lives, the implementation of such programmes may sometimes prove problematic.

Principles of Various Programmes

Many safety and prevention programmes use similar principles to try to help children tackle difficult situations.

Children are often taught to say 'no' to things they do not like, particularly touch, and then to get away and find someone they can trust to tell. For non-disabled children, such advice has sometimes been used to good effect, but in the case of disabled children these principles do not take into account their specific impairments. Many may use different forms of communication of a non-verbal kind (see above). To say 'no' therefore may be very difficult, and to tell someone even more so.

This is compounded by the fact that many forms of augmentative communication systems, particularly symbol systems (where children use fingers or eyes to point to boards to indicate what they wish to convey), censor all use of words/symbols to describe genitals or sexual acts. What is required for even very young children using communication boards is that they include as a matter of course symbols which show anatomical body parts and genitals, so that if required they may discuss their worries and concerns. Some residential institutions (for example, Chailey Heritage, Sussex) are already changing policies concerning access to sexual symbols from an early age. Producing them at a later stage, for example, when required for investigative purposes, can be construed by defence barristers as 'leading' in the investigative interview.

Children who use symbols boards and access these by either finger-pointing or eye-pointing may furthermore only be understood by one or two key people. The potential danger for children who use alternative means of communication and who have a limited number of people whom they can tell needs to be borne in mind, since these same people may be the abusers.

Children may not be able to find someone who can understand what they are saying, since even some teachers cannot understand the children they teach. This can be true of some deaf children who have a greater fluency in signing than their teachers. Deaf children who do not sign but who are being taught by the oral/aural method can be particularly difficult to understand, as they may have poor speech and intonation skills and limited grasp of language and words.

Children are often taught in safety programmes to try and get away from the harmful situation. Here we need to ask – how? For blind children, going might mean running into a road, wall or door, particularly if they have just been hurt or terrified by abuse, or taken to a strange place. Children with cerebral palsy may be able to go but at a slower pace using crutches or walking sticks. Children using wheelchairs may find it difficult to go if the room in which they are being threatened opens onto, say, two steps down, or if the door opens inwards. They may have muscular dystrophy and may not have the strength to propel their own wheelchair.

Children with learning disabilities often find these principles of safety and prevention programmes difficult to grasp. They may understand them within the classroom setting, but outside they may not be able to apply them. We need to be more aware of the fears and ambiguities these children may be prone to and to be more careful about explaining concepts and debriefing sufficiently. Excellent materials for these children have been produced by Ann Craft (National Association for the Protection from Sexual Abuse of Adults and Children with Learning Disabilities, NAPSAC) and by the Shepard School, Nottingham, which takes into consideration the cognitive abilities of learning-disabled young people.

Role plays can be helpful, but often children who are disabled find it scary if a teacher they know and trust becomes a 'baddie' in a role play. The idea of acting and pretending can be a concept beyond their grasp and may prove more frightening than helpful. Children who role play 'baddies' also need to know they are not in fact bad, but only acting. Equally, the audience will need to know this child actor is not bad either, only acting. Whilst aspects of such programmes may be 'easy' to explain to the non-disabled child, the experience, knowledge and understanding of disabled children may require a completely different approach.

Children are helped to understand touch they like and touch they do not like, and how to handle, especially, the unwanted, scary, hurtful touch. For many children with severe physical impairments, touch is a constant feature in their lives. Their body space has been invaded so many times for care and hygienic purposes that it seems in fact that their own body does not belong to them. A woman who had polio describes how constant invasion had confused her by the time a hospital porter abused her:

'The medical *experiences* I had made me very vulnerable to being abused; it just seemed the same as everything else that had been done to me, so I wasn't able to discriminate. There's no way you can say no to what a doctor does to you, they just damn well do it when you're a kid and you don't have any choice about it. I didn't say no to any doctor, the porter actually was to me doing absolutely nothing different at all that every doctor or nurse had ever done.' (Westcott, 1993.)

Marchant, however, found that children she cared for could discriminate between the sort of touch which was for personal hygienic necessity and the abusive touch. The child protection team at Chailey Heritage (a residential school for multiply disabled children where Ruth Marchant works) has designed both a children's rights charter, to help children understand their rights, and an intimate care policy so that staff can be more aware and careful about the intimate care they give to disabled children. The disabled children in Chailey are helped to overcome this confusion of touch by clear education concerning the different sorts of touch which are necessary, and what to do if there is touch which falls outside the remit of intimate care for hygienic/medical purposes.

Prevention and safety programmes can only work if the child receives sufficient information which will enable him or her to understand that their abusive experience need not be tolerated and that they have permission to tell.

Provided we are aware that some of the safety and prevention programmes and the principles taught to non-disabled children have their limitations and difficulties for disabled children, these programmes can still be utilised when adapted by skilled teachers or parents who understand the disabled children's particular requirements. To supplement programmes designed for non-disabled children, new material is being produced for the disabled child which is more relevant and appropriate. These include:

* *You Choose* by the National Deaf Children's Society, which utilises English, Sign Supported English and Signed English (see Figure 7.1).

Who could **help**?

Figure 7.1 *You Choose* Sign Supported English, Signed English and English (The National Deaf Children's Society).

* A set of books by the Shepard School, Nottingham, which utilises Makaton and English for learning-disabled young people (see Figure 7.2).

Paul is playing football

Figure 7.2 *Paul Plays Football*, Makaton over English (Shepard School, Nottingham). (Shortly to be reprinted by LDA, May 1994.)

- A set of books for learning-disabled young people called *Jenny speaks out and Bob tells all* (Sinason and Hollins).

At a time when very little material is designed specifically for disabled children, we can at least ensure that when we adapt existing materials we ask ourselves relevant questions. Marchant (1993) suggests a number of such questions:

1. Why might this message be confusing for a child who is disabled?
2. What kind of safety 'code' would make more sense for children who are disabled (or have a specific disability)?
3. What difficulties might there be in using these materials with children who are disabled?
4. How could these materials be made more inclusive?
5. *Representation*. Are children who are disabled included in the text and illustrations? Are they represented positively?
6. *Accessibility*. Is the material itself accessible? (For example, for children with sensory impairment; learning disability; physical impairment, etc.)

Points to consider. Complexity of language; use of signs; Braille; audio; large print; computer presentation; sub-titling or video, etc.

7.   *Content.* Does the message make sense for children who are disabled?
Does it rely on abilities that they have?
Does it talk about experiences they are familiar with?
Does it tackle all forms of infringements of disabled children's rights?
Does it confuse issues of intimate care?
Can the advice given be acted upon?
Does it address issues of oppression due to race, culture and disability?

We discovered in using *You Choose* that deaf children more readily absorbed the safety messages for one reason. There were more pictures of deaf children in the book. It seems that if the children in the books do not represent them, they do not believe the messages are for them. This has profound implications. Safety books which exclude visual representation of disabled children are regarded by them as 'not for us'.

Although access to safety and prevention programmes is a disabled child's right, it will take a commitment by agencies and policy-makers to ensure that appropriate materials are available and that these rights are fulfilled.

Children's Ability to Tell of Abuse

I have previously discussed how disabled children's lack of knowledge and access to safety and prevention programmes means that they may not readily be able to tell others about situations of abuse due to inappropriate or absent educational input. There are, however, other factors which may make it difficult for children to tell and for adults to be receptive to what they are indicating or saying.

Isolation and Risk

Children isolated in segregated residential schools are at far more risk of abuse (Marchant and Page, 1992; Westcott, 1993). There may also be a greater collective pressure not to tell in a residential situation. Ruth Moore (Morris, 1991) describes her experience in a hospital following the onset of Still's disease:

'I think I began to realise then how I was an object. I felt that for years, it was very very strict. I never dared to tell my parents what was going on, all our letters were censored and at the visits which we were allowed the staff were always around. My father gave me a doll for my eleventh birthday – I wanted this because I never had my own toys. I wasn't allowed to keep it.' (Morris, 1991.)

Using a different form of communication, having no access to a telephone (use of which may, indeed, be difficult due to physical impairment) and the isolation from family and friends provides fertile ground for abusive practices to go unchecked (see Table 7.4). A new minicom text telephone line has recently been installed in 'Childline' for Deaf children to use, a major step forward for at least one group of children.

Table 7.4 *Blocks to disclosure for disabled children.*

- they receive less information on safety and prevention programmes
- they may use other forms of communication such as British Sign Language, Sign Supported English, Makaton Rebus, Blissymbolics, Paget Gorman
- they may be isolated in segregated schools and residential care
- they may not have access to telephone helplines
- their disclosure may be disbelieved or misunderstood
- their communication system may be 'censored' of the words and phrases crucial to disclosure

Disabled Children's Trust of Adults

Children may be inhibited from disclosing depending on whether or not the adult is disabled and on his or her ethnic origin. Children who are disabled are more likely to have been abused by a non-disabled adult, and there will be a clear power and status imbalance. Disabled children who have been abused may believe that *all* non-disabled adults are not to be trusted and therefore would want to disclose to a disabled adult.

The issue of race and ethnic group of the abuser is important. I knew of 16 boys all from ethnic minority groups who had been abused by a white adult. These children had been multiply abused through disabilism, racism and sexual abuse. Many of them did not trust other white people, and the situation required very sensitive handling from the child protection team. It is difficult to know how to overcome these issues because an appropriate person may not readily be available, but it remains important to determine from the child who they want to be involved: a male or female worker, a black or white worker, or a disabled or non-disabled worker. Many disabled children are not asked or given this choice.

Receptive Skills of Adults

Adults may also be less receptive to disclosure from disabled children because denial about abuse of disabled children is very much stronger than it is for non-disabled children. No one wants to know that a disabled child has been hurt. We have these feelings with non-disabled children, but they are greater when it is a disabled child. There is also a great fear of not knowing what to do in such a situation, and it becomes easier to ignore rather than to face the issue.

Confusion of Signs and Indicators

Many children do not disclose by verbally telling their story, they are 'picked up' by adults who see behaviours or signs and indicators which worry them. Watching for certain behaviours, signs and indicators in disabled children which will alert to possible abuse is a more difficult task, since adults may be inclined to attribute all signs and indicators to the child's disability. It is important when we see bedwetting, fear of the dark or withdrawn behaviour also to consider the possibility that the child is being abused in his or her bed at night. Many workers with disabled children have not had child protection training (as it is believed that disabled children are not abused, and therefore training is not necessary). So when any signs of possible abuse occur, workers do not know how to make sense of them and attribute them automatically to behaviour stemming from disability.

It is precisely because we may be able to justify another construction based on 'signs and indicators' that signs from the abused disabled child may be missed because we attribute signs and indicators to the wrong cause. To be disabled and to be abused is to experience oppression, powerlessness, stigmatisation and traumatic sexualisation.

It could be argued that some of the more explicit signs of sexual abuse could never be confused with the effects of disability or a disabling society. Unfortunately, experience shows that even the more explicit signs have been so attributed. (BASPCAN Working Party on Disability and Abuse).

What is necessary within training programmes is for workers to begin to recognise the fact that they may confuse signs and indicators of abuse with those of disability. To overcome this tendency, workers need to be directed to explore all signs and indicators fully rather than making assumptions too quickly.

The Investigative Interview

The Memorandum of Good Practice on Video Recorded Interviews with Child Witnesses for Criminal Proceedings (MOGP, Home Office and Department of Health, 1992) lays down the protocol for interviewing children suspected of being abused. The MOGP states, 'each child is unique and the effective interview will be . . . tailored to the child's particular needs and circumstances' (page 2). It also notes, 'if the child has any disabilities, for example speech or hearing impediment (*sic*), or learning difficulties particular care should be taken to develop effective strategies for the interview to minimise the effect of such disabilities' (paragraph 2.10).

Certainly, the MOGP has recognised the presence of disabled children, but in actual fact the document does not really provide the help needed by those who will undertake the interview with disabled children. Throughout the document, reference is made to 'hearing' the child's evidence, indicating that verbal communication is assumed. They do know about deaf children using sign language, but there is no guidance on the level of skill, training or qualifications necessary in spite of the fact that there is official training which can been undertaken (Council for the Advancement of Communication with Deaf People, CACDP). There is an alarming suggestion that, exceptionally, it may be in the interests of the child to be *interviewed* (this is not interpreting, but interviewing itself) by an adult in whom he or she has already put confidence (2.24). Although it adds, 'provided that such a person is not party to the proceedings, is prepared to co-operate with appropriately trained interviewers and can accept adequate briefing'. This may lead to adults who are actually party to the abuse being used or to inappropriate people being used simply because 'they can sign'.

The lack of clear guidance here means that when children use other forms of communication virtually anybody can be used to 'interpret', 'facilitate' or actually carry out the interview itself. There is no acknowledgement or guidance concerning children using Blissymbolic, Rebus or other augmentative communication systems. Invariably, the child protection team turns to teachers to fill this role (a practice quite common with signing deaf children). There are many contraindications for using them in this role (see Table 7.5). These contraindications could also apply to any person who is in a position of authority and known to the child in another capacity.

Provided that certain ground rules are observed, the use of qualified (CACDP) interpreters in child abuse investigations is essential. There are a number of factors involved in the role of interpreters in this context which I shall now consider. (The reader is also referred to an excellent book by Baker *et al.*, 1991, which explores the role of interpreters of foreign languages in public services and sets out principles which can be usefully transferred to the situation of children who use sign language or other augmentative communication systems such as Bliss, Rebus and Makaton.)

> 'The interpreter's and facilitator's role is to convey the *meaning* of everything which is said or indicated. This does not mean literal word-for-word translation since it is impossible to word-for-word translate from British Sign Language to English or to translate from Bliss Board to English.' (Kennedy, 1993.)

In the *Abuse and Children who are Disabled (ABCD) Pack*, Kennedy (1993) has drawn up checklists (see below) for setting up interviews with disabled children and interpreters.

What the child protection workers (interviewers) will need to know of the interpreter/facilitator:

1. The extent of the training the person has received in that communication system.
2. The qualification the person holds.
3. The experience of that person working in the investigative context.

Table 7.5 *Contraindications for using teachers in the investigative interview.*

1. the child may fear being punished if she/he speaks out
2. blurred boundaries
3. teachers have limited signing skills/understanding of child abuse and no training in counselling
4. teachers lack knowledge of deaf culture
5. the child may identify school life with abuse
6. the child may want school to be the place where she/he can 'get away' from implications of assault
7. teachers not aware of legal implications
8. an easy option for professionals – little choice for child
9. difficult to separate pedagogic and therapeutic rules
10. the child feels 'watched', 'guilty', 'bare' and vulnerable
11. child may receive differential treatment and/or expect it
12. confound learning situations
13. contaminates relationships with teacher
14. the child may not disclose fully, to save teacher embarrassment
15. the child fears teacher's relationship with parents
16. difficult for teacher/child to put issues aside during school day
17. use of teacher may 'taint' evidence
18. can never be sure teacher not involved in abuse (if suspected in school setting)
19. the child has a right to an independent worker

(Source: Kennedy, 1992.)

What the child protection workers (interviewers) will need to know of the child:

1. The level and understanding the child has reached regarding language (receptive and expressive).
2. The use and extent of vocabulary the child has acquired.
3. Whether the child has words for body parts and sexual activity. (Some systems exclude these words and the child may not be able to name body parts.)
4. How the child communicates.
5. How the child accesses his/her augmentative signing/symbol system (finger points, eye points).
6. The implications of that communication system (how it functions) on the investigative process and whether it will allow for language and concepts that may arise at interview.
7. Whether the child favours male/female interpreters/facilitators.
8. Whether the child favours a white or black worker/interpreter or facilitator.

The investigative team should make clear to the interpreter or facilitator:

1. The identity of the people involved and their relationship with each other.
2. The purpose of the conversation to be interpreted. This may include relevant background information about the case.
3. The worker's own objectives and desired outcomes, where appropriate.
4. How long the interpreting process is likely to last.
5. Any difficult language or concepts which are likely to arise.
6. Any difficult behaviour which may be encountered (e.g. anger, tearfulness, withdrawal) and how the interpreter should respond.
7. Any difficulties or misunderstandings which might arise between interviewer and interpreter/facilitator and how to overcome these. (Kennedy, ABCD Pack, 1993.)

Much work has been done in child protection for learning-disabled children (Craft), deaf children (Kennedy) and children with complex disabilities (Marchant). Readers are directed to the relevant agencies at the end of this chapter for further advice and guidance. The National Deaf Children Society's Keep Deaf Children Safe Project has a child protection course which trains interpreters who are already qualified in sign language and keeps a register of interpreters who have undergone this training. Marchant and Page (1993), in *Bridging the Gap*, show very clearly the dynamics of using a facilitator for children using augmentative communication boards. It is worth reproducing here what they observed:

> 'Over the course of several interviews we observed how the flow of communication between the interviewer, the child and the interpreter appeared to move through several stages as the interview progressed. We have found it most helpful to conceptualise these stages as progressing through different 'triangles' of communication, as follows.

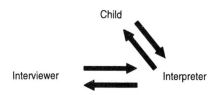

Child

Interviewer   Interpreter

Stage 1

In the first stage all communication tends to be routed through the interpreter. The interviewer may find it difficult to address the child directly for a variety of reasons and the child is unlikely to direct his or her responses towards an unfamiliar adult who clearly does not yet know about his or her communication systems.

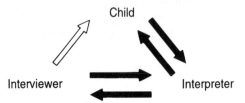

Stage 2

In the second stage some communication begins to move directly between the interviewer and the child, as the interviewer begins to have confidence that the child is understanding what is being said, and begins to address the child directly. The child is likely to continue to address his or her responses to the interpreter at this stage.

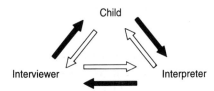

Stage 3

The third stage seemed to mark a turning point in most interviews: this is the point at which the interviewer begins to understand the child's 'yes' and 'no' responses for him/herself. At this point the child begins to address his or her responses directly to the interviewer and the first two-way direct communication is established.

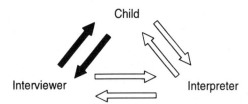

Stage 4

The final stage may not be reached in every interview. At this stage the interviewer has understood enough about the child's language ability and 'yes' and 'no' responses to have the confidence to communicate directly with him or her, and the child responds directly to the interviewer. The role of the interpreter becomes more of a fallback loop for clarification or if there are difficulties.

The main lesson for practice must be to place a very high priority on the interviewer learning and understanding the child's 'yes' and 'no' responses, as this seems to mark a point at which the interview can 'change gear' and enable direct, two-way communication to get underway. This also has an impact on the interviewer's ability to adjust his or her language and approach to the level of understanding of the child. We found that some interviewers tended to adjust their approach 'down' to their perception of the child's understanding, and would unnecessarily speak slowly and simply until they were receiving direct feedback that the child was understanding them.' (Marchant and Page, 1993, page 27.)

Unlike the above, where the child protection interviewer may establish direct communication with the child, communication with deaf children will always require going through an interpreter. The gender of the interpreter is crucial. Recently, a woman police officer telephoned me to tell me a 14-year-old girl failed to tell her everything because a male interpreter had been present. She wrote on a piece of paper after the interview, 'not all – could not tell all – man'. The police officer was rightly upset and concerned since the prosecution may fail because of this.

Interviewing disabled children who have been abused is fraught with difficulties not only because of communication issues. The Crown Prosecution Services are loath to take such cases to court, because in a great many cases the credibility of the child's statement is regarded as less reliable simply on the grounds of disability. The logic seems to be:

- this child must be 'disturbed' due to disability;
- this child may be lying due to lack of attention because of disability (attention seeking);
- this child is probably also learning-disabled.

This is discrimination and yet common practice. Recently, an excellent pack (Plotnikoff et al., 1993) was produced for child witnesses going to court which, although I would recommend it for non-disabled children, includes only three sentences of guidance – for parents – on disabled child witnesses:

'Being a witness at court is an experience no child finds easy. For children with a learning disability or other disability it can be even more difficult, especially if the disability affects the child's speech or hearing. Remember that your child may need extra encouragement and support both before and on the day of the trial'. (Plotnikoff et al., 1993.)

It would have been useful to have given more consideration to the needs of children who are disabled. Disabled children may have the following fears and worries.

- What if I know I'm about to have an epileptic fit?
- What if my hearing aid battery goes flat in the middle of my testimony?
- What if the lighting is poor and I can't lip read?
- What if I don't understand the interpreter?
- How will I know who everyone is? (blind child)
- What if I cannot get into the toilets? (child using wheelchair)

We know of instances where disability has been used to discredit a child's testimony. A partially deaf child who said he couldn't hear the defence barrister was brutally shouted at; 'Can't hear or don't want to answer my question?' The child burst into tears. This same barrister, with a child who was incontinent of urine and faeces due to emotional disturbance, said, 'Who would want to abuse a smelly, shitty child like you?' Such questioning of the child's integrity is damaging, and some preparation for the possibility of this occurring needs to be made. Children who are disabled should be able to give their account in open court, but more work is required to enable this to be an empowering process, not a disempowering one.

'Therapeutic' Services

The terms relating to services for disabled children following abuse are not helpful. There is a tendency to medicalise/pathologise the child who has been abused. For this reason, the ABCD training pack on disability and abuse (1993) uses the term 'survival process' in place of 'therapy/treatment'. This is the term which will be used here too.

Survival services are often denied to disabled children because, especially if they do not use speech, they are considered unable to benefit from counselling following abuse. Disability workers know little about issues of abuse, and child protection workers know little about the experience of disability. Often, instead of acknowledging that there are difficulties with the services offered, the problem is located in the child. Lack of commitment, time, knowledge or confidence on the workers' part becomes, 'she wouldn't have the understanding to cope with counselling'. Inadequacies in toilet facilities are translated into, 'he can't use our toilets'.

Before looking at the themes of survival work, one must look at the practicalities of doing this work. Workers need to ask themselves whether they can do the work on their own, or whether they need specialist help.

Workers can gain much help from co-working with speech and language therapists and/or specialist social workers in disability (e.g. social workers with deaf people or with learning-disabled people). There is advice available from Craft (NAPSAC) and the Keep Deaf Children Safe Project (deaf children). Sinnason of the Tavistock can offer advice on psychodynamic work with abused, learning-disabled people. Marchant of Chailey Heritage is available where multiply disabled children are concerned.

Intepreters or facilitators may be necessary for children who use other forms of communication, but their skills will need to be considered in relation to their experience in interpreting, and their awareness and ability to work in the area of child abuse. Some facilitators or interpreters could find the work too painful or stressful and may not have the training to support them through this. Sometimes it might even be necessary to use non-abusive family members as co-workers, or a person the child knows well (but this should be considered with utmost care for the reasons given previously in using teachers as interpreters and should only be considered as a last resort with the approval of the child).

For children who are disabled, the creative therapies such as art therapy, play therapy and drama therapy can be especially helpful, particularly for children who find voice/language a real difficulty. At the end of the day, the most appropriate worker is one who is able to be creative and take risks in trying new ways of implementing techniques previously used. The person who is imaginative and persistent is ideal.

Survival Work with Disabled Children

Children who are disabled and have been abused often ask, 'Was I abused because I am disabled?' The sad reality is that this is often the case. Even though we know many children are abused, we equally know disabled children are more likely to be targeted. The child is therefore faced with two very painful realities; they are disabled and they have been abused. It is vitally important that the worker appreciates both these aspects of the child's life.

For work to be truly empowering, one must acknowledge both the experience of being impaired in a disabling society, and the oppression of child abuse and how the child has been harmed, used and devalued. They cannot be separated (see Table 7.6).

A service offered by a disability worker may tend to focus more on the aspects of impairment, that offered by the child protection worker may focus more on the abuse. There is a very clear need for dual specialists (Kennedy, 1990). Until that time, co-working is essential where disability worker and child protection worker co-operate and offer services together to facilitate the empowerment/survival process.

Conclusion

This chapter has, in a sense, catalogued the deficiencies and the discrimination towards disabled children in the child protection domain. It reflects the general level of society's devaluation of disabled people and the low priority given to a group considered to be of less importance.

Child protection services, as they are structured at the moment, often do not suit the requirements of disabled children. Safety and prevention programmes, survival/empowerment facilities and investigative and criminal proceeding have never considered this group of children. Children who are disabled cannot be offered the same services as are offered to the non-disabled child. This is because they often have very different needs in relation to communication, mobility, dexterity, physical strength and cognitive abilities. Adapting the current ways of working with non-disabled children seldom works, for it fails to grasp the fact that disabled children's experiences are unique and sufficiently different to necessitate a new approach to service provisions. This new approach must take as its starting point the fact that a disabled child is not simply a child who happens to be disabled (and so we only need to adapt our current ways of working with non-disabled children), but a disabled child who requires a completely different input.

Requirements for disabled children include:

1. Intimate care policies which promote confidentiality and privacy and safety for disabled children.
2. Disabled children's rights policies which encourage and enable choice and decision-making.
3. Training which will challenge workers' stereotypes, disabilist attitudes and prejudices.
4. Assertion training for disabled children which promotes self-respect, high self-esteem and confidence.
5. Self-defence training for disabled children which addresses the issues of fight or 'flight' appropriately.
6. Safety and prevention programmes relevant to the additional requirements for children who are disabled.
7. Programmes for disabled children which explore and address issues of racism and disabilism.
8. Programmes for the disabled children which explore issues of sex, sexuality and gender.
9. Area child protection policies which address the specific needs of these children in relation to safety and prevention programmes, investigative interviews, empowerment/survival work and criminal proceedings.

Table 7.6 *The worker must understand the possible responses of two separate experiences.*

Disabling society/disability	Possible responses	Abusing society/abuse
'I've caused all the family problems by being disabled' 'My fault'	self-blame	'I've caused all the problems by being abused' 'my fault'
Against: family, educational system, society, God for being disabled *About:* missing information, feeling ineffective	anger	*against:* abuser, family, professionals, siblings
Hate: hearing aids, special schools, hospital visits, speech therapy	hatred	for abuser, family, sex/sexuality
'I can't hear' (deafness) 'I don't understand'	frustration	'how do I stop it?' 'how do I get away?'
'I'm useless, stupid' 'I've had enough – struggle is too great'	suicidal	'I'm bad, useless' 'I've had enough' 'the pain is too great'
Disability becomes the focus, not education	poor concentration	can't study in school distracted, preoccupied by abuse and possibility of future abuse
'I'm bad' 'I'm faulty'	lack of confidence	'I'm bad' 'I'm dirty'
For being rejected because disabled For being deaf For 'failing'	bitterness	for being 'used' for 'loss' of family care/protection
Of social situations Of not hearing (deafness) Of appearing stupid Of making a mistake Of failing	fear	more abuse touch/closeness injury/harm pregnancy someone finding out
No control over events, no choice	powerlessness	no control over events
'I can't keep up and I'm keeping away'	withdrawal	'I don't want anyone to know what's going on' 'I don't want to be noticed by abuser'
'I'm not the child my parents wanted'	guilt	'I've caused it' 'I'm abused because I'm disabled' 'I liked it'
'I'm not the child my parents wanted' 'They don't want me to be disabled – I have to be normal' (rejection of true identity)	rejection	'I'm only good enough for this' 'They don't love me'
'I'm not like everyone else' Feeling 'left out'	isolation	'I'm not like everyone else'

Table 7.6   *(contd.)*

Disabling society/disability	Possible responses	Abusing society/abuse
I'm useless' 'I'm stupid' 'I'm defective'	depression	'I hate myself' 'I'm bad/dirty'
'Nobody can help me'	false belief	'nobody can help me'
'Will I make bad/stupid mistakes? Confusion' 'Will I go completely deaf?'	anxiety (constant)	'when will it happen?' 'will I be harmed?' 'will he kill me?'
'What's happening?' 'Why am I disabled?'	confusion	'what's happening?' 'why is this happening?'
'Am I deaf or hearing?' 'Am I normal/abnormal?'	conflict (identity)	'am I child or partner?'
Pretending to be 'normal' Lip reading Concentrating (deafness)	fatigue	pretending all is okay keeping going

(Source: Kennedy, 1990.)

10. Programmes which take account of alternative forms of communication.
11. Programmes which take account of the child's physical strength, mobility, dexterity and impairments (visual or hearing impairment) and cognitive abilities.

To undertake any child protection work with disabled children demands that we as workers address our stereotypes, prejudices and attitudes towards disability. It also requires that we begin to value and promote the confidence and self-esteem in disabled children which have been eroded by oppressive practices, disablism and now abuse, and that we begin to develop a truly personalised service tailored to the exact requirements of disabled children.

References

Ammerman, R.T., Hersen, M., Van Hassett, V.B., McCongigle, J.J. & Lubetsky, M.J. (1989). Abuse and neglect in psychiatrically hospitalized multi handicapped children. *Child Abuse and Neglect 13(3)*: 335–343.

Baker, P., Hussain, Z. & Saunders, J. (1991). *Interpreters in Public Services*. Venture Press.

Degener, T. (1992). The right to be different: implications for child protection. *Child Abuse Review 1*: 151–155.

Department of Health (1990). *Children and Young Persons on Child Protection Register Year Ending March 31st 1989, England*. A/F 89/13. London: Government Statistical Office.

Doucette, J. (1986). *Violent Acts Against Disabled Women Toronto, Canada*. Dawn quoted in Westcott.

Garbarino, J. (1987). The abuse and neglect of special children: an introduction to the issues. In J. Garbarino, P.E. Brockhauser & J. Authier (eds): *Special Children – Special Risks: The Maltreatment of Children with Disabilities*. New York: De Gruyter.

Home Office, Department of Health (1992). *The Memorandum of Good Practice on Video Recorded Interviews with Child Witnesses for Criminal Proceedings*. London: HMSO.

Kelly, L. (1992). The connections between disability and child abuse: a review of the research evidence. *Child Abuse Review 1(3):* 157–167.

Kennedy, M. (1990). The deaf child who is abused. Is there a need for a dual specialist? *Child Abuse Review 4(2).*

Kennedy, M. (1992a). Not the only way to communicate: a challenge to voice in child protection work. *Child Abuse Review 1:* 169–177.

Kennedy, M. (1992b). The case for interpreters – exploring communication with children who are deaf. *Child Abuse Review 1(3):* 191–193.

Kennedy, M. (1993) *Language and Disability: A Guide through the Terminology Maze.* Abuse and Children who are Disabled (ABCD) Pack.

Kennedy, M. & Kelly, L. (1992). Inclusion not exclusion. *Child Abuse Review 1(3):* 147–149.

Marchant, R. (1991). Myths and facts about sexual abuse and children with disabilities. *Child Abuse Review 5(2):* 22–24.

Marchant, R. (1993). *Safety and Prevention Programmes,* Abuse and Children who are Disabled (ABCD) Training and Resource Pack.

Marchant, R. & Page, M. (1993). *Bridging the Gap,* Child protection work with children with multiple disabilities. NSPCC.

Mayes *et al.* (1986) *Child Sexual Abuse: A Review of the Literature and Educational Materials.* Psychology Department, University of Lancaster.

Morris, J. (1991). *Pride Against Prejudice. Transforming Attitudes to Disability.* The Women's Press.

Plotnikoff, J. *et al.* (1993). *The Child Witness Pack, Helping Children to Cope.*

Senn, C.Y. (1988). *Vulnerability, Sexual Abuse and People with Learning Disabilities.* G. Allan Roeher Institute, quoted in interagency information and awareness programme in child sexual abuse, Subiaco, Western Australia (1991).

Sobsey, D. & Varnhagen, C. (1988). *Sexual Abuse and Exploitation of People with Disabilities.* Unpublished manuscript quoted in Westcott (1993): *Abuse of Children with Disabilities.* NSPCC Policy Practice and Research Series.

Sullivan, P.M., Vernon, M. & Scanlon, J.M. (1987). Sexual abuse of deaf youth. *American Annals of the Deaf 3:* 256–262.

The Children Act (1989).

Westcott, H. (1991). *Institutional Abuse of Children – From Research and Policy a Review.* NSPCC.

Westcott, H. (1993). *Abuse of Children and Adults with Disabilities.* NSPCC Policy Practice and Research Series.

Westcott, H. and Cross, H. (1995) *Thus Far and No Further: Towards ending the abuse of disabled children.* Venture Press: forthcoming.

Wolfensberger, W. (1987). *The New Genocide of Handicapped and Afflicted People.* Syracuse, New York.

Useful Addresses and Information

ABCD (Abuse and Children who are Disabled). A training pack produced by the National Deaf Children Society, NSPCC, Chailey Heritage and Way Ahead Disability Consultancy. Comprises of trainer pack (exercises) and reader (specialist papers). The reader can be purchased separately. Pack can be ordered from Caroline Riley, Training Department, ABCD Pack, c/o NSPCC National Training Centre, 3 Gilmour Close, Beaumont Leys, Leicester LE4 1EZ. Cost £120.

British Association for the Study and Prevention of Child Abuse and Neglect (BASPCAN), 10 Priory Street, York YO1 1EZ.

Council for the Advancement of Communication with Deaf People (CACDP), Pelaw
  House, School of Education, University of Durham, Durham DH1 1TA (provides a
  list of qualified sign language interpreters).
Margaret Kennedy, 5 Albion Works, Sigdon Road, Hackney, London E8. Freelance
  Trainer/Consultant on Disability and Child Protection. Previously Founder and
  National Co-ordinator of the National Deaf Children Society's 'Keep Deaf Children
  Safe Project.'
National Association for the Protection from Sexual Abuse of Adults and Children
  with Learning Disabilities (NAPSAC), Department of Mental Handicap, University
  of Nottingham Medical School, Queens Medical Centre, Nottingham NG7 2UH.
Ruth Marchant, Child Care Manager, Chailey Heritage, North Chailey, Nr Lewes, East
  Sussex BN8 4EF.
VOICE, PO Box 238, Derby DE1 9JN.

II

Managing the Process of Child Protection

Working Together (HMSO, 1991) identified three stages in child protection cases: recognition and investigation; assessment and planning; implementation and review. The boundaries between these stages are flexible, but the chapters in this section can mainly be said to address aspects of the structures and processes of the first two stages which have been put in place in the UK in order to try and ensure the protection of children. Thus, the chapters analyse the frameworks (such as that provided by the law), the structures (such as joint investigations or case conferences) and the processes (such as assessment, monitoring and inter-professional co-operation) which have been developed for managing the stages of intervention in cases involving the protection of children.

In no other country in the world, with the possible exception of North America, have the legal and policy structures involved in child protection been so closely scrutinized as they have in this country. The discussion in the chapters in this section therefore reflects the rapid changes which have taken place in recent years, the detailed policy guidelines which have emerged, and the considerable amount of research which has been, and is still being undertaken. Partly as a result of this unprecedented level of scrutiny, practice in many of the areas of child protection considered here is changing rapidly, posing certain problems for those attempting to give a 'state of the art' account. However, where this is the case, the authors indicate areas in which they consider practice is most likely to alter in the foreseeable future. The ordering of the chapters loosely reflects the sequential stages of the child protection process, beginning with two chapters concerned with the frameworks of child protection.

In the opening chapter, Lyon focuses on the civil legal framework for protecting children, considering in some detail the provisions available to protect children under Parts IV and V of the Children Act 1989. A rather different kind of framework is that considered by Brian Corby in Chapter 11. He discusses inter-agency co-ordination, the merits and demerits of current inter-agency arrangements and reflects on the broader issues to be considered about this type of co-ordinated activity, such as the little that is known about the effectiveness of our current systems.

In Chapter 9, Corinne Wattam presents a critical review of policy and practice in relation to making referrals and conducting joint investigations. She brings together a number of research findings on the source of referrals, and reviews three approaches to staged interviewing, before analysing four areas of policy which are essential to the investigative process.

Following the likely sequence of child protection intervention, Olive Stevenson in Chapter 12 considers initial case conferences and the current state of knowledge about them in five dimensions: namely, content and purpose, process, inter-professional co-operation, parent/child participation and specific factors of importance. Although she recognises four areas of concern, she concludes encouragingly that inter-professional work in child protection case conferences is 'light years ahead of other comparable situations which require co-operative endeavour across agencies.'

In Chapter 10, Margaret Adcock discusses the complex issue of assessment in child protection, considering among other things issues involved in the assessment of risk and in following the guidelines for comprehensive assessments set out by the Department of Health.

In Chapter 13, Anne Peake addresses the concerns of teachers, whom she considers to have a key role in monitoring situations where there are concerns that a child may be the subject of abuse, and sets out a detailed monitoring schedule which teachers in primary and secondary schools could adapt for use in their own schools.

The three remaining chapters in this section focus on that point in the process where court proceedings are being implemented. Ann Head, in her chapter, considers developments in the role of the guardian under the Children Act, recent research studies on the role of the guardian, policy issues which arise from these and finally, the implications for practice. Mary Lane and Terry Walsh focus predominantly on practice in their chapter, considering the preparation of evidence, the role of the expert witness, the use of research findings in evidence and the skills involved in giving evidence in court proceedings. In the final chapter in this section, John Williams considers the impact of the criminal justice process on child victims of crime and the policy issues behind the law, and he explains the implications of these for the various professionals and individuals who have contact with child witnesses in the criminal courts.

8

Child Protection and the Civil Law

Christina M. Lyon

Introduction

This chapter considers the legal provisions in England and Wales intended to provide the framework within which a range of state and voluntary agencies are expected to work together to prevent children suffering or being at risk of suffering harm at the hands of those looking after or caring for them. These provisions are now contained within one piece of legislation – the Children Act 1989 (and its consequent Rules of Court, Regulations and Guidance), which was described by the Lord Chancellor as 'The most comprehensive and far-reaching form of child law which has come before Parliament in living memory'.

It is, however, essential to be clear about the scope of the Children Act 1989, since much mythology has already been built up around its provisions and interpretation in law and in practice. It is a statute which deals with a great deal, though by no means all, of the civil law relating to children in England and Wales. Adoption law, although it has been amended by the Children Act 1985 (s.85 and Sched. 10), remains a separate civil law code, and children are subject to a vast plethora of other civil law statutory provisions and case law which will impinge upon their lives in many different ways (see, for example, the Education Act 1944–1993, Child Abduction Acts 1984 and 1985, and the Child Support Act 1991).

Except for minor provisions amending the orders which may be made in respect of children in criminal proceedings under the Children and Young Persons Acts 1969 (s.90 and Sched. 15) and the criteria which must be satisfied before secure accommodation orders may be made (s.25), the Children Act does not deal in any way with the criminal justice system. Where, pursuant to a joint police and social services investigation, a child is believed to have suffered or to be at risk of suffering significant harm, within the meaning of the Children Act 1989 (s.31 (2) (a and b)), the decision whether or not to prosecute the adult or juvenile perpetrator is one for the public authority charged with making such decisions within the criminal justice system, the Crown Prosecution Service. The position of the child victim in the criminal justice system is considered in detail by John Williams in Chapter 16.

This chapter therefore focuses entirely on the civil legal framework for protecting children. It would, however, be wrong to confine ourselves to thinking in this area solely of the civil justice system, since the Children Act 1989 goes much further, at least in its underlying philosophies, than merely to define the terms upon which access to the courts may be sought (see Department of Health (DOH), 1989). Thus, as will be seen, there are provisions expressly designed to foster the development of preventive strategies and approaches, principally by local authority social services departments, but also by other agencies (s.17 and Sched. 2, Part i para. 1). There are also very important provisions in Parts VI to XII of the Act governing the duty of local authority social services departments to secure the welfare and protection of children in what-ever environment they are being looked after away from their own parents, whether this is in: local authority children's homes; homes run by voluntary organisations or private bodies; day nurseries or childminding facilities; private foster placements; independent boarding schools; residential health facilities run by private individuals; or in hospitals.

The legal framework provided by the Children Act 1989 is contained not only in the provisions of the statute but also now in Rules of Court and in a large number of Regulations referred to by lawyers as 'secondary legislation'. Such Rules of Court and Regulations are as binding as the Act itself upon those to whom they relate and in respect of those whom they seek to protect. (See, for example, The Family Proceedings Court (Children Act 1989) Rules 1991 and see also The Children's Homes Regulations 1991.) In addition, the legal framework provided by the Act, the relevant Rules of Court and the Regulations, is further supplemented by Guidance issued by the government departments most closely involved with issues of child protection, that is to say the Department of Health, the Home Office, the Department for Education (formerly the Department of Education and Science) and the Welsh Office.

Guidance on the Children Act 1989 now runs to many volumes, including most crucially *Working Together Under the Children Act 1989 – A Guide to Arrangements for Inter-Agency Co-operation for the Protection of Children from Abuse*, published in 1991, which significantly appeared under the imprimatur of all four government depart-ments referred to above. This guidance must be part of the working Bible of any professional working in the field of child protection. Such guidance from government departments is issued pursuant to section 7 of the Local Authority Social Services Act 1970, which requires local authorities in their social services functions to act under the general guidance of the Secretary of State. As such, the guidance does not have the full force of statute, but it *must* be complied with, unless local circumstances indicate exceptional reasons which justify a variation. It should also be noted at this stage that circulars issued by government departments concerning the implementation of the provisions of statutes or regulations occupy a similar position.

The Children Act 1989, the consequent Rules of Court, Regulations, Guidance and Circulars therefore provide the skeleton or framework for protection under the law. Putting the flesh on the bones of the skeleton is the task of the practitioners working together to achieve the greater protection of children, ranging from the field social worker struggling within limited resource allocations to support a family close to breaking point, down to the judges making orders under, or seeking to interpret the meaning of phrases in, the Children Act 1989.

Review of Literature and Research

Research on the impact of the new civil legal framework on aspects of child protection is still in its infancy. Even in the earliest days of implementation, however, the Department of Health was quick to respond to concerns about local authority social services departments failing to use the new court orders. It commissioned a study by the Social Services Inspectorate (SSI, 1992) from which it was quick to draw out lessons to be learned by local authorities seeking both to work within the new prevailing philosophy of the legislation, that is to say partnership, whilst at the same time continuing to emphasise that children should be and feel properly protected. The message extracted from this study was sent out in the first report on the Children Act entitled the *Children Act Report 1992* (see para. 2.21, DOH, 1993).

The Department of Health is further funding a number of research projects looking at the effect of the Act on child protection practice, including: one on 'the implementation of the 1989 Children Act in respect of children in need of protection', which focuses on the preventive provisions of the Act, directed by Dr June Thoburn at the University of East Anglia and which will report in September 1995; a second study entitled 'Statutory intervention in child care: the impact of the Children Act', which is looking at compulsory intervention in cases of child protection and its management by the courts, is directed by Hunt and Macleod at Bristol University and is expected to report in September 1995; and lastly a study entitled 'Guardians *ad litem*, expert evidence and child care proceedings', which aims to investigate the policy and practice of guardians *ad litem* with regard to the use of expert evidence in child care and related proceedings, and to examine the role of directions appointments in family proceedings courts as a mechanism for achieving the evidence, under the direction of Dr J. Brophy of the Thomas Coram Research Unit and expected to report by September 1996.

Never before has so much government money been directed to a more or less immediate evaluation of the impact of a piece of legislation and its procedures on the practice of all the professionals involved in the system. A number of other projects looking at the impact of the implementation of other areas of the Children Act 1989 are also being supported by Department of Health money, but those highlighted above relate specifically to the framework of child protection.

Theoretical analyses of the 'political influences shaping the civil legal framework of child protection developed in the Children Act 1989' can be found in the work of Fox-Harding (1991), but much more importantly in the work of Parton (1985, 1991). An analysis of the legal framework from the perspective of the many professionals who must work within it is provided by the socio-legal work of Lyon and de Cruz (1989, 1993) and, very importantly, the Children Act Advisory Committee established by the Lord Chancellor's Department and the Department of Health both now publish annual reports on the practical effect of implementation of the Act, the former Department from the courts' perspective and the latter from the perspective of the government department in overall charge of social services responsibilities under the Act.

The research work and the theoretical and socio-legal and practical analyses outlined above are but a small part of what must grow to be a huge body of work on the impact of the civil legal framework of child protection, not only upon those who work within it, but also and most crucially for the children who are intended to benefit from it.

The Civil Legal Framework

Prevention

Local authority social services departments are placed under a very wide-ranging duty by s.17 of the Children Act 1989 to safeguard and promote the welfare of children within their area who are in need; and, so far as is consistent with that duty, to promote the upbringing of such children by their families by providing a range and level of service appropriate to those children's needs. Pursuant to that, s.17 (2) of the 1989 Act goes on to provide that for the purpose of facilitating the discharge of their general duty under s.17, local authorities must have specific regard to their duties and powers set out in Schedule 2, Part I of the 1989 Act.

Under the provisions of Schedule 2, paragraph 1, a duty is imposed upon local authorities to take reasonable steps to identify the extent to which there are children in need within their area, and it is further provided that local authorities must publish information about services provided by them and by voluntary organisations, pursuant to their duty under Part III of the 1989 Act and that they must take such steps as are reasonably practicable to ensure that those who might benefit from the services receive the information relevant to them. Local authority social services departments all over the country have now published information leaflets setting out details of those children whom they regard as being in need and what services are available to support the families of those children in need.

The Act provides in s.17 (10) and (11) a very wide definition of children in need. Thus, a child shall be taken to be in need if he/she is unlikely to achieve or maintain, or have the opportunity of achieving or maintaining, a reasonable standard of health or development without the provision of services for him/her by a local authority under the Act; if his/her health or development is likely to be significantly impaired, or further impaired, without provision for him/her of such services; or if he/she is disabled, and for these purposes a child is disabled if he/she is blind, deaf or dumb, or suffers from mental disorder of any kind or is substantially and permanently handicapped by illness, injury or congenital deformity or such other disability as prescribed.

Section 17 (10) goes on to provide that development under the Act encompasses physical, intellectual, emotional, social or behavioural development and health encompasses both physical and mental health. As has been noted, this is indeed a very wide definition and many social services departments' information leaflets purport to restrict that all-encompassing definition in order to 'gate-keep' limited resources available to departments for prevention. In many of these leaflets a high profile is given to the local authority's duty to safeguard children, and it is made clear that children in need of protection will be given a high priority in the provision of services. (See Chapter 2 of the *Children Act Report 1992*, DOH, 1993.)

Building on this preventive approach, the 1989 Act goes on to provide in paragraph 4 of Schedule 2 that local authorities must take reasonable steps, through the provision of services under Part III of the 1989 Act, to prevent children in their area suffering ill-treatment or neglect. Further reinforcement of the local authority's duty to safeguard children is provided by Schedule 2, paragraph 7, which requires local authorities to take reasonable steps to reduce the need to bring care or supervision order proceedings with respect to children in their area. As if to emphasise the point that children who abuse are, potentially, equally to be viewed as children in need as those children who are abused, the local authority is also required to take reasonable steps to reduce the need to bring criminal proceedings against children within its area and to take reasonable steps to encourage children in its area not to commit criminal offences (Sched. 2, para. 7 (a and b)).

The methods by which local authorities establish which children require safeguarding services will depend upon the measures for inter-agency collaboration in the identification process laid down by Local Area Child Protection Committees pursuant to the guidance provided in chapter 2 of *Working Together Under the Children Act 1989* (DOH, 1991). As *Working Together* points out, 'Co-operation at the individual case level needs to be supported by joint agency and management policies for child protection, consistent with their policies and plans for related service provision.' (Chapter 2.4.)

A coherent prevention policy and plan is therefore necessary if local authorities are to take seriously their duty to safeguard the welfare of children within their area. (For a more detailed examination of this, see Lyon and de Cruz, 1993, chapter 4.2.) Other preventive measures can also be identified within the provisions of the 1989 Act. These include the provision in s.17 (3) that any service provided by an authority in the exercise of its functions may be provided for the family of a particular child in need or for *any member of his/her family*, if it is provided with a view to safeguarding or promoting the child's welfare. It is important to realise, therefore, that where an abused child is suffering at the hands of a family member, whether this is a parent, an older sibling or some other relative living in the family, it may be the case that the local authority will seek to provide services for those family members in order to attempt to safeguard the child who has suffered or is at risk of suffering significant harm.

Where it is felt desirable that an abusing member of the family should move out of the family home, the provision of Schedule 2, paragraph 5 to the 1989 Act could be used to encourage the perpetrator to move out of the premises and to provide accommodation for him or her. This, of course, will demand the co-operation of the perpetrator, and where one is considering the case of child perpetrators who may well have been abused themselves it may be more appropriate to consider the provision of the service of accommodation under s.20 of the 1989 Act, together with other necessary services such as psychiatric, psychological or social work assessment.

The use of both the service of accommodation under s.20 and other support services for such children will of course depend upon the level of co-operative partnership achieved between parents and workers. The necessity for the local authority social services to resort to s.20 may be obviated in situations where the department feels confident that the non-abusing parent will obtain protective measures in the form of domestic violence injunctions or orders, including exclusion orders or ouster injunctions under the provisions of the Domestic Proceedings (Magistrates' Courts) Act 1978 and the Domestic Violence and Matrimonial Proceedings Act 1976.

It has long been recognised, although it only seemed to be officially acknowledged for the first time in the Cleveland Report (Butler-Sloss, 1988), that removal of the perpetrator is far better than seeking to remove the child, and thus every support should be given to the non-abusing parent if they are prepared to seek remedial action using the domestic violence legislation in an effort to keep the child in the family setting. In those situations where police action has resulted in the removal of either an adult or child perpetrator, the necessity for the local authority to use the provisions of s.20 or Schedule 2, paragraph 5 will have been removed, possibly by the imposition of bail conditions in respect of an adult perpetrator, or in a remand to local authority accommodation in the case of a child perpetrator.

Given that the overriding philosophy in the 1989 Act is that children are best brought up by their families, the provision of services under s.17 and Schedule 2 in order to prevent children suffering from or perpetrating abuse is clearly the most desirable policy. Clearly, a major tool in achieving the prevention of abuse must also be education of children in adopting preventive strategies within settings in which they may be susceptible to abuse. One of the principal defects of the Children Act 1989 is that none of its provisions seem to be directed towards providing resources for children to be educated in adopting such preventive strategies. In an era of scarce resources, it would seem that we are probably misdirecting many of our resources to cure rather than prevention, and this is a major area which has yet to be tackled by the combined forces of the Department of Health and the Department for Education.

As has been noted above, the main problem with regard to the achievement of the goal of prevention is that it depends upon available resources which, following the implementation of the 1989 Act, are felt to be in very short supply (see Lyon and de Cruz, 1993, Chapter 4.2). The principal intention behind the preventive measures contained in the Act and highlighted in the guidance, whether these result in services being provided by local authority social services, health, education or voluntary organisations, is to improve both the position of children and the lot of families under stress so that the potential for the child suffering significant harm is diminished, if not totally eroded. Since it is now clearly recognised that, even in the most severe examples of child abuse, one is dealing with a continuum of abuse which may be becoming more and more serious rather than with single isolated incidents, even limited resource input by social services and the other agencies may prevent a situation turning into a case of serious child abuse. Local authorities, in particular, must therefore devote far more attention to prioritising resources in the direction of preventive services and this must include education, since, in the words of the old adage, 'prevention is better than cure'.

The process of identification and investigation

Suspicions about whether a child is suffering or likely to suffer significant harm may arise in a variety of ways. It should, however, be noted that where concern surfaces about whether a child is suffering or likely to suffer significant harm in family proceedings which are already before the court, the court has the power under s.37 of the 1989 Act to direct a local authority to investigate whether there is a need to bring care or supervision order proceedings in respect of such a child. While the local authority is conducting such an investigation, the court can consider whether it is necessary to make either an interim care or supervision order. (See below.)

More often than not, in situations where it is suspected that a child is suffering or is likely to suffer significant harm, the child is a member of a family with whom social services are already working or is already on the Child Protection Register (see below), or concerns about the child have already surfaced with a number of different professionals, all of whom are working with the child and the family. Dale et al. reported in 1986 that in well over 75% of cases which ultimately find their way into the courts, the family or the child was already known to the various helping agencies and was already the subject of considerable concern.

Pursuant to s.47 of the 1989 Act a local authority, in particular, is under a duty to investigate whenever it is provided with information which may suggest that a child living or found within its area is suffering or is likely to suffer significant harm, or where it is informed that such a child is the subject of an emergency protection order or is in police protection (see below). Where information is passed to the National Society for the Prevention of Cruelty to Children (NSPCC), a local authority may also undertake appropriate enquiries and investigations (see, e.g. s.44 (1)(c) and s.31 (1)(9)). To undertake such investigations the local authority, in particular, is required to consult with a range of other agencies to enable it to decide what action it should take to safeguard or promote the child's welfare. The local authority social services may also request other agencies to assist them in such enquiries and investigations. These processes are described in much fuller detail in Lyon and de Cruz (1993, chapters 4 and 5).

The meaning of 'significant harm'

The basis for deciding to embark upon an investigation or to invoke any of the procedures to be described hereafter is that the child about whom one is concerned is suffering or is likely to suffer 'significant harm'. The concept is therefore the trigger for much of what might follow in the way of investigation, and it is also the ground to which the concerned agencies and courts must look when deciding whether to apply for orders, to exercise any special powers, or in the case of the courts, to make orders.

Harm is defined by s.31 (9) of the 1989 Act as meaning 'ill-treatment or the impairment of health or development'; development is defined as meaning 'physical, intellectual, emotional, social or behavioural development'; health is defined to include 'physical or mental health' and, finally, ill-treatment is defined as including 'sexual abuse and forms of ill-treatment which are not physical'. When looking to satisfy the criterion of harm, it would appear to be the case that the court may be satisfied that the child is suffering from harm if any one of the three types of harm envisaged in s.31 (9) is present. This is indeed the guidance offered by the Department of Health, which states that these three types of harm are 'alternatives' and that only one of these conditions needs to be satisfied, but that the proceedings may 'refer to all three' (DOH, 1991, para. 3.19).

The grounds for intervention can thus be seen to be very wide and, indeed, the Court of Appeal in Newham London Borough Council v AG [1993] FLR 281 at 289 has emphasised that the words of the Act must be considered but were not meant to be unduly restrictive when the evidence clearly indicated that a certain course of action should be taken to protect a child, a point reiterated by Thorpe J. in Re A (a minor) (Care Proceedings) [1993] 1FCR 824.

The condition as to significant harm is drawn with reference to the child concerned, so those conducting the investigations, and the courts who may be called upon to make orders, must look at the position, characteristics and needs of each particular child. The criteria which may trigger off an investigation and subsequent making of orders are intended to cover both situations, where the child has suffered, or is likely to suffer, significant harm and the two may be linked together. Clearly, an investigation relating solely to past events is unlikely to proceed much further unless it is being linked in some way to the evidence that the harm is likely to continue (see Re M (A Minor) (Care Order: Threshold Conditions) ([1994] 2 FLR 577). It was stated very clearly in that case that a court could make a care order on the grounds that a child was suffering significant harm if the child had suffered such harm up to the point at which the local authority initiated protective action.

As to looking at the likelihood of the future possibility of harm, as indicated by the words 'likely to suffer significant harm', the investigating agency, in consultation with other professionals concerned with the child, must seek to establish that there would be a greater risk to the child in leaving him/her in his/her current situation than by seeking to provide the services to ameliorate the situation or, in the worst case, by seeking the child's removal through an application for court orders.

The harm suffered or apprehended must be 'significant' and, where this turns on the issue of health or development, the child's health or development will be compared with that which could be expected of a similar child (s.31 (10)). As far as the word 'significant' is concerned, the Department of Health and Social Security (DHSS) *Review of Child Care Law* (DHSS, 1985) stated that minor shortcomings in the healthcare provided, or minor deficits in physical, psychological or social development, should not give rise to compulsory intervention unless they are having or likely to have 'serious and lasting effects upon the child' (para. 15.15). The Lord Chancellor also stated prior to implementation of the Act that, 'unless there is evidence that a child is being, or is likely to be, positively harmed because of failure in the family, the State whether in the guise of a local authority or a court, should not interfere.' (Lord Mackay, 1990.)

The comparison to be made with a similar child is not without problems, however, since one is required to compare this subjective child with that hypothetically similar child. This issue came up for consideration by the court in the case of Re O (a minor) (care order: education: procedure) [1992] 2FLR 7, where Ewbank J. took a very robust view of what constituted a similar child. In this particular case he was dealing with a young girl who had been truanting from school and the issue was whether she had suffered harm compared with another child. In Ewbank J's view, a similar child in this case meant 'a child with equivalent intellectual and social development, who has gone to school, and not merely an average child who may or may not be at school' (page 12). Clearly, if a child is disabled in some way and that has affected his or her health and development, the investigating agency must ask itself what state of health or development could be expected of a child with a similar disability.

As to whether 'similar' connotes any consideration being given to the child's background is doubtful since, according to the Lord Chancellor, 'the care that a parent gives to his child must be related to the circumstances attributable to that child in the sense of physical, mental and emotional characteristics' (*Hansard*, 1989). While the child protection agencies, when investigating issues of significant harm, will have to be sensitive to racial, cultural and religious issues (see more on this in Lau, 1991), what the Lord Chancellor was clearly indicating was that the agency must clearly focus on the needs of the particular child.

Processing the investigation further

The provisions in s.47 of the 1989 Act, which go on to deal with processing the investigation by social services, provide that enquiries must in particular be directed towards establishing whether they should make any application to the court or exercise any of their powers under the 1989 Act which could include the provision of services pursuant to s.17 of the Act. Such alternative action may well be considered in the context of a child protection conference (see below).

Section 47 provides for a range of measures to be taken to enable the local authority to pursue its investigation, including provisions to allow it to gain access to property in order to see the child or in terms of engaging the assistance of other agencies to help it further carry out the investigation.

Where the local authority's investigation under s.47 is impeded or frustrated in any way by the unreasonable refusal of access to the child, it should be noted that such refusal may constitute grounds for a local authority seeking an emergency protection order under s.44 (see below) or invoking the assistance of a police constable to exercise police powers of protection (see below).

It should be noted that by this stage of the investigation, as many details as possible relating to the child should have been gathered, including the child's name, address, names of parents, names of others in the household, name of the family's GP, details of any nursery or school which the child attends, and details of the family's or child's social worker, if there is one. The next step will be to check with the Child Protection Register. The purpose of this register is to provide a record of all children in the area who are currently the subject of an inter-agency child protection plan and to ensure that the plans are formally reviewed every 6 months at least. All social services departments normally maintain such registers and the key information to be held on the Child Protection Register is detailed in Appendix 4 of *Working Together*.

Wherever there is time, as well as checking the Child Protection Register, the agency involved may also check with the health visitor, school, education welfare department, the probation service, family GP, the police and the NSPCC. All such checks provide essential information, but it might be that speed is of the essence and therefore action is required without being able to make all the desired enquiries.

The child protection conference

It may therefore be the case that while the next step in a non-urgent situation would be discussions within a child protection conference setting, such discussions may actually have to be postponed until after the taking of emergency action. In a non-emergency situation where there is felt to be a risk of harm which has not yet materialised, there may well be ongoing work with the family which has identified a looming, potential crisis. In such circumstances, it may be possible to convene a child protection conference with all the relevant personnel. An opportunity is thus provided for giving measured consideration to taking further legal steps, such as obtaining a Child Assessment Order (s.43 of the 1989 Act) or the institution of proceedings for an interim care or supervision order (see s.31 and 38 of the 1989 Act).

Where more measured consideration is possible, the child protection conference may have recommended that it is more appropriate to engage in formal social worker involvement with the family together with the provision of additional services from a range of other agencies. The provision of such services is made possible by s17 of the 1989 Act, and if services from other agencies are to be provided this may require the invoking of s.27 of the 1989 Act.

Under s.27, a local authority may request the help of one or more other agencies including health, education and housing in performing its duties to provide services under Part III of the 1989 Act, and those agencies must comply with such requests unless they can prove that it is not compatible with their own statutory or other duties, or it unduly prejudices the discharge of any of their functions. The recommendation to provide services and monitoring of the provision of such services in terms of the effects on the family does, of course, leave open the option of taking more formal legal action through the institution of proceedings for a care and supervision order if and when this might be required.

It should be noted that the child protection conference's only decision-making power is to place a child on the local Child Protection Register and, if registration is agreed, to allocate the key worker. The key worker must be a worker from either the social services department or the NSPCC. Upon registration of a child, consideration will be given to the provision of a written child protection plan which will be dependent upon a full assessment of the child and family having been undertaken. The child protection plan must include consideration of the wishes of the child and the parents, local resources, the suitability of specialist facilities, their availability for addressing the needs of the child and his or her family.

Working Together points out that, 'special attention will need to be given to ensuring services provided under the plan are co-ordinated, structured and ethnically and culturally appropriate for the child and the family, with built-in mechanisms for progress review and crisis management' (see paras. 5.16. and 5.17). The decision to register a child and formulate a child protection plan is a formal process but, in the same way as with more informal social worker involvement and provision of services, where things go wrong or emergencies intervene, consideration may have to be given to more formal legal action.

In certain cases, however, the recommendation of the case conference may be that more formal court action is required immediately.

Emergency action

Where, therefore, there is reasonable cause to believe that a child is likely to suffer significant harm if either the child is not removed to accommodation provided by or on behalf of the applicant, or does not remain in the place in which he/she is then being accommodated, *any person* may make an application for what is termed under the Children Act 1989 s.44 an 'emergency protection order'. Such an application can be made by any person pursuant to s.44 (1)(a) of the 1989 Act, and may be made *ex parte* (i.e. without the other parties being present) to a single magistrate. Such *ex parte* applications for emergency protection orders may also be made by any of the relevant child protection agencies using s.44 (1)(a).

Local authority social services and the NSPCC are given additional rights to apply for orders under s.44 in cases of emergencies. Thus, in the case of an application made by a local authority, s.44 (1)(b) provides that where enquiries are being made with respect to the child in pursuance of an investigation, and those enquiries are being frustrated by access to the child being unreasonably refused to a person authorised to seek access, and the applicant's social worker has reasonable cause to believe that access to the child is required as a matter of urgency, the court may make an emergency protection order authorising the removal of the child to accommodation provided by social services or the child's detention in the place in which he/she is being accommodated. Almost identical provision is made with respect to officers employed by the NSPCC.

A great deal of detail with regard to the duration of emergency protection orders, conditions which may be attached to them, and provision regarding application to be made for discharge of the orders are provided in sections 44 and 45 of the Act.

In addition to the provisions for any person or local authority or the NSPCC being able to seek court orders authorising the removal or detention of a child from or in a specified place, the Act also provides the police with the ability to exercise police powers of protection without resort to the courts. These powers are exercisable by any police constable under the provisions of s46 and may be exercised for up to 72 hours. This gives the police a very wide power to remove children from dangerous situations in which they might find them on being called out to cases involving domestic violence, disturbance or in response to any other information being laid before them. The police further have a role in assisting with the execution of emergency protection orders if it is felt to be necessary to have to obtain a warrant to enter premises if need be by force (s48).

It should be noted that the general principles governing the making of decisions by the court concerning the upbringing or welfare of children apply to the making of emergency protection orders. Thus, the court's primary consideration has to be the welfare of the child, although the court is not required to have regard to the welfare checklist provided under s.1 (3) of the Act, as this is held not applicable to orders under Part V of the Act. In addition, it should be pointed out that no court should make an order under the Act unless it considers that doing so would be better for the child than making no order at all (s.1 (5) – termed by the author the 'positive advantage' principle).

Acting on suspicions that the child is suffering or likely to suffer significant harm

Where there are merely concerns or suspicions that a child is suffering or likely to suffer significant harm, the local authority or the NSPCC may now seek an order, usually from the family proceedings court, known as the Child Assessment Order (s.43, 1989 Act). Before granting such an order, the court must be satisfied the applicant has reasonable cause to suspect that:

1. the child is suffering or is likely to suffer significant harm;
2. an assessment of the child's state of health or development or the way in which he/she has been treated is required to enable the applicant to determine whether or not the child is suffering or is likely to suffer significant harm; and
3. it is unlikely that such an assessment will be made, or be satisfactory in the absence of a Child Assessment Order.

Since an application for such an order is likely to be a planned response to concerns, court rules provide that the application must be made on notice and this underlines the fact that the order should not be made in emergencies (see Family Proceedings Courts (Children Act 1989) Rules 1991, r.4 (1)). The Child Assessment Order must specify the date by which the assessment is to begin, can nominate the person who is to do the assessment, and can have effect for such period not exceeding 7 days beginning with the date specified in the Order.

It should, of course, be pointed out that where suspicions of abuse arise in certain situations the local authority may have the power to simply remove the child rather than being required to go to court to obtain an order to do so. This would be the case where the child is being 'looked after' pursuant to s.20 of the 1989 Act or pursuant to a care order made under s.31 of that Act, and concerns about the child have developed as a result of care in a particular children's home or other residential placement, or where the child is being cared for by foster parents.

Suspicions about the child suffering significant harm may also surface in the course of any family proceedings brought in the family proceedings court, the county court or the High Court. In such family proceedings, a court welfare officer may have been requested to investigate the child's circumstances and returned to court indicating that there was a degree of concern about the possibility of the child having suffered or being likely to suffer significant harm. In such circumstances, s.37 of the 1989 Act provided the Court with the power to direct a local authority to undertake an investigation of the child's circumstances where it appears to the court that it may be appropriate for a care or supervision order to be made.

Where the court gives a direction under this section, the local authority is required, when undertaking the investigation, to consider whether it should apply for a care order or a supervision order with respect to the child (s.37 (2)). When the local authority decides that there are grounds for the institution of care or supervision order proceedings, those proceedings may be commenced in the same level of court as the original family proceedings.

It should be noted that while all family proceedings courts are of equal standing under the 1989 Act, the county court's jurisdiction has been classified according to the nature of the case being brought. Thus, county courts have been classified into Divorce County Courts, Family Hearing Centres and Care Centres by the Children (Allocation of Proceedings) Order 1991, article 2. The judges who can hear the proceeding in the designated trial centres and the types of proceedings to which they are restricted are provided in the Family Proceedings (Allocation to Judiciary) Directions 1991 and 1993. Where an application for a care or supervision order, or any associated orders, arises from a direction to conduct an investigation made by the High Court or county court under s.37 of the 1989 Act, then, provided that the court is a county court Care Centre, the application can be made there or in such a Care Centre that the court that directed the investigation may order. Where a s.37 direction is made by the High Court, it has jurisdiction to proceed to hear the application for the care or supervision order made by the local authority.

It should be noted that the general principles governing the making of decisions by the court concerning the upbringing or welfare of children apply to the making of child assessment orders. Thus, the court's primary consideration has to be the welfare of the child, although the court is not required to have regard to the welfare checklist provided under s.1 (3) of the Act, as this is held not applicable to orders under Part V of the Act. In addition, it should be pointed out that no court should make an order under the Act unless it considers that doing so would be better for the child than making no order at all – the 'positive advantage' principle referred to above.

Application for care or supervision orders

Where concern over actual or potential harm has not escalated suddenly, consideration should be given instead to initiating care or supervision order proceedings by way of issuing an application for such an order in the family proceedings court. Such action may also be taken following on from an emergency protection order, the exercise of police powers of protection, the result of a s.37 investigation or the obtaining of evidence pursuant to an assessment done under the provisions of a child assessment order.

An action applying for a care or supervision order is one brought under Part IV of the Children Act, and thus for the first time in this chapter we must consider the application of the welfare checklist. This is provided for by s.1 (3) of the Act, and s.1 (4) provides that this is only applicable to applications to make, vary or discharge s8 orders and any other orders under Parts I and II of the Act, and also to any orders made under Part IV of the Act. As was noted earlier, therefore, the welfare checklist does not apply to any applications being made to the court for emergency or other protection orders (see above).

It should be remembered that care proceedings are civil proceedings and the standard of proof required will be proof on the balance of probabilities. Thus, under the terms of s.31 of the 1989 Act, the applicant would be required to 'prove on the balance of probabilities' that the particular child involved is suffering, or is likely to suffer, significant harm (for discussion of this see above) and that the harm or likelihood of harm is attributable to:

1.   the care given to the child or likely to be given to him/her if the order were not made, not being what it would be reasonable to expect a parent to give to the child; or
2.   that the child is beyond parental control.

As was noted earlier, in considering whether or not to make an order the court can look not only at the care actually being given to the child but also to look at the care which is likely to be given to the child if the order was not made and set that against the standard of care which it would be reasonable to expect a parent to give to the child.

In addition to satisfying the grounds laid down in s.31 (2) of the 1989 Act, the court is required, when making such orders or an interim care or supervision order under the provisions of s.38, to be satisfied that making an order is better for the child than making no order at all – the 'positive advantage' principle provided by s.1 (5). It may also be of the view, perhaps as a result of the guardian *ad litem*'s report, that the making of a care or supervision order would actually be the wrong order to make. The provision of s.1 (4) enables the court to decide whether to make one of a range of orders which are available under the 1989 Act, including the making, where relevant, of any of the s.8 orders which could be made in conjunction with the supervision order. (The s.8 orders available under the 1989 Act include a residence order, a contact order, a specific issues order and a prohibited steps order. The provision of s.8 should be consulted for the precise scope of these orders as space considerations do not permit detailed consideration herein.)

Any of the s.8 orders can be made, however, in conjunction with a supervision order. Thus, the local authority may have applied for a care order in respect of a child, and the guardian *ad litem*'s report may recommend the making of a residence order in favour of grandparents or other relatives and the making of other s.8 orders in respect of the parents, such as a contact order in favour of the mother and a prohibited steps order in respect of the father. Where the local authority or the court considers that contact should be supervised in any way, this should be done by means of an s.16 family assistance order (see the comments of Booth J. in Leeds City Council v C [1993] 1FLR 269).

In order to determine that any order which the court makes is in the paramount interest of the child, the court is required to consider the terms of the welfare checklist set down in s.1 (3) of the 1989 Act. This provides the court with a very extensive checklist relating both to the background and circumstances of the individual child, as well as to the capability of any persons that might be seeking orders in respect of the child or relation to whom the court is considering making any one of the orders available under the Act.

Where the court is proposing to make a care order, the local authority should, under the provisions of s.34 (11), further submit to the court the arrangements which are being proposed for the child to have contact with members of his or her family. Where the court is proposing that there should not be contact, or the family or child do not agree with the arrangements being proposed, an application will have to be made to the court to determine issues of contact under the provision of s.34 (see Lyon and de Cruz, 1993, chapter 8).

In addition, the position of a guardian *ad litem* has been mentioned frequently, and it should be noted that the provisions of the Children Act dealing with both child protection issues and issues to do with applications for care and supervision orders provide for the appointment of an independent social worker to investigate and report to the court on the basis of what action the court may take in the child's paramount interest (s.41, Children Act 1989; see also Head, Chapter 15). In addition to the child being represented by a guardian *ad litem*, the court must further consider whether the appointment of a solicitor for the child should also be made (s.41). This unique system of the dual representation of a child, by a solicitor representing what the child wants (where he/she is capable of giving such instructions) and of the guardian *ad litem* representing what is in the child's best interests, has been considerably strengthened by the provisions in the 1989 Act and the relevant Rules of Court.

Where, in a final hearing for a care or supervision order, the court is determined that one or the other order should be made despite the availability of other orders, then the provisions of s.31–33, s.36 and Schedule 3 will have to be consulted in detail. These provide respectively for the effects of the making of a care order or a supervision order, and in the provisions of Schedule 3 the additional conditions which may be attached to a supervision order.

Additional protection available through the courts

Whereas in most situations the making of a care or supervision order will be sufficient to guarantee the protection of the child suffering, or at risk of suffering, significant harm, there may be situations in which the local authority will need additional protection for the child, or specific guidance in relation to some aspects of the care of the child. Where this is necessary, and where it is not possible by any other means (including the use of the provisions of the 1989 Act) to acquire such protection, the local authority may have to use the inherent jurisdiction of the High Court to obtain the relevant orders (see s.100, Children Act 1989).

Since a local authority which has a child in its care is unable to use the provisions of s.8 to obtain a prohibited steps order or a specific issues order (see s.9 (1) of the 1989 Act), although the court can grant such orders of its own motion under s.10 (b), the local authority will have to apply to the High Court to be given leave to make an application for an order providing relevant protection under s.100. The High Court may only grant leave where it is satisfied that the result that the authority wishes to achieve could not be achieved through the making of any other order under the provisions of the 1989 Act and there is reasonable cause to believe that if the court's inherent jurisdiction is not exercised with respect to the child, the child is likely to suffer significant harm (s.100 (4)).

The sorts of situations in which it is envisaged that the High Court's inherent jurisdiction may have to be invoked by the local authority include those situations where an injunction is required to prevent an abusing parent or child from going near or having contact with the child in need of protection (as in Re S (Minors) (Inherent Jurisdiction) (Ouster) 1994 IFLR 623) or, where some operative procedure is required in respect of the child, the child's parents are refusing to give consent and the relevant authority is concerned about accepting the consent to operative treatment provided by the local authority holding the care order (see Lyon and de Cruz, 1993).

Appeals in care and contact order proceedings against the magistrates' decision to make or refuse to make any order (s.94 (1)) – by the child, or by the parents, or by any other persons who have been made parties to the proceedings – goes from the magistrates' court to the Family Division of the High Court, except in the following situations, where there is no right of appeal.

1. Appeals against the making or refusal to make an emergency protection order, the granting of an extension of or refusal to extend the effective period of an emergency protection order, the discharge of or refusal to discharge the emergency protection order, or the giving or refusal to give any directions in connection with the order (s.45 (10) as substituted by the Courts and Legal Services Act 1990, s.116 and Sched. 16, para. 19).
2. Cases where the magistrates' court has exercised its powers to decline jurisdiction because it considers that the case can more conveniently be dealt with by another court s.94 (2).
3. Appeals against decisions taken by courts and questions arising in connection with the transfer or proposed transfer of proceedings except as provided by orders made by the Lord Chancellor (under s.94 (10) and (11)).

On hearing the appeal, the High Court (Family Division) can make such orders as may be necessary (s.94 (4)), including such incidental consequential provision as appears to be just (s.94 (5)) in order to give effect its determination of the appeals. Any order of the High Court made on appeal, other than one directing a re-hearing by the magistrates, shall, for the purposes of the enforcement, variation, revival or discharge of the order be treated as if it were an order of the magistrates' court from which the appeal was brought and not an order of the High Court (s.94 (9)). The role and powers of the appellant courts and the court structures generally are considered in much greater detail in Lyon and de Cruz (1993, chapters 3 and 6).

An appeal from a decision of a judge in a county court Care Centre or in the High Court is made direct to the Court of Appeal and there are no special rules relating to such appeals.

Protecting children in care

In order to cater for a large number of difficult situations with regard to the standard of care exercised in respect of children being looked after by a local authority, the 1989 Act provides for a system of reviews of cases to enable the child complainant's voice to be heard (s.26 (1) (2)). Where a child is complaining about harm occurring in either a residential home provided by the local authority, a home provided by a voluntary organisation or a foster home, then *Working Together* (para. 15.19.1– 15.20.10) advises that social services must take such complaints seriously and investigate in the same way that they would for abuse occurring within the family setting.

Working Together states that, 'Children in accommodation provided for them are entitled to the same level and standards of protection from harm as is provided for children in their own homes'. It goes on to point out that:

> 'It must be clear that whether a child is placed with a foster parent or living in a residential home or school, the agency's actions must take place within the agreed child protection procedures, even though other procedures such as an agency's internal disciplinary procedures or wider considerations about the future of an establishment may need to be pursued in parallel.'

Both the system of reviews and the new representations procedure (established by local authorities under s.26 (3) of the 1989 Act) are intended to ensure that children's complaints are brought to the surface, particularly in the wake of residential child care scandals such as Leicestershire, Ty Mawr, Castle Hill, St Charles, Melanie Klein and Kincora. Where a child or young person does wish to make a complaint about the treatment he/she is receiving in any accommodation provided by or on behalf of a local authority, he/she may have to obtain information about the local authority's, voluntary organisation's or children's home's complaints procedure. Such a procedure is required to be established for considering any representations and the procedure is a two-stage process. These procedures are considered in greater detail in Lyon and de Cruz (1993, chapter 9 and see also Lyon and Parton (1995, chapter 3)).

Conclusion

What has been provided here is only the briefest sketch of the provisions available to protect children under Parts IV and V of the Children Act 1989. As was indicated in the introduction, the provisions in Parts VI to XII of the Act also seek to extend protection to children in whatever environment they are being looked after, but in many situations if there are concerns about the child suffering harm, resort will have to be made to the orders contained in Parts IV and V of the Act.

To many working with children and families, resort to the court will be seen as a failure of all the agencies and systems designed to prevent children suffering harm. Whilst to a certain extent this may be true, it must also be acknowledged that there are simply situations in which resources, however plentiful, will simply make no difference, or where serious and sudden outbursts of violence towards children can neither be predicted nor, in many cases, prevented.

Much does, however, remain to be done in the field of educating children so that they might develop their own preventive strategies, and little effort has been put into this area either by central or local government and particularly not in schools. Slogans such as 'information is power' and 'forewarned is forearmed' spring readily to mind when considering the plight of many youngsters who have to act in ignorance of what could be achieved if only they had been taught appropriate strategies. Of course, this raises the concern that discussing strategies and raising the profile of the issue of child abuse may encourage a proliferation of unfounded allegations, but the evidence now being provided by research into the incidence of child abuse and the testimony of adult survivors must make it all the more certain that we should work towards the notion that prevention is always, but always, better than cure.

In respect of the implementation of the Children Act 1989 in England and Wales, one has to ask whether the Government can really state affirmatively, in response to questions as to whether we have implemented the United Nations Convention on the Rights of the Child, that it has, in accordance with Article 19.1, taken all

'appropriate legislative, administrative, social and *educational* measures to protect the child from all forms of physical, or mental violence, injury or abuse, neglect or negligent treatment, maltreatment or exploitation, including sexual abuse, while in the care of parents, legal guardians, or any other person who has the care of the child' (emphasis added.)

Article 19.2 goes on to provide that:

'Such protective measures should, as appropriate, include effective procedures for the establishment of social programmes to provide necessary support for the child and those who have the care of the child, as well as for *other forms of prevention* and for identification, reporting, referral, investigation, treatment and follow-up of instances of child maltreatment and as appropriate for judicial involvement' (emphasis added).

In respect of both these provisions of article 19, it must be admitted that both the law and the practice implemented by the Children Act 1989 *fail*.

References

Butler-Sloss, Lord Justice E. (1988). *Report of the Inquiry into Child Abuse in Cleveland 1987*. Cmnd. 412. London: HMSO.

Dale, P., Davies, M., Morrisson, T. & Waters, J. (1986). *Dangerous Families – Assessment and Treatment of Child Abuse*. London: Tavistock.

Department of Health (1989). *The Care of Children – Principles and Practice in Regulations and Guidance*. London: HMSO.

Department of Health (1991). *Children Act 1989 – Guidance and Regulations*, vol. 1, *Court Orders*. London: HMSO.

Department of Health (1993). *Children Act Report 1992*. London: HMSO.

Department of Health and Social Security (1985). *DHSS Review of Child Care Law*. London: HMSO.

Fox-Harding, L. (1991). *Perspectives in Child Care Policy*. London: Longmans.

Hansard (1989). *Hansard Debates Committee*, vol. 503, col. 355.

Home Office, Department of Health, Department of Education and Science, Welsh Office (1991). *Working Together under the Children Act 1989 – A Guide to Arrangements for Inter-Agency Co-operation for the Protection of Children from Abuse*. London: HMSO.

Lau, A. (1991). Cultural and ethnic perspectives on significant harm – its assessment and treatment. In Adcock, White & Hollows (eds): *Significant Harm*. Croydon: Significant Publications.

Lord Chancellor's Department (1992). *The Children Act Advisory Committee Annual Report*. London: HMSO.

Lyon, C.M. and de Cruz, S.P. (1989) *Child Abuse* 1st edn. Bristol: Jordans.

Lyon, C.M. & de Cruz, S.P. (1993). *Child Abuse*, 2nd edn. Bristol: Family Law.

Lyon, C.M. & Parton, N. (1995). Children's Rights and the Children Act 1989. In Franklin (ed.) *Children's Rights: Comparative Policy and Practice*. Routledge

Mackay, Lord Chancellor (1990). *The Joseph Jackson Memorial Lecture*, 139 NLJ 505 at 508.

Parton, N. (1985). *The Politics of Child Abuse*. London: Macmillan.

Parton, N. (1991). *Governing the Family – Child Care, Child Protection and the State*. London: Macmillan.

Social Services Inspectorate (1992). *Court Orders Study – A Study of Local Authority Decision-Making about Public Law Court Applications*. London: Department of Health.

9

The Investigative Process

Corinne Wattam

'It is never enough simply to comply with the letter of the state of procedures . . . . There is always an overriding professional duty to exercise skill, judgement and care.' (Kimberly Carlile Inquiry, Department of Health (DOH), 1991*a*).

Introduction

The investigative process is directed by local procedures, all of which cover the requirements stated in *Working Together Under the Children Act 1989* (DOH, 1991*b*). Such procedures can only offer a broad outline, they cannot convey every aspect of the investigation. Like all rules they have to be applied. The recipe for application – skill, judgement and care – is a good one. However, these attributes are something of a moving feast. How do practitioners know when they get it right? The standards by which they are judged appear to veer from interventionist to non-interventionist, doing too much or doing too little. Practitioners involved in the social aspects of welfare, and particularly child protection, must daily confront these difficulties. Is it better for the child to remain with his/her natural parents in a potentially dangerous situation, or to remove him/her and risk the longer-term effects that family separations can cause? What constitutes a dangerous or 'at risk' situation, 'significant harm' or long-term effects? The exercise of judgement is in itself a skill, which includes weighing up information from research, literature, experience and training. The indications are, however, that practitioners make little use of the research (Giller *et al.*, 1992). In addition, it appears that they may get caught up in ways of working that are led less by judgement and more by the requirements of their organisation and that of the legal process (King and Trowell, 1992; Wattam, 1992).

Crucial decisions are made early on in the process of intervention upon which the quality of a child's life may depend. The investigative process is therefore important, and it is surprising that relatively little attention has been paid to its content in terms of skill, judgement and care. This chapter aims to review some of the research in relation to five specific areas which might inform decision-making. It also considers the official guidance which must be attended to, and some of the practice implications which result from this.

Review of Recent Research and Literature

Where do referrals come from?

Table 9.1 summarises the results from recent studies[1]. It can be seen from Table 9.1 that the child is generally not the referrer. This places practitioners in a difficult position from the start. The subject of their investigation generally has not voluntarily come forward. The onus is on the investigator to establish what, if anything, has happened. Thus, from the beginning there is a particular emphasis. It is that of establishing the validity of an allegation, rather than a comprehensive needs assessment of the child. The parents may see the intervention as intrusive, the child may not be willing, or ready, to talk further. From the point of referral the right to protection must be carefully balanced against the rights of privacy and self-determination.

Schools are a major source of referral, which suggests that training, including training concerning issues of reporting, is important. One study which interviewed teachers who had been involved with cases of children who had or might have been abused found that teachers generally reported their concerns. However, the length of time taken to do so varied. A key factor in taking the matter further was the 'confidentiality trap' (Wattam, 1989). The interaction required to break a confidence was complex and not a matter easily addressed by procedures which merely state that

Table 9.1 *Summary of the source of referrals from recent studies*

	Study		
Referrer	Conroy *et al.* (1990)	Denman and Thorpe (1993)	Wattam (1991)
Parent	27%	23%	28%
Friend/relative	14%	17%	5%
School	16%	13%	10%
Health	11%	8%	8%
Public/anon	–	18%	17%
Child	–	12%	3%
Other	31%	10%	28%

[1] All the studies in this chapter are located in child protection. However, two differences are relevant if they are to be compared. Firstly, their location: Denman and Thorpe (1993), Gibbons *et al.* (1993) and Giller *et al.* (1992) are all based on local authority social service departments. Conroy *et al.* (1990) was based in a Special Sexual Abuse Project, and Wattam (1991) in the NSPCC and social services. Secondly, their client group: Denman and Thorpe, Gibbons and Giller *et al.* analysed all child protection referrals. Conroy *et al.* and Wattam examined sexual abuse only.

abuse should be reported. Teachers found the experience difficult and three methods of getting out of the trap were identified: attempting to get the child to tell someone else; attempting to get the child's permission to tell someone else; and asserting the right to tell others by telling children it would be in their best interests. Whilst these methods were ultimately successful, the time between the child's first account and the report varied from immediate referral to a wait of 1 year.

A small percentage of referrals are anonymous or from the general public. These comprise many of the no further action cases (Wattam, 1991; Denman and Thorpe, 1993). There is a suggestion that anonymous referrals need careful screening on the basis of such findings (Besharov, 1988). However, a policy which refuses to accept them is incompatible with protecting children (DOH, 1991a), and the anonymity of referees should be respected (Carlile Inquiry, 1987).

Joint working

There is a very clear mandate that the police and social services should work together in the investigation of child abuse (DOH, 1991b). The anticipated benefits of such a model have been outlined as:

- A reduction in the number of occasions children are interviewed.
- Establishment of a clearer understanding of individual worker's roles.
- Increased co-ordination in the delivery of services.
- Establishment of group support for difficult decisions.
- Increase in effective communication between professionals (Conroy et al., 1990).

The benefits of combining the roles of child protection and criminal justice in the investigation are, on the surface at least, quite evident. If both needs can be met from one investigation, this saves resources and reduces the level of intervention, which should mean an improvement for children and families. However, there is no research which supports the view that the outcome for children and families is better under a joint working approach (Kelly and Regan, 1990). Conversely, there is some concern that joint working has actually made the process more intrusive. If the police and social workers are involved at the very early stages of investigating a report, it immediately highlights the potentially criminal nature of the allegation. The investigation and resolution of child abuse requires a sensitive and careful balancing of these two aspects. Such balancing is dependent on the relationship which exists between the police and social services. Where one is more powerful, the balance may not be in the child's interests. It is this concern that has led to accusations of children being secondarily victimised by the process of investigation (Blagg and Stubbs, 1988).

In relation to the involvement of other agencies, an important source of information has been the review of child abuse inquiries (DOH, 1991a). Inquiries noted the need for the local authority to liaise with a number of relevant agencies. Amongst those identified are home care and day care staff, who have an important contribution to make in terms of information about the child's development and initial identification of abuse. Some reports comment on the usefulness of liaison with the housing department, particularly in terms of case conference attendance and subsequent planning. Health practitioners, such as health visitors and midwives, also have a crucial role to play. The Doreen Aston Inquiry noted:

'. . . some conflict in philosophy and expectation of the health visitor, on the one hand facilitating and supporting individuals and families requiring an open, honest and direct relationship with parents whilst ensuring other professionals were kept fully informed. On the other hand, because a health visitor is usually afforded easy access to the home there is a social policing role in relation to early identification of abuse with a view to protecting the child. This can lead to loss of parental confidence and trust. A balance must therefore be maintained between these two approaches.' (DOH, 1991a, page 12.)

This is a difficult balance to strike, and one which is also faced by social workers who must work within the principles of partnership with parents and parental responsibility. It can be helped by viewing such an assessment in terms of weighing up risks.

Initial risk assessment

The investigative process inevitably involves a certain degree of risk assessment. This topic is addressed in Chapter 10. However, it is worth looking at how risk assessment might operate in the early stages of investigation.

Practitioners must have some knowledge of risk factors in order to carry out the investigation. However, they must also be cautious about reacting to a situation on the basis of risk factors alone. Research has shown that certain factors may predispose a situation to be harmful or injurious to a child. Parental features include the parent's relationship history, including their own experience of abuse, marital status (single, cohabiting, reconstituted), immaturity, alcohol and drug use, criminal history, and social and economic factors, such as isolation and poverty. Factors to do with the child include previous history of abuse, weight and physical appearance, separation from parent, feeding difficulties, prematurity at birth and physical or mental disability (Greenland, 1987; Browne and Saqi, 1988; Parton, 1989).

Analysis of this research and repeated studies have also revealed that such factors do not necessarily mean that a child will be abused. Many of these attributes have been derived from studies of reported and/or registered abuse. Caution should be expressed for two reasons. Firstly, it is generally accepted that there is a level of under-reporting, and we therefore know very little about the characteristics of unreported abuse and perpetrators. Secondly, correlation is not a cause. The nature of child abuse is complex, and it can have many causes (see Corby, 1993, for a review). It may be that some of the more salient predictors of potential abuse have not yet been identified.

One approach for the investigative process can be derived from Brearley's work on risk (1982). This model considers the probability of harm or injury in terms of hazards and dangers. Hazards are existing actions, events, circumstances. Dangers are the expected outcomes of hazards. Thus, the existing hazard of, say, domestic violence has the danger of possible injury to the child. Hazards are not just specific to the child and family, they can also involve the support network and professional context, for example, lack of supervision, over-intensive intervention, and so on. Cooper and Ball (1987) advocate a systematic cataloguing of risk factors in terms of hazards and strengths. An example might be the following, which concerns the decision to remove a child on an Emergency Protection Order after an allegation of sexual assault by her stepfather.

Hazards (pre-disposing/situational)	*Strengths*
Father: Schedule 1 offender	Mother very supportive of child
Alleged perpetrator strongly denies offence	Alternative accommodation for alleged perpetrator is available
Domestic Violence	Intensive therapeutic support available

(Adapted from Cooper and Ball, 1987, page 75.)

Interviewing

There has been a great deal of research activity into the abilities of children to recall witnessed events accurately (for a review, see Spencer and Flin, 1993). Much of this has been laboratory-based, and its application to real-life investigations has yet to be evaluated (Doris, 1991). Encouraging children to recall events freely appears to give the best quality of information, but the quantity varies with age (Dent, 1990). In relation to children's ability to tell the truth, the Pigot working group noted that,

> '... contrary to the traditional view, recent research shows that untruthful child witnesses are comparatively uncommon and that, like their adult counterparts, they act out of identifiable motives.' (Home Office, 1989.)

The conclusion to be drawn from the psychological research is that children are an important source of information on witnessed events if they are questioned carefully.

For this reason, research has also been directed at developing interviewing techniques with children. It is agreed that most interviews should follow a staged approach (Vizard, 1991) and this is reflected in the *Memorandum of Good Practice* (Home Office, 1992, see below). Alternative approaches vary in terms of techniques used to aid recall, the way in which relevant events are focused upon, and the number of times a child should be interviewed. Three approaches are reviewed briefly here: stepwise; the cognitive interview; and the systematic approach to gathering evidence (SAGE).

Stepwise.   This approach provides the framework for the *Memorandum of Good Practice*. It has been applied and evaluated in Canada (Yuille, 1988) where it is found to be useful. Essentially, the model (which is considered in more detail later in this chapter) includes, in its British application, four phases: rapport, free narrative, questioning and closure. The stepwise approach is often associated with Statement Validity Analysis (SVA) or Criteria-Based Content Analysis (CBCA); techniques which can be applied to witness statements to test their credibility. For example, if children spontaneously give new information in the free recall stage which is detailed, specific and consistent with other information, their statements would be rated as more reliable than that of a child who only gave short replies to leading questions. These, of course, are two extremes. Most interviews fall somewhere between the two. Criticisms of the stepwise approach centre on what it does not do, rather than on what it does. It has to be acknowledged that most child witnesses will be victims of child harm and injury. A proportion of these may be disturbed by their experiences, reluctant to talk (Vizard, 1991; Wattam, 1992) and also have special needs (Westcott, 1993). For such children, free narrative is likely to be difficult and this automatically undermines the credibility of their account. It is because of this difficulty that techniques are being developed and researched that might be used within the stepwise approach. One of these is the cognitive interview.

The cognitive interview.   This approach uses techniques developed in cognitive psychology to aid recall of events. Such techniques include paying attention to the context of the event, the sequencing of the event and the perspective of others on it. The focus is still, therefore, on a witnessed act, or series of acts. There is some debate as to how effective these techniques are in relation to children (see Bull, 1993, for a review and Westcott, 1992). In summary, young children may have problems with sequencing and taking a different perspective. There is some evidence, however, that the approach is useful if the child is prepared by familiarisation with the principles (McCauley and Fisher, 1992).

Systematic approach to gathering evidence (SAGE). This model aims to provide a structure for interviewing children who are unable or unwilling to give spontaneous information about an event (Roberts, 1992; Glasgow, 1993). It may be because the event(s) is/are complicated by external factors (such as a divorce between the parents) or internal factors (such as the age or ability of the child). The focus of this model is on the child's world and what is relevant to the child, rather than a specific event. The approach is 'modular' and may involve a series of interviews which focus on different aspects of the child's life. The advantages of SAGE are that it collects a wealth of potentially relevant information which cannot be known from the outset, and it is more likely to result in an assessment which will address the child's needs. The disadvantage is that it does not fit neatly into evidential requirements, primarily because it demands a series of interviews, and accusations may be made that the child's evidence has been contaminated in the interim. However, given that it is those children who find it difficult to talk who are most unlikely to enter into the criminal legal process, this approach means that their needs can be more comprehensively assessed, and also that the possibility of prosecution remains. The practice implications of alternative approaches to interviewing are discussed further below (see Interviewing the child).

Decision-making

Finally, we should be aware of general patterns. It may be that there are wider influences on the investigation process which cannot be detected in individual cases. For example, recent research shows that many cases result in no further action. When the factors which operate in the decision-making process are viewed in this wider context some patterns begin to emerge. It is important to understand these patterns, as they may be operating in ways which are not intended or are inappropriate.

Table 9.2 below summarises the results of four studies and shows the proportion of cases which get filtered out of the process during the investigation.

Table 9.2 *Summary of proportion of cases filtered out during investigation.*

	Study			
	Conroy *et al.* (1990)	Denman and Thorpe (1993)	Gibbons *et al.* (1993)	Giller *et al.* (1992)
Investigated	81	100	1368	1129
Conferenced	21	30	438	489

Each of these studies shows that a considerable amount of filtering goes on during the investigation stage which results in many cases dropping out of the system. The criteria identified by this research as significant in decision-making include:

- moral judgements about parental competence – are they 'good' parents?
- whether the child was compliant or responsible in some way;
- whether there is evidence of harm or injury which could form the basis of a legal case;
- whether there is another motive for referral;
- whether the parents co-operate or corroborate the allegation.

From this it is clear that the decision-making process needs further inspection. These criteria may not be the most appropriate, and they are primarily focused on proving or disproving an allegation rather than addressing children's needs, whatever they may be.

Analysis of Policy Issues

There are four essential areas of policy which are relevant to the investigative process: The Children Act 1989, *Working Together under the Children Act 1989* (DOH, 1991*b*), the Criminal Justice Act 1991 and the *Memorandum of Good Practice on Interviewing Children* (Home Office, 1992), and the UN Convention on Children's Rights. A summary of the relevant aspects of policy is given below.

Working together under the Children Act 1989 (DOH, 1991*b*)

This document combines the relevant sections and principles of the Children Act 1989 with guidance on inter-agency co-operation, management of child protection and the investigative process. All Area Child Protection Committee (ACPC) child protection procedures should conform to the guidance provided in *Working Together*. ACPCs tend to supplement the information to provide more detailed guidance for local use. All practitioners involved in child protection should be familiar with *Working Together* and the advice it contains. The following analysis derives from relevant sections of the Children Act 1989, combined with the more detailed guidance in the *Working Together* document.

The Children Act 1989 provides a framework for care and protection. Under section 47 of the Act, local authorities have a general duty to make enquiries to enable them to decide what action should be taken to safeguard and promote the child's welfare. The crucial principles relate to the child's welfare being of paramount concern, no order being made unless it would be better for the child, and partnership with parents who retain parental responsibility.

The court has powers to concern itself with assessment at emergency or interim stages and with children's contact with their parents. There are a range of orders which can be brought into the investigative process to enforce social work intervention. Three orders were created by the Act in relation to the investigative process: an emergency protection order, a child assessment order, and a recovery order. In addition, the police have powers to take children at risk into police protection, and to obtain warrants to search premises.

An emergency protection order can be granted if the court is satisfied,

> 'that there is reasonable cause to believe the child is likely to suffer significant harm or the authority is investigating under section 47 (i.e. reasonable cause to suspect significant harm) and access is frustrated.' (DOH, 1991*b*, 5.7, page 26.)

The court can specify how long it will have effect, up to a maximum of 8 days (extendible in certain cases).

A child assessment order can be applied for after investigation under s.47, where an emergency situation is not identified but the parents are not co-operating. It has to be shown that 'all reasonable efforts were made to persuade those caring for the child to co-operate and that these efforts were resisted'. The order can last for a maximum of 7 days. Assessment should be designed to secure enough information to decide what further action, if any, is necessary. The child may refuse to consent to assessment.

A recovery order can be made to assist the recovery of a child who is in care, under an emergency protection order or in police protection, where there is reason to believe that the child has been unlawfully taken away, or is missing for some other reason.

The Children Act sets out issues which courts will have to take into consideration. It is therefore important to take these issues into account during the investigation, so that if a case ever gets to court it can be shown that they have been attended to. In any event, they are fundamental principles and practitioners are advised to use them to underpin their work. They include:

- the ascertainable wishes and feelings of the child;
- the child's physical, emotional and educational needs;
- the likely effect on the child of any change in his/her circumstances;
- the child's age, sex, background and other relevant characteristics;
- any harm which the child has suffered or is at risk of suffering;
- how capable the parents are of meeting the child's needs;
- the range of powers available to the court.

Most cases do not go to court. If they do, before the case is heard there can be an initial hearing called a directions appointment. This will give directions to everyone concerned about how the case should proceed and can include: agreement on a timetable for the case; appointment of a guardian *ad litem*; decisions about whether the case should be transferred; consideration of attendance of the child; and other directions as appropriate, for example, contact or assessment.

The tasks in the investigative process are:

- to establish the facts about the circumstances giving rise to the concern;
- to decide if there are grounds for concern;
- to identify sources and level of risk; and
- to decide protective or other action in relation to the child and any others.

Staff undertaking investigations should be competent and trained. The focus should be on the child and efforts should be made to make him/her feel at ease. In addition, the child and family should be given as much information as possible about the process (for a useful publication for older children and parents, see NSPCC/FRG (Family Right's Group), 1992). A particular point is made in *Working Together* that the special needs of children and parents with communication difficulties must be attended to.

The Criminal Justice Act 1991 and the *Memorandum of Good Practice* (Home Office, 1992)

The 1991 Criminal Justice Act builds on reforms introduced by the 1988 Act. These were concerned with making the process of giving evidence easier for children and young people, and included the introduction of video links in some Crown Court centres. In 1987 a working group issued a report, generally referred to as the Pigot report, which commented on extending provisions for child witnesses. Recommendations made by the group were as follows:

- The competency requirement should be abolished.
- Child witnesses should be interviewed as soon as possible after the event and the interview should be video-taped.
- Cross-examination of children should take place in chambers.
- Full committal proceedings should be abolished.

These recommendations were intended to make the process easier for children, and to reduce the need for children to have to give their testimony in open court.

The 1991 Criminal Justice Act abolished the competency requirement, allowed for committal proceedings to be bypassed under certain circumstances, and permitted video-recorded evidence to be admitted, but only for evidence in chief. This partial implementation of the Pigot recommendations has meant that the child still has to go to court to be cross-examined, and that more children are eligible to go to court. This, combined with the admissibility of video evidence, has served to intensify the focus on the child victim as a potential witness.

Justice Pigot recommended a Code of Practice for practitioners. This came in the wake of criticisms of social work interviews with children following Cleveland (Butler-Sloss, 1988) and the widely publicised trials in Rochdale and Manchester (for a review, see Wattam, 1992). As a consequence, the Home Office published the *Memorandum of Good Practice* (MOGP) (1992). This document provides advice on video-recorded interviews with child witnesses for criminal proceedings. The MOGP builds on the *Working Together* approach, in particular the need for the police and social services to investigate jointly cases of child abuse in order to combine 'the interests of the child and justice'.

The offences which apply to the making of video-recorded interviews cover physical abuse, cruelty, neglect and sexual abuse. The interview should equate with a 'witness statement of the first detailed account given to the police and should be conducted as soon as is practicable'. There are three reasons for this. Firstly, there has been much controversy over the possible contamination of evidence by practitioners and parents prior to the initial interview. Secondly, it is considered better to get as recent an account as possible from the child in the light of research on memory and recall. Thirdly, a recent complaint has more validity in law. As a consequence, video interviews have now become an important consideration early on in the investigative process.

Whilst the legislation does not prescribe particular equipment and facilities for videoing, a number of criteria must be met. These are outlined in the MOGP and include the need for privacy and comfort, facilities for the disabled, high-quality audio and visual sound, and the need for the court to see the circumstances in which the video was made.

Planning and assessment of the child's development, circumstances, background, competence and availability for cross-examination are emphasised prior to the interview. It is advised that the child's agreement to video should be sought, and if they are too young to understand, that the views of parents or carers should be listened to. Written consent is not necessary.

The interview itself should go at the child's pace, but as a 'rule of thumb' should last for less than an hour. The document is, however, entirely voluntary. Thus, it is possible to conduct more than one interview where the circumstances justify it. The interview will be phased following a model based on the stepwise approach, as follows.

Rapport. This stage helps the child to relax and supplements the 'base line' knowledge obtained in planning. Crucially, it allows the interviewer to explain the ground rules for discussion, such as the need to tell the truth and the acceptability of saying 'I don't know' or 'I don't understand'.

Free narrative. The child is asked to recall everything they can remember about the alleged offence in their own words. Prompts can be made about information mentioned by the child, for example: 'Did anything else happen?'

Questioning. This stage begins with open-ended questions and progresses to specific, non-leading questions, closed questions and, as a last resort, leading questions. The aim is to ask as few questions as possible, to elicit as much free narrative as possible and to avoid leading questions which are likely to be edited out and invalidate the interview.

Closure. It is essential to make sure that the child is not in distress at the end of the interview. Neutral topics can be returned to, the child should be asked if they have any questions, and a contact name and telephone number should be given.

The MOGP emphasises that these are not therapeutic interviews, and that once they have been completed it should be possible for 'appropriate counselling and therapy' to take place. The Crown Prosecution Service should be informed about this. The legal constraints to conducting the interview are clearly outlined, and practitioners are advised to abide by the basic rules of evidence. These include: avoidance of questions which assume disputed facts or suggest an answer (leading questions); steering away from talk about previous statements or what others have said (hearsay); avoiding references to the character of the accused.

There are a number of administrative and organisational issues relevant to recording, access, storage, copying and handling of tapes outlined in Part 4 of the *Memorandum.* In principle, copying should be avoided, access restricted, and storage and handling carefully monitored.

UN Convention on Children's Rights

This convention was ratified by the British Government in 1991. It is relevant to the investigative process in at least two ways. Firstly, it sets out basic rights that pertain to all children. These are broadly covered by the Children Act and include the advice that:

- all actions concerning the child should take full account of his or her best interests;
- the rights and responsibilities of parents are respected;
- the child has a right to express an opinion and to have that opinion taken into account in any matter or procedure affecting him or her;
- the child has a right to obtain and make known information and express views unless they violate the rights of others;
- the child has a right to protection from interference with regard to privacy, family, home and correspondence, and from libel/slander;

- the State has an obligation to protect children from all forms of maltreatment perpetrated by parents or others responsible for their care.

Secondly, a number of investigations may concern the assessment of behaviour which is alleged to be bad for the child. In this context, it should be noted that the following rights apply.

- The child's right to freedom of thought, conscience and religion, subject to appropriate parental guidance and national law.
- The child's right to meet with others and to join or set up associations, unless the fact of doing so violates the rights of others.

Practice Implications of Research and Policy

The purpose of the investigation

There are competing needs and interests in the investigation, to do with rights, responsibilities, protection, prosecution and justice. All of these must be balanced, and quite clearly, the welfare of the child is paramount. However, these are broad issues and general terms. Individual workers will have to make judgements in each particular case, and within different working arrangements. Much hinges on the relationship in the field between social workers and the police when trying to achieve a balance between protection and prosecution. In addition, a great deal depends on the moral and cultural framework within which individual practitioners operate, particularly in relation to children's rights, parental competence and participation. The implications for practice are two-fold. Firstly, that decision-making should be guided by the needs of the child, and not the balance of power in working relationships. Secondly, that practitioners need opportunities to review and be objective about their decision-making criteria, in order to learn how these might affect the investigation and its outcome.

Ultimately, the purpose of the investigation must be to find out what, if anything, has happened to a child and what should be done about it. The emphasis in practice appears to be on the former, with the result that very little attention seems to be paid to services for the child, the family and the alleged abuser once the investigation is complete.

Collating information and collective planning

If the courts are involved there will be a need to plan work with their timescales in mind. An early strategy discussion is essential – this can be over the telephone – between police and social services to plan the role of each agency and the extent of joint investigation. The welfare of the child must be of first importance.

It is important in the context of both the *Memorandum* and the Children Act 1989, where there is increasing emphasis on evidence, that the investigation is carefully planned. This planning must take account of as much available information as possible. Where feasible, this should include developmental assessment (school, health visitor, parents, psychological services, where there has been previous contact). The purpose of this information is to inform the interview strategy and decision-making on the validity of the allegation. For example, knowledge of the child's reading age will determine what written information can be given. Information on motor skill development can be judged against an account where the allegation concerns something it is claimed the child has done, for example, walked into a fire. Relevant information would also include the child's relationship context: friends, relatives with whom the child has contact, other significant people in the child's life. Clearly, it is also important to know of any relevant medical history, cultural issues – particularly language and identity – special needs and day-to-day routine. This information will assist in deciding who should conduct the investigation, what help they will require, when the child can be seen, and so forth.

The timing of the medical is a further consideration. Reasons for having it prior to the interview include the child's need for immediate medical attention, or loss of forensic evidence if a medical is not carried out as soon as possible. In the majority of cases an immediate medical will not be necessary.

All information must be documented and the decisions made at the strategy meeting recorded. A form which structures the planning process is advisable, since a record could, at some later date, be required by a court. One of the things the court will be interested in is how the interview was planned, whether this plan was diverged from, and if so why.

Treating children's accounts forensically

There is an increasing emphasis on obtaining evidence for both criminal and care proceedings, and the impetus of the investigation is to establish the validity of an allegation. In practice, it appears that children's accounts are judged by the everyday criteria used in any situation to establish whether any person is telling the truth. These are concerned with how people are categorised in terms of their reliability – are their behaviours characteristic of someone who is telling the truth? Certain features make an account appear more valid. If the information is specific, detailed, consistent, without motive and can be corroborated, these features lend validity. The problem arises where children, especially those who have been subjected to long-term repeated abuse in a close relationship, cannot meet these criteria. Investigators can help by pre-empting the need to show such features and by skilfully guiding interviews with the child to account for them.

Confidentiality

Child protection requires a close working relationship between agencies at individual and joint agency and management policy level. Practitioners from other agencies are not only carrying out their own agency functions, they are also helping the local authority to discharge its child protection duty. In terms of sharing information, there is often concern about confidentiality. *Working Together* includes the following advice:

1. Any information exchanged should be treated in confidence and cannot be disclosed for any other purpose without consulting the person who provided it.
2. In relation to medical information:

   '. . . if a doctor has reason for believing that a child is being physically or sexually abused, not only is it permissible for the doctor to disclose information to a third party but it is a duty of the doctor to do so.' (DOH, 1991b, page 12.)

3. In relation to nurses any decision to withhold or disclose information should be able to be justified. Practitioners should always take the opportunity to discuss the matter fully with other practitioners, and explore the ramifications of their decisions.
4. In relation to social workers, they should:

'recognise that information clearly entrusted for one purpose should not be used for another purpose without sanction.' (DOH, 1991b page 12.)

Social workers can only divulge information with the consent of the client, unless there is evidence of serious danger to the client, worker, or others in the community. They must make clear to those providing information that confidentiality may not be maintained if the withholding of the information will prejudice the welfare of a child.

Interviewing the child

It can never be assumed that something has for certain happened to a child. Important decisions have to be made at the strategy stage in order to weigh up whether or not it is necessary to conduct an interview under the MOGP. Practice experience shows that this is not always in the child's interests, particularly if:

- the child does not consent;
- the child is exhibiting life-threatening behaviour and needs immediate therapeutic support;
- the child is not yet ready to discuss details of the alleged offence.

The style of interview will depend on the age and characteristics of the child and the nature of the allegation. For those who have suffered long-term abuse and who are traumatised by events that have occurred, a more sensitive and gradual approach may be required, such as SAGE (see above).

The status of the *Memorandum* is quite clearly voluntary. However, there is a tendency in practice to interpret the guidance strictly, largely owing to a fear of repercussions from the defence if a case ever does get to court. The fact is that very few cases ever reach prosecution, and the interests of the child must be paramount, particularly in relation to protection through the civil process. Decisions about how to interview, and when to divert from the *Memorandum*'s stepwise, non-leading approach, can be justifiable in terms of the child's welfare. High standards are required by both jurisdictions, and the principles of the *Memorandum* are applicable to both in as much as children should not be pressured or led by questioning into giving false information. If leading questions are to be used, very skilful handling of the replies and information leading from the replies is required. Readers are directed to Jones and McQuiston (1989) for further information on this point. With regard to using alternative techniques such as the cognitive interview or SAGE, similar advice pertains. These are techniques which have yet to be evaluated sufficiently to justify their inclusion in the *Memorandum*. If it is felt that more information would be obtained from a child by using them, which can be the case, then the principles of evidence should be borne in mind.

Finally, bearing in mind the potential evidential usefulness of the first substantive interview, professionals coming into contact with the child prior to the interview must be extremely careful that they do not question the child about the alleged offence. The

Memorandum guides practitioners to listen and carefully record any spontaneous account.

Some key issues

Recording.   Records must be accurate and clear, reflect all the work which is being done and all information known regarding the family.

> 'They should contain clear details of the investigation, assessments, the decisions agreed, the basis on which they were made and the plan on which work is based.' (DOH, 1991*b*, page 26.)

Records are accountable. They may be used by the court and are increasingly called for by the defence as undisclosed material. They can also be accessed to clients, and they may be scrutinised under case review procedures. Distinctions must therefore be made between fact, opinion and hearsay, and confidentiality of source information should be respected. For example, if a teacher gives information about a child which is to be recorded, it should be explained that the information will be attributed to the named individual. If teachers do not wish for their names to be divulged, this could be respected by the use of an anonymous category such as 'teacher'. Practitioners must be careful that people cannot be identified by other means as they would be, for example, in the case of 'Jane's class teacher'. Failure to respect confidentiality and to underestimate the future importance and use of records may result in an unwillingness on the part of others to offer significant information.

Use of anatomically complete dolls.   These dolls have traditionally been used in interviews with children where sexual assault has been alleged. Some controversy surrounds their use, and it has been suggested that they have evoked responses which can appear to confirm an allegation but which actually may be just a normal reaction to the dolls and the interview situation. Whether this is true or not, it has led to scepticism within the legal profession, and for this reason their use is not advised unless the interviewer is skilled and trained in their use and misuse.

The medical examination.   Definitive physical signs and symptoms of sexual assault are rare (Royal College of Physicians, 1991). Although it is possible that medical findings are present in less than half the cases where children have been sexually assaulted (Glaser and Frosh, 1988), even where medical findings are present it is difficult in many cases to state categorically that these signs are conclusive evidence of abuse. Cases of physical assault and chronic neglect or failure to thrive are more likely to have medical evidence. However, in some cases the sign or symptom may appear to be quite minor, such as small fingertip bruising on the face or back. The social and historical context of the injury is therefore essential and should be obtained before the medical is conducted.

Medical evidence is important for three reasons: to reassure the child and family that there is nothing physically wrong; to ensure that the child receives appropriate treatment wherever necessary; and to obtain forensic evidence for use in court proceedings.

Once again, the general principle of obtaining the informed consent of the child and family applies. This means that the process of the examination should be carefully explained to the child, in an age-appropriate way. Where the parents do not consent, but the child does, the 'Gillick' principle[1] applies. The gender of the examiner is

[1] The Gillick decision affirmed the right of a competent child to take decisions about their own medical treatment.

important and children should be given a choice. There has been some concern that the medical examination can contribute to a feeling of 'secondary abuse' for the child, however sensitively the practitioner may handle it, particularly in cases of sexual assault. When consent is refused, an emergency protection order or a child assessment order can be applied for. However, in such cases the grounds for carrying out a medical need to be very clear.

Recent research suggests that the distinction between forensic and medical evidence is not always clear (Wattam, 1992). This is an important distinction, because cases may fail to proceed on the basis that there is no medical evidence, and forensic evidence tends not to be sought. In cases of child assault, evidence is narrowly defined in terms of the results of the alleged actions on the body. However, other forensic evidence which might corroborate a child's account can sometimes be present, such as fibres on clothing, bedding, and so forth. The child's sense of what happened to him or her needs to be fully explored, and not dismissed merely because the adult interpretation does not give a medical sign consistent with it.

Conclusion

This chapter has presented a critical review of policy and practice in relation to making referrals and conducting joint investigations. From this it is clear that the investigation process is essentially an information gathering and an information sharing exercise. It is also a process which requires skill of judgement in order to assess and balance the immediate and long-term interests of the child, the need for prosecution and justice, and the need for intervention and respect for individual privacy and freedom.

As a consequence of recent research and changes to legislation there are national concerns surrounding child protection practice. Much of this centres on the investigative process, as it has done ever since Cleveland. Tensions generally arise in three areas. Firstly, defining the right of the state to intervene in family life, and the prevailing principle of non-intervention. Secondly, the demands of civil and criminal jurisdictions and the difficulties of reconciling them. Thirdly, the focus of intervention which is strongly biased towards investigation.

The investigative process has a certain amount of variance across the country, with a nominal division into exclusive and inclusive practices. These are two extremes and most authorities fall somewhere between the two, veering towards one end or the other of what could be described as a continuum of levels of intervention. The exclusive approach is characterised by decision-making which seeks to exclude children from the child protection system. There is a focus on minimal intervention; doing what has to be done for accountable purposes. Reasons for this approach can include a high referral rate, under-resourcing, an imbalance of the power in joint working relationships between the police and social services, and a strong influence from the legal process. Philosophical and professional justification for this approach derives from two standpoints. Firstly, that child abuse is a crime and should be investigated as such, and that the state has no right to intervene unless crimes are being committed. Secondly, that intervention is bad for children and families, and should be kept to a minimum. An inclusive approach is characterised by decision-making which seeks to include as many children as are referred. It is characterised by the 'no smoke without fire' and a 'play safe' viewpoint. As a consequence, in some areas many cases filter out early on, whilst in others cases linger on. Both outcomes are of potential detriment to the child. Practice could alter, towards a more comprehensive assessment, which takes account of possible outcomes and is needs-based rather than allegation-based.

There is a clear tension between the civil and criminal domains of law. This is played out in the investigation in both joint working relationships and also decision-making around the *Memorandum of Good Practice*, particularly about when to divert from it. Both jurisdictions have different interests and work towards different outcomes, yet it is left to practitioners to marry these interests on behalf of the child. Such a reconciliation is often difficult to achieve in practice, and current debate centres on how far government guidance should go. The *Memorandum* is entirely voluntary, but its interpretation is often more stringent in practice owing to fear of the repercussions of diversion, not least from the defence at court.

Finally, with regard to the 'bias' in intervention towards investigation it is becoming clear that the process is focused by legal requirements (King and Piper, 1990). The accountable actions in a case are those which must be justified to the organisation. Increasingly, these are prescribed by the law and official guidance. The emphasis is on protection rather than prevention or longer-term well-being. It could be argued that whilst therapeutic support and outcomes in terms of the well-being of children are not subject to legal sanction, this dominant focus on investigation will continue.

All of this points to one conclusion. If the investigative process is to be child-centred, it requires a comprehensive needs assessment of the child which takes account of the Children Act principles. Whilst this is easy to recommend on paper, the practical realities will remain complex and on occasions present conflicts that are not amenable to resolution.

Further Reading

Children's Rights Development Unit. (1992) *The United Nations Convention on the Rights of the Child*. London: CRDU.
Includes a background to the convention, full text and unofficial summary of main provisions.

Department of Health (1989). *An Introduction to the Children Act 1989*. London: HMSO.
Clarification of terminology, overview of the act, and indications of previous legislation which is now altered.

Department of Health (1991a). *Child Abuse. A Study of Inquiry Reports, 1980–1989*. London: HMSO.
Review of 19 inquiry reports. Summary of the issues raised in relation to: agency functions, issues for management, inter-agency working and management of individual cases.

Department of Health (1991b). *Working Together Under the Children Act 1989*. London: HMSO.
Comprehensive advice on the management and conduct of child protection investigations and procedures.

Home Office (1992). *Memorandum of Good Practice*. London: HMSO.
Detailed guidance on the organisation and conduct of video-recorded interviews with child witnesses for criminal proceedings.

Jones, D., Pickett, J., Oates, M. & Barbor, P. (1987). *Understanding Child Abuse*. Basingstoke: Macmillan.
A good introduction to child abuse, its assessment and presentation, investigation and continuing work with the family.

Spencer, J. & Flin, R. (1993). *The Evidence of Children: The Law and the Psychology*. London: Blackstone.
A comprehensive review of psychological research and legal issues in relation to child witnesses and interviewing children.

Wattam, C. (1992). *Making A Case in Child Protection*. Harlow: Longmans.
A review of research and practice in relation to obtaining evidence in child protection work.

References

Besharov D.J. (1988). The need to narrow the grounds for state intervention. In D.J. Besharov, (ed.): *Protecting Children from Abuse and Neglect: Policy and Practice*. Springfield, Illinois: C.C. Thomas.

Blagg, H. & Stubbs, P. (1988). A child centred practice? Multi-agency approaches to child sexual abuse. *Practice 2 (1)*.

Brearley, C.P. (1982). *Risk and Social Work*. London: Routledge & Kegan Paul.

Browne, K. & Saqi, S. (1988). Approaches to screening for child abuse and neglect. In K. Browne, C. Davies & P. Stratton (eds): *Early Prediction and Prevention of Child Abuse*. Chichester: John Wiley.

Bull, R. (1993). Innovative techniques for the questioning of child witnesses especially those who are young and those with learning disability. In M. Zaragoza (ed.): *Memory and Testimony in the Child Witness*. London: Sage.

Butler-Sloss, E. (1988). *Report of the Inquiry into Child Abuse in Cleveland 1987*. London: HMSO.

Conroy, S., Fielding, N. & Tunstill, J. (1990). *Investigating Child Sexual Abuse: The Study of a Joint Initiative*. London: The Police Foundation.

Cooper, D.M. & Ball, D. (1987). *Social Work and Child Abuse*. Macmillan: Basingstoke.

Corby, B. (1993). *Child Abuse: Towards a Knowledge Base*. London: Open University Press.

Denman, G. & Thorpe, D. (1993). *Family Participation and Patterns of Intervention in Child Protection in Gwent*. A Research Report for the Area Child Protection Committee, Gwent. Lancaster University.

Dent, H.R. (1990). Interviewing. In J. Doris (ed.): op. cit.

Doris, J. (1991). *The Suggestibility of Children's Recollections: Implications for Eyewitness Testimony*. Washington DC: American Psychological Association.

Gibbons, J., Conroy, S. & Bell, C. (1993). *Operation of Child Protection Registers: Report to Department of Health*. University of East Anglia: Social Work Development Unit.

Giller, H., Gormley, C. & Williams, P. (1992). *The Effectiveness of Child Protection Procedures: An Evaluation of Child Protection Procedures in Four ACPC Areas*. Manchester: Social Information Systems Ltd.

Glasgow, D. (1993). *Interviewing Children Who May have been Sexually Abused: A New Application of an Established Methodology*. Available from the Department of Clinical Psychology, Liverpool University.

Glaser, D. and Frosh, S. (1988) *Child Sexual Abuse* Basingstoke: Macmillan.

Greenland, C. (1987). *Preventing CAN Deaths: An International Study of Deaths Due to Child Abuse and Neglect*. London: Tavistock.

Home Office (1989). *Report of the Advisory Group on Video Evidence*. London: HMSO.

Jones, D. & McQuiston, M. (1989). *Interviewing the Sexually Abused Child*. Gaskell: The Royal College of Psychiatrists.

Kelly, L. & Regan, L. (1990). Flawed protection. *Social Work Today 21 (32)*: 13–15.

King, M. & Piper, C. (1990). *How the Law Thinks About Children*. Aldershot: Gower.

King, M. & Trowell, J. (1992). *Children's Welfare and the Law: The Limits of Legal Intervention*. London: Sage.

McCauley, M. & Fisher, R. (1992). *Improving Children's Recall of Action with the Cognitive Interview*. Paper presented at the meeting of the American Psychology–Law Society, San Diego.

NSPCC/FRG (1992). *Child Protection Procedures – What They Mean for Your Family*. London: NSPCC.

Parton, N. (1989). Child abuse. In B. Kahan (ed.): *Child Care Research, Policy and Practice*. London: Hodder & Stoughton.

Roberts, H. (1992). *Gathering Evidence from Children: A Systematic Approach*. Paper presented at the British Psychological Society Symposium, Harrogate, 26 March.

Royal College of Physicians (1991). *Physical Signs of Sexual Abuse in Children: A Report of the Royal College of Physicians*. London.

Vizard, E. (1991). Interviewing children suspected of being sexually abused. A review of theory and practice. In C.R. Hollin & K. Howell (eds): *Clinical Approaches to Sex Offenders and their Victims*. Chichester: John Wiley.

Wattam, C. (1989). *Teachers' Experiences with Children who have been or may have been Sexually Abused*. Occasional Paper No. 5. London: NSPCC.

Wattam, C. (1991). *Disclosure: The Child's Perspective*. Research Report for the NSPCC. Available from NSPCC Hedley Library.

Westcott, H. (1992). The cognitive interview: a useful tool for social workers? *British Journal of Social Work 22*: 519–533.

Westcott, H. (1993). *Abuse of Children and Adults with Disabilities*. Policy, Practice and Research Series. London: NSPCC.

Yuille, J. (1988). The systematic assessment of children's testimony. *Canadian Psychology 29*: 247–262.

10

Assessment

Margaret Adcock

Introduction

It is an accepted principle that good assessment is the foundation of good child protection work and planning (Department of Health (DOH), 1989). The research suggests, however, that it is questionable whether agreement exists as to what constitutes good assessment and whether or not it does actually happen in practice. In a recent study of child protection in four areas of Wales, Giller *et al.* (1992) found that over 75% of children dropped out of the child protection system at a point between referral and the decision of a case conference to register the child or not. The researchers claimed that there were no qualitative differences between the cases which dropped out and those which were ultimately registered. Decisions on registration were not guided by policy documentation or research findings. The researchers asserted that, 'In the absence of clear guidelines to document acceptable and unacceptable levels of risk, subjective evaluations emerge.' Moral judgements were made by staff on such issues as normal chastisement and parental respectability which influenced the likelihood of the child's name being placed on the register.

Registration itself did not guarantee thorough assessment and planning. There seemed to be no Departmental guidance or formats for assessments. There was no discussion in any of the documentation on different models of assessment, nor on the possibility of linking the type and depth of assessment to the severity of the case. As a result, staff were left to formulate their own views on the purposes and methods of assessment.

Other research on assessment points to different approaches in short-term assessment and decision-making, depending on whether the case is physical or sexual abuse (Corby, 1993). Assessments in cases of physical abuse tended not to be based on research findings and resulted in decisions favouring non-removal of children. The opposite seemed to be true in child sexual abuse cases, but there has been no detailed research since Cleveland.

In assessment of the long-term outlook for the child and the kind of intervention needed, both Dale *et al.* (1986) working with physical abuse, and Bentovim *et al.* (1988) working with sexual abuse, claim some success with their methods of assessment and intervention in difficult and complex cases. They emphasise the need to focus on assessment of the carer's capacity to acknowledge the abuse. Corby takes the view that statutory agencies cannot replicate the highly skilled and detailed assessment and intervention practice described by these authors. He suggests that the issue for policy-makers, if these kinds of approach are desirable, is who should implement them and how they should be resourced.

In the guidance on the Children Act 1989 there is an attempt to deal with some of the issues raised by the research. In *Working Together* (DOH, 1991) responsibility for investigation and initial assessment is given to the police and social services. A comprehensive assessment is recommended following the registration of a child. This assessment should include contributions from all relevant agencies to cover social, environmental, medical and developmental circumstances. The assessment must be planned and structured, and decisions have to be made about who will undertake the assessment and where it will be undertaken (para. 5.16.1 and 2). The importance of reference to research evidence is stressed. Research evidence is one of the two criteria by which a finding of 'significant harm' is to be made for the purposes of registration (para. 6.39).

The aim of this chapter is to describe the investigation and comprehensive assessment model recommended in the statutory guidance, to consider some of the practice issues involved in the process, and to link these to the relevant research findings.

Legal, Policy and Practice Issues – the Children Act 1989

The Children Act 1989 is more specific than previous legislation as to when a local authority must investigate or may assess a child's circumstances. The duties of investigation and assessment are set out in Part V of the Children Act and include the requirement for a court direction in respect of medical or other assessments when there is an emergency protection or an interim care order. They should be considered in conjunction with the guidance in *Working Together* (DOH, 1991).

All work where significant harm to a child is suspected or confirmed requires an assessment to be made, both of the risks to health and development of the child's needs. Because both Part III (Local Authority Support for Children and Families) and Parts IV and V (Care and Supervision and Protection of Children) refer to significant harm through the impairment of health or development, there is often a grey area where the professionals are not clear what the statutory basis of an investigation or assessment is. Assessments may take place in order to offer services to a family where there is a child in need (s.17) or as part of the child protection process (s.37, 47, 38, 43 and 44). It is very important that families, as well as all the professionals involved, understand the legal basis on which they are being asked to work with the local authority. Child protection investigations and assessments should not take place under the guise of an assessment for services under s.17.

All professionals engaged in statutory investigation and assessment need to bear in mind that the process may also reveal cases where there is no cause for concern. White (1994) identifies key points where it may be appropriate to decide not to proceed on a child protection basis; in particular after checking and reviewing initial information, after investigation, and before or after the child protection conference. In each of these circumstances there may still be a basis for offering services under s.17 (10) and Schedule 2 of the Act.

Differing Values

It is important for practitioners to be aware that the research suggests that, although there is agreement between the different professions and with the general public about what constitutes child maltreatment, there is often disagreement about the relative seriousness of it as a criterion for intervention. Boehm (1962) found that social workers, doctors, clergy, nurses and teachers were more likely to perceive the need for intervention than lawyers and businessmen. She suggests that the explanation may be that the latter are more likely to value individual freedom, legal rights and minimal intervention.

Giovanni and Bercerra (1979) found that amongst the general public there were marked ethnic and social class differences in the perceptions of the relative seriousness of different kinds of maltreatment. For example, black mothers rated matters pertaining to supervision and basic child care as more serious than other respondents. Hispanic mothers were more concerned about sexual abuse and sexual mores. Amongst white respondents, lower education and lower income were related to ratings of greater seriousness. They state that the notion that the labelling of maltreatment by white middle class professionals as simply an imposition of their values on lower class people and those who are not white is clearly oversimplistic.

The Definition of Assessment

All professionals who become involved in child protection work are engaged in assessment of some kind in their daily work. It is highly likely, however, that their definitions of assessment and the purposes for which it is used are all different. Trowell (1993) suggested that there is often a failure when professionals come together in multi-disciplinary work in child protection to share and clarify definitions. Misleading assumptions are then made about other colleagues' meanings and activities. This can lead to confusion, antagonism and lack of co-operation. As a consequence, children and families may not receive the protection and help they need.

The following examples of different professional assessment activities and aims were shared in a group which was looking at working together in multi-disciplinary assessments.

Midwife
- Assessment of the well-being of the unborn baby and health of the mother.
- Purpose to ensure live healthy mother/child and safe environment.

Health visitor
- Assessment of family functioning and any areas of stress, either ante- or postnatally.
- Purpose to assess needs and mobilise any necessary resources.

Family centre worker
- Assess family functioning and parenting skills.
- Purpose to prevent family breakdown and assess whether child/ren can stay at home.

Social worker
- Assessment of family problems and any deficits in the care of the child/ren.
- Purpose to identify any unmet needs of the child and any risk of harm, and to offer appropriate services.

Speech therapist
- Assessment of feeding and communication skills in relation to child development and functioning in the family.
- Purpose to identify and address any communication problems.

Health visitor
- Assessment of ongoing development and health of children.
- Purpose to assess any cause for concern.

Social worker
- Assessment of parents' ability to protect child.
- Purpose to contribute to statutory investigation of significant harm and subsequent child protection decisions.

All these activities contribute to the promotion of the welfare of children and their protection from significant harm. Most of these assessments will not, however, be undertaken with the primary aim of contributing to social services child protection investigations and decisions, although they may all contain material which could at some stage be highly relevant to child protection decisions. All professionals, therefore, need to understand what information is needed for child protection assessments and decisions. They also need to understand each other's roles and functions, and what part their particular assessment could play in protecting children.

Working with Families in Partnership

Before looking at the detail of the process of assessment, consideration needs to be given to the context in which it should take place. Under the Children Act, working in partnership is an integral part of all work with families. It must form the basis of all assessment work.

Working Together (DOH, 1991) states that,

'As parental responsibility for children is retained notwithstanding any court orders short of adoption, local authorities must work in partnership with parents, seeking court orders when compulsory action is indicated in the interests of the child but only when this is better for the child than working with the parents under voluntary arrangements.' (Para. 1.4.)

'All staff working in the area of child protection should be aware of the welfare checklist in s.1 of the Act and should use these principles to underpin their work which should always be sensitive to the culture and background of the child and family.' (Para. 1.5.)

'Under s.22 the local authority looking after a child or proposing to do so must give consideration, having regard to the age and understanding of the child, to his wishes and feelings, religious persuasion, racial origin and cultural and linguistic background. This is in addition to the wishes and feelings of the parents and others with parental responsibility.' (Para. 1.6.)

It is against this background that agencies should operate the child protection provisions of the Act, which are designed to promote decisive action when necessary to protect children from abuse or neglect, combined with reasonable opportunities for parents, the children themselves and others to present their points of view (para. 1.7).

Agencies should ensure that staff who are concerned with protecting children from abuse understand that this assumption in the Act of a high degree of co-operation between parents and local authorities requires a concerted approach to inter-disciplinary and inter-agency working (para. 1.8).

The difficulty for many professionals is in knowing what exactly is meant by partnership in child protection work. There is an absence of a clear definition in the Act which has led to confusion. It has resulted in individual professionals having to formulate their own definitions. These vary considerably and are not necessarily shared with families or other agencies. It has often been assumed that working in partnership means that work should be undertaken on a voluntary basis.

In the first Children Act Report to Parliament (DOH, 1992) some clarification was offered. The report stated,

> 'there is a belief that the no order principle requires authorities to demonstrate that working in partnership has broken down or been exhausted before an order will be made. This was not the intention of the legislation. Where a local authority determines that control of a child's circumstances is necessary to promote his welfare then compulsory intervention, as part of a carefully planned process will always be the appropriate remedy. Local authorities should not feel inhibited by the working in partnership provisions of the Children Act from seeking appropriate court orders. Equally the existence of a court order should not of itself impede a local authority from continuing its efforts at working in partnership with the families of children in need. The two processes are not mutually exclusive. Each has a part to play, often simultaneously, in the case of management of children at risk.'(Para. 2.20.)

In a discussion about partnership, the Family Rights Group (1992) commented that respect for statutory rights and the attitudes of professionals were perceived by families as all-important. These rights and attitudes need to be incorporated into all assessment work.

Under the Act parents are entitled to:

- information/consultation about procedures, planning and decision-making;
- involvement in child protection conferences;
- access to complaints procedures;
- exercise parental responsibility, subject to the limitations of s.47, 37 and 31;
- withdraw children from accommodation.

Attitudes should reflect the following principles (Adcock, 1991).

Respect for persons.   This is possible even in difficult situations. Salter (1988) describes this in relation to sex offenders. She says, 'the critically important factor is the simultaneous capacity of the worker to extend respect to people as human beings, to empathise with their pain, and to believe in their capacity to do better in future while not colluding with the sexual abuse a single inch'.

Willingness to allow and encourage the expression of anger. Anger is almost inevitably present when restrictions are placed on an individual parent's freedom of action. The worker needs to express empathy and then to explain which areas are non-negotiable and which are areas where the client still has free choice (cf. Rooney, 1988, for further discussion).

A sense of fairness and natural justice. Morrison (1990) describes this as comprising the opportunity of advance warning, of prior consultation, of being heard to object, of representation, of knowing the full circumstances of the decision and of appeal.

Honesty, directness and openness combined with empathy and support. Crittenden (1991) points out the similarities between parental failure to care for and protect the child and the failure of society to protect its weaker and more vulnerable members from poverty, victimisation and discrimination. She warns against ignoring the victimisation of most maltreating parents by their own parents and by a culture that devalues them. If parents are treated in the same coercive manner in which they were treated as children and now treat their own children, treatment providers become part of the dysfunctional approach they are trying to correct.

The Nature and Process of Assessment under the Children Act

Working Together (DOH, 1991) identifies the following stages of work in individual child protection cases:

- Referral and recognition;
- Immediate protection and planning the investigation;
- Investigation and initial assessment;
- Child protection conference and decision-making about the need for registration;
- Comprehensive assessment and planning;
- Implementation, review and, where appropriate, deregistration.

It states that to be effective, co-operation between agencies providing protection to children must be underpinned by a shared agreement about the handling of individual cases (para. 5:10). *Working Together* (DOH, 1991) also states that the basis of an effective child protection service must be that professionals and individual agencies work together on a multi-disciplinary basis, with a mutual shared understanding of aims, objectives and what is good practice. This should take into account the sensitive issues associated with gender, race, culture and disability.

Within the legal framework and the guidelines in *Working Together*, assessment in child protection can be described as a continuing process which involves different activities for different purposes at different stages of the legal and casework process. It is important for families and all the professionals to know what is meant when the word is used, and for everyone involved to identify the purpose and nature of an assessment in a specific case. The purpose and method will depend on the nature and stage of the case (Adcock *et al.*, 1994).

Risk Assessments

Risk assessment is a term that is frequently used without practitioners being clear exactly what is meant or when it should take place. Often the initial investigation is described as a risk assessment. It may be seen as an alternative to a comprehensive assessment. A risk assessment should be defined as the systematic collection of information to determine the degree to which a child is likely to be abused or neglected at some future point in time (Doueck *et al.* 1992). It should be linked to the question of whether the child is safe in the current living situation. It could be argued that assessment of risk should be taking place throughout the child protection process.

There are various models of risk assessment. Often workers are presented with checklists of so-called risk factors and an additive approach is adopted, whereby the more worrying factors there are, the more risky the case is thought to be. Doueck *et al.* (1992) describe and evaluate three models which are widely used in the USA. All the models include risk factors which relate to the child, the care givers and the maltreatment. All three models stress that there are connections between treatment planning and identified risk factors, and that assessment of risk should be based on interactions among factors present in any given situation and not on a single risk factor. It should be noted that all three models also claim that they promote comprehensive assessments. Doueck and colleagues conclude that there should be caution about the overall utility of risk assessment systems. First, questions remain about the reliability and validity of most models. Second, research indicates that there are problems about the adequate implementation of the models. Third, these models cannot replace competently trained staff. All the models Doueck reviewed required a staff trained and knowledgeable in human growth and development, parenting practices, the causes and effects of mistreatment and family dynamics.

Nevertheless, Jones *et al.* (1993) make the important point that one of the major advantages of risk assessment systematisation may lie less in the content than in the process which is involved in applying it.

> 'When they (the workers) have to apply some sort of matrix to the problem they are faced with, the problem itself is broken down into more manageable bits. The process allows the worker to consider different elements of the situation, rather than being overwhelmed by one striking component of a child abuse case. I would argue that the all-important process of maintaining neutrality can be enhanced by such a process of analysis and consideration of the different elements of risk.' (Jones *et al.*, 1993.)

Jones *et al.* advocate the system, described above, of weighing positive and negative factors identified by research. They conclude, 'the advantages of examining risk along a series of damages and considering the positive and negative elements are primarily rooted in the effect this has on worker confidence and process, such that it is argued that there is an increased objectivity and opportunity for the essential stopping and thinking through using this approach, which outweighs the disadvantages.' This approach will be incorporated and described in more detail later in this chapter.

Undertaking the Assessment

The process of assessment

The process of assessment as a sequence is shown below. Regardless of the point in the sequence at which an assessment takes place, reference should always be made to the information gathered in the preceding stages. If this is not available, it may be necessary to obtain it before undertaking new work with a different purpose.
The process of assessment.

Assess:

- What is the cause for concern in the child or his/her upbringing?
- Is there significant harm or the likelihood of it?
- What is the harm, e.g. ill-treatment or impairment of health or development?
- What is the risk and can the child be protected by the parent/s or current carers?
- What is the explanation for the harm or likely harm?
- What are the child and family's needs as a consequence of the harm?
- What needs to change to resolve the harm and prevent it occurring in the future?
- What is the prognosis for the child and family?
- What intervention and treatment needs to be provided for the child and family?
- What will the process of change involve?
- What will the criteria for success be?
- What is the time-scale for the child within which changes must occur?

The process of reassessment. Reassessment may take place as part of the child protection plan to evaluate change and/or provide a basis for future decisions.

Assess:

- What changes, if any, have occurred in the child and the family? How far do they meet the requirements previously specified?
- What patterns of interaction now operate between the parent/s or carers and the child, and within the family as a whole?
- Do the parent/s (or carers) accept responsibility for what has happened to the child or the risks of what could have happened?
- What are the child/s needs?
- Do the parent/s (or carers) understand the child's present and future needs?
- Is significant harm still occurring or likely to occur?
- Can the child now be kept safe within the family or be returned safely to the family?
- What further changes need to take place?
- What further intervention/treatment is required?
- What is the time-scale for the child within which change must take place?

Investigation and initial assessment. This will take place as a result of the local authority's duty to investigate suspected significant harm under s.47 of the Children Act 1989. The purposes of the investigation are to:

- establish the facts and decide if there are grounds for concern;
- identify sources and levels of risk to the child and all other children at the same address;

- decide upon protective or other action for the referred child, other children and adults in the household (Social Services Inspectorate, 1993).

Jones *et al.* (1993) make similar points about the aims of investigative interviewing in a context of alleged sexual abuse. They stress first the need to obtain as clear and unequivocal an account as possible about what, if anything, has happened or is happening to a child. An assessment should be made as to whether the child is, or is likely to be at risk of significant harm, or whether services are needed to promote the child's welfare. Immediate help (including protection or medical treatment) should be provided where necessary, and plans made for protecting and promoting the child's welfare in the future. An important overall aim is to contribute effectively (e.g. by providing evidence) to any legal proceedings resulting from the investigation.

Investigations and preliminary assessments conducted in accordance with these guidelines should enable the professionals to formulate preliminary answers to the first five items in the process of assessment above, i.e. to identify whether there is cause for concern for the child, to assess whether this is significant harm or likely harm, to obtain a preliminary explanation, if there is one, of what has happened and to decide whether any immediate protection for the child is necessary.

Because the way in which professionals intervene can itself affect the outcome of a case either positively or adversely (Jones, 1991), a process of local authority involvement must be established which will prejudice or impede later interventions on behalf of the child as little as possible (Adcock, 1993). The section on 'Investigation and initial assessment' in *Evaluating Performance in Child Protection* (Social Services Inspectorate, 1993) draws attention to specific areas and sets out the following criteria for the required standards and methods of working.

Procedures.

- All investigations are carried out without delay and in accordance with agreed procedures.
- The recording of interviews is accurate and distinguishes between hearsay and opinion.
- Written records of interviews are contemporaneous.
- The appropriate people are informed in writing about the outcome of the investigation including when no cause for concern was revealed.

Treatment of children and parents.

- Consideration is given to providing a separate worker specifically for the parent/s or care givers.
- The investigating social worker interviews the child and interviews or gathers information from those people who are personally and professionally connected with the child.
- The number of investigative interviews or examinations of the child is kept to the minimum necessary to understand the child's situation.
- During the investigative interviews the child is helped to relax and feel at ease. Consideration is given to having an appropriate parent/carer, relative, friend or supporter present.
- The interviewer listens carefully to what the child has to say and communicates with him/her in a responsive and receptive manner.

- The interviewer works at the child's pace, using language or means of communication the child can understand and enables the child to talk about and give a clear account of the events which were a source of concern.

The whole process should be conducted in a non-discriminatory fashion. The need for careful checking and evaluation of information should be recognised in both procedures and practice. All professionals should be aware of the stage in the investigation when this will take place. White (1993) stresses the need for supervisors to ensure that alternative explanations have been thoroughly checked out before firm conclusions are drawn, and to ensure that the information gathered has not been limited to that necessary to confirm a particular explanation of the facts.

The importance of obtaining and evaluating factual evidence as a basis for decisions and subsequent assessments cannot be sufficiently stressed. The research undertaken by Parents Against Injustice (PAIN) (Prosser, 1992) suggests that a careful evaluation of the evidence is not always undertaken early on. Important decisions are then made on the basis of unverified assumptions at great cost to children and their families. An example of this was a case where children were thought to have had burns from cigarettes. After many months of separation from the parents a diagnosis was finally made that the children had been suffering from impetigo!

Comprehensive Assessment

This assessment is a process of collecting information and generating understanding about significant harm or likely significant harm to a child. It will involve a series of meetings between the professionals and the family, individually and together, and may well take 3 months to complete. *Working Together* states that a social worker should be appointed as key worker, but that the assessment should include contributions from all relevant agencies to cover social, environmental, medical and developmental factors.

A detailed guide to the content and process of a comprehensive assessment is to be found in *Protecting Children – Guide to Comprehensive Assessment* (DOH, 1988). This guide was prepared by a working group of social work practitioners set up by the Department of Health in 1987 following a Social Services Inspectorate report on the handling of child abuse cases in nine local authorities. A major finding of the inspection had been that initial assessment was providing a good basis for short-term planning and protection of the child, but that comprehensive assessments for the purpose of long-term planning were largely conspicuous by their absence. The Inspectorate recommended that a working group should prepare a practice guide on assessment and long-term case management.

The guide suggests that a comprehensive assessment is likely to take place when:

- a child's name has been placed on the Child Protection Register; or
- a court has ordered an assessment in care proceedings; or
- children are already the subject of a care order and decisions about their future need to be made;
- professionals have been involved with a family for some time but standards of parental care have not improved and the professionals feel 'stuck'.

The working group who prepared the guide saw the function of a comprehensive assessment as being much more than the collection of detailed information about a family. They saw it as an opportunity for professionals to try and engage with a family in a dynamic process which would give them all the opportunity of gaining more understanding of the causes of concern about the child, of what changes would be needed to resolve these and the potential for change. The assessment should offer parents and children an opportunity for reflection and consideration of their family functioning and the degree to which the children's needs are being met. The purpose of the assessment is therefore to provide:

- an understanding of the nature of the causes of concern about the child or his/her upbringing and the level of future risk;
- an explanation and understanding, to which, if possible, both professionals and the family subscribe, of why the harm occurs or is likely to occur;
- information about family and individual functioning which identifies strengths as well as areas of difficulty;
- a view of the level of responsibility taken by the parent/s or carers for what has happened, and their capacity to protect the child in the future;
- a view of their responsiveness and ability to change;
- detailed information about the child's needs;
- identification of what needs to change;
- a basis for a prognosis for the child and family and for decisions about intervention and treatment.

Managing the Process of an Assessment

Planning the assessment

Before the assessment begins, consideration needs to be given to who should be involved in an assessment and how the work will be planned and managed. The more care that is taken and the more preparation that is done at this stage, the less there are likely to be irretrievable difficulties in the assessment work with the family.

Since the assessment is likely to take place only in situations of existing or likely significant harm, the gravity of the situation for the child and his/her development needs to be recognised. The nature of the existing harm or the likely future harm and information already available about the child, the parents and their responses to professional intervention should form the basis of the planning. The planning team needs to think about how best to establish an appropriate context for the work, to enable the workers to engage with the family and to process the work appropriately.

First, as far as possible, the child/ren need to be safe. A preoccupation with a high level of continuing harm or likely harm makes it very difficult for everyone to focus on developing understanding and explanations about what is going on in the family.

Second, the context for the assessment must be created. As Morrison (1991) says, 'families are often defensive and reluctant to look at the real issues. The motivation for change is often far greater in the agencies than in the family. Assisting families with deeply entrenched patterns of dysfunctional behaviour to make a serious commitment to change requires considerable skill, patience and effort.' Motivation to change comes from an interplay of internal and external factors. Families need, therefore, a clear message from the social services department about the concern for the child and the need for an assessment.

If this is done by a manager, in some cases in writing, and with a copy to the parents' solicitor, the social worker's task will then be easier. It will be harder for the individual worker to be resisted or scapegoated and easier for them to engage with the family on a basis that, if the members of the family so wish, s/he is there to work with them on the task already identified by the agency.

In the case of some families, the possibility of legal action may need to be considered. A direction from the court under an interim care order, specifying the details of the process and who will need to be seen, can be used to provide a clear framework. This is particularly important if the harm is serious and the adults are denying any involvement or responsibility or are likely to be hostile or resistent to an assessment.

Parents/carers have a right not to participate in an assessment, although they need to understand the consequences of such a refusal. Professionals have the right to say that they cannot undertake an assessment with a particular family because there is no real co-operation. Spending time identifying and discussing these difficulties openly may then facilitate genuine co-operation.

One social worker is unlikely to have the requisite knowledge and skills to carry out an assessment alone: other social workers and members of other professions may be needed. For example, a different professional or a specialist may be necessary to assess drug and alcohol problems or learning difficulties or a sexual or violent abuser. Medical involvement is likely to be essential in cases of acute injury, and also in cases where regular monitoring of the child's development is an essential part of gathering the evidence.

Race, gender and the circumstances of the case clearly need consideration. It may be that different workers should work with individual family members. For example, if there has been violence between the parents as well as harm to the children, the mother may need a female worker. The father or abusing male may respond better to a male worker. Care may also be needed in ensuring the right worker for the child. A severely sexually abused girl may be quite unable to feel safe with a male worker. Situations in which there has been very distressing harm and trauma may need more than one worker in order to minimise the stress for the child. If the family is likely to have continuing crises throughout the assessment or feels extremely angry about the initial investigations, it may be better for one worker to hold the case responsibility and for another to undertake only the responsibility for the assessment.

Involving Families

Before beginning the assessment, the worker/s need to ask themselves the following questions devised by Wynne (1993).

1. Within the legal framework how can I empower the family, address power issues and maintain a sensitive balance between care and control?
2. What is the position of this child in this family? Have I considered the risks and how the child can be protected?
3. Am I the right person to do this assessment in terms of gender and race. Have I addressed my own racism?

4. Do I have the appropriate knowledge and understanding for this family?
5. What has been their previous involvement and experience of social services? How will this affect their ability to participate in an assessment?
6. Can I be honest and open and work in partnership with this family, sharing concerns, goals and expectations?
7. Have the family understood what an assessment involves? Have I checked this out with them by asking them to tell me what they understand we will be doing, and why?

Social workers need to discuss these issues with their supervisors and with any members of other disciplines who will be working with them on the assessment. They need to consider throughout the case what feelings and thoughts it triggers for them in terms of their own experiences and what effect this may have on their work.

The experience of professionals who have undertaken assessments is that the initial negotiations with families to involve them and obtain their agreement to participate are crucial. Difficulties are likely to arise during the process if an assessment is started without the family understanding what an assessment is, why it is needed, and how they might benefit from the outcome.

The first question to consider is when to inform a family about the possibility of a comprehensive assessment. The parents are likely to comprehend very little if they are only told at the end of a case conference – after they have been informed of a decision that the child's name will be placed on the Child Protection Register and that legal proceedings may be commenced – that a social worker will undertake a comprehensive assessment. The idea could more helpfully be suggested when the social worker is preparing the family for the case conference, or it might be discussed after the conference. What is important is that a time is chosen when the family is not too upset or angry to hear what is being said.

The language that is used is also extremely important. The term 'comprehensive assessment' is likely to mean very little, and even an explanation of what will be discussed is not in itself sufficient. The social worker needs to be able to explain simply what a comprehensive assessment is, why it is needed and what its purpose is, before going on to explain the process.

Thought also needs to be given as to what the family might gain from an assessment and to discuss this with them. This will vary depending on the circumstances. For example, for some parents the return of their child is all-important. For another, the goal may be to remove the child's name from the Register. It must always be made clear that participation in the assessment does not guarantee the desired outcome for the parents, but it is recognised that this is what will be attempted.

It can be helpful for professionals to try and draft a statement or a letter for the family inviting them to participate in an assessment, using language they can understand. The statement should explain the cause for concern, why an assessment is needed and what they might hope to gain. An example of such a statement might be:

Dear Mr and Mrs A,
As you will know, your son Michael is at present being looked after by foster parents as a result of three unexplained fractures to his leg and arms. These are regarded as very serious injuries for a baby of his age and the social services department has applied to the court for a care order in order to protect Michael.
    I know that you have been very upset by all that has happened and that you are

very concerned about Michael being away from you and that you would like him to come home. It is the policy of this department to try and return children to their families if we can be sure that they will not suffer other injuries and they will be safe. I am sure that, although you have not been able to explain what has happened to Michael, you do not want him to be hurt again.

I am writing to ask you, therefore, if you would be willing to work with the social worker and the staff at the family centre on what is called a comprehensive assessment. This is something recommended by the Department of Health to help social workers and families to try and understand more about the way in which parents care for their children and behave with each other and any difficulties they may have. This would help us all to understand any changes that might be needed to make Michael safe in the future and whether we could offer you services to help achieve these changes.

The social worker would want to arrange a series of meetings with you together, with you and Michael, and with each of you separately. She would want to find out the things that work well in the family, as well as any problems you may have.

It would take about 8 to 10 weeks to do the assessment but in the meanwhile you will be able to go on seeing Michael as you are at present – 4 days a week at the family centre and twice at the foster home.

We want to ask the court for an order to do this work. Perhaps you would let me know if you would be willing to work with us on the assessment. I would be very happy to give you any more information you may want. You may want to talk to your solicitor about this.

Yours sincerely
Team Manager

Once there is some agreement about an assessment, it is very useful to have a written agreement, carefully negotiated with the parents, and the child, if this is appropriate. The agreement can set out the content and the process, and can include important details such as who will see the finished report. Such agreements both provide families with necessary important information and increase their sense of participation and having some control over the process.

The assessment is usually undertaken by involving the relevant family members individually and in combinations, in a series of activities and questions that seem appropriate for their circumstances and abilities. *Protecting Children* (DOH, 1988), recommends, for example, the use of genograms and ecomaps and asking families to do homework between sessions, e.g. talking together in order to identify family rules. The workers need to be able to elicit and observe interactions within the family and between the family and the professionals, and to share these observations with the family. All these activities may lead to some change within the family as members are encouraged to interact or behave in new ways or to talk, often for the first time, about the causes for concern in the child, and the possible outcomes, or painful areas in past or present relationships. The worker needs to be alerted to the moments when change is happening or realisation is dawning and to make constructive use of them. An example of this was a mother, who at the end of the sessions focusing on the child, suddenly said that she could see that she had no attachment to her and had always disliked her since the unwanted pregnancy.

Components of the Assessment

Protecting Children (DOH, 1988) lists eight components of a comprehensive assessment:

1. The causes for concern.
2. The child:
    i.   parents' perceptions;
    ii.   routine and care;
    iii.   early history;
    iv.   subsequent history;
    v.   emotional development;
    vi.   growth and development;
    vii.   child's perceptions;
    viii. social worker's perceptions.
3. Family composition.
4. Individual profile of parents/carers.
5. The couple relationship and family interactions.
6. Networks.
7. Finance.
8. Physical conditions.

All these components are important, although space only permits discussion here of three elements.

Causes for concern

It is important in most cases to start by exploring with the family what they think are the causes for concern about the child and his or her upbringing. The parents may have a different view from the professionals, and their concerns may be very relevant. They may not understand what the professionals' worries are. Giving parents an opportunity to discuss their own concerns may enable the professionals to help parents realise why other people are concerned.

An example of this was a 3-year-old girl called Sharon, who was thought by the paediatrician and health visitor to be developmentally delayed and not making progress because her mother did not stimulate her or exercise appropriate controls. The mother was seen as hysterical and unhelpable. The social services department became involved after Sharon's father beat her severely for her defiant behaviour. During the assessment, the mother revealed that she had thought there was something wrong with Sharon from the time of her very difficult labour and forceps delivery. Sharon had been a very difficult baby to care for, she was very unresponsive to her mother and then, when she finally became mobile, was restless and lacking in concentration. The mother had no support because her own parents were in Ireland. The next baby, born 2 years later, had no problems and this confirmed the mothers' fears about Sharon. After the mother had discussed her perceptions, these were shared with the paediatrician. The latter agreed that Sharon might have some minor residual damage as a result of her birth but then reassured the mother that with help Sharon could now make good progress. This enabled the mother then to look at what she and her husband could now do differently to help Sharon.

In *Protecting Children* (DOH, 1988) there is a list of all the forms of abuse, neglect and ill-treatment that a child might experience. It is suggested that the social worker, having asked the parents a general question initially about their understanding of the causes for concern, should then discuss these individual items and invite the parents to consider whether any of them are relevant either to the past, the present or the future of their child. The parents should be asked which they think are the most serious problems, when they came to light and what caused the problems. They should also be asked what they think will happen if things do not change.

It may be necessary for the worker both to provide factual information, to correct any misapprehensions and to explain fully the concerns of other professionals. The parents may sometimes be quite ignorant of the significance of various forms of harm. Hooper (1992) suggests, for example, that mothers in her research sometimes did not realise that certain sexual behaviours were abusive. The social worker herself/himself may need to discuss the significance of a particular condition for a child with other professionals before they talk with a parent. They may also want the other professional to talk to the parent at some stage.

Discussions about the causes for concern will enable the professional to begin to make an assessment of two factors which will need to be explored further in the discussions with the parents/carers about the child's perceptions, and about the parents/carers as individuals and the adult family relationships. The first is the non-abusing parent's willingness and ability to protect the child in the future. This is a key part of any assessment, particularly in cases involving sexual abuse or violence. Account needs to be taken of how recently the non-abusing parent has learnt about the abuse, what supports have been provided, and what have been the consequences of the disclosure, e.g. the abuser has left the home. Attention should be given to the parent's relationship with the abuser, e.g. there is a high likelihood of future violence to the non-abusing parent or, alternatively, there is some degree of collusion between the parents. The second factor is what responsibility the parents/carers take for the harm that has occurred, or is likely to occur, and whether they are willing to work with the professionals to resolve the consequences and to see that the child is protected in the future. It is unlikely that many parents/carers will take complete responsibility for what has happened or may happen for some considerable time. Indeed, one of the main aims of treatment is to help them to do this. It is important to see, at the outset, however, whether any responsibility is taken, even in terms of agreeing that parents have a responsibility to try and ensure that their children do not come to harm.

The causes for concern in the child or his/her upbringing i.e. what is happening or is likely to happen to the child, the parents' perceptions of the child and the child's perceptions of what has happened (if he or she is old enough) should then provide a continuing point of reference for the assessment. The social worker should make use of these discussions in order to explore with the parents and develop with them an explanation of why it is that harm was/is occurring or is likely to occur. Talking with the parents about the early history of the child, the circumstances of the pregnancy and birth, the child's development, personality and behaviour will help some parents in this process, particularly if attachment difficulties are the major cause of concern. For some parents it may be their first opportunity to think in some depth about the child and his/her needs, or to share with someone else the difficulties they have had in caring for him/her.

An example of this was Darren, aged 9, who frequently had unexplained bruises, seemed to be scapegoated within the family, and whose behaviour was uncontrollable at school and at home. In looking at his history, it became clear that the pregnancy had been unplanned, that he had been born at a time when the mother was looking after the maternal grandfather, who was dying, and that his sister had been born 10 months later. The parents realised that they had never really had an opportunity to bond with Darren and that they had resented his demands. Father had, as a child, been expected to be quiet and obedient and had been severely chastised for any naughtiness and he had continued the same pattern with Darren. The parents were then able to use the social worker's help to promote the development of attachments and to modify Darren's behaviour.

The child

A full assessment of the child should be based on the child's perceptions, wishes and feelings, attachments and developmental history, the effect of any harm that has already occurred, the changes that are needed to resolve this and to ensure healthy future development, and an estimate of the child's ability to change.

The child's perceptions, wishes and feelings. The child's statements about his/her situation and what has happened are a very important source of information both for the assessment and its outcome. When shared with the parent/s, they can be a powerful lever for creating change within the family or a source of evidence that change is unlikely.

Wishes and feelings can be ascertained through observation and play, through talking with older children, and by gathering reports from those closely involved with the child, e.g. teachers and current carers.

Child development and attachments. It is very important to assess the child's attachments and developmental progress. The importance of a secure attachment for a young child cannot be overemphasised. It provides the child with a secure base from which to explore the world and to which the child can return when anxious or distressed. Fahlberg (1991) states that attachment helps the child to:

- attain his/her full intellectual potential;
- sort out what he/she perceives;
- think logically;
- develop a conscience;
- become self-reliant;
- cope with stress and frustration;
- handle fear and worry;
- develop future relationships;
- handle jealousy.

Children who experience moves and separations may have defective or disordered attachments which will affect their behaviour and development. It is important, therefore, to chart moves and to find out who the child feels close to, as well as the quality of the attachment. Children may be ambivalent about a particular carer, or they may show considerable affection for an abuser, or they may feel they have to look after a brother or sister. These feelings need to be taken into account, together with the need to provide the child with secure attachment when plans are made for placement and contact.

Professionals need to understand the various categories of attachment and the stages of child development. Jones *et al.* (1991) suggest that, 'The developmental perspective emphasises the unfolding of the individual over time, in physical, social and psychological spheres of life. The process consists of a series of basic tasks, which once achieved by the child, remain critical for the individual throughout life. Each critical task of development interrelates and influences the other.' Key tasks of social and emotional development have been described as:

- The baby's achievement of a balanced state, e.g. feeding, sleeping and elimination (during the first few weeks of life).
- The development of a secure attachment with a caretaker (0–12 months of age).
- The development of an independent sense of self (12–30 months).
- The establishment of peer relationships (30 months–7 years).
- The integration of attachment, independence and peer relationships (7–12 years).

The authors go on to state that, 'Few single influences on development, including severe abuse have an inevitable future consequence, and all factors have the potential to affect future outcome in the direction of good or less good states of adjustment. Additionally, the sum as well as the direction of such influences may alter over the individual's life course, so that a disturbed child can change, if there is sufficient change in the positive and negative influences bearing on him/her.' (Jones et al., 1991, page 117.)

The effects of harm.   These are likely to be reflected in the child's behaviour, development, play and communication with other children and adults. Close observation and the provision of opportunities for the child to play and talk may be necessary in order to ascertain how the child is. Terr (1990), writing about post-traumatic stress, suggests that there is often a tendency for adults to concentrate on the child's apparent recovery, e.g. 'she doesn't talk about it' and to ignore signs of continuing distress.

Assessments of children should be undertaken by a professional who is experienced in observing and communicating with children and who has, or can gain access to, knowledge about the possible effects of the particular harm the child has suffered or is likely to suffer. If the assessment is likely to take several sessions, consideration will need to be given to the relationship that develops between the worker and the child, and what the child is encouraged to express. An abrupt withdrawal of a new, important relationship in which the child has exposed a lot of hurt, anger and grief may reinforce previous experiences of abuse and loss.

The possibility of change.   The child's healing is most likely to be achieved by the provision of 'good enough' parenting. Changes in the parent/s or a move to a different placement will help to secure this. However, some children may also need additional individual help to enable them to make progress. These are likely to be children with attachment problems, severe health or development or educational problems, or an experience of sexual abuse or other violence, or post-traumatic stress. This needs to be considered during the assessment.

The individual adult and the couple relationship

In working with the parents to compile these profiles, there are a number of areas that it is important to look at. Practitioners doing the assessment will wish to see how the parent/s perceive themselves, whether this matches up to how others see them, and what value and self-esteem are displayed. It is very important to identify positive attributes and coping abilities as well as exploring difficulties both in order to obtain an overall picture and because these qualities are likely to be the basis for future change.

Killen Heap (1991) has developed categories and criteria for investigating and evaluating parental functioning and potential. These are similar to those in the Department of Health Guide.

They include stress factors in the parents' childhood, adolescence and early adulthood, stress factors related to pregnancy and birth, socio-economic factors, social networks and relationship factors; immaturity, which encompasses dependent and demanding behaviour, lack of impulse control and lack of ability to postpone satisfaction of needs, to think in time perspectives, to observe the connection between actions and consequences, and lack of empathy. Unresolved problems which were considered to affect the parent – child interaction negatively were marital conflict, conflict from an earlier divorce, current separation or divorce conflict, life stage/role crisis, unwanted pregnancy, anxiety/aggression problem, unmet dependency need, and alcohol or drug problem. Seven central parental capacities were identified:

- Capacity to perceive the child realistically.
- Capacity for realistic expectations as to the needs a child may satisfy.
- Capacity for realistic expectation as to the child's coping and achievement.
- Capacity for empathy with the child.
- Capacity for involvement with the child.
- Capacity to give priority to the child's developmental needs.
- Capacity to restrain aggressive behaviour towards the child.

Killen Heap (1991) analysed a group of abused and neglected children and their parents using these categories and followed them up 5–6 years later. She found that immaturity was of greater importance for parental dysfunctioning than emotional problems such as anxiety or depressive states or uncontrollable anger. The mothers who scored highest on immaturity also had the highest number of stress factors in childhood, adolescence and early adulthood. She concluded, 'the high covariation between stress factors in childhood, adolescence and early adult life is of note. The findings underline the need for a thorough investigation of the interaction in the family, the child's role in it, the parents' background, their level of maturity, emotional problems, and their central parental capacity.' (Killen Heap, 1991, pages 261–273.)

Clearly, their own childhood experiences will have an effect on how parents care for their children. This is explained by Bentovim (1991) as a process 'whereby the families of origin of such parents may provide a "training ground" for interpersonal violence and reduced social competence, through exposure to stressful and traumatic life events. This means they are ill prepared for the stresses of parenting, and their adaptation means that the child is seen as a cause of anger, frustration and arousal. Abusive patterns are triggered and these become part of the inflexible maladaptive breakdown state of the family.' (Bentovim, 1991, page 56.)

Not all parents, however, who were themselves abused and neglected go on to maltreat their own children. Egeland (1988) says, 'Our findings indicate that about one-third of parents who were abused as children are at risk for abusing their own children. . . . The most compelling findings were in the area of relationships, where we found that mothers who broke the cycle of abuse were as children most likely to have an emotionally supportive relationship with another adult and were as adults more likely to have an emotionally supportive husband or boyfriend.' (Egeland, 1988, page 97.)

The possibility of change

Difficulties in any of the areas included in the assessment may contribute to the maltreatment of a child. Most practitioners now subscribe to a multi-dimensional causal model of child ill-treatment. However, it is important to consider the nature of the harm or likely harm to the child, and what this may indicate about the parents and the possibility of successful intervention. Gelles (1992), who has written and researched widely on family violence, has stated, 'our research clearly indicates that there is not a "continuum of abuse" with severe abuse occurring because of increased stress and disadvantage. Instead there seem to be distinct categories of maltreatment. Thus parents who inflict severe injuries on their children or kill them, are categorically different from those parents whose maltreatment does not involve life-threatening harm.' He suggests that in such cases, 'child protection and child advocacy needs to replace family reunification as the guiding policy of child welfare agencies.'

The research suggests that a number of characteristics in the parent, in the parent-child interaction, in the child, in the nature of the abuse, in the social setting and in the professional help offered are associated with a more positive or a more negative prognosis (Jones, 1991).

Negative factors include: continuing parental denial of abuse or impairment; parents who refuse help or do not co-operate with professional help; severe parental personality problems – antisocial, aggressive or inadequate; parental mental handicap with accompanying mental illness; persistent parental psychosis with delusions involving the child; abuse in childhood not recognised as a problem; severe physical abuse, burns, scalds, failure to thrive, mixed abuse; pervasive lack of empathy for the child; severe sexual abuse, involving penetration, and of long duration; sadistic abuse or that which includes slow premeditated infliction of pain and suffering; certain types of abuse cases, e.g. Munchausens by proxy, deliberate poisoning, scalding and burns.

Positive factors include: a non-abusive partner; acceptance of the problem and taking of responsibility; compliance; a normal attachment; parental empathy for the child; less severe forms of abuse; a good corrective relationship for the child; professional outreach to the family and partnership with parents; more local child care facilities and volunteer networks.

The various factors in a case will need to be weighed relative to one another and a prognosis estimated in the light of the research findings and the likely ability of the parents to work with professionals and make use of any intervention. Most experts in the field would be likely to advocate the use of court orders to protect the child in cases with a poorer prognosis.

Completing the Assessment

By the end of the assessment the following questions should have been answered:

1. Is there an explanation for the significant harm or cause for concern?
2. What are the patterns of interaction which operate within the family and with the professionals?
3. Have any changes occurred during the assessment?
4. Do the circumstances which gave rise to the harm or likely harm/cause for concern still exist?

5. What are the implications of the answers to the above questions for the child and family and their future? (DOH, 1988.).

If practitioners have been able to involve the family fully in the assessment, the parents will have an understanding of the answers to these questions and they will be aware that they need to decide whether they wish to pursue any further changes that have been recommended and to continue working with professionals. Whilst the assessment is in process, family members should be given feedback and invited to comment on their understanding of what has been happening and to share responsibility for any blocks or lack of progress. Sometimes a parent, if invited to give an opinion on what an outsider or a court would consider to be their strengths and difficulties, will give a view that very much accords with that of the professionals. No change and no understanding, despite repeated efforts to engage family members, will provide evidence of the difficulty in preventing future harm if the child remains within the family.

The evaluation of an assessment and the resulting decisions should, wherever possible, be made by a group of professionals which should include those who participated in the assessment as well as some with experience in the work but no direct involvement in the case. The longer and the more closely involved a professional has been with a family, the harder it is likely to be for them to have the necessary detachment to make an objective assessment.

Annotated Reading List

Adcock, M., White, R. & Hollows, A. (eds) (1991). *Significant Harm: Its Outcome and Management.* Significant Publications.
A collection of papers by social workers, child psychiatrists, a lawyer and a paediatrician which explore the concept of significant harm and its assessment and treatment under the Children Act 1989, consider cultural and ethnic perspectives, and discuss the implications for work with children and families.

Briere, J. (1992). *Child Abuse Trauma; Theory and Treatment of the Lasting Effects.* London: Sage.
A detailed analysis of the trauma of child abuse, with special reference to sexual abuse. There is discussion of the long-term impact of abuse, of assessment and treatment, and of relevant research. A child maltreatment schedule for clinical assessment is included.

Department of Health (1988). *Protecting Children. A Guide for Social Workers Undertaking a Comprehensive Assessment.* London: HMSO.
This is a guide to the comprehensive assessment of children and families after the completion of initial child protection investigations. The components of a comprehensive assessment are set out. There are suggestions about summarising and evaluating the information gathered and using this as a basis for planning and decision-making.

References

Adcock, M. (1991). In M. Adcock, R. White & A. Hollows (eds): *Child Protection – A Training and Resource Guide to the Children Act 1989.* National Children's Bureau.

Adcock, M., White, R. & Hollows, A. (1991). *Significant Harm: Its Management and Outcome*. Significant Publications.

Adcock, M. (1993) Investigation and assessment in child protection. In Adcock, M., Hollows, A. & White, R. (Eds) *Child Protection Update*, National Children's Bureau.

Bentovim, A., Elton, A., Hildebrand, J., Tranter, M. and Vizard, E. (1988) *Child Sexual Abuse within the Family*. London: John Wright.

Bentovim, A. (1991). Significant harm in context. In M. Adcock, R. White and A. Hollows (eds): *Significant Harm: Its Management and Outcome*. Significant Publications.

Boehm, B. (1962). An assessment of family adequacy in protective cases. *Child Welfare 41*.

Corby, B. (1993) *Child Abuse: Towards a Knowledge Base*. Milron Keynes: Open University Press.

Crittenden, P. (1991) Treatment of child abuse and neglect. *Journal of Human Systems 2; 3–4*.

Dale, P., Davies, M., Morrison, T. & Waters, J. (1986) *Dangerous Families*, London: Tavistock.

Department of Health (1988). *Protecting Children. A Guide for Social Workers Undertaking Comprehensive Assessment*. London: HMSO.

Department of Health (1991). *Working Together. A Guide to Agency Co-operation for the Protection of Children from Abuse*. London: HMSO.

Department of Health (1992). *Report on the Children Act*. London: HMSO.

Department of Health (1993). *The Care of Children. Principles and Practice in Regulations and Guidance*. DOH Social Services Inspectorate. 1993. *Evaluating Performance in Child Protection*.

Doueck, H.J., Bronson, D.E. & Levin, M. (1992). Evaluating risk assessment implementation in child protection. *Child Abuse and Neglect 16*.

Egeland, B. (1988). Breaking the cycle of abuse; implications for prediction and intervention. In K. Browne, C. Davies & P. Stratton: *Early Prediction and Prevention of Child Abuse*. Chichester: John Wiley and Sons.

Fahlberg, V. (1991). *A Child's Journey through Placement*. Perspectives Press.

Family Rights Group (1992). Unpublished communication to the author.

Gelles, R. (1992). Family re-unification versus child protection. Update. *National Center for Child Prosecution. 5(8)*.

Giller, H. *et al.* (1992). *An Evaluation of Child Protection Procedures in Four Welsh ACPC Areas*. Social Information Systems.

Giovannoni, J. & Bercerra, R. (1979). *Defining Child Abuse*. New York: Free Press.

Hooper, A. (1992). *Mothers Surviving Child Sexual Abuse*. London: Routledge.

Jones, D.P.H. (1991). The effectiveness of intervention. In M. Adcock, R. White & A. Hollows (eds): *Significant Harm: Its Outcome and Management*. Significant Publications.

Jones, D.P.H., Bentovim, A., Cameron, C., Vizard, E. & Wolkind, S. (1991). Significant harm in context. In M. Adcock, R. White & A. Hollows. (eds): *Significant Harm: Its Outcome and Management*. Significant Publications.

Jones, D.P.H., Hopkins, C., Godfrey, M. & Glaser, D. (1993). The investigative process. In: *Investigative Interviewing with Children*. Milton Keynes: The Open University.

Killen Heap, K. (1991). A predictive and follow up study of abusive and neglectful families by case analysis. *Child Abuse and Neglect 15(3)*.

Morrison, T. (1990). *The Professional Dilemma: Child and Family Participation at Case Conferences*. Unpublished paper given at Newcastle University.

Morrison, T. (1991). Change, control and the legal framework. In M. Adcock, R. White & A. Hollows (eds). *Significant Harm: Its Outcome and Management*, Significant Publications.

Prosser, D. (1992). *Child Abuse Investigations; the Families Perspective.* PAIN.

Rooney, R. (1988). Socialisation strategies for involuntary clients. Social casework. *Journal of Contemporary Social Work.* Family Service America.

Salter, A. (1988). *Treating Child Sex Offenders and Victims.* London: Sage.

Terr, L. (1990). *Too Scared to Cry.* Basic Books.

Trowell, J. (1993) *International Society for the Prevention of Child Abuse and Neglect.* Unpublished Paper, Chicago.

White, R. (1994). In Adcock, M. White, R. & Hollows A. (eds): *Child Protection. A Training Resource and Guide to Child Protection under the Children Act 1989,* 2nd edn. National Children's Bureau.

Wynne, M. (1993) Personal Communication.

11

Inter-professional Co-operation and Inter-Agency Co-ordination

Brian Corby

Introduction

The way in which various health, welfare and police agencies work together both at the individual and organisational level has been seen as *the* crucial factor in child protection work in England and Wales in recent decades. Almost all the public inquiries published since 1973 have highlighted failures of systems to act in a co-ordinated way and failures of individuals to co-operate and communicate effectively in events leading up to children's deaths. This chapter charts in detail how this emphasis on inter-agency co-ordination and inter-professional co-operation has developed during this period, then considers the merits and demerits of current inter-agency arrangements and ways in which those professionals engaged in child protection work can best co-operate within these arrangements. First, however, attention will be paid to research into and theorising about inter-agency co-ordination in a range of fields including child protection work.

Review of Recent Literature and Research

There is an extensive literature on collaboration between different professionals and agencies in the subject areas of management studies, organisation theory and public and welfare policy. This has been excellently summarised by Hallett and Birchall (1992), from whose work much of the material in this section is drawn. They point out that there are three terms that are used almost synonymously – co-ordination, collaboration and co-operation. All three activities are characterised by arrangements between two or more agencies or institutions to work together to achieve common goals. The differentiating factor between the three terms is the degree of formalisation involved in the arrangements. Thus, co-ordination is seen as the most formalised, involving agreement between organisations at the highest level and the use of specifically allocated co-ordinative machinery. Collaborative arrangements are characterised by looser, lower-level agreements, and co-operation is the least formalised arrangement of the three.

The attraction of co-ordinative activity for managers and policy-makers is that it has the potential for achieving more than merely the sum of the collaborating parts operating independently. It can create an extra dimension and, therefore, an increased pay-off. This, the most commonly held view about co-ordination, is termed by some writers as 'the optimistic tradition' (Challis *et al.*, 1988). Adherents of this viewpoint can see little fault in collaborative activities. They are considered worthwhile in terms of both outcome and process. There is, on the other hand, a 'doubter/sceptic' view, that which sees co-ordinating activity as having the potential to stifle individual creativity and initiative and impose unnecessary constraints. (Weiss, 1981). From this point of view, the assumption that co-ordination is inevitably the best way to achieve goals is questionable. Indeed, there is a distinct possibility that co-ordinative action can be misused as a substitute for shortage of resources.

There has been a good deal of research into those factors which enhance or inhibit co-ordinative activities in the field of public policy. Hallett and Birchall (1992), in their review of this research, stress the importance of the following factors. First, the external environment has to be supportive of such moves, and a perceived crisis is often needed to act as a catalyst. Second, there has to be a good degree of consensus between the collaborating agencies about the solution to the targeted problem. Third, there is a need for committed individuals to push ahead with collaboration. Fourth, co-ordination is assisted by the fact of different agencies having coterminous administrative boundaries, and fifth, there need to be financial incentives. Inhibitors include the reverse of the above conditions and other factors such as lack of trust between professionals, status and resource differentials, fear of loss of autonomy, and different agency priorities and working schedules.

Hallett and Birchall (1992) point out that most of the literature on the effectiveness of collaborative approaches emphasises the benefits. They refer to several studies of inter-agency approaches to child protection work which point to positive outcomes of co-ordination (Newberger *et al.*, 1973; Wallen *et al.*, 1977; Hochstadt and Hardwicke, 1985; Mouzakitis and Goldstein, 1985; Cohn and Daro, 1987; Gilgun, 1988). However, the usefulness of these studies is limited for a variety of reasons. First, they are all North American, and the projects being evaluated are often small-scale and time-limited and not directly comparable with the systems which we use. Second, they rely heavily on the views of professionals who are often more concerned with process than outcome and do not take into account users' views. Third, they concentrate on collaboration at the interpersonal level without consideration of structural and organisational factors. There are a smaller number of North American studies which point to negative outcomes of co-ordinating activities, such as over-reliance on group processes for decision-making, diffusion of responsibility and overuse of routinised responses (Bourne and Newberger, 1980; Byles, 1985).

There is comparatively only a small amount of British research specifically looking at the effects of co-ordination on outcome in the field of child protection. Those studies that do exist have concentrated largely on inter-professional communication at case conferences (Hallett and Stevenson, 1980; Dingwall *et al.*, 1983; Dale *et al.*, 1986; Corby, 1987) and have tended to focus on the dysfunctions. Other sources of information are public inquiry reports (Department of Health and Social Security (DHSS), 1982;

Department of Health (DOH), 1991a) (but inevitably they highlight errors and failures in communication) and Social Services Inspectorate reports which tend to concern themselves mainly with the formal nature of inter-professional arrangements.

All the factors and issues raised in this section should be borne in mind when assessing the nature and effectiveness of inter-professional work under the British child protection system.

An Analysis of Policy Issues

The issue of inter-agency co-ordination in child care work was recognised as early as 1945 when the inquiry into the death of Dennis O'Neill reported (Home Office, 1945). In that case, two young children had been hurriedly placed by one local authority in an unapproved foster home situated in the area of another local authority without proper agreement between the employees of either about their respective duties and responsibilities. Six months after the placement had been made, Dennis, aged 12, was beaten to death by his foster-father. In his report, Sir Walter Monckton was critical both of the systems and of the individuals involved:

'What is required is rather that the administrative machinery should be improved and informed by a more anxious and responsible spirit.' (Home Office, 1945, page 18.)

The need for better co-ordination between agencies involved with families whose child care standards were a cause for concern was also reflected in the 1950 Home Office circular which recommended to Health, Education and Children's Departments that they set up co-ordinating committees to review their work with such families (Home Office, 1950).

By the mid-1960s, 'baby battering' had been discovered, resulting in the issue of government department circulars in 1970 and 1972 encouraging more inter-agency collaboration.

The Maria Colwell inquiry

However, it was the comments on inter-professional co-ordination and co-operation in the Maria Colwell inquiry report in 1974 that were crucial in determining the future of child protection policy over the next 20 years (DHSS, 1974). Maria, aged 7, died as a result of neglect and beatings by her step-father. She was under a supervision order to one social services department, but was living in an area serviced by another. She was attending school. Thus, social workers, teachers and an education welfare officer were all involved with her in the last year of her life. So, too, were an inspector from the National Society for the Prevention of Cruelty to Children (NSPCC), a general practitioner, housing officials and police officers following allegations by neighbours of ill-treatment of Maria. While the report was critical of the work of individuals, most notably that of the social worker with responsibility for Maria's supervision order and that of the NSPCC inspector, its main conclusion was that:

'The overall impression created by Maria's sad history is that while individuals made mistakes it was the "system", using the word in its widest sense, which failed her.' (DHSS, 1974, page 86.)

In fact, there was no formalised inter-agency system for dealing with child abuse in most parts of the country at this time apart from the work of the co-ordinating committees set up in 1950 which tended to deal more generally with 'problem families'. Much was left to the initiative of individual workers. The child protection system, as we know it, was set up as a direct consequence of the Colwell report's findings. The structure which was established between 1974 and 1976 is essentially that which underpins today's child protection system. It consisted of three main components:

1. Area Review Committees (now termed Area Child Protection Committees) consisting of senior managers of all agencies with an involvement in child protection work: social services, police, health, education, housing and probation. The main function of these committees was (and still is) to oversee the establishment of the child protection system, and to monitor its operation. In addition, it was given responsibility for issuing procedural guidance to all practitioners and for identifying and meeting their training needs.

2. Non-accidental injuries registers (now termed child protection registers). These were instituted with the aim of highlighting for all agencies those children considered to have been abused or at risk of abuse.

3. Case conferences called to assess all allegations of child abuse unless they were considered of insufficient substance to warrant holding them. These conferences were to be attended by all agencies with an involvement with the family in question. A 1976 circular emphasised that the police should be present at all case conferences unless they felt that it was unnecessary to attend.

Thus, co-ordination between agencies was officially seen as the key to developing an effective system for dealing with the problem of child abuse. While in theory these mechanisms were joint and co-operative enterprises, in practice a great deal of emphasis was placed on the role of the social services departments and to a lesser extent on the NSPCC. It should be stressed that there were no legal requirements imposed on professionals either to report abuse (as is the case in the USA) or to attend conferences. Social services departments, the NSPCC and the police were the only agencies with responsibilities laid down by law. Thus, co-ordination between agencies with child protective functions was at this time an uneven and experimental activity looking firmer on paper than it was in actuality.

1973 to 1981

Between 1973 and 1981, there were 18 further inquiries into the deaths of children as a result of abuse (see DHSS, 1982). Most of the cases inquired into were dealt with under the new arrangements for child protection. Inevitably, therefore, in seeking an explanation for what had happened in these cases greater emphasis was placed on the individuals operating the systems. Failures by professionals to share information and to work together collaboratively were identified by the DHSS summary as key factors contributing to the failure to provide children at risk with sufficient protection:

'cases usually involve several professions and two or more agencies, but effective work is hampered by ignorance or misunderstanding of respective functions.'

'all workers need arrangements for exchanging information and, where there is an overlap of function or activity, a clear and common understanding of the extent and purpose of each individual's involvement in the case.'

'case conferences offer an important means of co-ordinating action, but they need to be called at appropriate junctures, to involve everyone with a contribution to make, and to be specific about who is doing what to what end.' (DHSS, 1982, page 68.)

Put more simply, it was felt that often professionals did not know who was responsible for what. This resulted in duplication of work, but, more seriously, in the belief that someone else was taking responsibility when in fact no-one was – the Darryn Clarke inquiry report demonstrated this very clearly (DHSS, 1979). In this case the police, social services department social workers and NSPCC inspectors all thought that an agency other than their own was taking responsibility for looking for Darryn whose relatives alleged that he was being seriously abused but did not know where he and his mother were living. In fact, none of these agencies was actively seeking out this child. The inquiry report found that this situation might well have been sorted out by better communication procedures or by holding a case conference.

Hallett and Stevenson (1980) outlined some of the reasons why this lack of co-operation was persisting. First, they pointed out that professionals in their training and practice developed separate identities and ways of working. They were often not trained to work in conjunction with other professionals on an equal basis. Second, they had different social statuses, levels of education and pay, which served to reinforce divisions. This was particularly obvious in the case of medical doctors. Third, there were major differences of perspective about child protection issues – at this time this was most evident in the contrasting views held by police and social workers. Fourth, there was no regular meeting point for ground-level professionals to air issues other than in the heat of the case conference. Hallett and Stevenson (1980) went on to stress that one of the ways in which professional workers coped with these differences and difficulties was to resort to stereotyping, which was a major barrier to the type of communication and good collaboration that child protection work required.

The early 1980s

The early 1980s saw few developments of note in the working of the child protection system. The main feature of this period was the fact that child protection work was becoming more and more dominated by social services department personnel. Studies of the working of the system (Dingwall et al., 1983; Dale et al., 1986; Corby, 1987) focused largely on inter-professional activity at case conferences. They found that decision-making was confused, and that there was little real progress in respect of inter-professional co-operation.

Nevertheless, the number of public inquiries diminished between 1981 and 1985 (DOH, 1991a), and statistics collected by the NSPCC (Creighton, 1984; 1989) pointed to a decline in the number of serious physical abuse cases being dealt with by the child protection system and to the overall number of child abuse registrations remaining constant. These factors suggested that the problem of child abuse was being reasonably well contained, and that despite its faults the co-ordinative machinery was achieving some measure of success.

The Beckford inquiry 1985

The inquiry report into the death of Jasmine Beckford (London Borough of Brent, 1985) shook the child protection system out of any complacency that it might have fallen into. This report was unequivocal in its view that the various statutory agencies should bear responsibility for what had happened:

> 'On any conceivable version of the events under inquiry the death of Jasmine Beckford on 5 July 1984 was a predictable and preventable homicide. . . . The blame must be shared by all these services (health, education, social services and magistrate's court) in proportion to their various statutory duties, and to the degree of actual and continuing involvement with the Beckford family.' (London Borough of Brent, 1985, page 287.)

Jasmine and her sister had both been seriously abused by Morris Beckford in August 1981. They had been made the subject of care orders and were returned to live with him and their mother in April 1982 after being in a foster home.

The report questioned both the wisdom of the decision to return these children and the way it was reached, i.e. at a case conference attended only by social services personnel and chaired by a line manager. It felt that a health visitor should have been present and that the consultant paediatrician who had been involved at the time when Jasmine and her sister had been hospitalised should have been invited to attend.

It went on to criticise the ongoing monitoring arrangements, particularly the lack of involvement of health professionals. During the first 6 months of Jasmine's 'home-on-trial' period there was no contact between the health visitor and the social worker. There were no checks on her and her sister's health and development at the local health clinic. At the case conference at which Jasmine and her sister were deregistered, neither the health visitor nor the general practitioner was able to attend. In January 1983, Jasmine was placed in nursery school. No mention was made to the head teacher of the school that Jasmine had been abused or that she was still on a care order. The social worker felt that there was no need for the school to be involved in monitoring Jasmine's health and welfare. When Jasmine's attendance at the school deteriorated, as soon it did, the head teacher did not, therefore, consider this a particular cause for concern. From the summer of 1983 until Jasmine's death in July 1984, she was seen only once by her social worker and not at all by the health visitor, despite many calls to the home. There was no liaison at all between these two workers.

There is little sign of good co-ordination of services in this case. The report paints a picture of social services personnel going it alone and not sufficiently involving other agencies. It is difficult to know whether this was what they wanted or whether they had low expectations of doctors' and health workers' readiness to become involved. Health workers may have felt that social workers had a lead role because of the care order and that it was therefore justifiable to leave the case to them. Regardless of the explanations, to judge by this case alone, the communication problem that had evidenced itself in the Maria Colwell case had not been much improved by the child protection system which it had generated.

In 1986, the DHSS issued draft guidelines in response to the Beckford inquiry. Among the recommendations for better inter-agency co-operation were the following.

1. That child protection case conferences should not be chaired by line managers already involved in the cases under scrutiny. Case conferences should set out protection plans and appoint key workers to manage them with the involvement

of other identified professions. Deregistration of children should only take place with the agreement of all those who attended the case conferences at which the registration decisions had been originally made.

2. That schools should be required to nominate teachers to undertake special responsibility for liaising with other agencies over child protection issues.

3. That Area Review Committees be retitled Joint Child Abuse Committees and be allocated funds from joint social services and health authority funding. (The intention was to try and widen the responsibility for child protection work with the particular goal of putting health authorities more fully into the picture.)

In addition to these administrative changes, it was proposed that legal regulations be passed requiring inter-professional consultations to take place before placing children 'home-on-trial'.

The Cleveland inquiry 1988

Before the shock waves of the Beckford report had died down, the Cleveland affair broke (Butler-Sloss, 1988). It, too, had considerable impact on child protection co-ordination.

Child sexual abuse had been a cause for concern for a small number of doctors and social workers (mainly female) in Britain since the early 1980s. By 1986, there were nearly 6000 children registered on the grounds of sexual abuse. Paediatricians in Leeds had been particularly active in detecting signs of anal abuse of young children (Hobbs and Wynne, 1986). A MORI Poll survey (Baker and Duncan, 1985) had reported much higher rates of sexual abuse than previously imagined. In this climate, two paediatricians in Cleveland, using the techniques pioneered by Hobbs and Wynne, diagnosed large numbers of children as having been sexually abused. They were fully supported in what they were trying to achieve by the child protection co-ordinator in Cleveland Social Services Department who had also developed a particular interest in the issue of child sexual abuse. Other agencies, however, most notably the police and police surgeons, were more sceptical about the new thinking on sexual abuse and thus a major split in the inter-professional network was created. Paediatricians diagnosed abuse and the social services department social workers, heavily influenced by post-Beckford developments, speedily removed children to places of safety. Meanwhile, the police and police surgeons dissociated themselves from what was happening. The following extract from the Cleveland report emphasises the full extent of the breakdown of inter-professional co-operation.

'A week later social workers referred another family of three as a result of the comments of the eldest child of 10 at school and the concern of her headmistress. Dr Higgs examined the first child with the consent of her mother, and found signs she felt were consistent with sexual abuse. Before she could examine the second child, the father arrived on the ward and removed the three children. He took them to a secret address. He was at the time required to report daily to the police who were unable to persuade him to divulge the whereabouts of the children. However, he agreed to the examination of the children by a police surgeon, and Dr Beeby was taken to the secret address. He examined the children in an upstairs room and found no abnormality. They were then returned home by their father, removed on a place of safety order obtained by Social Services and taken back to hospital. This time Dr Higgs examined all three children and diagnosed sexual abuse in respect of all three. The following day Dr Irvine (police surgeon) examined the three children and agreed with the conclusions of Dr Beeby. Two weeks later, Dr McCowen, paediatrician from Northallerton, considered the signs suspicious and later in June Dr Roberts (police surgeon) and Dr Paul considered there was no abnormality.' (Butler-Sloss, 1988, page 16.)

The conflict was not confined to the actions of the professionals on the ground. The Cleveland report closely examined the working of the Joint Child Abuse Committee which had replaced the Area Review Committee in line with the recommendations of the Beckford report. It pointed out that this body had been entirely ineffective in sorting out the chaos which reigned in the spring and early summer of 1987, and the reason for this was that it was not sufficiently recognised by senior managers in the different agencies as having any authority to do so. When the chips were down, agencies disowned the collaborative mechanism and pursued their own interests.

The Cleveland Report (Butler-Sloss, 1988, pages 248–250) had much to say about inter-professional co-ordination. It stated that:

'no single agency – Health, Social Services, Police or voluntary organisation has the pre-eminent responsibility in the assessment of child abuse generally and child sexual abuse specifically.' (Butler-Sloss, 1988, page 248.)

It went on to outline the need to set up specialist assessment teams consisting primarily of police, social workers and doctors to deal with problematic referrals of child sexual abuse. While this particular recommendation has been largely ignored, there can be little doubt that the Cleveland report has had a massive impact on inter-professional co-operation over the last 5 years, perhaps more than any inquiry report since that relating to Maria Colwell. It placed child protection work firmly back into the court of *all* the agencies and emphasised the need for more attention to be paid to careful inter-professional planning of intervention into suspected cases of child abuse. In particular, it recommended that police and social services department workers conduct joint interviews of children alleged or suspected to have been sexually abused. It also affirmed the need for inter-professional training for child protection work: 'For example police officers and social workers designated to inter-view children should have joint training in their approach to this task.' (Butler-Sloss, 1988, page 251.)

The Cleveland report also made recommendations about the treatment of children and parents that have had significant effects on inter-agency co-ordination. The most influential of these was the requirement that they be more closely involved at every stage in the investigative procedure, including attendance at case conferences. This recommendation, which together with all the other Cleveland recommendations was hastily inserted into the 1988 *Working Together* guidelines (DHSS, 1988), increased the pressure on agencies to improve communications with each other. They had to ensure a united front now that their decisions were being reached in a more public arena.

Implications for Practice

In this section, focus will first be placed on the current state of inter-agency co-ordina-tion in child protection work, and then consideration will be given to ways in which professionals can make best use of the systems within which they work.

The current functioning of the child protection system

The mechanisms and systems for developing inter-professional co-ordination have become far more sophisticated over the past 20 years, particularly so since the publication of the Cleveland inquiry report. The administrative/managerial functions of the child protection system still rest with what are now called Area Child Protection Committees (having been retitled yet again in the 1988 guidelines). These bodies have a crucial function in ensuring that co-operation and collaboration between all the agencies involved in child protection work is effective. The latest *Working Together* guidelines (DOH, 1991*b*) stress the need for all agencies to be represented at these committees by people of sufficient weight to commit them to agreed courses of action, and all agencies are required to contribute to the financial costs incurred by their work. While this requirement represents a major improvement on what went on before, these committees nevertheless still do not have full managerial authority over the child protection work carried out by constituent member agencies, and this is seen as a continuing weakness by several commentators (Stevenson, 1989; Walton, 1993).

The reporting of concerns about children at risk to either social services departments or the police is still not legally required of other agencies, but in reality, particularly as a result of Department of Health guidelines, such activity has become less and less subject to the discretion of individual workers. Once a child has been identified as being at risk, it is now the duty of local authority housing and education departments and of health authorities to assist in any ensuing inquiry (see section 47(9) of the 1989 Children Act). Some professionals, such as health visitors and general practitioners, have retained a degree of discretion about when to refer and what to refer, but they are now much more aware of child protection issues and much more involved in the child protection system than was the case even as late as the mid-1980s.

Child protection conferences are generally more focused and formalised than has been the case in the past. This is partly due to the appointment of child protection co-ordinators, usually social workers who have developed a good deal of expertise as specialist child protection workers. As already stressed, another important factor in this respect has been the involvement of parents and children in conferences. This has forced professionals to consider more carefully the format of the procedures and to be more explicit about aims and objectives (Thoburn, 1992).

There is greater emphasis on inter-professional discussion and contact outside the case conference forum. Following events at Cleveland and Rochdale, and more recently what happened in the Orkneys, professionals concerned about suspected cases of abuse have been encouraged to get together in more informal settings than those of the case conference to discuss intervention strategies.

In the post-case conference period, there is now a clear expectation that the key worker will involve other important professionals, parents and, in some cases, children in constructing the details of a child protection plan and implementing it. It should be pointed out, however, that there is little information about how this is working out in practice. Nevertheless, in many more ways than before and at several different stages inter-agency co-ordination and inter-professional co-operation has become the accepted way of working in child protection cases.

Referring back to the levels of co-ordination discussed by Hallett and Birchall (1992) at the start of this chapter, it is clear that by any set of criteria the child protection system, while not subject to legal regulations, is now at a relatively high level of formalisation. Communication and co-operation are essential requirements of child protection work, not merely forms of practice preferred by professional workers.

Inter-professional co-operation now

It is probably safe to say that the standard of inter-professional co-operation is now at its highest level since 1974. In this brief review, the current expectations of all the main professions involved in child protection work will be considered along with a commentary on the way in which they are carrying out their responsibilities.

The importance of the role of general practitioners is heavily emphasised in the 1991 *Working Together* guidelines, as is the need for them to receive child protection training. Since 1987, there has been clear guidance for GPs from the General Medical Council stressing their professional duty to disclose information when they consider a child is being physically or sexually abused. (Prior to this, there had been a good deal of uncertainty on their part about the ethics of breaking confidentiality in these circumstances.) On the debit side, general practitioners are still not regular attenders at case conferences and most have remained on the sidelines of child protection training and work.

Health visitors have now also clarified their position over the issue of confidentiality (Smart, 1992). The 1991 *Working Together* guidelines recommend that each health authority should identify a senior health worker (health visitor, community nurse or clinical medical officer) to oversee child protection issues and improve inter-professional communication and collaboration. Despite the views of the Beckford report and some commentators (Dingwall *et al.*, 1983) that health visitors should play a more central role in child protection work, particularly with regard to the under-fives, the profession has preferred to remain marginal (relative to social workers) in order to preserve good relationships with families, which it feels to be essential to the provision of community health care and advice.

Paediatricians have over the years been less equivocal over the issue of confidentiality than other members of the medical and health professions. They played a lead administrative as well as medical role in the early stages of child physical abuse rediscovery and, as has been seen, they were in the forefront of important developments in the field of sexual abuse detection as well. However, the Cleveland affair threw into doubt their credibility as expert witnesses in such cases, and while they are still key figures in child protection work their role has consequently diminished to some degree.

The role of the police in child protection work has changed dramatically in the last few years. Before the rediscovery of sexual abuse in the mid-1980s, police officers had only become directly involved with families in those physical abuse and neglect cases which were considered to be serious enough to warrant prosecution, and such cases were very much in the minority. Their other main function was (and still is) to furnish case conferences with details of relevant offences committed by adults suspected of abuse. They have developed a more central role in child protection work since the Cleveland affair which led to all Area Child Protection committees making arrangements for joint police and social work interviews of children alleged to have been sexually abused, and for joint training to facilitate this work.

This more prominent role for the police has been reinforced by the requirements of the *Memorandum of Good Practice* in joint interviewing (Home Office, 1992). Some commentators are sceptical about the benefits of the closer involvement of police and social workers in this sphere of activity and consider that social services departments' central role and approach is being threatened by the more crime-focused emphasis adopted by the police (Kelly and Regan, 1990). Others are convinced that these new developments have enhanced police–social worker relationships, resulting in a more consistent service to families and children (Wattam, 1990).

The role of schoolteachers and education welfare officers has not changed greatly over the past few years. As pointed out earlier, as a result of the Beckford inquiry report, all schools are now recommended to have a child protection liaison officer and in general there is greater awareness of the issues, particularly with regard to sexual abuse, as a result of media publicity and inter-disciplinary training. Many schools have developed sex and safety education programmes. School personnel are much more closely involved in child protection plans than before.

Social services department social workers, while subject to high levels of criticism throughout the whole period in which child abuse has been a prominent public issue, have nevertheless retained the key central role in the system. The 1991 guidelines recommend the employment of specialist child protection co-ordinators to oversee child protection systems. Social services department managers are seen as key figures in the administration of Area Child Protection Committees. Only social workers can assume the role of key workers, and it is their responsibility to manage the child protection plan agreed upon at the case conference. Social workers have key statutory responsibilities and resources in relation both to abused children and all other children in need.

The NSPCC still retains its long-established statutory powers in the area of child abuse detection and investigation. In practice, it is moving away from work in these areas and focusing more on therapeutic work with families in which children have been abused.

The probation service retains its responsibility to notify social services departments about discharged prisoners convicted of child abuse and to supervise offenders in the community. Probation officers have become increasingly involved in child sexual abuse work in relation to sexual offenders and have developed treatment programmes both for those in prisons and those on probation orders in the community.

Finally, local authority solicitors have been given a more central role in child protection work than before. The *Working Together* guidelines recommend their attendance at case conferences to give legal advice at as early a stage as possible.

Suggestions for improving inter-professional co-operation

It should be evident by now that good inter-professional liaison depends on the quality of systems, the quality of those working within them and the interplay between the two. It has been argued that there has been a concentrated effort since Beckford and Cleveland to improve the standard of child protection procedures, and that involved professionals as a whole are working together better than ever before. As long as we retain our present system for dealing with child abuse, with its reliance on agencies to work together in a voluntaristic way, it is crucial that the relevant professionals continue to develop open and trusting relationships in order to maximise their effectiveness. This has several implications for practice.

First, inter-professional training in child protection work should be obligatory at all stages of professional development: during training for qualification, and at in-service and post-qualification courses. (Clearly, there needs to be some distinction between the sort of training required for specialist child protection workers and for those for whom involvement in child protection work forms only a small part of their overall responsibilities.)

Second, practitioners need to maintain an awareness of the multi-disciplinary dimension of child protection work by ensuring that they have a clear understanding of the organisational requirements and duties placed on professionals from other agencies.

Third, there is need for regular dialogue between different professionals about what forms of behaviour they consider abusive (or seriously abusive) and why. Giovannoni and Becerra (1979) have demonstrated how occupational concerns and requirements can lead to widely differing definitions of abuse between different professional groups.

Fourth, there is a need to avoid stereotyping other professionals which, as Hallett and Stevenson (1980) have pointed out, serves only to create and strengthen separation and distrust.

Fifth, there is a need to be clear about who has responsibility for what in carrying out a protection plan and the need to check it out if in doubt.

All these issues can (and should) be addressed in training. Some can be aided by systemic changes, such as the clear delineation of responsibilities and expectations at case conferences. However, there is still a need for all individual workers to take professional responsibility in these matters over and above the stated requirements of the system. In addition, those in consultative or supervisory capacities over professional workers should be particularly attuned to the need for good inter-professional relationships as an essential ingredient of child protection work and ensure that it is high on their agendas.

Concluding Comments

While there have been considerable strides forward in the past few years in improving inter-professional co-operation within the child protection system that we have developed, there are still many outstanding broader issues to be addressed about this type of co-ordinative activity.

First, we still know very little about the effectiveness of our current system. Little attention has been paid to alternative ways of organising child protection work, such as the development of the specialist inter-professional teams which was recommended for consideration by both the Cleveland report (see above) and the Kimberley Carlile report (London Borough of Greenwich, 1987).

Second, as Hallett and Birchall (1992) point out, in our determination to make our system work, we run the risk of seeing only the positive aspects of inter-professional work and of thereby ignoring the possible dysfunctions. For instance, some commentators have argued that the bureaucratic arrangements needed to ensure inter-professional co-operation have led to more defensive decision-making (Harris, 1987; Howe, 1992) and the elimination of the use of professional discretion and judgement on the part of individual workers (Finkelhor and Zellman, 1991).

Third, there are factors such as costs and resources that have to be taken into account. The formalisation of the inter-professional system, particularly since 1985, has seen a major increase in the number of conferences held (DOH, 1992). These conferences are costly in themselves because of the amount of professional time that they consume and because the more comprehensive decisions being made at them entail the provision of more resources. For instance, a recent Social Services Inspectorate (SSI) report found 600 unallocated registered cases in the London area (SSI, 1990). The American system, which has experienced similar developments to our own, is seen by some to be so overloaded that it cannot achieve what it sets out to do (Krugman, 1991).

In the previous section, the focus was on what could be done at the training and practice levels to maintain and improve inter-professional co-operation. These broader practice and policy concerns also need to be taken into account in the development of our child protection arrangements. While we have achieved a tighter and more carefully managed approach which has the strength of utilising a wide range of professional knowledge, expertise and perspectives, we need to ensure that these arrangements do not eliminate flexibility and innovation in decision-making, that there are sufficient resources to meet identified needs, and that we pay attention to outcomes as well as to inputs.

Annotated Reading

Corby, B. (1987). *Working with Child Abuse*. Milton Keynes: Open University Press.
This is an empirical study of social work practice in child protection work which incorporates issues of inter-professional co-operation at case conferences (chapter 5, pages 63–82) and in ongoing work with families (see pages 96–101).

Dale, P., Waters, J., Davies, M., Roberts, W. & Morrison, T. (1986). *Dangerous Families: Assessment and Treatment of Child Abuse*. London: Tavistock.
This is an action study of child protection work carried out by the NSPCC with a view to deciding whether children who have been seriously abused by their parents should be rehabilitated to them following removal from their care. The authors focus specifically on how professionals conflict with each other (particularly at case conferences) and become 'stuck' over how to work with families. Drawing on the experience of family therapists, they suggest the use of network meetings involving families and professionals to overcome these problems and therefore to ensure safe rehabilitations. (See particularly chapter 2, pages 26–50.)

Department of Health (1991a). *Child Abuse: A Study of Inquiry Reports 1980–89*. London: HMSO.
This study looks at 20 inquiry reports and draws together the various recommendations under different themes. The first section (pages 3–22) considers the roles of different agencies – social services departments, the NSPCC, health and education authorities, the police and the probation service. There are also relevant sections on case conferences (pages 44–47) and inter-agency procedures (pages 50–53).

Department of Health (1991b). *Working Together under the Children Act 1989 – A Guide to Arrangements for Inter-Agency Co-operation for the Protection of Children against Abuse*. London: HMSO.
These are the current government guidelines for carrying out child protection work. They place particular emphasis on the need for close liaison between all agencies and professionals involved in child protection work.

Dingwall, R., Eekelaar, J. & Murray, T. (1983). *The Protection of Children: State Intervention and Family Life*. Oxford: Blackwell.
This is an empirical study of child protection work in the late 1970s which takes into account the functioning of a wide range of relevant agencies. The authors identify conflicts between agencies and professionals in the decision-making process, but to some extent consider this to be an inevitable outcome of the liberal-democratic nature of our society and its child protection concerns.

Hallett, C. & Birchall, E. (1992). *Co-ordination and Child Protection: A Review of the Literature*. London: HMSO.
This is a comprehensive study of a wide range of issues affecting inter-professional co-ordination in child protection. It starts with a review of relevant organisational theory, provides an in-depth account of the roles and duties of various agencies and professionals, surveys British and American child protection studies and pays particular attention to the effectiveness of inter-professional arrangements.

Hallett, C. & Stevenson, O. (1980). *Child Abuse: Aspects of Inter-professional Co-operation*. London: Allen and Unwin.
This is an in-depth study of a small number of child abuse case conferences which the researchers observed and followed up by interviewing the different professionals that attended them. There is a good deal of relevant theoretical material on small group processes, stereotyping and professional identity which is of considerable use in understanding social-psychological barriers to good inter-professional co-operation.

Stevenson, O. (1989). Multi-disciplinary work in child protection. In O. Stevenson (ed.): *Child Abuse: Public Policy and Professional Practice*. Hemel Hempstead: Harvester Wheatsheaf.
This chapter provides a thoughtful survey of up-to-date issues in inter-professional co-operation. It looks at the structure and function of Area Review Committees, professional status and power issues, the impact of organisational priorities and constraints, case conference dynamics and the difficulties of obtaining agreed definitions of child abuse and what to do about it in a complex and multi-cultural society such as ours.

References

Baker, A. & Duncan, S. (1985). Child sexual abuse: a study of prevalence in Great Britain. *Child Abuse and Neglect 9*: 457–467.

Bourne, J. & Newberger, E. (1980). Interdisciplinary group process in the hospital management of child abuse and neglect. *Child Abuse and Neglect 4*: 137–144.

Butler-Sloss, Lord Justice E. (1988). *Report of the Inquiry into Child Abuse in Cleveland 1987*. Cmnd. 412. London: HMSO.

Byles, J. (1985). Problems in inter-agency collaboration: lessons from a project that failed. *Child Abuse and Neglect 9*: 549–554.

Challis, L., Fuller, S., Henwood, M., Klein, R., Plowden, W., Webb, A., Whittingham, P. and Wistow, G. (1988). *Joint Approaches to Social Policy – Rationality and Practice*. Cambridge: Cambridge University Press.

Cohn, A. & Daro, D. (1987). Is treatment too late? What ten years of evaluative research tell us. *Child Abuse and Neglect 11*: 433–442.

Corby, B. (1987). *Working with Child Abuse*. Milton Keynes: Open University Press.

Creighton, S. (1984). *Trends in Child Abuse*. London: NSPCC.

Creighton, S. (1989). *Child Abuse Trends in England and Wales 1983–1987*. London: NSPCC.

Dale, P., Waters, J., Davies, M., Roberts, W. & Morrison, T. (1986). *Dangerous Families: Assessment and Treatment of Child Abuse*. London: Tavistock.

Department of Health (1989). *Survey of Children and Young Persons on Child Protection Registers, Year Ending 31 March 1988, England*. London: HMSO.

Department of Health (1991*a*). *Child Abuse: A Study of Inquiry Reports 1980–89*. London: HMSO.

Department of Health (1991*b*). *Working Together under the Children Act 1989 – A Guide to Arrangements for Inter-Agency Co-operation for the Protection of Children against Abuse*. London: HMSO.

Department of Health (1992). *Survey of Children and Young Persons on Child Protection Registers, Year Ending 31 March 1991, England*. London: HMSO.

Department of Health and Social Security (1974). *Report of the Committee of Inquiry into the Care and Supervision Provided in Relation to Maria Colwell*. London: HMSO.

Department of Health and Social Security (1979). *The Report of the Committee of Inquiry into the Actions of the Authorities and Agencies Relating to Darryn James Clarke*. Cmnd. 7739. London: HMSO.

Department of Health and Social Security (1982). *Child Abuse: A Study of Inquiry Reports 1973–1981*. London: HMSO.

Department of Health and Social Security (1986). *Child Abuse – Working Together. A Draft Guide to Arrangements for Inter-Agency Co-operation for the Protection of Children*. London: HMSO.

Department of Health and Social Security (1988). *Working Together – A Guide to Inter-agency Co-operation for the Protection of Children Against Abuse*. London: HMSO.

Dingwall, R., Eekelaar, J. & Murray, T. (1983). *The Protection of Children: State Intervention and Family Life*. Oxford: Blackwell.

Finkelhor, D. & Zellman, G. (1991). Flexible reporting options for skilled child abuse professionals. *Child Abuse and Neglect 15:* 335–341.

Gilgun, J. (1988). 'Decision-making in interdisciplinary treatment teams.' *Child Abuse and Neglect 12:* 231–239.

Giovannoni, J. & Becerra, R. (1979). *Defining Child Abuse*. New York: Free Press.

Hallett, C. & Birchall, E. (1992). *Co-ordination and Child Protection: A Review of the Literature*. London: HMSO.

Hallett, C. & Stevenson, O. (1980). *Child Abuse: Aspects of Inter-Professional Co-operation*. London: Allen and Unwin.

Harris, N. (1987). Defensive social work. *British Journal of Social Work 17:* 61–69.

Hobbs, C. & Wynne, J. (1986). Buggery in childhood – a common syndrome of child abuse. *The Lancet:* 792–796, 4 October.

Hochstadt, N. & Hardwicke, N. (1985). How effective is the inter-disciplinary approach? A follow-up study. *Child Abuse and Neglect 9:* 365–372.

Home Office (1945). *Report by Sir Walter Monckton on the Circumstances which Led to the Boarding-Out of Dennis and Terence O'Neill at Bank Farm, Minsterley and the Steps Taken to Supervise Their Welfare*, Cmnd. 6636. London: HMSO.

Home Office (1950). *Children Neglected or Ill-treated in Their Own Home*. Joint circular with the Ministry of Health and the Ministry of Education. London: HMSO.

Home Office, Department of Health (1992). *Memorandum of Good Practice on Video Recorded Interviews with Child Witnesses for Criminal Proceedings*. London: HMSO.

Howe, D. (1992). Child abuse and the bureaucratisation of social work. *Sociological Review:* 491–508.

Kelly, L. & Regan, L. (1990). Flawed protection. *Social Work Today 21(32):* 13–15.

Krugman, R. (1991). Child abuse and neglect: critical first steps in response to a national emergency. *American Journal of Diseases in Childhood 145:* 513–515.

London Borough of Brent (1985). *A Child in Trust.* The report of the panel of inquiry into the circumstances surrounding the death of Jasmine Beckford. Brent.

London Borough of Greenwich (1987). *A Child in Mind: Protection of Children in a Responsible Society.* The report of the commission of inquiry into the circumstances surrounding the death of Kimberley Carlile. Greenwich.

Mouzakitis, C. & Goldstein, S. (1985). A multi-disciplinary approach to treating child neglect. *Social Casework 66(4):* 218–224.

Newberger, E., Hagenbuch, J., Ebeling, N., Colligan, E., Sheehan, J. & Mcveigh, S. (1973). Reducing the literal and human cost of child abuse: impact of a new hospital management system. *Pediatrics 51(5):* 840–848.

Smart, M. (1992). Professional ethics and participation – nurses, health visitors and midwives. In J. Thoburn (ed.): *Participation in Practice – Involving Families in Child Protection.* Norwich: University of East Anglia.

Social Services Inspectorate (1990). *Child Protection in London: Aspects of Management Arrangements in Social Services Departments.* London: HMSO.

Stevenson, O. (1989). Multi-disciplinary work in child protection. In O. Stevenson (ed.): *Child Abuse: Public Policy and Professional Practice.* Hemel Hempstead: Harvester Wheatsheaf.

Thoburn, J. (ed.) (1992). *Participation in Practice – Involving Families in Child Protection.* Norwich: University of East Anglia.

Wallen, G., Pierce, S., Koch, M. & Venters, H. (1977). The interdisciplinary team approach to child abuse services: strengths and limitations. *Child Abuse and Neglect 1:* 3559–3564.

Walton, M. (1993). Regulation in child protection – policy failure? *British Journal of Social Work 23:* 139–156.

Wattam, C. (1990). Working together. *Social Work Today 22(3):* 222–223.

Weiss, J. (1981). Substance vs. symbol in administrative reform: the case of human services co-ordination. *Policy Analysis 7(1):* 21–45.

12

Case Conferences in Child Protection

Olive Stevenson

'The child protection conference is central to child protection procedures . . . The conference symbolises the inter-agency nature of assessment, treatment and the managment of child protection'. (Department of Health (DOH), 1991, page 41: 6–1.)

Introduction

In the past decade, case conferences have increasingly been seen as a crucial element in the protection of children at risk. Advice on their conduct has been given by the Department of Health, most recently in *Working Together* (DOH, 1991). Criticism of their effectiveness has been made in various child abuse inquiries, including the cases of Jasmine Beckford (London Borough of Brent, 1985) and Stephanie Fox (Wandsworth Area Child Protection Committee, 1990). Most important for the purposes of this chapter is the recent substantial body of research throwing light on their content and process, and on the attitudes of professionals and parents towards them. Much water has flowed under the bridge since the present author (with Hallett) studied conferences in relation to inter-professional co-operation (Hallett and Stevenson, 1980). For instance, that work did not refer to sexual abuse or to the issue of parental participation at conferences. These examples remind us how quickly and profoundly the nature of child protection work has changed. Those participating in the conference, accordingly, have had to adapt to radical changes in both its content and process. During the late 1980s, there were a number of small-scale mainly local studies focused upon the issue of parental participation (Rousiaux, 1984; McGloin & Turnbull, 1986; Phillips & Evans, 1986; Shemmings & Thoburn, 1990). However, there is now much more comprehensive research available which places conferences in the more general context of child welfare practice, and it is upon this that much of the discussion which follows is based. The primary sources of reference in this chapter are to Farmer and Owen (1993), Hallett (1993) and Thoburn *et al.* (1993).

This chapter focuses upon initial conferences. There is, comparatively, a poverty of research concerning review conferences, and constraints of space do not permit their exploration here. However, their importance and the need for further work in this area should not be overlooked. The emphasis on initial conferences in the literature is in some ways symptomatic of the preoccupation with assessment of risk and relative neglect of 'protective planning', which will be later considered.

The case conference is not the only forum for discussion amongst professionals. Before the initial conference, *Working Together* (DOH, 1991) states:

> 'it is essential that there is an early strategy discussion, which may not require a meeting, between the statutory agencies, i.e. police and social services, to plan the investigation and in particular the role of each agency and the extent of the joint investigation'. (DOH, 1991, page 2: 5.3.i.)

Clearly, this envisaged the discussion as a 'management tool' and not as an occasion to 'stitch up' the conference, although some have feared this might happen. (We have no evidence of this from the research.) One notes that this discussion is envisaged as taking place between two agencies in particular, and it is easy to see how this may on occasion be perceived as 'too cosy' by other participants. (We refer later to the question of relationships between police and social workers.)

After the initial conference, but not in place of formal review conferences, 'core group' meetings are springing up in which the focus is on how to protect, and on managing and resourcing interventions. At present, these are relatively informal meetings. There are no clear-cut guidelines on who should chair them, whether parents should be present, or whether they should be informed of their occurrence. Hallett (1993) found that out of the 48 cases she studied, only six had established core groups. (It is likely, however, that their frequency has by now increased.) She notes that, where they existed, they were 'genuinely welcomed, both as a mechanism for sustaining inter-agency involvement and ensuring that plans were implemented'. (Hallett, 1993, page 207.) However, here again, some concerns about 'cosiness' were expressed. The core groups 'usually met without management input', and there was a danger of concentrating too much power in the hands of the key worker and the social services department (Hallett, 1993, page 208). Hallett cites one worker who feared that core groups were making decisions which were properly the responsibility of the case conference.

Perhaps all that can safely be said at present is that the evolution of core groups needs monitoring as an important part of the protection process. It would be unwise to discourage meetings which can give purpose and shape to inter-agency intervention, but a watchful eye needs to be kept on their power, especially in relation to the role of review conferences and to the involvement of parents in planning. The complex issues which arise in relation to the initial conference will be analysed under five headings:

- Purpose and content.
- Process.
- Inter-professional aspects.
- Parent/child participation.
- Specific issues.

Purpose and Content

The essential purposes of the conference seem to be generally agreed. The most important are said to be, first, to share and evaluate information; secondly, to make an assessment about the existence and levels of risk; thirdly, to decide if there is a need for registration and, fourthly, to recommend plans for protection when registration is necessary (DOH, 1991). *Working Together* (DOH, 1991) warns that the conference should not be used 'as a forum for a formal decision that a person has abused a child, which is a criminal offence' (page 1. 5:5:2). However, these apparently clear-cut purposes are not unproblematic when they are set in the wider context of child welfare work generally. Farmer and Owen (1993), in a comprehensive study of decision-making in child protection, found that 'the priority given to the child's protection meant that little attention was given to the broader issue of the childs' welfare'. (Farmer and Owen, 1993, summary, page 11.35.) Thus, other needs could be overlooked, both material and psychological. The treatment needs of sexually abused children were of particular concern, as was the relative neglect of consideration of material circumstances (see also Gibbons *et al.*, 1993). In evaluating the outcomes of the cases studied, Farmer and Owen suggest three criteria: whether the child had been protected; whether the child's development had been effectively enhanced, and whether the needs of the main caring parent had been met. They found that a high proportion (70%) were protected and their development enhanced (68%). But in less than a third of the cases were the needs of other family members met. It is beyond the scope of this chapter to discuss the broader issues of child welfare policy which these findings raise. However, it is important that the present definition of the objectives of the case conference are subject to scrutiny, not least because they have a bearing on the effectiveness of working in partnership with parents, and to consider how well the initial conference achieves its stated purpose.

Assessment of Risk in the Conference

Farmer and Owen (1993) discuss this at some length. They suggest that there were 'certain standard patterns of reasoning' which nearly amounted to 'alternative models of decision-making', although they can and were on occasion combined. These are described as: accumulating concerns; matching present and previous contexts; focusing on specific incidents of abuse or neglect (page 141). In the first of these, 'the conference members virtually pile concerns on top of each other' (page 142). In the second, the conference examines what is the likelihood of the abuse taking place again. In the third, the emphasis is on the gravity of a specific incident. Farmer and Owen point out that there was little evidence that the dynamics of the family situation and the social context were analysed in relation to the making of a protection plan. (However, Bell and Sinclair (1993) found that the making of such plans was sometimes left for a later meeting.) This finding may be related to the central deficiency which they discuss – the absence of theoretical content. They ask: 'in a case conference which is attended by well-qualified practitioners ... why is there so little reference to causal theories or to research evidence bearing on the aetiology of child abuse?' (Farmer and Owen, 1993, page 148.)

Elsewhere I have drawn attention to the difficulties surrounding the utilisation of theory (Stevenson, 1989). I argued at that time that social workers were trapped by a fear that explanations of behaviour in individuals and families lead to strategies which deny the significance of socio-economic forces.

However, research suggests that this is not borne out in practice. Farmer and Owen (1993) and Gibbons *et al.* (1993) found surprisingly little reference to material factors relevant to the family situation. Bell and Sinclair (1993) found that professionals became uneasy when parents introduced information about deplorable material circumstances. Hallett (1993) suggests that in practice most social workers operated 'on the basis of some concepts of individual and family malfunctioning'. This may in part reflect the impact of day-to-day experience upon workers in child protection, especially following the increase of sexual abuse referrals. The realisation that socioeconomic factors do not alone provide an adequate framework for understanding may have moved workers to a more pragmatic, less ideologically driven, position. Yet, as we have seen, such pragmatism is evidently not underpinned by clear theoretical formulations and it is, in a sense, the worst of both worlds if neither material circumstances nor family dynamics are adequately explored.

As will be discussed further below Hallett (1993) found a striking absence of dissent and conflict between the different professions. It may be that, in such highly charged matters, there is a tacit agreement amongst those present at conferences, which must produce action plans, that deeper differences in the way situations are perceived must be avoided. Furthermore, social workers, who may now be more willing to explore the dynamics of family functioning, find themselves with little confidence in, or understanding of, theories which might facilitate this. An exception to this concerns the application of feminist theory to sexual abuse, which has been incorporated into the thinking of many contemporary social workers. It is likely, however, that in practice many social workers 'lie low' in conferences lest too assertive a stance jeopardises the process.

The evidence therefore suggests that the conference is operating with little or no explicit content and with little discussion of 'causation', of whatever kind.

The danger of this is that implicit theoretical assumptions which influence decisions are not tested and, as Farmer and Owen (1993) point out, moral rather than professional judgements become central to the process. Most important, the formulation of a protection plan may not be meaningfully linked to the process of risk assessment. Farmer and Owen conclude that, in their study, 'good assessments were comprehensive and dynamic and used a variety of methodological approaches' (page 155). However, even so, 'they were assessments of *risk* rather than of *need*'. As earlier suggested, the very concept of risk assessment at the heart of the conference process may itself be limiting and even distorting to sound child welfare practice.

Registration

Gibbons *et al.* (1993) ask the question: 'Were the "right" cases placed on the register?' They conclude that, in cases of physical abuse, 'a substantial minority of apparently serious and substantiated cases . . . were not placed on the register' (page 95), whereas very few high-risk cases of sexual abuse were not registered. They also note that, although neglect cases were less likely to reach the conference, those that did so were more serious, a finding confirmed by Bell and Sinclair (1993). Despite this, a substantial proportion (nearly a quarter) were not registered. These findings mask marked variations between authorities in their registration behaviour. As Gibbons *et al.* remark, 'ideally the . . . conference would place *all* children with demonstrably great need for protection and *only* those children on the child protection register but to achieve this the state of knowledge about the need for protection itself would have to improve' (pages 98–99).

Practice varies as to whether parents are themselves consulted as to whether they themselves wish their child to be registered. It seems desirable that parents and children, if old enough, should be asked for their views. Sometimes it may be obvious that there must be registration, but on other occasions it may not be clear that it is necessary or desirable. In such cases the views of parents and children are a valuable addition to the information needed to make a decision.

At present, government guidance (DOH, 1991) is unclear as to whether registration is appropriate when a protection plan is needed but there is full co-operation by parents. Such cases may arise when the alleged abuser has left the home, but the child's sexualised behaviour leaves her or him vulnerable and in need of protection. Clearly, a decision not to register in such cases must imply great confidence on the part of the conference participants that the assurances given by the parent are 'safe', i.e. that they are not plausible or, even if sincere, unlikely in practice to be able to offer adequate protection. In this, as so many matters, the experience and skill of the conference chair will be vital.

Gibbons *et al.*'s findings also prompt reflection on the apparent variations in the number registered in the different categories. Farmer and Owen (1993) suggest that, 'one factor which strongly influenced the registration rate was the degree of frequency with which certain types of abuse reached the conference', 'sexual abuse cases were more likely to reach conferences because of their high public profile' (page 156). However, fewer may be registered because there may be no outstanding protection issues if the abuser was outside the family or has left the family. They also consider other factors, in addition to the severity of the abuse or neglect, which have a cumulative effect and may influence the decision to register. One of these is that in many cases registered under one heading, there was also concern about the other kinds of abuse. Apparently, mixed categories are rarely used so that official records 'under-represent the concerns' and do not reflect 'the way concerns are clustered together' (page 157). This is puzzling. It would seem highly desirable for registration to report all the areas of concern, not least because it may help to ensure that proper emphasis is given to all dimensions of risk.

Farmer and Owen (1993) and Bell and Sinclair (1993) also draw attention to the increased likelihood of registration if the family was previously known to agencies other than social services. This may be because other options have been tried and failed, or because more information was available at the conference. A further finding was that children were more likely to be registered if the mother was seen as responsible for the abuse or neglect. I return to this issue at the end of the chapter. It is also important to consider the factors which lead to a decision not to register. Farmer and Owen found that 'good reports' on parents, even if irrelevant to the matter in hand, or 'attractive' behaviour during the conference were relevant.

All this reminds us that the conference is a dynamic process in which decisions to register are taken in a web of complex factors: the policy (stated or unstated) of the different authorities, the 'accumulation of concerns' and the dynamics of the particular conference – all these and other factors play a part.

The issue of registration has, from its inception, been contentious and complex. Some now argue that, under the new legislation, registration should be tied to tighter definitions of 'significant' (or likely significant) harm. The act of registration certainly makes it more difficult to translate the ideal of partnership into reality. However, if the process were more tightly circumscribed, effective multi-agency work to support the family and to protect the child in a more general way *must* be legitimated, with an appropriate allocation of resources. It is well known at present that the act of registration unlocks resources. It would be disastrous if limits on registration resulted in a failure to help certain families effectively.

The Protection Plan

Both Farmer and Owen (1993) and Hallett (1993) found that risk assessment had so dominated the majority of conferences that the second crucial element, the protection plan, had come a poor second. Farmer and Owen found that in conferences, on average, only 9 minutes were devoted to the protection plan. In Hallett's study, workers differed in the extent to which they thought the conference was the appropriate forum for specifying the plan in detail. But Hallett found that inter-agency collaboration 'was much more highly developed up to and including the initial conference than it was thereafter' (page 275). That is to say, the opportunities for collaborative intervention in the protection plan were not effectively utilised. It would seem that, even if such plans need to be developed in other meetings (such as the core groups) after the initial conference, the conference is the place where sound foundations can be laid.

Farmer and Owen (1993) found that there was great variation in the quality of the plans made at the conference, from broad general statements to detailed specifications. In over a third of the cases studied, important aspects were, in the researcher's view, overlooked. It is also clear from both research studies that a very high proportion of the protective intervention suggested was in the hands of social services. Whilst such a finding is unsurprising and to an extent understandable, it prompts reflection on the extent to which other professionals at the case conference have sought to define a role for themselves or their agency beyond the stage of investigation.

The research demonstrates conclusively that the third aim of the conference, the delineation of a protection plan, is not at present effectively pursued. Whilst there may be legitimate differences as to the detail into which it is appropriate for conference to enter, it is clear that the conference mirrors a fundamental deficiency in much current work – the lack of clear, purposeful multi-disciplinary plans for intervention. This surely must be addressed in the next stage of the development of child protection work.

Selection of these issues does less than justice to the rich mine of information on the content of conferences which is now available. They serve to illustrate, however, that the respectability of the conference as a part of child protection and the widespread acceptance of their value (Hallett, 1993) must not encourage complacency concerning their essential purpose and the knowledge and skill brought in them to the understanding of the problem.

Process

The research now available tells us in general less about the dynamics of the conference than it does about the attitudes of the participants and the steps taken in reaching decisions and recommendations. (The exception to this is in relation to parental participation, considered below.) Yet the nature of the interaction between participants is clearly important, as was argued in my earlier work (Hallett and Stevenson, 1980). In that work, we drew attention to certain distinguishing features of the child protection conference as a 'group in action'. These included the degree of anxiety and intensity which these particular meetings engender and the uncertainties which professionals may have about each others' roles. Recently, there has been a growing insistence on what might be described as the 'instrumental' aspects of the conference process. It is suggested that meetings should be business-like and keep emotional content low. Bell and Sinclair (1993) suggest that the presence of parents dynamically affects the process. It may, for example, engender high anxiety and inhibit discussion. Do chairs tend to be more business-like in those circumstances? The idea of the conference offering mutual support in anxiety-provoking situations is not popular. Yet, in our early work (Hallett and Stevenson, 1980), we had accepted this as a valid part of the process, a view which is confirmed by Farmer and Owen (1993):

> 'At times this anxiety-sharing function was very apparent to us. The formality of the conference and the routinisation of the procedures, had the effect of distancing the participants from the emotional impact of some of the distressing information which had emerged during the investigation. It therefore became more manageable.' (page 71.)

What this suggests is that the business-like conduct of a meeting does not, and should not, rule out awareness and sensitivity to the underlying dynamics, especially on the part of the chair. Such sensitivity has two outcomes: first, it creates a climate in which, without sentiment or drama, workers sense that they are 'allowed' to have feelings; secondly, it opens the way to handle more effectively those situations in which feelings are 'getting in the way of business'. All this is perhaps of particular importance in some cases of sexual abuse which may, quite appropriately, raise initial feelings of disgust and anger.

An important finding related to the process is to be found in Hallett's (1993) work. She reports 'a high degree of inter-agency consensus in relation to conference decisions concerning both registration and the child protection plan' (page 182). This question is: is this consensus a cause for concern? Few of those interviewed by Hallett thought it was, but the dangers of shifting debate and of collusiveness are clearly potentially problematic (Dingwall *et al.*, 1983). Hallett found the degree of consensus surprising, given the literature on inter-professional work, and she asks why this might be so. She advances four possibilities: first, that 'the process is circumscribed, bureaucratic and technical rather than one in which sharp ideological differences surface' (Hallett, 1993, pages 280–281). This is interesting in the light of the 'atheoretical' stance discussed earlier. Secondly, the need for professionals to continue to work together may serve to limit disagreement. Thirdly, anxiety about 'getting it wrong' may encourage deference to those considered more expert. The fourth important suggestion is that, 'working within any system or organisation limits fundamental questioning of its dominant paradigm' (Hallett, 1993, page 281). If, as we have discussed earlier, the emphasis of the conference is largely upon 'fact-finding' concerning risk and upon the making of plans to reduce risk, and this is accepted as its primary objective, it is perhaps not surprising that disagreements do not surface. If conference participants are primarily asking 'what happened?' rather than 'why did it happen?', the room for disagreement is narrowed. It would be profoundly unhelpful if professionals were at war with each other but, as Hallett (1993) warns, 'if the culture . . . is so uniform that disagreement . . . is very rare, this may pose a threat to the civil liberties of some children and families' (page 83). Furthermore, as was pointed out in the early case conference research (Hallett and Stevenson, 1980), there is no guarantee that group decisions are better than individual ones.

It is now widely accepted that the role of the chair is crucial in achieving satisfactory conference outcomes. Research (Farmer and Owen, 1993) seems to indicate that the chairing role may be best carried out by someone who is outside line management in social services. The responsibility is indeed onerous. To manage 'the business' effectively requires a combination of instrumental and expressive skills for, as has been earlier suggested, the chair must be aware of the complex emotions (including his/her own) which 'bang about' in such meetings. If he/she does not do so, decisions may get skewed. However desirable it may be, the presence of parents has greatly increased the difficulties of chairing. The development of training courses for chairs, now increasingly common, is a welcome acknowledgement of their pivotal role. To be effective, they must concentrate on the detail of the process, giving chairs an opportunity to examine the minute-by-minute dynamics of the discussion. Of particular interest, in the light of the findings discussed above, is the chair's ability to facilitate the expression of dissent when it is hovering in the air but has not been articulated.

For more than a decade, there has been great discontent about an important aspect of conference process – the taking of minutes. Recent research simply adds fuel to the fire (Farmer and Owen, 1993; Hallett, 1993). Resources for this area may be inadequate. This is indefensible when so much money is poured into child protection work. The reasons are bound up with the traditional resistance of local authorities to provide a decent administrative infrastructure for its professional staff (Stevenson and Parsloe, 1978). However, the framing of minutes is not an easy task and even guaranteed resources do not guarantee satisfactory minutes. Hallett (1993) reports continuing debates about format, including the amount of detail provided, and she suggests that the lack of detailed government guidance on this point is surprising.

There can be no doubt that the way minutes are phrased and the emphasis which they give plays a part in firming up the attitudes and views of the conference participants. Furthermore, the increasing participation of parents who will receive minutes makes their drafting even more sensitive and complex than heretofore. For all these reasons, policy decisions about their format and the training of minute-takers is an essential part of satisfactory conference process.

Inter-professional Aspects

As Hallett's study convincingly demonstrates, the need for inter-professional work is now widely accepted. The conference epitomises this. Associated with this is the rise of inter-disciplinary training, often fostered by Area Child Protection Committees. There has been growing recognition that such training cannot consist solely of 'joint events' but needs to address the knowledge of, and attitudes towards, other professionals and their respective roles. The quality of the conference, which must be focused on the case in question, is much affected by the understanding which professionals bring to it. As has been shown earlier (Hallett and Stevenson, 1980), difficulties arise when there is 'an outer circle' of conference attenders who encounter child abuse less often and are less conversant with its implications, but who are expected to participate fully. Hallett's (1993) recent research reveals such a problem in relation to teachers, and this is confirmed by Bell and Sinclair (1993). They frequently attended conferences and other practitioners regarded them as having a key role in the identification of abuse. Yet they, and the teachers themselves, thought that their knowledge of procedures and of their potential role in child protection were inadequate. (However, Farmer and Owen, 1993, found that teachers actively contributed to case conferences.) The difficulties for teachers, with 'a large workforce in dispersed locations' are obvious, and these problems are made more difficult by recent structural changes in the education system. However, just as health visitors play a key part in the safety of younger children, so teachers are crucial in the case of school age children. Failure to integrate them effectively in inter-professional child protection means that a vital element in the system is missing.

Two further matters are deserving of particular comment. The first concerns the absence of general practitioners from most of the conferences. All the research reviewed here confirms this widely noted and lamented fact. The position is now as it always has been and has not changed significantly since it became customary to pay GPs a fee for attending. Practical steps, such as holding conferences out of surgery hours, make little overall difference. Similar and related difficulties are now widely reported by those in adult care seeking to implement community care arrangements. Hallett (1993) asks how indispensable they really are, whilst acknowledging that their contribution was thought by most of her respondents to be very important. In my view, there is a pressing need for government to define and enforce the duties and obligations of general practitioners in relation to these social aspects of their work. If attendance at child protection conferences is not to be given priority over other work, expectations regarding such conferences should be clarified – for example, whether a written report should be provided. While not denying that there are difficulties, for example, in relation to patient/doctor relationships and confidentiality, the roots of this problem lie in the terms of GPs' employment and the orientation of their training, which sets them apart from other professionals in this work.

The second, striking, matter concerns the trend over the past few years towards improved co-operative activity between the police and social workers, the evidence for which is supported by Hallett (1993) and Farmer and Owen (1993). The rise in joint investigative procedures (whether closely defined as joint interviewing or not, Hallett, 1993), notably in cases of sexual abuse, has altered the dynamics of some conferences, since both parties come to them on the basis of previously shared activity and, often, a shared view. The effect which this has had on both groups and their traditional mode and style of interviewing is outside the scope of this chapter, but it reminds us that British case conferences (unlike some other countries) take place parallel to consideration of criminal justice proceedings. The effect of this upon the conference is difficult to gauge. There is evidence that the police exercise considerable discretion, often walking a tightrope between 'welfare' and 'criminal justice' orientations. Hallett (1993) found that the majority of social workers did not appear concerned about the interaction of the two systems and the resultant shift of emphasis. Indeed, some felt that children and young people were not adequately protected by the criminal justice system, especially in relation to the decisions made by the Crown Prosecution Service, and that more prosecutions would be welcome. Yet a small minority argued that greater involvement by the police and criminal justice system was unhelpful. Some of these went so far as to argue that 'child abuse was better conceptualised as a symptom of individual or family malfunctioning . . . than as a crime' (Hallett, 1993, page 109).

These findings raise again the theoretical uncertainty about the etiology of child abuse and therefore about appropriate remedies. Parton (1991) has suggested that the discourse of the conference has changed from 'socio-medical' to 'socio-legal'. The research utilised in this chapter confirms a view of the process which emphasises the bureaucratic and administrative aspects of the conference process rather than a pooling of professional understanding. What precisely one understands by the term 'socio-medical', however, needs careful exploration, turning on definitions of 'the medical model' beyond the scope of this chapter. For our purposes, it is sufficient to point to a model of conference process in which the social and legal implications of the finding of abuse take precedence over discussions of etiology.

However this may be, it seems likely, however, that the price of improved co-operation between police and social workers may be an increase of tension between social workers and the medical and nursing professions, who see the element of 'socio-medical' discourse diminishing. The discomfort which some doctors (notably paediatricians) experience about the process is well described by Farmer and Owen (1993).

In summary, it is clear that much has been achieved in co-operative working in recent years, and there is quite a high level of professional satisfaction about it. There remains much to be done to consolidate and improve participation amongst particular groups such as teachers and general practitioners. More fundamentally, however, the extent, nature and implications of the alliance between social workers and police deserve closer scrutiny.

Parent/Child Participation

Some of the research on case conferences took place before the impact of the Children Act 1989 and the *Working Together* guidance was fully felt. The guidance is unequivocal: 'it is important that Area Child Protection Committees should formally agree the principle including parents and children in all conferences'. (DOH, 1991, page 43. 6:14.) The exclusion of parents from the conference should be 'exceptional'. Certain criteria have been formulated more recently. It is suggested that three criteria are needed: where there is risk of violence, where a potential participant has been diagnosed as suffering from psychotic behaviour, and where a participant arrives at the conference severely under the influence of drugs or alcohol.

A further 'exclusion' clause has been suggested – the wishes and feelings of the child or young person concerned. This reminds us of the need to consider their participation in conferences, which at present remains comparatively rare. The guidance and research is much more cautious on this point. Obviously, age plays a part but the literature reports general unease which goes beyond that, and suggests that children themselves may not be keen to attend (Farmer and Owen, 1993). Further research is needed on this matter. It is important, however, to note the difficulties which parental participation in the conference may create for some, especially older young people in allegations of sexual abuse, if they wish to attend. It is also hard to envisage many situations of this kind in which such young people could be frank about their experiences in front of a sizeable group of people, most of whom they have not met before.

Research by Thoburn *et al.* (1993) and by Farmer and Owen (1993) makes it clear that 'partial' exclusion of parents (other than in exceptional circumstances and for as short a time as possible), which has been favoured by some authorities, is probably the worst of both worlds from the parents' perspective. It seems that it increases the anxiety and distrust of parents, although Thoburn *et al.* suggest that the way this is handled by workers, in particular in giving parents a careful explanation, goes some way towards mitigating these feelings. Bell and Sinclair (1993) found that about a third of the professionals thought parents should leave at the decision-making stage of the conference, for example, when sexual abuse has been denied.

In general, the research shows that the fears and anxieties expressed by professionals at the outset have not been borne out in reality. Bell and Sinclair (1993) found that, contrary to expectations, such conferences were not less frequent, less well attended and did not lead to different registration outcomes. Professionals believed that conferences were better with parents attending than without; the quality of information was better, and the parental perspective better appreciated. Parents who attended were, in general, glad that they were able to be present and believed that it was right that they should be present. It should be noted, however, that a significant number of parents did not attend. Some had been excluded and some did not receive the invitation in time. Of course, some parents choose not to attend. That is their choice, although the sensitivity and helpfulness in the way they are approached clearly plays a part.

Is the debate over? There remain some thorny and important issues to be considered further. Farmer and Owen (1993) and Bell and Sinclair (1993) show that, although many parents were glad to have attended, the conference was often experienced as intensely painful and humiliating. Although some of this may be due to poor handling of the situation and poor preparation, the inexorable fact remains that the occasion is inherently highly stressful. Its very nature, which differs so markedly from other situations when professionals and parents meet, determines that it will be fraught for the parents. Furthermore, as Farmer and Owen (1993) point out, when the conference takes place the parents are 'in crisis', with all the implications which that term has for labile and confused emotions. One aspect of parental distress concerned the shame and embarrassment of seeing their lives 'on the table' in front of a group of perhaps ten people, some of whom they had never met before.

Farmer and Owen (1993) have estimated the parents' contribution to the conference discussion. Parents attended 71 conferences (out of 120 studied), although in only a small number were parents present throughout. In 44 cases, they found that the parents' contribution enabled the conference to learn about their situation. In 15 cases, 'the parents' contribution was extremely limited'. In only 11 cases were parents able to participate in an exploration of the relevant issues. Thus (taking into account the conferences where no parent was present), the ideal was realised in only 10% of cases (Farmer and Owen, 1993, page 104). Farmer and Owen argue for greater use of parent advocacy. Certainly, this offers possibilities for facilitating more effective participation, but it also carries the dangers (notably when the advocate is a lawyer) that the conference becomes an adversarial encounter. That this is one element in most initial conferences is obvious – and no good comes of denying it. If the object of the conference is simply to 'get at the truth', such a stance may not always be unhelpful, but it becomes much more difficult when the underlying intention is to establish 'partnership'. Thoburn *et al.*'s (1993) comment is apposite.

> 'In the early stages of child protection work, there are few cases where it is *possible* to involve parents fully as partners.' (Page 19.)

It is unhelpful to disguise the tension which exists between a primary focus of the conference on risk assessment, challenging as it does the capacities and motivation of parents and the current emphasis in child welfare on partnership with them. The more the conference focuses upon that element and disregards wider welfare needs, the less likely it is that the conference will be experienced as positive by parents. Let us be clear that professional satisfaction at gaining better information and parental satisfaction that 'they are not talking behind my back' does not mean that the present situation is acceptable. The agony of some mothers (not too strong a word) reported by Farmer and Owen (1993) about the event must cause us to search for every possible way of improving the process from investigation to the conference, including, of course, preparation for it, 'debriefing' and all the practical steps which can make it less awesome. But it will remain, for a good many parents, a nasty business, the very opposite of the cosy encounter which simplistic talk of partnership may suggest.

Specific Issues

Gender

Farmer and Owen (1993) throw light on a particularly important issue concerning gender. Not surprisingly, mothers attended case conferences more often than fathers. Thirty-five percent of conferences were attended by mothers only. They found that, whoever (male or female) was responsible for the abuse, 'the focus of work was almost exclusively on mother figures, and that the frequent association of child abuse with domestic violence to the woman was allowed to disappear from sight'. Furthermore, when the mother was responsible for the abuse, the child was more likely to be registered. It seemed that, 'social service departments were more willing to intervene in single-parent families than in two-parent households.' (Farmer and Owen, 1993, page 314.) The reasons for this are complex, but these findings raise a familiar and unresolved problem, now potentially exacerbated by the case conference itself, that responsibility for protection is most often perceived as the woman's responsibility. Farmer and Owen found that the mother's needs for support and understanding were often not met. Whilst much of this should take place outside the conference, this finding raises questions again as to whether a conference which focuses intensively on risk rather than on need can provide reassurance to these oppressed women. It further reminds us that conference participants are not immune to the influence of wider social attitudes. At present, much attention is focused on single mothers and ambivalence concerning their position is evident.

Ethnic minorities

The research findings reported here throw little light on matters of race, partly because of the small number of studies involved. Reference is made to problems with inter-preters at conferences (Farmer and Owen, 1993). Gibbons *et al.* (1993) found that black and Asian families were over-represented among referrals for physical injury and under-represented in referrals for sexual abuse. This raises important questions con-cerning cultural values and norms which are bound to arise in conferences. There is a widespread feeling of discomfort amongst the professionals that the addressing of cultural variations could be interpreted as racist, and there is uncertainty about the legitimacy of making 'judgements'. Bell and Sinclair (1993) found that more cases from ethnic minorities could be described as 'difficult' (not arbitrarily, but on defined criteria), and they suggest that among the factors contributing to the difficulty was the 'pervasive experience of racism' which affected the families' attitude to intervention, and which 'simultaneously disempowered the predominantly white workers' (page 16). General studies of the kind reviewed do not consider a sufficient number of cases to take these important matters further, and qualitative research is urgently needed to understand better the issues which arise in the management of child protection involving ethnic minorities.

Sexual abuse

During the 1980s, a striking feature of child protection work has been the increase in referral and investigation of cases of sexual abuse, for which the professionals involved were unprepared. The impact on all concerned has been profound, raising as these cases do, intense feelings about the exploitation of children in this way. Farmer and Owen (1993) show that there were a number of distinctive features in the management of such cases, including the decision, much more frequent than in other cases, to separate the abused child from the alleged perpetrator. In the conference, there is less often clear-cut physical evidence, and sometimes there are extremely uncomfortable situations in which an alleged dominant male perpetrator 'fights his corner', which defeats any objective of partnership. Whilst there have been situations in which injustices have been done to the men concerned, there are also situations in which social workers and other professionals have felt powerless to protect children, despite a strong belief that they have been abused. This is especially noticeable in cases where middle class parents are involved. For all these reasons, conferencing of sexual abuse cases can produce particular tensions and difficulties which have not yet been addressed as fully as they deserve. Again, the chair's role and training in this matter is important.

Conclusion

This chapter has reviewed the current state of knowledge about case conferences in five dimensions: namely, content and purpose; process; inter-professional co-operation; parent/child participation; and specific factors of importance. It acknowl-edges the progress that has been made in developing a relatively sophisticated mechanism for the sharing of information and the assessment of risk. It further acknowledges the good intentions and the promising start which has been made in encouraging parents to participate in conferences, in the context of the partnership ideal. Four warning notes are, however, struck. Firstly, excessive preoccupation with 'risk' to the detriment of wider welfare considerations is unlikely to lead to constructive and effective intervention. Secondly, the impact of dynamic 'hidden agendas' on conference decision-making should not be underestimated; the role of the chair in such matters is crucial. Thirdly, we should not be complacent about consensus, which may on occasion be counterproductive to good decisions. Fourthly, the painful position of parents, especially mothers, in the conference must not be glossed over, however desirable their presence may be. Further, and realistic, consideration needs to be given to the management of the process in which ideals of partnership jostle uncomfortably with the investigative process.

All that being so, it remains the case that inter-professional work in child protection conferences is light years ahead of other comparable situations which require co-operative endeavour across different agencies, such as those which arise in adult care. The concern, commitment and care shown by many professionals in this forum is little understood by many of those who criticise child protection practice.

Acknowledgement

The authors of the research described above have been generous in offering their comments on this chapter and I am very grateful to them.

Further Reading

The following include examples of small-scale research on parental participation in case conferences.

McGloin, P. & Turnbull, A. (1986). *Parent Participation in Child Abuse Review Conferences*. Greenwich Social Services Department.

Phillips, J. & Evans, M. (1986). *Participating Parents*. Bradford Family Services Unit.

Rousiaux, St (1984). *Parental Attendance at Child Abuse Case Conferences*. Coventry: NSPCC Special Unit.

Shemmings, D. & Thoburn, J. (1990). *Parental Participation in Child Protection Conferences*. Report on a pilot project in Hackney Social Services Department. University of East Anglia.

References

Bell, M. & Sinclair, I. (1993). *Parental Involvement in Initial Child Protection*. Conference in Leeds. University of York.
Department of Health, Home Office, Department of Education and Science, Welsh Office (1991). *Working Together under the Children Act 1989 – A Guide to Arrangements for Inter-Agency Co-operation for the Protection of Children from Abuse*. London: HMSO.

Dingwall, R., Eekelaar, J. & Murray, T. (1983). *The Protection of Children: State Intervention and Family Life*. Oxford: Blackwell.

Farmer, E. & Owen, M. (1993). *Decision-making, Intervention and Outcome in Child Protection Work*. Report to Department of Health. University of Bristol.

Gibbons, J., Conroy, S. & Bell, C. (1993). *Operation of Child Protection Registers*. Report to Department of Health. University of East Anglia.

Hallett, C. (1993). *Working Together in Child Protection: Report of Phase Three*. Report to Department of Health. University of Stirling.

Hallett, C. and Stevenson, O. (1980). *Child Abuse: Aspects of Inter-professional Co-operation*. London: Allen & Unwin.

London Borough of Brent (1985). *A Child in Trust*. The Report of the panel of inquiry into the circumstances surrounding the death of Jasmine Beckford. Brent.

Parton, N. (1991). *Governing the Family: Child Care, Child Protection and the State*. Basingstoke: Macmillan.

Stevenson, O. (1989). *Public Policy and Professional Practice*. London: Harvester Wheatsheaf.

Stevenson, O. & Parsloe, P. (1978). *Social Services Teams: The Practitioner's View*. London: HMSO.

Thoburn, J., Lewis, A. & Shemmings, D. (1993). *Family Participation in Child Protection*. Report to Department of Health. University of East Anglia.

Wandsworth Area Child Protection Committee (1990). *Report of Stephanie Fox Practice Review*.

—————————— **13** ——————————

Dealing with the Suspicion of Child Sexual Abuse: The Role of the Teacher

Anne Peake

Introduction

The role of the teacher in situations where there are suspicions that a child is being sexually abused may be pivotal. Teachers are the only professionals who are in regular daily contact with school-aged children, and they are in a unique position to monitor situations where there are concerns about a particular child. By dint of their training and the numbers of children in a particular age group with whom they have contact, teachers are also well equipped to identify those children whose behaviour, for whatever reason, falls outside the normal range. Yet there can be few problems faced by children that arouse teachers' anxiety quite like that of child sexual abuse. The distress of the children, the complexity of the problem, the difficulties of investigation and the often unhelpful media coverage of the issue, all contribute to the very understandable levels of anxiety and sense of vulnerability which they feel.

This chapter addresses some of these concerns by setting out in detail ways in which teachers are uniquely placed to monitor children where there are suspicions of abuse, and by identifying frameworks within which children can be monitored by teachers in primary and in secondary schools. It must be stressed at the outset, however, that although teachers can monitor children, the duty to investigate and take action always lies with the statutory child protection agencies. Once a child is known to be the victim of sexual abuse, the provisions of the Children Act 1989 and the guidelines contained in *Working Together* (Department of Health (DOH), 1991) must be brought into play, together with the child protection procedures laid down by the local authority, which should be followed without delay. Teachers therefore need to be aware of these and of the work of the statutory agencies, to liaise with them and adhere carefully to local child protection guidelines (Department of Education (DES) circular, April 1988).

Distinctive Features of Child Sexual Abuse

Teachers have had a longer time to adjust to the procedures with regard to the physical abuse of children and their role within the procedures than is the case with child sexual abuse. Thus, although the main features of child sexual abuse are dealt with in detail in Section I of this book, the main issues are summarised here because it is important to be clear at the start about the ways in which child sexual abuse differs from the physical abuse of children. Child sexual abuse is an essentially different phenomenon from the non-accidental injury of children. The difference rests on five basic features.

1. The incidence of child abuse is different from that of physical abuse. In child sexual abuse, the majority of the abusers are men (Finkelhor, 1984). A survey by Baker and Duncan (1985) has shown there to be no significant class or geographical differences, and the majority of the victims are girls. (This is discussed more fully in Section I by Creighton, Chapter 1 and Frosh, Chapter 4.)
2. The question of evidence sets sexual abuse apart from physical abuse. The nature of most sexual abuse is such that there is rarely, if ever, any evidence. Even in cases where there is evidence of abuse (Manchester, 1979), it is often impossible to prove the identity of the abuser. If we have learned one lesson from Cleveland, it is that even when professionals are confident that there is evidence of sexual assaults on children, the evidence will be challenged and professional competence questioned. With the exception of brittle bone disease, there is rarely such a high level of controversy about the evidence in cases of the physical abuse of children.
3. The issue of gender is central, not only in terms of the incidence of child sexual abuse, but also in terms of the intervention of professionals (Frosh, 1987). Traditionally, professionals have given insufficient attention to the significance of the gender of the worker. However, from the child's point of view, the gender of the adult can determine how safe they feel. Additionally, girls need to see their same-sex adult models in positions where sexual assault is seriously and effectively challenged. The issue of race needs consideration too, not least because of the position of women in some ethnic minority groups. Racism at both the individual and institutional levels of society places additional pressures on children from different ethnic/cultural groups which may affect their attitude to disclosure. The existence of positive adult models from their own communities who are active in child protection work may encourage children from ethnic minority groups to seek help.
4. The problems of obtaining hard and reliable evidence also have implications for the assessment of children. In the field of child sexual abuse, there is no equivalent to the regular medical examinations whereby a child's growth and physical well-being are checked after known instances of physical abuse. The professional dealing with suspected sexual abuse therefore has to face the problem of monitoring children without a specific baseline of checks that can be made. In addition, when someone who has been strongly implicated as an abuser but has not been convicted moves in with a family in which there are children, social services departments may be unclear as to the basis upon which they can judge whether the children in that household are safe or not, and how best to protect them.
5. Child sexual abuse raises professional anxieties and divides workers more than other problems (Furniss, 1983). It would be hard to imagine such an intense and

long-lasting debate about whether children exaggerate, fantasise or lie being conducted about other problems children present.

These features – the different incidence of sexual abuse, the question of evidence, the issue of gender, the difficulties of monitoring situations and the level of anxiety aroused – all combine to set child sexual abuse apart from physical abuse, and to make it a problem that saps the confidence of many workers. However, although the parameters of the problem are such that protecting children in such situations is not easy to resolve, particularly given the demands it makes for the co-ordination of different professional roles (see Corby's Chapter 11 for a detailed discussion of issues of inter-professional co-operation), the protection of the child where sexual abuse is suspected is of paramount importance in view of the suffering and damage it can cause.

The Role of the Teacher in Responding to Suspicions of Abuse

As a psychologist who has worked in both education and social services departments, I have frequently been approached by teachers seeking advice about the problem of suspected sexual abuse. Faced with this need for guidance, I began to think about detailing the ways in which teachers could make their own contribution to assessments concerning the child's safety. Not only are there particular features of the teacher's role which may make it very important but also, when abuse is suspected, the nature and sequence of professional involvement is critical. The following factors are of particular importance.

1. There is a need to collect evidence on which to base the need for professional intervention to protect the child, or perhaps to make a case for the prosecution of the abuser, or to allay anxieties about possible abuse.
2. There is a need to avoid warning the abuser of the fact that there are suspicions. If an abuser becomes aware of such concerns before child protection agencies are in a position to act to protect the child, the abuser can be made more powerful. He/she would be able to adjust his/her threats accordingly, and/or remove the child from the school setting, so that the capacity of professionals to act is diminished. He/she would also become more powerful in the eyes of the child because of his/her demonstrated capacity to resist efforts to intervene and to continue the abuse.
3. It is important that when professionals do intervene in the lives of children and families, they do so effectively. This involves not only collecting evidence and avoiding alerting the abuser, but also having a clear and co-ordinated programme of action to which those professionals involved are committed. It is therefore important that the child protection network has time to plan intervention carefully where sexual abuse is suspected. There is nothing more dangerous than hasty and ill-prepared intervention. In the event of failure, this leaves the child even more isolated and powerless, whilst the power of the abuser in the eyes of the child is increased and the child's capacity to trust in the action of the professionals is severely damaged.

Given these considerations, the nursery worker, class or form teacher in daily contact with children can have an important part to play in collecting information for those agencies who have a statutory role in regard to child protection. Teachers are the *only* professionals who are in regular daily contact with children about whom there may be concerns about possible sexual abuse. They are in a unique position for monitoring suspicion for three main reasons.

1. Training for teachers, particularly for the infant/nursery sector, includes work on child development which is a helpful basis for considering children whose present-ing behaviour is a focus for professional concern. This means that concerns about the behaviour of one child can be considered in the context of the normal develop-ment of children of a given age and ability.
2. Teachers are the only professional group in regular and almost daily contact with children about whom there may be concern. So a teacher may make detailed observations of a child in a variety of situations involving a variety of interactions with peers and adults. Teachers can also have close and trusting relationships with some children which may make them feel safe enough to reveal some of their deeper anxieties.
3. Most importantly, there is no professional group, other than teachers/nursery workers, who have regular daily contact with such large numbers of children of a given age group. They are therefore able to place their detailed observations of children about whom there are concerns in the context of both knowledge of child development and regular experience of the normal range of children's behaviour. Teachers will constantly be comparing one child with approximately 25 other children of the same age on the basis of daily contact. The observation by a teacher that a child is different from his or her peers in specified ways can therefore be a powerful statement.

In my work advising teachers who are worried about what to do when there are suspicions of child sexual abuse, it became plain to me that there is a need for a locally agreed system of monitoring which enables teachers to feel confident about their role in a field where professional anxieties are high. What was developed initially in conjunction with teachers was a standardised outline for monitoring children in school where particular situations or concerns suggested the need for further assessment. Two outlines have subsequently been developed, one for younger children and one for children in secondary schools. These have been agreed and accepted by one local social services department and may provide a workable base for considering the role of the teacher in dealing with the suspicion of child sexual abuse. More generally, they may also provide the basis for developing whole-school policies for dealing with child protection in conjunction with local social services departments, which fit in with area child protection guidelines.

Outline for Monitoring Younger Children in School

The following outline is suggested for teachers to use in monitoring children in primary schools and for those young children who have one class teacher all day every day who are either known or suspected to have been sexually abused. It is intended to be a basic outline which teachers can adapt in ways which suit the particular needs of the child about whom they are concerned and the features of the school situation in which they are working.

By way of introduction, it is important to stress that teachers should be alert to overt signs of abuse. In the event of a child displaying any of the following overt signs of child sexual abuse, the teacher should inform the head teacher who should contact the nearest social services office:

- a child saying he/she has been touched sexually;
- a third party saying a child has been touched sexually;
- a child with injuries to the genital area;
- a child giving clear evidence of an awareness of sexual behaviour, in drawings, play or talk;
- a child who masturbates excessively.

In such cases, monitoring is not an option to be considered, since the involvement of the appropriate child protection agencies is clearly justified. In suspected cases of child sexual abuse, however, systematic careful monitoring is essential. However, the following four points should be kept in mind when a programme of monitoring is undertaken.

1. Careful attention needs to be paid to observing children in both structured and unstructured settings. Children may well show few, if any, warning signs in a structured busy classroom which may be fully occupying their thoughts, so that feelings, memories and insecurities are less likely to surface. Additionally, of course, the close presence of adults in structured situations may well discourage children from acting out their inner feelings. The nature of child sexual abuse is such that there are enormous pressures on children not to reveal what is happening to them. Teachers' observations of children in unstructured settings such as playgrounds and playhouses in classrooms can also be very helpful, as can observations of behaviour during the usual classroom routines and activities.

2. It is important in recording any observations or comments about a child's behaviour that teachers also note the context in which it occurred. Context can be viewed in different ways, and therefore several examples are given.

    i.   The context could be the actual setting in which the behaviour was seen. Thus, for example, the recording might note that the behaviour was observed 'during 10 minutes free play in the playhouse', or 'in a concealed corner of the playground not normally used by children playing at break', or 'when all the class were asked to write and draw about the weekend in their diaries', etc.

    ii. The context could also be provided by the behaviour of other adults or children. For example, the behaviour may be noted as a reaction when 'a teacher (male or female) touched the child's arm', or 'another child who tends to be clumsy pushed him/her', or the note might describe how the child responds to the proximity of male adults. Attention must also be paid here to possible cultural differences in response, for example that of an Asian female towards an adult male.

    iii. The context can also be provided by the usual practices or routines in a given situation. For example, a child may exhibit unusual behaviour in response to the classroom routine for changing for PE, or when children are asked to sit on mats where they are close to each other for story time, etc.

    It is, of course, important always to be aware that many changes in behaviour which a teacher might notice may have nothing to do with sexual abuse and may be attributable to a wide range of other, less serious causes.

3. It is essential that any activities planned by teachers which may also be used for the purposes of monitoring should be balanced and open-ended. There should never be any room for the suggestion that a teacher might have led or biased a child's responses. For example, if children are asked to make a drawing depicting someone with sad/angry feelings, they should also be given the opportunity to depict glad/happy feelings with respect to the same person. This approach has two advantages. Firstly, it avoids leading children. Secondly, it reflects the reality of children's worlds, in which they often have ambivalent feelings, rather than clearly positive or negative feelings.
4. Child sexual abuse understandably arouses anxieties in adults concerned about children they suspect or know are being abused. Unlike the physical abuse of children which can sometimes necessitate urgent action, child sexual abuse is rarely life-threatening, so with children suspected of being victims of child sexual abuse it is better to begin a system of careful monitoring. This will enable professionals to clarify the basis for their concerns and, if necessary, to plan an effective form of intervention.

The quality of the monitoring of children about whom there is concern is clearly important and, where possible, is best carried out by the child's teacher. Regardless of who does this, however, it is of overriding importance that observations are objective, recorded systematically and without bias.

The headings outlined below constitute a range of parameters which teachers can use as a basis for monitoring children. Some ideas and explanations are given to help the teacher doing this for the first time. It may be best to record observations in a notebook which can be kept confidentially and in a secure place. Exercise books are probably best avoided for this purpose because of the obvious risk of confusion with other exercise books, resulting in the record falling into the wrong hands.

These headings can be put on separate pages, with examples of behaviours or incidents (including dates, times and the context) entered under the appropriate headings. The book will then contain a range of observations in chronological order organised under respective headings. This will provide a clear basis on which a teacher can give a structured report on a child to a social worker, police officer, or to a case conference. Systematic monitoring is a continuous process which can be time-consuming, since it may take weeks to establish a clear and detailed picture of a child's behaviour. Systematic and effective monitoring therefore requires both time and perseverance.

Once it is clear that a child is the victim of sexual abuse, the statutory child protection agencies are responsible for investigation and intervention, and the provisions of the Children Act 1989 and the guidelines contained in *Working Together* (DOH, 1991) must be brought into play, together with the child protection procedures laid down by the local authority, which should be implemented without delay. In the early stages of concern, however, the very special contribution of the teacher to any subsequent multi-agency work can be in terms of the quality of their monitoring of children believed to be at risk. The following are suggested as parameters which will help to ensure the quality of that monitoring.

Attendance

Details of dates and time are all-important, since patterns of absence can often be very revealing: for example, absences on a particular day may coincide with the presence or absence of a particular parent and/or caretaker; notes written to explain absences may always be written by one parent and not the other; children can be brought in late by one adult but on time by the other. It is possible that repeated reasons for absences given to the school are not being brought to the attention of the family's doctor and this can be checked out by the school nurse, where there is one.

Mood changes

Children may show changes of mood during the day, perhaps becoming quiet and tense towards the end of the day when home time is anticipated. Children's behaviour may also change if the adult who collects them from school is different from the one who brought them.

Contact with parents

The school's contact with parents may also shed light on a child's situation. Although there may be obvious and common-sense explanations, such as domestic arrangements or a parent's work pattern, details of which parent comes to the school and his or her responses to encouragement from the child's teacher to be involved in his/her child's education may be important. The interaction between parent(s) and the child's teacher can often be a lifeline for the non-abusing parent but a threat to an abuser. Teachers need to be aware of this two-edged effect.

Children's body language/behaviour

So often, and particularly with young children, body language can speak volumes. Observations can be made of children with their parent(s) and/or caretakers, and of any different responses of children to adults according to the gender of the adult. Children can also show signs of change in body language which vary with the time of day or the day of the week. For example, a child may well show signs of tense, or apathetic, or otherwise unusual behaviour towards the end of a school day. This may be because the child is anticipating returning to an abusive situation at home. Similarly, a child might show changed body language/behavioural change before and/or after weekends, which may coincide with access visits, staying with relatives, the presence of a baby-sitter in the home, etc.

Some children may display overt signs of distress such as marked changes in eating patterns (over-eating, refusing to eat, extreme faddiness) or a sudden onset of day-time, or reported night-time wetting and/or soiling. There may be a deterioration in a child's demeanour, with the child becoming increasingly unresponsive, aggressive, tense, etc., or children may display bruises, problems when walking and/or sitting on chairs or on the floor. Teachers noting such behavioural signs of distress should note the dates of these changes and any contemporaneous events in the life of the child being monitored.

Any sexualised behaviour is extremely significant and should be noted carefully, although it should be interpreted with caution. Children can only learn sexualised behaviour from others, either by being abused, by being present during adult sexual behaviour, or by watching sexually explicit or pornographic videos/films. However, children below the age of 8 displaying sexualised behaviour are unlikely to learn such detailed behaviour from seeing adult sexual behaviour (they usually think the adults are cuddling or wrestling). They are also unlikely to learn sexualised behaviour from pornographic videos or films, since with younger children, their short concentration span coupled with their limited capacity to grasp the details and meaning of what they see make it unlikely they will mirror what was on film in their play (although children aged 8 or over would certainly be able to concentrate and remember images and behaviour seen on video). In young children, therefore, the most likely explanation of sexualised behaviour is that they are or have been sexually abused.

Children's language

Young children are unlikely to verbalise what is happening to them in a clear way. This is because they may not have the language for body parts and sexual behaviour, or they may well be too young to speak about what is happening to them. Even very young children will have deduced or been told, tricked or threatened that what is happening to them must be kept secret. Therefore, they may not feel they have permission to tell, and so they will often speak in analogous terms about snakes that spit at them, tickling they don't like, monsters that gobble them, etc.

This should be recorded carefully, noting the exact words used by the child rather than adult equivalents. Unless teachers have been specially trained for such work, however, and are acting after consultation and with the agreement of the statutory agencies, they should not actively explore any such comments with a child.

Children's play

Teachers are the best judges of normal age-appropriate play because of their training in child development and their expertise with large numbers of children in given age groups. So, for example, an observation by a reception class teacher that a particular child was the only child in the class to play with a toy in a given way may be significant, as the teacher will be comparing the child with approximately 25 other children. No other professional is in a position to make such observations.

Obviously, there are many aspects of children's play which could be detailed here, and it is worthwhile to stress again the need to consider more obvious and less worrying explanations. However, any aspects of play which seem to be out of the ordinary should also be considered in the light they could possibly shed on a child's safety. A child can often act out with a toy ways which may mirror an abusive situation – for example, play with a teddy bear having breakfast and going to school, and then a child saying 'Teddy doesn't want to go to bed'. For many children it is easier to talk about teddy's fears than to talk about their own. Dolls, glove puppets, soft toys, playhouse corners and telephones can be useful. Any such incidents should be noted carefully, but the teacher should avoid becoming directly involved in the child's play or any attempt to investigate further.

Children's drawing/writing

Whilst teachers also need to be extremely cautious in forming conclusions on the basis of children's drawings and/or written work, children often express a great deal of themselves in this way. No one drawing or type of drawing, in terms of figures drawn or colours used, is necessarily indicative that a child is being sexually abused, and an enormous range of self-expression through such media is to be expected. However, on occasions children's drawings may be a useful index of their fears and feelings, and when children draw people with genitalia the possibility that this might be a cause for concern should be considered. Other kinds of drawings may also need careful consideration, such as children who draw themselves or small children in pictures where they are calling for help. Such evidence should be noted carefully and, if there are doubts about its possible significance, expert advice sought from an educational psychologist or from social services.

Many teachers make use of a weekly diary session for all the class. This can be a very useful way of monitoring a particular child. For example, a child's account of their weekend at home may reveal potentially important information about events and people which should be carefully recorded. If the class has a time for each child to write his/her own diary each week, it may well be useful to consider who in the family gets most mentioned and who doesn't, what are the times when different adults are alone with a given child, and does the child always write about being out of the house rather than in the house, etc.

Often a link can be made between drawing/painting and writing. For example, if a class is asked to draw and paint pictures of being happy/sad/angry in which work is done with the class on colours and lines in art, each child could then write about a time when they were happy/sad/angry, or the group of children can be helped to list words connected with being happy/sad/angry. The responses of the child being monitored could then be noted. The advantage of doing this as part of a class lesson is that the teacher is not singling one child out and suggesting that child is happy/sad/angry. Also, the responses of the child being monitored can be compared with those of a group of peers.

Medicals, PE

A child who is being or has been sexually abused may well react differently from classmates when the time comes for PE/games lessons and/or before a school medical. Teachers are now aware that PE/games lessons, where children undress, provide a useful weekly point to check children known to be at risk of physical abuse for tell-tale signs of injury. Teachers monitoring children who may be sexually abused should consider the extent to which they might also use this weekly opportunity for observation. Signs such as torn clothing, blood stains on clothes, the smell of semen on a child's skin or clothes, an unusual reluctance to undress, or an apparent shamefulness about being undressed, or a disinhibition which is out of keeping with the norm of the age group of children may be of some significance.

However, there are obvious dangers in making such observations, not least the risk that the teacher might be accused of taking an inappropriate interest in the child, and such opportunities for observation should only be taken after careful consideration and prior discussion with a senior colleague. Physical examination by a teacher should not, of course, be contemplated under any circumstances

Children who are being sexually abused may also often make veiled references to their plight in the guise of psychosomatic complaints. They may well present in school with headaches, stomach-aches and pains. A note should be kept of the frequency of such complaints, and the school nurse kept informed. An abusing parent/adult may well keep a child away from school when medicals are planned. If a child who is being monitored is away from school for a medical, this should be noted and followed up.

Finally

This outline is intended to help in situations where teachers suspect a child is being sexually abused, and to provide some practical guidelines about the important role they can play in providing systematic daily monitoring of a child. Teachers need always to remember, however, *that they should never shoulder alone their concern about a child they suspect is being abused.* The sexual abuse of children is a crime and needs to be reported to one of the agencies with statutory powers to deal with the problem, namely, social services, the NSPCC or the police. Where there is a suspicion that a child is being abused, advice might also be sought from an educational psychologist and/or education welfare officer, and social services should be informed.

Outline for Monitoring Children in Secondary Schools

Although in suspected cases of child sexual abuse, systematic careful monitoring is essential, teachers should be alert to overt signs of abuse. In the event of a child displaying any of the following overt signs of child sexual abuse, the teacher should inform the head teacher who should contact the nearest social services office:

- a child saying he/she has been touched sexually;
- a relative, neighbour, third party reporting a child is being sexually abused;
- a child with injuries to the genital area;
- a child who makes a suicide attempt;
- a child who is excessively sexualised, giving clear evidence of an awareness of sexual behaviour, or a child who sexually assaults another child/adult.

In such cases, monitoring is not an option to be considered, since the involvement of the appropriate child protection agencies is clearly justified. In suspected cases of child sexual abuse, however, systematic careful monitoring is as essential as it is with younger children.

The following is a suggested outline for teachers to use for monitoring children in secondary schools who are either already known or are suspected to have been sexually abused by someone known to them. One major way in which secondary schools differ from primary schools is that the children have several different subject teachers each year. They could have between four and eight different teachers in any one day. This raises the obvious question about which teacher should co-ordinate monitoring of a child about whom there are concerns. No one teacher in a secondary school will be in a position to shoulder the task of monitoring a child. A nominated teacher will therefore be needed to co-ordinate the contributions of all the teachers involved with that child, and there is no obvious answer as to who this should be. Options range from the form tutor, the year head, the teacher who sees most of the child, the teacher the child likes most, to the teacher with special responsibilities for special needs and/or child protection. In selecting the teacher to co-ordinate the monitoring, there are three particular issues to bear in mind.

1. Although there are obvious advantages to this being a teacher who has regular contact with the child about whom there are concerns, this may not always be possible and will depend to some extent on the organisation of the school. What is more important is that the co-ordination of the monitoring should be well-organised and effective, and this does not necessarily require a teacher who knows the child well. The co-ordinator must ensure that staff involved in monitoring are clear about what behaviours/incidents to record and how to record them. What is important is that the teachers actually making the observations are those who regularly interact with the child.

2. In addition to being suitable in other respects, the teacher who takes on the task should be willing to do so. As mentioned above, child sexual abuse can raise many anxieties about children and about the consequences of recognising abuse for the child, the family, the teachers and the school. For some, it also raises anxieties about their own attitudes to child sexual abuse, such as being able to accept that it does happen. Sadly, for some, it may also raise spectres from their own past, since some teachers are themselves survivors of child sexual abuse. This may make them more or less willing to undertake to co-ordinate the monitoring of a child. So for a variety of reasons, it is important that the teacher selected to co-ordinate the monitoring in a secondary school should be willing to do so.

3. The co-ordinator needs to have ready access to information on child sexual abuse and the support of other professionals to perform this task. Much relevant information, together with references which may be followed up, is contained in other chapters in this handbook. Additional information and support could also be sought by contacting: the member of school staff with overall responsibility for child protection; the local social services Child Protection Training Officer; and specialist agencies such as the NSPCC, Childline, etc. In some authorities, there are also special services for consultation which teachers are encouraged to use (Peake, 1991). The teacher who takes on this task also needs the personal and professional support of immediate colleagues.

The following is intended as a basic outline which teachers can adapt in ways which suit the particular needs of the child about whom they are concerned and the features of the school situation in which they are working. Since secondary schools differ widely in their organisation, it will also be necessary to adapt the ideas according to the pastoral care system of the school.

By way of introduction, it is important to stress the following points which should be kept in mind when a programme of monitoring is undertaken.

1. Careful attention needs to be paid to observing children in both structured and unstructured settings. Children, especially teenagers, who are socially aware and more able to control their feelings, may show few, if any, warning signs in structured busy classrooms. The demands of the timetable in terms of subjects, teachers and room changes may well fully occupy their thoughts and time, and feelings, memories and insecurities are less likely to surface. The close presence of adults in structured situations may also discourage children from displaying their emotions. It is also the case for some abused children that school is the one place where they can feel safe and their wish to appear like other children provides them with a relief from the pressures at home. Older children can also be skilled in behaving in ways which meet the expectations of staff. For some children this is a relief they will not readily abandon.

Also, with child sexual abuse there are enormous pressures on children not to tell what is happening, which for the teenager are particularly acute. Having kept the secret, quite possibly for some time, they feel implicated by their silence, and they are all too aware of society's condemnation of young people who have early sexual experiences, even the victims of child sexual assault. They are also more aware of the possible consequences of disclosure. Observations of children in different classroom settings (e.g. formal lessons, group work) and different responses to teachers of varying age and/or gender should be compared with observations in more unstructured settings such as games or leisure periods, etc.

2. It is important in recording any observations or comments about a child, that teachers also note the context in which the behaviour occurred or the observation was made. Context is particularly important in a secondary school setting, as children may move between several different situations in one timetabled day. The observations of differences in behaviour in different settings and with different adults can be extremely helpful, particularly if they are clearly recorded.

Context can be viewed in different ways, and therefore several examples are given.

    i.   The context could be the actual setting in which the behaviour was seen. Thus, for example, the recording might note that the behaviour was observed 'during the time when children gather before registration'; or 'in a formal English lesson with a middle-aged male teacher'; or 'when the class were asked to work in groups in a drama lesson on families'; or 'when all the class were asked to write about "the worst day I can remember" '; or 'in a concealed part of the play-ground by staff cars, where the children know they should not be', etc.

    ii. The context could also be provided by the behaviour of other adults or children. For example, the behaviour may be noted as a reaction 'when the teacher (male/female) touched the child's arm'; or 'when another child (gender/age) who tends to be aggressive toward quiet children pushed him/her'; or 'this child responded to the presence of male teachers in close proximity by . . .'; or 'when spoken to in a one-to-one situation in a member of staff's room this child . . .', etc.

    iii. The context can also be provided by the usual practices or routines in a given situation. For example, 'children always walked into assembly in this way', 'the PE teacher's routine for children changing for a lesson is', 'all children are told not to use the yard by the office', 'after school most children', 'if a child is late for school he/she is expected to', 'when letters are given out for parents' evenings', etc. Such contextual information should be followed by a description of the behaviour of the child being monitored.

3. It is essential that any activities planned by a teacher which may also be used for the purpose of monitoring should be balanced and open-ended. There should never be any room for the suggestion that a teacher might have led or biased a child's responses. If, for example, a class is asked to write a pen-picture of their fathers, they should also, at another time, be asked to write a pen-picture of their mothers. Similarly, if they are asked to write about the 'worst day they remember', they should also be given the opportunity to write about 'the best day they remember'.

This approach has two advantages. Firstly, it avoids leading children, which could have the effect of a child saying what he/she imagines will suit the teacher. Abused children are particularly sensitive to adult interest in their home life (maintaining a secret has made them thus). If an abused child feels an adult is taking too much interest, the child may withdraw and become even more guarded.

Secondly, this approach reflects the reality of children's worlds, which are that they often have ambivalent feelings about their situation, rather than feelings which are clearly positive or negative. They may well love their abuser and be reluctant to betray him or her. He or she may well detest the sexual abuse but may have moved on to be sexually active in a way which they *do* enjoy, or which they feel might compromise any disclosure they might have to make about the initial sexual abuse.

4. Child sexual abuse understandably arouses anxieties in adults concerned about children they suspect or they know are being abused. Unlike the physical abuse of children which can sometimes necessitate urgent action, child sexual abuse is rarely life-threatening, so with children suspected of being victims of child sexual abuse, it is better to begin a system of careful monitoring. This will enable professionals to clarify the basis for their concerns and, if necessary, to plan an effective form of intervention. However, child sexual abuse *might* become life-threatening if professionals intervene but fail to ensure the safety of the child, or if there is the threat of the child talking to an outside agency. Some children just run away in the face of possible attempts to help them disclose. This then places the child at even greater risk, and beyond the reach of much of the help that is available.

Most children who are being sexually abused and attend secondary school have been abused for some time and have developed strategies for achieving a precarious balance between being a victim of abuse and 'surviving'. There is a sense of strength in doing this, and adults should not challenge this without clear and effective plans to guarantee a child's safety and an end to the abuse. Careful monitoring enables professionals to become clear about the basis of their concerns and to plan an effective form of intervention, involving the agencies which can protect children. Schools are not able to offer such protection.

The teacher selected to co-ordinate the monitoring needs to collect information/observations systematically from all the teachers who have contact with the child about whom there is concern. The following sequential plan may well be useful.

i.   The support of the head teacher, or the special needs/child protection teacher, or the head of year is sought to determine a plan for monitoring the child.

ii. A meeting is arranged for all those who teach the child about whom there is concern. They are all given an opportunity to hear and discuss the concerns.

iii. All the subject teachers are given the heading from the monitoring outline and asked to make a written record of behaviour/incidents over a specified length of time. Teachers could be asked when recording their observation to do so using the following framework:

- details of the incident/behaviour;
- where it took place;
- when it took take place;
- with whom it took place;
- the duration of the incident or the intensity of the behaviour;
- the frequency of the behaviour;
- the sequence of the behaviour (following what/before what did the behaviour occur).

iv. At the end of the period of monitoring, the co-ordinating teacher collects the written records of the other teachers and assembles incidents/behaviours recorded by different teachers under the headings as listed. So, for example, for attendance there would be incidents/behaviours recorded by all the subject teachers under that heading.

v. The co-ordinating teacher may well see patterns emerging in the incidents/behaviours recorded by different teachers. The monitoring will then contain a range of observations in chronological order by different teachers organised under respective headings. This will then be a clear basis upon which the co-ordinating teacher can give a structured report on a child to a social worker/police officer, or to a case conference.

It is worth emphasising that, as with younger children, systematic monitoring is a continuous process which can be time-consuming, since it may take weeks to establish a clear and detailed picture of a child's behaviour. Systematic and effective monitoring therefore requires both time and perseverance.

Once it is clear that a child is the victim of sexual abuse, the statutory child protection agencies are responsible for investigation and intervention, and the provisions of the Children Act 1989 and the guidelines contained in *Working Together* (DOH, 1991) must be brought into play, together with the child protection procedures laid down by the local authority, which should be implemented without delay. Children who are sexually abused have a variety of needs – legal, medical, social, emotional and often educational – and so need the combined work of a variety of professionals.

In the early stages of concern, however, the very special contribution of the teachers to any subsequent multi-agency work can be in terms of the quality of their monitoring of children believed to be at risk. The following are suggested as parameters will help to ensure the quality of that monitoring.

Attendance

Details of dates and time are all-important, since patterns of absence can often be very revealing. For example, absences on a particular day may coincide with the presence or absence of a particular parent and/or carer. It may be that notes written to explain absences are always written by one parent and not the other. Repeated reasons for absences given to the school may not be being brought to the attention of the family's doctor. This can be checked by the school nurse, if there is one, whilst repeated complaints of headaches, stomach-aches or urinary tract infections should be followed up. Older children may well provide quite plausible explanations for absences or injuries, and often it is the frequency and/or pattern of absences that is revealing. A child may reveal anxieties by changes of moods within a school day or week, perhaps becoming tense and quiet towards the end of a day, when home time is anticipated. Such a child may well seek out opportunities to stay behind after school to delay going home.

Contact with parents

The contact between parents and secondary school teachers is less than that between primary school staff and parents, not least because secondary school children often travel unaccompanied to and from school. It is nevertheless important to be aware of the frequency and quality of the school's contact with parents and to consider the light this may shed on a child's situation. Although there may be obvious and common-sense explanations, such as domestic arrangements or a parent's work patterns, details of which parent comes to the school for parents' evenings and open days, and his/her responses to encouragement to participate in the child's education are important and should be monitored where practicable.

When letters are given out for children to take home to parents, the child's reactions/comments should be noted where possible. If the child and parent(s) are seen together in school, does the child's demeanour differ from what the teacher would expect, and in what ways does the child's demeanour alter? The interaction between parent(s) and the child's teacher can often be 'a lifeline' for the non-abusing parent, but a 'threat' to an abuser. An abused child will watch this interaction closely, since such children are sensitive to the moods and wishes of adults. Abused children need adults who are prepared to put children first and are seen to do so.

Children's body language/behaviour

Body language can communicate the existence of problems, but less so with older children than with younger children, since they often behave in a way which is designed to conceal the existence of sexual abuse. Observations can be made of a child with his/her parent(s)/carers, which may indicate different responses to adults according to the individual or the gender of the adult. For example, a child may shun proximity to men and/or be especially aggressive towards men. A child may show signs of tense, apathetic or other inappropriate behaviour which is most apparent on particular days. This may be because abuse is occurring at particular times of the week, or it may coincide with the visits of relatives, etc. Since children at risk are often the least able to express how they feel, or to seek out appropriate and effective help, frequently the only indication of their unhappiness is the existence of inappropriate behaviour.

The ethos of the school and the responses of school staff to children displaying inappropriate behaviour may influence the signals abused children use and the likelihood of their talking about any underlying unhappiness. Rudeness to a teacher may be dealt with as only attention- and confrontation-seeking and therefore as a disciplinary issue. If, however, the reasons for the rudeness are unhappiness stemming from abusive experiences, the child may find it more difficult to trust staff and to explain.

Helpful conditions for a child exist where school staff are visibly prepared to accept that children may have a variety of reasons why they misbehave, that the reason for the misbehaviour is sought from the child and discussed, and that staff are able to demonstrate that while some behaviours are clearly not acceptable, the children are accepted. Signals used by sexually abused children often include the following.

Suicide attempts/self-mutilation.   Surveys of adult survivor organisations indicate that the vast majority of survivors of child sexual abuse seriously considered or attempted to end their lives as teenagers. Teenage years are a time of rapid upheaval, physically, socially and emotionally, for all children. Most teenagers experience mood changes and periods of poor self-confidence. However, very few contemplate, talk about and/or attempt to kill themselves. Those that do are saying very clearly that their lives are intolerable and that they see no way out other than to end their lives. No suicide talk/attempt or incident of self-mutilation should be ignored or dismissed. Adults should not use their own perspectives on the child's suicide talk to attempt to judge the seriousness of the child's intentions. Children who attempt suicide, if not in contact with their family doctor, should be referred to the educational psychologist/education welfare officer/local social services office/child psychiatrist so that the causes, including the possibility of sexual abuse, can be explored.

Children who run away from home/school. Children, even teenagers, are entirely dependent on adults for their well-being and safety. Adults provide children with shelter, food, love, attention and guidance. No child casually or deliberately puts him/herself at risk for no reason, and children who run away are giving a clear cry for help. Such children are likely to be dealt with by the social services department or the police, and this is not primarily an issue requiring action by teachers. Such an incident should not be viewed in isolation, however, since it may assume added significance if other behavioural anomalies have been observed in school.

Relationship problems with peers and adults. Adolescence is a time when children begin to distance themselves from adults and to gravitate to their peer group. Children who have been or are being sexually abused tend to be isolated, however. The pressures on such children not to tell isolate them from other significant adults in their lives. A child may often want to tell a sympathetic teacher or school nurse, but the pressure to keep silent may be too great and militate against this. These pressures also isolate children from their peers. This is especially so for teenagers. If class mates are talking of first dates, how can a child who has been sexually abused for years want or be able to join in? The isolation goes still further, since the abuse may isolate children within their families, from their mothers and their siblings. It is this isolation that leads many abused children to believe that they are the only children to whom this has happened, and it underpins their problems in relating to both peers and adults.

A sexually abused teenager may well maintain a distance between him/herself and adults in school in a variety of ways, such as being very well-behaved, quiet and never in the forefront or available to adults; or by being so churlish and difficult that adults readily dismiss him/her as unworthy of any teacher's efforts; or by establishing contact with adults based on reasons which mask the child's real need for adult contact, such as excessive helpfulness or repeated health complaints.

Abused teenagers will often have few if any close or lasting peer friendships. Such friendships may well not be allowed by the child's abuser. There is a strength in children's closeness with each other which can be a challenge to the power of an abuser. So friendships are often discouraged or forbidden. The child may well not want close friendships, fearing rejection should the secret become known. Often abused children have such a poor sense of self-esteem and confidence that they do not believe they are worthy of friendships and do not attempt to make any, or the friendships they do make are with the more antisocial/disaffected groups where they feel they will be judged less harshly or where they can gain some status and positive regard.

Children do, of course, vary in this as in many other respects, and the existence of such factors on their own will not necessarily signify the existence of abuse. They may, however, be significant as a small part of a much larger pattern of behaviour and may provide important supplementary or confirmatory evidence.

Changes in mood, both gradual and sudden. Many teenagers display changes in mood as a result of normal hormonal changes and in any event, the usual secondary school situation makes it hard to monitor changes in mood in individual children. Subject, teacher or room changes affect the way children behave and feel during the school day. For any child, a double period of their least favourite subject, particularly on a Friday afternoon, may well account for a great deal!

However, careful monitoring may reveal that all teachers who take a child at the end of a day find that he/she is withdrawn and tense, perhaps indicating a fearfulness about home time. As discussed earlier, a weekly pattern of acting-out or withdrawn behaviour may well coincide with events at home such as access visits, weekends with grandparents, outings with an uncle, etc. Gradual changes in children are even harder to notice, particularly if teachers have daily contact with a child over several years. Checking previous school reports/records may reveal that a child's attendance, work patterns and/or behaviour have deteriorated over time.

Children who hurt or assault other children/adults.   Children who are confused, frightened or being hurt do often build up defences to protect themselves from further perceived threats. Older children are able to do this more effectively than younger children. Their capacity to contain their own emotions and be aware of the demands of others and of situations are such that many teenagers mask the warning signs of their own abuse. Teachers should be alert to the possibility that children who hurt or assault other children and/or adults are losing control of themselves.

Such behaviour may reflect a variety of factors, including poor role models at home, or involvement in a delinquent or gang subculture. However, the question needs to be asked why a child is behaving thus, rather than assuming we know the answer. Children can also hit out at other people because they are under pressure. They may hit out at people who have done nothing to hurt or frighten them because they cannot hit out at the people who *have* hurt and frightened them. Socialisation processes can lead to gender differences in children's reactions, so that sexually abused boys are more likely to hit out, acting out their anger and hurt. Details of any such assaults need to be carefully recorded, noting the date, time, age and gender of the victim, and the nature of the assault, including details of what was said and done.

Children's drawing/writing

Whilst teachers also need to be extremely cautious in forming conclusions on the basis of their students' drawings and/or written work, children often express a great deal of themselves in this way. No one drawing or type of drawing, in terms of figures drawn or colours used, is necessarily indicative that a child is being sexually abused, and an enormous range of self-expression through such media is to be expected. However, on occasions children's drawings may be a useful index of their fears and feelings, and teenagers are particularly adept at using drawings in metaphorical ways. Drawings will seldom be explicitly about child sexual abuse, but they may provide a basis for the teacher to be concerned enough to seek expert advice (from the educational psychologist or from child protection workers) and to consider whether the child should be monitored more closely.

Children will often respond to ideas for writing in very individual ways. It is helpful if programmes of work for helping children to express themselves include ideas or prompts which might be an opportunity for children to write about what is happening to them, although any such ideas should obviously be used in some overall curriculum context for a whole group or class.

The advantages of monitoring an individual child's drawing/writing in the context of a piece of work for the group/class is twofold. Firstly, the one child about whom the teachers feels concern is not singled out in ways which would suggest the child is happy/sad/angry/at risk, etc. So children who perhaps shun approaches by adults can be monitored as soon as there is any concern without unduly making them feel threatened. Secondly, the responses of the child who is being monitored can be compared with those of a group of peers. Such comparisons are often very helpful in alerting teachers to a child's fears and feelings.

Health complaints, medicals, PE

For many secondary school students, complaining about an ache or a pain is a way of avoiding unpopular lessons or activities, or it may be a normal part of adolescence, such as the onset of menstruation in girls. It may, however, be a more 'respectable' way to bid for attention than to talk of being unhappy and needing help. Certainly, going to an adult with a health complaint provides a cover to keep inquisitive peers at a distance. Children may often present with repeated and/or trivial health complaints, such as headaches, stomach-aches, pains, feeling sick, etc.

Whichever way children present with health complaints, they should be taken seriously, listened to, and offered advice and help. Some such complaints will be invented, but many will be related to real illnesses, and schools have a duty to be alert to the health of their pupils. Some real health complaints may well not seem to be founded on actual symptoms at all. Even if this is the case, the teacher and/or welfare assistant and/or school nurse if there is one, who listens carefully and is sympathetic, is showing a child that he/she takes what the child has to say seriously and is prepared to listen. This may be a child's first step to approaching adults outside the family, and the response with which he/she is met may determine future approaches from the child.

Many adolescents go through a period of not wanting to participate in physical activities, and this is often associated with the physiological changes which they are experiencing. However, a child who is being sexually abused may well react differently from class mates when the time comes for PE/games lessons. Teachers are now well aware that PE/games lessons, where children undress, provide a useful weekly point to check children known to be at risk of physical abuse for tell-tale signs of injury, and those monitoring children who may be sexually abused should consider the extent to which they might also use this weekly opportunity for observation.

However, there are obvious dangers in making such observations, not least the risk that the teacher might be accused of taking an inappropriate interest in the child, and such opportunities for observation should only be taken after careful consideration and prior discussion with a senior colleague. Marks are perhaps less likely to be seen on older children, and since abused children are often aware of the consequences of disclosure they are also likely to provide plausible explanations for any marks. For these reasons, it is all the more important that any obvious marks are noted, concern expressed and the child's responses noted. However, physical examination by a teacher should not, of course, be contemplated under any circumstances.

Medicals are also an opportunity to talk to children about their well-being, and although teachers are not directly involved in these, visiting medical staff should be alerted to any concerns. A child may well feel more able to talk to someone with a medical background whom he/she does not see everyday. Notes on a child's absences and health complaints should also be shared and discussed with visiting medical staff, and if a child who is being monitored is away from school during a medical this should be noted and followed up.

Finally

As with the previous outline, the above is also intended to help in situations where teachers suspect a child is being sexually abused, and to provide some practical guidelines about the important role they can play in providing systematic daily monitoring of a child. Teachers need always to remember, however, that they should never shoulder alone the concern about a child they suspect is being abused. The sexual abuse of children is a crime and needs to be reported to one of the agencies with statutory powers to deal with the problem, namely, the social services, the NSPCC or the police. Where there is a suspicion that a child is being abused, advice might also be sought from the educational psychologist and/or education welfare officer, and social services should be informed.

It is also important that whenever a decision is made to undertake monitoring of a child in a school setting, a record is kept of the process of monitoring which includes details of timing, discussions with colleagues, follow-up action taken and dates set for further reviews. The notebook in which the notes relating to the monitoring of the child's behaviour are kept should contain a record of these.

Issues Arising from Using a System of Monitoring

The monitoring guidelines outlined above have been welcomed by both education workers and social services workers. Several issues have arisen as a consequence of the outlines being used on a regular basis. The debate around these issues has served to define and clarify views both within the profession and between professionals about the role of the class teacher. The issues that have arisen are as follows.

Parental involvement

Most child protection procedures usually, and quite rightly, include the need for early discussion of concerns with parents. The Children Act 1989 lays great emphasis on partnership with parents, and there has obviously been much debate about the stage at which the practice of monitoring children at school should be discussed with parents. This clearly needs to be decided in consultation with senior colleagues and child protection workers.

As discussed earlier, if a discussion with parents is held too soon this may only serve to alert the abuser and make him/her more skilful. For example, to explain that sexual abuse is suspected because of a child's drawing of a man with genitalia is to provide the basis for future threats to that child, not only about telling, but also about what he or she draws in school. This makes it possible for the abuser's threats to become more specific, but also for him/her to appear to have knowledge of what the child does in situations separate from him/her. This can make him/her seem more powerful and can seem to the child to be a betrayal by other adults in his or her life. Such a precipitous warning to an abuser could result in that child never doing such a drawing again.

Obviously, the aim of the monitoring guidelines is not to undermine the rights of parents. What is clear is that most arguments about the rights and civil liberties of parents/adults cut across the needs that some children have for protection, given the simple fact that the majority of children who are sexually assaulted are assaulted by adults who are in their families or known to their families beforehand. It is obvious, therefore, that some kind of balance needs to be struck.

Where there are specific grounds for suspecting abuse, it would seem in everyone's interest that those grounds are refined and made more specific, so that they can be discussed with parents by the appropriate authorities, while at the same time providing a basis for effective protective action if necessary. It needs to be remembered that these outlines for monitoring children in school are specifically designed to be useful in situations where there are suspicions of child sexual abuse which need to be substantiated or eliminated. It is in the interests of everyone that when such concerns are aired, there is clarity about the evidence on which they are based. These guidelines are one way of achieving this clarity.

Local authority open records

Many local authorities are now adopting the system of open records, to which parents have access. The advice to teachers in the monitoring outlines is that they record their observations in a notebook, but it is quite clear that the matter is not one for the child's record at that stage. It is important that any record of discussions involved in planning the monitoring of a particular child should include specific decisions made about the nature of the record of the monitoring which is to be kept, and the stage at which the school's concern would be discussed with the child's parents, entered on the child's record and discussed with professionals from other agencies.

The timing of monitoring

It has become increasingly evident that there need to be parameters to the timing of any arrangements for monitoring a child. It is clear, however, that when a teacher suspects that a child in his or her class is being sexually assaulted, these concerns should be discussed immediately with the head teacher and with a member of the local social services department, e.g. the duty officer at the local office, or the allocated social worker if the family is already known to social services, or the child protection co-ordinator for that authority. If the suspicions are unclear, the discussions may well centre around the ways in which the outline for monitoring can be adapted to clarify the situation.

It is also important to remember that where the evidence is quite clear – for example, a child is displaying overtly sexualised behaviour in a way which is out of keeping with the normal range of behaviour for a child of that gender, age and ability – then the decision could well be that monitoring by the school would not be an appropriate course of action on its own, and that an investigation of possible abuse should be initiated according to the local area child protection guidelines. So the decision to start monitoring needs to be made first and foremost on the basis of the level of concern about the risk to the child.

A second consideration in the decision to monitor a particular child is to determine the period of time over which monitoring takes place. Monitoring must take place over a reasonable period of time, and it must be geared to the level of concern about the child and to any difficulties envisaged in establishing an effective and comprehensive system. Thus, where the level of suspicion is quite high, the decision with regard to monitoring may well be to monitor the child more intensively over a shorter period of time.

Any decision about the length of time over which monitoring takes place should also include a decision about when the monitoring should be reviewed and by whom, and arrangements made accordingly. The central point is that monitoring needs to be a flexible system which, while providing a standard framework, remains sufficiently flexible to meet the needs of individual children and the level of professional concern about these children.

One issue that has arisen from the use of the outline by teachers has been the need to stress that monitoring is not an activity in itself which protects children. It is one means of aiding the work of other professionals to do just that. So there is no virtue in monitoring a child about whom there is concern if the results are not communicated to local child protection workers. There is also a danger that monitoring, which provides a specific and clear role for teachers, can be seen as an end in itself and used as a means to avoid the difficulties of implementing local procedures with regard to child protection. It is therefore always important to distinguish between situations where monitoring is sufficient and those where action is needed.

The important point is that monitoring should have a clear start and end. The duration of the monitoring should be geared to the level of concern about an individual child, and there should be consultation between professionals at all stages. Decisions made should be clearly recorded.

Professionals' use of the monitoring guidelines

Obviously, the above outlines for monitoring were written specifically for teachers, and in using them many have demonstrated their skills and expertise in ways which have contributed greatly to the protection of many children. Given a specified role in the collection of information, teachers are extremely skilful in the observations they make, and in their capacity to place those observations in the context of daily contact with children and also the range of normal behaviour of children.

The outlines have also been found to be useful by social workers or educational welfare officers. It is often the case that the initial concerns about possible risk to a child do not arise in school, but rather arise in the context of family work done by social workers or educational welfare officers. These professionals frequently need to obtain information about a child in different settings from those in which they see the child, and they will often approach the child's teacher to ask for additional information which may clarify their concerns. The outlines have been useful for them in clarifying what they can expect from, and the basis on which to approach, a teacher. This has led to a greater level of consistency within the authority that uses the outlines in terms of what social workers and educational welfare officers ask of teachers.

Teacher confidence

Currently, the confidence of teachers is at a very low ebb, partly because of their vulnerability to being accused of sexually abusing their own students, and because of the pressures involved in delivering the National Curriculum. Some reluctance to take on what might be seen as a social work role is therefore, perhaps, to be expected. The introduction of this system of monitoring has, however, resulted in an increased level of teacher confidence. The outline recognises the ambiguities of any situation where there is the suspicion of child sexual abuse and the levels of professional anxiety that this produces. In asking teachers to take on the specific role of monitoring children in school, it is helpful to be able to give them a standardised outline which can then be modified to take account of their particular concerns, the particular situation within their school, and the child about whom there is concern. The fact that there is something specific for the teacher to do often helps to reduce their understandable reluctance to get involved.

Increased levels of teacher confidence have been particularly apparent in child protection conferences. Teachers who attend, having previously been given the outline for monitoring children in school, are usually quite clear about the information that has been collected. Often the information the teacher has been able to provide has encouraged discussion of the roles of other professionals and other basic information which has to be collected.

The outlines have also made clear where the contribution of the teacher ends and where the work of statutory child protection workers begins. However, a note of caution needs to be sounded. The introduction of a monitoring system for use by teachers brings with it the challenge of court work. Evidence from monitoring by teachers will increasingly be used in courts, and teachers are going to need training, reassurance and support to do this work. However, the signs are that when teachers do present the results of balanced and careful monitoring, the courts are more able to protect children.

Inter-agency conflict

Other chapters in this section of the book address the issue of inter-professional relationships in some detail. However, the introduction of a system of monitoring where child sexual abuse is suspected has helped to reduce inter-agency conflict. When teachers are clear about the role they can play in child protection work, their anxieties about children are less likely to lead to tensions between themselves and workers from other agencies. Those who have participated in case conferences know all too well the way in which such tensions can be generated by a lack of awareness of others' roles, responsibilities and authority. The outlines enable teachers to become a more integral part of the child protection process in which the emphasis is on multi-disciplinary teamwork, based on clear and realistic expectations of the roles of all concerned.

Conclusion

The sexual assault of children by adults known to them is a difficult situation which arouses anxiety in all who care about the welfare of children. My message is that teachers have a key role in dealing with the suspicion of abuse, but that this role needs to be clarified. Given clear parameters for monitoring, teachers can make a powerful contribution to the assessment of risk. The essential point is that teachers can monitor the situation of a particular child, but the duty to evaluate their observations and take action always lies with the statutory child protection agencies. Teachers need to be aware of the work of these agencies, liaise with them and adhere to local child protection guidelines (DES circular, April 1988).

Recommended Further Reading

David, T. (1993). *Child Protection and Early Years Teachers*. Milton Keynes: Open University Press.
This is an extremely useful book for teachers, covering the different forms of child abuse. It has a helpful first section on understanding child abuse which sets out clearly the historical, social and legal contexts to abuse. The book then goes on to look at how schools and teachers respond to child abuse both in terms of concerns about individual children and also in terms of developing a whole school approach to child protection. The book contains information, practical advice and some attention to the feelings this difficult work raises for teachers.

Peake, A., Rouf, K. & Michaels, M. (1995). *Working with Sexually Abused Children*. London: Children's Society and Oxford Brookes University. (In press.)
This is a resource pack for professionals, parents and children. It contains nine practice papers for professionals on a range of areas in the field of child sexual abuse: suspicion, assessment, group work, one-to-one work and consultation. There is a very comprehensive set of INSET materials for teachers in schools who may wish to develop their knowledge and understanding of child sexual abuse. The pack has accompanying leaflets and books for parents and children which can be ordered separately.

Brown, H. & Craft, A. (1989). *Thinking the Unthinkable*. Family Planning Association Education Unit.
This is a collection of papers on the problems of child sexual abuse for people with learning difficulties. The papers cover a range of topics from the need for safeguards, keeping safe programmes, to issues to do with the law and sexual abuse of adults with learning difficulties. It is a helpful set of papers, seeking to begin to chart a very difficult area of work. The book is useful in that at the end of each paper there are a set of key questions for professionals wanting to make practice-based developments to protect children and adults with special needs.

Rouf, K. (1991). *Into Pandora's Box*. London: Children's Society.
It is important in our work in the field of child sexual abuse to listen to the voices of children. This is a collection of poems and drawings by a young Asian woman about what it means to be abused and to be black. The complex and conflicting emotions contained in the poems remind us all of the dilemmas for children who are abused by trusted adults. Without such brave reminders, our practice would be impoverished and irrelevant.

References

Baker, A.W. & Duncan, S.P. (1985) Child Sexual Abuse: A Study of Prevalence in Great Britain. *Child Abuse and Neglect 9*: 457–467.

Department of Education and Science (1988). *Working Together for the Protection of Children from Abuse: Procedures for the Education Service*, London: HMSO.

Department of Health (1991). *Working Together under the Children Act 1989 – A Guide to Arrangements for Inter-Agency Co-operation for the Protection of Children against Abuse.* London: HMSO.

Finkelhor, D. (1984). *Child Sexual Abuse: New Theory and Research.* New York: Free Press.

Frosh, S. (1987). Issues for men working with sexually abused children. *British Journal of Psychotherapy 3*: 332–339.

Furniss, T. (1983). Mutual influence and interlocking professional–family process in the treatment of child sexual abuse and incest. *Journal of Child Abuse and Neglect 7*: 207–223.

Herman, J. (1981). *Father Daughter Incest.* Harvard: Harvard University Press.

Manchester, A.H. (1979) The Law of Incest in England and Wales. *Journal of Child Abuse and Neglect. 3*: 679–682.

Peake, A. (1991). Consultation: a model for inter-agency co-operation in child sexual abuse. In J. Ussher (ed.): *Gender Issues in Clinical Psychology.* London: Routledge.

14

Court Proceedings

Mary Lane and Terry Walsh

Introduction

Many professionals believe that good child protection practice means avoiding courts as far as possible – a view echoed in the initial guidance from the Department of Health. The new legislation of the Children Act 1989 was, however, informed by the findings of major child abuse enquiries, especially that social workers allegedly fail to use their legal powers to protect children, or abuse families with these powers. Accordingly, the Act takes many decisions away from social workers and gives them to courts, to be determined by the 'due process' of law. Courts were also given new powers to examine and intervene in professionals' plans for children.

It is therefore now more likely that social workers, health professionals, teachers and carers will testify in court, and so it is vital that they have the court skills which are required. This chapter gives practical and realistic guidance in preparing for court proceedings and giving evidence competently. Families also often find courts frightening and daunting, and many professionals agree that they are far from being user-friendly. The advice in this chapter is based upon the premise that knowing more about what happens in court and why, and how lawyers approach their tasks, will better equip witnesses for court.

It is perhaps unsurprising that lawyers and 'helping' professionals have some difficulty working together. Lawyers often regard social workers as 'vague, unrealistic, starry eyed', and social workers often regard lawyers as 'self-serving and unscrupulous' (Bell and Daly, 1992). With open minds, however, experience and knowledge of each other's work usually overcome such inaccurate views.

However, the legal profession is undeniably steeped in tradition and has adapted only slowly to modern life. In spite of moves towards reform at the highest levels, judges are still predominantly white, middle class, middle-aged to elderly men, and most magistrates have conservative life experiences. The judiciary may therefore be thought to regard those who come before them stereotypically: for example, women projecting unconventional images of femininity may have their evidence devalued, and the prejudice experienced by members of ethnic minorities generally may also be present for professionals in court. However, stereotypes are not always unhelpful. Female witnesses giving evidence about children may have the advantage of more credibility, at least initially, than their male colleagues. All witnesses with qualifications and experience will have enhanced status in court, whatever their gender or race, especially if they have the qualities consistent with professionalism – detached and informed competence and commitment to their child client's welfare.

When in Rome . . .

Witnesses must be realistic about the way courts are, rather than considering how they might want them to be. The court is a forum with its own culture and etiquette. It is not the place to challenge what may be regarded as unnecessary ritual and formality with hostile or dismissive behaviour. Witnesses should give evidence on the basis that they are not in court for themselves, to proselytise their own world view, but to achieve a particular result for a child. Two particular aspects of the legal system are now outlined to assist readers' understanding, if not forgiveness. Since both solicitors and barristers have rights of audience in most family courts, the word 'advocate' is used throughout to mean the lawyer in court.

The adversarial method

A social work academic has criticised courts as, 'a context in which winning is more important than an exploration of all possibilities and options. Social workers seek to have their plans ratified on the basis of selected and selective evidence' (Ryburn, 1992). Social workers are trained to seek co-operation and consensus, not take sides. However, when courts are used to resolve child protection disputes, a partisan approach is largely unavoidable because the conduct of most British court hearings follows the adversarial method. That is, justice is achieved through ritualised verbal contest between two or more advocates, each challenging the other's version of events and presenting their own in the best light to persuade an independent arbitrator to decide in their favour.

At the time of writing (autumn, 1993) there has been a spate of cases where the adversarial nature of care proceedings has been called into question. However, to date only the strict application of the law of evidence has been eroded by these cases, so that the family court now has the power to order disclosure of legally privileged material, e.g. a psychological report commissioned by one party but excluded from evidence because it was not favourable to them. Those hoping that this case law signals the beginning of the end for cross-examination will be disappointed. Care proceedings are still adversarial in the sense that each party is entitled to be represented by an advocate, entitled to be heard according to formal rules, and to challenge opposing evidence. The position at this time might be paraphrased as: care proceedings are adversarial, but should not be conducted in an adversarial way.

Despite the surge of change brought about by new legislation and enormous pressure for family courts to be 'non-stigmatic responsive institutions employing conciliatory procedures' (Murch and Hooper, 1992), the combatant nature of court hearings has not been destroyed, only tempered, and for the foreseeable future an adversarial approach to the preparation and presentation of evidence will still be taken by lawyers. Once in court, however, witnesses may find hearings much less 'red in tooth and claw' than anticipated. Nonetheless, before the hearing it is still necessary to prepare, mentally and evidentially, for battle, especially for challenging cross-examination and the need sometimes to risk wounding others by saying things in their presence which compassion would leave unspoken.

The power of oral evidence

In most family proceedings, disclosure of each witness's evidence is required in advance of the proceedings. However, detailed knowledge of what will be said in court does not make the outcome of a proceeding certain – the judiciary make their decision after witnesses have been seen and heard. Oral evidence provides them with much more than words on paper. Demeanour, appearance and attitude are all part of assessing witness credibility, and in family matters assessment of the characters of those contending for the care of a child are vital ingredients in the judiciary's decision-making.

Qualities in a witness such as respect, clarity, audibility, sincerity and steadfastness sway hearts and minds in court. Conversely, inept performance in the witness box can weaken or even destroy good evidence. In other words, convincing testimony is a matter not only of the evidence given, but the way it is given.

Preparing Evidence

A textbook on the law of evidence contains the story of a judge, exasperated by constant interruptions from advocates, asking, 'Am I never to hear the truth in this matter?' The answer came back from one of them, 'No, my Lord, you will hear the evidence.' Advocates must not lie or mislead the judiciary, but they do not give an all-inclusive, balanced exposition. They select and shape the information provided by their clients into evidence, presenting the court with that which is persuasive in their favour, and dissembling that which is not.

Turning information into evidence

Professionals instruct solicitors (tell them what is wanted and why), and solicitors advise and represent, without accepting instructions uncritically. Solicitors should identify weaknesses, give realistic appraisals of the likelihood of success, or suggest viable alternatives.

During first meetings between solicitor and witness, the history of the case should be discussed. Whilst a comprehensive knowledge of all aspects of the case is needed, teachers of advocacy skills suggest that the preparation of evidence should concentrate on identifying six or seven of the strongest and most crucial points, the 'pillars' on which the case is constructed, others being discarded as weak or peripheral. Once these are established, the next exercise is to play devil's advocate by trying to predict the points and arguments which might be advanced from the other side to demolish these pillars, and to predict what the other side's own pillars might be.

Bearing in mind that solicitors may be coming completely new to the matter, witnesses should give them as much detailed information as possible, including, where appropriate:

- a family tree, a diagram of the members of the family, their names, dates of birth and relationships to each other;
- a chronology in date order, of events, including the beginning (and end) of witnesses' involvement with the case. Solicitors will value advice about the emotional, educational or medical impact of events (e.g. repeated admissions to care, changes of school, shaking a young baby) and welcome guidance in linking facts to theory and research, e.g. the effects of abuse, known risk factors, etc.;
- names and addresses of other potential witnesses, e.g. previous health visitors or colleagues who witnessed a crucial incident, and if possible, opinions as to their likely attitudes to and experience of giving evidence.

Sometimes even the most professional workers make errors or omissions. These may be used to attack witnesses, so it is vital to explore information in the privacy of interviews with the witnesses' own solicitors, so that they can be identified, taken into account and their harmful potential defused – forewarned is forearmed.

Expert witnesses

Experts are those whom the judge or magistrates decide are experts in the particular circumstances of the case and after reading or hearing about their qualifications and/or experience. Paper qualifications are not always necessary to establish expertise – for example, a person with lengthy fostering experience can give an expert opinion on that subject.

Professionals should consider with their solicitors their own perceived level of expertise and whether effective presentation in court requires support from others, such as specialist practitioners. Offence should not be taken if solicitors raise this, and witnesses could suggest someone amongst their colleagues. Strategy may also require a weighty 'outside' expert to counter someone called by the other side. Galling though this may be, the reality is that doctors and psychologists with strings of qualifications are given much greater status in court than 'mere' social workers, and to attempt a David and Goliath match in court is foolishness rather than valour.

Leave of court for expert evidence

The court must give permission for experts to examine or assess children for legal proceedings, or to have sight of the papers. This rule applies to in-house experts who have not previously been involved, as well as those in other services. Without leave, the evidence may be excluded.

Research evidence

Research evidence backing up witnesses' views will be welcomed by advocates during the preparation of the case, but research offering alternative views should also be mentioned. It is not sufficient, and could be dangerous, for witnesses simply to preface their oral evidence with 'Research says . . .'. Bearing in mind that the Law Society has established a panel of child care solicitors who receive specialist training, and that a competent barrister is capable of becoming an instant expert on any subject, a cross-examiner may know the research and challenge such vague references. Witnesses should be able to quote authors and publications, as well as deal with contradictory research which might be thrown at them in the witness box.

Child abuse enquiries

Every professional giving evidence in a child protection matter should be able to recount the main recommendations of the Cleveland report in particular, and other relevant published reports of child abuse enquiries. Failure to do so is lethal to the credibility of the most able professional witness. The Cleveland guidelines on the reliability of children's evidence, although not law, are regarded by the courts as expert evidence of best practice, and therefore their benchmark in assessing professional conduct. Other essential reading includes the 'orange book' – the Department of Health (DOH) guide to assessments (DOH, 1988) – and the *Memorandum of Good Practice* on videoing children's evidence (DOH, 1992), which is particularly relevant to avoiding asking children leading questions or coaching them for court.

Written evidence

Procedural rules require that written statements or affidavits are prepared of the evidence to be given by all witnesses and submitted to court in advance of the hearing. The intention is to facilitate 'cards on the table' litigation – to ensure that as much evidence as possible can be agreed between the parties, that oral evidence is adduced only on disputed matters, and that each party knows what they have to challenge or counter.

Statements and affidavits are legal documents and are usually prepared by solicitors. The language may therefore be rather legalistic and could appear too cryptic or blunt compared with the witnesses' preferred style. It is important for witnesses to check carefully, before signing, that the contents are truthful and not misleading, since the sanction of perjury applies. Affidavits are sworn, by reciting the oath or affirmation, before independent solicitors or court officials.

Evidence not provided in statements or affidavits can only be given at the hearing with the leave of the court. Solicitors should be informed immediately of new evidence, so that leave can be requested. When all the written evidence is received, witnesses can fine tune what they will give in oral testimony by seeing where their evidence fits in with the rest.

Using written evidence in court

Giving oral evidence is not a test of memory and however well witnesses prepare, they may need to remind themselves of certain events or dates whilst testifying, especially if a cross-examiner tries to confuse them. Witnesses could take their files into the witness box, but this is not recommended – fumbling through a pile of papers during the course of evidence can fluster a witness and does not look professional. More importantly, the witness risks falling foul of the rule of evidence about 'memory refreshing documents'. If used in the witness box, files or other records must, at the request of opposing advocates, be submitted for their scrutiny, and this has potential dangers.

Witnesses should, however, take their statements into the witness box. Well-written statements conclude with the main points in support of the case. If statements do not include a summary of the main points, these should be noted down prior to going into the witness box, thereby providing an *aide-mémoire* under pressure. Underlinings, highlighting and handwritten notes on witnesses's personal copies of statements are acceptable, but nothing should appear on them which amounts to new and undisclosed evidence, or that witnesses would be unhappy for opposing advocates to see.

Directions Hearings

These are relatively informal discussions, before a judge/district judge or magistrates' clerk, in the weeks or months before the final hearing to decide procedural matters, including leave for expert evidence, deciding the appropriate level of court and timetabling to ensure delay is minimised. Decisions can also be made at directions about which evidence can be agreed or remains in dispute, therefore requiring witness attendance at the final hearing.

It is unusual for witnesses to give oral evidence at directions hearings, but crucial parties should attend (the guardian *ad litem* must attend unless excused) to give instructions to their advocates on the directions being requested or disputed, and they should bring their diaries to agree on dates.

Personal Preparations for Court

Never underestimate the importance of dress and appearance – it should be smart and sober – the kind of clothes worn to an important interview. Dressing casually to try to lessen the ceremonious or intimidatory nature of court will be seen as disrespect. Formal clothes may also increase witnesses' confidence and sense of occasion. Lapel badges espousing political or other causes risk damaging the witnesses' acceptability – the judiciary assessing the witnesses may hold different views. Unless there are religious constraints, female witnesses should wear skirts, not trousers, and males a shirt and tie with jacket and trousers, or suit. Keep make-up and jewellery toned down. Witnesses should read over their evidence the night before court but not burn the midnight oil.

The Day of Court

Avoid going into the office first – it is easy to be late because of last-minute telephone calls. Get to court in time – at least half an hour before the start of the hearing (most final hearings begin at 10.00 a.m.; directions hearings can be earlier – always check!). Before the hearing starts, advocates may need to discuss points, and witnesses need time to compose themselves and feel comfortable.

Witnesses who are unavoidably delayed should ensure that their advocates are notified so that an adjournment can be requested. An advocate will not start a hearing with vital witnesses absent. On arrival at the court building, find an usher (clipboard and black robe or badge) if you are uncertain about where to find the right courtroom.

Viewing the courtroom

Another good reason to arrive early is to have a look at the empty courtroom before the hearing starts, to become familiar with the layout – e.g. where the witness box is in relation to the door – and to check the acoustics and any steps, or other possible 'affronts to dignity', which might spoil that all-important walk into the witness box or chair. Ushers will usually oblige by showing witnesses around.

Feeling nervous

Apprehension is normal for court witnesses but, up to a reasonable level, it can be conducive to good performance. Blasé or over-confident witnesses may perform badly. Nerves can be reduced by deep rhythmical breathing, the yoga exercise of tensing and relaxing muscles, or just chatting to others. Alcohol and other relaxing drugs are not recommended – they interfere with coherent thought! It may be of comfort to know that even experienced advocates get anxious before court, even if they know how to conceal it in public.

It frequently happens, for a number of reasons, that on the morning the hearing is to start all is suddenly agreed 'at the court door', or the hearing is unexpectedly adjourned. Whilst this means a day or more of unpleasantness avoided, it can leave witnesses feeling frustrated – sometimes because they have just spent a sleepless night psyching themselves up, and sometimes because a court hearing is cathartic. Use the unexpected free time to do something relaxing and come back down to earth.

Waiting to start

Beware of being overheard when discussing cases outside the courtroom – valuable clues to strategy can be picked up in this way. Key workers with main responsibility for cases will usually be allowed to stay in court throughout the proceedings, both before and after giving their evidence. Expert witnesses also usually sit through all the proceedings, but other witnesses are not usually allowed into court until it is their turn to testify.

Having a book to read will relieve the tension and boredom of a long wait outside court, and it will help to avoid conversations with witnesses for other parties who are sharing the same waiting room. Ushers can help if there is any unpleasantness – they can find alternative places to wait.

Order of examination of witnesses

The applicant for the order which is the substance of the court case is the first to call witnesses to give their evidence, and all the applicant's witnesses are examined at this stage. Each witness is examined in chief, first by his/her own advocate, then he/she is cross-examined by the advocate(s) for the other parties, and he/she is finally re-examined by his/her own advocate. Those challenging the application call their witnesses next, and all their witnesses are also examined at this stage. Children's evidence is usually the last to be heard. Guardians *ad litem* and their witnesses (and/or very occasionally the children) are examined at this stage.

If witnesses are being cross-examined when there is a break in the hearing, for lunch or at the end of the day, they are forbidden by the rules of evidence from speaking to their advocates or other witnesses about their evidence, and they may be questioned on their return to the witness box to check compliance. Witnesses in this position should therefore ensure that they leave the court building and lunch alone.

Final speeches and announcing the decision

When all the witnesses have been heard, advocates give an overview of their evidence and make points of law, often citing previously decided cases, to the judiciary. The magistrates/judge may give their decision and their reasons at the end of the hearing, or retire and give their decision later. Judgment can also be reserved to another day, or handed down in writing.

Giving Oral Evidence

Witnesses can make a good start by walking confidently and purposefully into the witness box, thus conveying the impression of an experienced witness. All eyes, including those of advocates for the other parties, are on the witness at this point, and observation of body language can reveal a lot.

Taking the oath or affirmation

Witnesses promise to speak the truth either by oath or affirmation (non-religious promise). Affirming with dignity and a sense of occasion is as acceptable as taking a religious oath, but whereas the religious oath card is always to hand, often the card with the affirmation words has to be found, therefore jarring the smooth flow of proceedings in a way which might distract attention from the witness's evidence. Hence, witnesses wishing to affirm should warn the usher or clerk in advance, or better still, memorise the words so that the card is not needed. The oath or affirmation should be unrushed, pronounced with sincerity and solemnity, and with eye contact with the judiciary.

Christian oath. Taking the Bible/New Testament in the right hand:

'I swear (in the magistrates' court 'promise') by Almighty God that the evidence I shall give shall be the truth the whole truth and nothing but the truth.'

Affirmation. Practise saying this as the phrasing is awkward:

'I do solemnly and sincerely and truly declare and affirm that the evidence I shall give shall be the truth the whole truth and nothing but the truth.'

Non-Christian oath. If a non-Christian form of religious oath or other ceremony is required, the usher should be told before court starts so that the necessary book or equipment can be obtained, or witnesses could bring their own. Such witnesses might also consider affirming.

Sit or stand?

After the oath/affirmation, the judge or magistrates may invite the witness to sit – do not do so until invited. Thereafter, sitting or standing is for each witness to decide, whichever feels right according to the setting. Witnesses of small stature giving evidence in the high-sided witness boxes in some formal courts should consider standing so that they can be seen and thus maximise their presence in court! Whether sitting or standing, avoid slouching – be upright and alert.

Body language in court

Witnesses are giving evidence to magistrates or judges alone – it is they who must be convinced by it. Witnesses may look at the advocates when listening to questions, but should look to the judiciary when giving the answers. This breaks the normal rules of conversation, and seems awkward at first, but although evidence is given to the court by way of questions and answers, it is not conversation (there is more on this point later). Eye contact with the judiciary should be maximised – it helps credibility. The occasional smile – in appropriate places – is a good way of establishing rapport with the bench. It is important to speak clearly and pace speech to take account of the fact that most judges and magistrates make handwritten notes.

If you are in any doubt about the judges' or magistrates' titles, listen to how the advocates address them – a judge or magistrate's title can be used to effect by a witness (see below). Their titles are:

- *The Family Proceedings (Magistrates') Court:*
  'Your Worships, Sir or Madam';
- *County Court/Care Centre:* the judge, male or female, is 'Your Honour';
- *High Court:* the judge is addressed as 'My Lord/Lady or Your Lordship or Ladyship'.

Qualifications and experience

The first a court hears about a witnesses is his or her occupation, professional address, qualifications and experience. These details should be stated briefly and clearly from a previously prepared CV – every professional should know how many years they have been a social worker, health visitor or teacher without having to count them up in the witness box! Witnesses should give the full title of qualifications, not just the initials, e.g. 'CQSW' or 'RSN'. Witnesses should think carefully about whether any aspect of their CV needs emphasis (or playing down) for a particular case. If employed in a capacity or by an organisation which the judiciary may not know (e.g. community link worker, family centre staff), witnesses should give a short explanation. Senior positions should be mentioned – modesty is out of place in a court, the aim is to impress.

Examination-in-chief

The first evidence witnesses give is via questioning by the advocate acting for them, the purpose being to put before the judiciary – who will be hearing it for the first time

– the evidence in support of their case. In essence, evidence-in-chief is an oral repetition of witness statements, and some suggest that this stage should be dispensed with to save time. However, by giving full evidence-in-chief, witnesses can achieve several desirable objectives, including adding power to the written word, e.g. statements referring briefly to poor domestic hygiene can be brought to life with graphic details!

Also, during this easier stage of giving evidence via a friendly advocate asking the questions, witnesses can show (apparent) confidence and competence, thereby establishing credibility with the court, and settle into the role of giving evidence before coming under attack during cross-examination.

The technique of giving evidence-in-chief

Evidence-in-chief is teamwork – it involves an exchange of questions and answers between witness and advocate, with the flow relaxed and rhythmic, like the movement of a metronome, and which seems like conversation. Good advocates use their skills to ask questions in a way that elicits the evidence with convincing impact on the court, emphasising the facts and details (the 'pillars') which are essential to proving the case. Witnesses give answers to the judiciary, but occasional eye contact with their advocates during the evidence-in-chief maintains the feeling of teamwork.

Leading questions

A leading question only has one answer. For example, if a child said to a witness that she did not want to see her father, a leading question would be, 'Is it right that she told you she didn't want to see her father?' Rules of evidence prohibit an advocate asking leading questions during examination-in-chief, hence the need for advance preparation so that witnesses will know what their advocates are aiming at if questions sound obscure, or if several are needed to reach the same point that leading questions reach directly!

The clue to the answer to a non-leading question may lie in key words, such as: 'When you saw her, did she *say* anything to you about her *father*?' Although witness and advocate know the answer, no leading question has been asked. In family courts, the rule excluding leading questions during evidence-in-chief is often relaxed or even ignored, but that will not become apparent until the actual hearing, and witnesses should be aware of it as part of their preparation for evidence-in-chief. Leading questions can be asked during cross-examination, however, and frequently are in order to try to put words into the witness's mouth!

Cross-examination

This is without doubt the aspect of giving evidence which causes the greatest apprehension. Psychologist Rhona Flin argues that 'torturing' witnesses by cross-examination is hardly an effective way to ensure that the truth emerges (Flin and Spencer, 1990). Many advocates would disagree with her, and cross-examination is a time-honoured and central element of the adversarial method.

The aim of cross-examination

This is to destroy or weaken the evidence given 'in-chief' by attacking or undermining it or the credibility of witnesses, and introducing evidence favourable to the other party – usually in the form of alternative explanations or re-interpretations of what the witness has said.

In family courts, cross-examination is likely to be less ferocious than in criminal courts, and the bullying advocate who reduces the witness to tears risks alienating the judiciary and giving witnesses the sympathy vote. However, if aggressive cross-examination is successfully denting the credibility of a witness or the evidence, i.e. the sympathy of the court is not with the witness, it may be allowed to continue.

All aspects of witnesses or their evidence might be challenged, devalued or negated by a cross-examiner, including their qualifications, experience and memory, or by attempts to demonstrate bias or misunderstanding. Cross-examiners may try to make witnesses muddled, lose confidence or contradict themselves. Curiously, and possibly because they feel guilty about being part of the adversarial process, many 'helping' professionals regard cross-examination as something to be endured passively, but there is no rule that witnesses, professional or otherwise, should submit to cross-examination without defending themselves and their evidence. It is not discourteous to fight back, and indeed, witnesses on behalf of a child have a duty to meet the challenge of cross-examination, although this should at all times be polite and dignified. Cross-examination is verbal chess – it can be intellectually stimulating and even exciting. Witnesses can make it an experience in which they control and succeed.

Surviving cross-examination

Witnesses who have worked with families competently and made adequate recordings should have little to fear under the searchlight of cross-examination, and an obviously honest witness can be difficult to undermine. The essential key to surviving cross-examination, however, is preparation. Having well-organised evidence, with potential weaknesses covered and crucial points to hand in the witness box, will help the witness avoid becoming muddled or being thrown off balance.

Giving evidence-in-chief with confidence and panache may assist survival during cross-examination because all advocates watch witnesses during this stage. Witnesses who appear vulnerable may attract more challenge than strong ones.

Don't take it personally!

Cross-examination may feel like a personal attack, but it is not. Goading witnesses into getting angry or upset is part of an advocate's tactics. Seeing it as such, and maintaining professional dignity and emotional control, will help witnesses to rise above it. Cross-examination is not always aggressive. A wheedling, cajoling or falsely flattering style can be equally difficult to cope with, unless that too is understood as strategy. Some advocates use tedium to wear witnesses down, although these are not always planned tactics!

Body language during cross-examination

This should be as calm and confident as during evidence-in-chief. Backing away into the farthest corner of the witness box will signal that the witness is on the defensive. Witnesses should always look at the judiciary to give their answers. In fact, it is not necessary to look at the cross-examiner at all. Witnesses feeling threatened by cross-examining advocates can help themselves by not looking in their direction, even during the questions. Not only does this prevent intimidation by the advocate's body language, scowls, etc., but it conveys an unspoken message to the judiciary that they are of no importance and as such their antics can be ignored.

Beat the rhythm!

Conversation is a face-to-face, mutually supportive exchange of questions and answers. Giving evidence is not. Like politicians, witnesses can become experienced in saying what they want to be heard, whatever questions they are being asked (while at the same time remaining polite!) During evidence-in-chief, the witness and advocate work together using flow and rhythm, like a conversation only more planned. During cross-examination, witnesses should try to avoid advocates setting the pace or establishing a rhythm, because they thereby gain control and can push and pull witnesses in dangerous directions.

Witnesses should interrupt a smooth exchange of questions and answers, giving long answers when short ones are expected (and vice versa), asking for questions to be repeated, taking time to think about the answer, or drinking water.

Pausing for effect

There are times in giving evidence when witnesses may need to pause or emphasise some particular aspect of their evidence, especially when a cross-examiner is making damaging inroads on their evidence. The witness should use the judiciary's title, addressing them directly, e.g. 'Your Worships (Honour, etc.), that's the fourth time I've been asked that question . . .', or 'Your Lordship, please may I finish giving my answer . . .'. This guarantees that for the next few minutes a cross-examiner's tirade must stop, and the witness regains control.

If an advocate insists on a 'yes' or 'no' answer, a witness could give it, and then, just as the cross-examiner moves on to the next question, elaborate or add an explanation, therefore weakening or negating the impact of the first answer. Alternatively, witnesses addressing the judiciary could say that in their opinion such a simple answer is inadequate, and they could then go on to give the appropriate answer. Whenever possible, in answer to cross-examination questions, witnesses should seize opportunities to restate to the court the main points of their evidence-in-chief (ideally set out in front of them in their witness statements) so that the court's attention is drawn back to them, rather than to the cross-examiner's distortions.

Multiple cross-examination

In each court hearing one advocate is on the witness's side and will conduct the examination-in-chief and the re-examination. All the other advocates, representing other parties in the case, are each entitled to cross-examine.

The Children Act 1989 provides for more multi-party hearings in which a witness gives evidence-in-chief once, but could be cross-examined four, five, six or more times! This may not be the nightmare it seems at first because some, or even most, of the advocates in a multi-party case will be on the same side as the witness they cross-examine, sharing on behalf of their clients the witness's view about what the court's decision should be.

When preparing for court witnesses should therefore ascertain from their own advocates, and from reading witness statements, which of the other advocates is 'friend' or 'foe', or in a complex case 'friend' on some issues and 'foe' on others. Witnesses then have the advantage of the rule permitting leading questions during cross-examination. They can allow themselves to be led in their evidence, in the knowledge that the interests of the witness and the cross-examiner coincide.

Questions from the judiciary

At any point in giving evidence witnesses may be asked questions by the judge or magistrates directly. These are good opportunities to explain vital points of evidence in the sure knowledge that they, the only audience that matters, are listening.

Re-examination – Repeating or Repairing Evidence

After the magic words 'no further questions' from the last cross-examiner, witnesses may be tempted to relax and let down their guard, but they should remain alert – re-examination by their own advocate is next. If, during cross-examination witnesses became confused or their credibility was shaken, questions during re-examination will be directed at untangling the confusion, correcting misunderstandings and putting the evidence 'back on the rails'.

Alternatively, advocates may ask witnesses to remind the judiciary of important points so that the last words they hear from witnesses are a restatement of their evidence-in-chief given before being dented by cross-examination. Leading questions cannot be asked in re-examination, so questions may again be indirect. Witnesses should re-establish eye contact with their advocates to facilitate the communication and teamwork.

After Giving Evidence

Witnesses are usually permitted to remain in court after giving testimony, and much can be learnt by observing entire hearings, but the judiciary will usually release witnesses on the request of advocates if all parties agree.

Witnesses remaining in court can assist their advocates by making notes of other witnesses' evidence when their own advocate is cross-examining. They can also give further instructions as other evidence unfolds, by passing notes to their advocates or whispering – but not so frequently that this causes distraction or creates the impression that the advocates were poorly instructed in the first place. When listening to evidence, witnesses should sit in an impassive but respectful manner, not making disapproving noises or facial expressions.

After the Decision

The judiciary's judgement should be received calmly and with dignity. Professional witnesses should bear in mind that their next appearance in court may be before the same bench, and unprofessional behaviour will be remembered. Witnesses may feel tired and sad after a court hearing, even if they get the decision they wanted, partly because of adrenalin draining away, but mostly because child protection decisions inevitably involve loss to one person or more. This is a time to seek support from trusted colleagues and, if an appeal is contemplated, to sleep on it first.

Conclusion

It is said that there are no short cuts to anywhere worth going to. Developing skill and confidence as a court witness requires practice and experience. Some of the most valuable lessons are learnt from mistakes, and confidence grows with each court appearance. A respect for, and acceptance of, the unique rules and procedures of the judicial process is a good beginning. Whilst social workers and other professionals start from a very different position to lawyers there is no reason why teamwork cannot be achieved, with roles being complementary and skills melded, thus ensuring that the right decisions are made for those children who need the protection of the courts.

Additional Reading

Because of the dearth of literature in this particular area, no additional reading has been suggested.

References

Bell, M. & Daly, R. (1992). Social workers and solicitors – working together? *Family Law* 22: 257–61.

Department of Health (1988). *Protecting Children – A Guide for Social Workers Undertaking a Comprehensive Assessment*. London: HMSO.

Department of Health (1992). *Memorandum of Good Practice on Video Recorded Interviews with Child Witnesses for Criminal Proceedings*. London: HMSO. (Although this is concerned with criminal proceedings, a witness who interviews a child because of an allegation of abuse for any purpose, on video or not, may be asked about compliance with these guidelines.)

Flin, R. & Spencer, J.R. (1990). *The Evidence of Children: The Law and Psychology*. Oxford: Blackstone Press.

Murch, M. & Hooper, D. (1992). *The Family Justice System*. Bristol: Family Law.
Ryburn, M. (1992). Contested adoptions. *Adopting and Fostering Journal 16(4): 29–38.*

15

The Work of the Guardian *Ad Litem*

Ann Head

Introduction

The decision of a social services department to institute care proceedings is clearly a very serious one, which may result in a child's compulsory, and even permanent, removal from his or her family. In addition to the procedures described in the preceding chapters, there is a further safeguard for the child in the court's appointment of a guardian *ad litem* (hereafter referred to as a GAL), a person independent of the local authority, whose prime duty is to safeguard the interests of the child. The appointment of guardians *ad litem* and their duties under the Children Act 1989 are matters dealt with under section 41 of the Act and in the Rules of Court. The assumption is that a GAL will be appointed in the great majority of public law cases.

'for the purpose of any specified proceedings the court shall appoint a guardian *ad litem* for the child concerned unless satisfied that it is not necessary to do so in order to safeguard his interests.' (Children Act 1989, section 41(1).)

The concept of a GAL, in the sense of a person appointed by a court to safeguard the interests of a child in the course of legal proceedings, has been known in adoption proceedings since the Adoption Act 1958. The extension of the concept to the field of public law resulted from a need for the child in care proceedings to be represented by a voice independent of the local authority bringing proceedings and of the child's parents. This was highlighted by the Field Fisher inquiry into the death of Maria Colwell (Department of Health and Social Security (DHSS), 1974), a child who had been returned from foster care with relatives to her mother and step-father, and who subsequently died at the hands of her step-father. The inquiry report drew the conclusion that an independent social worker's views of Maria's best interests would have been helpful to the court in that case. A further pressure to secure an independent voice came from David Owen's Children Bill 1974, which directed attention to the need for independent legal representation for children.

'In any proceedings relating to a minor in any court, separate representation should be considered and, if appropriate, the child should be made (if not already so) a party of the proceedings.' (Children Bill, 1974, clause 42.)

The Children Act 1975 reflected both these identified needs and the views of the Houghton Committee (1972) on adoption, in making provision for courts to appoint GALs in care proceedings. Full implementation of the provisions had to wait until 27 May 1984, when it became mandatory for local authorities to establish panels of GALs and reporting officers (ROs) who would be available to act in the full range of care and related proceedings, as well as in adoption and freeing for adoption cases. The task of the reporting officer is to interview parents who wish to consent to an adoption order, and to advise the court whether the consent is given freely and with the full understanding of its implications.

Early studies of the work of GALs drew attention to the wide variations in the number of appointments in care and related proceedings, consequent upon the degree of discretion allowed in the 1975 Act. Murch and Bader (1984), for example, commented as follows:

'Diversity is a theme which runs throughout the scheme: diversity between local authorities of comparable size in the number of cases which came to court; diversity in courts' practice, concerning both the criteria used in order to separate representation in the first place, and the stage at which this is done, that is, on application after the initial hearing; diversity between courts with comparable workloads in the proportion of cases in which GALs are appointed.' (Murch and Bader, 1984.)

The Children Act 1989 addressed this question of diversity and it extended the range of work to be encompassed by GALs. It also directed that the courts were to appoint a GAL, unless they were satisfied that it would not be in the child's interest to do so. The duties which now fall to the GAL, which are set out in the *Manual of Practice Guidance* for GALs and ROs (Department of Health (DOH), 1992*a*), are to advise the court on the following matters:

1. Whether the child is of sufficient understanding for any purpose, including the child's refusal to submit to a medical or psychiatric examination, or other assessment that the court has power to require.
2. The wishes of the child in respect of any matter relevant to the proceedings, including the child's attendance at court.
3. The appropriate forum for the proceedings, basing the criteria for the transfer of cases on:
   i.   exceptional complexity, importance or gravity;
   ii. the need to consolidate with other proceedings, for example, adoption and contact applications;
   iii. urgency.
4. The appropriate timetabling of the proceedings, or any part of them, always bearing in mind the dictates of the Children Act, section 1(2) regarding the avoidance of delay.
5. The options available to the court in respect of the child and the suitability of each such option, including what order should be made in determining the application.
6. Any other matter on which the Justices' Clerk or the court seeks the guardian's advice, or concerning which the guardian considers that the Justices' Clerk or the court should be informed. (DOH, 1992*a*.)

In practice, the GAL's duties will involve appointing a solicitor for the child, (Family Proceedings Court Rules 1991, rule II (a)), identifying to the court any person whose party status in the proceedings would help to safeguard the child's interests (rule II (6)), accepting documents on behalf of the child (rule II (8)) and conducting a full investigation of all the circumstances of the case (rule II (9)) which will lead to the production of a written report (rule II (7)) making recommendations as to the course of action which will best promote the child's interests. The GAL is bound by the court's obligation to reduce delay and to have regard to the matters set out in the welfare checklist (see Chapters 8, 14 and 16)).

The duties of the GAL are many and varied. It is perhaps helpful to consider the type of tasks involved, which I suggest are as follows.

Practical. As laid out in the court rules: appointing a solicitor, aiding the swift and efficient conduct of the proceedings, advising on matters to be considered by the court.

Investigative. Gaining a full picture of the case from documentation and from those professionally and privately involved with the child.

Analytical. Teasing out the issues from conflicting arguments and reaching reasoned conclusions, based on experience, research findings, expert advice and a detailed consideration of the facts of the case.

Representational. Promoting in court the child's best interest as perceived by the GAL and the child's wishes and feelings, and defending his or her conclusions in the face of challenges by other parties.

Explanatory. Interpreting the process of investigation in a sensitive manner to the child.

Research

The role of the GAL in family proceedings is a new one, although comparable systems in Scotland (the curator *ad litem*) and in the USA predate the setting up of panels in the UK.

Early studies of panels of GALs and ROs focused on the wide variations there were between local authorities in the size of the panels, the personnel appointed and the use made of the service by the courts. Those acting as GALs, the overwhelming majority of whom are experienced social workers, are either freelance, fee-attracting, local authority employees offering a service to a neighbouring authority's panel on a reciprocal basis, or employees of another agency, usually a voluntary agency or a probation service. In Coyle's study of the works of GALs (1987), of 130 GALs interviewed, 54% were employed full-time with a voluntary or statutory agency and 29% were self-employed; a further 14% were self-employed with voluntary or statutory agencies (Coyle, 1987). The figures quoted in the Children Act Report 1992 for panel membership at 31 March 1992 show that the numbers of fee-attracting or self-employed GALs had risen to 56.6% – local authority employees accounted for 28.1%, and probation officers and members of voluntary organisations accounted for a further 15.2% (DOH, 1992b).

It is clear from the change in the figures over 6 years and from the reduction in overall numbers of GALs (2366 in 1989–90 to 1327 in 1992) that there has been a general trend away from large numbers of workers doing a small amount of work each, in favour of smaller, more work-intensive panels, composed primarily of self-employed

GALs. There is some evidence of a North/South divide, with reciprocal panels composed of local authority social workers being more common in the north of the country, and panels of mainly or solely fee-attracting GALs predominating in the south of the country.

Feedback from the courts has been generally enthusiastic about the work of GALs. Justices' Clerks interviewed in the course of Coyle's (1987) study commented favourably on the help given by GALs to the courts in resolving difficult cases, and on the quality and general acceptability of the reports produced. Many of the clerks were, however, concerned about the delay in concluding cases where a GAL had been appointed. There is no clear evidence, however, about whether GALs contribute significantly to delays and if so, in what ways. As the Social Services Inspectorate (SSI) have argued, further research is needed before the causes and effects of delays in making decisions about the future of abused children become clearer (SSI conference report: *Avoidable Delay in Child Care Proceedings*, 1993).

Several studies have described the weight given to recommendations made by the GAL. As a recent SSI report comments, 'Courts put great weight on the GALs' contributions and followed their recommendations in over 90% of care and related proceedings in the sample' (SSI, 1990). A case which went to appeal not long after the establishment of GAL panels called forth the following comment from Sir John Arnold, then president of the Family Division.

> 'It is well established in relation to appeals from magistrates that if they fail to follow the advice which they receive – for example from a probation officer, without any justification for that failure, then the appeal will ordinarily be allowed. Exactly the same consideration must apply, in my judgement, to the views of the Guardian *ad litem*.' (Devon County Council v. Clancy, May 1985.)

I am not aware of any research conducted amongst the children represented by GALs or their families. It is true that the appraisal of the work of GALs is a subject which has exercised the Department of Health and panel managers. Most panels have introduced appraisal systems, requiring GALs to be interviewed about their work and to produce examples of written reports, and advice about the GAL's competence is sought from courts and solicitors.

Since the Department of Health's issue of guidelines to panel managers, there has been an expectation that panels will be organised on similar lines across the country, and that mechanisms for appointment, appraisal and dismissal of GALs will be in hand, guided by a panel advisory committee. It is acknowledged that panels will have different compositions, but there is some argument that a relatively small, well occupied but flexible panel works best (DOH, 1992b). Evidence also suggests that qualified and experienced social workers are most likely to have the knowledge necessary to be a GAL, and that GALs must keep abreast of research and practice developments by having access to high-quality training and adequate support.

Policy Issues

A number of policy issues have arisen in studies conducted into the work of GALs, and I propose to address these individually.

Independence

A key quality of the GAL system, as envisaged in the 1970s, was independence. It was seen as essential that the GAL should be independent of the social services department bringing proceedings, and of the child's parents or other relatives. Care has been taken from the inception of the role to ensure that the person appointed as GAL has no prior knowledge of the case, unless, of course, it is a reappointment for the same child in fresh proceedings. Thus, it has been seen by every study as a major flaw that the GAL service continues to be a responsibility of social services departments. As the joint ADSS/ACC/AMA* officers stated in their report, dated April 1986:

'Almost all sources doubted whether true independence of GALs/ROs can be compatible with a local authority's responsibility to set up, administer, train and finance the panels.' (Quoted in Coyle, 1987.)

Similarly, Independent Representation for Children in Need (IRCHIN) commented:

'If panel members are to work independently and are to be seen to be working independently, they must be free from outside pressures and constraints. This is extremely difficult unless they have an independent administrative structure from which to operate . . . the difficulty with the present arrangement is that panels are funded and administered by the local authorities.' (IRCHIN, 1985.)

Following the implementation of the Children Act 1989, attempts have been made to distance the administration of panels from the managerial structure of social services departments by the appointment of panel managers working with advisory committees which have independent representation, and by the setting up of complaints boards, again with independent representation.

These attempts to organise panels of GALs separately from the structure of social services departments, whose work it is the responsibility of GALs to appraise, are clearly to be welcomed. However, to most outside professionals and, more importantly, to many families involved in family proceedings as a result of allegations of child abuse, such improvements do not detract from the fact that GALs are paid by social services departments. That the government has allocated funds specifically for the administration of panels does not answer the widespread objections to the service being located within social services departments.

In November 1991, Cornwall GALs took the issue of budgetary independence to Judicial Review, following an attempt by the Director of Social Services to impose time limits on the amount of work that could be done by a GAL on a particular case (R. vs. Cornwall County Council, 1992). The President of the Family Division, Sir Stephen Brown, found in favour of the GAL: 'This case underlined the importance of guardians *ad litem* being seen as officers of the court whose professional decisions should not be constrained by the administrative dictate of social services.' (Quoted in Murch and Hooper, 1992.)

The case did, however, illustrate the vulnerability of the GALs, who work very much as individuals and who, in the Cornwall case, had to request personal donations from other guardians across the country in order to cover their costs in bringing the action to Judicial Review.

* Association of Directors of Social Services, Association of County Councils and Association of Metropolitan Authorities.

Resources

GALs have been criticised for making unrealistic recommendations about the plans which should be made for children, suggesting the use of resources which are not available and thereby causing dissatisfaction and disappointment to children and their families. It is not difficult to envisage the basis for such complaints, particularly given the aspirations of the Children Act to ensure the co-operation of all the authorities concerned with children and their families (section 27) and to provide a wide range of services to children in need (section 17).

Should the GAL be recommending an ideal or a realistic course of action for the child? Many other professionals concerned with children may have asked themselves what aspirations for children are reasonable. To take an example, should the GAL recommend that a mother and baby be kept together in a therapeutic and educational environment even though no such facility exists in the area, or should the discussion focus on what might be the next best solution – perhaps the placement of the baby in foster care with liberal contact for the mother? I take the view that it is the responsibility of the GAL to consider all the options, discussing the merits and disadvantages of each, and making it clear why certain options are unlikely to be viable. It is only by making clear statements about the absence of necessary resources that GALs will be able to build up a case to show the negative, and often ultimately costly, effects of lack of provisions.

A further argument about resources concerns the diversion of finances and skilled personnel away from hard-pressed social services departments into the GAL service. It is undeniable that social workers and front-line professionals like teachers and health visitors are under extreme pressure as a result of increasing demands for their services and cut-backs in local and central government funding. GAL panels have undoubtedly taken some experienced workers from actual or potential posts in social work teams. As the National Children's Bureau's submission to the House of Commons Social Services Committee states:

> 'One further cost . . . has been to deprive existing child care teams of senior members. It is important that ways are found to encourage such experienced personnel to return to local authority child care work after a period as guardians, bringing back with them the additional expertise gained from working as a guardian.' (National Children's Bureau, 1988.)

However, the issues involved in child abuse cases which come before the courts are extremely serious, and the GAL system does ensure that each case is looked at by an experienced social worker with specialist expertise, whose sole perspective is the welfare of the child. It is clearly important that the expertise of the GAL service is fed back into the work of social services departments in a constructive way. It may also be the case that a substantial number of freelance GALs have been attracted to the work specifically because it can be done flexibly and accommodated with other responsibilities, professional or personal. The SSI report (1990) made this point:

> 'The growth in the number of freelance members has been marked. They were a previously untapped source of scarce, skilled labour, and have provided a flexible workforce useful in meeting the uneven demand for the service.' (SSI, 1990.)

Financial constraints

There is likely to be continuing tension between GALs and local authority social workers in the area of finance. To social workers, it can appear that the GAL has no financial constraints and can do work which the key social worker cannot do, either because of lack of time or because a directive from management forbids it. GALs do have a great deal of personal freedom to decide how much work to do on the child's behalf, and this freedom has received legal sanction in the Cornwall judgement mentioned earlier.

However, both social workers and GALs are committed to providing optimum services for children and their families at a time of reduced public finances, and there is a responsibility on panel managers to ensure that the resources of their members are used economically. GALs are gaining confidence in limiting their work, underlining good local authority practice where it is observed, restricting their work where a case is overwhelmingly made out and reserving major pieces of intervention for those cases where the issues are complex or very finely balanced, or where there appear to be major flaws in the local authority's or parents' cases.

It is incumbent upon the GAL to seek the views of all those who may have a contribution to make relevant to the child's future, and frequently the GAL is able to talk to important people whose views have not previously been heard. A class teacher at the child's school (or a playgroup or nursery worker for a younger child) may have a very particular account to give of the child's activities, behaviour or friendships. These workers may not have had a chance to attend a case conference. Equally, a relative living at a distance or friends from a previous home area may have important views to contribute but may not have been interviewed by the local authority social worker.

Sometimes workers from other disciplines and relatives and friends of the child are very relieved to be able to speak freely to the GAL, appreciating her position of independence, particularly if they have reservations about the local authority's case, or if they have had previous unfortunate experiences with a social services department. It is therefore essential that the GAL should be at liberty to research any views which may be pertinent to the child's future. Some critics have referred to the unfairness of a 'Rolls Royce' service being offered to some children and not to others, but the emphasis, particularly since the implementation of the 1989 Act, on bringing before the court only those cases which have been impossible to solve in any other way, perhaps indicates that these cases involve the children who deserve the most thorough examination of all the circumstances and options. As the IRCHIN *Training Notes* (1985) state:

> 'Firstly – and most fundamentally – is (the point) summed up by Brenda Hoggett in her book *Parents and Children*, "any child whose future has to be decided in litigation has already been deprived of his best interests." ' (Hoggett, 1985.)

Another financial constraint on a service composed largely of self-employed individuals is the absence of back-up for essential resources needed by the GAL. GALs are responsible for their own office administration, training, library and professional support. There is a sense in which this is right and proper if they are to function as independent professionals, but the inevitable consequences are an unevenness in the resources at the disposal of individual GALs, and a reluctance amongst many to involve themselves in training and organisational events when these have to be paid for and when they represent a serious loss of earnings.

Causes of delay

One of the early concerns about the appointment of GALs in care proceedings, as mentioned earlier, was that this would cause a delay in dealing with child care cases coming before the courts. Murch and Bader (1984), in their early survey, report the views of many Justices' Clerks: 'cases chosen for GAL reports now take much longer to complete, both in the preparatory stages, and in the trial itself.' (Murch and Bader, 1984).

This is echoed in the SSI report published 6 years later: 'The demand for the service has increased and GALs and ROs have generally taken longer to complete cases than had been anticipated.' (SSI, 1990.) There is a danger in assuming that all delay is harmful to the child. Clearly, there are some cases where an adjournment of the final hearing for a specific purpose, for example, to allow a piece of intensive work to be undertaken with the parents or to allow a child to build up a link with an absent relative, can be very beneficial to the child.

There is also a view that the potential increase in the number of parties, following the implementation of the Children Act 1989, has of itself added to delays. The GAL has a clear responsibility to locate and interview quickly anyone who may have a right to be appointed as a party, and to advise the court of the benefits or otherwise to the child. Recent case law suggests that party status is unlikely to be given to relatives whose case is very similar to that of another party (see G. vs. Kirklees M.C., 31 July 1992, Booth).

Delays in appointing a GAL to the proceedings continue to be a problem in some parts of the country. The Cleveland inquiry drew attention to the unwarranted delay caused by the need to appoint a GAL (DHSS, 1988), and the more recent SSI report (1990) concedes that there is still cause for concern:

> 'Although there was some evidence of improvement in the time taken between request and appointment of GALs and ROs, long delays were still common. Undoubtedly this has been detrimental to the interests of many children because they have had to wait too long for major decisions about their lives to be made.' (SSI, 1990.)

There are some indications that delays in appointment of GALs occur more frequently in those panels which rely heavily on GALs who are social workers for a neighbouring authority. Where panels employ a majority of freelance guardians, or those who work exclusively as GALs, delays are not apparent and an appointment can usually be made in time for the GAL to be present at the first interim hearing of the case, or at an emergency protection order hearing. Many panels now operate a duty system to ensure that even hearings held at very short notice can benefit from a GAL's attendance.

The trend towards long, drawn out hearings is a concern, but it is perhaps a consequence of a desire to hear the maximum amount of evidence in the most complex and bitterly contested cases. Justices' Clerks who complained that, 'sometimes more information merely serves to confuse the issue' (Coyle, 1987) would surely not suggest that information should be withheld in child abuse cases merely to expedite the outcome. There is a responsibility for the GAL to make a clear summary of the issues and to indicate which particular matters are central and disputed. If these are clearly set out at a directions hearing, and a proper timetable for the filing of reports is made and adhered to, delays should be kept to a minimum. However, the GAL is, above all, the child's representative and should sanction or request delay where this is essential to ensure that the child's needs are met. As the *Manual of Practice Guidance for Guardians Ad Litem and Reporting Officers* states:

> 'The purpose of their liaison and communication with the court is not to ease the passage of the case through the courts as an end in itself, but to secure the welfare of the child by so doing.' (DOH, 1992*a*.)

Implications for Practice

Understanding and interpreting the child's wishes and feelings

Communicating effectively with children and interpreting their wishes and feelings is perhaps the central task of the GAL. It is far from being easy, given the time limits of the GAL's role and the number of people with whom the child may already have had to communicate prior to the guardian's arrival. As Masson and Shaw (1986) have commented:

> 'The notion (central to the function of the guardian *ad litem*) of an independent person coming in to take a fresh look at a child's situation runs into difficulties in the face of the reluctance of most children to confide readily in unfamiliar adults.' (Masson and Shaw, 1986.)

Nevertheless, the GAL has a unique opportunity to spend time with the child playing, talking and observing, in order to put forward as comprehensive a view as possible of his or her wishes and feelings. Most GALs have developed a wide repertoire of games, stories and toys to engage younger children, and a variety of techniques to explore the feelings and views of older children. Some children, although young, can offer a sophisticated account of their history and family members as well as clear wishes of their own, whilst others can do little more than indicate where their feelings are very raw, or where they are strongly attracted to a particular person.

Often children's behaviour is a more powerful indicator of their feelings than what they actually say. For example, a child may insist that he or she definitely wishes to return home, but on being told that this is not thought by the court to be in his or her best interests, may respond with relaxed and settled behaviour in his or her foster home and at school.

Some commentaries on the Children Act 1989 suggest that it puts undue emphasis on the child's wishes and feelings, at the expense of a proper consideration of the child's best interests. This is illustrated by a recently reported private law case in which a 12-year-old child who, having spent her whole life with her mother, was made the subject of a residence order in favour of her father after a brief court hearing during which she had expressed a preference to live with her father. An unidentified psychiatrist commented that:

> 'The Act completely misunderstands child psychology. In a case like this, the child's comments should obviously be taken very, very seriously. But, that's not the same as acting upon them without proper evaluation.' (Phillips, 1993.)

In the even more complex arena of child abuse, it seems to be crucially important that the GAL, whilst listening carefully and sympathetically to the child's views, does not put more responsibility on the child than is appropriate.

Legislation allows for the child to put his or her own views directly to the solicitor appointed, and for the solicitor to take instructions separately from the child if those instructions differ from the GAL's. To take instructions from the child alone, the solicitor must decide on the child's capacity so to do. The *Guide for Guardians* Ad Litem (DHSS, 1984) in the juvenile court sets out the position clearly.

'Court rules provide that the GAL gives instructions to the solicitor except where the solicitor considers, having taken into account the views of the guardian, that the child wishes to give instructions which conflict with those of the guardian and is able, having regard to his age and understanding, to give instructions on his own behalf. In these circumstances the solicitor has a clear duty to act on instructions from the child.' (DHSS, 1984.)

This is, in my experience, a rare occurrence, but even in these circumstances there is provision for the court to hear both about the child's wishes and feelings and an independent view as to his or her best interests.

Consulting widely on the child's best interests

As has been stated earlier, it is difficult to talk in terms of the child's best interests when his or her future has to be decided by a court. One is generally looking at the least detrimental alternative among possibilities which are much less than ideal. The early DHSS guidance to GALs, which reflects the wording of the Court Rules to Magistrates 1970, stated that, 'The guardian *ad litem*'s first and paramount consideration must be the need to safeguard the child's best interests *until he achieves adulthood*.' (DHSS, 1984; italics added.)

This was a high, perhaps impossible, expectation and the wording has not been included in subsequent legislation, although the *Code of Ethics* produced by NAGALRO (National Association of Guardians *ad litem* and Reporting Officers) has a similar aspiration (1991). There are issues on which it is very difficult to determine the best long-term interests of the child. Disputes over contact for a child who is in the care of the local authority can be particularly difficult. It can be argued with equal force both that an abused child is distressed and unsettled by contact with the abusing parents, and that it is in the child's long-term interests to retain contact with his or her natural family. In such finely balanced decisions, it seems important to have a reasoned view expressed by an independent person who will be biased neither towards the understandable aspirations of the parents, nor towards the equally understandable views of substitute carers, but who is seeking to determine the best interests of the child.

Judith Timms of IRCHIN, sums up well the task of the GAL in reconciling different views as to the best interests of the child:

'Panel members can be presented with numerous different interpretations of the child's best interests, as viewed by the local authority, the social worker, the solicitor, other involved professionals, the natural family, the foster parents, and – most importantly – the child. It is in attempting to balance these differential interpretations that panel members will be confronted with the most onerous aspects of their role, while bearing in mind that "best" interests can quickly become "vested" interests in an adversarial situation.' (Timms, 1985.)

Evaluating conflicting evidence

Following on from the last issue, the GAL, in completing the investigation may have to reconcile conflicting evidence from equally well-qualified professionals, or from apparently equally convinced private parties. GALs will inevitably have to take into account their own observations and attempt to test their hypotheses. Masson and Shaw (1986) offer an interesting comment on this issue:

> 'Perhaps the most marked difference of approach we noted is between those guardians who tend to take the "facts" of the case as given, and those who adopt a more creative approach, testing and to some extent re-working the material to see if there is scope for changing the facts. For example, is a child's opposition to parental contact a fact to be respected or one to be explained and possibly modified? Is lapsed parental contact to be taken as given or should the guardian attempt to discover the reason for this lapse or perhaps propose a contract approach to restoring contact.' (Masson and Shaw, 1986.)

I would suggest that, faced with conflicting evidence on important issues, GALs have no choice but to make their own clear observations known, if necessary setting up situations in which hypotheses can be tested.

It is clear that the GAL's case will be very influential in court, particularly when other professional views are polarised. It is an important part of the role of the GAL to indicate the wide range of opinion there may be in relation to a particular case, before making clear the grounds for his or her own opinion. Other parties may omit or gloss over pieces of evidence which do not fit comfortably with their case, but the GAL has an obligation to put the whole picture before the court.

Promoting good practice

The preceding paragraphs make clear that the GAL needs to be particularly well-informed in the face of conflicting evidence and opposed views on the child's best interests. Sometimes a particular case will require an enormous amount of research, and in other cases knowledge of professional viewpoints and an ability to evaluate the merits of each will be required. The GAL has an advantage in having a constant workload of very different cases, and he or she is likely to have had considerably more concentrated exposure than the social worker. This is particularly true of problems and syndromes which are on the increase or which are newly recognised – for example, drug addiction, AIDS, Munchhausen's syndrome by proxy and sexual abuse.

There is a responsibility on GALs to seek to promote good practice in the care of children, by disseminating research findings, questioning poor practice and validating examples of good practice. The SSI report *In the Interests of Children* (1990) states that the GALs support the local authority's case in 84% of cases. This does not take account, however, of those instances where the GAL's involvement may cause the local authority to modify their application or their plans, or to withdraw unfounded applications completely. Research is awaited on the influence of GALs on local authority practice from the point of view of both parties.

It must be said that the GAL's viewpoint is restricted to a brief period of time, and the longer time perspective of the social worker and others should never be underrated. However, a re-evaluation of a well-known situation by an independent person can sometimes identify a new way forward which merits consideration.

Summary and Conclusions

Situations of child abuse which are brought to a court for consideration will involve the appointment of a GAL, an independent person who is almost always an experienced social worker. The GAL appointed will have the task of representing to the court the child's wishes and feelings, and recommending a course of action which will be most likely to promote the child's best interests. In order to fulfil this task, the GAL will need to get to know the child as well as possible in a defined period of time and conduct a thorough investigation of all the circumstances of the case, consulting widely and using his or her experience and knowledge to evaluate conflicting opinion and research evidence.

Court proceedings, when a family's problems and relationships are exposed to public scrutiny, can be traumatic and distressing, and it is an important responsibility of the GAL to ensure that the case is properly and expeditiously carried forward, and that the child's welfare is paramount. It is to be hoped that the involvement of exclusively child-centred workers will lead eventually to improvements in the legal system which will reflect the needs of children as well as adults and which will ensure that children who have been abused in their own families are not further abused by the court process.

Annotated Recommendations for Further Reading

Adcock, M. & White, R. (ed.) (1985). *Good Enough Parenting*. (British Agencies for Adoption and Fostering).
This book contains useful chapters on the assessment of parenting (Margaret Adcock) and an invaluable discussion on 'good enough', borderline and 'bad enough' parenting (Christine Cooper).

Adcock, M. White, R. & Hollows, A. (1991). *Significant Harm: Its Management and Outcome*. Croydon: Significant Publications.
This collection of papers focuses on assessment of harm against the background of the 1989 Children Act. The contribution of David P.H. Jones on the effectiveness of intervention is particularly helpful to GALs in deciding whether rehabilitation of an abused child to his or her family is likely to be viable, and there is also a useful chapter by Annie Lau on cultural and ethnic perspectives.

Aldgate, J. & Simmonds, J. (ed.) (1988). *Direct Work with Children*. London: B.T. Batsford Ltd.
Although this collection of papers is aimed primarily at social workers, its themes of listening to children and helping them to make sense of their past experiences, as well as planning for the future, are relevant to the work of GALs. Case examples are taken from the work of students on the Advanced Diploma in Social Work with Children

and Families at Goldsmiths' College, and, in that the work of the students was strictly time-limited, it offers useful suggestions for the intervention of GALs.

Department of Health and Social Security (1985). *Social Work Decisions in Childcare*. London: HMSO.
A useful summary of research relevant to child care decision-making, based on nine research reports. (See DHSS, 1991, for an update of this report.)

Department of Health and Social Security (1991). *Patterns and Outcomes in Child Placement*. London: HMSO.
This is an update of the DHSS (1985) report on similar focuses and messages from research, but against the background of the Children Act 1989.

King, P. & Young, I. (1992). *The Child as Client*. Bristol: Family Law.
This book was written specifically for solicitors who represent children, but it covers the principles which must govern the work of a GAL, and it deals in considerable detail with the partnership between the GAL and the solicitor. The book discusses the practical steps which are necessary in order to ensure that the child's case is properly put, and it also covers ethical issues and problems of communication and assessment.

References

Coyle, C. (1987). *The Practitioner's View of the Role and Tasks of Guardians* Ad Litem *and Reporting Officers*. London: Barnardo's Research and Development Section.
Department of Health (1992a). *Manual of Practice Guidance for Guardians* Ad Litem *and Reporting Officers*. London: HMSO.
Department of Health (1992b). *Children Act Report*. London: HMSO.
Department of Health and Social Security (1984). *Guide for Guardians* Ad Litem *in the Juvenile Court*. London: HMSO.
Department of Health and Social Security (1974). *Report of the Committee of Inquiry into the Care and Supervision Provided in Relation to Maria Colwell*. London: HMSO.
Department of Health and Social Security (1988). *Report of the Inquiry into Child Abuse in Cleveland 1987*. London: HMSO.
Hoggett, B. (1987) *Parents and Children (3rd Edn)* London: Sweet and Maxwell.
Independent Representation for Children in Need (1985). *Representing Children*.
Independent Representation for Children in Need (1985). *Training Notes for Guardians* Ad Litem *and Reporting Officers*. Heswall.
Masson, J. & Shaw, M. (1986). *Guardians* Ad Litem *in Care Cases*. University of Leicester: Centre for Law and Social Work Research.
Murch, M. & Bader, K. (1984). *Separate Representation for Parents and Children: An Examination of the Initial Phase*. University of Bristol Family Law Research Unit.
Murch, M. & Hooper, D. (1992). *The Family Justice System*. Bristol: Family Law.
NAGALRO (1991). *Code of Ethics, Code of Practice for Guardians* Ad Litem *and Reporting Officers; Statement of Policy in Regard to Equal Opportunities*. NAGALRO.
National Children's Bureau (1988). *Review of Progress on Children in Care*. Submission to House of Commons Social Services Committee.
Phillips, M. (1993). *Ninety Minutes to Lose a Daughter, The Guardian*, 13 February.
Social Services Inspectorate (1990). *In the Interests of Children, an Inspection of the*

Guardian Ad Litem *and Reporting Officer Service*. Department of Health. London: HMSO.

Socio-Legal Centre for Family Studies, University of Bristol (1993). *Avoidable Delay in Care Proceedings*. Conference report. Department of Health.

Timms, J. (1985). The task of the guardian *ad litem*. In *Training Notes for Guardians* Ad Litem *and Reporting Officers*. IRCHIN.

16

Child Protection and the Criminal Justice System

John Williams

Introduction

This chapter considers the plight of children as witnesses in the criminal justice system. It does not discuss children as accused persons in criminal proceedings, but rather those who are called upon to give evidence either as victim witnesses or bystander witnesses in child abuse cases. Many areas of the civil law process have addressed the issues surrounding the appearance of children as witnesses. Although falling far short of perfection, child care proceedings endeavour to recognise the vulnerability of children and to make appropriate allowances. Until recently, however, very little had been done to make the criminal courts less threatening to children giving evidence, and the interest shown in this area indicates the concern of professionals, parents and children regarding the potential for further abusing children by exposing them to a system which fails to recognise their special status. The chapter considers the policy issues behind the law and explains the implications for the various professionals and individuals who have contact with child witnesses in the criminal courts.

Review of Literature and Research

The impact of the criminal justice process on child victims of crime is a burgeoning area of research. Although initial interest was merely an offshoot of the increase in awareness of the plight of victims in general, it has now developed into a discrete area of research. The work of Hardin on the potential for the use of a guardian *ad litem* (GAL) in America provided an impetus for research in this country (Hardin, 1987; see also Spencer, 1990). The study of child victims conducted by Morgan and Zedner (1992) provides a basis for exploring ways of enhancing the plight of child victims, revealing the shortcomings of the present ad hoc response to the needs of child victims. Similarly, the provisional findings of Plotnikoff and Woolfson highlight the disturbing fact that even after the reforms outlined below, there is still delay in bringing cases to court. It therefore appears that the reforms have not met the objectives of the legislation (Institute of Judicial Administration, 1993 and Plotnikoff et al., 1995).

Plotnikoff (1989) has also developed a package for use by those working with child witnesses, whilst Morgan and Williams (1992) have made a number of suggestions as to how procedures could be improved. They point out that the reforms should not be seen as a panacea – children may still suffer avoidable trauma even with the changes accomplished by the Criminal Justice Act 1991 (Morgan and Williams, 1992, 1993). Importantly, research findings dispel the myth that children are unreliable witnesses and compulsive liars, or are unable to distinguish fact from fantasy (Goodman and Helgeson, 1985; Davies et al., 1986; Jones, 1987). This has done much to remove the prejudice against child witnesses.

Such studies are only the beginning of what must be an ongoing review of child witnesses in the criminal justice process. The National Society for the Prevention of Cruelty to Children (NSPCC), as part of its Justice for Children Campaign, stress the need to review how the system meets (or fails to meet) the needs of children. Although the reforms are welcomed, research indicates that they are the beginning rather than the end of the process.

Analysis of Policy Issues

When considering the approach of the law to child witnesses in criminal proceedings, a number of policy issues are encountered. The subject is a focal point for a study of the interface between the civil and criminal processes so far as they relate to children. Within the civil system, children benefit from provisions designed to minimise harm, whereas under the criminal justice system those same children may be exposed to the full rigours of an adult-based adversarial process. At this interface, a number of apparently irreconcilable conflicts present themselves which can lead to the argument that nothing can be done.

Such defeatism ignores the progress made in joint investigation of child abuse by the police and social services. Morgan and Zedner (1992) found in their study that a number of difficulties have arisen, mainly because of the different philosophies of the two agencies. However, despite their different cultures and statutory frameworks the two agencies have succeeded in developing a more integrated approach to interviewing children. The success of joint investigation is illustrated by the fact that it has been developed in the majority of police forces in England and Wales (Conroy et al., 1990). It should not, therefore, be impossible to create a workable *rapprochement* between the civil and criminal processes. It is essential that the differences between the two systems are recognised and not ignored. It is also necessary to ensure that children are prepared for these differences.

One important area of conflict between the two systems is the different objectives which each seeks to achieve. In general terms, the criminal justice system seeks to determine guilt or innocence. It also provides safeguards for the accused by, for example, placing the burden of proof on the prosecution, and by the laws of evidence. Civil law child protection proceedings are designed to safeguard and promote the welfare of children (see s.1, Children Act 1989). These different objectives are illustrated by the different standards of proof required by each system. Under criminal law, the standard of proof is that of beyond all reasonable doubt; in civil proceedings, it is on a balance of probabilities. However, it is interesting to observe that in certain types of care proceedings the civil standard of proof is more variable than is often assumed. Lyon and de Cruz (1993, pages 212–219) identify a trend in recent case law to move either side of this traditional formulation of the standard of proof depending upon a number of different factors.

Perhaps the principal difference between the two systems is the weight which each gives to the welfare of children. The application of the welfare principle in care and related proceedings is dealt with elsewhere (see Lyon, Section II, Chapter 8). For present purposes, a brief summary will suffice. The Children Act 1989 imposes a duty on the courts to regard the welfare of the child as the paramount consideration (see s.1). The 1989 Act also lays down a welfare checklist which courts must refer to in care and related proceedings. This list requires the court to give appropriate consideration to, amongst other matters, the wishes and feelings of children, their physical, educational and emotional needs, and the likely effect that any change of circumstances may have on them (see s.1 (3)).

The Act also enhances the role of GALs, who have a general duty to act as an independent voice to safeguard and promote the welfare of children. In the advice given to GALs, the Department of Health (DOH) envisages their appointment early on in the proceedings and emphasises their 'full and active role in advising courts on issues of case management', along with a 'proactive role with regard to the conduct of proceedings, including timetabling and offering advice to the court on the range of orders available.' (DOH, 1991a, para. 2.2.) Other attributes of care proceedings found in the 1989 Act are the presumption of no delay, the drawing up of timetables which must be adhered to, and the ability to hear cases at the most appropriate level in the judicial hierarchy. No such protection exists for the child witness in the criminal process. Hardin (1987) and Morgan and Williams (1992, 1993) argue that greater provision should be made for child witnesses in the criminal process, and they advocate the use of a support person to perform a role similar to that of the GAL.

The Pigot report (1989) made a number of important recommendations for the improvement of the plight of child witnesses, and many, but by no means all, of the recommendations have been introduced by the Criminal Justice Act 1991. Guidance on the way forward was also provided by the Butler-Sloss report on the events in Cleveland (Butler-Sloss, 1988).

Implications for Practice

Pre-trial

There is little indication that children are properly prepared for giving evidence. Any assistance given is invariably of an ad hoc nature and will vary from case to case. Flin (1990) points out that, 'The question of children's stress during the pre-trial period is extremely significant because prosecutors may decide whether to proceed with a case on the basis of the child's emotional fitness to testify.' (Flin, 1990.) Preparing children cannot involve coaching as it may well destroy the value of any evidence. Preparation should, however, involve informing children, in an appropriate manner, what is happening. Information such as that contained in *The Child Witness* (Plotnikoff, 1989) should be made available to adults who have the responsibility for guiding child witnesses through the system. Similarly, children may find publications such as *Susie and the Wise Hedgehog* (Bray, 1989), *Going to Court* (Crown Office and Procurator Fiscal, 1989) and *The Child Witness Pack* (Home Office, 1993) useful in seeking to find out about what is going to happen when giving evidence. A visit to the court may be of value, as will liaising with the court officer as to the likely time at which a child witness will be called. Morgan and Williams reflect that,

> 'At present preparation and support for child witnesses is carried out on an *ad hoc* basis in England and Wales. Advice and practice vary considerably around the country. Although the provision of support both before and during the trial has been advocated, no one inside or outside the criminal justice system has a clear responsibility to provide information about the court process to child victims and their families; to liaise with others about the child's needs; to assist the child required to give evidence (for example, by arranging an advance visit to the court or by reading the child's statement); to support the child in court, or to explain the court's verdict.'

Morgan and Zedner's research (1992) shows that support, where offered, is often marred by lack of continuity or by the inexperience of those providing it. To a large extent, the responsibility for pre-trial support for child witnesses rests with professionals, such as social workers, since no agency within the criminal justice system will undertake responsibility. Child witnesses will be children in need as defined by s17 (10) of the Children Act 1989, and as such will be entitled to support.

The welfare of the child

The welfare principle as found in the Children Act 1989 does not apply within the criminal justice system. However, s.44 of the Children and Young Persons Act 1933 requires the criminal courts to 'have regard' to the welfare of any children 'brought before it', which arguably includes those children brought before it as witnesses. However, in applying this provision, the criminal courts will be conscious of their duty to protect the interests of the accused and to ensure that 'justice' is done. Nevertheless, the Court of Appeal in R. v X., Y. and Z. ([1990] 91 Cr. App. Rep. 36) emphasised that judges must ensure that the system operates fairly, 'not only to the defendants but also to the prosecution and also to the witness.' This may involve making special concessions to the fact that the witness is a child.

There are examples of judges being sensitive to the special needs of child witnesses. Indeed, the Court of Appeal in R. v X., Y. and Z. endorsed, with some reservations, the presence of a support person in court. Lord Lane CJ recognised the possibility of social workers sitting alongside child witnesses 'to comfort them when necessary'. He did, however, point out that this course of conduct has to be undertaken with considerable care, and that judges must ensure that no encouragement is given to child witnesses to tell anything other than the truth. Other things which judges might usefully do include checking that the child is not hungry or tired, and regularly consulting a social worker as to the child's welfare. In doing this, judges are not enhancing the credibility of the evidence, but rather they are improving the prospect of children giving evidence and minimising the harm which children will inevitably suffer from going into the witness box.

The problem is that not all judges recognise the special needs of child witnesses. Many will misinterpret enabling them to present their testimony with minimum distress as unfairly adding to the weight and value of their evidence. Such attitudes are an obstacle to the evolution of appropriate conditions for child witnesses in the criminal process and partly explain why statutory intervention was and, it is submitted, still is required. Justice must surely require that the best available evidence is presented to the court. To place child witnesses, who in cases of child abuse are probably the most crucial witnesses, in a position which is disadvantageous solely because of their tender years is tantamount to denying them the protection of the criminal law.

A number of practical difficulties arise when children are required to attend courts to give evidence. Courts are not designed with the welfare of children in mind. They are invariably unfriendly and crowded, and they lack the basic amenities needed for children and their carers. As part of its Justice for Children Campaign, the NSPCC highlights the danger of child witnesses bumping into the alleged abuser in the court buildings. Clearly, this is highly unsatisfactory and underlines the needs for specially equipped safe rooms to be made available for child witnesses. As yet, such facilities are not readily available and it will often be left to the responsible social worker to 'negotiate' with the court official for provision to be made.

Considerable thought must also be given as to who will be responsible for looking after child witnesses when present in the court building before they are called to give evidence. A support person for child witnesses present in court buildings is essential if the trauma of the experience is to be minimised. Parents may be inappropriate because they are often either the accused or are to be called as witnesses. Social workers and other professionals, such as teachers, who have worked on the case are unsuitable if they are going to be called to give evidence.

Although the Lord Chancellor has advocated the use of court ushers as support persons, this fails to recognise the impracticality and undesirability of such a proposal, not least because they have many other duties to perform and lack the necessary training. Again, the provision of support persons for child witnesses depends upon the willingness of professionals and others to make sure that it happens, perhaps through the use of appropriately trained volunteers. Unless somebody takes the initiative, there is no formalised procedure, as there is in care proceedings, for ensuring that appropriate arrangements have been made.

Wards of court

Special provisions apply when seeking to interview children who are wards of court. Before interviewing wards, the leave of the wardship court must be obtained. If granted, the order should give leave for any number of interviews to take place. An *ex parte* application may be desirable if it is considered necessary to interview a child without letting the alleged offender (or some other person) know that police inquiries are being carried out. If practicable, notice should be given to the GAL.

There may, however, be situations where the police have to deal with a complaint immediately, for example, if a ward has been raped and a medical examination to collect forensic evidence must be carried out immediately. In such cases, the investigators can proceed without prior approval of the wardship court, although it should be apprised of the situation at the earliest possible opportunity. Parents, foster parents and other appropriate adults should be notified so that an adult has the opportunity of being present at the interview. If possible, the GAL should be notified and a record of the interview should be supplied to him or her.

Leave of the court is not required for wards to appear as witnesses. However, no evidence or document in the wardship proceedings, or information relating to them, should be disclosed in criminal proceedings without leave of the wardship court. (See Practice direction (ward: witness at trial (No. 2) [1988] 1 WLR 989.) Where the defence wishes to call a ward to give evidence, leave to interview is necessary, and the practice direction procedures should be followed. In Re R (a minor) (wardship: witness in criminal proceedings) ([1991] 2 WLR 912), the Court of Appeal ordered that the ward could be interviewed by the father's solicitor in the presence of a representative of the official solicitor on condition that the father was not present. It was stated that it would be inappropriate for the ward to be interviewed by the defence if he or she was to be a prosecution witness.

Unsworn evidence and competence of children as witnesses

Section 52 of the Criminal Justice Act 1991 inserts s.33A into the Criminal Justice Act 1988 which states that,

1. a child's evidence in criminal proceedings shall be given unsworn;
2. a deposition of a child's unsworn evidence may be taken for the purpose of criminal proceedings as if that evidence had been given on oath;
3. in this section 'child' means a person under 14 years of age.

Thus, children under 14 years will now give evidence unsworn.

The question as to whether a child is competent to give evidence is one that must be addressed early in the investigative process. Prior to the Criminal Justice Act 1991 children under the age of 14 years were presumed to be incompetent witnesses unless the contrary was proved. Before young children could give evidence, courts had to undertake an examination as to whether or not they understood the difference between telling the truth and telling lies. Now, by virtue of s.52 (2) of the Criminal Justice Act 1991, 'the power of a court in any criminal proceedings to determine that a particular person is not competent to give evidence shall apply to persons of tender years as it applies to other persons'.

The courtroom environment

In many courts, little effort is made to place child witnesses at ease. Those trappings which supposedly portray the majesty of law will, to children, render the experience that much more traumatic. Judges and counsel should remove their wigs and gowns, softly spoken children should be allowed to use a microphone, and thought should be given to the seating arrangements in the court. Under s.37 of the Children and Young Persons Act 1933, courts may, in cases concerning decency or morality, direct that the courtroom be cleared of members of the public when children or young people give evidence. *Bona fide* members of the press may not be excluded under this provision.

Committal proceedings

Committal proceedings enable magistrates acting as examining justices to test the evidence against accused persons before the full case is heard by the Crown Court. The prosecution must show that a *prima facie* case has been made out. Although written statements may be used at these proceedings, witnesses may be required by the defence to attend the committal proceedings and give evidence in person and be cross-examined. Section 53 of the Criminal Justice Act 1991 introduces a procedure whereby certain cases involving children may be transferred to the Crown Court without a committal hearing. This procedure applies when a person is charged with an offence to which s.32 (2) of the Criminal Justice Act 1988 applies and the Director of Public Prosecutions (DPP) is of the opinion that,

1. the evidence of the offence would be sufficient for the person charged to be committed for trial;
2. a child who is alleged
   i. to be the victim of the offence, or
   ii. to have witnessed the offence,
   will be called as a witness at the trial; and
3. for the purpose of avoiding any prejudice to the welfare of the child, the case should be taken over and proceeded with without delay by the Crown Court.

There is no appeal against, or court review of, the DPP's decision to issue a notice of transfer. However, the defence may apply to a Crown Court judge who may dismiss the charges if it appears that the evidence is not sufficient for a jury to convict (see s.53 and Sched. 6 of the Criminal Justice Act 1991).

The use of screens

The Court of Appeal in R. v Smellie ([1919] 14 Cr. App. Rep. 128) held that where there was a fear of a witness being intimidated, he or she could give evidence out of sight of the accused. The argument against such arrangements was that the accused had the right to face his or her accusers. It is doubtful whether such an absolute right ever existed. The use of screens erected to prevent child witnesses seeing or being seen by the accused was approved by the Court of Appeal in R. v X., Y. and Z., which recognised that measures could be taken to prevent children from being intimidated by the presence of the accused in the court. A request for the use of screens may be made by the police, parents or social workers. The introduction of live television links and pre-recorded video interviews does not mean that screens are no longer an alternative method of giving evidence. Some children may prefer to give evidence using screens rather than using the alternatives.

Live television links

Live television links for child witnesses under the age of 14 years were introduced by the Criminal Justice Act 1988. A number of important amendments to this provision have been made by the Criminal Justice Act 1991. Child witnesses using this facility are seated in a separate room in front of a television monitor and answer questions from counsel who is in the courtroom. The testimony is relayed on a monitor in the courtroom. Child witnesses using the live television link may be accompanied by a person who is acceptable to the court (see Crown Court Rules 1982 and Magistrates' Courts (Children and Young Persons) Rules 1992). Interestingly, this is the only statutory reference to the right of child witnesses to be accompanied by another person when giving evidence.

Initially, this facility was only available in the Crown Court, but it has now been extended to the new youth courts. The facility may also be used in appeals to the criminal division of the Court of Appeal. Leave of the court is required before use can be made of live television link facilities (for the procedure for applying for leave see r.23A of the Crown Court Rules 1980 and r.23 of the Magistrates' Courts (Children and Young Persons) Rules 1992). Where leave is given in a case to be heard before the youth court and suitable facilities are not available at the court-house in which it is able to sit, the court may hear all or part of the case at any place where these are available. This can include a place outside the court's petty sessions area (see s.32 (3A) of the Criminal Justice Act 1988).

Under s.32 of the Criminal Justice Act 1988, a person other than the accused may give evidence through a live television link if:

1. the witness is a child, or is to be cross-examined following the admission under s.32A of the Criminal Justice Act 1988 of a video recording of his or her testimony (see below for s.32A); and
2. the offence is one of those listed in s.32 (2) of the Criminal Justice Act 1988 (See s.32 (1)(a) and (b) of the Criminal Justice Act 1988.)

The offences listed in s.32 (2) of the Criminal Justice Act 1988 are divided into offences of violence and sexual offences. This list is important not only for live television links, but also for other parts of the legislation.

Offences of violence.   These include those which involve an assault on, or injury to, a person and offences under s.1 of the Children and Young Persons Act 1933 (cruelty to persons under the age of 16 years).

Sexual offences.   These include offences under the Sexual Offences Act 1956, the Indecency with Children Act 1960, the Sexual Offences Act 1967, s.54 of the Criminal Law Act 1977, or the Protection of Children Act 1978.

This list also includes attempting or conspiring to commit, or aiding, abetting, counselling, procuring or inciting the commission of any of the above offences. The distinction between violent and sexual offences is important in determining who can use the live video link. The Criminal Justice Act 1991 extended the availability of the link to witnesses under the age of 17 years in certain cases. Where the offence is one of violence, witnesses under the age of 14 years may use the link, but in sexual offences the link may be used by witnesses under the age of 17 years. Slightly different age restrictions apply when the link is used to cross-examine witnesses whose evidence has been given by pre-recorded video interview. These are considered in the next section.

Pre-recorded video interviews

The law.   The most radical development in the treatment of child witnesses was the change in the law which made pre-recorded video interviews with child witnesses admissible as evidence-in-chief – that is, evidence presented by the party who called the witness (see Lane and Walsh, Section II, Chapter 14). This follows the recommendation by Pigot (1989). The Criminal Justice Act 1991 inserted s.32A into the Criminal Justice Act 1988 which states the conditions for the admissibility of pre-recorded interviews. Police and social workers engaged in joint investigation will need to be fully aware of the requirements surrounding the admissibility of video interviews. If they fail to adhere to these, the video may be inadmissible and the case may be abandoned or the child required to give testimony in the traditional way – there is little opportunity to correct errors at some later stage.

If the video is used at Crown Court, it must be produced and proved by the interviewer or any person present at the interview (see Practice direction [1992] 1 WLR 839). Children should have explained to them the purpose of the video recording and be fully informed in a manner appropriate to their age and understanding. In the case of children mature enough to understand, consent should be given, although it need not be written consent. The views of carers and parents should be listened to, but care should be taken to avoid pressure being put on children to refuse to be video interviewed. At this stage, the specimen interview sheet (see Annex H of the *Memorandum of Good Practice*, Home Office and DOH, 1992), or a variation of it, should be handed to the parents or carers. Children should also be given information, and use may be made of some of the children-based publications mentioned above.

Section 32A of the Criminal Justice Act 1988 applies to the following proceedings.

1. Trials on indictment for any offence mentioned in s.32 (2) of the Criminal Justice Act 1988 (see above).
2. Appeals to the criminal division of the Court of Appeal and references under s.17 of the Criminal Appeal Act 1969 in respect of such offences.
3. Proceedings in youth courts for any such offences and appeal to the Crown Court arising out of such proceedings. (See s.32A (1)(a) and (b) of the Criminal Justice Act 1988.)

In these proceedings, a pre-recorded video interview between an adult and a child (who is not the accused) may, if certain conditions are satisfied, be given in evidence. The reference to a 'child' is slightly different from that used for the purposes of the live television link noted above. The distinction between violent and sexual offences applies – in the case of an offence of violence the witness must be under the age of 14 years, or if he or she was under that age when the recording was made, under the age of 15 years. For sexual offences, the witness must be under the age of 17 years, or if he or she was under that age when the recording was made, under the age of 18 years. (See s.32A (7) of the Criminal Justice Act 1988.)

Before pre-recorded interviews can be admissible, the following conditions must be satisfied:

1. The evidence must relate to any matter which is in dispute in the proceedings.
2. The child will be available for cross-examination.
3. Leave of the court has been obtained. (See s.32A (2) of the Criminal Justice Act 1988.)

Condition 1 is self-explanatory. As far as point 2 is concerned, this goes against the proposal in Pigot (1989) to allow pre-recorded cross-examinations to take place which would have avoided the need for the child to attend court. The Government argued that the Pigot proposal would lead to children being exposed to more interviews in order that further questions could be put to the child as new evidence emerged during the trial. A better approach, the Government argued, was to allow for the cross-examination of the child through the live television link referred to above. The position is, therefore, that child witnesses must be present in the court and available for cross-examinations either in open court (with or without screens) or, subject to s.32, through the live television link. If the link is to be used, the extended age limits referred to above apply.

Any party to the proceedings may apply for leave, including the defence. Leave will not be granted if the child witness will not be available for cross-examination. Nor will it be admissible if the court considers that this would be contrary to the interests of justice. It is not clear what is meant by the interests of justice as the Criminal Justice Act 1988 does not define the term. The *Memorandum of Good Practice* (Home Office and DOH, 1992) states that it will be for the court to decide the matter in the light of all the circumstances (page 36). Presumably, it is intended to apply to cases where admission of the video would be unduly prejudicial to the accused.

However, it is always possible to seek the exclusion of parts of the video (see below). Applications for leave must follow the form laid down in Schedule 7 of the Crown Court Rules 1980. They must be accompanied by a copy of the video and include information connected with, amongst other matters, the name and address of the defendant and the offences charged, the name and date of birth of the child, and a statement that the recording complied with r.23C (4) of the Crown Court Rules. The reference to the Crown Court Rules requires a detailed statement of the following:

1. the times at which recordings commenced and finished, including any details of interruptions;
2. the location at which the recording was made and the usual function of the premises;
3. the names, ages and occupations of any person present at any point during the recording;
4. the description of any equipment used (e.g. fixed, mobile, number of microphones, etc.)
5. the location of the master tape and details of when and where copies were made.

These requirements emphasise the importance of a logical and planned approach to interviews with child witnesses. Accurate records of the above information must be kept so that it can be included in an application for leave. Failure to comply with the provisions of the rule to the satisfaction of the court will mean the refusal of the application for leave (s.32A (3)(b) of the Criminal Justice Act 1988).

A completed notice must be sent to the court officer and every other party to the proceedings. Copies of the video must be sent to any party who has not already been served with one. However, in the case of defendants representing themselves, videos must not be sent but must be made available for viewing. The judge has a general discretion whether to determine the application with or without a hearing. However, where one of the parties objects to the application and wishes to be represented a hearing must be held. The judge may grant or refuse to grant leave for the video to be admitted. Alternatively, the judge may, if he or she considers it to be in the interests of justice, exclude parts of the video. The power either to refuse leave or to exclude certain parts of the video emphasises the importance of conducting the interview in the correct manner.

The Memorandum of Good Practice (MOGP). The experience of the use of pre-recorded videos in wardship cases is not a very happy one. A series of cases reported in [1987] 1 FLR highlighted some of the problems involved for the legal process when considering pre-recorded video interviews with children. To overcome these problems, the Home Office in conjunction with the Department of Health published the *Memorandum of Good Practice* (1992), although its status is not that of a code, as was recommended by Pigot. Instead, it is voluntary, 'but should be followed whenever practicable to try to ensure that a video recording will be acceptable in a criminal court' (MOGP, page 1). A key theme in the *Memorandum* is the need to further develop the inter-agency skills acquired following the Butler-Sloss report and the revised version of *Working Together* (DOH, 1991*b*) in the light of the new law outlined above. Practitioners will need to prepare carefully, 'in order to make the best use of the reforms, both in the interests of the child and of justice.' (MOGP, page 2.)

Interviewers must have clear objectives which are consistent with the main purpose of the interview. That main purpose 'is to listen *with an open mind* to what the child has to say, if anything, about the alleged event.' Interviews are not to be referred to as therapeutic interviews, nor as disclosure interviews (MOGP, page 3). The requirement that child witnesses be available for cross-examination may unfortunately delay full therapeutic work until after the trial. Although the *Memorandum* states that counselling and therapy may take place after the interview, it also points out that the defence may wish to know what form it has taken, which unfortunately may be an inhibiting factor. This problem makes the idea of a pre-trial hearing all the more attractive. Practitioners must familiarise themselves with the detail of the *Memorandum* in its entirety. The following account merely highlights some of the main issues.

A pre-recorded video interview is part of the evidence which child witnesses present to the courts, and as such it is subject, so far as is realistically possible, to the laws of evidence. The most common difficulty is how to avoid asking a leading question. These may be perfectly proper in other types of interview, but as evidence before the court they may attract, at best, adverse comment by the judge and at worst be excluded. Although courts may take a relatively sympathetic view of leading questions used when interviewing child witnesses, this is by no means certain and it is essential that their use is minimised or avoided altogether. For detailed guidance on leading questions see Parts 3A and para. 3.51–3.55 3B of the *Memorandum*. Guidance is also offered on the use of previous statements (paras. 3.56–3.60) and references to the character of the accused (para. 3.61–3.63).

Great care has to be taken in choosing the venue for the interviewing of child witnesses. Ideally, purpose-built facilities should be available, and special arrangements must be made for children with disabilities. Suspect interview rooms should not be used. Appropriate amenities should be provided (refreshments, toilets, waiting areas, etc.). In the case of younger children, toys should be available in the waiting area, although the *Memorandum* stresses that genitalled dolls are unsuitable. Although the *Memorandum* and the Criminal Justice Act 1988 do not specify the type and quality of the equipment to be used, practitioners must bear in mind that faulty or inadequate equipment may render the video inadmissible. Technical guidance is to be found in Annex F of the *Memorandum*. Courts will require detailed information about the equipment and the venue. The *Memorandum* suggests that ideally practitioners should strive to achieve the same quality as the live television link used in courts.

Part 2 of the *Memorandum* deals with procedure before the interview and exhorts the interviewers not to conduct an interview without adequate planning, even when the interview has to be conducted at short notice. One important feature of planning is to understand what information is required for the purposes of the alleged offence; Annex D provides guidance on these matters. The *Memorandum* lists a number of developmental factors which the interview team should consider. These should cover assessing the child's development, use of language, social and sexual understanding, concepts of time, ideas about trust, the child's present state of mind, cultural background and any disabilities (see paras. 2.3–2.10).

The length and duration of the interview is important and should, so far as is possible, be planned in advance. Ideally, only one interview should be conducted. However, there may be cases where a further interview is thought to be needed. A supplementary interview should only be carried out if the investigation team is fully satisfied, following consultation with the Crown Prosecution Service, that it is needed. It should be video-recorded. Interviews should proceed at the child's pace and not that of the interviewers.

Where there are breaks, these should be carefully noted as they will have to be accounted for when applying for leave. Reasons for any breaks, and their duration, will need to be recorded, and the court may want to be satisfied that child witnesses are not coached during the recess. Regard must always be had to the normal routine of children (e.g. their normal bedtime – see paras 2.17–2.21). On the question of who should be interviewers, the *Memorandum* suggests it should be a person who has, or is likely to able to establish, rapport with the child, can communicate effectively with him or her, and who has a proper grasp both of the rules of evidence and the elements of criminal offences (see para. 2.23).

Police officers and social workers should be flexible and willing to respond to particular situations. The presence of a second member of the interviewing team during the interview will be helpful, although it is desirable that only one member interviews during any single phase. Guidance is given on when children can be interviewed by somebody who is not part of an interviewing team. (See para. 2.22–2.26.)

Part 3A recommends a four-phase approach to the interview:

Phase	Designation	Purpose
Phase 1	Rapport	To settle the child and relieve anxiety
Phase 2	Free narrative account	To enable the child to give account in own words
Phase 3	Questioning	To find out more about the alleged offence
Phase 4	Closing the interview	To ensure the child has understood the interview and is not distressed

Again, the *Memorandum* provides detailed guidance on the conduct of each of these four phases, and it should be studied closely by practitioners.

One final point must be borne in mind by practitioners. This is that judges have a general power under s.78 of the Police and Criminal Evidence Act 1984 to exclude any evidence if they think it would have an adverse effect on the fairness of the proceedings. They may also, under the common law, exclude evidence where its prejudicial effect outweighs its probative value.

Summary of Key Issues

A number of key issues arise from the above account of the law and practice relating to child witnesses. The lack of any statutory framework for protecting and promoting the welfare of child witnesses prior to, during and following the trial means that initiatives must be taken by individual agencies and practitioners. Those who have responsibility for the welfare of children should be prepared to take the initiative and be proactive in seeking to achieve the best possible arrangements for the child.

Negotiation with court officials and others will be necessary to, for example, ensure that adequate provision is made for the child when attending court. Child witnesses will need to know that support is available for them throughout the process. The judicial system must recognise the important role it has to play. The interests of justice will not be defeated by easing the potential trauma for child witnesses and enabling them to tell their story. Simple things such as removing wigs and gowns may help. A greater understanding on the part of lawyers responsible for questioning child witnesses would also be helpful.

Those responsible for the investigation of the alleged offence will need to be fully informed of the legal and practice issues surrounding interviews with child witnesses. The central theme running through the *Memorandum* is the importance of careful planning and getting it right first time. There is little opportunity for going back and starting again – mistakes may well result in the case not proceeding, or the child having to appear in court. The importance of good inter-agency work is essential. The excellent progress already made in joint investigation must be further developed. Close working relationships with the Crown Prosecution Service must be cultivated. Education and health professionals and the voluntary sector will also have key roles to play. Practice and procedure must be carefully developed.

Conclusion

For children, the prospect of giving evidence in whatever form will potentially be a traumatic and distressing experience. The above procedures provide a means by which that trauma and distress can be minimised. They do not, however, represent a panacea and should never be considered as such. It is imperative to listen to child witnesses. What do they want? Do they want to use live television links or pre-recorded video interviews? Would they prefer to give evidence in open court? How do they feel about giving evidence? What are the specific fears of each individual child? Only by listening to children can we really prepare them for giving evidence by whichever method is decided upon. Hopefully, the above provides a basis for more reforms designed to protect children from being further abused by an adult world.

Further Reading

The literature on child witnesses is growing. Those wishing to reflect on the broader policy issues surrounding child witnesses are advised to read the Pigot report (1989). The information provided by the NSPCC as part of their Justice for Children Campaign examines the working of the law and identified some of its defects. Morgan and Zedner's study (1992) of children as victims identifies many of the problems experienced by child witnesses and provides an excellent account of the shortcomings of the system. Jones (1987), Davies *et al.* (1986) and Goodman *et al.* (1985) are all useful reading when seeking to address the argument that child witnesses are unreliable. The *Memorandum of Good Practice* (Home Office and DOH, 1992) is essential reading for those involved in pre-recorded video interviews. Lyon and de Cruz (1993) provide an excellent overview of the legal and practical issues that arise in working with child witnesses. Professionals should also familiarise themselves with the literature aimed at informing children and their parents of what actually happens in the court (see Bray, 1989; Home Office, 1993).

References

Bray, M. (1989). *Susie and the Wise Hedgehog.*

Butler Sloss (1987) *Report of the Inquiry into Child Abuse in Cleveland, 1987.* London: HMSO.

Conroy, S., Fielding, N.G. & Tunstill, J. (1990). *Investigating Child Sexual Abuse: The Study of a Joint Initiative.*

Crown Office and Procurator Fiscal (1989). *Going to Court.*

Davies, G., Stephenson-Robb & Flin, R. (1986). The reliability of children's testimony. *International Legal Practitioner:* 95.

Department of Health (1991a). *Guardians* ad litem *and Other Related Issues,* vol. 7, *The Children Act 1989 Guidance and Regulations.*

Department of Health (1991b) *Working Together.* London: HMSO

Flin, R. (1990). Child witnesses in criminal courts. *Children and Society 4(3):* 264.

Goodman, G.S. & Helgeson, V.S. (1985). Child sexual assault: children's memory and the law. *University of Miami Law Review 40:* 181.

Hardin, M. (1987). Guardians *ad litem* for child victims in criminal proceeding (1986–87). *Journal of Family Law:* 687.

Home Office (1993). *Child Witness Pack.* London: HMSO

Home Office and Department of Health (1992). *Memorandum of Good Practice on Video-Recorded Interviews with Child Victims in Criminal Proceedings.* London: HMSO.

Institute of Judicial Administration (1993). *Annual Report 1992–93.* University of Birmingham.

Jones, D.P.H. (1987). *The Evidence of a Three-Year-Old Child.* Crim. L.R. 677.

Lyon, C. & de Cruz, P. (1993). *Child Abuse,* 2nd edn. Bristol: Family Law.

Morgan, J. & Williams, J. (1992). Child witnesses and the legal process. *Journal of Social Welfare and Family Law:* 484.

Morgan, J. & Williams, J. (1993). A role for a support person for child witnesses in criminal proceedings. *British Journal of Social Work 23:* 113–121.

Morgan, J. & Zedner, L. (1992). *Child Victims: Crime, Impact and Criminal Justice.* Oxford: Clarendon Press.

Pigot, T. (1989). *Report of the Advisory Group on Video Evidence.* London: Home Office.

Plotnikoff, J. (1989). *The Child Witness.* Childright.

Plotnikoff, J. & Woolfson, R. (1995) *Prosecuting Child Abuse: An Evaluation of the Government's Speedy Progress Policy.* Blackstone Press.

Spencer, J.R. & Flin, R.H. (1993) *The Evidence of Children: The Law and the Psychology.* London.

III

Intervention

The chapters in this third section of the *Handbook* focus, broadly speaking, on those aspects of the child protection process which follow comprehensive assessment and case conference decisions and recommendations: namely, the implementation of the child care plan in out-of-home care for the child, or the provision of a variety of helping services for victims of abuse, whether as children, adolescents or adults, and their families. In this introduction, we shall, before reviewing the content of the section chapters, briefly consider issues concerning policy and practice in the provision of therapeutic services, some of which are raised separately in the four chapters specifically addressing the provision of therapeutic help.

The Children Act 1989 places a duty on local authorities to provide a range of services to safeguard and promote the welfare of children within their area who are in need, or to facilitate the provision of such services by others, in particular by voluntary organisations. Such services include help given at family centres and a range of therapeutic interventions.

As has been pointed out earlier in this *Handbook*, and is reiterated again in this section by Stephanie Petrie and Adrian James, policies and resources concerning child maltreatment have focused to a large extent on that part of the process which involves identification and investigation, and the immediate steps which need to be taken to protect the child. But despite the fact that more children since the Act are remaining in the care of their birth parents or extended families, there is no evidence of any transfer of resources from investigation to the provision of a range of helping services. Indeed, again as Petrie and James point out, there is some evidence of a diminution in such services (Trinder, 1993.)

A further assault on such provision has come about as a consequence of changes in the role of social workers as a result of the Community Care and Nation Health Service Act and the Children Act 1989. In the former, the Government makes an explicit commitment to a flourishing independent sector, with social services authorities as 'enabling' agencies. Although this is less clearly spelt out in the Children Act 1989, here too there is an emphasis on the development of a mixed economy with local authorities using and co-operating in the provision of a range of services. Although it will still be possible for services to be provided from within the statutory agency itself, in practice both Acts are likely to enhance the purchaser/provider split, with the local authority and health service acting as purchaser or facilitator of services and with a commensurate development in the private or not-for-profit sector. The underlying rationale for such changes may be seen to be the need not only for a more systematic and needs-led provision of services, but also greater clarity and hence control concerning the cost of each service. In relation to the provision of therapeutic services, such changes have a number of implications, which are now considered.

Whereas historically social workers have themselves undertaken much of the therapeutic help provided (and indeed, major therapeutic innovations have derived from social work practice), the division under the two Acts into purchasers and providers suggests an increased emphasis on the role of social worker as case manager, involving the dual role of assessor and enabler with the 'ability to make a proper assessment of need and to ensure that a range of services is available to meet that need' (James and Wilson, 1991).

Such a role is of course not new. However, the changed emphasis is likely to be marked by a commensurate lessening of involvement on the part of workers in statutory settings in the undertaking of therapeutic work. Therapeutic help, such as that described in the ensuing chapters, is increasingly likely to be offered by health workers or social workers in settings such as family centres or family service units. This has two important implications. First, the skills involved in undertaking assessments and in drawing up care plans which include therapeutic work need to be clarified. Second, the current haphazard pattern of providing services needs to be recognised and changed. There is very little information concerning the effectiveness of different therapeutic approaches with different problems and at different stages in children's lives, and services within a locality usually seem to have developed piecemeal and are dependent on the individual interests and talents of the individual practitioner. There is a need for research which would both help develop a more systematic framework of provision and guide practitioners in referral decisions. In the absence of this, the material in the chapters in this section will assist the practitioner in developing plans for children.

The first two chapters address issues which relate to all aspects of the child protection process, i.e. issues of partnership and communicating with children: but are seen to have particular relevance to this part of the process. Petrie and James (Chapter 17) explore the nature and meaning of the concept of partnership with parents in the context of its history and other requirements for working in partnership (with children and with other agencies) which are embodied in the Children Act. They suggest that definitions of partnership are elusive, but that there is a consensus that for true partnership to exist there must be an element of power-sharing: partnership is then most difficult to achieve in compulsory intervention. Nonetheless, the small amount of available research suggests that the absence of parents from decision-making is usually detrimental to children. In the context of a section which focuses on services provided under Part III of the Act (i.e. 'less compulsory' forms of intervention) but which includes a focus on out-of-home care, this finding is important, suggesting as it does the principles which should inform all such intervention.

The following chapters concern the provision of help to victims of abuse either as individuals or in the context of families or in groups. The first chapter on individual work with children (Crompton, Chapter 18) considers a broad range of interventions which may be undertaken, exploring the professional principles that need to inform all communications with children, and a variety of means, such as life story books, music, drama and storytelling, to enhance these.

In the following chapter, Virginia Ryan provides a detailed discussion of one particular approach to therapeutic work with children, that of non-directive play therapy. This approach will be familiar to many readers from the work of Axline, who adapted Rogerian client-centred therapy with adults to child therapy. However, its theoretical and practice base, described here, has recently been more rigorously developed. We selected this particular approach for inclusion in the *Handbook* from a range of possible child therapies because it offers a robust and relatively brief method of working with children, particularly in statutory settings.

Katy Cigno's chapter on behavioural work, which follows, explores the different ways in which this approach may be used in work with troubled children and their families. She considers three applications of the approach, namely parent–child interaction, parent training and work with children who have failed to thrive, where research suggests this way of working may be particularly effective.

In Chapter 21, Tilman Furniss and Liza Bingley Miller discuss therapeutic work with abusive families, exploring the distinction between family therapy approaches and family approaches, and highlighting a range of practice issues, such as those relating to the stance of the therapist, work with the parental dyad, the mother–abused child dyad, and, a focus that is all too often forgotten, the needs of the siblings. Although they review the application of family systemic techniques, space clearly does not allow for a detailed discussion of these, and readers not familiar with the practice of systemic work are referred elsewhere for more basic guidance. They also consider the use of family work in conjunction with other methods of intervention. It should be noted that although the application of much of the discussion to working with other forms of abuse is considered, the focus in much of the chapter is on working with sexual abuse. As we suggest in the Introduction to the *Handbook*, this in part reflects the current emphasis in practice: developments particularly in family therapy in the last 5 years have notably been concerned with this form of abuse, doubtless reflecting the particular difficulties afforded by the patterns of secrecy and obsessional behaviour which characterise it. Whether or not this emphasis is because this has been a developing area of practice and will therefore give way in time to other emphasis, or because the difficulties are in fact greater, is as yet, in our view, unclear.

In the fifth chapter on therapeutic work, Anne Bannister and Eileen Gallagher (Chapter 22) describe the use of groups in child protection settings. They review issues in relation to planning and conducting groups for children and adolescents, and they give detailed practice suggestions. In a separate section, they consider particular problems and styles of working appropriate for groups of adults, both for adult perpetrators who may be mandated by the courts and for adult survivors of abuse.

The needs of this last group form the focus of the final chapter concerning approaches to helping, namely that of helping adult survivors of child sexual abuse. It considers individual and group approaches to this, and in particular the important early stages of contact. It is probably unnecessary to justify the inclusion of a chapter on working with adult victims in the *Handbook*, since many child protection workers currently do involve themselves in this as a spin-off of their other work. However, if justification is needed, Liz Hall and Siobhan Lloyd (Chapter 23) point out that an understanding of the potential long-term effects derived from this work can be helpful in working with abused children and can improve our understanding of the nature of child sexual abuse and the ways in which children of different ages cope with the experience of abuse. As with the chapter on family work, the fact that this chapter is concerned solely with problems occasioned by sexual abuse reflects current practice. The long-term effects of other forms of abuse are relatively neglected in research literature and in practice initiatives, and as Hall and Lloyd suggest, it seems likely that the needs of adult victims of such abuse are in many cases still unaddressed.

In the final chapter in the section, that on out-of-home placements, June Thoburn (Chapter 24) provides a detailed review of research findings on the placement of children in residential care, foster care and with adoptive families, emphasising what they can tell us about how practice might be improved. She highlights the importance of assessment and decision-making about placements, and, linking with discussions in the earlier chapters in this section, discusses the provision of other services which are most likely to ensure that the short- and long-term needs of children are met.

References

James A. & Wilson, K. (1991). Marriage, social policy and social work. *Issues in Social Work Practice 10(1, 2):* 92–111.

Trinder, L. (1993). *Reviewing the Reviews: Day Care for Children in Yorkshire and Humber-side.* West Yorkshire: Yorkshire and Humberside Regional Childcare Group.

Partnership with Parents

Stephanie Petrie and Adrian L. James

Introduction

Principle of partnership

Partnership is one of the principles underpinning the Children Act 1989 (for the remainder of this chapter referred to as the Act). Within the Act the concept of partnership is not restricted to partnership with parents, but also extends to partnership with children and between agencies. However, following the implementation of the Act on October 14 1991, the words 'partnership with parents' leapt into the vocabulary of those working with children and their families as though it was a new activity that stood alone without reference to the framework in which it was placed.

The word partnership does not occur in statute and is not defined, although it is frequently referred to in guidance. There is therefore considerable potential for different assumptions to be made about what this might mean in practice, and for these assumptions to remain implicit, unworkable and unchallenged.

Partnership with children, with parents and between agencies

Whilst the Act is certainly not a children's charter, the welfare checklist (s.1 (3)) and the opportunity for a child to be a full party to proceedings (s.10 (8)), to challenge an emergency protection order (s.45 (8)(a)) and to make representations (including complaints) (s.26) can all be seen to represent forms of partnership.

Partnership between agencies, on the other hand, rests on the fact that much of the Act is addressed to the whole of the local authority, not just social services departments, and there are also many specific requirements for agencies and departments to work together. Such duties as are contained in s.19 (day care review), s.27 (co-operation in provision of services for children in need) and s.47 (duty to investigate possible significant harm), amongst others, highlight this.

Partnership with parents, however, has attracted the greatest debate and controversy.

In part this is because the parameters to partnership are even more difficult to identify. The notion of partnership with parents derives from the Act's provisions on parental responsibility (defined in ss.2–3) which remains whether or not a care order has been made, and the local authority's duty to promote the upbringing of children by their families specified in s.17, as well as crucial requirements related to the provision of accommodation (s.20 (7) and (8), s.22 (4) and (5)(c)); promotion of contact (s.34, Sched. 2, Part II, para.15); shorter orders and more rights of challenge. Guidance in official advisory documents does, however, spell out the requirement for partnership with parents more directly. For example, Home Office Circular 65/1991 states that:

> 'The Act rests on the belief that children are generally best looked after within the family *with both parents playing a full part* and with legal proceedings being a last resort to protect a child's welfare.' (Para. 3; italics added.)

Partnership in practice

The nature and meaning of the concept of partnership with parents is not clear, therefore, despite the frequency with which these words are used by practitioners and managers alike. It can only be understood in the context of its history and alongside the other demands for working in partnership contained in the Act.

The aim of this chapter is therefore to outline the policy background to the issue of partnership; to clarify the nature of partnership; and to review evidence about parents' experience of welfare professionals and the impact on children of parental involvement (or lack of it) in decision-making. Finally, the implications of these for practitioners and agencies are considered in the light of the wider partnership framework.

The Policy Background to the Children Act 1989

Pre-war

The place of parents in child welfare decision-making has had a long and varied history. Attempts to both involve parents and exclude them have swung like a pendulum, but with no consistent rhythm. For example, Dr Barnardo's view was that, 'parents are my chief difficulty everywhere; so are relatives generally ... because I take from a very low class' (cited in Holman, 1988). He reflected the nature of welfare provision in the latter half of the 19th and early 20th century, which worked against any form of partnership as the parents of needy children were believed to be a pernicious influence on their offspring.

Since the Second World War, however, there have been several swings of the pendulum away from this perception of parents, and back again, which have been linked to economic conditions and social values rather than changes in family behaviour.

Post-war to the 1970s

The immediate post-war period saw a significant change in attitudes towards parents. The knowledge gained of the effects on children of separation from their parents as a result of wartime evacuation was a key factor, together with a social consensus that a more liberal and humane welfare system was desirable (see Frost and Stein, 1989). Local authorities were required by the Children Act 1948 to 'endeavour to secure that the care of the child is taken over' by a parent or guardian, relative or friend. (Part I, s.1 (3).)

Recognition of the importance of family life to children was subsequently reflected in the development of services designed to prevent children coming into care. The Ingleby report (1960) stressed the value of family work in the prevention of both deprivation and delinquency, and the subsequent Children and Young Persons Act 1963 empowered local authorities, by virtue of s.1, to give assistance to families, including cash, to prevent children coming into care. Two further White Papers *The Child, The Family and the Young Offender* (1965) and *Children in Trouble* (1968) firmly established the link between child welfare and juvenile offending and led to the Children and Young Persons Act 1969.

The 1970s to the 1980s

This consensus in child welfare ideology began to shift in the 1970s as professional and public attitudes changed and conflicting perspectives emerged. Economic problems led to growing disillusionment with theories that concentrated on interpersonal issues and family failure and ignored the impact of structural factors, such as inner city deprivation and unemployment, on child-rearing (see Frost and Stein, 1989).

The Barclay report (1982) re-emphasised many of the recommendations of the Seebohm report (1968) which had not been implemented. The thrust of both of these reports was to bring services nearer to clients and communities. Many social services departments moved towards generic neighbourhood-based teams (see Hadley and McGrath, 1984) and decentralised services. Partnership with parents was seen as better served by advocacy, welfare rights and community work services rather than by individual casework. Services were primarily adult-focused and aimed at keeping children out of care.

Simultaneously, other influences were emerging alongside community welfare approaches that were pushing child protection services in a different direction. The Maria Colwell inquiry (Department of Health and Social Security (DHSS), 1974) had exposed the dangerousness of some families and their ability to evade and manipulate child protection systems. This, together with research including that drawing attention to the numbers of children drifting in care (Rowe and Lambert, 1973), influenced the Children Act 1975 which gave local authorities increased powers to permanently separate parents and children once a child was in care.

Front-line services were therefore focused on keeping families together, but once a child was in the system the pressure was on to achieve 'permanency' as quickly as possible. This was usually interpreted to mean some form of placement in an altern-ative family rather than any form of 'shared care'.

The 1980s to the 1990s

This view gradually came to dominate child care services. The criticism made in the course of the Lucy Gates inquiry in 1982 (London Borough of Bexley and Greenwich and Bexley Health Authority, 1982) reflected an increasingly common concern that:

'The rights of parents appear to take precedence over the rights of children. There is confusion over what the rights of children are. There is currently strong pressure on professional workers to keep children with their parents at almost any cost.' (Department of Health (DOH) 1991, page 5.)

The series of child abuse inquiries of the 1980s were significant in reinforcing this perception by focusing attention and resources on the investigation and identification of child abuse. Child protection and permanency services became increasingly specialised and separated from other services to children and their families. The sheer volume of work resulting from increasing statutory intervention led to a 'child rescue' culture dominating most social services departments, and systems developed that largely excluded parents (see Parton, 1985, 1991). This in turn led to increasing criticism of local authorities for heavy-handed and inappropriate intervention, particularly during subsequent child sexual abuse controversies, most significantly in Cleveland in 1988.

Concentrating attention solely on the abusive experiences of children also meant their other needs were often overlooked. Little attention was paid to issues of race and culture within families and its importance to children throughout this period, not only in child protection practice but even in the inquiry reports themselves (of which there were 19 between 1980 and 1989).

'Despite the fact that seven of the inquiries relate to black and minority ethnic children, issues relating to the recruitment of black staff are barely touched upon, despite contemporaneous encouragement by the Department of Health and others to take positive action.' (DOH, 1991, page 37.)

Yet on the other hand, although there were criticisms of the responses of local authorities and other agencies to parents and families in these situations, concern was also being expressed that local authority powers to intervene to protect children were not strong enough.

'There is a popular feeling, commonly expressed that children must be protected from danger. The simple fact is that under legislation existing in 1986 and 1987 children were not offered protection from danger.' (Doreen Aston inquiry 1988; cited in DOH, 1991, page 4.)

The Children Act 1989 – protection and prevention

As a result of these dual pressures, professional behaviour prior to the Act tended to fall into one of two camps – those in favour of protecting children and those in favour of keeping families together. Although not incompatible or mutually exclusive, they often became polarised, particularly when feelings were running high and both themes were evident in the pressure for legislative change (see Dickenson *et al.*, 1991).

The Children Act 1989 tries to recognise the tension that exists between the right of children to be protected, and the rights of children and their parents to their own family life. Workers and agencies have to balance these conflicting imperatives for each child at risk as part of the partnership with parents. Local authorities have been given increased powers to protect children, through new orders and greater powers attached to orders, but at the same time their actions have been curtailed through strict time limits and more rights of challenge.

The Act therefore offers a framework within which parents have a place:

'Parents should be expected and enabled to retain their responsibilities and remain as closely involved as it is consistent with their child's welfare, even if that child cannot live at home either temporarily or permanently.' (DOH, *The Care of Children* 1989, page 18.)

Parental responsibility

The Act promotes a 'new model of parenthood' (Open University, 1991) through the concept of 'parental responsibility'. This is not a simple concept (see Eekelaar, 1991), however. Parental responsibility itself is only defined as a set of rights and duties, and it is recognised that more than one person (not necessarily the biological parents) can share it; the local authority does not automatically acquire it when 'looking after' children; and it is a lifelong responsibility.

Such a framework draws us away from the fetters of short-term child rescue models to a more mature appreciation of the long-term benefits parents can offer. The benefits to children of early decision-making are distanced from the cost benefits to agencies of early adoption, since under the Act it is much harder for local authorities to sever links between parents and children, or to avoid responsibility for the long-term welfare of children in care. The concept of parental responsibility together with the welfare checklist and definition of 'significant harm' (limited as that may be) give greater clarity to the criteria against which parents are to be measured, and for the first time a local authority, as proposed holder of parental responsibility, may be weighed in the balance *alongside* parents.

Race, culture and religion

The value to a child of parental identity is also enshrined in the requirement to take into account racial origin, cultural and linguistic background and religious persuasion when providing day care (Sched.2, para.11) and when looking after children (s.22). This is a crucially important step not only because anti-discriminatory care is enshrined in law but because difference is positively recognised. This provides a framework for respecting the unique elements of each child's family, and of the individual characteristics which are of significance to all children.

Parental rights

Parents have also acquired very real rights under the Act, both to information and to challenge, during judicial and administrative processes. Rights only become meaningful, however, if they are exercised and this is likely to depend on the development of good advocacy networks for parents and children.

This in turn depends on the ability of child protection agencies to accept and even encourage challenge (in the interests of sound decision-making) without becoming defensive, and on the willingness of other agencies, including the voluntary sector, not to flee from active involvement as soon as child protection issues emerge.

Children in need

Part III of the Act spells out the sort of assistance parents can expect if they are experiencing difficulties bringing up their children. Whilst there are undoubted resource problems in providing these services, identifying them does give a starting point for negotiation and parents are less at the mercy of individual perceptions of what constitutes 'help'. Even acknowledging formally that the service needed is not available can be helpful, particularly if parents wish to test out the obligations due to a 'child in need'.

However, even with this framework there are still many issues that need to be explored when considering partnership with parents in the context of child protection.

The Nature of Partnership

Definitions of partnership

Although the word 'partnership' is now commonly used, little attention has been given to its meaning and whether it is a legitimate description of the relationship between professionals and 'clients'. One way of understanding partnership is to consider it as part of a continuum of power relationships (see Arnstein, 1969).

8. Citizen control	
7. Delegated power	degrees of citizen power
6. Partnership	
5. Placation	
4. Consultation	degrees of tokenism
3. Informing	
2. Therapy	non-participation
1. Manipulation	

This typology suggests that partnership involves a high degree of power-sharing and requires more than helping, informing, consulting and co-operating.

Partnership is an elusive concept, however, because it refers to elements of both the *process* and the *status* of a relationship. For example, Jordan (1988) distinguishes between *co-operation* and *partnership*:

> 'people co-operate because there is some mutual advantage. . . . Partnership, however, implies a good deal more than co-operation. It implies a kind of pooling of resources, and fairly close integration of roles, as in the marital relationship, or in a commercial firm. It implies trust, and a good deal of potential or actual agreement on common goals, and the means of achieving them.' (Jordan, 1988, page 30.)

Jordan goes on to say that although co-operation is necessary for the process of partnership it is not sufficient in itself to assume the status of a relationship. Furthermore the barriers to co-operation (let alone partnership) are many and include lack of trust, imbalance of power and, related to these, different levels of knowledge. Parents are disadvantaged not only by their lack of knowledge – of the law, procedures, etc. – but also by their inability to control what information is gathered and the way it is interpreted during assessment and decision-making.

> 'It is a convenient myth – for doctors and lawyers, as well as for other would be professionals – that knowledge is their source of power. Rather it is the other way round – that the measure of their power is their ability to control what is seen as relevant for their work . . . this power is licensed by the state.' (Jordan, 1988, page 32.)

Such ideas were also developed by other commentators, such as Timms (1989), Sainsbury (1989) and Rees (1991). Sainsbury focused on participation, which might be described as another *process* implied by partnership:

> 'it is variously associated with freedom of individual conscience and action, with the extension of choice, with the containment of repressive controls, and with ideals of democracy (however defined).' (Sainsbury, 1989, page 96.)

So although concepts of partnership vary, a universal theme is that for true partnership to take place, some degree of power-sharing must occur.

Partnership and power-sharing in the Children Act 1989

There are two differing notions of partnership underpinning the Act, one based on empowerment (involving de-professionalisation, decentralisation, community politics and anti-oppressive practice), the other based on consumerism (emphasising power of choice, quality assurance through market forces, rights of the individual and minimising state intervention). Even though these ideas of partnership are quite different, they both presuppose the user has or can acquire power.

Since the interests of adults and children do not always coincide, the first model poses the critical question, 'whom are we seeking to empower?' There is also perhaps a danger that this vague aim prevents an honest appreciation of some real contradictions. As Rees (1991) points out, all of the 'rhetoric about empowerment has given the term an aspirin like quality, as though it is a pill for all seasons, to "reverse the process of disempowerment or oppression" '. (Rees, 1991, page 4.)

The rise in consumerism and the growth of service provision through purchaser/provider structures is even more problematic. Who is the consumer? The child, the parents or the purchaser of services? Being a consumer implies a choice of services and the power to decide between them. This is rarely the case for either children or their parents and, in reality, the purchaser of services is increasingly likely to be the local authority.

Partnership and child protection in the Children Act 1989

Not surprisingly, in view of such complexity, there has been no consensus about the appropriate level of parental involvement in the provision of child care services in general and child protection services in particular, even before the Children Act 1989. Wherever else power-sharing in child care decision-making might be possible, however – and we should not ignore the professional cultures that work against this – it is much more difficult during compulsory intervention:

> 'Child protection is the area where family participation leads to most anxiety and where the term partnership is most stretched. When an agency takes a decision to intervene through court proceedings, partnership may seem a meaningless concept. Power is very much concentrated on one side.' (Family Rights Group 1991, page 18.)

In child protection decision-making, therefore, partnership can only be perceived as a *process* that begins with information, involvement and participation before leading, ideally, to the *status* of partnership, which involves a sharing of power. (See Social Services Inspectorate/DOH, *Partnership with Families in Child Protection – Practice Guide*, pre-publication abstracts, 1992.)

Review of Recent Literature and Research

Views of parents

Parents are acutely aware of the nature of the power system with which they are involved and they have expressed dissatisfaction not only with the absence of power-sharing but also with the processes offered to them. As long ago as 1978, Robinson, writing as both a client and an academic, proposed that:

> 'a major step forward can only be achieved if clients are taken into something like full partnership by professionals . . . [it means] accepting that the client, too, has an expertise and a potential, albeit different from the professional's – an expertise and a potential of equal importance.' (Robinson, 1978, pages 60–61.)

The powerlessness of 'the client' and disillusionment with the helping professions were threads running through many aspects of social policy in the 1980s, and evidence of consumer dissatisfaction with social work has been accumulating since the work of Mayer and Timms (1970) and Timms (1973) in the early 1970s. The study by Rees (1978) starkly revealed clients' confusion, uncertainty and even fear they sometimes felt in the context of their contacts with social workers.

Subsequently, Rees and Wallace (1982) reviewed research spanning two decades, drawing attention to the fact that, 'the low expectations and passivity of the most powerless groups has been a strong theme in much literature' (Rees and Wallace, 1982, page 17), and that feelings of suspicion or fear are common amongst people with child care difficulties: 'This is particularly the case amongst clients who associate social work departments with law enforcement agencies and courts. . . No matter how 'caring' a children's department, it always potentially has the power to be coercive.' (Rees and Wallace, 1982, pages 31–32.)

One study (Fisher *et al.*, 1986), however, was able to describe practice which was experienced by family members as helpful. This was a ' "cards on the table" business-like approach, a consistent showing of concern and an exhibited desire for their involvement in the decisions and activities of care.' (DOH: *Social Work Decisions in Child Care*, 1985, page 29).

Nevertheless, problems continued to emerge when professionals and families were thrust together at times of child protection decision-making. This was highlighted particularly in the report of the Cleveland inquiry (Butler-Sloss, 1988), which identified that parents were alienated by: 'The lack of basic understanding of the unique features of each family as a family and unwillingness to see their point of view.' (Cited in DOH, 1991*a*, page 82.)

Confirmation of the continued pervasiveness of such issues comes from a recent study by Prosser (1992). Although there are qualifications which must be made about the methodology of this research, the study identifies many important issues. Parents felt they were perceived as being guilty from day one, and that they were in a 'no win' situation in which, no matter what they said or did, their activities would be miscon-strued. They said they were either not informed when case conferences were to take place and consequently did not attend, or they were only able to attend parts of the conference, usually the beginning and the end. Because conferences needed to be arranged quickly, doctors and teachers who knew the parents well were often unable to attend.

Parents also believed that communication was inadequate, and that they were not informed of procedures, codes of practice, evidence or views presented at conferences, their rights or the alternatives that might be open to them. Criticism encompassed all professionals with medical practitioners, in particular, being identified as being both powerful and 'arrogant' (Prosser, 1992, page 14).

Quality of decision-making when parents are excluded

Apart from considerations of natural justice, there are other reasons why parents should be involved, as there is an unfounded complacency about the quality of decision-making when parents are excluded. In a study of case conference decision-making, Higginson (1990) noted a number of concerns which included:

- distortion and omission of evidence;
- decisions made on the basis of moral judgements;
- professionals contradicting their own evidence and silencing one another.

She concludes:

'Parents were judged to be dangerous according to whether they were thought to have transgressed community values. This led to perceptual distortions and evidence was interpreted to support stereotypic views of parental behaviour. (DOH *Patterns and Outcomes*, 1991*b*, page 72.)

As Rowe points out, these comments applied to all professionals, not just social workers, and are corroborated by the findings of recent Social Services Inspectorate (SSI) reports (ibid.).

Involvement of parents for the benefit of children

Since the purpose of parenthood (and therefore the purpose of partnership with parents) is to promote the welfare of children, the surest indicators of sound decision-making are children themselves, and we know of the benefits to children of continued parental involvement in their lives. Child care practice has been subject to a great deal of scrutiny throughout the 1980s, from the many child abuse inquiries to research about the impact on children's lives of decision-making and the experience of care (see DOH, Social Work Decisions, 1985).

'By the mid 1980s there was cumulative research from both the USA and Great Britain showing that the well-being of children being cared for by social agencies is enhanced if they maintain links with parents and other family members. Unfortunately, other research showed that all too often links were not being maintained.' (DOH, *Patterns and Outcomes*, 1991*b*, page 24.)

Many studies and inquiries reveal the absence of the family, both adult and children, as key players in decision-making. Undoubtedly, children were not heard, and that omission will be dealt with elsewhere, but the lack of adult involvement had three main negative effects:

- all relevant information was not available or was lost over time;
- the strengths of other family members were not exploited;
- realistic plans that met the needs of the child(ren) were difficult to make and carry out.

Partnership with parents post-Children Act 1989

How, then, has the situation changed since the implementation of the Act, if at all? A recent study (Flynn, 1992) concluded that, 'Around one-third of parents were taken by surprise by information at case conferences', indicating that a substantial percentage of practice outside conferences has not changed, despite recommendations that openness should pervade the entire investigation and assessment process and not just during the conference (see DOH, 1991a, page 43).

Thoburn's study of parental attendance at case conferences (Thoburn et al., 1991) also showed that there are few examples of parental involvement near to full partnership, and the majority of parents are given information but are not involved. Flynn (1992) found that significantly fewer professionals from outside social services attended case conferences when parents were present.

Ironically, agencies have devoted considerable time, effort and resources to improving inter-agency communication, focusing in particular on multi-agency conferences, without giving the same attention to communication between families and professionals, despite parental attendance at conferences. One reason is that information gathered from family members is seen as less reliable than that gathered from professionals, perhaps because the former are seen as 'stakeholders'. A corollary of this is that professional information is seen as more objective and accurate, yet professionals are stakeholders too:

> 'Information from clients, family and neighbours might be particularly unreliable as they
> may have reasons for painting rosier pictures than the facts may warrant. But so too, do
> workers' perceptions of the case need checking on the basis of fact rather than opinion.'
> (DOH, 1991a, page 80.)

Sadly, most professional discussion has concentrated on how to maintain the same kinds of meetings with parents present, rather than a radical rethink of how decision-making can be improved with the help of parents. Thoburn et al. (1991), whilst acknowledging there are few situations where true partnership is possible at the beginning of an investigation, urge agencies to consider why parents should attend conferences: 'Some [agencies] think they [parents] are there because it is their right, others because the government has ordered it. But parents are there because they are the experts in their own families.' (CC 15 October 1992.)

Despite this gloomy picture of parents' experience of partnership, statistics at the end of the first year of the Act's operation (DOH, Children Act Report, 1993) suggest 'that the diminishing number of episodes under court orders has been balanced by an increase in "voluntary provision" reflecting increasing co-operation with parents and decreasing recourse to the courts as the Act intended.' (2.36–22.) This confirmed the results of an early study of four local authorities during the first 6 months of the Act's operation, which claimed that one reason for the decline in the use of care orders was successful involvement of parents on a voluntary basis. (*Children Act 1989; Court Orders Study*, 1992.)

However, the Department of Health also expresses concern that there seemed to be a mistaken belief 'that the "no order" principle requires authorities to demonstrate that working in partnership has broken down or been exhausted before an order will be made. This was not the intention of the legislation.' (Lord Chancellor's Department, 1993, 2.20–21). The DOH goes on to point out that compulsory intervention as a first step may sometimes be the appropriate remedy.

These comments suggest a confusion of practice which is worrying. Despite many professional reservations about the concept of partnership in child protection prior to the implementation of the Act, this area of practice shows the most noticeable impact of changing professional behaviour. This may be reflecting the development of partnership, but it could equally reflect a professional inactivity which is abandoning children to their fate, or adaptive professional behaviour that is finding covert rather than overt ways of exercising power. Whatever the reasons for these trends, all professionals and agencies need to monitor and scrutinise decision-making patterns as they emerge to inform the development of policies and practice which truly promote the welfare of children.

Implications for Practice

Models of partnership with parents

We do have some models of good partnership in practice to draw on. There is a growing body of research drawn from respite care schemes for children with a disability, and from work with adoptive parents and non-family carers which gives additional emphasis to the conclusions drawn by Fisher et al. (1986).

Packman (1989) summed up the qualities and approaches parents found helpful. Understanding the family's point of view and honesty about the nature of the power relationship were very important, and workers who offered practical help as well as sympathy and support were particularly valued: 'Above all most parents wish to participate in decisions about their children and to be included as important partners in negotiations.' (DOH, *Patterns and Outcomes*, 1991, page 47.) As Robinson (1978) argued, the best way forward is 'Some notion of a team of co-partners but with the client more centrally placed than at present.' (Robinson, 1978, page 73.)

Identifying partners

Partnerships, as previously mentioned, are not restricted to those with biological parents. Section 8 orders are already being widely used by other family members (Lord Chancellor's Department, 1992), and there is anecdotal evidence that local authorities are encouraging applications for residence orders by relatives rather than initiating public law proceedings (Lord Chancellor's Department, 1993, 2.17, page 19).

Both research and child abuse inquiries have consistently shown the importance to children of family involvement and specifically the benefits of placements with relatives (Rowe et al., 1984). Even children who spend long periods in care eventually live with one family member or at least re-establish contact and receive some practical help from them (Stein and Carey, 1986; Farmer and Parker, 1991). It is essential, therefore, that children's real (as opposed to notional) families are acknowledged and involved.

Partnership is not short-term, although agreements may be

We cannot therefore make assumptions about who will be partners, how many there will be, or even if there will be more than one partnership simultaneously or sequentially. It has been recognised that quality outcomes for children are more appropriately planned as a series of steps, 'a linked sequence of outcomes representing stages towards some more general and long-term goal would certainly fit into the current emphasis in the new Children Act upon planning, monitoring, review and, if necessary, revision' (Parker *et al.*, 1991), and therefore that appropriate agreements must be made at each stage.

Power relationships within families

When identifying partners, it is also important to be alert to power imbalances within the family, particularly in situations involving domestic violence. Concern was expressed prior to the implementation of the Act that the concept of parental responsibility would further weaken the position of women and children in these circumstances. The local authority may need, on occasion, to be actively partisan and form an open and stronger partnership with one parent in order to safeguard the welfare of the child, rather than adopting an even-handed approach. In the Tyra Henry inquiry (London Borough of Lambeth, 1987) the local authority was criticised for failing to assist the mother and grandmother to protect Tyra from her father: 'It would have performed the task which, instead, was invidiously left to Claudette and Beatrice Henry, of warning Andrew Neil off.' (DOH, 1991*a*, page 82.)

Power need not be total

Many professionals have found themselves pondering the wisdom of decisions to remove children from their homes in light of their subsequent care experience, and it is certainly one of the potential benefits of partnership with parents that decision-making for children should move away from an 'all or nothing' approach. More effective partnerships at an earlier stage can ensure family care is 'good enough' to enable the child to stay at home and, whilst it would be wrong to return to an 'all care is worse than family care' outlook, partnership with parents offers real possibilities of compensating for the deficiencies of the 'corporate parent'.

We know that the parenting standards of local authorities are not high. For example, children need vigilant and constant attention to matters of health and education, yet as Wolkind sadly points out, 'it is very easy for a child to go through care with no one knowing whether they are right-handed or left-handed' (Bamford and Wolkind, 1988).

Parents can provide continuity of love and identity, they can be the guardians of history, culture and religion and they can be a watchdog on behalf of their child's welfare. There are many parents and family members who can and want to play a greater part in their child's life, even if they cannot provide full-time care. As Jordan (1988) argues, developing partnerships requires 'negotiations on which power is shared, rather than monopolised by one side' (Jordan, 1988, page 33), and with careful thought it is nearly always possible to ensure that parents have a significant voice in many decisions affecting their children – routines, clothing, hairstyles, education, leisure pursuits and health all require parental decisions. One of the burdensome responsibilities of parenthood is that of making such decisions all the time, and the hardest switch to make is from overload to exclusion – which very quickly closes a child's place within the family.

Encouraging parents to retain as much responsibility as they can may create other problems, however. Carers may feel they are being asked to perpetuate child care practices that are less successful than their own, or to respond to parents for whom they have little respect. Other agencies may be left feeling confused as to who has the main responsibility for the child. Previewing such consequences with those likely to be involved and continuing to review the partnership in practice in an open and clear manner is the only way to ensure quality care for children.

It is to be hoped that the increasing specialisation and separation of children's and adult services does not restrict the possibility of transferable learning. Although the challenge of how to involve children has attracted careful thought from child care workers, most of the discussion and skills investment in partnership with adults has taken place within the developing framework of 'community care'. Much work has already been done on involving adults in decision-making and quality assurance, particularly those with learning disabilities and the frail elderly. Many of the issues of compulsion and limits to choice are similar for these user groups as they are for parents involved in child protection processes and could usefully be developed.

In the long-term, it is clear that when parents and family continue to play a part children do better, and therefore parents and families are a resource no agency can afford to discard.

The need for realistic planning

The main message from Thoburn et al.'s research (1992) is that child protection policies should be aimed at the vast majority of those parents who try (but fail) to care adequately for their children and not just the 'really dangerous ones'. She also points out that long-term planning is needed, and that abused children are likely to need support services, at least episodically, whether they are with their natural families, relatives, or living with other carers. But what should these support services be?

Bebbington and Miles (1989) draw attention to the shocking but perhaps not unexpected conclusion that deprivation was even more closely related with entry into care during the 1980s than in the 1962 study by Packman. Stone's recent study (1990), however, showed that social workers considered that three-fifths of the children of all ages had experienced abuse or neglect at some time (DOH *Patterns and Outcomes*, 1991*b*, pages 6–7), indicating that professionals see the issues as primarily family-centred.

Yet there is emerging evidence to show that children of mixed racial parentage are two and a half times more likely to enter care than white children (ibid.), and young children of mixed racial parentage were also more likely to experience multiple admissions (Rowe *et al.*, 1989).

It is clear, therefore, that many families who are involved in child protection systems are at the mercy of structural pressures. Realistic plans can only be made, therefore, if there is some convergence between the needs parents feel they have and the needs workers perceive. This means not just placing them within a hierarchy of risk factors or stereotypes indicative of possible abuse (Prosser, 1992), but respecting parents' own views of what is required for change, and recognising in particular the real impact of poverty.

In the main, parents experiencing difficulty are asking for services, for help in bringing up their child(ren). After all, just keeping children and their families together at times of extreme stress without some positive intervention is unlikely to achieve anything. Webb (1990) has identified respite services as 'central to the principles of partnership' notwithstanding confusion as to the definition of respite and lack of a conceptual model (DOH, *Patterns and Outcomes*, 1991b, page 48), and our own common sense tells us this is so.

Partnership as an agency issue

Much of what is written about partnership simply reiterates that it is a 'good thing', and it must be remembered that the identification of dangerousness may not be quick or easy. Nevertheless, effective partnerships depend on a multi-agency policy framework which reflects understanding of the full range of factors affecting child-rearing practices in our society, not just pathological ones. Professionals and families must agree on the type of services required and some, at least, must be accessible to families.

There will always be a range of agencies involved which need to agree on a number of issues: their definition of partnership; what constitutes a family; acceptable ways of sharing information; whether to act as advocate on behalf of a family and whether this would imply taking sides; how to deal with aggression and threats to workers; and how to deal with differences of opinion – with families and with colleagues. Parents are acutely conscious they are dealing with a power system, and agencies must also recognise that system and agree operational definitions of partnership that are open and changeable.

Such issues also need to be addressed before the process of decision-making begins. This should be possible, as most key players – e.g. consultants, head teachers, voluntary and private sector providers, etc. – will be known in advance. Failure to be clear will cause confusion, suspicion and hostility and make the transition towards true partnership almost impossible.

Agreements are therefore required at all levels of operation; strategic, middle management and practitioner (see Shaw *et al.*, 1991). For example, at the moment partnership with parents can involve general statements about parental attendance at case conferences at strategic level, with very little agreement on the resource implications at middle management level or agreement about implementation between practitioners.

Deployment of resources and prioritisation is crucial, as child protection is more than investigation and identification. The trend, unfortunately, is to split the early part of child protection decision-making from longer-term planning, and the focus on specialisms and the move towards a purchaser/provider split is likely to reinforce this. Inevitably, children and families are likely to experience several changes of worker during a comparatively short time.

This makes it difficult for agencies to plan together during the 'long childhood', and there is a tendency for plans and emphasis to change with a change of worker. Agreements are made on behalf of agencies, not workers, and if an agency defaults the client must have redress. Promises made must be realistic (and likewise demands of parents), and managers must look at agreements with consumers before withdrawing resources.

Consequently, agencies must acknowledge that the Act was not written just for social workers. Resource constraints make it impossible to develop partnerships with parents and families without recognising the resource implications for other agencies and undertaking strategic planning: 'The report considered it scandalous that Lambeth was unable to provide one of its own dwellings to enable Beatrice Henry to do the council's own job of keeping Tyra well and safe' (DOH, 1991a, page 9).

As a result, we also have to take account of sensitive political implications. We no longer have a social consensus about the level of support we wish to give children and their families, and the public are unlikely to be happy with a situation where 'culpable' parents are given priority for scarce resources. Frequently, however, the benefits to children of home-based services are also cost-effective if costed out throughout a child's life and set against the total costs to society as a whole. The issue is rarely one of pragmatism but of ideology, yet identifying and attempting to secure necessary resources is still too often a matter of negotiation between individual workers.

Strategic planning is proving very difficult, however. Services under Part III of the Act, for example, are clearly going to be part of many child protection agreements where children remain with their families. The Act not only envisages partnership with parents in decision-making relating to their children, but as consumers relating to the services they use. The day care review requires education and social services departments to review and plan, together with service users and providers, the development of day care services for the under eights and specifically to address the provision made by the local authority under s.18 (duty to provide day care for children in need).

Recent research across 11 local authorities in Yorkshire and Humberside revealed that, 'No report included an estimation of children in need in their area' (Trinder, 1993, page 43). By the publication of the first review, it was clear that even the accumulation of basic data was a problem for most authorities, and joint planning of scarce resources was, in the main, a new concept. Definitions of children in need were still being written and, 'There was little speculation as to whether, once the numbers of children in need had been identified, there would be enough places, in the right areas, with the right type of provider, and, crucially, having regard to the different racial groups to which children in need belong' (Sched. 2, Part I (11)).

Families need advocates

An area of potential conflict, therefore, is the right of parents (and of course children) to challenge those in authority. Merely informing people of their rights is not good enough. Actively securing advocacy on their behalf is essential. This may be through relatives, friends, user or advice groups, other agencies willing to perform this function or part of one's own agency. The rules need to be clear. The main consideration is that the advocates' contact with the children places no greater responsibility on them than that of a good citizen, and their part in the child protection decision-making processes can be whole-heartedly focused on the parents.

The parental advocate should be able to arrange good legal advice, support use of the complaints procedure, organise transport, assist with changes to benefit, explain any documents, attend meetings alongside parents and access any necessary translation.

They must feel able to do this whether or not they believe the parents have abused their child(ren) and they must be able to avoid being drawn into any other role by families or other professionals. It is quite unrealistic to expect agency workers with clear statutory power to also discharge the full agency responsibility for laying the foundations of partnership at the beginning of an investigation. This is clearly a corporate issue, and commitment must be demonstrated to open and challengeable processes across all the agencies involved.

Without better partnerships between all sectors and agencies at all levels – strategic, middle-management and practitioner – partnership with parents is unlikely to succeed. The basic questions which therefore must always be asked are: Who are the partners? Is this the right partnership for ensuring that the child's best interests are met? How fully can this partnership be developed? What is the time-scale? What resources are needed and who will provide them?

Summary of the Main Issues

Partnership with parents is not a new concept. However, the Children Act 1989 has major implications for the notion of partnership; partnership with children, with parents and between agencies. Partnership is not mentioned or defined in the Act itself, although it is frequently mentioned in guidance. It is to be inferred, however, through activities outlined in Statute.

In the last 20 years, two main themes have emerged in practice, and increasingly in research. Firstly, the recognition of the importance of families to children, and secondly, the recognition that some families are unsafe and that children need to be protected. The Act tries to balance these imperatives and promote a 'new model of parenthood' through the concept of 'parental responsibility'.

Definitions of partnership are elusive. There is a consensus that for true partnership to exist, there must be some element of power-sharing, and this is most difficult to achieve in compulsory intervention. Research (of which there is little from the perspective of parents, and even less from that of children) does reveal, however, that the absence of parents from decision-making processes is usually detrimental to children. Early evidence post-Children Act indicates there has been a drop in court activity related to child protection, although the reasons for this are not yet clear.

Effective partnerships must reflect the differing religious, racial, cultural and linguistic characteristics of families, the complex nature of family membership and the power relationships within families. The dynamic nature of families indicates that there will have to be a series of agreements over time to meet changing circumstances. Agencies need to agree operational definitions at all levels (strategic, middle management and practitioner) to establish a sound foundation for open, accountable, child-focused decision-making. The principle of partnership underpinning the Act is unlikely, however, to become more than a good idea without an investment by society as a whole in accessible, quality services for children.

Conclusions and Policy Implications

The Children Act 1989 became caught up in the tension between national and local government. The delay in implementing the National Health Service and Community

Care Act 1991 meant that many local authorities expected the Children Act to be similarly delayed, and so they did not prepare adequately. Resource issues had become such a major preoccupation that even in areas of practice where it was not the overriding issue, the possibility of change was hampered by what appeared at times to be an attitude of sabotage.

This has been particularly evident in the area of child protection. Prior to implementation, many managers and practitioners were appalled by the prospect of change, and there were dire predictions of the court system collapsing under the weight of applications, a flood of complaints and appeals, and great numbers of rejected applications as workers desperately tried to protect such children. Such fears were ill-founded. There has been a reduction in court activity, and numbers of children on the Child Protection Register have fallen (Lord Chancellor's Department, 1993, pages 22–24).

Correspondingly, the wider family has acquired more involvement as indicated by the increase in s.8 orders (ibid. page 19). The figures are so dramatic that concern is now being expressed, by the Department of Health amongst others, that 'partnership' has gone too far and children are at risk from a lack of action!

If more children are remaining solely within their parents' control, however, one might expect a planned transfer of resources from interventionist strategies to home-based services. Yet services provided under Part III of the Act also appear to be diminishing (Trinder, 1993, pages 52–54). Additional resources have, however, been drawn into the administration of day care, which is acquiring the same characteristics (i.e. concentration on agency safety and minimal agency risk-taking) that has bedevilled child protection services, very often to the detriment of children. Local authorities are reducing their provision, either through closure or limiting criteria for support. Community groups are finding new regulations difficult to meet, especially with the loss of national funding opportunities although private sector provision is increasing rapidly.

Protecting children is not a specialist activity – it is the duty of every citizen. Preventing and dealing with the consequences of abuse may well require specialists, but the foundations of any partnership must be rooted in social consensus. If we believe that children are solely the responsibility of their parents, who should not expect help if they encounter child-rearing difficulties, then we cannot expect professionals to turn partnership into a meaningful activity on our behalf. For any society to care for its children requires an investment in their nurturing, education, health and leisure, whatever the capability of their parents. Ultimately, it is for us to decide if we will embark on this fundamental partnership with parents for the benefit of all our children.

Acknowledgement

The authors wish to acknowledge their debt to Diana McNeish for ideas and information contained in an unpublished paper, *Parental Participation in Social Work Decision-Making: Impact of the Children Act 1989 on Policy and Practice* (1991).

Annotated Reading

Adcock, M., White, R. & Hollows, A. (1991) *Child Protection Training Pack.* ISBN 0–90–281762–0. London: National Children's Bureau.
Although designed primarily for local authority workers, this is an easy-to-use, multi-method pack focusing on child protection decision-making using a case study. It has very useful exercises on issues of race and culture and voluntary agreements versus a statutory framework.

Department of Health, (1989). *The Care of Children – Principles and Practice in Regulations and Guidance.* ISBN 0–11–321289–5. London: HMSO.
A useful summary of the main principles of the Act drawn together in a series of operational statements.

Department of Health (1991a). *Child Abuse: A Study of Inquiry Reports 1980–1989.* ISBN 0–11–321391–3.
An overview of the lessons learned from the main child abuse inquiries from 1980 to Cleveland. Although specific inquiries are difficult to locate, due to layout, it does draw together key messages for all agencies, including the failure to work constructively with parents and other family members.

Department of Health (1991b). *Patterns and Outcomes in Child Placement.* ISBN 0–11–321357–3. London: HMSO.
A compilation of recent research, including results of studies on the pattern of entry into care, impact of care on the health and educational achievement of children, decision-making in case conferences, and partnership with parents and carers. An excellent and illuminating publication with work sheets attached.

Department of Health (1993). *Children Act Report 1992.* ISBN 0–10–121442–1. London: HMSO.
Preliminary statistics and observations of the working of the Children Act 1989 during the first year of its operation. Direct comparisons with activity before the Act are difficult because of the change in methods of data collection and definitions. Nevertheless, a very important snapshot in time.

Family Rights Group (1991). *Working in Partnership with Children and Families and Communities.* ISBN 0–11–321447–2.
Although this multi-method pack does not concentrate on child protection, and indeed rather evades some of the more difficult issues, there are some useful papers and model agreements to consider. Designed primarily for social workers.

Frost, N. & Stein, M. (1989). *The Politics of Child Welfare: Inequality, Power and Change.* New York: Harvester Wheatsheaf.
An interesting analysis of the concept of childhood from early times to date and society's changing response to children and their needs. Of particular importance when considering our current concept of partnership with parents are the shifts in child welfare policy since the end of the Second World War.

Holman R. (1988). *Putting Families First: Prevention and Childcare.* Basingstoke: Macmillan Education.
For many years Holman has represented the voice of the poor from a community

development perspective. Although this approach has become rather unfashionable during the growth of specialist services in child protection, he gives powerful expression to the reality of many people's lives and their limited choices.

Lord Chancellor's Department (1992). *Children Act Advisory Committee: Annual Report 1991–92.* London: HMSO.
More statistics from the perspective of the courts, with very interesting information on the interface between public and private law and the reduction in court activity.

Macdonald, S. (1991). *All Equal Under The Act? – A Practical Guide to the Children Act 1989 for Social Workers.* ISBN 1–873912–01–3. Race Equality Unit. London: Joint publishers Race Equality Council (REC) and National Institute of Social Work (NISW).
Although also aimed at social workers, this is an extremely useful workbook with exercises and information designed to test out the stereotypes we use when making judgements about children and their families.

Parton, N. (1991). *Governing the Family: Child Care, Child Protection and the State.* London: Macmillan Education.
A must for those who wish to gain insight into the social and political influences that led to the Children Act 1989.

Thoburn, J., Lewis, A. & Shemmings, D. (1992). *Family Involvement in Child Protection Case Conferences.* University of East Anglia: Social Work Development Unit.
The most comprehensive study of parental involvement so far from a well-respected researcher. Highlights a range of operational issues, including lack or inappropriateness of agency policy as well as practice issues.

References

Arnstein, S. (1969). A ladder of citizen participation. *American Institute of Planners Journal 35:* 216–224.

Bamford, F.N. & Wolkind, S.N. (1988). *The Physical and Mental Health of Children in Care.* ERSC: Research Needs.

Barclay report (1982). *Social Workers – Their Role and Tasks.* Report of a working party under the chairmanship of Mr Peter Barclay. London: Bedford Square Press.

Bebbington, A. and Miles, J. (1989). The background of children who enter local authority care. *British Journal of Social Work 19(5).*

Butler-Sloss, Lord Justice E. (1988). *Report of the Inquiry into Child Abuse in Cleveland 1987.* Cmnd. 412. London: HMSO.

The Child, the Family and the Young Offender (1965) Cmnd. 2742, London: HMSO.

Children in Trouble (1968). Cmnd. 3601. London: HMSO.

Department of Health (1989). *The Care of Children: Principles and practice in Regulation and Guidance.* London: HMSO.

Department of Health (1991a). *Child Abuse: A Study of Inquiry Reports 1980–1989).* London: HMSO.

Department of Health (1991b). *Patterns and Outcomes in Child Placement.* London: HMSO.

Department of Health (1993). *Children Act Report 1992* London: HMSO.

Department of Health and Social Security (1974). *Report of the Committee of Inquiry into the Care and Supervision Provided in Relation to Maria Colwell.* London: HMSO.

Department of Health and Social Security (1985) *Social Work Decisions in Child Care: Recent Research Findings and their Implications.* London: HMSO.

Department of Health and Social Security and the Welsh Office (1988). *Working Together: A Guide to Arrangements for Inter-Agency Co-operation for the Protection of Children from Abuse.* London: HMSO.

Dickenson, D., Stainton-Rogers, W., Roche, J. & Jeffrey, C. (1991) *The Children Act 1989: Putting it into Practice.* Milton Keynes: The Open University Press.

Eekelaar, J. (1991). Parental responsibility: state of nature or nature of the state. *Journal of Social Welfare and Family Law 1:* 37–50.

Farmer, E. & Parker, R. (1991). *Trials and Tribulations: Returning Children from Care to Their Families.* London: HMSO.

Fisher, M., Marsh, P., Phillips, D. & Sainsbury, E. (1986). *In and Out of Care: The Experiences of Children, Parents and Social Workers.* London: Batsford.

Flynn, L., (1992). *Parental Participation in Child Protection Conferences: Report of the Avon County Pilot Project.* Bristol: Research Section Avon SSD.

Frost, N. & Stein, M. (1989). *The Politics of Child Welfare: Inequality, Power and Change?* New York: Harvester Wheatsheaf.

Hadley, R. & McGrath, M. (1984). *When Social Services are Local: The Normanton Experience.* London: Allen and Unwin.

Higginson, S. (1990). Distorted evidence. *Community Care:* May *814,* 23–25.

Holman, R. (1988). *Putting Families First: Prevention and Childcare?* London: Macmillan Education.

Ingleby report (1960). *Report of the Committee on Children and Young Persons* Cmnd. 1191. London: HMSO.

Jordan, B. (1988). What price partnership? Costs and benefits. In A. James & D. Scott (eds): *Partnership in Probation Education and Training.* London: Central Council for Education and Training in Social Work (CCETSW).

Jordan, L. (ed) (1989) *The Children Act 1989: An FRG Briefing Pack.* London: Family Rights Group.

London Borough of Lambeth (1987). *Whose Child?* A Report of the Public Inquiry into the Death of Tyra Henry

Lord Chancellor's Department (1993). *Annual Report: Children Act Advisory Committee 1991/92.* London: HMSO.

Mayer, J.E. & Timms, N. (1970). *The Client Speaks.* London: Routledge.

Parker, R., Ward, H., Jackson, S., Aldgate, J. & Wedge, P. (eds) (1991). *Assessing Outcomes in Child Care.* London: HMSO.

Parton, N. (1985). *The Politics of Child Abuse.* London: Macmillan.

Parton, N. (1991). *Governing the Family: Child Care, Child Protection and the State.* London: Macmillan.

Prosser, J. (1992). *Child Abuse Investigations: The Families' Perspective.* Oxford: Evaluation Unit, Westminster College.

Rees, S. (1978). *Social Work Face to Face.* London: Edward Arnold.

Rees, S. (1991). *Achieving Power: Practice and Policy in Social Welfare.* North Sydney, Australia: Allen and Unwin.

Rees, S. & Wallace, A. (1982). *Verdicts on Social Work.* London: Edward Arnold.

Robinson, T. (1978). *In Worlds Apart: Professionals and their Clients in the Welfare State.* London: Bedford Square Press and the National Council for Social Service.

Rowe, J. & Lambert, L. (1973). *Children Who Wait.* London: British Association for Adoption and Fostering.

Rowe, J., Cain, H., Hundleby, M. & Keane, A. (1984). *Long-Term Foster Care.* London: Batsford/BAAF.

Rowe, J., Hundleby, M. & Garnett, L. (1989). *Child Care Now.* BAAF Research series 6. London: BAAF.

Sainsbury, E. (1989). Participation and paternalism. In S. Shardlow (ed.): *The Values of Change in Social Work*. London: Routledge.

Seebohm Report (1968). *Report of the Committee on Local Authority and Allied Personal Social Services*. Chairman F. Seebohm Esq. 1968 Cmnd 3703.

Shaw, M., Masson, J. & Bocklesby, E. (1991) *Children in Need and their Families: A New Approach. A Manual for Managers on Part III of the Children Act 1989*. Leicester: University of Leicester School of Social Work and Faculty of Law and the Department of Health.

Social Services Inspectorate/Department of Health (1992). *Partnership with Families in Child Protection: A Practice Guide*. Pre-publication abstracts. London: HMSO.

Stein, M. & Carey, K. (1986). *Leaving Care*. Oxford: Blackwell.

Stone, J. (1990). *Children in Care: The Role of Short-Term Fostering*. City of Newcastle-upon-Tyne Social Services. Adoption and Fostering Unit.

The Child, the Family and the Young Offender. (1965). Cmnd. 2742. London: HMSO.

The Children Act 1989; Court Orders Study. (1992). London: HMSO.

Thoburn, J., Lewis, A. & Shemmings, D. (1991). *Family Involvement in Child Protection Conferences*. University of East Anglia: Social Work Development Unit.

Timms, N. (ed.) (1973). *The Receiving End*. London: Tavistock.

Timms, N. (1989). Social work values: context and contribution. In S. Shardlow (ed.): *The Values of Change in Social Work*. London: Routledge.

Trinder, L. (1993). *Reviewing The Reviews: Day Care for Children in Yorkshire and Humberside*. Yorkshire and Humberside Regional Childcare Group.

Webb, S. (1990). Preventing reception into care: a literature review of respite care. *Adoption and Fostering 14(2)*.

White, R., Carr, P. & Lowe, N. (1990). *A Guide to the Children Act 1989* London: Butterworths.

18

Individual Work with Children

Margaret Crompton

Introduction

'You are mistaken if you think we have to lower ourselves to communicate with children. On the contrary, we have to reach up to their feelings, stretch, stand on our tiptoes' (Korczak, 1925; in Lifton, 1989, (page 172).

The CCETSW *Guidance Notes* for teaching about child care in the Diploma in Social Work (DipSW) courses emphasise that, 'The Children Act 1989 requires that the wishes and feelings of children should be considered in all decision-making. The Cleveland inquiry report (1988) gave the profession a salutory reminder about the importance of treating children as people, not objects.' Maintenance of 'that perspective of the child as client' requires development of 'skills in communicating directly and honestly with children, young people and adults, recognising the need to take time and not to compel . . . clients to talk' (CCETSW, 1991, page 18).

The implications of regarding the child as a client and of direct, honest and unpressured interaction must form the base of any work with children, together with avoidance of labelling by symptom. Only attention to the whole, individual child by the whole, individual worker can lead to communication. Whatever the agency and context of the interaction, it is essential to respect children and to be clear about the purpose of contact for *each* child.

A nursery nurse, in a voluntary agency specialising in help for abused and neglected children summarises thus:

'If you centre on the whole child she goes away from the sessions as a stronger person with increased confidence because she knows what's going on. If you centre totally on the abuse, on what actually happened, where is the rest of the child? You can give the child the impression that only the abuse is important' (Crompton, 1980, page 12).

There are many kinds of abuse and many reasons for referral. The observable scars of children who have been subject to physical abuse (including neglect and sexual assault), are accompanied by wounds to the emotions, mind and spirit. Children also suffer invisible assault, unaccompanied by visible clues but nonetheless desperately needing careful attention from adults. Physical and emotional abuse attract far more attention than cognitive and spiritual abuse.

The main focus of this chapter is an introduction to some ways of communicating with children, including an account of work with a 10-year-old boy. Material is largely drawn from texts focusing on work with children who have been referred to agencies because of observed abuse. However, the aim of the chapter is to discuss individual work with children who have, as part of their experience of life, suffered abuse, as distinct from 'abused children'.

Emphasis is on straightforward, uncluttered, simple methods and approaches. Children and workers have neither time nor energy for elaboration and the most effective interactions are those in which child and adult *meet*, with minimal accessories, material or verbal.

The chapter is organised in three main sections:

1. The professional background to individual work
2. Some methods of communication
3. Work with a 10-year-old-boy

The Professional Background to Individual Work

The idea of working with, and not only on behalf of, children is far from new. Kastell (1962), Winnicott (1964) and Holgate (1972) were among influential writers and teachers in the UK, while in the USA the texts of Axline and Oaklander were first published in 1947 and 1964, and 1969 respectively. Social workers in field and residential agencies understood the importance of play and the skills of listening, seeing, waiting and communicating. It is irritating to workers who are still far from decrepit to read of 'new emphasis on the concept of "communicating with children" ' (Wells, 1989, page 45). Stevenson (1991) regrets that the CCETSW guidelines 'could not have been available earlier before innumerable wheels all over the country were re-invented!' (page 5.)

However, Stevenson (1991) emphasises the need for continuing efforts towards good practice (page 5), not least because of deficiencies in social work training, which has lacked rigour and placed too little emphasis on 'knowledge and well-researched evidence . . . Because a social work qualification is a licence to practise measurable standards should be set and adhered to'. Decisions about individual work, regarding philosophy, models of human development and intervention, and efficacy of such intervention, should be well-founded (CCETSW, 1991, page 10).

Training should be a respected specialisation, with academic and practical work on many aspects of childhood, including the history of politics and philosophy in the legislation of education, employment, religion, health and social welfare, together with the day-to-day culture of school, leisure, fashion, family and peer group. Students should spend time in playgrounds and discos and read teenmagazines and children's literature (Crompton, 1992, pages 5–6). Familiarity with a range of models of development and behaviour, and of approaches to helping is also essential. Thompson and Rudolph (1988) and Shapiro (1984) provide excellent introductions.

Communicating with children requires professional rigour, including clear definition of the purpose and aims of every interaction. Stevenson's comment, 'Prompted in particular by concern about sexual abuse, social workers have rushed to observe children's play with little open discussion of the justification for the inferences drawn' (page 6), illustrates the confusion of undertaking action without a sound philosophical grounding.

The decision to offer helping interaction to an individual child requires careful thought, understanding of what such interaction might entail, and commitment by both worker and agency, before the offer is made. O'Hagan (1989) is anxious that focusing on the individual may 'exacerbate the crisis generated by the disclosure' (page 116), and Furniss (1991) points out that seeing children individually is not automatically synonymous with individual counselling or therapy. Disciplined definition is required, with an understanding of possible difficulties for workers (Stone, 1990, page 33).

Moore (1992), whose chapter 'Face-to-face work with the abused child' is down-to-earth and useful, is clear that, 'An abused child has the right to be the primary client, to be facilitated in a face-to-face way, to make sense of what has happened and, in spite of the trauma, helped to become a survivor' (page 127). She advises that:

> 'What we can offer is warm, friendly, personal help, aimed at enabling [the children] to come to terms with themselves and their actual situation . . . . The only way for an abused child is forwards. We must help them understand and mature through the awful experience . . . . The role of a worker is to help children get in touch with the suffering part of themselves: to reassure them that they are understood and respected, so that they can move on, leave the baggage behind and start living for themselves' (Moore, 1992, pages 130–131).

Such help cannot and should not erase memories of 'awful experiences'. Moving on involves the whole person in the real world, where the 'actual situation' and the problems of life have to be met again and again. The most important aim is to develop strength with which to face and manage challenges and suffering.

However, as Bagley and King (1990) note in their review of therapeutic philosophies, 'many children do not receive treatment for the traumas that child sexual abuse involves, during their childhood years. These principles of healing are equally relevant for "the hurting child" who may still be part of the adult personality' (page 133).

Glaser and Frosh (1988) note that individual work may accompany, replace or succeed time-limited group experience and comprise contact with 'a professional, usually their social worker, teacher or counsellor' (page 146). Decisions about what kind of help can be offered depend not only on an assessment of what should be available, but also of agency resources and may be quite arbitrary. Workers should be clear about constraints.

The purpose of providing opportunities for communication directly between children and professionally caring adults may be simply defined as 'assessment' and 'help'. 'Assessment' includes, for example, all activities leading to writing reports, making recommendations to courts and planning for future accommodation. Tasks include gathering information, communicating to children information about possibilities and constraints, learning about feelings, perceptions, preferences and plans. 'Help' comprises provision of an environment conducive to developing self-awareness, confidence, self-esteem and the ability to trust wisely, to make realistic plans and decisions, and to form relationships which contribute to the well-being of all involved. Tasks include helping children to recognise and manage external realities (past events, present accommodation, future relationships) and inward experiences (memories, perceptions, feelings), and to co-operate in forming realistic plans. It is important to be clear about the primary purpose of interaction, particularly when considering such communicative activities as those reviewed in the second part of this chapter.

The implications of such concepts as self-esteem need analysis (see Roberts, 1993). Trust, too, should be carefully considered (see Cooper and Ball, 1987, page 103; Crompton, 1990, pages 53–62; Doyle, 1990, page 41; Furniss, 1991, pages 23, 43).

Another word used frequently and loosely is 'therapy'. It is not always clear whether practitioners and authors associate 'therapy/therapist' with their original connotations of disease and healing. More important is the need to be clear about the distinction between 'therapeutically informed intervention' by social workers and long-term therapeutic work which requires more specialist skills. Therapy within social work interactions should not be confused with psychotherapy (see Glaser and Frosh, 1988, pages 56, 161; Doyle, 1990 page 32). A distinction should also be made between this and such specialisations as art, drama, music and play therapies. Wilson *et al.* (1992) differentiate between 'the use of play in play therapy and in activities . . . which are used by an adult to explain, clarify, prepare or for other purposes work on an area which the adult has identified as one of concern', defined as 'play-related communication' (page 13).

Professional rigour requires semantic and conceptual precision. If individual, group or family-based help is available, the reason for choosing one approach rather than another should be clear. The exclusive attention of one adult offers the best chance of a peaceful, private and relaxed period, away from the immediate pressures of family relationships or identification in a group with a label, and the child can use this kind of interaction freely.

Workers' principal skills must be *really* to *see* and to *listen*. This necessitates leaving all fears and assumptions behind, and endeavouring to engage with the world of the child, both internal and external. Moore advises: 'Communication is a reciprocal giving and receiving of thoughts and feelings. The worker's body posture and tone of voice must convey empathy and understanding' (Moore, 1992, page 132). Mearns and Thorne (1988), following the Rogers, person-centred model, define *empathy* as 'a continuing process whereby the counsellor lays aside her own way of experiencing and perceiving reality, preferring to sense and respond to the experiences and perceptions of her client' (Mearns and Thorne, 1988, page 39). *Empathy* is currently a popular and overused word. The concept is useful but should be approached with care. It is easy, for example, to confuse it with sympathy or with recognition of a similar experience in the worker's own life, or to become dangerously immersed in the child's feelings. (For further references and discussion, see Crompton, 1992, chapter 6).

The endeavour to engage so intimately with children's inner lives carries with it the danger of intruding on their privacy. Care should be taken to avoid 'pressing the bruise' or expecting too much response (if any). Even when respecting the right not to speak, it is easy to stimulate thoughts and feelings which are difficult and painful and which continue to have an impact long after the end of immediate contact between child and worker (Crompton, 1991).

Children often give clues that they do not wish to pursue a particular line or activity; moving to another toy, running around, changing the conversation. This is in itself a form of communication. Workers should notice the triggers to withdrawal and judge whether the reaction is to the particular topic or activity, perhaps associated with some memory, or to a communication by the worker.

Pressing too hard for overt responses may lead to distortion, even lying. Conversely, apparent failure to respond may mask unexpressed internal activity or alterations of behaviour elsewhere. Dorfman (1951) writes of an aggressive and abusing 13-year-old boy who spent most of his regular and protected hour ignoring her. After ten sessions, he was told that although the hour was saved for him, he need not continue to attend. His response was, 'Whaddya mean, not come any more? I'll come till the cows come home!' His behaviour outside the worker's room had greatly improved. Only to the worker did he give no overt hint of the positive use to which he put the unpressured hour with her (Dorfman, 1951, pages 244–245).

Respect for *privacy* and non-intrusion is essential but Doyle (1990) notes that avoidance of discussing abusive activities may result from the inability of adults to tolerate children's pain. Interviews may remain superficial and 'the child left feeling that he or she has been involved in something so dreadful that it cannot be discussed. Children should be allowed to talk about the abuse and examine what it has meant for them' (Doyle, 1990, page 34). Only real attention to individual children, including *waiting* for their own timing, enables them to respond as they wish.

An aspect of privacy demanding special care is *confidentiality*, which cannot be guaranteed, for example, because a worker fears that the child client, or other children, may be in danger. Children should be 'assured that only people who are in a position to help either them or other children will be allowed to know what the child does or says in a session' (Doyle, 1990, page 42). Some authorities suggest that confidentiality may represent a potential danger, mirroring the secrecy which characterises child sexual abuse cases (Glaser and Frosh, 1988, page 72). It is most important to give children clear information about any limits to confidentiality, including, for example, whether any other staff member knows about interactions between child and worker and, if the worker should be unavailable at any time or leave the agency, whether colleagues know about the child's situation, feelings and attitudes. Such clarity can offer good experiences of honesty and plain dealing by the worker and opportunities to exercise choice and control about speaking and keeping silent.

Danger, or at least confusion, may be represented by the physical privacy of one-to-one work for children whose experience of private engagements with adults has entailed abuse. Some writers suggest that workers risk seductive behaviour and allegations of abuse by children but Doyle (1990) regards the latter as unlikely, because 'few youngsters tell lies about sexual abuse.' However, workers should be alert to the possibility of misunderstanding by children whose experience of adults has not led to the development of wise trust, and children should not be exposed to feeling 'isolated and trapped' with workers (Doyle, 1990, pages 35, 39).

Nonetheless, common sense, good training, professional discipline and efficient agency organisation should ensure that such problems, confusions and dangers are prevented, and that every child for whom it is appropriate has the opportunity for individual, protected, private contact with a worker.

Some Methods of Communication

This discussion is necessarily selective and brief. No reference is made to such electronic aids as videos and computers, and the main focus is on work with the minimal material facilities usually available to workers, including drawing and writing equipment, books and a car. The most important constituents of communication are the individual people concerned, within time and space dedicated to the child.

Choice of activity and equipment is negotiated between child and worker, having regard to both preferences and explained, understandable constraints. For example, when working with a 10-year-old boy, without access to any room, my age and abilities precluded communication via football or swimming but we were able to share simple art work and walking. Equipment was kept in a carrying box which I took to every meeting and gave to him at the end of our contact. Shelter was provided by a café and my car. Co-operation in developing an activity may help to increase self-confidence and, thus, strength in managing everyday life.

Although some reference is made to 'therapy', examples illustrate activities which may be undertaken by non-specialist (but trained) workers. For example, a section on play therapy follows (page 354), but there are innumerable ways in which play, interpreted very broadly, can be used as both a vehicle and an environment for communication by non-specialist practitioners.

Bannister (1989) is one of many writers to stress that workers should not seek to interpret the process and/or product of children's creative activity, for not only may such interpretation 'be incorrect or irrelevant' but, most important, 'the child has expressed feeling and, maybe, found a solution' (Bannister, 1989, page 84). (See also Oaklander, 1978; Crompton, 1992).

Although the phrase 'face-to-face with children' is often used of direct work, play activities essentially provide opportunities for interaction without being face-to-face, so that eye contact need not be sought or forced, and verbal conversation may play only a small role.

Agencies sometimes produce information packs containing ideas for play activities, and a compendium such as Redgrave (1987) forms a useful reference base. However, Redgrave himself warns that:

> 'It would be quite wrong for anyone to issue a working pack for people who wished to undertake *direct work*, and to provide sets of questionnaire cards and things of that sort. In my practice, and that of my colleagues, the *games* are being constantly adapted to the needs of the individual child. I have attempted to provide *examples* and to state a few principles, but each worker must draw upon his or her imagination and make up new *games*' (Redgrave, 1987, page 6).

The environment

A satisfactory physical and psychic environment, including safety and privacy, is essential. Whether meetings take place in playrooms or cafés, hospital wards or cars, workers are themselves part of the environment. For example, clothes should be appropriate for sitting on the floor, painting, cuddling or walking. It is important not to insult children by dressing in a slovenly fashion. Dress should reflect care and respect. It may even be possible to avoid wearing colours which are known to be particularly disliked by an individual child.

Anxiety about laddering tights or creasing trousers may be regarded by children as anxiety about being with them, for workers' feelings also contribute to the environment of the interaction. If adults are exhausted, anxious, unhappy, angry, depressed or ill, energy available for the children is limited and they may sense the emotionally charged or depleted atmosphere. Similarly, if adults are fit and fully able to concentrate on the children, the emotional environment will be clearer and more spacious.

Workers with abused children may communicate their feelings about the abuse too, for example, anger towards the abusers, horror about the events and sympathy with the children. It may at times be preferable to postpone a contact than to expose a child to the feelings of the worker.

Yet postponement itself can be perceived as rejection or evidence of the child's lack of worth. Meticulous courtesy and attention to punctuality and reliability are essentially aspects of the total environment and the messages given and received. Children should not be kept waiting or let down because 'something has come up'. Khadija Rouf, 1989) writes that she:

> 'got a social worker, Sue. She was okay but because our family had gone past crisis point she never came round. That is to do with big caseloads, I know, but we did *all* need someone to talk to . . . [Workers should] remember that a lot of children are on their own. Don't let them down. If you arrange to go out, then go out. If you say you'll be in court, then for God's sake be there. Abused children have been let down enough' (pages 9–10).

Attention should be given to the duration of interactions. Respect for the whole child includes recognition that life continues outside the playroom. The child may have other appointments, friends waiting or a favourite television show which will be missed if workers do not honour agreed stopping as well as starting times.

Enthusiastic work with a boy led to extended hours spent in the sitting room of the foster home. In one case, belated recognition that this delayed teatime and kept the family from the television led to better discipline and timekeeping by the worker. Beginnings and endings of not only individual sessions but also the entire period of contact are especially important (Crompton, 1990).

Contacts should never be interrupted by telephone calls or enquiries from colleagues. Discussions with the agency director or court appearances would not be interrupted for the worker to take a message. Working with children requires concentration and continuity.

The physical environment is in itself a form of communication, indicating to children attention to their welfare. Some agencies provide well-stocked playrooms where workers may ensure a period of uninterrupted ownership of protected space. Many workers create defended space, for example, in 'empty broom-closets and in the back of gymnasiums' (Shapiro, 1984, page v).

It may help children's sense of being individual and cared-about if workers keep their materials in separate, particular bags, indicating that they are not just other 'cases'. Attention to materials is important; for example, folders used for life story books could be chosen in the child's favourite colours. Shopping together is not always possible, so care shown by a worker in demonstrating choice on behalf of the child is beneficial.

A personal set of coloured pencils, which only the child has a right to use or not to use, may offer some sense of control. If the favourite colours are constantly used, while others are neglected, children can see how their own choices affect the world, even in the form of only one coloured pencil. No other child is interfering and workers can protect this aspect of the child's environment by keeping the containers and equipment themselves and bringing them, regularly and intact, to appointments, thus indicating that the individual child is remembered and respected during the intervals between contacts. Similarly, children may keep their own equipment. This offers opportunities for them to demonstrate control and the ability to protect important possessions. The equipment can become a symbol of the continuity and reliability of contacts with workers.

Protecting and respecting material property which children share with workers indicates respect for, instead of abuse of, children. It helps to establish wise trust and encourages children to feel that, through those material extensions of themselves, they have worth.

Much important communication occurs indirectly through such aspects of every-day life as clothing and food (Crompton, 1990, pages 102–111). Respect for a child's personal preferences and cultural traditions is essential and lack of such respect can be a form of abuse (Ahmed *et al.*, 1986; Gardner, 1987).

Kenward (1989) illustrates the powerful symbolism of food for Anna (8 years): the availability of food had 'been dependent upon her being sexually co-operative'. When her foster mother offered her food, Anna said, 'I'm hungry and I want it. I can't make my hand take it'. The foster family helped, partly by giving Anna control of serving food (Kenward, 1989, page 32). Offering, receiving and sharing food can provide opportunities for children to exercise choice and control, and to experience ordinary routines of social interaction (see also Crompton, 1990, chapter 10).

Anxiety can be raised in a child who feels unable to conform to adult expectations of everyday behaviour. Kenward (1989) quotes John (11 years), following a visit to new foster parents: 'I liked them very much but they didn't know how I am inside . . . I don't know what they want me to do or how to do it and I'm afraid in case I make them angry and they hurt me' (page 32). Such clear expression of inner confusion is rare and illuminating.

Whatever the physical environment and activity, workers themselves define the immediate environment. On a walk, for example, the adult provides a boundary within which the child may choose the path, the speed, whether to stop and look down a rabbit hole or run across a field, leaving the worker behind. The child's freedom is safely within the context of the contact with the worker. Such freedom is not abandon-ment or lack of caring and boundaries are not arbitrary obstacles. Workers are the providers of space, time and interest. They set limits and ensure that doors are safely closed, so that there will be no interruptions. The environment must be non-threaten-ing and safe, offering opportunities for choice, control, stimulus and peace.

Art

Workers do not have to be skilled artists to share artistic activity with children. Inadequacy may even be helpful if a child can discover and demonstrate greater competence than an adult, maybe taking the superior role of teacher. Simple, cheap materials are easily transported for spontaneous use. Drawing, painting and model-ling provide opportunities for absorbing and relaxing activity. Children who have been subject to the stresses of abuse and investigation may find respite in a holiday from words, within space and time provided by a non-pressurising adult. Clues about feelings may be implied through choice of subject, colour, materials, use of space, concentration and response to making a mess, and it is interesting to note what is done with the product. For example, a picture may be given to the worker, taken home to a parent, treasured or destroyed.

Materials need not be used for obviously creative purposes. A nursery nurse noted that a 5-year-old used clay to dunk in a bowl of water, saying, 'I'm drowning the clay', soon after her sister had been accidentally drowned in her presence (Crompton, 1990, page 42).

Sharing artistic activity may help to relieve tension, for example, when awaiting a court appearance or on a journey.

Drawing may be included in making life story books with children (see below). An artistically unskilled worker may manage at least matchstick people or may be able to draw simple outlines to be coloured in, at will, by the child, or the child may draw all the pictures. Shapes of houses, people, animals, cars and so on can easily be cut from sheets of coloured paper and stuck onto paper or card. Very young children can be fully involved in choosing colours, gumming, choosing the position for shapes, and older children can also draw and cut. Pictures can be cut from magazines but young children may not appreciate the difference between photographs of models and of themselves: an attempt to teach a young boy about his life as a baby, using a photograph from an advertisement, led to confusion as he thought the picture was of himself.

Allan (1988, pages 64–92), Bannister (1989, pages 84–89) and Jones (1992, pages 40–42) discuss drawing by children who have been sexually abused, including useful illustrations (pictorial and narrative) and analysis of method.

The rosebush-guided fantasy, based on Stevens (1971), is a method of encouraging self-expression through drawing and verbal exposition. Children are invited to imagine themselves to be rosebushes, then to draw and explain the picture. Allan (1988) comments that it 'may be a useful screening device for detecting children who have been or are being sexually abused', but advises great caution and specialised training and supervision (pages 82–83). (Since this is a specialised discussion by a Jungian psychoanalyst, readers are recommended to study the original text.)

Oaklander (1988), using a gestalt approach, writes of Gina (8 years) who, suffering from much anxiety, said, 'I can grow easier if I don't have roots; if they want to replant me it will be easier. I always have buds'. Her adoptive parents had separated, causing much anxiety for the child. Oaklander found the rosebush work very helpful to Gina (page 35).

The same technique was used by Seymour (1990), a social worker, with Trevor (10 years) who had been removed from home because of neglect and, following the end of an adoptive placement, awaited a 'permanent family'. Trevor's rosebush, like that of Gina, had no roots: they 'would not grow because nobody took care of it.' However, there were 'lots of thorns on it so that it would hurt anyone who tried to touch it' (pages 1, 10; see also Crompton, 1992, pages 177–178).

Workers interested in this technique are advised to refer to Oaklander (1988) and Stevens (1971). Further discussion of art as a communicative activity can be found in Crompton, 1980, chapter 7 and Crompton, 1992, chapter 9.

Music

Music may be overlooked as a communicative activity, especially when workers are shy about their own abilities. Musical instruments may be too large to transport but equipment in playrooms and residential units could include percussion, piano or keyboard, recorders and guitars, and a cassette/record player. Many cars are equipped with radios and cassette players.

Music may contribute to the total communicative environment; for example, children or workers may choose some recorded music to accompany an activity. Workers should be aware of the impact of such choices. A child might use a very noisy disc to overwhelm or distract the worker, or might respond with distress to the worker's choice of some melody intended to be calming. A piece of music or a sound may have important resonances which stir memories (possibly disturbing). A child who has suffered abuse may respond with anxiety to a record which was popular during the period of abuse or a favourite of the abuser, or even played during sexual or violent episodes and/or assaults on the emotions and spirit. Choice of background music offers children some control and a ground for negotiation about duration and volume.

Children may like to play instruments alone, perhaps finding relief and release in pounding a drum or piano, or finding relaxation in devising apparently formless, meditative melodies. The presence of the worker is important, protecting space, time and activity, and demonstrating acceptance and attention.

Playing an instrument or singing may be shared by child and worker and can bring relaxation and enjoyment, also providing opportunities for children to demonstrate abilities which can attract praise and encouragement for further development, invaluable when self-respect has been demolished.

Listening to music together can demonstrate the worker's ability to attend to the child, without pressure on the child to buy that attention with words (answering questions, offering revelations) or actions (collusion in abusive acts).

Words may be included in the form of songs, composed by the child or in the form of recorded or sung music, offering a clue to the child's feelings. 'Laurel', after confinement in a secure unit for unruly behaviour, chose to play again and again a record with words of loss and bewilderment. She did not seek to converse with the quietly attentive adult but recognition of the presence of that adult suggested that the choice of record was made partly in order to express something about herself (Crompton, 1992, page 186).

Dance offers opportunities for relaxation, expression of feeling, concentration on the music or shared enjoyment and a break from the need for speech. Further discussion of music may be found in Crompton, 1980, chapter 6 and Crompton, 1992, chapter 10.

Stories

Telling a story can provide an environment of comfort, particularly if the child can be cuddled. The child, too, may be the storyteller. 'Luke' (6 years) would lie on the settee in his foster home. While not very articulate, at these times he would tell a story about a recent experience, the words tumbling out with great feeling as he relaxed. When these stories were carefully written out, his rapidly spoken words and lively tales helped Luke gain a sense of himself existing in some relationship to the past, present and future. Also, he learned that the stories were of enough value for an adult to listen, write out between sessions and return to him. Joint illustrations used matchstick figures and outlines which Luke could colour in, and his own drawings (Crompton, 1992, pages 153–156).

Marion Burch (1992) has drawn on her experience as mother to five adopted children and 30 years fostering to produce a guide, *I Want to Make a Life Story Book*, which includes a model for such a book, photographs, stories and other ideas.

Redgrave (1987) includes a substantial, practical and illustrated discussion of life story books, warning against routine and the unimaginative imposition of such an activity (pages 43–62). Donley (1975) advises that the product of life story, or any other, activity belongs to the child and that social workers should beware of themselves becoming attached to such products (page 28). Crompton (1980, 1992) discusses communication through both life stories and other forms of narrative. Oaklander (1988) includes sections on writing, poetry and books (pages 91–104). Allan (1988) describes serial story writing with a physically abused adolescent (pages 199–211).

Printed books may be useful as aids to communication but, as with any pre-packaged material, there are difficulties. Non-fiction books about feelings or experiences may be dull and/or confusing. Reading a story about experiences similar to the child's own may be reassuring demonstrating that the child is not unique and that feelings about such experiences are known to other people. However, published stories usually have neat plots and endings, whereas real experience is continuing and complex. Adults should not expect 'identification' with fictional characters.

The most influential books are usually those chosen by the individual child and it is useful to be aware of children's favourite or least favourite texts. Responses may be very different from those expected by adults. As a child, I hated pictures of a menacing genie, an exploding witch and a little naked boy floating down a stream alone. These represented terrifying power and powerlessness to the child, but to adults they were only illustrations of charming stories.

Published material may most usefully form an aid to relaxation and to learning about ways of managing the challenges of life through the eyes of other people. However, a programme of planned and guided reading may be devised, aiming to give support and modify behaviour, and known as *bibliotherapy* (Marshall, 1981).

Bibliographies of focused texts are sometimes produced by libraries. Mills (1988) reviews fictional treatment of sexual abuse (pages 166–170). Thompson and Rudolph (1988) include a bibliography of fictional texts about sexual and other abuse (pages 298–301, 322).

Particularly interesting and potent aspects of storytelling are found in myths, legends and fairy tales. Apparently simple stories may hold different meanings for different individuals. A black American boy (8 years) told the tale of 'Missy Red Riding Hood', wagging an admonitory finger with great glee. Polish students found the message of that story and of *Snow White* to be that they should not trust people. Yet for Julia (8 years), who had suffered from severe neglect by her mother, 'Snow White provided an opportunity to enact the part of the wicked (step)mother, "Only in this story, she doesn't win", Snow White is queen' (Hunter, 1987, page 28). *Rapunzel* represented comfort and security to an American 5-year-old when he learnt that his grandmother, who often cared for him, was to enter hospital. Bettelheim (1976) suggests that he learnt, 'That one's own body can provide a lifeline', just as Rapunzel's hair was used as a ladder: 'if necessary, he would find in his own body the source of his security' (Bettelheim, 1976, page 17). A girl who had problems with body images was helped through *The Ugly Duckling* (Bannister, 1989, page 83).

Janusz Korczak regularly told the children in his orphanage (many of whom had been abused by physical and/or emotional assault or neglect and, in pre-war Warsaw, were certainly socially abused) such old tales as *Puss in Boots*. He considered that, 'children who feel worthless in a society that doesn't value them, who feel angry and powerless because their parents . . . can no longer protect them, need to believe that there are magic forces that can help them overcome their difficulties'. (Nazi occupation is far from being the only condition necessary for children to feel unvalued, angry and powerless.) Such traditional tales, full of difficulties and obstacles requiring perseverence and strength of will, were 'close to life' (Lifton, 1989, page 74). Further discussion of myths and stories may be found in Crompton, 1992, chapter 7.

Drama

Drama (including role-play) is perhaps one of the most difficult and potentially dangerous methods and, I suggest, should not be used by non-specialist workers without opportunities for consultation. The feelings and memories stimulated may have repercussions for both child and worker. For example, the experience of wielding power when playing a role may be frightening for a powerless child, and new ideas about family relationships may be stimulated but not expressed, leaving a child in a state of bewilderment.

Bannister (drama therapist, psychodramatist and social worker), writing of work with sexually abused children (1989, pages 82–83), describes how Michelle (7 years), whose father had died, revealed that he had sexually abused her. Through acting based on *The Lion, the Witch and the Wardrobe* (Lewis, 1950), she began to gain strength and autonomy. She took the parts of, first, a child who rescues the Lion, and then the Witch, 'a very powerful person who had control over everyone'. After this, she could take the role with which she really identified – the Lion, whom she played as 'strong and brave and able to help others'. When his friends had rescued him, 'they thanked him for allowing himself to be caught because this protected them' and they 'admired Michelle's strength and power and also her kindness. The Witch was dead so the Lion dug a hole and buried her. Michelle's healing had begun' (Bannister, 1989, page 94).

This recalls the *Snow White* theme explored by Julia with psychotherapist Margaret Hunter. Julia could explore aspects of her feelings and history by enacting roles from the story, including that of the stepmother (see Stories above) (Hunter, 1987, page 28).

A toy may provide a third ear and voice through which child and worker may communicate. May (6 years) wanted to name a large glove puppet 'May' but was dissuaded by her social worker, who felt that three-way conversations in which two participants had the same name would be confusing. May then chose her own second name and the puppet became 'Jessie'. Jessie became a regular participant in conversations, was always physically, even if silently, present, and at times behaved in such ways that May accused her of being naughty and put her outside the door (Crompton, 1990, page 97).

The worker sometimes felt in danger of losing control and noted, 'don't let materials run away with you – I felt the glove puppet begin to take me over, began to lose focus on the child and to enjoy the game too much'.

A nursery nurse, Elaine, also recorded role-playing interaction which was difficult and disturbing. Selma (6 years) attended a voluntary agency weekly, with the aim of learning strategies for coping with her bizarre and neglecting mother. Although doing well at school and in good physical health, Selma appeared to be emotionally abused. During the fourth session, she began to act as mother to a doll and Elaine took the role of Selma, who then 'became' her own mother. They walked to a pile of teddies at one end of the playroom:

'Selma/mother had been very aggressive but now she changed her whole voice and manner and asked Elaine/Selma "would you like a present?" in a very soft stroking way. She gave Elaine/Selma all the teddies, then took her to the other end of the room to give another, enormous bear. Elaine/Selma said, "I can't carry it". Selma/mother immediately became annoyed, "you will have it. I've bought it for you".

Elaine/Selma found the difficulty was in coping with the "gentle mum". She felt frightened and puzzled: "what have I done that's made her nice?" She waited for aggression to return, to be punished for the Selma/mother's being "nice".'

Selma did not want to leave the role of mother and had enjoyed the power and control. Both she and Elaine 'needed a great deal of debriefing and cuddling'. Elaine wondered whether it had been a good idea to give her that taste of control, and she was also aware that 'Selma had let Elaine in on her world and feelings but then had to go home again to all the real stresses' (Crompton, 1990, pages 12–13). Elaine was well supported by a colleague with whom she could share such anxieties. Such work should not be undertaken unless consultation is available.

Anatomically correct dolls

Attention must be drawn, briefly, to the anatomically correct dolls (AC dolls) debate, summarised in the opinion of psychiatrist David Jones (1992):

'it has yet to be demonstrated that AC dolls help sexually abused children more than other, regular dolls. We do know that toys and materials in general help children to convey their memories accurately, but no convincing evidence exists for the superiority of AC dolls over other materials. By contrast, they cause confusion to professionals when interpreting the meaning of child's play. There is no evidence that they cause harm, though, *per se*, or abnormally sexualise the child, or are the source of major errors of recall. Professionals are generally poorly trained in their use and there is wide variability in the interpretation of findings from AC doll interviews' (page 44).

Further discussion may be found in Furniss (1991, pages 208–213), Glasgow (1987, pages 70–80), Doyle (1990, page 42), Bagley and King (1990, page 143) and O'Hagan (1989, pages 117, 130). Wells (1989) stresses the danger of seeking to replace real contact with techniques, representing 'the struggles of adults to bridge the gap of language and experience between themselves and children' (page 48).

Work with a 10-year-old Boy

This account of work with 'Mark' (10 years) illustrates some of the ideas mentioned above.

Mark was a member of a family in which sexual abuse had taken place and had been placed in a series of short-term foster homes. I was employed as an 'extra' social worker to help him emerge from the 'fog' in which he seemed to live, learn about the events which had brought about the break-up of his home and prepare for a so-called 'forever' home. Although not the direct victim of physical abuse, as a sibling, his life was irrevocably changed, for example, because of his removal from home. I was engaged to offer intensive, weekly, time-limited contact, in co-operation with the regular social worker. Contacts were substantial, usually about 90–120 minutes.

My aims were to offer Mark a structure of protected and reliable space and peacefulness, time which was all his own and interactions in which he had my whole attention. I hoped that we could really *meet* each other and that he could show me how, if at all, I could help him. There was no reason why he should like or trust me, or even give me his time. There was no reason why I should be able to make contact with him. My one guideline was *wait*, combating the urge to be seen to be successful within a short period of time, (in the same way that workers are beset by pressures to produce results within set times by senior officers, case conferences and court schedules).

Since most of our meetings were after school, when Mark was tired, it was particularly important to find ways in which we could be relaxed and have a place of our own. We had no access to an office or playroom but found a hospitable café. When Mark moved to yet another short-stay foster home, we found a river bank where we could park in privacy and he could choose one of several walks and activities. He could either walk with me or run ahead, he could share his discoveries, we could watch a ship together or walk peacefully apart.

Mark was never greedy. In the café he never asked for extra food or drink but relished his two weekly milkshakes. He had choice and (with my money) ordered the refreshments – an opportunity to gain social confidence too.

We worked hard. Every week, Mark dictated a story about recent events and I wrote, fast and illegibly. Then he drew an illustration, demonstrating ability and enjoyment. He taught me to draw such impossible objects as a bicycle, enjoying both his own achievements and the satisfaction of his superior skill (particularly important for a child with poor self-image). This pattern emerged from our first meeting when, on a walk, we had an adventure with a goose which became an excellent story and illustration when we next met. We thus immediately had shared experience and continuity.

Between meetings, I wrote out the week's story very carefully, using coloured pens or the word processor. My care and the continued existence of the story demonstrated that Mark himself had continued to exist for and with me and that his words had substance and were worthy of my time. With his own pictures, the stories built into a book recording the important events of his life. Finding a beautiful feather, getting lost, visiting a park – everyday events which had been important in themselves – became the focus for communication between us and were records of his past.

Darker aspects were regarded in the same way. When Mark wanted to discuss the abuse events and the reasons for his own removal from home, he asked his regular social worker for an explanation. At our next meeting, we wrote down this part of his story. Remembering that children should not feel defined by abuse or any other event or symptom, writing the story demonstrated that Mark's life included but was not confined to this aspect of his history.

His scattered parents and siblings could be gathered with stories, descriptions and drawings, helping Mark to decide how he foresaw his future, whether to be placed with a sibling or alone, and in what kind of family and place.

A whole day was spent visiting the scenes of his early life, including the maternity hospital and court. When a site on which he had loved to play and of which he had vivid memories was found to have been tarmacked and fenced by high wire, he asked, 'Why do things have to change?' We called at the museum to which Mark had gone on a recent school outing, and the castle, where he bought presents for his foster family and himself – his own choice was a cuddly toy (which, with a similar gift from his mother, became both a useful focus for and the medium of discussion of painful subjects, and a comforter). Writing, drawing, meals, silence and fun contributed to this important day.

Mark and I looked forward to seeing each other. I think he gained confidence, control, a sense of continuity and of himself. However, I felt that I failed him. The social services department failed to provide a 'forever' home. I had been asked to visit weekly but, after 5 months, at a distance of 40 miles, mileage was abruptly axed. When telling Mark that I could no longer visit him, I selfishly allowed my own anger and frustration to show and Mark, not understanding that my feelings were not directed at him, withdrew and asked, 'Can I go now?' If I had realised and controlled my self-absorption, it might have been better to have ended the day's contact early than to give Mark his full time, but spoil it. I would have valued support for myself, but I worked from home and did not wish to bother Mark's busy social worker.

We said goodbye in McDonald's, Mark's choice. I gave him all the materials we had used during our meetings and a strong carrying case, demonstrating that I had kept his possessions safe and that those aspects of his life which they represented were now in his own keeping. I had taught him to trust me and to enjoy being himself. It was important that in parting he should not feel abandoned, lest all my care become only another form of abuse.

We used physical activity, storytelling, writing, drawing, sending and collecting postcards, food, drink, car rides, toys, visiting places, conversation, explanation and silence. I tried to respect Mark's privacy and to be sensitive to his non-verbal messages, to be clear, straightforward and honest, and to give Mark opportunities for choice, control and the development of self-confidence. Everything was important for its own sake and I was (usually) careful to avoid interpretation traps.

It was frustrating that I could not complete the work for which I had been contracted. Mark had been abused at second hand by his family, and directly by the failure of the department to provide appropriate care. The financial cost was a small price for the attempt to help a hurt and bewildered child and more resources should have been available routinely (including, perhaps, the use of part-time, experienced specialist workers to undertake this kind of intensive time-limited contract). Working with Mark was not a luxury but there are many 'Marks' for whom no such help is available.

Conclusion

This survey of individual work with children has, of necessity, been swift and superficial. Nonetheless, it is hoped that readers will consider the questions raised, slowly and in depth.

One of the main strands has been the importance of achieving and maintaining good standards of practice based on well-focused, substantial training, and supported within equally well-focused agencies. Clarity of thought, demonstrated through, for example, precision of language, definition of role and task, and self-knowledge, is combined with loving care for every individual child.

Children must not be labelled by symptom or experience. Effective help can be offered only by a whole, individual worker to a whole, individual child, taking into account the whole life of the child, together with the resources and constraints of the agency.

Really *meeting* a child may be helped through many kinds of communicative activity, but no materials or techniques can produce communication if the worker has no wish, or skill, to engage in such interactions.

Shared activities can offer opportunities for children to develop strength and confidence, to experience achievement, choice and control, and to share unstressed time with an adult who does not threaten or pressure and who gives reliable and courteous attention.

Annotated Further Reading

Theory and practice of individual work

Dryden, W. (ed.) *Counselling in Action.* Series. London: Sage.
Although not focusing on work with children, this series is invaluable, including texts on feminist (Chaplin, 1988), Freudian (Jacobs, 1988), gestalt (Clarkson, 1989) and person-centred (Mearns and Thorne, 1988) approaches. Books in the series conform to a pattern and include case illustrations.

Shapiro, L.E. (1984). *The New Short-Term Therapies for Children: A Guide for the Helping Professions and Parents.* New Jersey: Prentice-Hall Inc.
A compilation of approaches to working with children, with a sense of the author as a real person and practitioner in the real world, and with real children. (Unfortunately, this book was out of print in 1992 but is still available through libraries. The British agent is Simon and Schuster).

Thompson, C.L. & Rudolph, L.B. (1988). *Counseling Children,* 2nd edn. Belmont, California: Brooks/Cole Publishing Co.
Excellent, well-organised and well-written accounts of models of counselling and approaches to working with children. Substantial summaries include lively vignettes of the originators (e.g. William Glasser, Fritz Perls, Carl Rogers) and notes on 'The nature of people', 'Theory of counseling', 'Counseling methods', a case study 'Research and reactions', and references for every approach.

A chapter on 'Counseling children with special concerns' includes sections on child abuse (pages 270–276) and a bibliography of fiction and other books written for children (pages 296–324) with reference to child abuse (pages 298–301) and sexual abuse (page 322).

Collections of papers

Ahmed, S., Cheetham, J. & Small, J. (1986). *Social Work with Black Children and their Families.* London: Batsford/BAAF.

Aldgate, J. & Simmonds, J. (1988). *Direct Work with Children.* London: Batsford/BAAF.

Holgate, E. (ed.) (1972). *Communicating with Children.* London: Longman.
Collections of papers by practitioners and academics discussing direct experience in direct work, and offering invaluable insights and ideas.

Individual approaches

Allan, J. (1988). *Inscapes of the Child's World: Jungian Counseling in Schools and Clinics.* Dallas: Spring Publications Inc.
Accessible and comprehensive account of theory and practice with stimulating Foreword by psychoanalyst James Hillman and chapters on use of, for example, art and story, and illustrations from children's work.

Burch, M. (1992). *I Want to Make a Life Story Book.* University of Hull: Department of Social and Professional Studies.
A4-size guide to life story writing. The author has five adopted children and 30 years' experience of fostering. Full of photographs, line drawings and ideas.

Crompton, M. (1990). *Attending to Children: Direct Work in Social and Health Care.* Dunton Green: Edward Arnold.

Crompton, M. (1992). *Children and Counselling.* Dunton Green: Edward Arnold.
Material from a range of approaches, practitioners and literature, including novels and children's books, focusing on communication between child and worker as whole people, and discussing such aspects as privacy, silence, spirituality and truth. Also includes use of, for example, art, environment, music, play and storytelling. Aims to stimulate further reading, and discussion and individual development of approaches and skills.

Oaklander, V. (1988). *Windows to our Children: A Gestalt Approach to Children and Adolescents.* New York: The Center for Gestalt Development.
Packed, stimulating and accessible account of ideas and practice with materials for a wide range of communicative activities, and with illuminating examples.

Redgrave, K. (1987). *Child's Play: Direct Work with the Deprived Child.* Cheadle: Boys and Girls Welfare Society.
Compact and practical introduction to many activities and ideas, based on the author's experience. Clear and accessible.

Work with children who have been abused

These texts include substantial reference to direct, individual work, ranging from a few paragraphs to papers focusing on a particular aspect.

BAAF (1989). *After Abuse: Papers on Caring and Planning for a Child who has been Sexually Abused.* London: BAAF.
See chapter by H. Kenward, 'Helping children who have been abused', pages 30–33.

Bagley, C. & King, K. (1990). *Child Sexual Abuse: The Search for Healing.* London: Tavistock/Routledge.
See chapter 7, 'Healing the child survivor', pages 133–156.

Doyle, C. (1990). *Working with Abused Children.* Basingstoke: Macmillan/BASW.
See chapter 3, 'Individual work with children', pages 32–49.

Feminist Review (1988). *Family Secrets: Child Sexual Abuse.* No. 28, Spring.
See J.C. Mills, 'Advising the young', pages 163–174.

Glaser, D. & Frosh, S. (1988). *Child Sexual Abuse*. Basingstoke: Macmillan/BASW.
See pages 53–162.

Lindsay, G. & Peake, A. (eds.) (1989). *Child Sexual Abuse: Educational and Child Psychology*, vol. 6(1). Disley: The British Psychological Society.
See K. Rouf, 'Journey through darkness; the path from victim to survivor', pages 6–10.

Moore, J. (1992). *The ABC of Child Protection*. Aldershot: Ashgate.
See chapter 8, 'Face-to-face work with the abused child', pages 127–139.

O'Hagan, K. (1989). *Working with Child Sexual Abuse: A Post-Cleveland Guide to Effective Principles and Practice*. Milton Keynes: Open University Press.
See chapter 8, 'Starting afresh; the case of Sarah and Elizabeth', pages 110–141.

Stone, M. (1990). *Child Protection Work; A Professional Guide*. Birmingham: Venture Press.
See 'Children and social work; the child as client', pages 30–36.

Wattam, C., Blagg, H. & Hughes, J.A. (eds.) (1989). *Child Sexual Abuse: Listening, Hearing and Validating the Experiences of Childhood*. Harlow: Longman/NSPCC.
See A. Bannister, chapter 5, 'Healing action – action methods with children who have been sexually abused', pages 78–94; D. Glasgow, chapter 9, 'Play based investigation assessment of children who may have been sexually abused', pages 138–151; J. Wells, chapter 3, 'Powerplays – considerations in communicating with children', pages 44–58.

Children in hospital

Jolly, J. (1981). *The Other Side of Paediatrics: A Guide to the Everyday Care of Sick Children*. Houndmills: Macmillan.
The author's experience in nursing and social work combined in a thoughtful and practical book full of 'real' children.

Müller, D.J., Harris, P.J. & Wattley, L.A. (1986) *Nursing Children: Psychology, Research and Practice*. London: Harper & Row.
Much useful material for medical and nursing staff, but also for social workers.

Shelley, J.A. (ed.) (1984). *Spiritual Needs of Children*. London: SPCK.
Excellent collection of papers, originating in the USA, on aspects of children's spiritual development, needs and care. Written by and for practitioners (nurses, hospital chaplain, etc.) and parents. The focus on children in hospital has wider implications. (Now out of print).

A church response

Armstrong, H. (ed.) (1991). *Taking Care: A Church Response to Adults, Children and Abuse*. London: NCB.
Published by the National Children's Bureau as a practical guide to helping non-professionals to develop awareness of, and ways of responding to, abuse in various manifestations.

References

Ahmed, S., Cheetham, J. & Small, J. (eds.)(1986). *Social Work with Black Children and their Families.* London: Batsford/BAAF.

Allan, J. (1988). *Inscapes of the Child's World: Jungian Counselling in Schools and Clinics.* Dallas: Spring Publications Inc.

Axline, V. (1947). *Play Therapy: The Inner Dynamics of Childhood.* Boston: Houghton Mifflin.

Axline, V. (1971). *Dibbs: In Search of Self.* Harmondsworth: Penguin.

BAAF (1989). *After Abuse: Papers on Caring and Planning for a Child who has been Sexually Abused.* London: BAAF.

Bagley, C. & King, K. (1990). *Child Sexual Abuse: The Search for Healing.* London: Tavistock/Routledge.

Bannister, A. (1989). Healing action – action methods with children who have been sexually abused, pages 78–94. In Wattam *et al.* (eds).

Bettelheim, B. (1976). *The Uses of Enchantment: The Meaning and Importance of Fairy Tales.* London: Thames and Hudson.

Burch, M. (1992). *I Want to Make a Life Story Book.* University of Hull: Department of Social Policy and Professional Studies.

CCETSW (1991). *The Teaching of Child Care in the Diploma in Social Work: Guidance Notes for Programme Planners: Improving Social Work Education and Training, No. 6.* London: CCETSW.

Cooper, D. & Ball, D. (1987). *Social Work and Child Abuse.* Houndmills: Macmillan/BASW.

Crompton, M. (1980). *Respecting Children: Social Work with Young People.* London: Edward Arnold.

Crompton, M. (1990). *Attending to Children: Direct Work in Social and Health Care.* Dunton Green: Edward Arnold.

Crompton, M. (1991). Invasion by Russian dolls: on privacy and intrusion. *Adoption and Fostering. 15:* 31–33.

Crompton, M. (1992). *Children and Counselling.* Dunton Green: Edward Arnold.

Donley, K. (1975). *Opening New Doors.* London: BAAF.

Dorfman, E. (1951) Play therapy pages 235–277. In C.R. Rogers (ed.): *Client-Centred Therapy: Its Current Practice, Implications and Theory.* London: Constable.

Doyle, C. (1990). *Working with Abused Children.* Houndmills: Macmillan/BASW.

Feminist Review (1988). *Family Secrets: Child Sexual Abuse.* No. 28, Spring.

Furniss, T. (1991). *The Multi-Professional Handbook of Child Sexual Abuse: Integrated Management, Therapy and Legal Intervention.* London: Routledge.

Gardner, R. (1987). *Who Says? Choice and Control in Care.* London: National Children's Bureau.

Glaser, D. & Frosh, S. (1988). *Child Sexual Abuse.* Houndmills: Macmillan/BASW.

Glasgow, D. (1987). *Responding to Child Sexual Abuse: Issues, Techniques and Play Assessment.* Liverpool: Mersey Regional Health Authority.

Holgate, E. (1972). *Communicating with Children.* London: Longman.

Hunter, M. (1987). Julia: a 'frozen' child. *Adoption and Fostering 11(3):* 26–30.

Jones, D.P.H. (1992). *Interviewing the Sexually Abused Child: Investigation of Suspected Abuse.* London: Gaskell/Royal College of Psychiatrists.

Kastell, J. (1962). *Casework in Child Care.* London: Routledge and Kegan Paul.

Kenward, H. (1989). Helping children who have been abused, pages 30–34. In BAAF: *After Abuse: Papers on Caring and Planning for a Child who has been Sexually Abused.* London: BAAF.

Lewis, C.S. (1950). *The Lion, the Witch and the Wardrobe.* Harmondsworth: Penguin.

Lifton, B. (1989). *The King of Children*. London: Pan.

Lindsay, G. & Peake, A. (eds). (1989). *Child Sexual Abuse: Educational and Child Psychology, vol. 6(1)*. Disley: The British Psychological Society.

Marshall, M.R. (1981). *Libraries and the Handicapped Child*. London: André Deutsch.

Mearns, D. & Thorne, B. (1988). *Person-Centred Counselling in Action*. London: Sage.

Mills, J.C. (1988). Putting ideas into their heads: advising the young. *Feminist Review* 28: 162–174.

Moore, J. (1992). *The ABC of Child Protection*. Aldershot: Ashgate.

Oaklander, V. (1978). *Windows to our Children: A Gestalt Approach to Children and Adolescents*. New York: The Center for Gestalt Development. (first published Moab, Utah: Real People Press, 1969.)

O'Hagan, K. (1989). *Working with Child Sexual Abuse*. Milton Keynes: Open University Press.

Redgrave, K. (1987). *Child's Play: 'Direct Work' with the Deprived Child*. Cheadle: Boys and Girls Welfare Society.

Roberts, J. (1993). The importance of self-esteem to children and young people separated from their families. *Adoption and Fostering 17(2)*: 48–50.

Rogers, C.R. (ed.) (1951). *Client-Centred Therapy: Its Current Practice, Implications and Theory*. London: Constable.

Rouf, K. (1989). Journey through darkness: the path from victim to survivor, pages 6–10. In G. Lindsay & A. Peake (eds): *Child Sexual Abuse: Educational and Child Psychology*, vol. 6(1). Disley: The British Psychological Society.

Seymour, C. (1990). *Counselling Children*. Unpublished paper. Durham University: Centre of Counselling Skills.

Shapiro, L. (1984). *The New Short-term Therapies for Children: A Guide for Helping Professionals and Parents*. New Jersey: Prentice-Hall Inc.

Stevens, J. (1971). *Awareness: Exploring, Experimenting and Experiencing*. Utah: Real People Press.

Stevenson, O. (1991). Preface, pages 5–7. In CCETSW: *The Teaching of Child Care in the Diploma in Social Work: Guidance Notes for Programme Planners: Improving Social Work Education and Training* No. 6. London: CCETSW.

Stone, M. (1990). *Child Protection Work: A Professional Guide*. Birmingham: Venture Press.

Thompson, C.L. & Rudolph, L.B. (1988). *Counseling Children*. Belmont, California: Brookes/Cole.

Wattam, C., Blagg, H. & Hughes, J.A. (eds.) (1989). *Child Sexual Abuse: Listening, Hearing and Validating the Experiences of Childhood*. Harlow: Longman/NSPCC.

Wells, J. (1989). Powerplay – considerations in communicating with children, pages 44–58. In Blagg *et al.*

Wilson, K., Kendrick, P. & Ryan, V. (1992). *Play Therapy: A Non-Directive Approach for Children and Adolescents*. London: Ballière Tindall.

Winnicott, C. (1964). *Child Care and Social Work: A Collection of Papers Written Between 1954 and 1962*. Welwyn: Codicote.

Winnicott, D.W. (1971). *Therapeutic Consultations in Child Psychiatry*. London: Hogarth.

19

Non-Directive Play Therapy with Abused Children and Adolescents

Virginia Ryan

Introduction

Current professional interest in play therapy has been heightened by the need for more effective help for the increasing numbers of abused children and adolescents referred for professional intervention. It is also due to an increased awareness by professionals of the seriousness of abused children's emotional difficulties. One particular approach, non-directive (or client-centred) play therapy, has recently been advanced as a viable, non-intrusive and relatively short-term method of working with abused children (West, 1992; Wilson *et al.*, 1992).

After giving an overview of this method's therapeutic approach and its historical background, non-directive play therapy's theoretical foundation in modern developmental theory will be summarised. Relevant evaluative research will also be briefly discussed. Non-directive play therapy also has relevance to policy issues of child protection, to care decisions and court proceedings, and to helping child witnesses. The last part of this chapter will give a more detailed analysis of the rationale for using non-directive play therapy to meet the emotional needs of abused children. A case history of a 13-year-old girl who was sexually abused will illustrate the method in practice.

Overview, Historical Background and Research

The most significant way in which non-directive play therapy differs from other play interventions and therapies is in its 'non-directive' nature: that is, the choice of issues, contents and actions in the playroom is determined by the child rather than the adult, within certain basic limits set by the therapist. The non-directive method assumes that the child will instigate therapeutic changes and achieve therapeutic insights him or herself without needing the therapist's overt directions, suggestions or interpretations. The therapist's primary role is to reflect the child's current feelings and emotions accurately and to provide optimum environmental conditions for therapeutic change. The child can then freely utilise the playroom and the therapist to resolve emotional difficulties at his or her own pace.

The method of non-directive play therapy was developed primarily by Axline (1947, 1987), who adapted Rogerian client-centred therapy with adults to child therapy (Rogers, 1951). Children's play rather than, or in addition to, children's verbalisations had already been established in psychodynamic practice by M. Klein and A. Freud as the primary medium for therapeutic help with children (Wolff, 1986). Axline and to a lesser extent other practitioners (e.g. Moustakas, 1953, 1959; Ginott, 1961) relied heavily on clinical examples to illustrate the practice of a non-directive method of play therapy, rather than developing non-directive play therapy's theoretical underpinnings or specifying its procedures rigorously. This atheoretical and aprocedural stance was a deliberate one, which early practitioners believed was needed to counteract the rigidity and convoluted or simplistic theorising they disagreed with in psychoanalytic and behavioural interventions.

Begun originally in North America, this approach also became known in Britain, where it seems to have been practised in relative isolation at child guidance and treatment centres. A few unconnected developments in non-directive play therapy, which took on their own separate characteristics, also emerged in continental Europe, most notably in Germany and Holland (van der Kooij and Hellendoorn, 1986).

These earlier proponents of non-directive play therapy, due largely to their generally atheoretical stance, failed to develop the method into a major school of therapy. Techniques were often not completely specified or directly linked to theoretical principles. Practice sometimes became questionable, and there was a tendency to drift into other therapeutic techniques. As a result, there are deficiencies in non-directive play therapy which are only now beginning to be addressed. First, there has been a notable lack of specification of how other therapeutic techniques with children, such as the World Technique, psychodrama, puppetry, art therapy and structured exercises, to name several discussed in earlier chapters of this book, could be incorporated into non-directive play therapy. (See Wilson et al. 1992, for a further discussion.) Nor has non-directive play therapy's relationship to other therapeutic interventions, particularly psychoanalytic and behavioural approaches, been explored sufficiently. Second, while earlier practitioners did begin to address the use of non-directive play therapy in group treatment (Axline, 1987; Ginott, 1961), other issues, such as the place of individual and/or family therapy or group therapy in statutory settings, as discussed earlier in this Handbook, are only now beginning to be explored (Wilson and Ryan, 1992). In addition, essential practice distinctions in statutory settings, such as differences in referrals for play therapy and referrals for the purposes of assessment, validation or preparation for a life event (for example, preparation of children as witnesses for court proceedings, or children's preparation for a change of foster placement) are also only now beginning to be specified (Wilson, 1993).

Besides addressing these current issues, the practice of non-directive play therapy itself has recently been reviewed and updated, as well as more rigorously specified, both theoretically and procedurally (Guerney, 1984; West, 1992; Wilson et al., 1992). This includes a recognition of its value in court proceedings and in pre-trial interventions with child witnesses (Ryan and Wilson, 1995a). Very recently British play therapy has also developed its own professional organisation (see end of chapter for details), and an extended training programme in non-directive play therapy is being planned.

Because of the earlier piecemeal and largely unco-ordinated approach to non-directive play therapy described above, the extant research on non-directive play therapy is somewhat disappointing. There is a great need for more tightly specified process and outcome research to assess its longer-term effectiveness and the effectiveness of its techniques. The existing research literature, reviewed by Guerney (1984) generally demonstrates that non-directive play therapy can indeed be practised as a technique (e.g. non-directive play therapists make more reflective comments than non-reflective play therapists). However, the research literature fails to specify practice skills completely enough to make replication studies possible. The literature also fails to address other important process issues, for example, at which points in therapy significant moments of therapeutic change occur (Mahrer and Nadler, 1986).

Existing research is also inadequate in failing to investigate current issues of ethnicity, class and gender in the practice of non-directive play therapy. Guerney (1984) stated that no differential process issues or results have been reported for any of the above areas of concern. However, the research she reviewed was not specifically designed to investigate these issues and is therefore not definitive. In fact, particular difficulties have been noted, for example, regarding the therapist's gender in working with sexually abused children and adolescents in non-directive play therapy (Wilson et al., 1992). Therefore, carefully designed studies to investigate these practice issues are much needed.

As well as process research and research on the influences of both the therapist's and the child's gender, class and ethnicity, non-directive play therapy is also in need of more thorough outcome research. While Guerney herself has conducted more extensive research on filial therapy, an offshoot of non-directive play therapy, and continental European psychologists have conducted outcome research on a combined method of directive and non-directive play therapy (e.g. Schmidtchen, 1986), adequate outcome research in non-directive play therapy, particularly research within a statutory setting, is yet to be conducted. However, the current renewal of interest in this approach, its more rigorous specification, and its special applicability to children in statutory settings will most probably contribute towards generating support for and interest in more adequate evaluative research.

The Theoretical Basis of Non-directive Play Therapy

As an approach, non-directive play therapy has a firm foundation in current child development principles (Wilson et al., 1992; Ryan and Wilson, 1995b). These principles are compatible with earlier organismic principles loosely defined by Axline and others. Therefore, some aspects of the organismic principles outlined below will also be familiar to practitioners in education, child health and child welfare.

Within a broad developmental framework of adaptation, as used by Piaget, all of a child's activities are assumed to further a child's adaptation to his or her environment (Wilson et al., 1992) The active internalisation of experiences by a child, or assimilation, is a child's most basic activity, more elementary than a child's other main adaptive function of accommodation, or adjustment of his or her activity to the requirements of the environment.

One universal and highly assimilative activity for a child is symbolic play, upon which non-directive play therapy is based. A child who is engaged in symbolic play, either under everyday conditions or during non-directive play therapy, spontaneously assimilates his or her personally meaningful experiences into internal, personal mental structures called schemas. A child's personal mental schemas are assumed to consist of affective, motor and cognitive components. While conceptually separate, these components are experientially inseparable for a child. During symbolic play, a child can largely ignore external, environmental constraints on mental activity at the same time as freely assimilating personal experiences.

Using this framework, abused children can be viewed as having been subjected to environments in which they were required to accommodate their personally salient experiences to their abusive environments, rather than freely assimilating these experiences to personal schemas. This over-accommodation to the environment is needed for abused children's emotional or physical survival. However, over-accommodation necessarily results in distortions or arrestations in abused children's play, in their relationships with significant adults, and in their own mental and emotional development (Crittenden, 1992; Wilson et al., 1992).

In normal development, unlike the development of an abused child, the large majority of the child's personally significant experiences with a parent are positive ones. Negative experiences, while present, are not as emotionally salient or nearly as frequent as positive ones. In this context, it is noteworthy that Judy Dunn (1988) proposes that normally a young child's cognitive, as well as his or her emotional development, is furthered by affectively charged verbal exchanges within his or her family which have arisen out of the child's thwarted self-interest. That is, 'a child's egoism, in the context of family relationships, motivates him *to understand others'* (Dunn, 1988, page 82). With abused children, however, the affective, motor and cognitive components of their personal schemas are necessarily more distorted, conflicting and/or dissociated from one another than normal because of the strongly negative experiences they have had with their parent(s), along with their more positive experiences. As a result, abused children's personal schemas will not be as easily assimilated to one another, and a more intensive realignment of personal schemas, such as occurs in non-directive play therapy, may be required.

Take the example of a verbal argument between child and parent over whether the child may leave the house, which ends with the abusing parent kicking the child away from the door. This child may not be able to readily assimilate this emotionally and physically painful experience into other more positive personal schemas connected with the abusing parent. In contrast to the non-abused child engaged in verbal conflicts described by Dunn (1988), an abused child may not be able to use assimilating devices such as repetition, imitation and/or symbolic play as readily. For emotionally troubled and abused children, then, personal schemas do not seem to be easily accessible to symbolic representation. This seems to be due to these schemas having been distorted, arrested or isolated from other schemas during their development (Harris, 1989).

Within this theoretical framework, the practice of non-directive play therapy is clarified. A permissive, enhanced play environment which immediately suggests symbolic play and other symbolic activities to an abused, troubled child is required. When this stable environment is coupled with the therapist's focus on the child's feelings, as well as the therapist setting certain limits to behaviour, a child experiences the following changes.

1. Thoughts and feelings previously outside the child's awareness are made conscious and given symbolic representation.
2. Because of the child's increased symbolic assimilation during therapy, the internal organisation of a schema changes, and connections with other personal schemas also alter.
3. Schemas become more mobile in assimilating new events to past experiences, resulting in changes of the child's mental organisation and structure (i.e. personality change) and changes in the child's behaviour.

The method of non-directive play therapy, therefore, has a theoretical basis in current developmental principles and research. It relies on interconnections and interdependencies among theory, rationale and procedures for its practice (see Wilson *et al.*, 1992, for a more extended discussion). Therefore, in order to ensure its effectiveness in helping abused children, non-directive play therapy needs to be utilised as a systematic, coherent approach, rather than being used, as sometimes documented in the literature, in an idiosyncratic or abbreviated manner (Guerney, 1984). When used systematically, as detailed below, it seems to be more effective than behaviour modification techniques or directed interventions aimed at one or two isolated aspects of an abused child's emotional problems (e.g. programmes on the enhancement of self-esteem, on how to say 'no' and keep safe, etc.). It will usually be a shorter intervention than most psychodynamic approaches, which also deal with deeper emotional difficulties. But unlike a psychodynamic approach which employs direct interpretation of symbols and psychological defences to the child, non-directive play therapy allows a child to keep his or her other psychological defences intact until the child is ready to change internally. Non-directive play also assumes that by using symbolic means of expression, a child can rework emotionally troubling experiences both verbally and non-verbally with the help of the therapist's verbal reflections, but without the therapist's verbal interpretations. Non-directive play therapy therefore addresses an abused or troubled child's overall emotional damage, yet it also allows the child to restructure internal personal schemas at his or her own pace.

Broader Policy Considerations and Non-directive Play Therapy

All therapeutic interventions, including non-directive play therapy, with abused children must be practised alongside consideration of child protection issues. No individual therapeutic intervention with a child can protect that child adequately if his or her environment is currently an abusive one. Indeed, in such a case this kind of therapeutic intervention is contraindicated and child protection issues must take priority. There are several reasons for this. First, a child who is already scapegoated or identified as the sole problem in an abusing family may be further scapegoated by being singled out for intervention. Second, the child may be unable to make substantial therapeutic changes because his or her emotional energy needs to be channelled primarily into emotional and physical survival. Third, if a child does, despite these difficulties, make therapeutic changes – say, by becoming overtly angry when the abusing parent makes unreasonable demands – the child may in this way put him or herself at greater risk of harm in an already abusing environment. And fourth, the child will often compare the therapist and the therapeutic relationship with other significant ongoing relationships. If the child's intimate relationship with carers is already seriously inadequate and cannot meet the child's needs, or if it is unsafe, the child may become overly and unrealistically attached to the therapist. The therapeutic relationship will then tend to be misused by the child to fulfil needs which can only be adequately met for him or her on a daily, long-term basis by carers (Glaser, 1991; Wilson et al., 1992). Therefore, the child's environment, for individual therapeutic work to be safe and productive must, at the very least, be minimally adequate for the fulfilment of the child's physical and emotional needs.

The practice of non-directive play therapy also has relevance for care decisions and court proceedings concerning a child. Often it is through individual sessions which are utilised by the child freely, rather than in sessions which are directed by an adult's agenda, that the child's current concerns and the intensity of these concerns are discovered. This information is of great importance in making care decisions and in presenting evidence in court based on the 1989 Children Act. Evidence from non-directive play therapy sessions can be quite different from, but as equally valid as, evidence derived from other means, such as direct questioning and family assessments, of the child's needs, wishes and feelings (Ryan and Wilson, 1995a). While the contents of play therapy sessions must be kept as confidential as possible, important themes emerging in the sessions will usefully inform care decisions concerning the child. Evidence of further abuse of an already abused and thus more vulnerable child may also emerge in non-directive play therapy sessions (see 'Non-directive play therapy with abused adolescents' below). This in turn will further inform care decisions and the necessary protection of the child.

Finally, there is currently professional concern about the conflict between meeting the therapeutic needs of children when court proceedings require that a child give evidence in court, and simultaneously meeting legal requirements for non-contamination of the child's evidential statements. Therapeutic interventions are not automatically ruled out for child witnesses in the UK, but they are at the court's discretion. There have been grave legal concerns, especially in sexual abuse cases where the child is often the only other witness to events besides the accused, that the child's evidence will be contaminated by a therapist's suggestions and interpretations. As discussed above, non-directive play therapy differs from psychodynamic approaches because it does not use interpretation in its practice. The therapist instead keeps to the metaphors and symbols used by the child to reflect the child's ongoing feelings. The non-directive method also employs therapeutic suggestion in a much more curtailed and circumspect way than other therapeutic methods (Ryan and Wilson, 1995a). Most importantly for the child's therapeutic needs, this method – more than any other therapeutic method – enables the child to set the pace for examining painful current material and memories. As well as addressing the child's best interests by providing therapeutic help as soon as possible, research also seems to demonstrate that children who have been traumatised by damaging personal experiences make better witnesses if they have been able to examine and work through on an emotional level their 'worst moments' prior to giving evidence concerning these events (Pynoos and Eth, 1984). Non-directive play therapy therefore has the advantage with child witnesses of preserving the child's own perceptions of these traumatic events. The child's evidence in court is not invalidated from undue therapeutic suggestion, directions or interpretations. And most crucially, the child will be able to receive therapeutic help immediately, rather than having therapy delayed for some time until after a criminal trial.

Child Abuse and Non-directive Play Therapy

Turning from the advantages of employing non-directive play therapy in statutory settings, non-directive play therapy, as stated above, is effective with abused children and adolescents because it is directed at the underlying emotional damage they have sustained. The short and long-term emotional effects of abuse on children and adolescents within a family context have already been discussed in an earlier chapter (see Hanks and Stratton, Chapter 5). Although these effects will vary, and even though a number of abused children do seem to recover from their abusive experiences (Finkelhor, 1992; Hall and Lloyd, 1993), the experiences themselves are inevitably emotionally damaging to children's development (Wilson et al., 1992). Also, it is generally recognised that children who have been abused need increased levels of care either from their own families or from their new care givers (Downes, 1992; Thoburn, Chapter 24). These increased levels of care often extend to children's relationships with professionals in positions of authority, such as teachers and social workers. Abused children often make greater demands on professionals' as well as carers' capacities for limit setting, appropriate physical and emotional closeness, and individual attention, even after the abuse has stopped.

Abused children, as mentioned earlier, have developed damaged, overly accommodating emotional responses to abusive experiences – responses such as passivity, peer aggression and regression to less mature levels of functioning, to name a few. This is because the child's responses to ongoing abusive experiences result in relatively permanent mental schemas on all three cognitive, motor and emotional levels of functioning. These schemas incorporate not only the child's carers (as described in 'The theoretical basis of non-directive play therapy' above), but simultaneously incorporate the most fundamental aspects of a child's own schemas about the self as well. Personally significant interactions, then, always involve the development of schemas concerning the self *and* significant others. And abused children's overly accommodating responses will necessarily involve disturbed personal schemas concerning both the self and carers. Repeated abusive experiences, or even one traumatic experience, may lead a child to develop strongly negative or conflicting personal schemas about him or herself and significant others. A highly compensatory environment may not be sufficient to enable a child to abandon these previously adaptive, persistent mental schemas, or to transform them into more positive ones. Children often need an intensive, corrective experience such as non-directive play therapy in order to re-enact their emotionally damaging experiences on a symbolic (mental) level. Children must rework their schemas concerning the self and significant others into more adaptive schemas once their abuse has ended.

A sexually abused child or adolescent, for example, may have developed a mental schema which contains strong feelings of fear and anger towards his or her carer along with other positive feelings of trust and affection. The cognitive component of this schema may also contain discrepancies concerning a parent who treats the child as an adult sexual partner and yet restricts that child's freedom as a parent in other ways. Relatively permanent cognitive explanations – usually deliberately fostered by the abusing adult (see Wyre, 1991) – such as 'I am unusually sexy, that's why my father/mother can't help being sexually attracted to me' may develop. Motor level conflicts are also common: sexual abuse involves parts of the child's body, usually both the child's intimate body parts as well as body parts such as the hands and mouth which are normally involved in non-sexual activities for a child. A child will have difficulty assimilating sexually abusive bodily sensations and motor responses which are experienced into existing motor schemas involving normal motor experiences. Take a motor schema related to physical care: a child having his or her hair brushed by the carer, for instance, would usually have developed a motor schema for hair-brushing associated with feelings and personal experiences of nurturance. But in sexual abuse, hair-brushing for this child may have emotionally powerful sexually abusive connotations as well.

Non-directive play therapy is of particular value for abused children and adolescents who have sustained this kind of emotional damage. This is because the mental organisation of personal experiences is inherently private, highly affective and predominately assimilative. A child or adolescent in non-directive play therapy is given time and privacy to address these deeper mental levels of personal experiences using symbolic play accompanied by the therapist's focus on reflecting the child's ongoing feelings. Symbolic play, as stated above, is a natural vehicle children use to assimilate and express their personal experiences. The abused child actively directs his or her own process of symbolic re-enactment of personally meaningful experiences, thus automatically individualising and personalising the practice of the method of play therapy itself.

Another feature of abuse, that is its co-existence with other forms of abuse, is also addressed in this way. Very often the separate effects of neglect, emotional, sexual and physical abuse may be difficult to unravel (see Chapter 5). Because of its highly individualised approach, non-directive play therapy can readily adapt to whatever additional issues emerge during therapy for the child. Besides the possibility of other forms of abuse, it is likely that the child will also be able to symbolically recreate and explore the 'worst moments' in his or her traumatically abusive experiences (Pynoos and Eth, 1986). These personally traumatic experiences may include the sudden, inexplicable abandonment of the child during a special, happy outing arranged by the usually abusive parent, or in another case, a child finding out that the abusing parent had lied to the child about the child's much valued toy being stolen when, in fact, the parent had deliberately sold the toy and kept the money him or herself. Another feature of abuse, that abused children often understate the extent of their abuse initially, can also be discovered in non-directive play therapy. (The implications for child protection issues when further abuse is disclosed in therapy are discussed in 'Non-directive play therapy with abused adolescents' below, and in Wilson et al., 1992.) In all these instances, the therapist recognises the feelings the child is expressing in the non-threatening environment of the playroom and reflects these feelings back to the child. This reflecting process, as discussed at greater length by Wilson et al. (1992), does *not* include praising, parroting, questioning or passivity, all of which are not conducive to accurate reflection of the child's ongoing activities, thoughts and feelings.

Returning to symbolic play, this type of play necessarily involves all the motor, emotional and cognitive levels of functioning together for a child, thus enabling a child to integrate and rework all these levels of abusive experiences. Furthermore, besides an immediate symbol a child may be consciously aware of, there may be many more remote or more threatening meanings to a symbol of which the child is unaware. Because the child determines the contents and issues of play therapy sessions, the child is able to give symbolic expression to thoughts and experiences which are less threatening to him or her, but which also connect with and activate more threatening schemas. In this way, non-directive play therapy does not raise the child's anxiety by dealing directly with highly self-threatening experiences or by dealing directly with the coping mechanisms a child has developed to protect him or herself from anxiety, such as denial, dissociation or displacement. The child him or herself breaks down his or her own barriers to self-threatening experiences with the help of the therapist's reflections, using the natural and fundamentally non-threatening activity of play.

Non-directive play therapy, therefore, is based on real choices of content and issues which are made by the child rather than by the adult therapist. This feature of the method is especially important in work with abused children. Control over the child's important personal experiences has been exercised abusively by the adult carer to meet the adult's emotional needs for power, aggression or sexual gratification, and not to fulfil the child's own needs. By the reintroduction of choice over personally meaningful experiences in non-directive play therapy, the lack of choice and previous adult coercion is directly counteracted. It is when the abused child or adolescent has control over the content of his or her sessions and the pace of therapeutic change that compliant or reactive mental schemas and overt behaviours that were developed in response to adult demands are minimised. As a result, the child's awareness of his or her own personal thoughts, feelings and responses is enhanced. Additionally, because the therapist follows the child's activities, thoughts and feelings and reflects these back, the child begins to realise that his or her own external and internal actions during the sessions are of importance to the therapist and, therefore, must be of value internally as well. In practising non-directive play therapy, the therapist's own needs and emotions have to be subordinated to the child's. But the therapist must also be consciously aware of internal emotions, especially those generated in the therapist by specific interactions with the child. These emotional reactions, which must be separated from personal and private emotions by the therapist, must then be used by the therapist to help clarify and give primacy to the child's expressed feelings.

This general subordination of personal emotions, thoughts and needs by the therapist is a necessary part of the practice of non-directive play therapy. It is an artificial enhancement of a feature of a normal adult–child nurturing relationship. The subordination of adult needs to those of the child in normal development, for example, the adult waiting to eat until the hungry child has been fed, is made workable because the adult parent's primary need, using Erikson's model, is for generativity, or caring for others (Erikson, 1963). But a recurring feature of abusive experiences for children is that this normal adult–child relationship pattern has been damaged, and adults have put the fulfilment of their own emotional and physical needs before those of their children. This helps account for the extreme adaptations and vacillations observed in abused children's emotional reactions. In normal development, children's needs are adequately met and they gradually learn to wait and to subordinate some of their own needs to others' needs. But abused children often over-subordinate their own needs to others, or else become desperate and frantically out of control in an attempt to have their own needs fulfilled. Even when their needs do begin to be met in a more appropriate manner, abused children often retain a learned fear that these needs will remain unmet.

In non-directive play therapy the therapist participates in sessions at the child's pace and direction with great predictability, thus subordinating his own or her own adult needs. But at the same time the therapist maintains an adult guiding role. The therapist needs to respond congruently with appropriate, healthy adult responses to the child's expressed behaviours, thoughts and feelings. For example, if a sexually abused child attempts to thrust some play dough down the front of a therapist's trousers, the therapist must respond congruently by saying that the therapist would not feel comfortable because that place is private and stop the child's action. But at the same time, the therapist needs to help the child express these feelings and perhaps perform these actions in a more socially acceptable way, say to a doll.

The above example illustrates that although the overall emphasis in non-directive play therapy is permissive and child-centred, it is essential that therapeutic limits are established by the therapist in his or her adult role. Indeed, both therapeutic limits and emotionally healthy adult responses are an essential component of this approach. In these adult interactions with the child, the therapist enables the child to develop emotionally healthy responses to necessary adult limits on the child's behaviour. More generally, the therapist also makes understandable and predictable to the child normal adult–child interactions (Ryan and Wilson, 1995b). In this way, an abused child is able to correct previously self-destructive and antisocial adaptations developed in response to abusive experiences.

The practice of non-directive play therapy therefore entails creating an enhanced play environment in which the toys and materials provided are conducive to symbolic play (see Wilson et al., 1992, for a further discussion of the appropriate setting and equipment). This equipment remains the same at each session. The sessions themselves take place at the same time each week, for a pre-determined time period, usually for an hour's duration. We have suggested that a short-term, time-limited intervention, say of ten sessions to begin with, with a review and the possibility of ten more sessions is a workable arrangement. (Again, see Wilson et al., 1992, for an extended discussion of preparation and planning issues.)

This regularity of time and place is adhered to in order to promote an emotionally troubled child's relaxation and confidence in a strange environment. More important still, the therapist, in addition to the environment, must convey familiarity easily to the child in their initial sessions. The therapist needs to communicate appropriate responsiveness to the child through his or her friendly, yet non-directive and non-intrusive stance during each session (Ryan and Wilson, 1995b).

These sessions are non-directive in the sense that the child is allowed to choose the content, issues and actions of the hour him or herself, in contrast to a more directive approach in which the therapist introduces his or her own topics of concern and asks the child questions. The non-directive therapist does, however, broadly structure the sessions for the child. As well as preparing the room with largely symbolic play materials, the therapist also directs the child's attention to his or her ongoing, spontaneously expressed feelings and emotions at a pace which is non-threatening to the child.

This core practice skill of reflection of ongoing feelings differs from a stance of passivity or of praising the child. It also differs from a psychodynamic approach because it does *not* include verbally interpreting the child's actions or verbalisations to the child him or herself. (But hypothesising and interpreting are a necessary aspect of the therapist's internal tasks. See Ryan and Wilson, 1995a.) In accurately reflecting the child's expressed feelings, the non-directive therapist is trained to use certain of his or her own feelings which arise in response to the child. These feelings are used congruently by the therapist to ensure that appropriate, normal adult responses are made to the child's behaviour and expressed feelings.

The practice of congruence can be illustrated in conjunction with another essential practice skill, the setting of therapeutic limits. If, using our earlier example, during their session together the child attempts to thrust play dough down the front of the therapist's trousers, the therapist needs to set a limit to the child's behaviour and not allow him or her to carry out this action. The therapist uses his or her own feelings congruently, in that this action invades a private place on his or her body. In addition, she reflects the child's ongoing feelings, such as, perhaps, his or her feeling of power over the therapist.

In summary, the practice of non-directive play therapy can be characterised as follows:

- Careful preparation and planning, to promote the child's confidence in trusting him or herself to therapy.
- The development of a trusting, accepting relationship with the child.
- The reflection of the child's feelings by the therapist in a non-threatening manner.
- The use of feelings congruently by the therapist to reflect back to the child appropriate responses to his or her expressed behaviour and feelings.
- The establishment of appropriate therapeutic boundaries.

Non-Directive Play Therapy with Abused Adolescents

Before illustrating the practice of non-directive play therapy with themes emerging in sessions with a 13-year-old sexually abused girl, a consideration of the appropriateness of this technique with adolescents is necessary. It has been generally accepted by earlier practitioners that children aged 12 and over of normal intelligence are unsuitable for non-directive play therapy. Case studies for early adolescence have seldom been documented, and an adult counselling relationship is advocated. The suitability of non-directive play therapy for older pre-adolescent children has also been questioned, and a different, more realistic set of games and activities is often made available by play therapists for this age group (Guerney, 1984; West, 1992).

In our recent book, we have discussed this issue at some length, arguing that non-directive play therapy is both an effective and theoretically justifiable therapeutic method with troubled adolescents. Briefly, non-directive play therapy can help an adolescent to integrate earlier childhood experiences, present concerns and future more adult concerns into the adolescent's developing sense of unique personal identity. Children and adolescents who have been abused have particular problems in integrating experiences which have been abusive into an emotionally healthy sense of self, as discussed above. When their personal mental schemas have been arrested or distorted, abused adolescents find it difficult to rework schemas of their childhood selves and apply them to emotionally healthy ways of functioning in more adult relationships. Not only will their earlier emotional development have been damaging, and parental role models unhealthy ones, but abused adolescents may also have developed difficulties in peer relationships and difficulties in their desire to and ability to integrate into wider adult society in an emotionally healthy manner.

Non-directive play therapy can be used therapeutically to help abused adolescents integrate emotionally damaging experiences into their current identities. In order to work effectively with this age group, however, certain practice issues must be considered throughout. While a few more highly structured materials may be desirable for this age group, most materials should still lend themselves to unstructured symbolic activities and play. As with younger age groups, materials (such as art materials, puppets and staging) should be selected that can be used at the highest potential level of adolescent functioning as well as materials that can be used for much younger, regressive play. Both types of materials should be made freely available for the adolescent's use. Adult-sized furniture also immediately demonstrates to the adolescent that the room is used by a range of ages to both sit and talk in and to play in. These preparations are needed for adolescents because the therapist must be aware of an adolescent's heightened sensitivity and negative reaction to being treated only as a child. In introductory meetings as well, the therapist must ensure that the adolescent is not alienated by the therapist's failure to respect his or her age. But at the same time, as with younger children, the therapist must enable the adolescent to feel a sense of permissiveness in the room which extends to whatever thoughts, activities (or non-activities) and materials the adolescent him or herself chooses.

Furthermore, concerns over privacy and confidentiality are often greater for adolescents than for younger children. A private room without any outside interruptions and which is not overlooked is particularly necessary for adolescents, who may be more self-conscious of other's reactions to their sessions and will only manage to engage freely with the materials and therapist in private. Another related area of concern to the adolescent may be anxiety about peers' and other outside adults' interest in therapy sessions, and others' possible misuse of this information by teasing or labelling the adolescent as different or deranged. Again, the therapist must be sensitive to arranging sessions at times which minimise this potential intrusion (for example, lunch-time or after school). With abused children and adolescents, however, privacy may be an even more sensitive issue. Too much privacy in one-to-one interactions may be reminiscent of abusive experiences, or may direct an adolescent's attention too painfully to the large discrepancies in his or her other significant adult relationships. In these cases, individual therapeutic intervention may not be possible, and other interventions may be more appropriate initially, such as group work or family work.

Another important related concern is the extent to which the therapist can assure the adolescent that the content of sessions will remain private. (It is essential, however, that abused children and adolescents are given permission explicitly by the therapist to reveal whatever contents of sessions the child or adolescent chooses to others. Otherwise, again, the therapeutic relationship may too closely mirror a previously abusive one.) It is impossible, and indeed misleading, for therapists to guarantee complete confidentiality. All therapists must consider issues of confidentiality because of their professional obligation to report disclosures of abuse made within therapy sessions. Added considerations for therapists working in statutory settings include the kind of communication to establish with the carer, the type of information from sessions which will be shared with a referring agency through case conferences and reports, and the level of detail to reveal in court proceedings (Wilson et al., 1992; Ryan and Wilson, 1995a).

While younger children may have more difficulty understanding the circumstances under which the therapist must discuss their sessions with others, adolescents are usually able to understand these issues. However, adolescents may also feel a heightened need for confidentiality from the therapist. And abused children and adolescents in particular may want complete confidentiality, having often been previously subjected to different forms of threats and coercions by abusing adults to ensure the secrecy of the abuse, and thus the abuser's freedom from detection and punishment. This need for security and exclusivity can be generalised to any close relationship with an adult, including individual therapy. It is imperative, then, that the therapist discusses confidentiality issues and recording procedures with the adolescent (and with young children, in keeping within their understanding) at the beginning of their time together. If this discussion is omitted, the adolescent may falsely believe, in keeping with his or her needs, that the therapist is offering complete confidentiality. The adolescent may then be less guarded and justifiably, feel betrayed when the therapist must report general sessional themes or specific abusive incidents to others. With abused adolescents (and children) mistrust of adults or overly trusting responses are already likely to be a crucial feature of their emotional difficulties. The therapist will increase this emotional damage if issues of confidentiality are not addressed honestly and sensitively from the start.

Working in Non-Directive Play Therapy with a Sexually Abused Adolescent

Patricia was 13 years old at the time of referral for play therapy sessions. Her initial appearance was of a self-assured, verbally aggressive and articulate older adolescent. She was physically mature, attractive and careful about her appearance. Patricia had disclosed sexual abuse by her uncle and later by her stepfather as well, but she was disbelieved and blamed for the resulting investigation by her family, which included her mother, stepfather, 16-year-old sister and 6-year-old half-brother. Patricia's extended family had already been investigated for sexual abuse. From the case notes on file, the atmosphere in these related families seemed to be highly sexualised, with a blurring of adult–child role boundaries and a failure to maintain sexual boundaries between generations. When Patricia began to attend play therapy sessions, which took place for an hour once a week over a 3-month period (15 sessions altogether), she had been separated from her family and placed in foster care because of the continuing risk to her of sexual abuse. Several key themes which were important to Patricia emotionally emerged during her play therapy sessions. These themes illustrate many of the points raised earlier about the value of non-directive play therapy in working with abused adolescents and children. Two important themes for Patricia in her sessions, to be discussed below, include: the therapist's trustworthiness; and the reworking of childhood memories and distortions of bodily image arising from sexual abuse. (For a more extended discussion of these themes, see Ryan and Wilson, forthcoming.)

Theme one: the therapist's trustworthiness

A key theme throughout her sessions for Patricia was whether the therapist was a trustworthy and reliable adult. This issue seemed to have strong emotional salience for Patricia because of her emotional development within an abusive family atmosphere. She shared her family's mistrust of and anger with any professional in a role of authority and was particularly vehement about social services' interventions which investigated sexual abuse. Patricia repeatedly blamed social services for removing her from home, yet she also began to express surprise during her sessions that her statements about sexual abuse had been believed in spite of her family's denials.

Another conflict for her was that while she desperately wanted to return home, and later in therapy expressed a longing to return to her pre-school existence within her family, she was at the same time deeply hurt by her family's rejection of her. In the process of therapy, Patricia began to consciously acknowledge to herself that her family often distorted information given to her, to other family members and to professionals, as well as keeping secret from her much about the extended family's complicated and disturbed relationships. Patricia's growing ability to examine her family's attitudes was made possible by the permissive atmosphere of her sessions, but also by the therapist's predictable and caring responses to Patricia's verbal statements and the therapist's reflection of Patricia's quickly changing and conflicting feelings. Patricia seemed to use the therapist as an anchor for thinking about her family and herself.

Confidentiality was an important, recurring theme for Patricia and an important element in the development of a trusting relationship with the therapist. Patricia tested out with the therapist the confidentiality of her sessions with other professionals, often aggressively challenging the therapist on whether her social worker would be informed of what she was doing in the sessions. Towards the end of their sessions together, when Patricia's level of trust in the therapist had increased, she confided in the therapist that she had not earlier told the therapist about several of the dangerous games she had been playing with peers because she had enjoyed having secrets from the therapist and, besides, she was certain that the therapist would have told her social worker or the police. The therapist reflected Patricia's feelings that it was fun to feel more powerful early on by having secrets from adults who were trying to know just about everything about you. The therapist also acknowledged that Patricia was right. The therapist as an adult would have tried to prevent Patricia from seriously harming herself and others, and she may also have had to tell others.

Patricia also spent an inordinate amount of time talking about other younger children who used the room. While this was related to Patricia retrieving her childhood memories, which are discussed below, she also seemed both intrigued and challenged by the therapist's rule of confidentiality regarding other children's use of the playroom. Patricia returned to this topic often, used a variety of persuasive arguments, and even resorted to a younger child's wheedling tone in her attempts to test out the therapist's resolve in keeping this rule. The therapist repeated that she must maintain silence, thus enforcing a necessary therapeutic limit, and she also reflected Patricia's varied feelings, including a genuine interest and concern for the younger children and a belief that if she was persistent, the therapist would weaken and do something the therapist felt was wrong. Patricia's use of more abstract thinking on this issue allowed the therapist to reflect Patricia's feelings back to her at each occurrence, to subordinate her own feelings of harassment to Patricia's need to adopt extreme means in an attempt to weaken the therapist's resolve, to state her own position to Patricia clearly and to give reasons for her position that Patricia at 13 years could understand. Using this non-directive approach, Patricia actively engaged in a process common to normal adolescence, but usually engaged in with lesser intensity. That is, Patricia was in the process of examining and understanding her own values and how these differed from both the values of the therapist and the values of her own family. The therapist for Patricia, therefore, represented the adult world of values in a very direct sense, and Patricia gradually developed a somewhat grudging trust in the therapist.

Theme two: the reworking of childhood memories and distortions in bodily image resulting from sexual abuse

While the first theme seems to rely heavily on non-directive counselling skills rather than play therapy *per se*, it is important in understanding Patricia's progress in therapy to note that from her first session onwards Patricia was purposeful in choosing an activity to perform with her hands while she talked. Patricia seemed to have no difficulty accepting the play setting or materials as appropriate for her age. (Her initial worries instead centred on her own use of the materials, which she considered to be inept and 'babyish', and on being ridiculed by peers for needing therapy at all.) She decided to use the clay and spent her early sessions, and a few sessions towards the end of her 15 sessions, modelling in this medium. Her early work in clay consisted of forming simple clay figures and using her hands to work them into smooth curves and then squeezing them shapeless again as she concentrated on verbal exchanges with the therapist.

After her initial play with the clay as an adjunct to her conversation, Patricia began to concentrate more intently on her ongoing activity using her hands, and her verbalisations lost prominence. Motor activities and sensations became central, and Patricia began to cover her hands completely with smooth wet clay, allowing it to harden before washing it off and restoring her hands to their usual clean, well-manicured condition. The therapist reflected Patricia's feelings and hypothesised to herself (and not to Patricia, as a psychodynamic therapist may have done) that perhaps Patricia was beginning to rework on a motor and affective level using symbolic means, the abusive masturbatory experiences she had disclosed during her earlier investigative interview. Along with the clay, Patricia also began to use the play dough in the room and to remember several happy times in her earlier childhood when she had enjoyed similar play and felt well looked after by her mother.

Following these play sequences, Patricia began to experiment with finger paints, first covering her hands with bright, vivid colours and then coating them repeatedly with more colours until they turned stickily dark brown. This process of covering her hands in thick layers of sticky paint lasted for several sessions, with Patricia using her whole body in a diffuse, sensual way. The therapist reflected Patricia's feelings of how good the process felt at the beginning; but then Patricia never stopped there and had to make her hands messier, even though they weren't as nice as at the beginning. She also reflected Patricia's disgust with her transformed hands by the end of her play, followed by her anxiety over needing to quickly make her hands perfect again.

Patricia's actions became less frantic and of shorter duration as she continued to rework what appeared to be her abusive experiences on this symbolic level. The therapist made occasional reflections, but Patricia, while continuing her activities without constraint, did not herself verbalise her feelings and actions during this time. However, she did verbally express great concern that the therapist would keep the paints ready for her use as long as she needed them. After several sessions, however, Patricia had finished completely with the finger paints and chose to return to her earlier medium of clay. This intense play sequence with finger paints paralleled changes in Patricia's appearance. She became more casual in her dress, decided to change her hairstyle and generally looked younger and more similar to other young adolescents.

By reworking her abusive experiences on a motor and affective level in symbolic play, Patricia seemed to have transformed her previously distorted mental schemas involving her body and its actions into more appropriate ones.

Summary

Non-directive play therapy is an effective method of intervention for children and adolescents who have been abused. Because the method is non-directive, during sessions children themselves direct the issues and contents to be explored in symbolic play. As discussed above, symbolic play is a normal means children use to express highly personal, complex emotional experiences. In non-directive play therapy sessions, children's abusive experiences are reworked into healthier patterns of responses on all mental levels (i.e. emotional, cognitive and motor levels) of functioning simultaneously. This reworking of experiences by children using symbolic play occurs within the context of a trusting, permissive atmosphere that the therapist and child have established. This relationship, while permissive, is also kept within the therapeutic limits needed by the child.

Adolescents in non-directive play therapy will commonly combine symbolic play with verbalising to the therapist, who needs to employ non-directive counselling skills more intensively for older age groups. A core skill in working with both children and adolescents is the therapist's ability to reflect the child's or adolescent's feelings during sessions in an accurate, yet non-threatening manner. The therapist must also have developed a coherent, personally meaningful and viable theoretical framework for therapeutic practice, as outlined in this chapter, to allow the use of personal feelings congruently in making appropriate, emotionally normal responses to the child's or adolescent's expressed behaviour and feelings.

Conclusions

It has been demonstrated in this chapter that non-directive play therapy provides the practitioner with a theoretically rich and coherent system of therapy based on developmental principles. This theoretical framework is useful in explaining the rationale for using non-directive play therapy in working specifically with abused children and adolescents. It also serves to guide the therapist in developing necessary non-directive play therapy practice skills, such as reflection of feelings, congruence and the setting of appropriate therapeutic boundaries. A strong need has been expressed for more definitive research on process and outcome issues in non-directive play therapy, especially in statutory settings. The development of a more extensive training programme in non-directive play therapy is also needed and being planned.

Professional Organisation (including Training Information)

Association of Play Therapists
c/o Lyn Bennett
Bucklands Cottage
Wallingford Road
Cholsey OX10 9HB

Recommended Further Reading

Axline, V. (1947). *Dibs: In Search of Self*. New York: Ballantine Books.
A moving account of a young boy's experience in non-directive play therapy.

Axline, V. (1987). *Play Therapy*, revised edn. New York: Ballantine Books.
A general introduction to play therapy, including Axline's eight principles.

Guerney, L.F. (1984). Client-centred (non-directive) play therapy. In C. Schaefer & K. O'Connor (eds): *Handbook of Play Therapy*. New York: Wiley and Sons.
An overview of research theory and practice.

Rogers, C. (1951). *Client-Centred Therapy*. London: Constable.
Roger's explanation of client-centred therapy, as well as Dorfman's application of his approach to play therapy.

West, J. (1992). *Child-Centred Play Therapy*. London: Edward Arnold.
A recent practical guide to working with children in non-directive play therapy.

Wilson, K., Kendrick, P. & Ryan, V. (1992). *Play Therapy: A Non-Directive Approach for Children and Adolescents*. London: Baillière Tindall.
An updated extension of theory and practice in non-directive play therapy.

References

Axline, V. (1987). *Play Therapy*, revised edn. New York: Ballantine Books.

Crittenden, P.M. (1992). Children's strategies for coping with adverse home environments: an interpretation using attachment theory. *Child Abuse and Neglect 16:* 329–343.

Downes, C. (1992). *Separation Revisited: Adolescents in Foster Family Care*. Aldershot, Hants: Ashgate.

Dunn, J. (1988). *The Beginnings of Social Understanding*. Oxford: Basil Blackwell.

Erikson, E.H. (1963). *Childhood and Society*. New York: Norton and Co.

Finkelhor, D. (1992). Child sexual abuse: recent developments in research. Paper presented at 'Surviving Childhood Adversity Conference', Trinity College, Dublin

Ginott, H. (1961). *Group Psychotherapy with Children: The Theory and Practice of Play Therapy*. New York: McGraw-Hill.

Glaser, D. (1991). Therapeutic work with children. In K. Wilson (ed.): *Child Protection: Helping or Harming*. University of Hull: Papers in Social Policy and Professional Studies, No. 15.

Guerney, L.F. (1984). Client-centred (non-directive) play therapy. In C. Schaefer & K. O'Conner, (ed.): *Handbook of Play Therapy*. New York: Wiley and Sons.

Hall, L. & Lloyd, S. (1993). *Surviving Child Sexual Abuse: A Handbook for Helping Women Challenge their Past*. London: Falmer Press.

Harris, P.L. (1989). *Children and Emotion*. Oxford: Basil Blackwell.

Mahrer, A.R. & Nadler, W.P. (1986). Good moments in psychotherapy: a preliminary review, a list and some promising research avenues. *Journal of Consulting and Clinical Psychology 54(1):* 10–15.

Moustakas, C. (1953). *Children in Play Therapy*. New York: McGraw Hill.

Moustakas, C. (1959). *Psychotherapy with Children: The Living Relationship*. New York: Harper and Row.

Pynoos, R. & Eth, S. (1984). The child as witness to homicide. *Journal of Social Issues* 40: 87–108.

Pynoos, R. & Eth, S. (1986). Witness to violence: the child interview. *Journal of the American Academy of Child Psychiatry 25(3):* 306–319.

Rogers, C. (1951). *Client-Centred Therapy: Its Current Practice, Implications and Theory.* London: Constable.

Ryan, V. & Wilson, K. (1993). Non-directive play therapy: therapeutic intervention with children and adolescents. In G. Bradley & K. Wilson (eds): *The Family, The State and the Child.* Papers from the Four Nations Conference. Hull: Department of Social Policy and Professional Studies, University of Hull.

Ryan, V. & Wilson, K. (1995*a*). Child therapy and evidence in court proceedings: tensions and some solutions. *British Journal of Social Work.* 25: 157–172.

Ryan, V. & Wilson, K. (1995*b*) Non-directive play therapy as a means of recreating optimal infant socialisation patterns. *Early Development and Parenting, 4(1):* 29–38

Ryan, V. & Wilson, K. (forthcoming) *Case Studies in Non-directive Playtherapy.* London: Baillière Tindall.

Schmidtchen, S. (1986). Practice and research in play therapy. In R. van der Kooij & J. Hellendoorn (eds): *Play, Play Therapy and Play Research.* Lisse: Swete and Zeitlinger.

van der Kooij, R. & Hellendoorn, J. (eds) (1986). *Play, Play Therapy and Play Research.* Lisse: Swete and Zeitlinger.

West, J. (1992). *Child-Centred Play Therapy.* London: Edward Arnold.

Wilson, K. (1993). The healer and the carer. *Community Care: 978:* 27.

Wilson, K., Kendrick, P. & Ryan, V. (1992). *Play Therapy: A Non-Directive Approach for Children and Adolescents.* London: Baillière Tindall.

Wolff, S. (1986). Childhood psychotherapy. In S. Block, (ed.): *An Introduction to the Psychotherapies,* 2nd edn. Oxford: Oxford University Press.

Wyre, R. (1991). Working with sex offenders. In K. Wilson, (ed.): *Child Protection: Helping or Harming.* University of Hull: Papers in Social Policy and Professional Studies, No. 15.

20

Helping to Prevent Abuse: A Behavioural Approach with Families

Katy Cigno

Introduction

In 1982, Sheldon wrote that it was impossible for one practitioner to open his or her mouth or put pen to paper without making another despise him or her for having got it wrong. This was because social workers and other professionals were looking for the approach to end, or encompass, all other approaches. This attitude to practice simplifies – dangerously so – the therapeutic task, particularly with regard to working with vulnerable people, as in child protection. A comparable view has been recently expressed in a paper on direct work with children (Ronen, 1993).

We have moved some way since then, and this chapter is part of a volume which addresses issues concerning child protection from many perspectives, giving examples of different theoretical and practice approaches to intervention. The question now to ask is not 'which approach?' but 'what evidence is there that this or that approach works, in specified circumstances, with this client with this problem?' (Cigno and Wilson, 1994.) The aim of this chapter is therefore to consider the circumstances in which a behavioural approach, using social learning theory, can be useful in helping to protect children by preventing abuse through improving child–parent interaction. This emphasis on prevention is advocated by Cohn and Daro (1987) in their review of the research on treatment effectiveness, and the issue has been recently readdressed on this side of the Atlantic by Hollows and Wonnacott (1994).

Some concepts associated with social learning theory and a behavioural approach have been incorporated into the Children Act 1989 (see below). Some have informed recent social work practice and education, as in the current emphasis on observable competencies in the Central Council for Education and Training in Social Work's Paper 30 (CCETSW, 1991). Teachers and health visitors have also long been aware of the importance of positive reinforcement and modelling in child development and skill acquisition. Ronen, while commenting that social work was founded upon a psychodynamic approach, nevertheless writes:

> 'Social workers have always been concerned with effective treatments, the definition of clear goals and the clarification of client needs. These features link social work to cognitive–behavioural therapy.' (Ronen, 1994, page 273.)

In short, there is now too much evidence of the effectiveness of behaviourally based approaches (Sheldon, 1986; Macdonald *et al.*, 1992) for these not to be part of a practitioner's repertoire (Hudson and Macdonald, 1986; Sutton, 1994; Webster-Stratton and Herbert, 1994).

The Current Policy Context of Intervention

Some key concepts which have emerged to inform the policy context for social services, social work, health and education of the late 1980s and early 1990s are:

- clarity and openness, verbally and in record-keeping;
- service user empowerment;
- partnership with service users and with other professionals;
- setting goals, monitoring and evaluating services.

Examples of recent legislation which set out guiding principles for practitioners and incorporate such concepts are the Access to Personal Files Act (1987), the Children Act 1989 and the National Health Service and Community Care Act 1990.

The idea of client or patient access to files initially aroused opposition from both the medical profession (Timmins, 1987) and other practitioners and officials (Cohen, 1982; Hennessy, 1988) who were unused to promoting an open agenda with service users and who were often unclear as to who, in fact, was the client and in whose interests the records were kept (Cigno and Gottardi, 1988, 1989). The same writers found that the more task-centred practitioners were clear on these issues and had, prior to the legislation and preceding Government circulars, worked openly on problem-solving and behavioural goals with their clients, many of whom were parents. More recent research has shown that parents involved in child protection investigations prefer social workers and others to be honest and direct with them (Hepworth and Larsen, 1990; Sutton, 1994).

The Children Act 1989 and the National Health Service and Community Care Act 1990 both stress the need for contracts, or working agreements, with clients. In the case of the former, however, this is implicit rather than explicit, but the Department of Health's document *Working Together* (DOH, 1991) spells this out more clearly. The use of contracts is long-established in behavioural work (Sheldon, 1979). It is clear from both these Acts that practitioners are to carry out careful, detailed assessments (essential in behavioural work) and empower clients by, for example, getting them to participate in writing records ('needs-led' user profiles, in the case of the National Health Service and Community Care Act).

The notion of partnership with parents for the benefit of the child is, again, implicitly incorporated in the Children Act 1989 (Herbert, 1993). It is, however, elucidated in such documents as *Protecting Children* (DOH, 1988), *The Care of Children* (DOH, 1989) and *Working Together* (DOH, 1991). These guidelines also stress that the child's interests are paramount. Behavioural workers have always been aware that intervention in the home, however well planned and child-centred, will fail unless the parents or carers are informed and involved (Herbert, 1987a; Corby, 1993; Webster-Stratton and Herbert, 1994). This is because they are important mediators for many types of intervention, and in any case spend far more time with their children than the practitioner.

In sum, a behavioural approach would appear to incorporate the principles of good practice embodied in current legislation affecting service users and, more particularly, families. In addition, because of its lack of mystique and its objectives of working with clients on specific, agreed goals, it is arguably also both ethical and anti-oppressive (see Hudson and Macdonald, 1986, page 20, for a full statement of the ethical guidelines of the Behavioural Social Work Group, UK).

Effective Intervention: Research and Practice

The intention here is not to address every area where a behavioural approach might be adopted. Space precludes this. Instead, the discussion will focus on specific, important and well-documented areas where the use of this approach has been particularly successful in work with families where risk to the child's well-being or safety has been identified. These include:

- working with families on child–parent interaction where child behaviour problems have been identified;
- training for parents, particularly to help them cope better where children have severe behavioural problems or where parents have difficulty in controlling their anger;
- intervention where the child is failing to thrive.

Writers and therapists in these areas are from different helping professions, publishing monographs and articles in a variety of professional journals. As might be expected, however, psychologists have been at the forefront in research on behavioural intervention in families (e.g. Herbert, 1987a and b, 1989; Gibb and Randall, 1989; Webster-Stratton and Herbert, 1994). Nurses have also made important contributions to the case study literature on child abuse (e.g. Gilbert, 1980). One important text on behavioural family therapy has been written by a psychiatrist (Falloon, 1988). Social workers have also, particularly recently, produced case study research (e.g. Bunyan, 1987; Bourn, 1993), while Sutton (1979, 1987, 1994) is one of a group (including Sheldon, 1982, and Hudson and Macdonald, 1986) with a background and qualifications in both social work and psychology who have written on theory and practice in a variety of settings, including child abuse and neglect.

Mention has already been made of the importance of working openly in partnership with families. However, a recent research study (Thoburn et al., 1991) indicates that, sadly, few practitioners fully involve and inform family members in child protection work. The authors conclude that policies aimed at client participation and empowerment are unlikely to be effective unless workers make constant, concerted efforts to involve the family in the process of protecting children. Corby (1993) also concludes that programmes which empower and include parents are likely to be more effective.

Theoretical Principles

The advantage of a social learning approach as a framework for effecting change is that working closely with family members to whose actions and words close attention is paid and who are considered partners in therapy is intrinsic to anti-oppressive intervention. As Sutton says, in a useful statement which includes both a definition and evaluation:

> 'Social learning theory comprises a large body of concepts which, happily, are recognised by researchers in the disciplines of both psychology and sociology. It concerns how children and adults learn patterns of behaviour, as a result of social interactions, or simply through coping with the environment . . . it suggests how to focus upon the practical rather than the pathological, upon people's strengths and potentials rather than upon their weaknesses or shortcomings, and upon how to empower those with whom we work.' (Sutton, 1994, pages 5–6.)

A behavioural approach, as the name implies, is aimed at altering patterns of behaviour which are dysfunctional and therefore requires the practitioner to focus on the detail of interactions between parents and children. Consequently, a starting point for behavioural assessments is usually an ABC (antecedents, behaviour, consequences) analysis of these interactions. Briefly, the questions to ask when using such an analysis in assessment are:

Antecedents
- What are the circumstances in which the behaviour takes place?
- What happens just before the behaviour in question?

Behaviour
- What is the actual behaviour?
- What does the child/person do?

Consequences
- What happens immediately after the behaviour?

Parents, and children where possible, are encouraged to look at the relationship between the three. Webster-Stratton and Herbert (1994) give many short examples of using the ABC format in family assessment. An example of the use of this format in child protection practice is given in the following section.

Working with families in the home

There is now a substantial body of studies evaluating behavioural intervention with families in non-clinical settings. What is striking about them is their careful, detailed, descriptive approach, attention to method, recording and use of observable criteria for success. Earlier studies contrast behavioural intervention with the prevailing psychodynamic approach. For example, Petts and Geddes (1978) point out essential differences and evaluate, by means of a chart and a descriptive account, the results of teaching child management to single-parent mothers as part of a strategy to improve family life. Seheult (1985) discusses the use of parents as their children's therapists and emphasises the importance of relieving stress which the whole family suffers when a child exhibits severe behavioural problems.

Therapeutic benefits to the pre-school child and the alleviation of family stress are also discussed by Bidder *et al.* (1981) who, from a medical school child health department, carried out a series of home interventions with nine children where there were similar problems to those reported by Bunyan (1987) and Bourn (1993), whose case studies are discussed below. Theirs was a carefully designed study which used a control group and aimed at achieving results over a short period. They found that the 'treated children' improved considerably, their behaviour becoming similar to those of the control group children after four to five visits. At 6 months, the improvements were maintained. They conclude that 'brief behavioural intervention has considerable potential and is reasonably economical in terms of staff time' (Bidder *et al.*, 1981, page 21).

Increasingly, programmes are multi-disciplinary and multi-faceted. Research has shown that practitioners need to pay attention to many factors in the family's environment and networks, using an ecological approach (Gambrill, 1983). Specific interventions should be undertaken within a framework of the use of other resources (e.g. a family centre or a nursery – see Cigno, 1988; Gill, 1989; Cigno and Wilson, 1994) and a warm rapport (Hudson and Macdonald, 1986). Gill, a social worker working with health visitors, reports a high level of parental satisfaction with support groups where participants were actively involved in devising and implementing strategies for change appropriate to them (Gill, 1989).

An example of such a multi-disciplinary, multi-faceted approach is given by Carter *et al.* (1981). A teacher, social worker and educational psychologist successfully intervened in the case of Alan, a 10-year-old boy who was glue-sniffing, aggressive and truanting. His parents had attempted to control his behaviour by physical punishment. They used a contract with the boy and his parents (see also Webster-Stratton and Herbert, 1994, for examples of contracts), targeted positive reinforcement and paid particular attention to working with the family to devise a strategy for maintaining improvements after programme termination. All targeted behaviours improved – for example, Alan began attending school again – but the authors claim only modest success and observe that 'time will tell' if the maintenance strategies devised will be effective.

In two articles, Ronen (1993, 1994) discusses direct therapeutic cognitive–behavioural intervention with children, mainly from a social work point of view. She is concerned with, among other matters, crucial issues of child involvement and careful choice of target and approach for intervention. She discusses important misconceptions about the selection of treatment methods; for instance, that the child who is lacking in verbal skills and has many problems is usually referred for long-term, dynamically oriented play therapy, while the child 'who suffers from a specific deficiency or problem and wishes to eliminate it is referred to short-term behaviour therapy'. (Ronen, 1993 page 593.) Echoing aspects of what is stressed elsewhere in this chapter, she urges practitioners to carry out careful assessments in order to find out where best to intervene and with which method, referring the child to another therapist if necessary.

Finally, two case studies describe the use by practitioners working in social services departments of the ABC format outlined earlier. Bourn (1993) gives an account of an intervention in the home where two children were put on the Child Protection Register after over-chastisement by the mother. The central problem was identified as child non-compliance and defiance towards a mother who was lacking in child-management skills. Bourn's analysis of 4½-year-old Scott's problem behaviours includes the following.

Antecedents
- Background of poor housing and socio-economic disadvantage.
- Active, restless child.
- Non-compliance worse at home and with mother, during the week.
- Mother tired and busy.
- Scott refuses to eat breakfast or get dressed.
- Mother gives unclear instructions, then demands immediate compliance with the implicit or actual threat of aversive consequences, e.g. 'Pack it in! Now!'

Behaviour
- Scott fails to comply.
- Twirls around with his trousers on his head instead of getting dressed.
- Swears at mother.

Consequences
- Mother makes threats which she is unable to carry out.
- If punishment given – e.g. if Scott sent to his room – he amuses himself there.
- Mother 'gives up', or over-chastises child in attempt to control him. (Adapted from Bourn, 1993, pages 488–489.)

Intervention included specifying the rules for positive reinforcement; using role-play in the settings where the behaviour was likely to occur to enable mother to practise how to reinforce Scott positively, both materially and socially; and getting mother's partner to encourage and socially reinforce her for using the programme.

Another useful example of an ABC analysis followed by behavioural intervention is given by Bunyan (1987), where a child at serious risk of abuse presented problems of defiance, aggression, destructiveness and sleep irregularity. Both Bourn and Bunyan stress the importance of thorough assessment. In both accounts, the intervention was aimed at increasing child compliance, improving parental management skills, reducing aversive interaction between parent and child using positive reinforcement (e.g. by praise, hugs, a sticker, small material rewards) and parent training.

The reported results are encouraging. In both families, there was a positive improvement in the child's behaviour and an increase in parental self-esteem and management skills as charted and observed by the practitioners. Bunyan followed up at 6 months and Bourn at 11 months. The results in both cases showed that the improvements in the target behaviours had been maintained, there was no symptom substitution, and the parents were relieved and more relaxed.

Parent training

It is often difficult to separate this from a 'working with families' approach described above, since it is often used as a strategy in family-centred interventions such as those considered in the previous section. However, Herbert (1987b, 1989) and Webster-Stratton and Herbert (1994) give many examples of parent training, which they refer to as a parent–therapist collaborative process. They include a review of the literature in this area as well as a detailed account of group work with parents.

Scott and Stradling (1987) and Scott (1989) have also carried out group parent training programmes in two connected areas: with parents of children with severe behavioural problems, and with parents who cannot benefit from such training, largely because they have difficulty in controlling their anger. The authors observe that the training can also work with individual parents. Scott's programme is based on six to eight sessions which include discussion, direct teaching of behaviours, role rehearsal and homework assignments. He stresses the importance of feedback and making sure that principles and instructions are understood. Where anger is a problem, parents can usefully be taught to relax before starting training (Barth et al., 1983).

Scott uses 'before and after' measures to evaluate how well new behaviours are learned, as well as a control group. Evaluation takes place at 3 and 6 months via home observation and role-play tests. He reports a significant decrease in frequency and intensity of child behaviour problems, and in parental depression and irritability (Scott, 1989). Whiteman et al. (1987) also report good results from cognitive–behavioural intervention aimed at reducing anger in parents at risk of abusing their child.

Webster-Stratton and Herbert (1994) stress the significance of empowering parents and giving them self-confidence in training sessions. It is also important to make sure that parents will have support and reinforcement for good parenting once the sessions are over, such as monthly 'booster shots' with the therapist. Many practitioners and researchers in this field refer to Patterson's (1976) earlier work, on which they base their intervention. Patterson also reported that parent training is an effective way of changing a child's disturbed behaviours. Frosh and Summerfield (1986) review the effectiveness of parent training, stressing that such intervention has an educative as well as a treatment role, a point which could be made of much behavioural therapy.

As community care policies are implemented, involving the emptying of hostels for adults with learning difficulties (many of whom came originally from long-stay hospitals), increasing attention has been given to the ability of such adults to cope in the community, even with the help of social services support workers. More particularly, there has been a focus on the ability of those who choose to have children to provide 'good enough' parenting. Dowdney and Skuse (1993) ask whether parents with a learning disability (they use the still current American term 'mental retardation') display competent parenting, and, if not, whether they can be taught parenting skills. This is an important area attracting increasing attention in terms of both research and practice. They report that the small amount of research so far available on the subject is conflicting, and that there are many factors to take into account. However, they conclude that intervention, within a relationship of rapport and trust, is usefully directed at teaching basic caretaking and play skills.

Where there is neglect or abuse, behaviour modification programmes can improve parenting. The authors suggest that imitating role models is a good way to acquire skills, which should be broken down into small steps (in a way similar to Portage methods used in families where there is a child with a learning difficulty; see, for example, Lloyd, 1986). Non-specific counselling in this area of work is not useful. The authors go on to say that training needs to be long, rewards are effective for establishing and maintaining behaviours, and that more success is obtained where the goals are clear and individualised.

Booth and Booth (1993) also review the research evidence in their study of 20 families where one or both parents have learning difficulties. Their conclusion is that parenting skills can be improved by training, despite some reservations about the focus of North American research and the (largely unmet) need for long-term skill reinforcement. They rightly consider the place of parent training and behaviour modification techniques generally in a broad environmental context which often discriminates against people with a learning disability. Practitioners are urged to take note when planning intervention that 'good parenting' models are necessary in order to be able to learn good parenting. Although not made explicit, the reference to the importance of social learning theory for intervention is clear.

Intervening where a young child 'fails to thrive'

Major research into cases of non-organic failure to thrive has been undertaken by Iwaniec and colleagues and has been reported in two parts (Iwaniec et al., 1985a, b). Part I considers psychosocial factors and Part II describes the intervention. A detailed description of the characteristics of such a child is given (see also Iwaniec, 1987, and Budd, 1990). Briefly, the child is below average height, thin with a large stomach, cold to the touch, intellectually and speech delayed. She or he appears sad and lethargic, refuses to eat and often vomits.

The intervention of Iwaniec and colleagues, based on social learning theory, has essentially three parts to it. It is often preceded by teaching the mother how to relax, since mothers of non-organic failure-to-thrive children tend to be tense and anxious. The workers:

- use modelling, role rehearsal and advice to restructure the way in which the mother feeds the child (how to touch, smile at and talk to the child at mealtimes);
- gradually work to improve mother–child interaction on a wider front (e.g. in play), involving other members of the family, including the father;
- concentrate on positive parent–child interactions; give frequent and regular support to the family (e.g. by telephone calls as well as visits) in order to give positive reinforcement to the mother for her efforts.

The writers stress that the child also needs to go to nursery school as an added safeguard. Physical aspects of the child's well-being need constant control. Intervention is terminated only when the practitioner has observable evidence that the child's health and development have improved. An average intervention lasts 10 months. Immediate and long-term evaluation has shown positive results.

Herbert's case study of a 2-year-old twin suffering from failure to thrive follows similar lines (Herbert, 1987a). He refers to theories of operant and classical conditioning to explain the child's behaviour, as well as theories of depression and learned helplessness (Seligman, 1975) to explain the mother's behaviour. The subject of the study had been hospitalised five times because of feeding problems and weight loss. With such serious threats to health, very careful monitoring and evaluation is essential. As well as self-monitoring by the mother and evaluation by the therapists, follow-up assessments by a paediatrician, nutritionist and health visitor were used to confirm progress.

Summary of Key Issues for Practitioners

Working under the Children Act 1989 often poses a dilemma for practitioners: how to work in partnership with parents *and* keep the child's interests central to the intervention. Here, the notions of thorough assessment, careful monitoring and evaluation of intervention should help. Further, as this chapter has underlined, in cases where the welfare of a child is of primary concern, a combination of techniques and services may be used to advantage, but the outcome criteria must be *observable*. That is, the practitioner is looking for positive behaviour change in the child and parent or carer; visible and audible improvement in child–parent interaction; and, in cases of failure to thrive, improvement in the appearance, weight, height and general health of the child. Practitioners need to become keenly observant of detail as well as conscious of the importance of the wider environment in assessment.

There is a need for open approaches which clients can understand and participate in, where family members feel empowered by being treated as individuals. The use of a written contract to state precise goals parents need to achieve, desired reciprocal behaviour patterns between a child and his or her parents (as in 'contingency' contracts) and/or responsibilities of clients and practitioner (as in 'service' contracts) can seem coercive if badly drafted (as many are) by those with insufficient training. In experienced hands, however, such a document is the clear, honest result of negotiation. It will make clear to parents and others, in simple language, what they need to do to make the child safe; how to improve child–parent interaction; what resources are available to support them in this (e.g. practitioner home visits, toy library, playgroup); when the contract will be reviewed; and what the consequences are for non-compliance of the responsible adults. (For further comments on the use of contracts in cases of child abuse and neglect, see Sutton, 1994, pages 215–216, and pages 174–175 for an example of a contract adaptable to many situations in one-to-one and family work; for rules for writing contracts, see Herbert, 1993, pages 172–173.)

It is particularly important in cases where parents feel they are failing in some way with their child that their views and feelings are carefully attended to, and that they are clear about the goals they need to achieve in order to demonstrate 'good enough' parenting. In some cases, service users need to know what they have to do in order *not* to be involved in intervention!

Gambrill's (1981) checklist for behavioural intervention in child abuse and neglect, although apparently basic, is still pertinent today and thus worth repeating. It provides a summary of key points to bear in mind, but also provides useful guidance for practitioners working with children and families about how to prevent abuse occurring. The checklist appears below in an abbreviated form.

1. Looking as well as talking.   Direct observation of parent–child interaction is essential. Identify specific behaviours, their antecedents and consequences. Assess in natural settings, such as the home and school.

2. Looking rather than inferring   Do not presuppose particular associations between behaviour and environmental events. Directly observe interaction.

3. Being specific rather than global   Identify specific objectives – what should be done, by whom, in what situation, with what frequency, duration or intensity? Describe clearly what assessment and intervention procedures are to be used.

4. Practising in addition to talking   Arrange for clients to practise new behaviours at home.

5. Focusing on overt behaviour   Identify observable outcomes against which progress can be measured.

6. Measuring rather than inferring progress   Identify objective and subjective measures of progress. Identify clearly what the desired outcome is.

7. Taking advantage of available resources Find out what the intervention costs in terms of time, effort and materials. Use resources already available and find out about suitable training material through publishers' lists, etc.

8. Training material for clients Use self-help manuals, written rules, instructions, reminders, pamphlets, tapes.[1] (Adapted from Gambrill, 1981, pages 18–20.)

Conclusion

Practitioners have a duty to do their best for their clients, especially for those, like young children, who cannot demand a service for themselves. Unless workers keep themselves well-informed – for example, through reading and seminars – and make efforts to increase their skills through practice under supervision, then values expressed in such terms as 'anti-oppressive practice', 'working together' and 'empowerment' will be meaningless. Children and parents have a right to competent intervention.

There are many approaches described in the literature for working with children and families. It should not be a question of choosing a favourite and sticking to it unquestioningly throughout one's professional life. First, the empirical evidence must be considered: how successful is this approach, with which people, with which problems? Has the approach or the service been evaluated at all? As a recent Royal College of Nursing report on nursing and child protection revealed, there is a 'worrying lack of co-ordination' in the wake of the NHS purchaser–provider split; a danger of service fragmentation, putting children at risk; and 'haphazard, inadequately planned, inconsistent services [which were] neither evaluated nor monitored' (Friend and Ivory, 1994, page 3).

Second, in each particular case, we 'start where the client is', looking at their priority needs. In the field of preventing child abuse, this must mean that our concern is to make improvements in the family situation so that the child is safe from harm, is able to play, go to school, enjoy contact with carers, etc. As Sutton (1994) points out in her review of intervention evaluation in child abuse, 'the research in this area should make us cautious'. Referring to Cohn and Daro's (1987) overview of treatment programmes for child abuse and neglect, she reminds us that recorded cases of neglect 'seemed particularly intractable' (Sutton, 1994, page 113).

On the whole, the evidence suggests that a multi-faceted approach where, for example, parent training is one of several services families receive, is more likely to lead to success. Moreover, concentrating on protecting children by preventing abuse happening or escalating could be a better way of tackling the problem (Cohn and Daro, 1987) and is certainly more beneficial to children and families (Hardiker *et al.*, 1989; Cigno and Wilson, 1994; Francis, 1994; Hollows and Wonnacutt, 1994). The evidence also makes it clear that social learning theory and behavioural intervention can make a significant contribution to the effectiveness of strategies for working with children and families.

---

[1] Many behavioural practitioners compile their own material. One useful, published booklet is *Seven Supertactics for Superparents* by Wheldall *et al.* (1983).

Further Reading

Hudson, B.L. & Macdonald, G.M. (1986). *Behavioural Social Work: An Introduction.* Basingstoke and London: Macmillan Education.
Written for social workers, the book is an excellent introduction to the behavioural approach for any practitioner needing a basic understanding of social learning theory and how to go about behavioural intervention. It also covers cognitive–behavioural procedures. Part I deals mainly with theory and methodology; Part II with different client groups and problems. There is a chapter on working with parents and younger children.

Iwaniec, D., Herbert, M. & McNeish, A.S. (1985*a*). Social work with failure-to-thrive children and their families. Part 1. Psychosocial factors. *British Journal of Social Work* 15: 243–249.

Iwaniec, D., Herbert, M. & McNeish, A.S. (1985*b*). Social work with failure-to-thrive children and their families. Part 2. Behavioural social work intervention. *British Journal of Social Work 15:375–389.*
These two articles are important for the understanding of failure to thrive. The description of the assessment and intervention is clear and detailed. The research is relevant to practitioners from different professions.

Sutton, C. (1994). *Social Work, Community Work and Psychology.* Leicester: British Psychological Society.
Many practitioners will find this book useful for its clear explanation of social learning theory and its applications in a variety of settings. The author is concerned with multi-disciplinary working and emphasises that different professions can learn from one another. Particularly relevant to child protection are the chapters on human development, children and families, child abuse, and values and ethics. The rich amount of case material is multi-cultural and deals with such issues as communicating across language and cultural barriers.

Webster-Stratton, C. & Herbert, M. (1994). *Troubled Families – Problem Children.* Chichester: Wiley & Sons.
The subject is child conduct disorders. The authors discuss family-based approaches and assessment, with an emphasis on working with parents. Part 1 is concerned with understanding child conduct disorders and their impact on the home and community, while Part 2 offers a detailed guide for therapists. There are many case examples and discussions of specific behavioural procedures, such as the use of 'time out' and contracts.

References

Barth, R.P., Blythe, B.J., Schinke, S.P. & Schilling, R.F. (1983). Self-control training with maltreating parents. *Child Welfare 62(4):* 313–324.
Bidder, R.T., Gray, O.P. & Pates, R.M. (1981). Brief intervention therapy for behaviourally disturbed pre-school children. *Child: Care, Health and Development 7:* 21–30.
Booth, T. & Booth, W. (1993). Parenting with learning difficulties: lessons for practitioners. *British Journal of Social Work 23:* 459–480.

Bourn, D.F. (1993). Over-chastisement, child non-compliance and parenting skills: a behavioural intervention by a family centre social worker. *British Journal of Social Work 23:* 481–499.

Budd, J. (1990). Falling short of the target. *Community Care:* 15 November, 12–13.

Bunyan, A. (1987). Help, I can't cope with my child: a behavioural approach to the treatment of a conduct disordered child within the natural home setting. *British Journal of Social Work 17:* 237–256.

Carter, B., Low, A. & Winter, S. (1981). A technology to replace an art. *Community Care:* 20–21.

Central Council for Education and Training in Social Work (1991). *Rules and Requirements for the Diploma in Social Work.* Paper 30, 2nd edn. London: CCETSW.

Cigno, K. (1988). Consumer views of a family centre drop-in. *British Journal of Social Work 18:* 361–375.

Cigno, K. & Gottardi, G. (1988). Il diritto dell'utente all'informazione e alla riservatezza: l'accesso dell'utente alla documentazione del servizio. *La Rivista di Servizio Social 4* 33–56.

Cigno, K. & Gottardi, G. (1989). Open files and data protection: serving the client's best interests? *International Social Work 32:* 319–330.

Cigno, K. & Wilson, K. (1994). Effective strategies for working with children and families: issues in the provision of therapeutic help. *Practice 6:* 285–298.

Cohen, R.N. (1982). *Whose File is it Anyway?* London: National Council for Civil Liberties.

Cohn, A.H. & Daro, D. (1987). Is treatment too late: what ten years of evaluative research can tell us. *Child Abuse and Neglect 11:* 433–442.

Corby, B. (1993). *Child Abuse: Towards a Knowledge Base.* Buckingham: Open University Press.

Department of Health (1988). *Protecting Children: a guide for social workers undertaking a comprehensive assessment.* London: HMSO.

Department of Health (1989). *The Care of Children: principles and practice in regulations and guidance.* London: HMSO.

Department of Health (1991). *Working Together: a guide to arrangements for inter-agency co-operation for the protection of children from abuse.* London: HMSO.

Dowdney, L. & Skuse, D. (1993). Parenting provided by adults with mental retardation. *Journal of Child Psychology and Psychiatry 34:* 25–48.

Falloon, I.R.N. (1988). *Handbook of Behavioural Family Therapy.* London: Guildford Press.

Francis, J. (1994). Cruellest cut of all. *Community Care:* 7 April, 14–15.

Friend, B. & Ivory, M. (1994). Fragmentation leads to chaos. *Community Care:* 17 March, 3.

Frosh, S. & Summerfield, A.B. (1986). Social skills training with adults. In C.R. Hollin & P. Trower (eds): *Handbook of Social Skills Training,* vol 1. Oxford and New York: Pergamon Press.

Gambrill, E. (1981). The use of behavioural procedures in cases of child abuse and neglect. *International Journal of Behavioural Social Work and Abstracts 1:* 3–26.

Gambrill, E. (1983). *Casework – A Competency-Based Approach.* New Jersey: Prentice-Hall.

Gibb, C. & Randall, P. (1989). *Professionals and Parents: Managing Children's Behaviour.* Basingstoke and London: Macmillan Educational.

Gilbert, M.T. (1980). Child abuse: a behavioural approach. *Nursing Times:* November, 828–831.

Gill, A. (1989). Putting fun back into families. *Social Work Today: 20:* 14–15.

Hardiker, P., Barker, M. & Exton, K. (1989) Perspectives on prevention. *Community Care 'Inside'* 7 December, i–ii.

Hennessy, P. (1988). Secrecy: the virus in the bureaucrats' blood. *The Independent,* 4 July, page 4.

Hepworth, D. & Larsen, J. (1990). *Direct Social Work Practice: Theory and Skills*, 3rd edn. Belmont, California: Wadsworth.

Herbert, M. (1987a). *Conduct Disorders of Childhood and Adolescence: A Social Learning Perspective*, 2nd edn. Chichester: Wiley & Sons.

Herbert, M. (1987b). *Behavioural Treatment of Children with Problems: A Practice Manual.* 2nd edn. London and Florida: Academic Press.

Herbert, M. (1989). *Discipline: A Positive Guide for Parents.* Oxford: Basil Blackwell.

Herbert, M. (1993). *Working with Children and the Children Act.* Leicester: British Psychological Society.

Hollows, A. & Wonnacott, J. (1994). Protected by prevention. *Community Care:* 30 April, 22–23.

Hudson, B.L. & Macdonald, G.M. (1986). *Behavioural Social Work: An Introduction.* Basingstoke and London: Macmillan Educational.

Iwaniec, D. (1987). Assessment and treatment of failure-to-thrive children and their families. *Behavioural Social Work Review 8(2a):* 9–19.

Iwaniec, D., Herbert, M. & McNeish, A.S. (1985a). Social work with failure-to-thrive children and their families. Part I. Psychosocial factors. *British Journal of Social Work 15:* 243–259.

Iwaniec, D., Herbert, M. & McNeish, A.S. (1985b). Social work with failure-to-thrive children and their families. Part II. Behavioural social work intervention. *British Journal of Social Work 15:* 375–389.

Lloyd, J.M. (1986). *Jacob's Ladder: A Parent's View of Portage.* Tunbridge Wells: Costello.

Macdonald, G.M., Sheldon, B. & Gillespie, J. (1992). Contemporary studies of the effectiveness of social work. *British Journal of Social Work 22:* 615–644.

Patterson, G.R. (1976). The aggressive child: architect of a coercive system. In L. Hamerlynk, L. Hardy & E. Mash (eds): *Behaviour Modification and Families*, vol. 1. New York: Brunner Mazel.

Petts, A. & Geddes, R. (1978). Using behavioural techniques in child management. *Social Work Today 10(5):* 13–16.

Ronen, T. (1993). Adapting treatment techniques to children's needs. *British Journal of Social Work 23:* 581–596.

Ronen, T. (1994). Cognitive–behavioural social work with children. *British Journal of Social Work 24:* 273–285.

Scott, M.J. (1989). *A Cognitive–Behavioural Approach to Clients' Problems.* London: Tavistock/Routledge.

Scott, M.J. & Stradling, S.G. (1987). The evaluation of a group parent training programme. *Behavioural Psychotherapy 15:* 224–239.

Seheult, C. (1985). Using parents as their children's therapists. *Update:* 15 February, 309–318.

Seligman, M.E.P. (1975). *Helplessness.* San Francisco: Freeman.

Sheldon, B. (1979). *The Use of Contracts in Social Work: A Practice Note.* Practice Note Series 1. Birmingham: British Association of Social Workers.

Sheldon, B. (1982). *Behaviour Modification: Theory, Practice and Philosophy.* London: Tavistock.

Sheldon, B. (1986). Effectiveness experiments: review and implications. *British Journal of Social Work 16:* 223–242.

Sutton, C. (1979). *Psychology for Social Workers and Counsellors.* London: Routledge.

Sutton, C. (1987). *A Handbook of Research for the Helping Professions.* London and New York: RKP.

Sutton, C. (1994). *Social Work, Community Work and Psychology.* Leicester: British Psychological Society.

Thoburn, J., Lewis, A. & Shemmings, D. (1991). *Family Involvement in Child Protection*

Conferences. East Anglia: Social Work Development Unit, University of East Anglia.

Timmins, N. (1987). 'Doctors divided over patients' right to know' and 'Open files would spell the end of surgical witticisms'. *The Independent,* 5 May, page 12.

Webster-Stratton, C. & Herbert, M. (1994). *Troubled Families – Problem Children.* Chichester: Wiley & Sons.

Wheldall, K., Wheldall, D. & Winter, S. (1983). *Seven Supertactics for Superparents.* Windsor: NFER-Nelson.

Whiteman, M., Fanshel, D. & Grundy, J.F. (1987). Cognitive behavioural intervention aimed at anger of parents at risk of child abuse. *Social Work 32:* 469–474.

21

Working with Abusing Families

Tilman Furniss and Liza Bingley Miller

Introduction

In recent years, family work in child abuse has changed from a mainly psychodynamic approach to a much clearer concept of family work in a wider systemic context. The relationship between therapeutic work and statutory contexts has been clarified and developed in the work at the Hospital for Sick Children, Great Ormond Street, London, in Rochdale and elsewhere (Dale *et al.*, 1986*a*, *b*; Bentovim *et al.*, 1988; Furniss, 1990). The function of family centres, which traditionally provided little more than a holding environment, is now much more structured and goal-oriented and stresses aspects of responsibility, self-help, autonomy, strength and resourcefulness of families and family members (Asen *et al.*, 1989).

Family work with abusive families has started to differentiate between families with physical abuse and neglect, and families where sexual abuse has occurred (Crittenden, 1988; Stratton, 1991; Hanks, 1993). Work with families where children have been emotionally abused is much less developed, and the focus is largely still on defining the core concepts involved (Crittenden and Ainsworth, 1989; Erickson, 1989; Glaser, 1993; Hobbs *et al.*, 1993).

This chapter explores the role of family work and family therapy with families where child abuse has taken place and it falls into two main parts. The first part of the chapter is concerned with all forms of child abuse and addresses a number of conceptual, planning and practice issues relevant to working with families where physical, sexual or emotional abuse or neglect has taken place. The second part focuses on child sexual abuse in order to highlight the specific considerations which need to be addressed and to allow the exploration of one area of child abuse in more depth.

Within the first part of the chapter, the scene is set by a brief review of some of the relevant literature on family therapy and the links with child abuse. Next, some conceptual and planning issues are considered which relate to working with abusing families. These include: the differences between family therapy and consultation; the distinction between a family approach and a family therapy approach to family work with abuse; issues of motivation; indicators for involving the whole family; and the differing emphasis given to change and growth in work relative to the different forms of abuse and neglect. A range of practice issues relating to family work and family therapy for all forms of child abuse are then covered, and several family therapy techniques are described which can be useful in work with abusing families.

The second part of the chapter focuses on families where child sexual abuse has taken place. A distinction is made between child sexual abuse and other forms of abuse, highlighting the therapeutic importance of some key aspects of the family work which is required, including the evaluation of suspicion of child sexual abuse and the handling of disclosures, trauma work and work with siblings.

Family therapy as an intervention is then considered more specifically. The steps which need to be taken for effective family therapy are laid out, as well as a range of family therapy techniques which can be useful at different stages of work with families. The chapter finishes with a closer look at perhaps the most difficult aspect of the therapeutic process – the conducting of the first family meeting. The content, process and organisation of such sessions are addressed in some detail because of the challenge they present to many professionals.

Working with Abusing Families – Child Abuse and Neglect

A brief look at the literature

This chapter is based on a family systems approach to working with abusing families. It looks at family therapy specifically as one form of change-oriented intervention with families and refers to a number of family therapy interventions and techniques. It is therefore important to map briefly the family therapy context in which this chapter is located and point to a few of the key themes in the family therapy literature for readers who are not familiar with the field.

Family therapy is a form of intervention which focuses on the whole family, including the relationships between family members, as the unit requiring attention. Family systems theory is used as a framework, both to make sense of the problems and difficulties encountered by individuals, subgroups or the family as a whole, and to shape the therapist's work with families. Systems theory (von Bertalanffy, 1968) forms the basis of family systems theory, in which the family is viewed as a system with specific properties. These include the structure of the family, its boundaries, patterns and processes of communication, the relationship between different subsystems within the family and between the whole family and the outside world, family rules and belief systems, and the way the individual family members give meaning to their experiences (Bingley et al., 1984; Burnham, 1986; Barker, 1990).

The family can be seen as a group of persons related by biological ties and/or long-term expectations of loyalty, trust and commitment, and comprising at least two generations (Loader, 1982). There is a social expectation that the family performs certain functions and tasks. For example, the family can be seen as being expected to take responsibility for the physical and emotional well-being and socialisation of the children, and to provide for the maintenance of the emotional well-being and the personal growth of the adults.

The tasks linked to the fulfilment of these responsibilities differ according to the various stages in the life cycle of the family, so that when the children are young, for example, the focus is likely to be on physical safety and nurturing, whereas by adolescence the emphasis is shifting towards helping the children to establish themselves as relatively independent and secure adults (Carter and McGoldrick, 1989).

The way in which families carry out these tasks varies greatly, because it is affected by the culture, ethnic group and religion to which the family belongs, their social and economic grouping, the balance of power within the family, and the values, attitudes, traditions and past experiences of adults in the family (Ahmed *et al.*, 1986; Walters *et al.*, 1988; Ahmad, 1990; Perelberg and Miller, 1990). All these dimensions influence how family members relate to each other and to the outside world.

These responsibilities, functions and tasks are carried out in a social context, and they are shared with other people and institutions such as the extended family and friends and the wider framework of educational, medical, social services and social security and law enforcement services. These institutions provide a context for the family which is usually likely to be experienced by families as supportive and complementary, but which can be experienced as hostile and threatening, as is often the case with families where child abuse has taken place.

The family is understood by family therapists as being a system which has a tendency towards equilibrium, which is achieved by the family responding to the need for change over time (morphogenesis), and as a system where the whole is more than the sum of its parts (von Bertalanffy, 1968; Carter and McGoldrick, 1989; Burnham, 1986).

Family therapists vary in the emphasis they give in their work to the different properties of the family as a system, and in this chapter we refer to a range of techniques from several different schools of family therapy. It may therefore be helpful to distinguish between some of these various family therapy approaches, although it is important to note that there is considerable overlap among them.

Structural family therapists work on creating change in the structure of the family system by paying particular attention to the boundaries around the different subsystems (parent–child, parent–parent, partner–partner, and so on) and the communication between them (Minuchin, 1974; Fishman & Rosoman, 1991). The therapist initially seeks to 'join' the family and will then use a range of techniques to 'challenge' the family's usual pattern of behaving and communicating or, as Minuchin and Fishman put it, 'how things are done' (Minuchin and Fishman, 1981). The therapist then actively works to provide the family with an experience of alternative ways of perceiving the family relationships and of behaving towards each other. The therapist reinforces any changes, thus 'restructuring' the family system into one more likely to enhance the development of family members.

Strategic family therapy focuses on devising strategies to solve the problems of the client or family (Haley, 1976, 1980; Madanes, 1982; Hayes, 1991). A wide range of direct and indirect strategies are employed, one of which is to give the family tasks to carry out together between sessions. The tasks are designed to redefine the problem situation in the family and to shift the way the family organises itself. Problems are often framed in terms of the family (as a system) needing to find a way of negotiating a move (or transition) to the next stage of the family life cycle (Carter and McGoldrick, 1989).

Systemic family therapy, as developed by the Milan group (Palazzoli *et al.*, 1978, 1980, 1982; Boscolo *et al.*, 1987), understands the problem presented by the family as an integral part of the system in which it occurs, and it is therefore regulated by the rules that govern that system. Thus, 'the way to eliminate that symptom is to change the rules' (Palazzoli et al., 1978). The Milan group initially emphasised the need for the therapist to remain 'neutral', although this has shifted more recently. The therapist, while avoiding taking sides with any part of the family, carefully gathers information about the way in which the family operates through techniques such as 'circular questioning'. This involves asking one family member about the relationship between two other family members, and then checking that perception. In this way, the therapist and the therapeutic team develop a picture of the myths and 'rules' which govern the family as a system, usually implicitly rather than explicitly, and the experience and meaning of family relationships for family members.

Interventions come in the form of statements offered to the family by the therapist which tie together the positive benefits or functions the symptom has for the family (reframing and positive connotation), with the negative price or 'sacrifice' the family has to pay to maintain it. Once the ambiguity around the 'symptom' has been identified, clarified and challenged, it is often unacceptable to the family to continue in their old pattern, and change takes place. Systemic family therapists, in common with some of the strategic family therapists, make use of tasks, rituals, paradox, metaphor and storytelling in their interventions with families (Campbell and Draper, 1985; Boscolo et al., 1987).

While many family therapists focus their attention on working with the current pattern of communication and relationships in families (the 'here and now'), other approaches seek to unravel the influence of significant past events, experiences and relationships on current family relationships. The work of Byng Hall (1973, 1990) links past patterns of attachment and authority structures to the family myths and scripts, attachment relationships and management of authority issues in the current family. A range of different ways of using genograms has been developed to highlight the pattern of intergenerational relationships (Satir, 1967, 1972; Liebermann, 1979; Carter and McGoldrick, 1989). McCluskey (1987) has developed an existential approach to family therapy which focuses on the emotional life of the family, using a theme to anchor the work.

The focal family therapy workshop at the Hospital for Sick Children, Great Ormond Street, London, developed a format for integrating and assessing information about significant past events and relationships, the meaning given by individuals to these experiences, and the impact those meanings have on current family interactions and relationships (Bentovim, 1979; Glaser et al., 1984). The focal formulation also enables the therapist to track and evaluate changes achieved during therapy (Kinston & Bentovim, 1983; Furniss et al., 1983). Bentovim (1992; Bentovim and Davenport, 1992) has developed the focal approach further in his work on trauma-organised family systems. McCluskey and Bingley Miller have combined focal family therapy and theme-focused family therapy to address the past in the present. Their approach gives adults the opportunity to re-edit the past and gives the children a voice to articulate their present concerns and feelings in relation to their experience of being in a family (McCluskey and Bingley Miller, 1995).

Recent developments in family systems theory have seen constructivist ideas coming to the fore (de Shazer 1984, 1989). The focus is on how individuals explain their experience to themselves by constructing a 'reality', or view of events, which is made up of elements of objective facts seen through the filter of that person's perception and experience of the world. Family therapists using a constructivist framework see the way in which family members construct their sense of reality as being integral to the distress or difficulties which bring them into therapy. The focus in therapy is to facilitate shifts in the constructed reality created in families which in turn produce changes in their expectations and enactment of family relationships.

De Shazer's solution-focused therapy (de Shazer, 1982) emphasises the solution to perceived problems and working with the self-organisation of the family towards realising that solution. It is future-focused, and looking at traumatic and salient past events in the life experience of family members is positively discouraged.

The fast growing area of trauma therapy (Eth and Pynoos, 1985; Figley, 1990; Bentovim, 1992; Herman, 1992), on the other hand, particularly stresses the need to work with the facts and the objective reality of traumatising events, or events over time in the case of chronic trauma. Therapeutic work involves tracking the details of the content and context of the event(s), with the aim of providing the individual family with a cognitive map of the traumatic event so that family members can recognise and integrate both their thoughts and feelings about the trauma into such a map.

These different strands in the field of family therapy, with an emphasis on constructed reality and solution-focused therapy, on the one hand, and on trauma and trauma work on the other, produce tensions and dilemmas in terms of practice for the clinician or practitioner working with abusing families. The authors of these papers argue that an integrated approach which brings together both aspects of therapeutic work is crucial to effective work with abusing families. Therapists need to help families and individuals deal with the trauma they have experienced. Families also need to look at the relationship between the traumatic experiences they have had as individual family members and the solutions they have evolved as families, and at the impact of both on the way family members now relate.

Nevertheless, while the objective reality of the trauma of abuse is an essential focus for therapeutic work with abused children and other family members, it is also the case that the individuals concerned have had to make sense of their own experience, and they have constructed their own psychic sense of causality – the meaning they give to that traumatic experience. This 'constructed reality' of individual family members or the family as a whole may hinder the growth and development or recovery of the family members, and therefore require therapeutic intervention. The approach to working with abusing families discussed in this chapter enables the therapist both to attend to the facts of the abuse and the meaning family members have given to that abuse, and also to focus on solutions families and family members will have to find for themselves.

These new developments in family therapy have given rise to other significant tensions and dilemmas for practitioners working with abusing families. The psychologically and developmentally damaging effects of child abuse fuel the responsibility of social service and legal systems to evaluate the risk to the child and the actual harm resulting from child abuse and neglect, and to act on that assessment in their work with abusing families. It informs the need for them either to bring about change in the relevant patterns of family relationships, or to provide alternative care outside the family for the abused or at risk child.

This linear relationship between the family and the statutory agencies responsible for child protection work is, however, sometimes seen as incompatible with the therapeutic relationship between therapist and family in family therapy, where there is a greater emphasis on the need for the therapist to remain neutral and adhere to the concept of circular rather than linear causality, which some see as inevitably blurring the issue of individual responsibility. Thus, professionals have been concerned about using a family therapeutic intervention with abusing families because of these apparent tensions. Furniss first introduced an integrated therapeutic and legal framework for working with abusing families (Furniss, 1990; Sheinberg, 1992; Sheinberg *et al.*, 1994), and this is further developed in this chapter.

In this chapter, we describe an approach to working with abusing families in a way which allows therapeutic work to progress within the legal framework of child protection without denying the reality of the abuse, splitting the professional network, or cutting across the work of the various professionals who form the child protection network or team around an abused child.

Conceptual and Planning Issues

Family therapy and consultation

The increased understanding of the context and greater clarity of aims of family work with abusive families has led to a clear distinction between family therapy which occurs as a result of a free contract between the family and the therapist and conditional family work in the context of statutory decision-making. Family work with abusing families does not constitute therapy in the traditional sense. Family members do not come to therapy of their own free will, and the basic contract is not between therapist and family, but between therapist and the statutory agency, on the one hand, and between the statutory agency and the family on the other.

This means that the basic rules of confidentiality do not apply, and therapists therefore need to distinguish carefully between therapy where these rules can apply and therapeutic work with abusive families as part of consultation to statutory agencies. Family work in child abusing families can therefore only take place with close and open co-operation between therapist and statutory worker. Family therapists must not accept abusing families for 'therapy' independently of the professional child protection system, because this creates the danger of inducing damaging splits in the professional network between the therapist as the 'goodie' and the statutory worker as the 'baddie'.

All therapeutic work which therapists undertake with abusing families needs to relate to the requirements of decision-making processes by statutory agencies regarding the future of the family concerned. In that sense, family work with abusive families is part of a consultation process to social services departments or courts, in which the social services department or the court are the clients rather than the families. All therapeutic work needs to take place in the context of consultation with these institutions.

The nature of the therapeutic family work as part of consultation to social services and courts needs to be made explicit to the family, either by having the social worker present during family sessions or by referring explicitly to the link between therapist and statutory agencies. In a family session, we might therefore say, 'What would the social worker/the court say about the change you have achieved so far in these sessions? Do you think they would feel it is safe for your child to live with you again or not?' This sentence not only reminds the family of the context of consultation, it also helps therapists to remind themselves that any family work with abusive families is part of consultation and not traditional family therapy.

This distinction is indicated in Table 21.1.

A family approach and a family therapy approach to working with abusing families

A family approach uses a family systems theory framework to conceptualise the dysfunctional aspects of abuse at a family level and in the context of family relationships. Using a family systems perspective helps to keep the central family process and the child's need for carers in mind, while opening up the options for different, concurrent forms of therapy in addition to family sessions. It also provides a unifying rationale for a range of protection, care planning and therapeutic tasks which need to take place when attending to the welfare of the abused child and family.

Thus, a family approach to working with abusing families, in contrast to a family therapy approach, encompasses work on different levels using concurrent forms of therapy, including individual, group and family sessions as well as family–professional sessions.

For example, although with physical abuse and neglect, and even perhaps emotional abuse, conjoint family sessions may be the only form of therapy, with sexual abuse concurrent forms of therapy are always required. Abusers always need some additional individual and/or group work for dealing with the abusive cycle. Mothers as non-abusing parents need individual help with the crisis of emotional turmoil, loss and practical problems that come with disclosure (Hooper, 1992), and the support of a group to counteract the isolation, disempowerment and low self-esteem associated with living in a family system shaped by the abuser's enactment of child sexual abuse as a syndrome of secrecy and addiction (Hildebrand, 1988).

In cases of child sexual abuse, the aim of therapy for the child needs to be the therapeutic transformation from secrecy into privacy (Furniss, 1990). Although family sessions deal with the secrecy of child sexual abuse by the shared experience of disclosing the secret thus creating a reality anchor, family therapy sessions alone do not give the child the necessary space to experience adequate privacy and to develop self-worth, self-respect, autonomy and individuation. This is achieved by individual sessions or group sessions which provide the individual space for self-experience (Wilson and Ryan, 1994). However, individual and group sessions alone can transform the confidentiality of the individual or group session into renewed secrecy if con-

Table 21.1 *Therapy and consultation.*

Therapy	Consultation
Intervention directed towards:	
1. Family	Professionals
2. Relationships	Decision-making
3. Boundaries	Functions
4. Family conflicts	Conflict by proxy
5. Therapist is a free agent with respect to family (independent professional responsibility towards family)	Therapist is consultant in the service of other professionals and agencies (responsibility towards hierarchy of consulting institution)

current family work does not guarantee a complementary domain of openness which keeps the abuse in the shared family domain.

The successful outcome of the concurrent use of different forms of therapy does not depend on the different forms of therapy themselves. Successful outcome depends on the willingness and the quality of co-operation between therapists, and on the ability of therapists to conceptualise their own form of therapy as part of a differentiated systemic framework of different concurrent forms of therapy.

Issues of motivation

Our skill needs to lie in knowing why abusing families are not motivated to be helped, and how we can motivate them to feel that they want help. The distinction between therapy and consultation in family work with child abuse underlines the fact that families are not primarily self-motivated to seek help as a result of emerging family problems. They are motivated to co-operate because of the danger of family break-up, and because of the openly stated preconditions for rehabilitation or for keeping their children at home.

The basically negative contextual framework of coercion in family work in cases of child abuse needs to be positively reframed by an explicit therapeutic contract which states openly the required aims and goals of family work. Some systemic approaches already make the development of the required aims and goals of treatment part of the treatment process itself. Questions like, 'What do you think needs to change in your attitude and behaviour towards your child in order for social services/the court to be satisfied that it is safe for you to continue living with your child?', or, 'What do you think social services/the court needs to know from you for them to trust your word when you say you are able to understand and satisfy the needs of your child without abusing him/her?' A systemic approach to family work can help to link issues of statutory responsibility and control with therapeutic aspects of required family func-tioning. The process of defining the aims for family work can help to motivate family members towards a wish for therapeutic change if we create a context where families take part and are co-responsible for the development of explicit, understandable, operationalised and detailed goals for therapy.

Indicators for or against involving the whole family

Family work needs to be undertaken in all forms of child abuse cases where rehabili-tation is considered. There are basically only two reasons for curtailing conjoint family work. The first is a situation where the child is additionally harmed by the process of conjoint family work itself. Whether or not conjoint family work becomes harmful to the child depends on the skills of the professionals and the chosen form of the intervention, on the one hand, and on individual and family characteristics of the abusing family on the other. However, professional variables and family variables are so complex that it is difficult to define valid general indicators for cases where conjoint family work should be suspended. This is likely to remain the case, even when clearer patterns emerge about which families are likely to respond to therapeutic help for general abuse as well as sexual abuse (Dale *et al.*, 1986a; Jones, 1987; Crittenden, 1988; Elton, 1988; Bentovim, 1992).

If a family worker or a family therapist has reservations about conducting conjoint family work which involves including a sexual abuser, for example, these reservations will influence the process of the family session itself and the way in which the abused child will experience the session. Equally, if a family worker is frightened of a violent father, conjoint family sessions will become counterproductive. Professionals therefore have to take their own parameters of personal attitude, professional skill and contextual support seriously in deciding whether to conduct conjoint family work in any particular case of abuse.

As long as family rehabilitation or any direct contact between the child and the family is still on the agenda, conjoint family work should take place, although family sessions may need to be accompanied by parallel individual work, group work or dyadic work with the child, non-abusing parents and abusers.

The second contraindication for conjoint family work in abusing families are cases where it has been decided that new permanency arrangements need to be made for the child away from the present family.

Change versus growth in work with abusing families

In child abuse work, we need to distinguish between therapeutic change work and growth-oriented work. Especially in cases of physical abuse and neglect, family work often contains a considerable amount of growth work, including the development of new skills in handling crisis situations and relationships.

Growth work in cases of physical abuse and neglect is often best carried out in family centres, which give family workers the chance to do specific goal-oriented change work and growth work during stressful day-to-day activities such as mealtimes, playtimes, toilet times and other situations where parents feel acutely overburdened by specific elements in their interactions with the child. Asen has described a structured family day clinic model, which includes educational elements as well as therapeutic growth and change work in an integrated goal-oriented family approach (Asen *et al.*, 1989).

Family work in child sexual abuse cases is usually more change-oriented with fewer educational and skill elements. It can therefore usually be undertaken in conventional family therapy outpatient settings.

Practice Issues

Family therapy techniques in work with abusing families

In cases of physical abuse and neglect, the use of educational techniques can be the main modality of treatment. Professionals may have to assist in direct ways, introducing new ways of coping in high risk situations. Giving encouragement, modelling, mirroring a parent's behaviour, other behavioural methods and video feedback can complement educational techniques in growth and change work.

In physical abuse work, where families have to learn to cope with high risk situations, structural techniques with the aim of achieving new problem resolutions in the here and now are often more appropriate than indirect strategic or Milan-systemic ways of working. Structural techniques have the advantage that a problem can be tackled in the presence of the therapist, who can assist in the development of new problem-solving techniques within the time frame of the session. This gives the therapist the chance to protect the change process and to work with immediate feedback within the session.

In a family where a child of 6 years had been physically abused by his father, the parents had great difficulty in setting down clear guidelines for acceptable behaviour for their child, and in responding early enough and with any consistency when the child behaved in an unacceptable way. Thus, the child had little sense of the 'rules' and was not treated consistently when he broke them, so that the situation often arose where one or other parent would explode with rage after quite a long period of his testing out how far he could go. Working with the parents' handling of his noisy, persistent, distracting interruptions within the sessions allowed for the development and practising of a new way of parent–child communication about actions which had been part of the escalating dialogue leading to physical injury.

Homework

Giving homework can play an important part in family work with all forms of child abuse. This usually takes the form of giving the family tasks to complete in between family sessions, and these tasks can be given for a range of purposes. Homework may be aimed at gathering information about specific crises and high risk situations at home, which can then be addressed in the family session. It can also focus on consolidating and enlarging areas of change already achieved during the family session. Homework can be used to highlight the family's own strengths and problem-solving abilities by asking family members to implement at home areas of change which they have developed and discussed in the family session.

In cases where parents have difficulties in managing their children's behaviour, a homework task in which children are asked to continue to show problem behaviour, in order to give their parents time to study the unwanted behaviour and to practise newly found skills, can be extremely effective. Symptom prescriptions, such as requesting children to have at least three very big temper tantrums before the next session or requesting them to eat no more than five spoonfuls of food at mealtimes so that parents can understand and describe the events of the problem situation in detail, can do miracles.

Time out arrangements, where parents are asked to give their children 'time out' apart from them when their behaviour deteriorates and techniques which give children symptom control, such as asking them to exhibit unwanted behaviour at a particular time of the day every day, can also lead to rapid behavioural control in the interaction between children and parents.

Working with Abusing Families – Child Sexual Abuse

In this half of the chapter, we focus specifically on child sexual abuse and the work that needs to take place with families where child sexual abuse has occurred. We start by distinguishing between child sexual abuse and other forms of abuse, and we look at how these differences inform the family work and family therapy that needs to take place. The evaluation of suspicion, trauma work and work with siblings are the areas of family work discussed. This is followed by a detailed examination of the steps or stages in family therapy which need to be addressed. A range of family therapy techniques which are useful at different stages of this work are outlined. The chapter ends with a consideration of the content, process and organisation of the first family meeting with and without the abuser.

Differences between child sexual abuse and other forms of abuse

For practical purposes, we can describe child sexual abuse as distinct from other forms of abuse as a syndrome of secrecy for the child, the family and the abuser, and as a syndrome of addiction for the abuser and sometimes the child. Aspects of secrecy and addiction in cases of sexual abuse create a family in which it is much more difficult to protect the child and to achieve effective therapy, especially if the abuser and the sexually abused child are living under one roof during the process of treatment.

The context of secrecy and the habit-forming sexual nature of sexual abuse raises issues of control and relapse prevention as central tasks in any family intervention. This usually leads to the exclusion of either the child or the abuser from the family. Either children are taken into care in cases where mothers join with the abuser, usually with no family work taking place at all, or the abuser leaves and family work is undertaken with mother and children only, and with the abuser being excluded. Issues arising from the exclusion of family members from integrated family work only rarely occur in other forms of child abuse, where conjoint family work has become much more established.

In addition, there is a strong body of opinion which states that in child sexual abuse cases conjoint family work including the abuser should only happen following group work, individual work and dyadic work, and towards the end of therapy. This therefore has the function much more of apology sessions or reconciliation sessions between the abuser and the rest of the family. However, this approach has not been shared universally, and we have conducted parallel work using group or individual work and family work right from the beginning with families where child sexual abuse has taken place (Furniss, 1990).

Up to now, a common underlying reason for the exclusion of sexual abusers from conjoint family work was certainly that we as therapists had little knowledge and confidence about therapeutic work with sexual abusers. We also feared whether we could survive conjoint family sessions with them, and especially whether we could protect children from secretly or openly threatening and undermining messages from the abuser.

Family work in child sexual abuse

In child sexual abuse cases, as with other forms of abuse, the way early interventions are handled can have therapeutic potential for a good longer-term outcome or can be positively anti-therapeutic. The way the evaluation of suspicion in child sexual abuse is approached, and the effective handling of any disclosures, can have an important therapeutic effect. Because child sexual abuse is a syndrome of secrecy, good work in the event of a disclosure can create a 'reality anchor' which establishes the facts of the sexual abuse as a family reality and as a precondition for any further family work.

Trauma work is the second step in therapeutic family work in child sexual abuse cases. Family work, run in parallel with group or individual sessions, needs to address the basic issues of trauma in child sexual abuse. There are several features of trauma work which are particularly significant for child sexual abuse.

1. Trauma work in cases of child sexual abuse needs to help families to find appropriate and emotionally neutral words to name anatomical parts and to address sexually abusive actions which families usually have no words to describe.
2. In trauma work, the child and other family members need to be allowed to relate their feelings about the events in order to deal with a potentially very traumatic experience.
3. Trauma work needs to address issues of who believes the child, and what is believed, and issues of activity, responsibility, participation, guilt, blame and power regarding the abuse. The distinction needs to be made between children's feelings of responsibility, which flow from the experience as active participants in the abuse, and the fact of responsibility which, because of the structural dependence of children on parents, can never lie with the child.
4. Trauma work needs to deal with the question of whom the child could turn to and who would believe the child's communications if there was a threat of sexual abuse in the future or if it occurred. This work does not only address issues of preventing re-victimisation. Children can often only allow themselves to open up for trauma work and therapy if they feel the work is conducted in a protected space where they feel emotionally secure and safe from further abuse.
5. Finally, trauma work needs to address feelings of guilt, shame, embarrassment, social isolation and stigmatisation of different family members through public knowledge of sexual abuse having taken place in the family.

In other forms of trauma, like death or illness, trauma work can usually be appropriately dealt with by the family and the wider social environment of the child. With child sexual abuse, trauma work requires professional involvement right from the beginning. This is due to the fact that in cases of sexual abuse, family members often cannot imagine what has really happened, they do not have the appropriate language to address what has happened, and they feel torn by feelings of loyalty, anger, disappointment, guilt and shame.

It is for these reasons that, although not all sexually abused children need therapy, all these children need specific professional help with specific and limited aims and goals in the adaptive task of trauma work which families of child sexual abuse cannot achieve by themselves.

Siblings in family work on sexual abuse

It is important to consider the effects of professional interventions on the siblings of sexually abused children. In the initial crisis after disclosure, all the attention is usually focused on the abused child, and siblings are easily forgotten in the process. Siblings need to be involved in the family work from the beginning of the disclosure process for the following six reasons.

1. Brothers and sisters of sexually abused children may have been sexually abused themselves. In many cases only one child discloses initially, and siblings need to be included in the evaluation in order to assess the possibility of multiple abuse of other children in the family.

2. In cases of long-term sexual abuse, siblings often know what has happened. If asked, they will not necessarily admit to it because they know that they are not supposed to know. In addition, witnessing the sexual abuse of a sibling, or even only knowing about it, can in itself be extremely traumatic. Children may for their own emotional protection want to pretend they do not know what they know.

3. Some siblings do not know that sexual abuse has happened in cases of long-term abuse in the family. These siblings are nonetheless much affected by child protection and legal investigations and by other events in the family from the moment of the initial disclosure. Non-abused children often suffer the consequences of family breakdown, placements in care and separations as much as sexually abused children. Siblings may experience the sudden departure of the father/abuser. They may see sisters or brothers being taken into care with great panic and haste, and they may be frightened that they themselves may suddenly be removed and taken away from the family.

   Siblings need to know why these drastic actions are taken, and they need to be able to adapt to the changes in the family. Brothers and sisters are often not told, and they are forced to make sense for themselves of very anxiety provoking situations without explanation or support.

4. One of the important functions of therapeutic family intervention is to avoid scapegoating of the abused child by other family members. Sexually abused children are often blamed by brothers and sisters for the removal of the abuser and for sudden family breakdown.

   Siblings of sexually abused children need to be present at the first family meeting – concerning responsibility – where the issue of responsibility for the abuse and for the consequences of disclosure are dealt with.

5. In some cases, non-abused children are excessively protective of their abused brothers or sisters. They can become very over-protective of and over-involved with sexually abused siblings. They may feel entirely responsible for the abuse and blame themselves for not having been able to prevent the abuse from happening.

   Older siblings who knew of the abuse can develop severe symptoms and become very disturbed. The symptoms can relate to their failed attempts to protect the sibling. An 11-year-old sister of a 6-year-old sexually abused girl became extremely obsessive and developed panic attacks and severe obsessional checking behaviour. Sexual abuse of her younger sister was revealed, and it emerged that the girl had witnessed the abuse. She was very protective of her younger sister and desperately tried to keep male adults under control. Another boy who had known of the abuse of his older sister tried to attack several boys in her peer group with knives in order to protect her from men. Over-protective siblings need to be included in treatment in order to deal with their guilt feelings, and with their inappropriate sense of responsibility for the sexually abused child.

   Some sexually abused older siblings have borne their own abuse in secrecy until the onset of sexual abuse of a younger sibling drove them to overcome their fear of disclosing despite unchanged and continued threats by the abuser.

6. Finally, we need to keep in mind that all the attention in the family is usually focused on the abused child, and the emotional care of siblings can be severely neglected. The phenomenon of relative emotional deprivation of siblings is well known from siblings of children with severe and life-threatening illness. It needs to be prevented as part of the family intervention in cases of child sexual abuse.

After the disclosure, siblings of sexually abused children need to be involved in further family meetings which deal with the effects of the abuse itself and of the disclosure on each family member and on the family as a whole.

Family therapy and child sexual abuse – steps in therapeutic family intervention

In therapeutic family intervention, the actions of all agencies involved, from police to therapists, need to relate to the overall aims and steps of the intervention. The basic aims and steps of therapeutic family intervention will remain similar for all families of child sexual abuse cases, but the sequence in achieving particular goals can differ according to the specific family situation. The family process and the family perspective always need to remain central to the interventions made, although the means, the setting, the context and the techniques may change according to the different requirements of each case. Earlier steps may be taken later and *vice versa*.

The following seven aims and treatment steps form the basis of therapeutic family intervention:

Preventing further sexual abuse. Since child sexual abuse is an interlocking syndrome of secrecy and addiction, the first step in therapy needs to be to prevent further sexual abuse. This often requires an initial and temporary separation of abuser and child during the crisis after disclosure until a time when professionals are convinced that the child, the abuser and the family will not relapse into secondary secrecy and denial, and until the abuser has made sufficient progress in therapy to be trusted to live with the abused child again. As a rule, the abuser and not the child should leave the family, and therapeutic and legal agencies need to co-operate to achieve this first treatment step.

Although the removal of the abuser should always be considered first, there are sometimes reasons why it may be important for the abused child to leave the family, such as when older adolescents do not want to return home, or when rejection and scapegoating of the abused child by the mother and other family members make it safer to find an alternative placement after disclosure. Nevertheless, we always need to work towards approaches where the child can stay at home.

Removing the child in the early stages of the intervention bears the serious risk of secondary traumatisation. Therefore, any removal needs to be rooted in a therapeutic family intervention, and careful steps need to be taken to guarantee continued and free access for the abused child to the mother, to siblings and to other important attachment figures in order to create a protective environment which prevents secondary psychological damage, especially for older children and adolescents.

Establishing the facts of abuse and the abuse as family reality. The second step needs to establish the facts of the abuse. This is in order to establish the abuse as a psychological fact and as a family reality. In the treatment of child sexual abuse as an interlocking syndrome of secrecy and addiction, we need to help the child and the family to find an appropriate explicit sexual language, something they may well not have available. They may have to describe events for which they have no words or language to communicate, and it is important to give the family explicit licence to talk openly about the abuse. By introducing the appropriate sexual language, professionals give the family the message that they, too, can talk about this difficult topic in front of the family without being ashamed, dismissive, punitive or upset.

Abusers taking responsibility for the abuse. As a basis for further therapy, the abuser needs to take full and sole responsibility for the sexual abuse itself. This does not mean that the abuser was the only active participant in the abuse, or that the child was entirely passive, or that the mother may not have known about the abuse. All abused children are active participants in the abuse (which is not to say they choose to be so), and in some cases of long-term sexual abuse children may at some stage even play a maintaining role. Whatever the child does in the abusive interaction, and whatever the mother knows, the responsibility for the sexual abuse itself can never rest with either the child or the non-abusing parent. It always and under all circumstances lies solely with the abuser.

The moment an abuser accepts sole responsibility for the sexual abuse from a paternal position, he becomes a true parent to the child and this is the precondition for the child being able to return to the position of being a child. The change in the paternal position from pseudo-partner to responsibility-taking adult relieves the child of his or her sense of responsibility for the abuse. It also establishes the future possibility of the abuser becoming a responsible carer in a parenting role. The 'responsibility session' with the abuser should take place even if the abuser is not the father or stepfather and, if possible, even in cases of extrafamilial abuse.

Parent's responsibility for general care. It is important that both parents are present at the first family meeting in which the abuse is discussed. Although the abuser is solely responsible for the abuse, both mother and father need to take equal responsibility as a parenting couple for the general care and well-being of their children. Establishing the fact of their responsibility as parents towards their children does not confirm them as marital partners. Issues concerning them as partners need to be addressed later. Initial work needs to concentrate on the intergenerational issues and on the parenting function, not on the marital relationship or partnership.

It is very important to differentiate between the parental and the marital couple. The couple can stop being partners. They will always remain parents, even if they are inactive parents in families of separation and divorce. It can be vital to keep these two distinct functions quite separate. Parents in conflict often use arguments between them as partners to avoid issues of parental responsibility, just as they may use parental arguments to avoid facing problems they have as partners when marital issues are addressed.

We need to acknowledge to the parents that partner conflicts have indeed to be addressed, especially the question of separation and divorce, but that parenting issues need to come first. We need to ask whether both parents want to remain involved as parents, and whether they want to take responsibility for the parental care of their children irrespective of their present or future position as partners. One of the most paternal acts of the father can then be to agree to leave the family and not to take part in the daily care of the child, but to give the child the chance to stay at home and feel safe until the abuser can be trusted to return again. Correspondingly, one of the most maternal reactions can be not to pursue instant divorce proceedings, even if from her point of view as a partner the mother may want to do so. This can give the child the space to deal with the abuse and the consequences of disclosure without additional confusing and potentially traumatising divorce proceedings at an early stage.

Work on the mother–child dyad. The next step in family work needs to focus on the relationship between the mother and the child. The work on the mother–child relationship is both therapeutic and preventative. It aims at making the non-abusing parent a more emotionally central and protective person, whom the child can trust to be believed when she tries to find protection in the event of renewed and further abuse.

In the work on the mother–child dyad, two central problem areas often emerge. The first concerns maternal guilt feelings about the failure to prevent the abuse and the child's need to be able to trust that the mother will listen to what has happened.

Only a very few mothers are actively involved as sexual abusers themselves, and not many know openly about the abuse and allow it to continue. However, mothers in cases of long-term sexual abuse have often at some stage been told in some form by the child, or have known in other ways about the abuse but were unable to take it in or to respond to the knowledge. Children's previous attempts to disclose usually emerge in therapy when issues of maternal care and the child's disappointment at not having been protected come into focus. Mothers need to learn to identify and to appreciate the child's emotional and protective needs in general and in relation to the abuse.

The second problem area is that at times there is a strong rivalry between mother and child. This does not only happen between mothers and adolescent girls. Mothers can feel strongly rivalrous also towards very young children. One mother of a 3-year-old girl who had been sexually abused by her father for over a year put it in a typical way, 'I am really angry with her. She is so precocious. She did not come to me and I just blame her'. She then talked about how she could appreciate intellectually how inappropriate her reaction was, but that nevertheless she was very angry and felt very rivalrous towards her 3-year-old child.

On one occasion, a 14-year-old girl pulled out letters from her father, saying triumphantly, 'Who does he really love, her or me?' Another 15-year-old girl in a session suddenly said, 'And who has the nicer breasts, Mum or me?' These moments, as well as times when mothers are accused by children for not having protected them from the abuse, are situations where mothers can become very depressed and suicidal or angry and rejecting. At this point, mothers often need considerable help and support as parents, and as people in their own right.

Work with parents as partners.   Once parenting issues have been dealt with, problems which the couple have as partners can be addressed. During marital work, the split between the couple's emotional and sexual expectations of each other forms a main focus of the work. In order to avoid conflicts as partners about sexual and emotional problems, both parents may join together in attempts to scapegoat the child as morally bad and to hold him/her responsible for every family problem.

It is important to keep in mind that in the initial crisis after disclosure, mothers often tend to decide to go for an instant divorce. This is the result of their own confusion of the parenting role and the partner role, and their reaction to their own moral shock and to the moralistic expectations of relatives and professionals. If a mother does demand instant divorce at this point as a parent, she may, as a partner, remain as intensely attached and 'married' to the abuser as ever.

As a result of the confusion of parenting role and partner role in professionals and parents alike, instant requests for divorce are often welcomed by all sides. However, a mother will often only realise her continuing attachment to the abuser when the initial shock of disclosure has subsided. Under moral pressure from relatives, friends and professionals, she is unable to admit openly to this enduring attachment and to understandable feelings of loss and loneliness. She can find it impossible to allow herself to miss the abuser as co-parent openly, both as co-partner and as material provider for the family.

Professionals need to check their own moral attitudes. They may find it difficult to fulfil the important therapeutic task of differentiating between parenting role and partner role. Professionals need to point out to the mother that the initial rejection of the abuser can be very helpful in fostering her protective role as a parent. It is equally important to give the mother permission to miss the abuser as a partner openly, even if she rejects this thought in the initial crisis after disclosure. Unless we do this, we risk the very common situation that parents secretly get back together again behind our backs and collude with renewed secrecy against the professionals, often successfully jeopardising any therapeutic family intervention. Giving the mother open permission to miss the abuser as breadwinner, co-parent and partner needs to be seen entirely separately from the final outcome of therapy, which may well conclude in a therapeutic divorce of the parents as partners.

In partner work, the main issue for abusers is to face up fully to their wives for their sole responsibility for the abuse. Abusers may initially express regret for what they have done. But the initial responsibility taking is often followed by attempts to minimise the abuse and its effects on the child and other family members. Abusers may even accuse their partners of having driven them to the abuse by perceived sexual or emotional shortcomings in the partner relationship. Sexual abusers often find it very difficult to own up fully to their responsibility with their wives and partners. They may employ strategies of seduction, accusation, minimisation and other defensive moves which show that psychologically they still deny the abuse and their own role in it. This can happen even in legally established cases in which they have admitted to the abuse in the courts. We therefore need to distinguish between the initial and external admission by the abuser and his fully owning up psychologically, which only happens towards the end of therapy.

Work on the abuser–child dyad.   Once the issues in the mother–child dyad and in the parent and partner dyad have been dealt with, it is much easier to return to the abuser–child dyad and to renegotiate the abusive relationship between the father figure and the child.

After disclosure, some children go through phases of anger and rejection of the abuser. The anger is often also an expression of a continuing strong attachment of the abused child to the abuser, which we find especially in cases of long-term sexual abuse.

Intensive and psychologically damaging attachments are nevertheless often very strong attachments, and it can be difficult for any professional to acknowledge possible positive aspects in the abuser–child relationship. If the child is to be treated professionally and therapeutically, rather than becoming a ready object for the personal projections, prejudices and moral judgements of professionals, the exploration of positive aspects in the attachment between the abuser and the child need to be allowed and fostered as much as the more obvious negative aspects.

It is important for the emotional development of sexually abused children that they be allowed to address their disappointed expectations of good and emotionally caring relationships with father figures. Sexually abused children need to be able to build and rebuild emotional relationships to adult men and father figures without the fear of renewed abuse. The child's experience of non-sexual and trusting emotional relationships with men is as important for the child's ability to develop trusting male relationships in adulthood as is the development of trust in emotional care and protection by maternal figures for the development of trusting adult relationships with women.

Family therapy techniques in work with sexual abuse

This section looks at family therapy techniques which are useful in therapeutic work in child sexual abuse cases. Different techniques need to be used for different situations in the treatment of abusing families according to specific areas of required change in the family process.

Direct intensification: the first family session in acknowledged abuse cases. Direct structural techniques which intensify underlying conflicts, and which deal openly and directly with structural issues of responsibility and intergenerational boundaries within the session, are extremely helpful in the first family sessions. The task of the first family session as a reality-creating responsibility session is to break the secrecy and to establish the full facts of the abuse, and by doing so to establish the abuse as an open family reality. The first session also needs to deal with the issue of the abuser's sole responsibility for the abuse. In openly admitted cases of child sexual abuse, the use of indirect strategic or systemic techniques would be unhelpful and would ignore central features of child sexual abuse where external reality and conflict are never openly and directly named and confronted as such. Reality avoidance in sexual abuse cases and the linear element of responsibility require the use of direct and intensifying reality-oriented techniques in the initial responsibility sessions. The secrecy of child sexual abuse needs to be removed. The facts of the abuse need to be told. The abuse as a family reality needs to be established, and children need to hear directly and openly, from the abuser him or herself, in front of all other family members, that sexual abuse has in fact happened and that he or she takes responsibility for it. To achieve these goals, the use of structural techniques can be eminently helpful.

Anticipatory problem-solving questions: anxiety reduction in primary and secondary denial. The treatment of denial requires working in exactly the opposite way to the direct structural mode of the openly acknowledged responsibility session. We need to address the anxieties which have led to the denial, rather than aiming directly at the facts of the abuse itself. We will only get the facts if we postpone our wish to get the facts, and if we address the context of the abuse instead. Strategic and Milan-systemic techniques greatly facilitate possible indirect ways out of the trap of denial, and create hypothetical solutions to problems which are denied. The feared family disasters resulting from possible disclosure need to be addressed first, before we can focus on the content of the abuse.

In therapeutic denial work, we need to ask hypothetical questions such as, 'What would be the biggest disaster if sexual abuse had really happened?', 'How long would it take and in what situation would it be safe for it to come out?' and 'Would your father think that he had done wrong if sexual abuse had happened?' By asking anticipatory problem-solving questions, we can identify the trap for the child, for the abuser and for the family which prevents family members from disclosing.

The stronger the denial, the more important is the use of increasingly indirect strategic and Milan-systemic methods. In cases of strong denial, we would put the possibility of disclosure into the indefinite future and say, 'Most likely you will never be able to disclose whether sexual abuse has happened, but if you were ever able to do so what would be the worst thing that could happen?'

Questioning of the hypothetical 'as if' level avoids symmetrical escalation and conflict. The anxiety-reducing effects of strategic and Milan-systemic techniques are precisely what is needed in denial work. In contrast to desirable intensifications in

structural moves of open disclosure and responsibility sessions, hypothetical questioning decreases potential conflict and decreases anxiety levels. It enables family members
to begin to think again about the future, and it can help children to find safer ways of
disclosing.

Similar methods can be used when families and family members relapse into
secondary denial after previous disclosure. We can ask, 'What would be the biggest
disaster if you were to repeat what you said before to so and so about what had
happened?' Again, with increasing degrees of denial we need to go for the worst
disaster, the longest time span until disclosure and the most peripheral family member.
Involving absent family members: family sessions by proxy. In family sessions without the abuser, or in family sessions by proxy with only the child, we can introduce
the absent family members by the use of strategic and Milan-systemic techniques.
We can include absent abusers by asking, 'What if your father were here? What
would he say? Would he say that he is responsible for the abuse or that you are
responsible? What would he say had happened between you and him?'. This way
of questioning can be followed up by circular questioning in the hypothetical mode,
such as, 'If your husband were here, who would he say has been most upset by what
has happened?'

*Hypothetical linking between family and professional networks: consultations with
professionals with statutory and legal responsibility.* Questioning in the subjunctive
mode can be very helpful in consultation sessions in which both the professional with
statutory responsibility and the family are present. Questions like, 'What would Mrs
X as a social worker with statutory responsibility have to know from you, Mr Y, for it
to be safe for your children to be with you on your own?' avoid the danger of collusion
by the consulting professional with the family against the professional with statutory
responsibility and prevents the split between the 'good professional' and the 'bad
professional'. At the same time, it involves family members actively in a problem-
oriented way, instead of making them receivers of orders from the higher authority of
social workers or courts. Elements of the consultation which address the professional–
family process can be conducted in hypothetical circular questioning of the family
about what professionals with statutory and legal responsibility would need to know
or would need to do in order to protect children and prevent further abuse.

*Decentralising and the 'one-down' position towards the family: maintaining a metasyste-
mic perspective as statutory and legal worker.* Legal and statutory workers can themselves avoid oppositional and symmetrical conflicts with abusers and families by
putting themselves under the higher authority of 'the law' or 'the guidelines'.

This process again requires hypothetical anticipatory problem-solving questioning
and circular questioning in the hypothetical mode. The statutory worker might say, 'I
am only here because the law requires me to be here, and I have to deal with the
situation because of the guidelines'. The worker can then continue by explaining the
law and the guidelines and (s)he can say, 'When do you think the law and the
guidelines would allow me to let your child return home?' and 'How much do you
think your mum and dad would have to be able to talk about their own problems, and
how much do you think your mum would have to learn to listen to you before the
courts would say that things have really changed in your family?'

Introducing the higher authority as a linear, statutory and legal element requires
the use of hypothetical and strategic techniques, which then allow the statutory worker
to decentralise him or herself and maintain a truly metasystemic stance. He or she can

become truly therapeutic and can remain a truly statutory worker at the same time. Hypothetical questioning and the mastery of strategic and Milan-systemic techniques in these circumstances are invaluable assets, and they form the basic requirement for the ability to maintain a truly metasystemic stance in child sexual abuse as a legal, statutory and therapeutic problem. The delegation of the linear and legal aspects of the responsibilities of statutory workers to the hierarchy of 'The Law' enables social workers and probation officers to conduct therapy without confusing their double role as controlling and at the same time helping agents for the family.

The first family meeting as reality anchor and as reality-creating responsibility meeting

A high priority in a therapeutic family intervention is to bring all the family members involved together in one or two conjoint family meetings ('naming events' meetings), in order to clarify the following five areas.

1. The first task of the family meeting is to establish the facts of the abuse and to clarify what really has happened. This is forgotten or is even actively avoided in many approaches at present. The child may have indicated in the past that abuse has happened. He or she may even have told the non-abusing parent and other family members, and he or she may never have been heard or believed. Each family member may have made separate statements to police, social workers, doctors, therapists and others. These statements may be of considerable length, and it may have taken hours or days to collect them. In addition, different professionals and agencies involved have often talked among themselves about the facts of the abuse at length. They may have exchanged lengthy written reports, and the abuse may have featured in the newspapers. In terms of family relationships, the sexual abuse remains a family secret despite all these activities. It has never been talked about openly among the persons most concerned: between the abuser, the mother and the children directly or indirectly involved.

   In the first family meetings as reality-creating naming events, everything written down beforehand needs to be spoken out loud. No fact should be taken as acknowledged or shared, least of all the fact of the sexual abuse itself, even if the abuser has been to court and has admitted to it. Admissions in court establish the abuse as an external and legal reality. Establishing the external reality of sexual abuse is the precondition for further therapeutic work, and in that sense the legal process is therapeutic. But creating legal reality does not automatically create relational reality for the abuser, the child and the family. Family reality is only created in a commonly shared family meeting, where the facts of the abuse are named aloud in the presence of all the family members.

   The family meeting as a naming event needs to introduce explicit sexual language which is neither embarrassing nor voyeuristic, pornographic, sexualised or inappropriate in other ways. The family meeting needs to establish the facts of the abuse, the circumstances under which it happened, where it took place, and where other family members were at the time. Words like 'sexual relationship' between father and child should be explicitly used to help the family to find an open way to approach the subject for which families do not have words and a language to communicate. It may not be necessary to go into more anatomical details of the sexual act itself than to mention words like 'intercourse' or 'putting his penis into the child's bottom'. The content has to be explicit but emotionally as neutral as possible. The aim is to establish facts in a non-persecuting and accepting way.

2. The second task for the meeting is to help the abuser to take sole responsibility for the sexual act itself in a way which is spoken out loud and which, in the presence of other family members and especially the mother, takes any responsibility for the abuse away from the child. The responsibility of the abuser needs to be very clearly established and named, because mothers tend to take the responsibility on themselves, and children are often blamed either for the abuse itself or for the family crisis after disclosure. Even if children are not blamed by others, they very easily hold themselves responsible for the abuse and for the consequences of family break-up after disclosure.

3. The third task is to help both parents to come to an agreement about the degree of their involvement as parents who are psychologically and in relationship terms equally responsible for the care and welfare of their children, independent of the legal status. Even if the mother has full and sole care and control, and even if the child will never live with the father again, the father will still remain the father of the child, however absent or inactive a person he is. The parents' attitude to their respective roles as attachment figures must be addressed, and the parental arrangements for the child need to be clarified.

4. The fourth task of the family meeting is to talk openly in front of everybody about separations in the family. Any separation needs to be put into the specific context of the child sexual abuse as an interlocking syndrome of secrecy and addiction, in order to make sure that possible therapeutic implications of any separation are understood by all the family members, and that any actual separation is not seen by the abused child as punishment for the abuse. Separation can involve marital separation, as well as the separation of the child when the child does not want to return home. If the father leaves home, it is important to clarify for the abused child and any sibling that the abused child is not responsible and not to blame for the father leaving. If the child leaves the family, discussion during the family meeting needs to make it understood that the child is leaving the family because the father has been irresponsible and cannot be trusted for the time being, and not because the child is being punished for the abuse and for secondary problems arising from the disclosure.

5. Finally, the fifth task is to clarify the degree of contact between family members, and to make visiting arrangements when children are separated from home. Which professionals will be involved, in what capacity, to what degree and intensity, and what the possible long-term plans for the family are must also be clarified for the benefit of all the family members.

When abusers admit to sexual abuse, a family meeting should take place as soon as possible and if possible within hours of the disclosure. The first reality-creating responsibility meeting is not meant to be a traditional family therapy meeting, but serves to create a reality anchor for the facts of the abuse and to establish the sexual abuse as a family reality as a precondition to any further trauma work and therapy. It can take place in a social services office, hospital, school, nursery or police station. It does not interfere with the legal process if the whole family can be taken to the police station as soon as the father has made a statement. A family meeting as a naming event can then be held, asking the abuser to do no more than repeat the statement he has just made to the police.

Once the fact of the abuse is shared in front of all the other family members and in the presence of someone outside the family, it will not be withdrawn again easily. An early family meeting as a naming event therefore fosters the legal process as much as it advances therapy.

The reality-creating responsibility meeting as a reality anchor for the abuse which is held immediately after the abuser has admitted to the abuse is especially therapeutic when the abuser is subsequently unavailable because of imprisonment and family break-up, or when the abuser is unco-operative during subsequent treatment. The first family meeting should therefore, if possible, always be part of the initial crisis intervention following disclosure, irrespective of the form any subsequent long-term family work takes.

Delaying these meetings can encourage primary denial, even when the abuser has assumed legal responsibility for the abuse. When these meetings take place several weeks, months or years after the initial disclosure, abusers are often too defensive to face the relationship facts of the abuse. The strength of psychological denial can make it necessary to resort initially to indirect techniques of denial work. It can be helpful to turn to the mother or to other siblings and to ask the question, 'What would we read in the police reports that your father has said he has done?' Or we can ask family members to guess what the abuser would really have to say if he said what he knows in the back of his mind has happened. Once other family members begin to talk openly about the abuse, abusers often begin to talk themselves and begin to help create the abuse as family reality.

Organising the first family meeting

Social workers with statutory responsibility and other professionals who are involved in the daily care of the child and therapists should, if possible, be present at the first family meeting.

If the first family session as a responsibility meeting takes place at a stage when the abuser or the child has left the family, brief meetings with the different family sub-units need to take place immediately before the conjoint session. The task of these brief meetings of 5 or 10 minutes is to explain the aim of the conjoint family meeting and state explicitly that the meeting may become very difficult but that this is normal.

The family needs to be aware that the therapist knows that different family members may be frightened of disasters during the session, and that they may fear the outcome and the consequences of the meeting. The anticipation of the anxieties and feared disasters as part of crisis work enables family members to subject themselves to situations of intense anxiety, which they would otherwise not dare to do. This holds especially for sexually abused children, and often also for the abuser.

In practical terms, it is helpful to ask the different family subgroups to arrive at slightly different times, and to provide different waiting areas so that family members do not have to wait together before the actual meeting. It is usually helpful to ask all the family members and professionals, but not the abuser, into the therapy room first, and to leave the chair next to the door free for the abuser. When everybody is seated and settled, and after any possible additional clarifications about the procedure of the meeting, the therapist can leave the room and ask the abuser to join the family.

This carefully chosen procedure avoids an increase of anxiety which otherwise can trigger the refusal of different family members to take part in the session. It also avoids uncontrolled and premature social contact between the abuser and the child. Uncontrolled social contact before the responsibility meeting can easily lead to renewed family secrecy and denial. In addition, the abuser could give direct or indirect threats and messages to the child to comply with his or her wish for secrecy.

Responsibility session by proxy

In child sexual abuse as a syndrome of secrecy, it is necessary for the child and other family members to establish, openly, the facts of the abuse, even when the abuser is unavailable due to imprisonment or when he or she has left and is unwilling to co-operate in cases of denial and extrafamilial abuse. The responsibility session by proxy is conducted in the absence of the abuser.

In the responsibility session by proxy, the professional who conducts the family meeting asks family members, especially the mother as the non-abusing parent, or both parents when the abuser is not the father, or he/she asks siblings and even the abused child what the abuser would say had really happened if he/she were present. In the responsibility session by proxy, the therapist always works on the hypothetical level, 'if the abuser were present, what would he/she say?' It is possible to establish on the hypothetical 'as if' level the facts of the abuse, and to deal with issues of responsibility, participation, guilt, blame and power.

If no responsibility session takes place, sexually abused children can still feel bound up in conflicts of loyalty. They often feel unable to deal openly with the abuse in therapy and keep it as a family secret unless a responsibility session by proxy has been conducted. The responsibility session by proxy often establishes for the first time the abuse as an acknowledged external reality for the child, the non-abusing parent and the family.

The responsibility session by proxy can be conducted with any family subgroup, and even with the abused child alone. This is especially important when the child has been removed from the family and taken into care.

Further Reading

Barker, P. (1992) *Basic Family Therapy*. Oxford: Blackwell Scientific Publications.
For the reader who wishes to learn more about the field of family therapy, Philip Barker's *Basic Family Therapy* provides a useful and accessible introduction. He writes clearly about the theoretical underpinnings of family therapy and a wide range of different models of assessment and treatment. The book has a strong practice component, exploring a variety of therapies and therapeutic techniques in some depth, and covering setting up and finishing therapeutic work with families, among many other practice issues, using case examples to illustrate the material. He also looks at teaching, research and ethical aspects of family therapy. The reader can therefore get a relatively comprehensive and eclectic view of the field of family therapy from this book.

Bentovim, A. (1992). *Trauma Organised Systems: physical and sexual abuse in families*. London and New York: Karnac.

In his book *Trauma Organised Systems*, Arnon Bentovim provides a systemic theoretical framework for understanding the impact of both physical and sexual abuse as traumatic experiences which can organise individual, family and professional systems. In particular, he links sociological, social-interactional and systems perspectives which describe how family systems become organised around the trauma of family violence, and he goes on to give a systematic account of trauma organised systems associated with different forms of family violence. Bentovim addresses the need to break the denial process inherent in trauma organised systems and presents a focal model which provides a systematic way of describing families and planning therapeutic work. The book is illustrated with numerous case examples and provides child protection professionals with a valuable framework for understanding and assessing families in which child abuse has occurred.

Furniss, T. (1990). *The Multi-Professional Handbook of Child Sexual Abuse – Integrated Management, Therapy and Legal Interventions.* London and New York: Routledge.
This book makes a more direct link between child abuse and family therapy. It takes further the material presented in this chapter and is therefore a good resource for readers who wish to look in more depth at working with families where sexual abuse has taken place. Using a systems approach, Furniss considers child sexual abuse as a syndrome of addiction and secrecy which requires a multi-disciplinary response. He presents an integrated approach to the management, therapeutic work and legal frameworks involved in the care and treatment of sexually abused children and their families, and shows how practical steps in therapy and management directly influence each other. The first part of the book outlines the principle ways and basic concepts used in dealing with child sexual abuse. The second part focuses on practical problems ranging from the evaluation of suspicion, the management of disclosure and inter-professional problems through to a wide range of treatment issues which relate directly to working with abusing families. The theoretical and practice sections are cross-referenced, so that the reader can use the conceptual framework to inform their therapeutic work in a direct and specific way.

Glaser, D. & Frosh, S. (1993). *Child Sexual Abuse.* London: Macmillan.
Danya Glaser and Stephen Frosh's very useful and accessible book *Child Sexual Abuse* is divided into two parts. The first part centres on understanding child sexual abuse and discusses the dimensions of child sexual abuse, ideas and research on sexuality and abusers, as well as the constellation of relationships, social circumstances and values which make it more or less likely that children are victimised. The authors also review the family systems model and offer a critique of its strengths and limitations. The second part on therapeutic practice addresses the management of suspicion and disclosure of child sexual abuse and the validation and decision-making process. It then focuses on therapeutic intervention, with the emphasis very much on practice. Glaser and Frosh are particularly helpful in linking up the overall aims of professional involvement with the specific therapeutic interventions that can be used to meet the needs of sexually abused children and their families, and they stress the need for a co-ordinated therapeutic approach.

References

Ahmad, B. (1990). *Black Perspectives in Social Work*. London: Venture Press.

Ahmed, S., Cheetham, J. & Small, J. (1986). *Social Work with Black Children and their Families*. London: Batsford.

Asen, G.E., Piper, R. & Stevens, A. (1989). A systems approach to child abuse. *Child Abuse and Neglect 13*: 45–58.

Barker, P. (1992). *Basic Family Therapy*. Oxford: Blackwell Scientific Publications.

Bentovim, A. (1979). Towards creating a focal hypothesis for brief focal family therapy. *Journal of Family Therapy 1*: 125–136.

Bentovim, A. (1992). *Trauma Organised Systems: physical and sexual abuse in families*. London and New York: Karnac.

Bentovim, A. & Davenport, M. (1992). Resolving the trauma organised system of sexual abuse by confronting the abuser. *Journal of Family Therapy 14*: 29–30.

Bentovim, A., Elton, A., Hildebrand, J., Tranter, M. & Vizard, E. (eds) (1988). *Child Sexual Abuse within the Family*. London: Wright.

Bingley, L., Loader, P. & Kinston, W. (1984). Research report: further development of a format for family description. *Australian Journal of Family Therapy 5(3)*: 215–218.

Boscolo, B., Cecchin, G., Hoffman, L. & Penn, P. (1987). *Milan Systemic Family Therapy*. New York: Basic Books.

Burnham, J. (1986). *Family Therapy*. London and New York: Tavistock Publications.

Byng Hall, J. (1973). Family myths used as a defence in conjoint family therapy. *British Journal of Medical Psychology 46*: 239–250.

Byng Hall, J. (1990). Attachment theory and family therapy: a clinical view. *Infant Mental Health Journal 2*: 228–236.

Campbell, D. & Draper, R. (eds) (1985). *Applications of Systemic Family Therapy: the Milan Approach*. London: Academic Press.

Carter, B. & McGoldrick (eds) (1989). *The Changing Family Life Cycle: A Framework for Family Therapy*. Boston, London, Sydney and Toronto: Allyn and Bacon.

Crittenden, P. (1988). Family and dyadic patterns of functioning in maltreating families. In K. Browne, C. Davies & P. Stratton (eds): *Early Prediction and Prevention of Child Abuse*. Chichester, New York, Brisbane, Toronto and Singapore: John Wiley and Sons.

Crittenden, P. & Ainsworth, M. (1989). Child maltreatment and attachment theory. In D. Cicchetti & V. Carlson (eds): *Child Maltreatment: Theory and Research on the Causes and Consequences of Child Abuse and Neglect*. Cambridge: Cambridge University Press.

Dale, P., Davies, M., Morrison, T. & Waters, J. (1986a). *Dangerous Families: Assessment and Treatment of Child Abuse*. London: Tavistock.

Dale, P., Waters, J., Davies, M., Roberts, W. & Morrison, T. (1986b). The towers of silence: creative and destructive issues for therapeutic teams dealing with sexual abuse. *Journal of Family Therapy 8*: 1–25.

de Shazer, S. (1982). *Patterns of Brief Family Therapy: An Ecosystemic Approach*. New York and London: Guildford.

de Shazer, S. (1984). *Keys to Solution in Brief Therapy*. New York and London: Norton.

de Shazer, S. (1989). Wrong map. Wrong territory. *Journal of Marital and Family Therapy 15*: 117–121.

Elton, A. (1988). Assessment of families for treatment. In A. Bentovim, A. Elton, J. Hildebrand, M. Tranter & E. Vizard (eds): *Child Sexual Abuse within the Family*. London: Wright.

Erikson, M., Egelend, B. & Pianta, R. (1989). The effects of maltreatment on development of young children. In D. Cicchetti and V. Carlson (eds): *Child Maltreatment:*

Theory and Research on the Causes and Consequences of Child Abuse and Neglect. Cambridge: Cambridge University Press.

Eth, S. & Pynoos, R.S. (eds) (1985). *Post-Traumatic Stress Disorder in Children.* Los Angeles: American Psychiatric Association.

Figley, C. (ed.) (1990). *Treating Stress in Families.* New York: Brunner Mazel.

Fishman, C. & Rosoman, B. (1991). *Evolving Models for Family Change: A Volume in Honor of Salvador Minuchin.* New York and London: Guildford.

Furniss, T. (1990). *The Multi-Professional Handbook of Child Sexual Abuse – Integrated Management, Therapy and Legal Interventions.* London and New York: Routledge.

Furniss, T., Bentovim, A. & Kinston, W. (1983). Clinical process recording in focal family therapy. *Journal of Marital and Family Therapy 9(2):* 147–170.

Glaser, D. (1993). Emotional abuse. In: *Baillière's Clinical Paediatrics,* vol. 1(1), pages 251–265. London: Baillière Tindall.

Glaser, D. & Frosh, S. (1993). *Child Sexual Abuse.* London: Macmillan.

Glaser, D., Furniss, T. & Bingley, L. (1984). Focal family therapy – the assessment stage. *Journal of Family Therapy 6:* 265–274.

Haley, J. (1976). *Problem-Solving Therapy.* San Francisco: Jossey-Bass.

Haley, J. (1980). *Leaving Home.* New York: McGraw Hill.

Hanks, H. (1993). Failure to thrive – a model for treatment. In C. Hobbs & J. Wynne (eds): *Baillière's Clinical Paediatrics.* London: Baillière Tindall.

Hayes, H. (1991). A re-introduction to family therapy – clarification of three schools. *Australian and New Zealand Journal of Family Therapy 12:* 27–43.

Herman, J. (1992). *Trauma and Recovery: From Domestic Violence to Political Terror.* New York and London: HarperCollins.

Hildebrand, J. (1988). The Use of Group Work in Treating Child Sexual Abuse. In: A. Bentovim, A. Elton *et al.* (eds) *Child Sexual Abuse within the Family.* London: Wright.

Hobbs, C., Hanks, H. & Wynne, J. (1993). *Child Abuse and Neglect: A Clinician's Handbook.* London: Churchill Livingstone.

Hooper, C.A. (1992). *Mothers Surviving Child Sexual Abuse.* London: Routledge.

Jones, D.P.H. (1987). The untreatable family. *Child Abuse and Neglect 11:* 409–420.

Kinston, W. & Bentovim, A. (1983). Constructing a focal formulation and hypothesis in family therapy. *Australian Journal of Family Therapy 4:* 37–50.

Lieberman, S. (1979). *Transgenerational Family Therapy.* New York: Croom Helm.

Loader, P. (1982). *Personal Communication.*

Madanes, C. (1982). *Strategic Family Therapy.* San Francisco and London: Jossey-Bass.

McCluskey, U. (1987). Theme Focused Family Therapy. In S. Walrond-Skinner & D. Watson (eds): *Ethical Issues in Family Therapy.* London: Routledge and Kegan Paul.

McCluskey, U. & Bingley Miller, L. (1995). Theme-Focused Family Therapy: The Inner Emotional World of the Family. *Journal of Family Therapy* (in press).

Minuchin, S. (1974) *Families and Family Therapy.* Cambridge, Mass.: Harvard University Press.

Minuchin, S. and Fishman, W. (1981) *Family Therapy Techniques.* Cambridge, Mass.: Harvard University Press.

Palazzoli, M. & Prata, G. (1982). Snares in family therapy. *Journal of Marital and Family Therapy 8:* 443–450.

Palazzoli, M., Cecchin, G., Prata, G. & Boscolo, L. (1978). *Paradox and Counter-Paradox.* New York: Jason Aronson.

Palazzoli, M., Checchin, G., Prata, G. & Boscolo, L. (1980). Hypothesising – circularity – neutrality: three guidelines for the conductor of the session. *Family Process 19:* 3–12.

Perelberg, R. & Miller, A. (1990). *Gender and Power in Families.* London and New York: Tavistock/Routledge.

Satir, V. (1967). *Conjoint Family Therapy.* Palo Alto: Science and Behavior Books.

Satir, V. (1972). *People Making*. Palo Alto: Science and Behaviour Books.

Sheinberg, M. (1992). Navigating treatment impasses at the disclosure of incest: combining ideas from families and social construction and family process. *Family Process* 31: 201–216.

Sheinberg, M., True, F. & Frankel, P. (1994). Treating the sexually abused child: a recursive multi-model programme. *Family Process* 33: 263–276.

Stratton, P. (1991). Incorporating circularity in defining and classifying child maltreatment. Human systems. *Journal of Systemic Consultation and Management* 2(3/4): 145–296.

von Bertalanffy, L. (1968). *General Systems Theory*. New York and London: Penguin.

Walters, M., Carter, B., Papp, P. & Silverstein, O. (1988). *The Invisible Webb: Gender Patterns in Family Relationships*. New York and London: Guildford Press.

Wilson, K. & Ryan, V. (1994). Working with the sexually abused child: the use of non-directive play therapy and family therapy. *Journal of Social Work Practice* 8(1): 71–78.

22

Group Work in Child Protection Agencies

Anne Bannister and Eileen Gallagher

Introduction

The efficacy of groups in medical and social settings has been well documented by Moreno (1934), Foulkes & Anthony (1957), and, more recently, by Williams (1991). Our further reading list gives other proponents and pioneers of group work in settings from a psychiatric hospital to a children's home.

An important task of a group in a child protection setting is to provide a safe place where clients may feel supported and may, if they wish, explore their own forbidden agendas. They may reveal mistakes, or make fresh mistakes, without being punished, and they may practise future behaviour or relationships without causing pain to existing family members. The worker can more easily assess clients' existing behaviour in a group, in order to encourage change, and the client may rehearse new behaviours where help is at hand to assess these.

Benson (1987) feels that the purpose of groups generally is to develop a sense of identity, to establish trust, to use power, to develop roles and values, and to create boundaries. When applied to child protection, the most relevant task from this list is probably to create boundaries. Many people who have suffered abuse, or who have become abusers, are afraid of the power of their feelings, which they have not been helped to contain by their carers as part of their normal development. The group can act as a therapeutic container which will allow expression of feelings in a safe way. Of course, the establishing of trust needs to occur first. Workers can use their power to empower members which, in turn, will lead to the development of a sense of identity and increased use of different roles and values.

Writing specifically about group work with children and adolescents, Dwivedi (1993) points to the fact that children and adolescents may find that groups more closely simulate the real world than one-to-one therapy. He reminds us of the power differential between adult and child and feels this is diffused in the group setting. He also points out the ability of the group to help children with their personal identity and to enable roles to be practised. For children who have been abused, this issue of their lack of personal power is crucial to their future development and behaviour. An abused child may need to be supported and empowered to a certain extent before being able to join a group. Once this is accomplished, however, the healing provided by the group may prevent years of suffering for both child and family.

Agencies, Resources, Policies

Resources in child protection agencies have always been limited. After the implementation of the Seebohm report in 1974, when several different agencies amalgamated to become a generic social services department, there was a concern that the specialised needs of specific groups were not being addressed and therapeutic groups were set up in an effort to meet these needs. The probation service, social services, child guidance clinics and other health departments set up groups (sometimes working inter-agency) for their clients who appeared to have similar problems. Self-help groups were also springing up at this time. These were usually supportive rather than therapeutic in nature.

Inter-agency co-operation is essential, especially if referrals are taken from several sources. Referring a client to a group run by another agency does not mean that responsibility ends for the referrer. The group member will receive most benefit if their worker is supportive (possibly providing transport or bus fares), as well as co-operative, in liaising with other family members if necessary. Co-operation across agencies can also be helpful in providing an accessible meeting place or facilities for groups with special needs.

It is sometimes thought that group work is very economical of staff resources since a number of people can be seen at one time. However, groups require careful planning, selection and assessment, recording and supervision, if they are to have a successful outcome and these processes are time-consuming. With practice, though, group workers do become more efficient at planning and selection, and at this stage the resource benefits may be felt in the agency.

One of the key functions of a group is to provide a place where members can experience a different way of interacting with others. They also have a ready-made setting for practising new ways of behaving. It is therefore vital that the group facilitators fully understand the dynamics of abuse. If the workers are new to group work, it is particularly important that they meet for several weeks (or longer) before the group starts with an experienced supervisor or consultant who can prepare them for the situations they are likely to face. This consultant should also be prepared to meet with them on a regular basis throughout the life of the group.

It is vital that an experienced person outside the group should provide a viewpoint to help the workers to understand the transferential feelings expressed by group members and the counter-transference experienced by the workers. In addition, the consultant can see how the co-workers react to each other and how their relationship is likely to impact upon the group. Sometimes an experienced person will run a group alone, but in the child protection field this is unusual. The reason is because workers need the support that a co-worker can provide, otherwise the personal stress can be too much to bear.

An experienced consultant will also help to monitor the power positions within the group as a whole. A group should never reflect the abusive situation with which its members may be familiar. Great care should be taken to ensure that the potential abuses of power within gender, ethnicity, disability, age, etc. are recognised by the workers so that group members can be encouraged to support and assist each other, rather than relying upon the workers.

Another potential conflict of power arises from the agency or agencies which are providing workers and premises for the group. Parents may feel oppressed in a group run by the statutory social services or National Society for the Prevention of Cruelty to Children (NSPCC), and the social worker facilitators may have a harder task to build trust. Likewise, young offenders may feel wary in a group run by the probation service. Nevertheless, these constraints may be used positively by group workers, and this is most likely to be effective in jointly run groups across the agencies. A psychiatric nurse and a social worker may be the most suitable people to run a group for mothers of abused children, for instance, and the presence of the social worker with statutory powers could be particularly helpful as a demonstration of how those powers could be used positively. It is vital, too, that the workers in a group for adolescent or adult perpetrators of abuse are very clear about the boundaries of the members' behaviour. For example, issues of current or recent abuse not previously known must be immediately addressed and child protection procedures instigated. Workers from the medical agencies would be strengthened by someone from the probation service; each agency could provide good 'modelling' for a discussion of boundaries, which could include the issue of 'care and control'.

The time spent planning a weekly group, preparing and running it, debriefing, recording and meeting with a consultant is likely to take up to 8 hours per week. It is unrealistic for workers to transport clients to groups because of the time involved. This also changes the group dynamics, since the group begins to function once two or more members are together, even on the journey to the group meeting. Consideration should also be given to the group setting, since some institutions (hospitals, police stations) can have unwelcome connotations for some members. This is not to say, of course, that highly effective groups cannot be run in a secure hospital or prison if the workers can use their skills to create a safe space where the members can address their forbidden agendas.

Initial Planning

Population

The initial planning decision concerns the population with which one wishes to work, and this may be determined by the need. The range of groups in child protection runs from children and adolescents who have been abused, through adolescent offenders, parents who have abused their children, non-abusing parents whose child has been abused, and adult survivors of abuse. Recently, young children who are abusing others have also been treated in groups. Groups for children and young people cannot be run without the full co-operation of their carers. Sometimes carers may be in parallel treatment groups (Frey-Angel, 1989, and also MacFarlane et al., 1986).

Workers

The next important decision concerns the group workers. We have already suggested that two workers are preferable to one, and that a consultant is also necessary. Unless the co-workers have previously worked together, they will need the consultant to help them look at their relationship before they begin.

Setting

The setting for the group is also important, and we would add to our previous comments on this that where confidentiality is important it is not wise for members to be drawn from one small geographical area. The place for the group would then have to be accessible from a wide area.

Size

It is usually considered that six to ten people is a suitable number for a group with two workers, and for children we would suggest the lower figure.

Type

Groups may be 'closed', where members join together and leave together, or 'open', where some members may join and leave at different times. A closed group is usually more suitable for children and adolescents and those for whom confidentiality is vital. A 'slow open' group is a compromise for adolescents and adults. This type of group starts with a fixed membership, but may agree to take more members at certain intervals and for some members to leave at specific times. A group for survivors of abuse would probably benefit from being closed because of issues of trust. Some adult groups, especially in residential settings, can cope with a 'slow-open' situation.

Length and duration

Time-limited groups are important to establish boundaries, especially for children. Many workers consider 12 weekly sessions to be ideal for young children. It is not advisable to have sessions less frequently than weekly for children. It may be that 20 sessions is a more realistic number in terms of measurable improvement in outcome. Certainly, for adolescents and adults it would be difficult to measure change in less than 16–20 sessions. An hour is a minimum length for a session; 1½–2 hours is more realistic, including time for consuming food and drink. This is usually provided at the beginning or halfway through a session.

Singer (1989) reports that men who have suffered childhood trauma appear to need a longer period in a group before progress can be made and maintained. From 6 months to a year is suggested, with members sometimes rejoining the group after a break. This is longer than the 6 months suggested by some authors for groups for female survivors, but it may reflect a tendency in the United States for such groups to be continued for a longer period. For instance, a group in Ohio for health professionals who had been sexually abused in childhood extended over 56 sessions (Kreidler and England, 1990).

Practitioners agree, however, that groups for adult sexual abusers cannot be effective unless they are continued over a considerable period. Although workers in Nottinghamshire (Cowburn, 1990) describe short intensive 'courses' for sexual offenders, most workers (Erooga *et al.*, 1990) agree that a year is a minimum time for such a group in the community. Short-term groups are sometimes run in prisons (Barnet *et al.*, 1990), and since such groups are totally dependent on the duration of sentences and the availability of suitable clients, it may be that a short-term approach is the only viable one. The authors mentioned above (Barnet *et al.*, 1990) were describing a group for women sexual offenders, and since there are far fewer women than men convicted of such crimes the availability of suitable group members may have been very limited.

Selection and Assessment

It is important for the health of the individual client and of the group that prospective group members are carefully selected. It is true that participation in a group may have an immediate attraction for someone anxious to overcome feelings of isolation. In our experience, though, some people may be unable to function within a group without prior individual work. Attention paid during the planning stage to issues of selection can increase the possibilities for the group to become an environment which is safe and healing.

Assessment of individuals for suitability for inclusion in a group varies widely, depending on whether the group is therapeutic and to be attended on a voluntary basis, or whether membership of the group is part of an order through the criminal justice system or child care system which mandates an individual to attend. With scarce resources, it makes sense to include only members who are able to benefit fully and who have demonstrated during an assessment period that they can make some progress. This can usually be done by the co-workers carrying out one or two interviews to test the motivation and potential for change of each proposed member. Inclusion in an adult sex offenders community-based treatment group may need to be mandated, and the client should be prepared for a highly structured setting with space built in to measure change and progress.

In groups where attendance is voluntary the idea of commitment to the group, from members and workers, should be introduced during selection. Unless a member is capable of some commitment, his or her presence could be unhelpful for the health and stability of the group.

Gender and sexuality

Groups offer an opportunity for people to learn different ways of relating to each other. A mixed-gender group may facilitate this best. A male and a female worker can also provide useful role models. However, in child protection treatment groups there are other important considerations. For example, female adolescent survivors of child sexual abuse need the support and safety of other girls and of women workers. We have some experience of groups for boys aged 8–11 who have survived sexual abuse, and also of groups for girls of a similar age. It seems to be important that groups for boys have co-workers who are male and female in order to reduce anxiety for boys who have been abused by men, and also to help them to look at their own worries concerning homosexuality. Young abused girls usually find it difficult to work on sexual abuse issues with male workers (unless they have had a male individual worker with whom they already have a good relationship and who has helped to prepare them for the group experience).

Age Range

For adults, life stages may be much more important to consider than age, but for children and young people fairly narrow age ranges are preferable, with developmental rather than chronological age being considered. Groups containing siblings can cross the age barrier more easily. Janice Frey-Angel (1989) describes such a group for children in violent families, usually where the father is violent to the mother. The children's ages range from 3 to 12 years, and although they often replay their parents' abuse, they can practise different behaviours in the group. They may form supportive, age-related subgroups across family boundaries.

Ethnicity

Race and culture need to be addressed. Workers should be aware of their own limitations in this regard. In groups for children and young people, care must be taken in selection to ensure that one child is not isolated because of racial or cultural differences. With adults, this possibility could be addressed directly with the potential group members during the assessment interviews. A group for black and white sexually abused children is described by Marie Lebacq and Zaffira Shah (1989). They keep to a narrow age band (from 5 to 8 years), but they mix boys and girls and members include black Asian, black Afro-Caribbean and white children. All the children are also described as British. The group is led by a black and a white worker. Their consultant is white, and they feel that if a suitable black consultant had also been available this would have been particularly helpful to both workers. The issues with which a black consultant could have assisted include exploring techniques to help black children move on from believing they were sexually abused because they are black to an understanding that sexual abuse happens irrespective of race. This reminds us that children who have been sexually abused are especially sensitive to abusive environments and discriminatory behaviour. Lebacq and Shah conclude that children of this age can work in mixed-gender groups on abuse issues.

Homogeneity

Groups are usually formed because of some thread of experience that is common to all members. This should not, however, become too narrow. For example, in groups for survivors of child sexual abuse the inclusion of survivors of intrafamilial and extrafamilial abuse can add a richness to the group. The sense of identity created by the group is not necessarily undermined by different backgrounds. Mothers of abused children, for instance, can form strong group cohesion because of their shared experience, although their personal histories are very varied.

Support

A high level of support outside the group is essential for members of a therapeutic group. This may not be so important in a group which is formed simply to provide support. Many young people require a great deal of practical help, which may include being transported to and from the group and the provision of a 'listening ear', in order to process material that is brought to consciousness in the group.

Motivation

Assessing motivation depends very much on the type of group. Often adults with a shared stated problem are highly motivated to meet in groups, and they often have difficulty in ending their involvement. Motivation can be very low for young offenders who are forced into groups as a result of court orders. However, even in mandated groups members can become highly motivated to remain and continue when they feel their needs are being met and where change is made possible for them.

Learning ability

This is particularly important to assess where groups have a formal structure with an educative input. Many rely on confrontational challenging of distorted cognitions, and group members have to be able to cope with this. Groups for members with learning difficulties would need to have a format more appropriate to their needs. For instance, the use of creative techniques such as art, drama and music could be emphasised instead of pursuits which required literacy or numeracy.

Running the Group

Although it is the responsibility of the group workers to plan carefully and to set the boundaries of their group, the workers must respect and trust the group to deal with any difficult dynamics which may occur. Benson (1987) likens this to the art of aikido, where the warrior never goes against his opponent's strength, but blends with and redirects the energy of the attacker. Benson continues with a helpful introduction to understanding group dynamics.

Workers have to be prepared to relinquish some of their power and control by trusting the group. This does not mean colluding with group repression of certain issues indefinitely, but it does mean respecting that the group may not yet be ready to address painful revelations.

Contracting

This trust of the group can be demonstrated by setting up a mutual contract with workers and members about confidentiality, commitment and caring for each other. It should also include an agreement to respect others, to be non-judgemental and to listen. If members are encouraged to contribute to the contract, this will set the tone for subsequent sessions. Groups for young children should also be approached in this honest and open way, so that members know why they are meeting. Members, including children, should be clear about the duration and structure of the group from the start.

Methods

Children

Young children who are sexually abusing others may benefit from a carefully structured group which uses the '12-step method' (MacFarlane and Cunningham, 1990). This is an adaptation of the method used by Alcoholics Anonymous. MacFarlane and Cunningham (1991) also incorporate the 'sexual abuse cycle', as devised by Connie Isaac and Sandy Lane (1990). They demonstrate how a child can work through the process through which he moved from thinking of himself as a 'bad boy' to his actual sexually abusive behaviour. It is vital that his parents or carers also attend a parallel group where they too can work through (perhaps also with a 12-step method) their process of facing up to the problem, accepting help, not blaming others and recognising that they may need to look at their own behaviour.

It is important that young children should not be confined in a very small room, but also that they feel cosy enough to foster group bonding. The room should contain art materials, toys, etc., according to availability and the group workers' expertise. Setting group boundaries, including issues of confidentiality, is just as important for children as it is for adults. In fact, it is often more important because parents often feel that their children should not have 'secrets' from them, and children similarly feel that adults will automatically tell their parents what they have said. Exemptions to confidentiality, such as issues of a child abusing another child or damaging him or herself, should not be avoided.

Each session should contain some educational material, and also some physical activity (even if it is only passing a squeeze round a circle), and each session should begin and end in ways which constitute a simple ritual which can be repeated each week. Educational input and physical activity must, of course, be sensitive to children with learning difficulties or physical disabilities. Naturally, no group member should be forced to talk about anything which has happened to them. It is enough that they acknowledge that they are part of a group which has suffered similar events. Most children will enjoy drama and role-play. All ages can have fun acting out their favourite fairy story or TV series. Older children will often spontaneously discuss the similarities in these stories with their own situation. For younger children, we can be sure that although the symbolism might not be overt, their expression of feeling as they rage against the 'monster' will be therapeutic.

Kinetic family drawings, making a collage of their family, or making a collage together which depicts the group, can be useful ways of working which children enjoy. Watching suitable videos together can also be helpful if plenty of time is allowed for discussion. Making up a story is a good exercise for older children. The worker starts a story and each group member adds a little to it.

Many children, both boys and girls, like to put on a puppet show, and animal puppets are useful in portraying all kinds of characters. Workers should take care when selecting puppets not to buy those which perpetuate racial or gender stereotypes. Even young children can participate in simple 'guided fantasy' sessions, and older children often find these most helpful. In particular, practising the fantasy of 'a lovely safe place' can be helpful to a child who is troubled by frightening dreams or nightmares.

From about the age of 7 years, writing games and exercises can be used. Sometimes this can take the form of writing letters which are not sent, or sometimes simply writing down lists of 'things that I am good at' to aid self-esteem. Drawing the outline of male and female bodies and naming the parts can be part of simple sex education for children of this age. These children can also be encouraged to write poems or design posters to 'help other children with the same problems'.

Other authors have described useful techniques for working with sexually abused pre-adolescent children (Corder *et al.* 1990; Berliner and Ernst, 1982).

Adolescents

Probation and social services departments have provided groups for young offenders to capitalise on the very powerful influences adolescent peers have on each other. One group is described (Bannister, 1983) which used drama therapy to enable young people to act out their frustration and to help them to face the more serious side of their offending behaviour.

Despite the links established between physical and emotional abuse of children, and acting-out/violence in adolescence, there is little in the literature on the use of therapeutic, preventative groups with these children or young people, and it is their antisocial or criminal behaviour which is then the focus of group intervention. For example, adolescent acting-out in one of its most serious forms can be sexual assault on children, and group work has become a central component of the treatment of this population.

Groups for teenage mothers have provided a good forum for education on health and parenting skills, and for some of its members a much needed source of support (Rosenwald, 1989).

Blick and Porter (1982) suggest that open therapeutic groups can be effective with adolescent girl survivors of child sexual abuse, with well-established members facilitating the integration of newer members. However, this same group of young people may also benefit from a closed, time-limited group with therapeutic aims. A detailed account of one such group is included at the end of this section.

An essential difference in treatment of survivors and sex offenders is that the latter are normally resistant to change and wish to 'protect behaviour that provides a significant sense of empowerment and adequacy' (Ryan and Lane, 1991). Adolescent survivors, on the other hand, come to group treatment desperately wishing to reduce their levels of fear, anxiety and sense of powerlessness. There are, however, some shared issues for these two client groups, one being the inability to trust, and change in this area must be a long-term goal for both groups.

Victim advocacy, which is also central to offender treatment, should be fostered in survivors, who are often lacking in concern for themselves.

The use of confrontation and support by peers is the basis of much offence-specific treatment in groups of adolescent sex offenders as described by Gail Ryan (Ryan and Lane, 1991). Identifying antecedents, patterns of abusive behaviour and high-risk situations for individuals is met with less resistance when done by peers.

A strong motivating factor to remain in such a group can be the realisation that the young person has patterns similar to other offenders in the group, and Ryan believes this provides a source of hope for many young abusers.

Description of an Adolescent Girl Survivors Group

The following is a description of a group co-led by two women workers, one of the present authors (an NSPCC child protection worker) and a health visitor within the same health authority (see Craig, 1990). Working across agencies enriches the group leader's skills and experiences, and improves communication at many different levels. It is, however, important for both agencies to feel that they own and contribute equally to the venture. As the group was held in the author's place of work, this meant that housekeeping, such as preparing the room and providing refreshments, was left to the worker 'on site'. Any feelings of resentment or irritation about being left to do these things can lead to distorted communication between the group leaders if it is not addressed.

The workers established criteria for the group as follows.

1. Girls between 14 and 18 years of age who have been sexually abused within or outside their families.
2. Potential members must have a stated wish to join the group.
3. Potential members need to be able to confirm openly their status as a sexual abuse victim.
4. All necessary steps must have been taken by the appropriate professionals and/or carers to ensure that the girl is protected and not at risk from any further abuse.
5. Presence of some stability in the girl's life. This does not exclude girls who are in crisis following disclosure where they are being cared for by a trusted and believing adult.

This group made particularly strong use of contracting, and in the planning process the workers for the referred girls entered into very clear written agreements with the group leaders. This facilitates the understanding of the group's aims and maximises support for group members from other professionals. This was also where very practical issues like who would transport girls to and from the group were agreed. Open negotiations with the worker prior to the group starting positively affected the process of making agreements with each girl within the group.

The group workers shared with group members their aims and objectives which were:

1. to reduce feelings of isolation and feelings of responsibility for their abuse and, in some cases, for the break-up of their family;
2. to reduce fear of their abusers;
3. to resist shame and stigmatisation;
4. to build self-esteem.

The two women group workers were provided with consultation by a woman psychotherapist. The gender of the co-leaders was a positive choice on the basis that at an early stage in treatment the presence of a male worker can be an inhibiting factor for this client group.

The group met weekly for 16 weeks, with the girls making a commitment to continue to attend the group after the first two or, at the most, three sessions.

The orientation phase, the first three or four sessions, was tightly structured using exercises designed to break down barriers between group members and provide opportunities for each girl to make contact with every other group member. Exercises done in pairs are particularly useful for this process. Rituals to begin and end each session also helped the girls to practise both giving and receiving positive feedback.

As the group became more cohesive, the leaders worked with material the girls brought, relating it to the framework stated earlier. Discussion for these girls was an invaluable part of the group process and an opportunity for learning words for some of their experiences. This provided a contrast to their abusive experience, which is often a covert, silent touching.

Some of the work on body image was only done once trust had been established. An exercise where girls draw around each others' bodies to produce a shape on paper provides much useful material. However, some of the girls found it too difficult to lie on their back and allow someone to touch and draw round certain parts of their bodies.

The use of cushions to promote 'safe' dialogue between a girl and her abuser provided opportunities to express feelings of sadness and anger. This often led to more open exploration of feelings of ambivalence towards an abuser.

Endings are always particularly difficult for young people in this situation, and therefore attention was paid to the last three or four sessions of the group where scenes of loss and death came to the surface as the girls were constantly reminded that the group was ending. One girl avoided the ending by not coming to the last two sessions, and a letter was sent reminding her of the formal end of the group, with some informed guesses about why she had not been able to join the rest in the ending. For the others, the ending to the group gave a very positive dimension through the verbal validation of the good things that they had had from each other during the life of the group.

This aspect of the ending was part of the evaluation which was also carried out more formally. Evaluation forms used in the ICEF programme in California (Giarretto, 1989) were completed by the girls and their workers or carers at the beginning and ending of the group and scores compared. Several of the girls improved their 'score' for their ability to focus anger towards the appropriate person. Also, there were changes for all the girls in their ability to express feelings about mothers. This professional assessment was used in concluding interviews with each girl's worker to make recommendations for future treatment. The verbal self and peer evaluation inside the group was valuable and also good fun. The short-term benefits seemed observable and tangible, but much longer-term follow-up would be needed to demonstrate any long-term benefits.

Adults

Groups for adults may be mandated by the courts (as in groups for sexual abuse perpetrators) or be purely voluntary, run by the adults themselves (as in groups for adult survivors of abuse). They may also not be strictly mandatory, but members can feel pressured if they agree to attend a group for physically abusing parents (the sanction being that otherwise their child might be removed from home). Although mandates are often seen as anti-therapeutic by some agencies, there is evidence to show that a mandate to attend a group can help an offender to work through his or her level of denial. Superficial denials will already have been addressed in the selection and recruitment process. Obviously, no one can work with a person who totally denies his or her culpability, but most offenders have some cognitive distortion which enables them to live with the consequences of their behaviour. The compulsory element of a group and peer pressure exert force on the member to address these distortions. (See Erooga *et al.*, 1990).

Cognitive distortions are also used as coping mechanisms by survivors of abuse. The abuser passes on his or her own distortions to a child and 'grooms' the child to believe that he or she is responsible for his or her own abuse. The guilt which ensues is a result of that distortion and may protect a child from facing his or her own fear. In a group setting, members can recognise the unjustified guilt of others more easily than their own, and so can facilitate an understanding of the process for themselves as well as others.

Yassen and Glass (1984), discussing their model of group work with adult survivors of rape, suggest similarly that witnessing the irrationality of others' guilt feelings can help group members to identify and face their own guilt. They also point out that members of such a group can go through an early stage where they suggest that their own rape was 'not so bad' or 'worse than' that of another group member. They see this as an attempt to validate members' own experience and to determine whether the group will meet their needs. This kind of comparison may therefore be useful in helping a survivor to place his or her own abuse in context, and to have witnesses who accept the nature of his or her experience.

Women who have physically abused their children often feel isolated and are frequently unsupported by partners or relatives. A group can reduce isolation, overcome stigma, provide an opportunity to work through childhood trauma and a practical forum for education on child care matters (Bannister and Prodgers, 1983). Such groups can work well on a 'slow-open' basis. This type of group would be unlikely to be mandatory, and there may be little pressure to attend but, as with all groups, a contract must be agreed between workers and members about attendance, confidentiality, group language and respect. A crèche may be provided, and it is important that boundaries are not broken by mothers crossing over into the crèche, or by children invading the mothers' group.

Groups for mothers who have physically abused their children can often contain a very high proportion of women who have been sexually abused in childhood. Often the group is the first place where they are able to share this. The main aims of such a group would be to improve the relationship between mother and child through insight and catharsis. There may not be sufficient time for members to work in detail on their own abuse, but they may then be sufficiently empowered to join a group for adult survivors.

Summing up a review of the literature on group therapy with adult survivors of abuse, Sheldon (1992) states that all the authors agree that group work is particularly suited to addressing the issues of secrecy, mistrust, isolation, low self-esteem, shame and self-blame. She goes on to show that the group work approach has been extremely effective with women who have been sexually abused in childhood. She states that in her experience such groups should run for about 20 sessions, each session should last for 1½ hours and should be 'closed' to new members. A new group is then started after a short interval, and some members may rejoin for a further 20 sessions.

Following the inter-agency model described earlier in this chapter, Sheldon, who is a psychotherapist, works with several other professionals from different backgrounds. She stresses the need for structure in survivors' groups, especially when they are just starting, but points out that this diminishes as the group progresses. She reminds us, however, that careful boundaries of safety remain the responsibility of the group facilitators.

Most groups for adults who have experienced traumatic childhoods take some time to develop trust and cohesiveness. However, the facilitators of a group for women who had been mistreated by pathological mothers (Roback *et al.*, 1981) felt that their group bonded immediately. They considered that this was because no one before had ever appreciated what the members' lives had been like, in particular how their childhood experience of abusing mothers had led them to build conflictual relationships with abusing men in adulthood.

This reminds us of the long-term damage that abusive parents can cause to children, both male and female. Groups for males who have suffered childhood trauma are less well-reported, but authors (Singer, 1989) report similar feelings of low self-esteem and difficulties in relationships amongst male survivors in groups.

There is very little in the literature to date on the necessity of male perpetrators of abuse receiving therapeutic work for their own experiences of childhood abuse. Most groups for perpetrators concentrate largely on the necessary behavioural treatment. Members learn about their own triggers for thinking about abusing and how to control their reactions. This is vital, but the work could perhaps be extended by running parallel groups for such perpetrators to work on their own trauma, whether it be physical, sexual or emotional. Sometimes, of course, this is done in individual therapy sessions, but it might be more productive for men who are already experienced members of their behavioural group to have another group as described. One of the main difficulties might be in keeping the boundaries of the two groups separate.

Mothers whose children have been sexually abused are often totally neglected by the child protection agencies who care for the children and by the agencies who treat offenders. Women in this situation are often desperate to talk to other women who have gone through, or are undergoing, this experience. Some authors (Print and Dey, 1992) feel that groups for such women rarely suffice as the only form of therapeutic intervention. They feel strongly that individual work should be offered to women who have difficulty in coping with this almost impossible situation. It is particularly difficult for women who have been abused themselves, and such women may well need some intensive individual work following practical intervention and support provided by social workers. A group, however, can provide another dimension in empowerment for women who have felt severely disempowered in their lives. Print and Dey also point out that mothers are generally the most important agents in ensuring that their children survive abuse and remain protected. A group can provide the essential support that women need for this demanding task.

Problems

Difficulties with a group can begin at conception unless careful negotiation is carried out within the agency and between agencies if necessary. Receiving suitable referrals may be dependent upon a trusting relationship which referrers have with group workers, so time spent in building this will be rewarded. Equally, a group can be ruined by jealousies or misunderstandings between co-workers, and it is here that a good consultant is invaluable. A group member who feels he or she has joined unwillingly may become a saboteur, so assessment of motivation is important.

In the case of children and adolescents, it cannot be emphasised too strongly that parents or carers should be carefully prepared for the group and also supported for its duration.

The birth of a group can be difficult if group members feel workers have not been entirely truthful as to the scope of the group or its purpose. Emergencies such as the illness of a co-worker should be discussed in advance, so that decisions can be made about groups being run with only one worker. Planned absences for holidays, for instance, can usually be managed successfully if the group knows what to expect.

Often people continue their most accustomed role in groups. This could be the scapegoat or victim, the 'wet blanket', the 'controller', and so on. It is unhelpful, not only for that person, but for other group members if this is allowed to continue for long. The most effective way to combat this is not to protect the scapegoat or discipline the controller, but to point out what seems to be happening and to allow the group process to take effect. In addition, group 'games' or exercises which give people a chance to practise other roles can be facilitating.

Group members who drop out may make the rest of the group feel rejected. They should be encouraged to compose a letter or to contact the members directly to sort out the problem. If the member does not return, the group will need to discuss the loss and to air grief and anger. Sometimes a group member may remain in the group but refuse to join in. The group workers should not use pressure to persuade the member to join in, but should try and encourage them to do so. If a facilitating move is not successful a discussion with the carer, in the case of a young person, or with the referrer may be helpful. If the problem persists it should be openly addressed within the group.

The difficulty of ending the adolescent girls' group has already been addressed, but closure may also be a problem for many other groups in child protection. Often members will have suffered abrupt and traumatic endings to relationships and may have been advised to 'forget' parents or others who have abandoned them. Allowing members to work through their grief and anger about closure of the group is an important part of healing. Closing rituals are also necessary for each session of a group. Children may decide for themselves that a particular game will always be played at the end of a session. Adolescents may prefer to make a single statement to the group about their feelings at the end. Some adults may accept a physical closure such as standing in a circle with hands touching.

Co-workers should ensure that they discuss their own issues about endings with their consultant.

Some people find closure so difficult that they leave the group prematurely or they invent reasons why the group must continue beyond its allotted span. Again, premature departure can be explained to the group so that they do not feel abandoned and their sense of loss at the ending of the group can be acknowledged.

Most 'group problems' have occurred before within groups, and an experienced consultant can help to allay fears that one's own group is particularly difficult. The worker's self-esteem can be easily undermined, so the worker should in addition allow sufficient time for preparation and debriefing, and be clear that this time is just as essential as the time spent actually running the group.

Summary and Conclusion

Therapeutic group work has a history which brings together the work of the pioneers in medicine, sociometry and social work. It can be used with good effect in many populations in child protection agencies. It requires careful planning, both from the agency and the workers, and there is a multiplicity of methods which can be applied according to the skills and experience of the workers and the group. Problems can be recognised and overcome.

Reports of groups run by practitioners seldom contain much information about evaluation. This may be because it is difficult to measure progress in an objective way. Hiebert-Murphy *et al.* (1992) made careful evaluations of groups for girls from 3 to 12 years which showed improvement in functioning and behaviour on measured scales. In our own groups, we have used evaluation forms as described in the section on 'Adolescents', and also questionnaires which we have devised ourselves. Groups for which we have acted as consultants have held post-group interviews for the purpose of filling in the evaluation forms. If this is done, care must be taken to advise members that this will be happening, otherwise some members may feel distressed to be contacted some months later. Dwivedi and Mymin (1993) give a thorough discussion of the literature on the evaluation of groups for adolescents and children, including the grid technique, assessment scales and self-report questionnaires. Benson (1987) reminds us that evaluation should be considered at the planning stage, and suggests that members should be encouraged to keep a group diary which could be used for a group evaluation.

Group work can be a successful mode of therapy for many people, but it is important to remember that some may need individual work first. Working with therapeutic groups can be frustrating and time-consuming. It can also be rewarding, for both members and workers, and extremely satisfying. In self-evaluations, the majority of members find groups to have been a nurturing, satisfactory experience which has brought long-lasting benefits.

Annotated Recommendations for Further Reading

Bach, G.R. (1954). *Intensive Group Psychotherapy*. New York: Ronald Press.
Describes a system of group development – helpful for a basic understanding of groups.

Benson, J.F. (1987). *Working More Creatively with Groups*. London: Tavistock.
A comprehensive practical guide to planning, running and ending a group, using many techniques such as gestalt, psychosynthesis, psychodrama, art therapy, drama therapy, etc.

Bion, W.R. (1961). *Experiences in Groups*. London: Tavistock.
Well-known theories on psychotherapeutic groups, basic to understanding process.

Brands, D. and Philips, H. (1978). *The Gamester's Handbook*. London: Hutchinson.
Dozens of useful ideas for group activities.

Brown, A. (1992). *Group work*, 3rd edn. Aldershot: Ashgate.
Brings the original 1979 edition up to date with new chapters on groups in residential settings and on the significance of race and gender in group work.

Dwivedi, K.N. (ed.) (1993). *Group work with Children and Adolescents*. London and Bristol: Jessica Kingsley.
A wide selection of chapters focusing on young people.

Dwivedi, K.N. & Mymin (1993). In Dwivedi, K.N. (Ed) *Group work with Children and Adolescents*. London & Bristol: Jessica Kingsley.

Ernst, S. & Goodison, L. (1981). *In Our Own Hands*. London: The Women's Press.
Full of empowering exercises and ideas for use in groups.

Tuckman, B.W. (1965). Developmental sequence in small groups. *Psychological Bulletin* 63: 324–399.
A good explanation of how groups behave, 'forming, norming, storming and performing'. Reassuring to know your group's behaviour is probably not unique. Simplifies Bach's original system of group development.

Whitaker, D. (1985). *Using Groups to Help People*. London: Routledge.
Broad scope, many kinds of group discussed. Particularly good on selection for a group, commitment of facilitators and problems when the group is ongoing. Hardly mentions consultancy, though.

Yalom, I. (1975). *The Theory and Practice of Group Psychotherapy*. New York: Basic Books.
A basic text for understanding group dynamics and psychotherapeutic issues.

References

Bannister, A. (1983). Dramatic recovery. *Social Work Today 14(18):* 14–15.
Bannister, A. & Prodgers, A. (1983). Actions speak louder than words. *Community Care* 472: 22–23.
Barnet, S., Corder, F. & Jehu, D. (1990). Group treatment for women sex offenders. *Groupwork 3(2):* 191–203.
Benson, J.F. (1987). *Working More Creatively with Groups*. London: Tavistock.
Berliner, L. & Ernst, S. (1982). Group treatment with pre-adolescent sexual assault survivors. In I. Stuart & J. Greer (eds): *Survivors of Sexual Aggression: Men, Women and Children*. New York: Van Nostrand Reinhold Company, Inc.
Blick & Porter. (1992). Group therapy with female adolescent incest victims. In Sgroi S.M. (ed.): *Handbook of Clinical Intervention in Child Sexual Abuse*. Massachusetts, Toronto: Lexington Books.
Corder, B., Haizlip, T. & Deboer, P. (1990). A pilot study for a structured, time-limited therapy group for sexually abused pre-adolescent children. *Child Abuse and Neglect* 14: 243–251.
Cowburn, M. (1990). Work with male sex offenders in groups. *Groupwork 3(2):* 157–171.
Craig, E. (1990). Starting the journey. *Groupwork 3(2):* 113–117.
Dwivedi, K.N. (ed.) (1993). *Groupwork with Children and Adolescents*. London and Bristol: Jessica Kingsley.
Erooga, M., Clark, P.L. & Bentley, M. (1990). Protection, control and treatment. *Groupwork 3(2):* 172–190.
Foulkes, S.H. & Anthony, E.J. (1957). *Group Psychotherapy: The Psychoanalytic Approach*. Harmondsworth, Middlesex: Penguin Books Ltd.
Frey-Angel, J. (1989). Treating children in violent families: a sibling group approach. *Social Work with Multi-Family Groups 12(1):* 95–107.
Giarretto, H. (1989). *Treatment and Training Manual*. ICEF programme, California.

Hiebert-Murphy, D. De Luca, R.V. & Runtz, M.N. (1992). Group treatment for sexually abused girls: evaluating outcome. *Families in Society* (April): 205–213.

Isaac, C. & Lane, S. (1990). *The Sexual Abuse Cycle in the Treatment of Adolescent Sexual Abusers.* Orwell, Vermont, USA: The Safer Society Press.

Kreidler, C. & England, D.B. (1990). Empowerment through group support: adult women who are survivors of incest. *Journal of Family Violence 5(1):* 35–42.

Lebacq, M. & Shah, Z. (1989). A group for black and white sexually abused children. *Groupwork:* 123–133.

Macfarlane, K. & Cunningham, C. (1990). *Steps to Healthy Touching.* Charlotte, N.C., USA: Kidsrights.

Macfarlane, K. & Cunningham, C. (1991). *Children Who Molest Children.* Safer Society Series. Orwell, Vermont, USA: The Safer Society Press.

Macfarlane, K. Waterman, J. Conerly, S., Damon, L., Durfee, M. & Long, S. (1986). *Sexual Abuse of Young Children,* London: Holt, Rinehart and Winston.

Miller, A. (1983). *For Your Own Good.* London: Faber & Faber.

Moreno, J.L. (1934). *Who Shall Survive? A New Approach to the Problem of Human Interrelations.* Washington DC: Nervous and Mental Diseases Publishing Co.

Print, B. & Dey, C. (1992). Empowering mothers of sexually abused children – a positive framework. In A. Bannister (ed.): *From Hearing to Healing.* Harlow: Longman.

Roback, H.B., Romfh, H., Bottari, M. & Lutz, D. (1981). Group psychotherapy for adult women mistreated as children by pathological mothers. *Child Abuse and Neglect 5:* 343–349.

Rosenwald, P.R. (1989). Wee care: reaching teenage mothers and changing their lives. *Children Today 18(3):* 28–30.

Ryan, G. & Lane, L. (1991). *Juvenile Sexual Offending, Causes Consequences and Correction.* Massachusetts: Lexington Books.

Sheldon, H. (1992). Working with adult female survivors. In A. Bannister (ed.): *From Hearing to Healing.* op. cit.

Singer, I. (1989). Group work with men who experienced incest in childhood. *American Journal of Orthopsychiatry 59(3):* 468–472.

Williams, A. (1991). *Forbidden Agendas.* London: Routledge.

Yassen, J. & Glass, L. (1984). Sexual assault survivors groups: a feminist practice perspective. *Social Work:* (May–June) 252–257.

23

Helping Adult Survivors of Child Sexual Abuse

Liz Hall and Siobhan Lloyd

Introduction

This chapter will examine a number of issues relating to work with adult survivors of child sexual abuse. It does not consider issues for adults who were abused in either a specific physical or emotional way, although it acknowledges that both of these forms of abuse often accompany sexual abuse. It is also worth noting that the long-term effects of these forms of child abuse have received rather less attention from research-ers and writers on the subject, and it may be the case that survivors of these forms of abuse have not had their needs met to the same (limited) extent as survivors of sexual abuse. It is important at the outset to explore the reasons for including a chapter on working with adult survivors in a book which deals primarily with issues relating to children. There are two main reasons to consider. Firstly, it is now recognised that childhood sexual abuse can have long-lasting psychological, emotional and physical consequences for a person well into adulthood (Browne and Finkelhor, 1986; Russell, 1986; Hall and Lloyd, 1993). An understanding of these potential long-term effects can be helpful in working with children whose distress manifests in ways which, with hindsight, may provide clues to these consequences. Table 23.1 gives a summary of the long-term consequences, and a full discussion is given in Hall and Lloyd (1993). Many survivors of sexual abuse have also experienced other forms of abuse, com-pounding their problems in later life. These long-term consequences are significant and have facilitated the recognition that prevention and early identification of child sexual abuse should be a high priority for all health and social service agencies.

Secondly, through the process of disclosing their childhood experiences, adult survivors are improving our understanding of the nature of child abuse and the ways in which children of different ages cope with being repeatedly sexually abused. This pool of knowledge has broken the secrecy surrounding child sexual abuse and in-creased our awareness of major trauma in a child's life. This chapter concentrates on survivors who have been sexually abused by an adult, predominantly by men. Individuals who have experienced physical and emotional abuse and neglect suffer

Table 23.1 *Summary of long-term consequences of child sexual abuse.*

Low self-esteem	Problems with trust
Confusion	Victim behaviour
Emotional reactions:	Further assault/revictimisation
– guilt	General fear of men
– anger and rage	Interpersonal difficulties:
– sadness and grief	– in relationships with men
– complete absence of emotional reaction	– in relationships with women
Depression	Sexual problems:
Anxiety problems:	– impaired sexual arousal
– generalised anxiety	– difficulties with orgasm
– panic attacks	– lack of sexual motivation
– specific fears and phobias	– lack of sexual satisfaction
– pronounced startle response	– guilt during sexual contact
Isolation and alienation	– vaginismus
	– pain during intercourse
Bad reactions to medical procedures:	Problems with touch
– hospital admissions	Parenting problems
– gynaecological procedures	Abuse of self:
– dental procedures	– self-mutilation and injury
Physical complaints	– suicide attempts
Sleep disturbance	Substance abuse:
Eating disorders:	– alcohol
– compulsive eating and obesity	– drugs
– bulimia	– tranquillisers
– anorexia	Compulsive and obsessional problems
Multiple personality disorder	Under-achievement in education and occupation
Dissociative problems:	Difficulty in sustaining positive experiences
– perceptual disturbances	
– flashbacks	
– nightmares/bad dreams	
– out of body experiences	

many of the same long-term consequences. These areas of child abuse are, as yet, under-researched. The majority of survivors currently seeking help are female, but an increasing number of male survivors are identifying themselves and literature is developing about them (Lew, 1990). In the future, it is anticipated that an increasing number of male survivors will ask for help, as well as survivors, both male and female, who have been abused by women.

Recent research on adult survivors of child sexual abuse has continued to examine the long-term consequences of such abuse and to refine our understanding of the factors influencing the severity of these consequences. It has been shown that a history of child sexual abuse is associated with an increased use of medical services (Cunningham *et al.*, 1988; Arnold *et al.*, 1990; Felitti, 1991) and psychiatric services (Shapiro, 1987; Krarup *et al.*, 1991; Waller, 1991). A number of studies are also now beginning to clarify the relationship between aspects of the child's experience and the nature of the long-term consequences. For example, Wyatt and Newcomb (1990) showed that the long-term negative consequences for an adult were related to the closeness of the relationship between the child and the perpetrator, the severity of the abuse, the extent of self-blame and non-disclosure as a child about the abuse. Leitenberg *et al.* (1992) have further suggested that the abused child's coping strategies of suppressing and avoiding emotions are associated with poorer adjustment in adulthood.

There is now a growing awareness of the similarities in response to events which are 'outside usual experience' (Colodzin, 1993), and there is a body of literature to support this (Herman, 1992; Scott and Stradling, 1992; Parkinson, 1993). These events include bombings, air disasters, industrial accidents and, in relation to sexual violence, rape, sexual assault, child sexual abuse and domestic violence. They can lead to hypervigilence, an increased startle response, depression, general anxiety, dissociation and flashbacks, sleep problems and the development of 'survivor guilt'. These consequences are a normal response to these traumas and are summarised in the phrase 'post-traumatic stress disorder' but, as Colodzin points out, it is not always useful to think of the person's pattern of functioning as a disorder. He suggests that the phrase 'post-traumatic stress' is more appropriate because this makes it easier to concentrate on the person who has lived through something overwhelming rather than on the symptoms of a medically defined disorder. This encourages a focus on the healthy responses and survival mechanisms rather than on what is 'wrong' with the person.

Seeking Help

Therapeutic work to overcome the effects of being abused as a child begins with a survivor's initial acknowledgement of the abuse. For some survivors, this acknowledgement is not possible for a number of reasons: memories of the abuse are not available; it is not the right time to disclose; the survivor does not feel safe enough with the helper or does not acknowledge that early experiences are having an effect on later life experiences. The survivor may, however, find that within the context of seeking help for another problem the history of sexual abuse emerges.

A survivor may come for help with a number of problems relating to the traumatic childhood experiences. Feelings of guilt, shame and helplessness, combined with fears of betrayal in close relationships may provoke a need to flee. The survivor can also fear disbelief, blame and rejection. From the outset, therefore, the helper should aim to establish a relationship that allows acceptance and a knowledge of being believed and being taken seriously. For the helper, this may involve suspending any preconceived ideas about sexual abuse, actively listening to the survivor, responding with warmth, support and interest, going at the survivor's pace and respecting the right to remain silent about any issue.

The specific aims of the work will vary according to the needs of the survivor and the setting in which it takes place. General aims include enabling the survivor to talk about childhood experiences so that an understanding of the long-term effects is reached, facilitating the safe release of emotions, exploring any losses resulting from childhood, breaking the secret of the past and gaining an acceptance of it so that the future can be faced with more optimism and hope.

When survivors make the decision to seek help, they are making an important step in coming to terms with the experience of childhood sexual abuse. It may have taken months or years to get to this point, and knowing what sources of help are available locally can be difficult. There are few specialist resources for survivors, but increasing numbers of helpers in statutory and non-statutory agencies are developing their work and training in this area.

In the statutory sector, family doctors are often the first person a survivor tells about the childhood experiences. The doctor's reaction can determine whether further help is sought or made available. Referral can then be made to a clinical psychologist, psychiatrist or psychotherapist working in the health service, or to a social worker or specialist worker in a voluntary agency. There are also therapists and counsellors in the private sector who work with survivors. Rape crisis centres and community mental health resources are also good local sources of help.

Professionals in nursing, social work, health visiting, community work, clinical psychology and psychiatry increasingly find clients disclosing a history of sexual abuse. It would not, therefore, be helpful to argue that only specialists in working with survivors are the most appropriate source of help. More realistic and helpful to survivors is training for these and other professionals; training which enables helpers to confront the difficult issues faced in working with survivors and building on skills which they already possess (Hall and Lloyd, 1993). Training should, at the very least, include input on the reality of sexual abuse and challenging the myths about abuse. It should also address practice issues relating to disclosure. Some principles and suggestions for training in work with survivors of sexual abuse are included in Hall and Lloyd (1993).

Knowing what resources are available locally can be the most difficult part of the search for help, and helpers who specialise in this area of work can find themselves overwhelmed by the demand for their skills. Until the survivor has reliable information about local resources, it is impossible to make an informed choice about an appropriate source of help. There are a number of questions which might be asked before deciding which route to pursue. These are listed in Table 23.2.

Table 23.2   *Questions to ask about sources of help.*

Can I refer myself?
If not, do I need to have a letter from my doctor?
Will notes be kept on my visits?
Who will see these notes?
Will information about me be sent to my doctor?
Can I see what is written about me?
Will I be able to get time off from work to attend for help?
Will I have to pay?
Are child care facilities available?
How regular will the sessions be?
How long will each session last?
Who will be present?
Where will we meet? (Hospital, own home, helper's office?)
Who else will my helper speak to about me?
Can I stop attending if it gets too difficult?
How will I know when it is time to end my contact?

A Framework for Working with Survivors of Child Sexual Abuse

In this section, key features of work with an adult survivor of child sexual abuse are considered, showing how the framework facilitates the recovery process and allows a survivor to reverse some features of the childhood experiences. This framework permits emotional growth and development through an understanding that links the survivor's experiences as a child with difficulties, strengths and resources as an adult. The key aim of the approach is to create a relationship with the survivor that acts as a partnership, with the survivor and helper using their collective resources to enable the survivor to come to terms with the past. Within such a framework, using a range of therapeutic methods becomes easier. It is essential, however, to start from the adult's childhood experiences and not to discount the very significant developmental effects that the experience of being abused may have had.

As a child who has been sexually abused grows into adulthood, feelings of power-lessness, lack of choice and control can continue, resulting in an expectation of betrayal by others. Issues of trust predominate and are obvious within a therapeutic relation-ship. The framework for therapeutic work should therefore address the key issues of power, choice, boundaries, understanding and trust. It is also necessary to consider issues relating to the silence and secrecy surrounding the abuse.

Power

A child has little or no power and is expected to obey the adult who is abusing him/her. The abuser, however, is misusing the position of power and responsibility he/she has over the child. When a survivor attends a helping agency in order to come to terms with the abuse, the helper is likely to be seen by the survivor as more knowledgeable, powerful, expert and important. This imbalance of power can reflect the survivor's view of authority figures and can also reinforce a lack of self-esteem. This is the reality of many therapeutic situations and, in order to redress this imbalance of power to some extent, the survivor's strengths, resources and courage should be acknowledged, valued and used within the helping situation. For example, if the survivor uses writing to describe feelings relating to the abuse and other childhood experiences, this can be used constructively to further an understanding of these emotional reactions. Ulti-mately, the survivor is the best judge of how he/she feels, even if the helper has to assist in finding the right words to describe these reactions.

The helper can empower the survivor primarily by listening, believing the disclos-ures about traumatic childhood experiences and showing acceptance without being judgemental. Acceptance by the helper will therefore enable the survivor to begin to value his/her strengths and resources, and to use them more constructively. In this way, the survivor is empowered to take control and regain a sense of personal worth and power.

Choice and control

A child has little or no choice or control over what happens in an abusive situation, although the abuser may have led the child to believe that he/she did have a choice. The therapeutic framework can reverse this by providing some choice over certain aspects of the helping situation. The most important relates to disclosure of details of the abusive experiences. Survivors should be given a choice about when, how much and to whom they choose to tell about the abuse. They often report feeling forced to tell a helper what happened to them as children, with no consideration given to the consequences this might have in terms of continuing contact after the disclosure and their possible need of support.

Although the choice of a male or female helper is not always available, the gender of the helper can be very important, because many survivors find it difficult to work with someone of the same gender as the abuser. For women who were abused by men, the initial choice is often for a female helper, but many discover that having a male helper can have beneficial effects in learning to trust a man. This can have positive implications for relationships generally.

Other areas where the survivor can have choice relate to the location and timing of sessions with the helper and other people available for support. Some survivors, for example, prefer not to meet the helper in the helper's office. Others might not be able to ask for time off from work to attend regular sessions and prefer to organise sessions during lunchtime or after work. Where possible, these preferences should be respected. The process of coming to terms with sexual abuse can be greatly facilitated if the survivor feels comfortable, unpressured and in control.

Boundaries

Normal physical and emotional boundaries between adult and child are violated when an adult sexually abuses a child. This can leave a child with problems in developing a clear sense of boundaries. Within the helping situation, it is essential that clear boundaries are established, so that there is no danger of the survivor being victimised again by the helping situation. Boundaries relating to confidentiality, the length and frequency of sessions with the helper, and the level of support available between sessions should be established early and may need regular review, especially at times of crisis or when the survivor is involved in a period of disclosure.

It is also essential that boundaries relating to touch are agreed. Holding the survivor's hand, using touch as a means of communication during disclosure, shaking hands on meeting or at the end of the work, or physical comfort at times of high distress may be acceptable to some survivors and not to others. The helper should not use touch in any of these ways without gaining the survivor's permission. Issues of gender are very important in this respect, and touch may be more acceptable from female helpers working with female survivors. Recent work suggests that some survivors are sexually abused by their helpers (Armsworth, 1989). Helpers need to be aware of any of their actions which might be felt by survivors to be abusive in any way. This clearly calls for a substantial degree of self-awareness on the part of helpers. The issue of confidentiality should be discussed openly, with the survivor's wishes respected in this matter. Information about the agency's policy concerning confidentiality should be given so that the survivor knows what the guidelines are. It is also important to indicate how much of the content of sessions with the helper will be recorded and how much, when and with whom the survivor may be discussed by the helper in supervision and support meetings, in meetings with other helpers, or with members of the survivor's family and wider support network.

Problems relating to confidentiality often arise when a survivor is being seen by a number of different agencies, or by several members of a multi-disciplinary team. In all these situations, it is important to inform the survivor of any policies regarding confidentiality, particularly about any information that may have to be passed to another helper. In this way, the helper can draw the boundaries clearly and explain them to the survivor.

Understanding

Children are unlikely to have any real understanding of what is happening during the abuse. They have no words, concepts or knowledge to allow them to describe the sexual abuse – even to themselves. A child may have feelings that range from extremes of love and respect for the abuser to acute terror, pain and hatred.

An important aspect of the framework for helping adult survivors of child abuse is to facilitate an understanding of how the experience of being abused has affected them, both as a child and as an adult. This could include recognising the ways the child used to cope with and survive the trauma. Linking the abuse with adult difficulties is central to work with adult survivors. It should enable survivors to recognise the relevance of the abuse to their development and facilitate the process of coming to terms with it. It also acknowledges and validates childhood experiences and the person's reaction to them.

Part of this aspect of the framework could include helping the survivor to understand the helping process. Predicting and managing potential crises, difficult times and the effects of doing certain aspects of the work can be shared with the survivor. This is likely to help the survivor to use her/his resources and the resources of any support network, including the helper, to minimise potential problems. For example, if the survivor is about to do some disclosure work, the possible short-term effects and difficulties can be anticipated and relevant support sought during this time. Thus, the survivor is more able to be involved in the helping process and can make appropriate choices which maximise the success of the work.

Trust

When children have been sexually abused by adults, they have been betrayed by someone who should have been protecting them from harm and danger. One consequence of this is that survivors may expect to be betrayed or let down by people in authority. This is compounded if a survivor's confidence in another person has been betrayed as an adult. Many survivors also come for help having had previous unsuccessful or unhelpful contacts with helping agencies. It is therefore important for the survivor to be given enough time to learn to trust the helper, and not to be pressurised to say more than he/she wants to. Building trust takes time, and this process can easily be disrupted by situations that seem unimportant to the helper. For example, if the helper fails to return a telephone call, a survivor may find it difficult to trust the helper. Trust is often experienced as 'all or nothing' by survivors.

Breaking the silence and secrecy

A child is often unable to tell anyone about the abuse for a number of reasons. The abuser may have used threats of violence or threatened the family. The child may also be unable to tell because of a sense of guilt and shame, or because there was no one to tell who might have believed. The child's coping mechanisms may complicate this further, as a child may deny, dissociate from, minimise or rationalise the abuse, so that telling someone becomes even more difficult. Finally, a young child does not have words and concepts to describe the abuse, thus making disclosure impossible.

The burden of keeping the secret can cause many psychological and physical problems that can be resolved through talking about these experiences (Lister, 1982). Disclosure requires sensitive handling and careful monitoring afterwards, as it can be both a very freeing and a painful process. Through disclosure, however, the survivor can discover that the abuser was responsible, that a child has a right to have protection and care from an adult, and that the emotional energy used to maintain the silence can become available for use in adult life. Many long-term problems can be resolved through talking about the abuse within a sensitive, believing and accepting environment. The helper will therefore have to be prepared to hear about the trauma of the abuse and its associated emotions, and be able to set aside preconceived ideas and myths about child abuse. For the survivor, being accepted by the helper even though the helper knows 'the worst' can lead to a significant improvement in self-esteem.

By addressing these issues within the helping process, the survivor is helped to gain control and power over current problems, and he/she develops an understanding of the relevance of the abusive experiences to their development. It also facilitates acknowledgement of the survivor's strengths and resources and, perhaps for the first time, to feelings of being valued and respected. The legacy of sexual abuse and the burden of responsibility for the abuse can then be shifted to the abuser. Within this framework, a wide variety of therapeutic methods can be used to address particular issues. By starting with the child's experience, the helping process immediately gives the sexual abuse a central place in the work, thus allowing for the potential for resolution of traumatic experiences.

Adult Survival Strengths

One of the main resources available in coming to terms with the abuse are those personal resources and strengths developed by the survivor in order to survive the abuse. A useful starting point can be the confirmation of the strength and courage involved in surviving into adulthood and in seeking help. There is a continuum of coping behaviours used by survivors. At one end are strategies like alcohol and drug abuse, unsuccessful suicide attempts and other types of self-injury. At the other end, there are survivors who channel all their energies into being high achievers in education or employment. Some survivors see their coping mechanisms as something to be ashamed of, and they may not wish to admit to some of them. It can also be difficult for the helper to confirm these strengths with the survivor when they are both working on difficult and painful memories and feelings.

Some coping mechanisms develop into clear strengths, such as becoming self-sufficient or being steady in a crisis. Others develop into self-destructive patterns of behaviour. There are also behaviours which have both healthy and destructive aspects – high achievement in academic matters may secure a college place or a good job, but it may lead the survivor into becoming more isolated from other people as energy is channelled into the pursuit of success.

The task for the helper here is to identify and examine the survivor's coping mechanisms, and to see which ones may still be useful. For example, writing can be a useful way of expressing the pain of childhood or disclosing aspects of the abuse which are difficult to express verbally. Other examples include work, educational or family achievements.

In recent years, the resourcefulness of survivors has been shown in the growth of published material written by survivors themselves in the form of poems, auto-biographical accounts, songs, letters and self-help books (Evert and Bijkerk, 1987; Sisk and Hoffman, 1987; Spring, 1987; Bass and Davis, 1988; Utain and Oliver, 1989; Finney, 1990; Maltz, 1991). These have been crucial in breaking the silence about child sexual abuse, and in educating professionals about the experience and effects of abuse in a very direct, accessible way. This literature has also played an important part in enabling survivors to see that they are not alone in their experience, that other survivors have struggled with similar difficulties, and that recovery is possible (Bass and Davis, 1988; Davis, 1990).

Identifying strategies which the survivor used as a child to cope with the immediate aftermath of the abuse is also important. Some of these strategies may need to be used during the therapeutic work. For example, a survivor could be encouraged to use a dissociative mechanism in order to control memories when he/she has to turn his/her attention to other aspects of his/her life.

Case Study

A case study is a useful means by which to look at the application of this framework in practice, with a particular focus on the first session between the survivor and the helper. In many ways, the framework provides a model for good practice for working with any client. Helpers often find after working with a survivor where the issues outlined in this framework are acknowledged and discussed, that their practice with other clients changes considerably.

Background

A 30-year-old woman – we shall call her Anne – attends a counselling agency for her first appointment. She was sexually abused as a child between the ages of 6 and 13 by her father, a successful businessman. He abused Anne at her home when her mother was out working night shifts as a nurse. He was physically violent to his wife and to Anne and her two younger sisters. Anne suspects that he sexually abused them too. She has never spoken about the sexual abuse to anyone. Her father died suddenly of a heart attack about a year ago, and the family have had problems in coming to terms with his death.

Anne works as a primary school teacher. She is married and has two young children. Her oldest child – a daughter – has just started school. Anne's husband does not know that she was abused as a child, but Anne thinks he would not understand how she feels. Over the last 6 weeks, Anne has been having nightmares, increasing problems in going to work and difficulties in her sexual relationship with her husband. She told her GP of these difficulties, but not about the abuse, and he suggested that she go to a counselling agency to talk over her problems. Anne feels that she will finally have to tell someone about the sexual abuse, as she is beginning to wonder if it is really the cause of her problems. She has misgivings about disclosing the abuse, particularly as she has no information about the helper she is to see. She is pleased to know that she will be seeing a woman.

First session

The helper encourages Anne to talk about what has brought her to the agency at this time. Anne tells her about current problems and a little of her family background. Anne does not feel pressurised and is surprised that the helper seems genuinely interested in her problems but does not come up with easy solutions that might have made Anne feel dismissed. Anne acknowledges that she was relieved to know that her helper is a woman.

She decides that she has to tell the helper about the fact that she was sexually abused and that her nightmares have been about these experiences, many of which she has forgotten. The helper listens without appearing shocked, surprised or disgusted by this information. She asks if Anne wants to talk more about the abuse during the session and congratulates her for sharing this information, recognising the difficulty that Anne may have felt before telling her. Anne feels that she cannot say any more at this stage, but says that she would like to talk more on a later occasion. Thus, the helper gives Anne choice and respects her decision not to say more at this stage, giving her as much control as possible within the helping situation.

Before the end of the session, the helper summarises their meeting, placing Anne's initial disclosure about the sexual abuse as a very important factor in the difficulties that she is having. Anne feels considerably reassured that she is experiencing similar problems to others who have been sexually abused. From the outset, the helper facilitates an understanding of the relevance of the sexual abuse to Anne's difficulties, indicating that the secret of the abuse can be broken when she is ready.

The helper offers Anne the opportunity to talk in further sessions about her problems, and about the abuse if she wants to. Anne agrees to this, and the choice is given to her to decide the most appropriate time for her next session. They agree that they will meet for four further sessions before reviewing the situation. Each session will last for approximately an hour and will, where possible, be held in the same room as the initial session. Anne comments that she is glad to be meeting the helper in the agency's office, as this assures her of anonymity which is not available to her in her GP's surgery.

The helper discusses confidentiality with Anne and says that she discusses her work on a regular basis with a supervisor. She assures Anne that although she may discuss Anne's case with her supervisor, any personal details which could lead to her being identified will remain confidential. Anne is concerned that her employer will be able to find out that she is attending for help, but is reassured that this information will not be shared. She feels she would like her GP to know, however, and agrees that she would like to tell him about the abuse but may need the helper's help in doing this.

The helper stresses that Anne has a choice about how much and when she wishes to discuss the abuse, but that it will probably be helpful to talk more at some point. However, her right to remain silent will be respected. She also tells Anne that she may experience strong emotional reactions now that she has disclosed her secret and suggests that she might look at available sources of support for herself before she returns for the next appointment. Anne does not feel that her husband will be very supportive, and she has a good friend whom she has supported in the past. This person knows about Anne's appointment with the helper.

In this way, the helper establishes the framework from the outset. She enables choice to be respected and indicates that choice and the range of issues to be covered will rest with Anne. She indicates the boundaries to their sessions and is clear about confidentiality. She respects Anne's decision to disclose the secret of the abuse and indicates that further discussion of the abuse may be necessary. She also confirms the place that the abuse has in Anne's difficulties. Throughout, the helper acknowledges Anne's strengths in disclosing but does not pressurise her for further information. By listening, believing and accepting Anne and not making light of her problems, she is validating Anne's experiences, and in so doing is empowering her to begin the process of recovery from the abuse.

Over the next year, Anne meets the helper on a regular basis, initially once a week and latterly at less frequent intervals. The focus of the work initially was to facilitate Anne's disclosure of her childhood experiences, and to examine the effects of the sexual abuse on her as a child. She identified that she still blamed herself for the abuse and was encouraged to look at the lack of choice, power and control that she had over her situation as a child. She had previously underestimated the effects of the fear generated by her father's violence and her need to protect her mother from any further problems. Her self-esteem improved as she placed responsibility for the abuse on her father and when she felt able to disclose details of the abuse, the nightmares and flashbacks she had been experiencing diminished significantly.

Eventually, she was able to tell her husband of her childhood experiences and was surprised to discover that he had already suspected the fact, as he had witnessed her nightmares. Together, they were able to look at the effect it had on their sexual relationship with guidance and support from the helper and by reading a number of useful books. These included *The Courage to Heal* (Bass and Davis, 1988), *Allies in Healing* (Davis, 1991) and *The Sexual Healing Journey* (Maltz, 1991).

By the end of the year, Anne felt that she no longer needed to come to the agency and was proposing to discuss gradually her experience of abuse with her sisters. She had also made plans to educate her own children realistically about child abuse, and to discuss introducing a child abuse prevention programme with colleagues at the school where she worked.

Therapeutic Contexts

A survivor also needs to consider whether a one-to-one setting or a group context with other survivors would be preferred. At some stage, some work with other family members or with a partner may be required. It is obviously preferable for a survivor to make use of resources located in the community, but sometimes an admission as an in-patient to a psychiatric hospital or unit may be necessary because the survivor is experiencing severe depression or suicidal feelings. Admission to hospital can give the survivor a period of rest away from the pressures of everyday life and a safe environment whilst difficult disclosure work is undertaken. There are a number of potential difficulties posed by a hospital admission, the main one relating to confidentiality and trust if the survivor is expected to talk to several members of staff about the abusive experiences.

One-to-one settings

Most survivors choose a one-to-one therapeutic situation, preferring the confidentiality and sense of security which it offers. Waiting times for an appointment can be a problem here, however, and this can sometimes leave the survivor feeling abandoned after having made the courageous first step in seeking help. There are a number of issues which can arise for both the survivor and helper in a one-to-one setting. It can establish a long-term trusting relationship with someone who believes the survivor, details of the abuse are confidential to one person, and the therapeutic work can be done at the survivor's own pace. Survivors can sometimes fear the intensity of the work, however, and a common fear is 'will I go mad if this carries on?' Survivors can also be concerned with burdening the helper with details of the abuse, and this can result in protecting the helper from their pain. For the helper, on the other hand, there may be concerns about over-involvement or dependency on the part of the survivor.

Survivors' groups

A survivor may decide to move on from an individual source of help to a self-help group whose members are survivors. Alternatively, a survivors' group can be the main source of help from the outset. Table 23.3 lists the main advantages and limitations of such groups.

Sgroi (1989) suggests that group members should plan to be seen individually by another helper outside a therapeutic group whilst the group is meeting. This, she suggests, will secure time for working through issues specific to the individual which have been triggered by the group experience.

Groups can be open-ended or closed, and there are advantages and disadvantages to each type. The former can provide immediate access when it is needed, and members at different stages can give each other encouragement and support. It is, however, difficult to build trust and to undertake planned work when group membership constantly changes. Variable attendance and issues relating to confidentiality are additional problems in open-ended groups.

Closed groups have the advantage of a more easily established climate of trust and

Table 23.3 *Group settings: advantages and limitations.*

Advantages	Limitations
Survivors share the burden of the abuse with others who have been through similar experiences.	Group setting may be too threatening for some survivors.
Emotional and social isolation is reduced when survivors realise they are not the only ones to have been abused.	Confidentiality may be more difficult to maintain.
It can help survivors to face the reality of what has happened.	Individuals may feel excluded or need more individual attention.
It can validate as normal a survivor's feelings of guilt, anger, grief, loneliness and other long-term effects.	Survivors may need more regular support than the group can offer.
More established members can acknowledge the progress they have made and can give hope to newer members.	Hearing about the experiences of others may be too painful.
Group can be a place of safety to express true feelings and emotions.	There may be a reluctance to participate in the group if the survivor feels he/she has not suffered as much as others in the group.

greater ease in establishing and maintaining a group culture. Members can also get to know each other over a period of time, and can move on together from one issue to another. One disadvantage is the difficulty of leaving if the group is not meeting the needs of the individual. There are three types of survivors' groups:

Self-help groups. These are formed by survivors themselves, without the support of professionals or volunteers. They usually operate without a formal leader, and the main difficulties they face relate to maintaining continuity and the powerful effects of hearing about the experiences of others before the survivor is ready for this. Their strengths are related to their immediate availability and the use of survivors' own strengths, resources and experiences to help each other.

Therapeutic groups. These are groups which are usually time-limited, more highly structured and facilitated by trained staff or volunteers. Potential members may be screened for membership, allowing the facilitator to assess the survivor's readiness for joining the group. The emphasis is on working together to understand, learn and move on from the experience of childhood sexual abuse.

Pressure/social action groups.   Here, the emphasis of the group is on raising the public profile of the issue of sexual abuse. Many survivors find these groups helpful when they are at a stage of wanting to do something to try to prevent sexual abuse happening to future generations of children. Organising such a group can be an empowering experience, and it is also a way of informing the local community about an issue of great social importance.

Working with partners

As more survivors seek help in dealing with issues from their past, a partner is often the first person a survivor tells about the abuse. This may be the result of feeling secure in a relationship, often for the first time, it can be the result of issues relating to pregnancy or children, or of difficulties which the couple experience in their relationship. It is not always possible, however, for survivors to work with their partners.

Partners themselves may need support during times of disclosure. They may find it difficult to understand the behaviour of a partner, and their relationship may experience significant change. There are three areas in which it can be helpful for partners to talk to someone: understanding the long-term effects of sexual abuse, gaining an understanding of the process of healing for the survivor, and consideration of the potential effects on the couple's relationship in the future. There are a number of helpful books which survivors can use with their partners, including *Allies in Healing* (Davis, 1991) and *Outgrowing the Pain Together* (Gil, 1992).

At some point, a survivor and his/her partner may wish to deal with the effects of the abuse on their sexual relationship. A useful book in this context is *The Sexual Healing Journey* (Maltz, 1991). There are also agencies, for example Relate and some clinical psychology departments in the NHS, that deal specifically with this area of work.

Conclusion

The partnership between survivors and their helpers has invoked a language to describe the child's experience in a way which has facilitated helpers to suspend any disbelief which they might have, and to dispel any remaining myths about sexual abuse. If helpers can listen to and hear adults who tell them about their experiences as children, this can facilitate a true understanding of their experiences. Throughout the last decade, the voices of survivors heard in prose, poetry, song, letters and novels have provided a powerful testimony of painful childhood experiences. Despite advances in devising appropriate methods for communicating with children when there is a suspicion that they have been abused, it has been and continues to be adult survivors who can convey a fuller knowledge of the child's experience. This can provide helpers with valuable information, and it provides a further justification, if one was needed, for working with adults.

Acknowledging the strengths of survivors in seeking help and working on issues from their past means taking a perspective which genuinely empowers the survivor and confirms that helpers acknowledge at the outset that the 'expert' view is that of the survivor, that survivors have power and control over the pace and depth of the work, and that helpers are facilitators and enablers rather than benefactors who 'help victims'. Survivors have many strengths, not least their courage in breaking the silence about sexual abuse. Although there may be times when survivors feel overwhelmed by the experience of recalling events which they thought were long-buried, the trauma of sexual abuse can be resolved, and survivors can begin to lead happier lives without being haunted by its legacy.

Coming to terms with the experience of childhood sexual abuse can be a long process. Many survivors are now embarking on that process, and they show great determination and courage in their ability to recover. Working with survivors is likely to challenge helpers in a number of ways. Methods of working may need to be reassessed, and long-held assumptions about the nature of the family and the status of childhood may need to be questioned. As a result, helpers will hopefully be able to listen to survivors in ways which are more appropriate to their needs. Being creative in the work, ensuring that there is good support and supervision, evaluating the work in the light of progress, knowledge and experience, encouraging survivors to write about their experiences and always being aware of the difficulty for a survivor in disclosing details of the abuse are all-important. Working with survivors can be slow, exhausting, sad, angry, despairing and tense. It can also be exhilarating, exciting, energising and rewarding work.

Annotated Further Reading

General books for working with survivors

Curtois, C.A. (1988). *Healing the Incest Wound: Adult Survivors in Therapy.* New York: Norton and Company.
A book for readers who are familiar with psychological concepts on the process of therapy with survivors

Dinsmore, C. (1991). *From Surviving to Thriving: Incest, Feminism and Recovery.* Albany: State University of New York Press.
An excellent book which acknowledges the strengths of survivors in overcoming the trauma of sexual abuse. There are good sections on the issues for women who are lesbian, on therapeutic issues and the area of memory recall.

Gil, E. (1988). *Treatment of Adult Survivors of Child Abuse*. Walnut Creek: Launch Press.
Looks at a wide range of issues, including prevalence, therapeutic work with survivors and specific issues including post-traumatic stress, multiple personality disorder and self-mutilation.

Hall, L. & Lloyd, S. (1993). *Surviving Child Sexual Abuse. A Handbook for Helping Women Challenge their Past*. London: Falmer Press.
A practice manual written for survivors and helpers. Covers the long-term effects of sexual abuse, disclosure, therapeutic methods, themes in working with survivors, training and issues for helpers.

Nelson, S. (1987). *Incest: Fact and Myth*. Edinburgh: Stramullion.
A classic – examines and refutes some of the commonly held myths about sexual abuse of children.

Personal accounts

Allen, C.V. (1980). *Daddy's Girl*. New York: Berkeley Book.
A first-person account of the author's experience of being sexually abused by her father. Gives a good insight into a child's ways of coping and the effects of the abuse on her subsequent development.

Evert, K. & Bijkerk, I. (1987). *When You're Ready*. Walnut Creek: Launch Press.
A personal account of coming to terms with sexual abuse by a mother. Especially helpful for a survivor who uses regression as a means of reawakening memories.

Sisk, S.L. & Hoffman, C.F. (1987). *Inside Scars*. Gainesville: Pandora Press.
An account of a woman's recovery from sexual abuse by her father. Gives a good insight into the process of therapy from the perspective of the survivor and her helper.

Spring, J. (1987). *Cry Hard and Swim*. London: Virago.
A personal account of a Scottish woman's journey in coming to terms with sexual abuse by her father. Describes the process of seeking and finding help, along with the difficulties she encountered. A moving and readable account.

Wilson, M. (1993). *Crossing the Boundary. Black Women Survive Incest*. London: Virago.
Looking at the situation of black women, the author focuses on the costs of survival and the strengths which sustain women. The book challenges the myth that sexual abuse is the norm in black communities.

Books written for survivors

Bain, O. & Sanders, M. (1990). *Out in the Open*. London: Virago.
A book for teenage survivors, written in a clear and readable style.

Bass, E. & Davis, L. (1988). *The Courage to Heal*. New York: Harper and Row.
An excellent book, packed with information, personal accounts and ideal for use in the recovery process from the experience of sexual abuse.

Davis, L. (1990). *The Courage to Heal Workbook*. New York: Harper and Row.
An excellent workbook to accompany *The Courage to Heal*.

Maltz, W. (1991). *The Sexual Healing Journey: A Guide for Survivors of Sexual Abuse*. New York: HarperCollins.
An excellent book for helping survivors deal with the sexual problems which might result from the experience of sexual abuse.

Books for male survivors

Lew, M. (1990). *Victims No Longer. Men Recovering from Incest and other Sexual Abuse*. New York: Harper and Row.
Written in the style of *A Courage to Heal*, this is a very helpful book.

Quinn, P. (1984). *Cry Out*. Nashville: Abindon Press.
Describes the abuse of a young boy and the consequences of the abuse in later life.

Books for partners and families

Byerly, C.M. (1985). *The Mother's Book*. Dubuque: Kendall/Hunt Publishing.
A useful, clearly written account of issues for women who discover that their children have been sexually abused.

Davis, L. (1991). *Allies in Healing*. New York: Harper and Row.
Full of essential information for partners and extended families of survivors.

Gil, E. (1992). *Outgrowing the Pain Together*. Walnut Creek: Launch Press.
An excellent book for survivors and their partners.

References

Armsworth, M. (1989). Therapy of incest survivors: abuse or support? *Child Abuse and Neglect 13*: 549–562.

Arnold, R.P., Rogers, D. & Cook, D.A.G. (1990). Medical problems of adults who were sexually abused in childhood. *British Medical Journal 300*: 705–708.

Bass, E. & Davis, L. (1988). *The Courage to Heal*. New York: Harper and Row.

Browne, A. & Finkelhor, D. (1986). Initial and long-term effects. A review of the research. In D. Finkelhor (ed.): *A Sourcebook of Child Sexual Abuse*. Beverley Hills, California: Sage.

Colodzin, B. (1993). *How to Survive Trauma*. New York: Pulse Station Hill Press.

Cunningham, J., Pearce, T. & Pearce, P. (1988). Childhood sexual abuse and medical complaints in adult women. *Journal of Interpersonal Violence 3*: 131–134.

Davis, L. (1990). *The Courage to Heal Workbook*. New York: Harper and Row.

Davis, L. (1991). *Allies in Healing*. New York: Harper and Row.

Evert, K. & Bijkerk, I. (1987). *When You're Ready*. Walnut Creek, California: Walnut Press.

Felitti, V.J. (1991). Long-term medical consequences of incest, rape and molestation. *Southern Medical Journal 84*: 328–331.

Finney, L.D. (1990). *Reach for the Rainbow*. Park City, Malibu: Changes Publishing.

Gil, E. (1992). *Outgrowing the Pain Together*. Walnut Creek: Launch Press.

Hall, L. & Lloyd, S. (1993). *Surviving Child Sexual Abuse: A Handbook for Helping Women Challenge Their Past*. London: Falmer Press.

Herman, J.L. (1992). *Trauma and Recovery*. New York: Basic Books.

Krarup, G., Nielsen, B., Bask, P. & Petersen, P. (1991) Childhood sexual experiences and repeated suicidal behaviour. *Acta Psychiatrica Scandinavica 83:* 16–19.

Leitenberg, H., Greenwald, E. & Cado, S. (1992). A retrospective study of long-term methods of coping with having been sexually abused during childhood. *Child Abuse and Neglect* 16(1): 399–407.

Lew, M. (1990). *Victims No Longer. Men Recovering from Incest and other Sexual Abuse.* New York: Harper and Row.

Lister, E.D. (1982). Forced silence: a neglected dimension of trauma. *American Journal of Psychiatry 139:* 872–876.

Maltz, W. (1991). *The Sexual Healing Journey: A Guide for Survivors of Sexual Abuse.* New York: HarperCollins.

Parkinson, D. (1993). *Post Trauma Stress.* London: Sheldon Press.

Russell, D.E.H. (1986). *The Secret Trauma: Incest in the Lives of Girls and Women.* New York: Basic Books.

Scott, M.J. & Stradling, S.G. (1992). *Counselling for Post Traumatic Stress Disorder.* London: Sage.

Sgroi, S. (1989). Healing together: peer group therapy for adult survivors of child sexual abuse. In S. Sgroi, (ed.): *Vulnerable Populations. Evaluation and Treatment of Sexually Abused Children and Adult Survivors,* vol. 2. Cambridge, Mass: Lexington Books.

Shapiro, S. (1987). Self-mutilation and self blame in incest victims. *American Journal of Psychotherapy 41:* 46–54.

Sisk, S.L. & Hoffman, C.F. (1987). *Inside Scars.* Gainesville, Florida: Pandora Press.

Spring, J. (1987). *Cry Hard and Swim.* London: Virago.

Utain, M. and Oliver, B. (1989) *Scream Louder.* Deerfield Beach, Florida: Health Communications.

Waller, G. (1991) Sexual abuse as a factor in eating disorders. *British Journal of Psychiatry 159:* 664–671.

Wyatt, G.E. and Newcomb, M. (1990) Internal and external mediators of women's sexual abuse in childhood. *Journal of Consulting and Clinical Psychology 58:* 758–767.

24

Out-of-Home Care for the Abused or Neglected Child: Research, Planning and Practice

June Thoburn

Introduction

Developments in the provision of out-of-home care for children who have been abused or neglected mirror more general developments in child and family policy, law and practice. When the emphasis has been on the importance of the natural family, greater efforts have been made to provide residential placements and foster carers who will support the family at times of stress by providing good care for the children and facilitating positive contact with family members so that they can return home as soon as possible. When a child-centred approach has predominated, an emphasis on rescue and a fresh start has led to more resources being available for the placement of children with permanent new families, preferably for adoption. This chapter starts from the premise that this either/or approach to child placement is detrimental to children whose protection or other needs require them to be placed away from home.

Like other aspects of service for children at risk of abuse or neglect, out-of-home placement has benefited from lateral thinkers and creative and adventurous practitioners, but it has also suffered when the work of the pioneers has been translated in a rigid way into practice, and has been expressed in jargonised language which has inhibited evaluation and adjustment. The two most obvious terms to which this statement apply in placement practice are 'permanence' and 'drift'. In the 1970s and 1980s, first in America and then in Britain, even to ask for a clearer definition of these words when applied to individual children was seen as condemning them to a life of impermanence or further abuse. The reader of the statement, 'the plan is permanence' at the end of a court report was led to believe that to plan for permanence was to achieve it. Little was said about the risks inherent in placement for adoption, which had to be balanced against the risks involved in children returning home or remaining in long-term care. As British research studies have evaluated permanence policies, the balance has shifted yet again, and, with the implementation of the Children Act 1989, we are embarking on a phase of more careful planning for each individual child who cannot remain at home. The Department of Health's introduction to the Children Act (DOH, 1989a, page 5) states:

> 'The Act seeks to protect children both from the harm which can arise from failures or abuse within the family and from the harm which can be caused by unwarranted intervention in their family life.'

This requirement to balance the consequences of different sorts of 'harm' arises from research findings which have shown that some children who were 'rescued' from their family homes were further harmed by the system which sought to protect them.

Other chapters in this *Handbook* have referred to research findings on the impact of abuse and severe neglect on the long-term health and well-being of children. The research findings discussed here on the outcome of a range of substitute placements indicate that 'love is not enough', that a substantial minority of children placed with loving and dedicated new parents will still need additional services if they are to overcome the harmful effects of their early experiences, and that a proportion will not totally recover and will remain emotionally vulnerable. The children who we most want to rescue are most vulnerable to the sort of adversities which can happen once they leave home, most obviously renewed abuse, multiple placements, and leaving care at the age of 18 without a secure base to provide the support they will need as young adults. (See Triseliotis, 1983; Bowlby, 1988; Thoburn, 1990, for detailed discussions of the concepts of 'a family for life' and a 'secure base'.)

In short, the early optimism of the 1970s and 1980s that, if restoration back home was not easily achievable, children could be placed successfully for adoption and thus be 'got off the books', has been shown in many cases to have been wishful thinking rather than a realistic appraisal of the child's long-term problems and needs. Even when strenuous efforts to prevent placement 'drift' were made, only a small minority of maltreated children were placed for adoption, and in a substantial minority of these cases the placements were not successful.

This chapter will summarise the research findings and place particular emphasis on what they tell us about how practice might be improved. It will highlight the crucially important tasks of assessment and making decisions about the type of placement and other services which are most likely to ensure that the short and long-term needs of the child are met. A discussion of the role of task-centred carers in providing a safe, nurturing and stable environment for assessment is followed by a consideration of the alternative long-term options for those children who cannot safely return to live with their parents.

The Literature on Out-of-Home Placement

There is an extensive literature on the placement of children in residential care, foster care and with adoptive families. For the busy UK practitioner, the most useful sources are the recent Department of Health publications which have accompanied the Children Act 1989. Guidance volumes 2 and 3 on family support and foster care placements, and volume 4 on residential care are based on the practice wisdom of the many writers and practitioners who have had an impact on what has become widely recognised as 'best practice'. *Principles and Practice in Regulations and Guidance* (DOH,

1989*b*) summarises the principles which should underlie all family social work, including the placement of children away from their families of origin. The British research which has been most influential is summarised in two volumes, *Social Work Decisions in Child Care* (Department of Health and Social Security (DHSS), 1985) and *Patterns and Outcomes in Child Placement* (DOH, 1991*a*). The surveys by Rowe and her colleagues (1989) of the extent to which over 10 000 placements met the desired aims, Bullock and his colleagues (1993) of 875 children, most of whom returned home from care, and Thoburn and Rowe of 1165 placements with permanent new families (in Fratter *et al.*, 1991) are complemented by a large number of smaller-scale studies which give a more detailed picture of child placement work in the UK. The literature review which was commissioned to accompany the review of adoption law summarises the research on this subject (Thoburn, 1992). The review document itself and the working papers which led up to it provide a very helpful summary of the legal and administrative structures which underpin the placement of children with permanent new families, including placements for adoption (DOH, 1992). Other overviews which consider research evidence and the practice literature are those of Maluccio and his colleagues (1986), which review the North American as well as the British literature; Thoburn (1994) and Roberts (1993), writing more specifically about foster care for children who have been abused or neglected. However, professionals who make recommendations about plans for specific children are advised to use these overviews merely as a starting point in the search for research literature which is relevant to any particular child, since the range of options to meet individual needs is wide, and some studies are more relevant to some types of need and placements than others. Oversimplification of research findings can lead to avoidable mistakes, the price of which will be paid by the children. I shall therefore consider the importance of assessing the needs of individual children, before considering the possible alternative placements which might be available to meet those needs.

Assessing the Placement Needs of Children who Cannot Remain Safely at Home

When plans are being made for the placement of a child who cannot remain safely at home, the following questions have to be considered.

- What sort of placement?
- For how long?
- What will be the appropriate legal status for the placement?
- What sort of contact will be appropriate, where and with whom?
- What services, support or therapy will be needed by all those involved in the placement – the child, the carers and members of their own families, the original family members and relatives?
- What financial help and practical support will be needed to maintain the placement?

The answers to all these questions must come from a view about the long-term aims which in turn have to be based on a painstaking and individually planned assessment process leading to a detailed statement of the child's needs and the ability of any of the adults who are currently a part of the child's life to meet those needs.

Professionals who are considering long-term plans for a child must have a clear idea of what they consider to be a successful outcome. It is worth noting that the review of adoption law suggests that any future legislation should stress the fact that the decisions taken at the time that adoption is being considered will have a lifetime impact on the child and other family members. Any placement must not only meet physical needs and offer protection, but must also meet the child's needs to give and receive love, feel secure and supported, and have the confidence to branch out and have new experiences. Professionals making decisions about children should have in mind the long-term aim of ensuring that as young adults they will have self-esteem and a positive self-concept which will allow them to make satisfying relationships and to provide in turn good enough parenting for any children for whom they may be responsible. Self-esteem grows out of mutual attachments to at least one parent figure – *a psychological parent* – who may be a birth parent or a substitute parent. Research has indicated that self-esteem is most likely to be enhanced if children have a *sense of permanence* in their relationships with their primary carers, and a *sense of identity*, and that these two must be kept in balance. Without a sense of permanence, the child will not feel secure enough to take the risks which go with new attachments, whether to new parents, siblings or friends. Without a sense of personal identity, which includes knowing and preferably being in contact with members of the birth family and important people from the past, racial and cultural identity, pride in appearance including skin colour, and being valued as the individuals they *are* and not measured against the persons their parents would like them to be, there is a risk that children will undervalue themselves in new relationships, or have the sense of being incomplete described by many adopted adults. Walby and Simons (1990) describe the groups which they facilitated for adopted people who movingly talk about these feelings. Mary, whom I interviewed 6 years after she was placed at the age of 12 with a permanent foster family, considered that her new parents had given her a great deal, including stability. However, she left home on New Year's Eve just before her 18th birthday, leaving a note for her foster mother saying, 'Mum, I'm sorry, I can't be the person you want me to be' (Thoburn, 1990).

The needs listed here are common to all children, but the way in which they are met will be peculiar to each individual child, including each member of a sibling group needing placement. One of the exercises in the Appendix of *Patterns and Outcomes in Child Placement* (DOH, 1991a) offers a framework for listing each of the child's needs and considering the 'job description' for the carers who are most likely to be able to meet the needs identified. During this assessment process, it will be essential for those responsible for making plans for and with the child to be aware of research findings. There is no point in identifying the perfect placement if research suggests that it is unlikely to be successful given the particular circumstances of this particular child. A second best solution which is likely to be successful in at least some respects may be preferable to the ideal solution which is highly likely to break down.

Research findings suggest that information must be collected about the characteristics, personality, aptitudes and any particular disabilities, whether emotional, behavioural, learning or physical, of each child. The age of the child is another important dimension, since age at placement has been associated by several researchers with outcome, with children who are older when placed being more likely to experience placement breakdown. The third dimension is the relationship of the child with significant others. This will involve a consideration of the child's attachments.

The child may be well-attached, ambivalently attached or not attached to birth mother, birth father, step-parent, siblings, relatives or the present foster parents, and these relationships must also be carefully considered when planning a new placement. The assessment must also consider whether the people who are significant to the child wish the child to continue to remain where he or she currently is, to return to them or to be placed elsewhere, and, if they have parental responsibility, whether they will consent to a particular form of placement but not to another form of placement. This occurs most obviously when a parent who acknowledges that the child cannot return home will consent to a placement with a view to a residence order (guardianship order in some countries), but not to a placement for adoption. The Children Act 1989 requires that the child, and all those who have parental responsibility, be consulted and due consideration given to their views, wishes and feelings. Whilst the wishes of important people, including the child him or herself, may sometimes have to be overruled, it is desirable to avoid this if accommodating their wishes will not clearly be detrimental to the child's long-term well-being.

Having formed a picture of the child's needs and relationships, and having consulted all those whose wishes and feelings must be given due consideration (Children Act 1989, section 22 and the welfare checklist, section 1), those considering the child's placement will be in a better position to answer the key placement questions listed above. Before considering alternative long-term placements, the key role of short-term or bridge carers will be discussed.

Bridge placements

The pendulum swings in child care policy and practice have already been noted. The emphasis and the value placed on short-term, bridge or task-centred foster placements have increased or diminished with these swings. In the 1950s and 1960s, many writers emphasised the value of short-term foster placements as an essential part of a family support service. The official guide to foster care practice which resulted from a working group set up after the inquiry into the death of Maria Colwell (DHSS, 1976) emphasised the particular skills and tasks of foster carers in facilitating good relationships between children and their natural parents. However, the concern about child abuse which followed that death and subsequent inquiries, together with a realisation that many children did not return to their natural families and remained in unplanned care (Rowe and Lambert, 1973), led to a greater emphasis on the placement of children in care with permanent new families, and to a concentration on the skills of permanent family placement to the exclusion of skills in recruiting, training and supporting short-term foster carers. The exception to this was the creative thinking and positive practice which went into the recruitment training and support of carers for teenagers, no doubt because the concern about child abuse at that period was rivalled only by concern about troublesome teenagers (Hazel, 1981; Shaw and Hipgrave, 1983).

This attempt to have a permanence policy without a well thought out and properly resourced foster care policy led to a new problem identified by the researchers whose work was reported in the Department of Health overviews. Drift, or lack of planning, ceased to be a significant problem, and was replaced by two equally serious problems: poor quality short-term foster care, which led to a succession of different placements while the child was awaiting a long-term placement; and poor and inflexible planning, which replaced a lack of planning. These two were inter-related, in that it is not possible adequately to assess the needs of children and undertake the work which is necessary with the parents, the child and the new family to prepare them for a permanent placement which is going to have a chance of succeeding, if the child is not in the interim period offered stable and skilled care by either residential workers or foster parents.

Rowe and her colleagues (1989) identified the tasks of short-term or bridge carers as temporary care (including short periods of planned respite care to alleviate family stress); emergency placements – to offer a roof for a very limited period; preparation for long-term or permanent placement, whether back home or with a new family; assessment; treatment; and a bridge to independence. Utting (1992) identified similar tasks for residential care.

The Children Act 1989 encourages the provision of accommodation as an important part of family support, to be used alongside day care when families are under stress and children are suffering as a result. When parents or older children ask for such help, or social workers consider a child's needs are not being adequately met and the child is suffering significant harm or likely to do so without an out-of-home placement, an early discussion of the sort of care which may be appropriate will alleviate the need for emergency placements and allow for better planning in more cases. Introductions can then be made, agreements about placement carefully negotiated, and the trauma of the separation minimised. In some abuse cases, it is inevitable that emergency action is taken. However, even here it is possible to minimise the harm by providing care for the whole family, or perhaps 'crash pad' facilities in residential care or family centres, so that time can be taken for a more careful decision about the placement of the child, or indeed about whether an alleged abuser is willing to move out temporarily and can be offered help to find accommodation outside the home.

A series of smaller-scale studies of foster care, most notably those of Berridge and Cleaver (1987) and Westacott (1988), preceded the more comprehensive study of placements of Rowe and her colleagues (1989). These authors studied a total of 5868 children from six English local authorities, who between them experienced over 10 000 placements between April 1985 and March 1987. They identified short-term placements which broke down without achieving their aims, and also those which were intended to be short-term but lasted longer than expected. Although 57% of the children had only the one placement in care, 8% had three or more during the 2-year period, and there were 38 children who had five or more moves. Six of these were aged under 5 years although most of those who had several moves were teenagers. Short-term placements had a lower breakdown rate than long-term placements, but the proportion breaking down (almost one in five in the Berridge and Cleaver study) is still alarming when one considers that they were only intended to last for up to 8 weeks. Few writers have measured outcomes other than placement breakdown for children who stay away from home for short periods. However, Packman (1986) found higher satisfaction rates amongst parents whose children *were* temporarily accommodated than amongst those whose request for care was refused. Stalker (1990) has reviewed the mainly positive but some negative effects of respite care for children with disabilities.

One explanation for those who were reported as staying too long in short-term foster care is that foster parents all too quickly come to see the children as 'theirs', and in subtle and unsubtle ways start to discourage contact between the parents and children, thus inhibiting the social worker's efforts to keep a space for child and parents in each other's practical and emotional lives.

What Sort of Placement?

Having already made the decision that a child may not safely remain at or return home, at least for the present, the alternatives will be placement with relatives or friends; foster family care; or placement in some form of group care which may be a children's home, boarding education, or a larger foster home such as those provided by the Children's Family Trust (Cairns, 1984).

A careful assessment should allow a decision to be made as to whether what is needed is a placement where the parent or parents will remain the 'psychological' parents, or whether new psychological parents are needed. Bullock and his colleagues (1993) demonstrate that up to 90% of children will eventually leave care and return either to their parents or relatives. The majority do so within the first 6 weeks, and almost all do so within the first 6 months. This 'leaving care curve' has been misinterpreted to imply that if a child is still away from home after 6 months, he or she is unlikely to return and should therefore be placed for adoption. The majority of the long stayers are not infants who will easily be placed with a new family, but are older children, many of whom have behaviour problems, and who are likely to return to their first families or at least, after leaving the local authority's care, drift back to their home neighbourhoods.

If it appears that the child will not be able to return home in the near future, but that there is a good attachment between parent and child, a placement is needed where the carers will *supplement* the care of the parent. The parent will remain the main attachment figure, and the placement carers will need to be chosen for their skills in facilitating this. If such a placement is likely to last for a period of years, and especially if the child is quite young, it may be that the birth parents and the carers will *both* fulfil psychological parenting roles. This most often happens when a child remains with a relative such as a grandparent, but there are cases when dual psychological parenting is appropriate for lengthy periods of time with children in foster care. In some cases, assessment will make it clear that the child needs new psychological parents, either because there is no attachment or a very destructive or ambivalent attachment with the birth parents, or the child is young and it is not feasible for him or her to remain psychologically attached to two sets of parents. In that case, substitute parents will be sought. These will normally be adoptive or permanent foster parents, but on occasion a young person may have been so hurt by early experiences within a family that he or she will request a group care placement. Some small children's homes, and group foster homes, are able to offer psychological parenting within a group care environment. Some older children who have been sexually abused may feel safer in such an environment, and skilled and loving carers are sometimes able to help them develop trust and indeed form long-term relationships with them which may offer a secure base from which to launch out into adult life.

For How Long?

Clarity is always needed about the approximate length of any placement, and this should be stated in the placement agreement. Where the situation is unclear, it is usually possible to estimate approximately how long might be needed for clarification. It is preferable in such cases to overestimate the time needed, and thus avoid a change of placement. If an older child has been harmed by earlier experiences, and assessment indicates that a permanent or long-term placement is needed, 18 months to 2 years is a realistic outer limit which allows for assessment followed by the search for the right placement and preparation for the move. Shorter time limits on task-centred placements merely result in unnecessary movements, as was demonstrated by Berridge and Cleaver (1987) and Cliffe and Berridge (1991) in their studies of the very much shorter-term foster placements favoured by some local authorities. If the intention is that the placement should be until the child is an adult, this should be clearly stated and recorded in the agreement.

What Legal Status?

The first option is for voluntary arrangements (accommodation is the terminology of the Children Act 1989) where parents retain full parental responsibility, but perhaps with the intention, if all are agreed, that the relatives or foster parents will make an application for a residence order once the child appears to be settled. In some cases where there is serious risk to the child, even though the plan might be to work towards rehabilitation, it may be appropriate for a residence order to be made at the onset of the placement to give legal security. This might also be appropriate if a parent is impulsive or suffers from a mental illness or an addiction associated with impulsive behaviour, or there is evidence from the past that an agreement may not be adhered to. Where there is evidence that a child is suffering or likely to suffer significant harm and an agreement cannot be reached to secure the child's placement in accommodation, or for the child to remain in a placement until a residence or care order is sought, it may be necessary to apply for an emergency protection or care order to secure the placement. If a permanent placement is being considered, the child may be placed directly under the Adoption Agencies Regulations, regardless of whether or not there has been a previous care order. Alternatively, the child may remain accommodated or in care as a foster child with the intention of an application for adoption or a residence order once the child is settled. Or he or she may remain as a foster child, in which case it will be important to have a very clear agreement that this is intended to be a *permanent* foster placement, especially if the child is placed under voluntary arrangements (see Thoburn, 1990, for a fuller discussion of the importance of ensuring that the child and the carers have a sense of permanence in such situations, and ways in which this sense of permanence can be facilitated). The Adoption Law White Paper (DOH, 1993) proposes a more secure residence order which will convey the status of *inter vivos* guardian on the foster parents or relatives until the child is 18. No application for a revocation of the order will be permitted without the leave of the court, and the guardians will be allowed to make provision for guardians for the child in the event of their death.

What Sort of Contact and With Whom?

The work of Millham and his colleagues (1986, 1989) played a major part in emphasising the importance of continued contact for children who are looked after by the local authority, not only with their parents but also with siblings if they are not placed together, and with relatives and friends. These authors also summarise previous research on the subject. Research on 'open adoption' and the issues surrounding openness when children are placed with permanent new families is summarised by the writers in Mullender's edited book on the subject (1991). There are circumstances in which face-to-face (or even more rarely indirect) contact cannot be safely achieved or is not in the interest of the child, but these are exceptions to be decided in each individual case. There is not sufficient space here to cite all the research evidence on contact with members of the birth family, whether or not the child is to return to them, but the cumulative findings can be summarised as follows. As far as I am aware, no large-scale study has concluded that face-to-face contact is associated with a higher risk of breakdown or other placement problems. One or two smaller-scale studies have pointed to problems resulting from specific factors such as inconsistency. Rowe *et al.* (1984) found that long-term foster children who appeared to be doing well were either regularly visited or had contact with parents at the start of the placement which had gradually diminished over time. Continued face-to-face contact with members of the birth family, especially birth parents, has been associated by one or more research studies with the following benefits.

- Increased likelihood of return home of the child (Fanshel and Shinn, 1978; Aldgate, 1980; Thorpe, 1980; Bullock *et al.*, 1993).
- A clearer sense of identity (Thoburn *et al.* 1986; Aldgate, 1990; Kelly and McAuley, 1995).
- Increased self-esteem in the child as he or she grows up (Weinstein, 1960; Fanshel and Shinn, 1978; Aldgate, 1980).
- Increased well-being, including higher educational performance (Fanshel and Shinn, 1978; Aldgate, 1990, provided that the child also has a sense of permanence).
- A diminished risk of placement breakdown (Berridge and Cleaver, 1987; Thoburn, 1990; Kufeldt and Allison, 1990; Fratter *et al.*, 1991).

Other benefits of continued contact which have been pointed out by research studies of a more qualitative nature include the following.

- It offers continuity, in that the members of the birth family offer some continuity of relationships to those children who experience a series of different placements whilst in care. For this reason, it is especially important that contact is maintained when a child is changing placements.
- It may help in a crisis or with a contingency if a placement in care breaks down and no suitable placement is available. On occasion in such circumstances, a reassessment may lead to the conclusion that the child may safely return home. On other occasions, members of the family, perhaps grandparents or relatives, may provide a bridge placement until a new placement can be identified.
- Continued contact will provide 'a family for life' for the child. If the child does settle well and form attachments with a substitute family, he or she may have the benefit as an adult of two 'families for life' if contacts have been maintained with the first family. If the placement in care does not lead to a good long-term attachment and a secure base, family members who have not been able to meet their children's needs when young may be able to do so when they are young adults. The particular importance of siblings must not be forgotten, since the relationship between siblings is potentially even more long-lasting than is the parent–child relationship.

This may apply to siblings born after the child left home, and there are many examples of siblings forming close friendships as adults, even if they never actually lived together as children.

The questions as to what sort of social work help and therapy will be provided and for whom will be discussed in more detail later in this chapter. Financial support can be available when appropriate through adoption allowances, residence order allowances, foster care payments, grants made under section 17 of the Children Act, settling-in grants and one-off grants, for example, if a child is particularly destructive.

In the next sections, the range of long-term placements which might be chosen following assessment are considered.

Respite, Long-term Shared Care and Placement with Relatives

Sometimes parents will themselves request out-of-home care to tide them over particularly stressful periods in their lives, or residential therapy for a child whose behaviour is particularly difficult. In some cases, the family may be most appropriately supported by the provision of regular planned periods of respite care in the same foster home or residential placement. In other circumstances, the family may be linked with a foster carer or residential placement which will provide accommodation at times of stress, as when a parent suffers from a debilitating physical illness such as AIDS-related symptoms, or a mental illness which recurs such as schizophrenia or clinical depression (see chapters by Fratter and O'Hara in Batty, 1993, and Aldgate and Bradley, 1995).

Mention has already been made of the importance of clarity about who is intended to play the psychological parenting role for a child living away from home. It has also been suggested that on occasions there will be dual psychological parenting. More often, however, the intention of using these options will be to maintain a strong attachment with the parents and other family members, including siblings. Longer-term shared care options are particularly appropriate when a parent and child are closely attached, but there is danger to the child if he or she continues to live at home. It is often possible to arrange for visits home to be fully supervised, or for the adult believed to be a danger to the child to be out of the home when the child returns home for visits. If this is not possible, a comfortable environment is needed so that the non-abusing parent and child can spend extended periods of time together.

Long-term Group Care Placements

In some cases, boarding education may be an appropriate way of maintaining the child's attachment to the natural parents. Some older children and their parents or step-parents are unable to live harmoniously together, but their fragile relationship can be maintained if they keep some distance between them, and may strengthen as the child becomes a young adult. In a study of 177 American adopted children with special needs, Nelson (1985) found that placement away from home or boarding education was a much valued service to adoptive families and made it possible for some placements under stress to survive. Grimshaw and Berridge (1995) have recently completed a study of boarding education for children with educational and behavioural difficulties. While they express concern at the potential risk of abuse of children placed in boarding education, they also note the positive role which such provision can play in the lives of children and families under stress. Aldgate (1980) noted that some parents found it very difficult to visit their children in foster care and were more able to remain in touch if they were placed in children's homes. Rose (1990) describes the therapeutic community approach to young people with serious behavioural difficulties.

Long-term Shared Care in Foster Homes

When long-term shared foster care is the placement of choice, particular attention must be paid to ensuring that the birth parents and the foster parents get on with each other well enough to share the parenting of the child. In some cases, the child will remain in accommodation on a voluntary basis, in which case the parents retain full parental responsibility, and the placement agreement must spell out which responsibilities are delegated to the foster carers, and the actions which all parties will take as contingencies if the arrangements break down. It is often small things such as a change in hairstyle which can cause trouble between the two sets of parents, and creative social workers and skilled foster carers must think ahead to pre-empt such difficulties. Even when there is a care order, the Children Act 1989 requires that the parents are enabled to retain as much of their parental responsibility as possible, and that the authority only takes away that much of their parental responsibility which is necessary in order to secure the child's well-being.

The major British sources of information about the success of intermediate or long-term foster care, residential placement and placement with relatives are found in the work of Rowe and her colleagues (1984, 1989); Berridge (1985), Millham *et al.* (1986) and Bullock *et al.* (1993) on residential care; Berridge and Cleaver (1987); Aldgate (1990); and Kelly and McAuley (1995). Recent North American studies are by Fein *et al.* (1990) and Kufeldt and Allison (1990). Hazel (1981), Shaw and Hipgrave (1983) and Caesar *et al.* (1994) have described and summarised the research on special placement schemes for adolescents, which normally aim to prepare them for independence and often endeavour to build bridges for them with their natural parents and relatives.

Most studies note that there is a higher breakdown rate of placements of teenagers, regardless of whether or not they are placed in specialist or professional foster schemes, in 'ordinary' foster homes, in lodgings or in residential care. Berridge and Cleaver (1987), however, noted a high breakdown rate amongst youngsters aged 7–11 years. Placements in residential care are least likely to break down. However, Colton (1989) compared the nature of caring in specialist foster homes and children's homes and concluded that, irrespective of the skills of the carers, those looking after young people in family environments are more able to be child-oriented than residential workers who can provide less individual attention. The voice of the children and young people is included in most of these studies, but is reported more fully by Fletcher (1993). Although breakdown rates are quite high, many adolescents speak well of their residential and foster carers, and it should be noted that adolescents are in any case a group of people 'on the move'. Studies using outcome measures such as health and educational progress are reviewed by Roberts (1993).

Turning to the research in more detail, Rowe and her colleagues (1989) compared the findings of her large-scale survey of foster placements with earlier studies. Twenty-seven percent of the 194 children placed in long-term foster care during the first year of the study had experienced breakdown between 12 and 24 months later. The proportion for those under four was 4%, for those aged between 5 and 10 years 23%, but for teenagers over 30% rising to 66% of those aged 16 or over. The authors concluded that two-thirds of the long-term placements were at least fairly successful. Most studies of educational progress of children in foster care have concluded that their education is negatively affected. However, Aldgate (1990) found that children in long-term foster placements were doing as well educationally, and in other aspects of their well-being, as were children who were on the social workers' preventive case loads but were not looked after by the local authority. They also note that increased well-being and satisfactory educational progress were associated with having a sense of stability and security within the foster home. The benefits of continued contact with members of the birth family have already been listed. Berridge and Cleaver (1987) found that more placements broke down if there was no contact, and Millham et al. (1986) showed how formal and informal barriers are often put in the way of contact, so that visiting is prevented or quickly tails off in the majority of placements.

To summarise, these studies show that the goalkeeping – 'care is bad for your health' or 'once they are in care, it is hard to get them back home' – attitudes and policies of the 1980s represented an over-simplification and must be adapted in the light of new knowledge. There is much in the studies to indicate how practice can improve to reduce the casualty rate even further, and to help identify the potential casualties, so that services (both when children are being looked after and when they leave) can be of a higher quality.

The fact that the majority of placements are reasonably successful should not, however, prevent us from recognising the extreme vulnerability of children who *do* become split off from their families of origin, and whose placements in care or for adoption are unsuccessful. Studies of homeless young people, and of young people in custody, indicate that a substantial proportion of these were originally abused, placed in care for their own protection and re-abused, or felt so unprotected or alone in care that they ran away and preferred to trust to their own devices.

Placement of Children from Minority Ethnic Groups

Most studies also consider whether placements of black children are any more or less successful than those whose parents are both white. It is generally considered that black children are over-represented amongst children in care. Rowe and her colleagues (1989) point out the dangers of over-simplification. Asian children are under-represented, and children, both of whose parents are African Caribbean, are over-represented amongst those in short-term placements but not amongst those in long-term placements. Children of mixed racial parentage, however, are over-represented amongst all groups of children in care. These authors found no difference in the pattern of placement of children whose parents were black, white, or of mixed racial parentage. They were equally likely to be placed in foster homes or in residential care, although black teenagers were more likely to be placed in specialist foster homes. Nor, in that study, were black teenagers any more likely than white teenagers to be in penal establishments.

Placement with Relatives

Rowe and her colleagues (1984, 1989) and Berridge and Cleaver (1987) are the major sources of information about children placed with relatives. All three studies note that such placements are more successful, whether measured in terms of breakdown rates or in terms of successfully achieving placement aims, than placements with non-related foster carers or residential placements when like children are compared with like. The Children Act 1989 strongly recommends placement with relatives in appropriate cases, even though social workers tend to be cautious about making such placements when children have been abused or neglected. Rowe and her colleagues (1984) found that relatives were particularly good at keeping the child in touch with both sides of the family, as well as offering long-term stability and good parenting to the children in their care. The point made earlier about the importance of well-negotiated agreements must be stressed here also, so that the child *does* have a sense of stability and security and is not afraid of impulsive removal, and also in order to ensure that the child is kept safe from renewed abuse when in contact with any relatives who were implicated in the original abuse.

Permanent Placement with Substitute Parents

It has already been noted that only a small proportion of the children cared for away from home will be placed with permanent substitute parents. In the study by Rowe and her colleagues (1989), long-term placements accounted for nearly 10% of all foster placements. However, the six authorities studied only made 261 placements directly for adoption or as foster children with a view to subsequent application to adopt (less than 3% of the placements studied). Only 16 of the 450 children who came into care in the cohort study by Millham and his colleagues (1986) were adopted or remained with their long-term foster parents until the age of 18 (3.5% of the total).

There have been many English language accounts of the permanent family placement of children in care over the last 20 years or so, both from practitioners and researchers. The American studies are summarised by Barth and Berry (1988), and the British research studies are summarised by Thoburn (1990).

The Psychology of Adoption

There have also been many studies over the years of the placement of infants for adoption which are also relevant to this volume, since some children are placed for adoption at birth if it is believed they are likely to be significantly harmed in the light of the experience of siblings. Space precludes a full consideration of the subject, but readers are referred to the work of Brodzinsky and Schechter (1990), who have brought together their own writings and those of other researchers and practitioners on the psychology and outcomes of adoption. Although care must be exercised when applying their conclusions to children adopted when older, these writers do throw light on the problems which adopted children and their new families may encounter. Their thesis is that the adoptive family faces additional challenges which result from the loss experienced by the child, and the loss for some adopters of the child by birth which they had hoped to have – the 'double jeopardy' theory. Additional challenges will be there if the child carries the scars of earlier harm, and if the child is of a different skin colour or cultural background from the adoptive family. These writers join Kirk (1964, 1981) in postulating that successful adopters are those who accept the special challenges of adoptive parenting which make it different from parenting a child born to them. They consider that an adoptive family is a dual identity family, in that it has to incorporate the original family of the child conceptually, even if there is no actual contact. Accordingly, they strongly support some form of contact between the birth family and the adoptive family, even if this is only by way of letters and photographs, partly because this reminds the adopters that they have extra parenting challenges to overcome, and partly because it avoids the risks of the child fantasising and idealising the first family, or the sense for the adopters of 'sitting on a time bomb' and wondering if and when the child will wish to seek out the natural family and what he or she may find when he or she does so.

This adoption research gives clues about the sort of family who is likely to be most successful with a child who has been abused or neglected. Since they have to be comfortable with the child's first identity, it is especially important that they can empathise with the parent who was responsible for the abuse or neglect. A child whose parent is a known abuser is likely to need help in establishing a positive sense of self, and this will not be helped if the adopters or foster carers make it clear that they have a low opinion or condemnatory attitude towards the first parents.

Permanent Placement of Older Children

Within the last few years, several outcome studies of permanent family placement of older children have been published, and their findings are generally similar. Some, such as the study of 1165 permanent placements with families not previously known to the child, use placement breakdown within 3–6 years of placement as the outcome measure (Rowe and Thoburn in Fratter et al., 1991). Other generally smaller-scale studies use a range of more subjective measures, such as the satisfaction or otherwise of the parents, the child, or other members of the family (Tizard, 1977; Macaskill, 1985, on the placement of children with a disability, and Thoburn et al., 1986; Rushton et al., 1988; Thoburn, 1990). Others use more objective measures, such as well-being scales, educational achievement or delinquency rates (see especially Rushton et al., 1988, for a particularly thorough study of the well-being of children and changes in their behaviour during the early years of placement). A series of studies of the work of Lothian Social Work Department, which set up a specialist section to place children in care with permanent new families, combines survey methodology using breakdown rates as the outcome measure with detailed studies of a small number of the place-ments using a range of other measures (Hoggan and O'Hara, 1988).

Some of these studies include children whose placement with a foster family with whom they were well established is confirmed as a permanent placement, whilst others only include new placements with parents who were previously unknown to the child. The first group are less likely to break down, since the new parents and child have already got to know each other before deciding that this should be a permanent placement (Lahti, 1982; Fein et al., 1983). Other variables which may affect outcome are the age range of the children placed, the quality of the social work support and the agency policies. The percentage of placements which had broken down between 18 months and 6 years after placement in the large-scale survey of 1165 placements made by voluntary agencies was 22% (Fratter *et al.*, 1991). However, it is not particularly helpful to have a global breakdown or success rate. All the studies identify the characteristics of the children which have an impact on the success or otherwise of the placement. Age at placement has been identified by all large-scale studies in Britain and America as associated with placement breakdown. Children who are younger and have disabilities might be hard to find families for, but once the family has been found these placements seem to be particularly successful. On the other hand, it is not too difficult to find families for sibling groups in the primary school age range, but these children do seem to be harder to parent than new families or social workers had anticipated. Around 22% of placements of 8-year-olds break down, and this rises to almost a half of the placements of 12-year-olds. One factor identified by most researchers as being associated independently with breakdown is that the child has been abused or neglected prior to the placement (Fratter *et al.*, 1991). Gibbons *et al.* (1995), in a study of children who were physically abused or severely neglected when under the age of 5 years, found that 8 years later the well-being of those placed for adoption or in foster care was, on average, no higher than that of children who returned home, and lower than a matched sample of children who had not been abused. Other factors associated with breakdown were the child being described as institutionalised, or behaviourally or emotionally disturbed. Several studies (Berridge and Cleaver, 1987; Borland *et al.*, 1990; Fratter *et al.*, 1991) found that placements where there was face-to-face contact with the birth parents after the placement were either less likely to break down or it made no difference.

Children, both of whose parents were black, were no more likely to experience breakdown than children of two white parents, but those of mixed-race parentage were significantly more likely to experience placement breakdown.

There was no difference in breakdown rate between those who were permanently fostered and those who were adopted. However, it should be noted that these children were all placed with the intention that the placement would be permanent, and the practice of the workers was aimed at giving them and the new parents a sense of permanence from the beginning of the placement. In that sense, they differed from long-term placements which at least early on were accompanied by uncertainty about the future. Some smaller-scale, qualitative studies have found that higher levels of satisfaction among the children and higher educational achievement were associated with placement for adoption rather than foster care (Triseliotis and Russell, 1984; Hill *et al.*, 1989). On the other hand, Thoburn (1990), Bullard and Malos (1990) and Kelly and McAuley (1995) noted that there are a group of children who are closely attached to their original families and wish to have the security of knowing that they will remain with a substitute family but do not wish to give up their legal attachments to their first family. The conclusion to be drawn from the studies is that the decision about legal status should depend on the wishes, attitudes and temperament of all concerned, especially the child. The apparent cost advantage of adoption should not play a major part in this decision, since it is likely that a high proportion of maltreated children who are adopted will need support through adoption allowances, and the costs of long-term post-placement support are likely to be incurred whatever the legal status.

Research studies differ in their findings about the sort of people who can successfully become substitute parents for children who have been abused or neglected. They agree in only one respect: that there is a high risk of failure if there is a younger child in the family who is within 3 years of the age of the child being placed, particularly if this younger child is of pre-school age. Most studies find that more experienced and older parents are more successful, but some studies (Hart, 1986; Wedge and Mantle, 1991) have found that younger childless couples have been particularly successful with groups of siblings. Moving away from these more obvious characteristics, writers agree about the attitudes, personal characteristics and skills of substitute parents who are more successful, and these will be discussed in the next section. Successful substitute parents have a range of reasons for undertaking this task. Provided that they enjoy being with children, and enjoy a challenge, research does not point to clear desirable or undesirable motivation.

The Task and Skills of Carers and Those Who Support Them

An overview of the social work task

There are several dimensions under which this work can be considered. Firstly, there are organisational decisions to be made about who will be primarily responsible for providing a social work service to the birth parents and their relatives, the child, and the carers and possibly members of their family. In some cases, it may be appropriate for the same worker to provide all these services. More often, a specialist worker will be responsible for the recruitment and approval process, and will support the carers or new parents whilst the worker for the child remains principally concerned with the child's welfare. If there is a conflict of interest between the child and the natural family, or strong disagreement about the plans which have been made, it will be appropriate for support to be offered to the parents by another worker or even another agency. The training, supervision and support needs of workers in group care settings are similar in some respects, but there are also differences. The emphasis here will be on those who care for children in their own homes.

It will be clear from the previous sections that the role of carers and, therefore, the skills and attributes needed are varied. Most obviously, carers fall into two groups: those who for a shorter or longer period or episodically will join with natural parents and social workers in caring for children in need; and those who will take on the prime parenting responsibility until the child becomes a young adult and beyond. The tasks of the social workers with these two groups are in many respects similar, but in other respects there are important differences. These tasks need to be considered in respect of the following stages:

- recruitment;
- selection and preparation;
- training;
- matching the carers with the child;
- preparing for the placement;
- providing support and, when appropriate, therapy for the child, the carers and the natural parents when the child is in placement;
- when appropriate, helping all those involved to ensure a smooth transfer back to the natural family or on to a new family.

Once approved, the Children Act 1989 requires that all foster families should be visited annually for the purposes of reviewing whether they are succeeding in undertaking the tasks which they wish to undertake, with the sorts of children and families with whom they have skills and can empathise. The review is also an opportunity for them to discuss their training and support needs, and the adequacy of the support service they have received over the previous year. It is also an opportunity for the agency to monitor how effectively they have discharged their obligations to the children placed with them during the year and to their parents.

All children who are away from home in respite or bridge placements should be offered a dependable relationship with the social worker who is responsible for the child's care plan. This area of social work practice has now been well documented, and a wide range of practice guidance is available. The term 'life story work' is most frequently used to describe some of the work undertaken with children away from home, but a classic article first published by Claire Winnicott in 1966, and reprinted by British Agencies for Adoption and Fostering in 1986, is still the best statement of the principles and values which must underpin such work. Aldgate and Simmonds (eds) (1987), Redgrave (1987), Aldgate *et al.* (1989), Fahlberg (1990, 1991) and Ryan and Walker (1993) are all useful sources on working directly with children in placement about the circumstances of their lives.

Useful practice texts on social work practice in foster care are those on group work edited by Triseliotis (1988) and on the support of short-term foster parents by Sellick (1992) and Triseliotis *et al.* (1995).

Task-Centred Carers

While a few of those who take children into their homes to provide a service on behalf of the agency will care for only one child, perhaps a young relative or a child who will have periods of respite over many years, the majority of task-centred carers must be able to care for a range of children with a variety of needs. Matching is therefore only possible in the broader sense of a particular age group, or children with particular characteristics or disabilities. Enjoying the company of children and feeling comfortable with them is an essential prerequisite, as are flexibility, negotiation skills and non-judgemental attitudes. Since some children will be placed before it becomes clear that they have been abused, all task-centred carers must be able to understand and empathise not only with the child who has been abused, but also with the parent who was unable to protect the child or was the abuser. If these characteristics are present, it will be possible to provide training and support both before and during placements, so that the special needs of each child and family can be met (Thoburn, 1991). Batty (1991) and Macaskill (1991) write specifically about the foster care task and the support needs of carers and children who have been sexually abused.

Substitute Parents

When children are placed with the intention that the new parents will become the psychological parents, many of the qualities required of them and the skills of the social workers are similar. There are, however, important differences, most notably that permanent carers will usually care for only one child, and will be selected and matched specifically with that child. A broad range of skills is less important than the matching of their skills and needs with the needs and potential of the child to be placed. The art of making permanent placements appears to be in learning what the new parents have to give, and what they will expect in return, and matching these with what the child can give and needs and is willing to take from the new parent. It would thus be a mistake to place with a childless couple who want to love a child who will love them in return, a youngster who has been so hurt by earlier experiences that it is not at all obvious that the child will be able to become fully attached to them. Such a child will be more likely to settle with new parents who have already had the rewards of successfully parenting their own children, are motivated by a love of children and the desire to help a youngster in difficulties, and can accept that the youngster may never grow to love them in the same way that their own children have grown up loving them from their early months. Assessing and matching, then, are the major social work tasks in permanent family placement on which can be built the later work of supporting the new family. Permanent placement work differs from work with task-centred carers in the sense that a family approved to take a child on a permanent basis should not have a child placed with them unless the match seems an appropriate one. For that reason, an even wider range of families may be approved. Indeed, many successful substitute parents have been turned down by foster care or more traditional adoption agencies as being unsuitable.

Another difference lies in the nature of social work practice. Once a child has been placed, most researchers have concluded that it is most appropriate for the long-term support of the placement to be undertaken by the specialist who undertook the home study and approval work. At the time of placement, the person who is most likely to help the new family to develop a sense of commitment and permanence is the worker in whom the substitute parents already have confidence. Many adopters or long-term foster carers have talked to researchers about their nervousness when visited by the child's worker. Children also report being made anxious by a visit from the worker who has been responsible for moving them around in the past. Thus, the child's worker is best seen as a caring presence in the background who arrives at the time when the placement is reviewed, but otherwise leaves the support to the new family's worker (Thoburn et al., 1986; Thoburn, 1990), or undertakes an agreed piece of work at the request of child, new family or the support worker.

The second of these studies which followed children through from their situation prior to placements to 6 years later found that therapeutic intervention in the early years when the child was settling in was not appropriate, although a continuation of the 'life story work', often undertaken jointly by the new family's social worker and the new parents, was particularly helpful at the appropriate moment. In the longer term, however, perhaps in the 3rd, 4th or 5th year after placement, when the new family felt established as a family, therapeutic intervention often became necessary with those children who had suffered abuse or neglect. It was sometimes appropriate in these circumstances for the therapeutic intervention to come from an agency other than the one which had made the placement. However, Howe and Hinings (1989) and the workers at the Post-Adoption Centre note that therapists must address themselves to the special nature of adoptive families.

Allegations of Abuse in Foster Family Care

Many children who have been abused are vulnerable to renewed abuse, whether physically, emotionally or sexually, and some children who have been abused in the past may make reference to abuse which may be misinterpreted as having been inflicted by the foster carer. Great sensitivity is needed when investigating allegations or suspicions of abuse when children are in foster care. It has been noted by some practitioners and foster care support groups that the incidence of unsubstantiated suspicion, and false allegation, is higher when children are in foster care. Procedures for investigating allegations must be followed but, as when children are living with their original families, they should not be removed without careful planning unless this is absolutely necessary for their protection. This is especially so if the placement is planned as a permanent substitute placement, and the child is becoming attached or is already attached to the new parents.

Summary and Conclusion

This chapter has emphasised that removal from home of a child who may be in need of protection may solve one set of problems but makes the child vulnerable to a new set of hazards. It has also referred to research findings which suggest that if temporary or permanent removal *does* become necessary, a course has to be steered between excess optimism and excess pessimism about the outcome for the child.

A succession of studies on permanent family placement and on the impact of abuse or severe neglect on children have indicated that it is the lucky or the temperamentally resilient minority who remain relatively unscathed. The majority will need more than replacement parent figures, no matter how much love they have to offer. Their fragile identities will require skill as well as love. If they cannot return safely home, their carers must work hard at understanding their past, and substitute parents must incorporate it into the life of the new family. Direct contact with members of the first family will usually be the best way of doing this, but a two-way exchange of letters and photographs may sometimes have to take the place of direct contact, sometimes for only temporary periods.

For those who help and support the children, their first families, their temporary carers or new families, the keys to success are good planning which adapts to the needs of each situation; imaginative and sensitively negotiated agreements and an adequate supply of 'bridge' carers with choices between family and group care settings. Above all, children need carers and professional workers who will go on fighting on their behalf but who can live with uncertain outcomes and the lack of tidy solutions.

Suggestions for Further Reading

The literature has been reviewed in the body of the chapter, and there are no short cuts when considering placement for a particular child. For the child protection worker wishing to get to grips with the issues the most useful texts are as follows:

On the principles underlying child placement and reviewing the research

Bullock *et al.* (1993); Department of Health (1985, 1989*b*, 1991*a*); Maluccio *et al.* (1986); Thoburn (1994).

On short-term placements

Berridge and Cleaver (1987); Millham *et al.* (1986); Sellick, (1992); Triseliotis *et al.* (1995); Rowe *et al.* (1989); Westacott (1988).

On residential care

Berridge (1985); Cliffe and Berridge (1991); Grimshaw with Berridge (1994); Rose (1990); Utting (1992).

On placement with relatives

Berridge and Cleaver (1987); Bullard and Malos with Parker (1990); Rowe *et al.* (1984, 1989).

On permanent placement with substitute parents

Barth and Berry (1988); Brodzinski and Schechter (1990); Fratter *et al.* (1991); Mullender (ed.) (1991); Rushton *et al.* (1988); Thoburn (1990, 1992).

On social work practice with children who are looked after

Aldgate and Simmonds (1987); Aldgate *et al.* (1989); Batty (1991); Fahlberg (1990, 1991); Triseliotis (ed.) (1988); Triseliotis *et al.* (1995).

References

Aldgate, J. (1980). Identification of factors which influence length of stay in care. In J.P. Triseliotis (ed.): *New Developments in Foster Care and Adoption*. London: Routledge and Kegan Paul.

Aldgate, J. (1990). Foster children at school: success or failure. *Adoption and Fostering* 7(2): 38–45.

Aldgate, J. & Bradley, M. (1995). *A Guide to the Provision of Respite Care*. London: HMSO. (In preparation.)

Aldgate, J. & Simmonds J. (eds) (1987). *Direct Work with Children*. London: Batsford.

Aldgate, J., Maluccio, A. & Reeves, C. (1989). *Adolescents in Foster Family Care*. London: Batsford.

Barth, R. & Berry, M. (1988). *Adoption and Disruption: Rates, Risk and Responses*. New York: Aldine de Gruyter.

Batty, D. (ed.) (1991). *Sexually Abused Children – Making their Placements Work*. London: British Agencies for Adoption and Fostering.

Batty, D. (ed.) (1993). *HIV Infection and Children in Need*. London: BAAF.

Berridge, D. (1985). *Children's Homes*. Oxford: Basil Blackwell.

Berridge, D. & Cleaver, H. (1987). *Foster Home Breakdown*. Oxford: Basil Blackwell.

Borland, M., Triseliotis, J. & O'Hara, G. (1990). *Permanency Planning for Children in Lothian Region*. University of Edinburgh.

Bowlby, J. (1988). *A Secure Base*. London: Tavistock.

British Agencies for Adoption and Fostering (BAAF) (1986). *Working with Children*. London: BAAF.

Brodzinsky, D. & Schechter, M. (eds) (1990) *The Psychology of Adoption*. Oxford: Oxford University Press.

Bullard, E. & Malos, E. with Parker, R. (1990). *Custodianship: A Report to the Department of Health*. University of Bristol.

Bullock, R., Little, M. & Millham, S. (1993). *Going Home*. Aldershot: Dartmouth.

Caesar, G., Parchment, M., Berridge, D. & Gordon, G. (1994). *Black Perspectives on Services for Children and Young People in Need and their Families*. London: National Children's Bureau.

Cairns, B. (1984). The children's family trust: a unique approach to substitute family care? *British Journal of Social Work 14*: 457–473.

Cliffe, D. & Berridge, D. (1991). *Closing Children's Homes*. London: National Children's Bureau.

Colton, M. (1989). *Dimensions of Substitute Care*. Aldershot: Avebury.

Department of Health (1989a). *Introduction to the Children Act 1989*. London: HMSO.

Department of Health (1989b). *Principles and Practice in Regulations and Guidance*. London: HMSO.

Department of Health (1991a). *Patterns and Outcomes in Child Placement*. London: HMSO.

Department of Health (1991b). *The Children Act 1989: Guidance and Regulations*, vols 2, 3 and 4. London: HMSO.

Department of Health (1992). *Review of Adoption Law: A Consultation Document*. London: HMSO.

Department of Health (1993). *Adoption: The Future*. London: HMSO.

Department of Health and Social Security (1976). *Foster Care: A Guide to Practice*. London: HMSO.

Department of Health and Social Security (1985). *Social Work Decisions in Child Care: Recent Research Findings and their Implications*. London: HMSO.

Fahlberg, V. (1990). *Residential Treatment: A Tapestry of Many Therapies*. New York: Perspectives Press.

Fahlberg, V. (1991). *A Child's Journey Through Placement*. Indianapolis: Perspectives Press.

Fanshel, D. & Shinn, E.B. (1978). *Children in Foster Care – A Longitudinal Study*. New York: Columbia University Press.

Fein E. *et al.* (1990). *No More Partings. An Examination of Long-Term Foster Family Care*. New York: Child Welfare League of America.

Fein, E., Maluccio, A.N., Hamilton, V.J. & Ward, D.E. (1983). After foster care: permanency planning for children. *Child Welfare 62(6)*: 483–558.

Fletcher, B. (1993). *Not Just a Name: The Views of Young People in Foster and Residential Care*. London: National Consumer Council.

Fratter, J. (1993). Positive options planning scheme. In D. Batty (ed.): *HIV Infection and Children in Need*. London: BAAF.

Fratter, J., Rowe, J., Sapsford, D. & Thoburn, J. (1991). *Permanent Family Placement: A decade of experience* London: BAAF.

Gibbons, J., Gallagher, B., Bell, C. and Gordon, D. (1995). *Development after Physical Abuse in Early Childhood: A Follow-up Study of Children on Child Protection Registers*. Norwich: University of East Anglia.

Grimshaw, R. with Berridge, D. (1994). *Educating Disruptive Children*. London: National Children's Bureau.

Hart, G.J. (1986). *Entitled to our Care: A Study of an Adoption Agency Placing Children with Special Needs*. Salford: University of Salford Department of Sociology and Anthropology.

Hazel, N. (1981). *A Bridge to Independence*. Oxford: Blackwell.

Hill, M., Lambert, L. & Triseliotis, J. (1989). *Achieving Adoption with Love and Money*. London: National Children's Bureau.

Hodges, J. & Tizard, B. (1989a). Social and family relationships of ex-institutional adolescents. *Journal of Child Psychology and Psychiatry 30(1):* 77–97.

Hodges, J. & Tizard, B. (1989b). IQ and behavioural adjustment of ex-institutional adolescents. *Journal of Child Psychology and Psychiatry 30(1):* 53–75.

Hoggan, P. & O'Hara, G. (1988). Permanent substitute family care in Lothian – placement outcomes. *Adoption and Fostering 12(3):* 35–39.

Howe, D. & Hinings, D. (1987). Adopted children referred to a child and family centre. *Adoption and Fostering 11(3)*.

Howe, D. & Hinings, D. (1989) *The Post Adoption Centre: The First Three Years*. Norwich: University of East Anglia.

Kelly, G. & MacAuley, C. (1995). *Foster Care in Northern Ireland*. London: BAAF. (In preparation.)

Kirk, H.D. (1964). *Shared Fate*. London: Collier-Macmillan.

Kirk, H.D. (1981). *Adoptive Kinship: A Modern Institution in Need of Reform*. Vancouver: Butterworths.

Kufeldt, K. & Allison, J. (1990). Fostering children fostering families. *Community Alternatives: International Journal of Family Care 1(17):* 1–17.

Lahti, J. (1982). A follow-up study of foster children in permanent placements. *Social Service Review*, University of Chicago.

Macaskill, C. (1985). *Against the Odds. Adopting Mentally Handicapped Children*. London: BAAF.

Macaskill, C. (1991). *Adopting or Fostering a Sexually Abused Child*. London: BAAF.

Maluccio, A., Fein, E. & Olmstead, K.A. (1986). *Permanency Planning for Children: Concepts and Methods*. London: Tavistock.

Millham, S., Bullock, R., Hosie, K. & Haak, M. (1986). *Lost in Care*. Aldershot: Gower.

Millham, S., Bullock, R., Hosie, K. & Little, M. (1989). *Access Disputes in Child Care*. Aldershot: Gower.

Mullender, A. (ed.) (1991). *Open Adoption*. London: BAAF.

Nelson, K.A. (1985). *On the Frontier of Adoption: A Study of Special-Needs Adoptive Families*. Washington: Child Welfare League of America.

Packman, J., Randall, J. & Jacques, N. (1986). *Who Needs Care? Social Work Decisions about Children.*, Oxford: Blackwell.

Redgrave, K. (1987). *Child's Play: Direct Work with the Deprived Child*. Cheadle: Boys and Girls Welfare Society.

Roberts, J. (1993). Abused children and foster care: the need for specialist resources. *Child Abuse Review 2:* 3–14.

Rose, M. (1990). *Healing Hurt Minds: The Pepper Harrow experience*. London: Tavistock.

Rowe, J. & Lambert, L. (1973). *Children Who Wait*. London: Association of British Adoption Agencies.

Rowe, J., Cain, H., Hundleby, M. & Keane, A. (1984). *Long-Term Foster Care*. London, Batsford.

Rowe, J., Hundleby, M. & Garnett, L. (1989). *Child Care Now – A Survey of Placement Patterns*. London: BAAF.

Rushton, A., Treseder, J. & Quinton, D. (1988). *New Parents for Older Children*. London: BAAF.

Ryan, T. & Walker, R. (1993). *Life Story Books*. London: BAAF.

Sellick, C. (1992). *Supporting Short-Term Foster Carers*. Aldershot: Avebury.

Shaw, M. & Hipgrave, T. (1983). *Specialist Fostering*. London: Batsford.

Stalker, K. (1990). *Share the Care*. London: Jessica Kingsley.

Thoburn, J. (1990). *Success and Failure in Permanent Family Placement*. Aldershot: Gower/Avebury.

Thoburn, J. (1991). Permanent family placement and the Children Act 1989: implications for foster carers and social workers. *Adoption and Fostering 15(3)*.

Thoburn, J. (1992). Review of research which is relevant to adoption. In Department of Health: *Review of Adoption Law: A Consultation Document*. London: DOH.

Thoburn, J. (1994). *Child Placement: Principles and Practice*. (Second Edition), Aldershot: Arena.

Thoburn, J., Murdoch, A. & O'Brien, A. (1986). *Permanence in Child Care*. Oxford: Basil Blackwell.

Thorpe, R. (1980). The experiences of children and parents living apart: Implications and guidance in practice. In J.P. Triseliotis (ed.), (1980). *New Developments in Foster Care and Adoption*. London: Routledge and Kegan Paul.

Tizard, B. (1977). *Adoption, a Second Chance*. London: Open Books.

Triseliotis, J.P. (1983). Identity and security in adoption and long-term fostering. *Adoption and Fostering 7(1): 22–23*.

Triseliotis, J. (ed.) (1988). *Group work in Adoption and Foster Care*. London: Batsford.

Triseliotis, J.P. & Russell, J. (1984). *Hard to Place: The Outcomes of Adoption and Residential Care*. London: Heinemann and Gower.

Triseliotis, J., Sellick, C., Ward, C. & Short, R. (1995). *The Theory and Practice of Foster Care*. London: Batsford.

Utting, W. (1992). *Children in the Public Care*. London: HMSO.

Walby, C. & Symons, B. (1990). *Who am I? Identity, Adoption and Human Fertilisation*. London: BAAF.

Wedge, P. & Mantle, G. (1991). *Sibling Groups and Social Work*. Aldershot: Avebury.

Weinstein, E. (1960). *The Self-Image of the Foster Child*. New York: Sage.

Westacott, J. (1988). *A Bridge to Calmer Waters*. London: Barnardos.

IV

Training and New Directions for Research and Practice

For many students and practitioners who consult this *Handbook*, from whatever profession, a section on training and research is unlikely to be the first to which they turn. For many, research will be regarded as a highly specialised and somewhat arcane activity pursued by others, usually academics, which although important, is at least one step removed from the concerns and priorities of practitioners. Similarly, training is likely to be something which they are either currently experiencing and which they are therefore less likely to objectify, or something which they experienced in the past and which now takes second place to the demands of the practice which it has helped to shape. However, training is a key determinant of the quality of practice and research is a key component of training. This in many ways highlights some of the complexities and dilemmas which have run through previous sections of this *Handbook* because research, training and practice are inseparable. They are bound up in a reflexive relationship in which one must be fed by the others.

We must therefore also acknowledge that research, practice and training are dynamic, both conceptually and in reality. In other words, not only are they constantly changing and evolving in response to a variety of internal and external pressures, but the very ideas about what constitutes research, practice and training are subject to the same pressures and processes of change. Thus, the main constituents of practice – the roles, tasks, skills and competencies – which come together to make practice are not static, any more than are the ideas about how to incorporate these into training. Equally, the potential and actual contribution of practitioners to the growth of knowledge and understanding requires a reappraisal and a broadening of more conventional perceptions of research, whilst the research agenda is constantly changing in the light of new knowledge and new challenges in practice.

Such reflections also raise some important issues concerning how we identify and define what constitutes quality in training and practice, so that we can then consider how to maintain and improve upon this. Much has been learned from the tragic consequences of earlier mistakes and shortcomings which have been revealed and commented upon in inquiry after inquiry, but there remains much still to learn.

Practice is defined by a number of parameters which therefore need to be encompassed in training. It is defined by the content of training, including the legal framework and a constantly changing knowledge base. It is defined by the context of practice, including the differing organisational contexts in which the professionals to whom this *Handbook* is addressed work, which have implications for the ethos and values, resources, management structures and accountability, and which establish definitive reference points for practitioners. We must also bear in mind throughout that practice is not entirely self-determining, or professionally defined, or defined by structural factors such as law and organisational issues. Practitioners respond daily to the various pressures and constraints imposed by parents and children and, in the age of 'the citizen's charter' and in the wake of the Cleveland and Orkneys inquiries, this is a dimension which is of increasing significance in shaping practice.

Having considered some of the factors which define and structure practice, we must consider some of the implications of these factors for the definition and structuring of training. An important determinant is the availability and perceived relevance of different or new areas of knowledge or theory – for example, the increasing popularity and perceived relevance over the last decade of family systems theory and learning theory have had a major impact on practice, both in terms of assessment and intervention. Changes in the legal context have also had an important impact on training – for example, the emphasis on developing working partnerships with parents in the wake of the Children Act 1989.

It is also clear, however, that the conceptual framework for training in general has shifted significantly away from the traditional bases provided by theory, values and knowledge/theory *per se* towards skills and competencies. This shift is of increasing importance in the training of all professionals, whether social workers, teachers, lawyers or those in the medical and allied professions. Such developments have major implications for the approach to and the content and structure of training.

These are reflected in developments such as the emergence of the National Council for Vocational Qualifications and the increasing concern with establishing vocational standards. Jocelyn Jones offers a critical appraisal of the implications of such developments, drawing attention to some of the problems inherent in such approaches and the dangers which these present in the person-centred professions. Of particular importance in the context of child protection is the fact that good practice revolves around effective inter-professional co-operation in the interests of the child, rather than being centred on the activities and competencies of an individual practitioner which are, by definition, the focus of competency-based training. Such approaches, she argues, may seriously impede the growth of knowledge, critical analysis and intellectual rigour which are the hallmark of a research-led profession and may impede the development of holistic and reflective understanding which is central to understanding and unravelling the complex web of relationships between families and professionals.

At another level entirely, in a chapter which complements this critique, John Simmonds explores the crucial importance of the worker's own perceptions and feelings on his or her ability to practise effectively. Of particular importance, he argues, are the worker's inner emotional resources and the need to understand the relationship between personal and professional experience, as well as the dynamic psychological processes which shape the responses of practitioners, and therefore the quality of practice. This then raises the key question of how best to help students to understand and work with such issues, which are marginalised by current approaches to professional education and training.

Building upon these contributions, the chapter by Kate Wilson, assisted by Jocelyn Jones, offers an overview of current training provisions with particular reference to training for social workers, focusing in particular on the importance of incorporating knowledge about adult learning into the way in which training is provided, on the provision of inter-professional training, and on the structure and content of training in the light of the current demands of practice.

The short straw in the compilation of this volume was drawn by Christine Hallett, who accepted the considerable challenge of offering an overview of the main issues to emerge from all of the previous chapters, and to consider the implications of these for the future development of child protection. In so doing, she usefully draws out important areas of deficiency in our current understanding of the causes, manifestations and consequences of child abuse which must be addressed if continued improvements are to be made in child protection practice. Of particular importance amongst these is the need to learn more about the interplay between structural and personal factors, since such understanding will be crucial in beginning to determine the proper boundaries between professional intervention and state provision in the search for solutions to the problems posed by the need to protect children from abuse.

What is clear from this overview is that the quality of both research and training lie at the very heart of good practice. Yet it is a sad fact that in these days of cash-limiting, research and training are often the first casualties in the battle for scarce resources, and that the ultimate casualties will be those children the abuse of whom remains undetected until it is too late.

25

Training for Child Protection Practice – A Question of Competence?

Jocelyn Jones

Introduction

This chapter begins with an examination of post-qualifying social work education and training policy for the 1990s. The section on literature and research discusses the moral and ethical decision-making context of child protection, the subtle psychological processes within families where a child death has occurred, and among the professional systems (Reder *et al.*, 1993*a,b*). It is argued that due to the complexity of practice, a reflected-on understanding, in which a practitioner is able to articulate a number of dimensions to their decision-making and action, is required. The more dimensions a practitioner can describe, the more understanding they have. Knowledge is thus seen as an 'interpretative resource' for a person (Ashworth, 1992, page 11), both enriching the account they can give of an ongoing situation, and linking it to other situations, for example, complex investigations where some parallels might be drawn.

Research on competence-based education and training is then considered, and it is shown that the current drive towards competence-based assessment fails to get to grips with the holistic nature of child protection practice. Many of the intuitive strengths of experienced practitioners are lost, as general concepts are disaggregated into elements and then further broken down into performance criteria. Due to resource constraints and the current political climate, it is feared that the educational and supportive functions of post-qualifying supervision will be overtaken by an increasing managerialism. The chapter concludes by questioning the current direction which post-qualifying training in the person-centred professions, particularly social work, seems to be taking.

An Analysis of Policy Issues

The aim of the Central Council for Education and Training in Social Work's (CCETSW) training continuum, based on National Vocational Qualification (NVQ) levels 2 to 4, the Diploma in Social Work qualifying award, and the post-qualifying and advanced awards is to 'ensure that consumers of personal social services receive the highest possible standard of service and care' (CCETSW, 1992, page 5). At the post-qualifying stage, some of the proposed changes include: the identification of two levels of competence, one at post-qualifying level and the other at advanced level; a concentration on learning outcomes; and the implementation of the framework through a network of consortia, educational institutions and agencies working together and covering the UK.

However, since the publication of the first edition of Paper 31 (CCETSW, 1990), the financial climate has worsened, with an even tighter squeeze on public spending affecting both local authorities and educational institutions, and many children's charities have also been struggling to protect their training budgets. In such a climate, it is doubtful whether the post-qualifying and advanced level requirements of Paper 31 will be implemented as speedily and thoroughly as once envisaged. In the meantime, the tasks and function of social work itself seem to be undergoing continual change, with the implementation of new legislation and devolved budgetary control to managers.

Substantial changes are also taking place in further and higher education as other professions adopt competence-based training and assessment models. The impact of NVQs in further education has already been felt, and over the next few years they will impact on higher education as further levels are added. In such a climate of change, the future shape of post-qualifying education and training in the person-centred professions, particularly for those employed in the challenging area of child protection, merits closer examination. It is vital that any system of education, training and assessment reflects the subject area and the nature of expertise at different professional levels.

The aim of the new social work post-qualifying framework (CCETSW, 1992) is 'to improve standards of service and care for consumers of personal social services 'in every setting and sector'. At the post-qualifying level, candidates are accountable for people's liberty and empowerment, and at the advanced level leadership and expertise need to be demonstrated. The documentation indicates that the framework takes account of the work of the National Council for Vocational Qualifications (NCVQ) and the Scottish Vocational Education Council (SCOTVEC), and requires the demonstration of learning outcomes which are to be assessed. At the time of writing, two draft working papers on child care at post-qualifying and advanced level are available which break down the general requirements into performance criteria (CCETSW, 1993a,b). There is also the final report from the CCETSW's Scottish Office on post-qualifying competence in child protection (CCETSW, 1993c).

The incorporation of National Vocational Qualifications (NVQs) and notions of competence into the education and training of other professional groups, such as teachers, nurses and youth and community workers, is now underway. It is the CCETSW's stated intention to develop multi-disciplinary training and joint validation agreements between themselves and other professional bodies (CCETSW, 1992).

Review of Recent Literature and Research

The complex nature of practice

The Department of Health document *The Care of Children: Principles and Practice in Regulations and Guidance* (DOH, 1989, page 1) spells out some of the current requirements of practitioners:

'It is essential that practitioners seek to combat racism in all its forms of discrimination against individuals and groups. The [Children] Act encourages this approach. Partnership, participation, choice, openness, parental responsibility, and every child's need for both security and family links are some of the major themes which are common to the principles and legislation.'

In order to assist practitioners and their managers in the development of such participatory practice, the document lists 26 principles which relate to individual children, young people and their families, and a further 16 which refer to agency responsibilities and 'systems'. When each principle is considered in turn, there is little to take issue with, but in combination their implementation becomes problematic and requires the capacity to weigh up moral and ethical dilemmas in relation to individual cases. The potential conflict between the needs and rights of parents as individuals, and their children's needs, wishes and feelings begins to become apparent (see Harris, Section I, Chapter 2). The document hints at some of the complexity in principle 35 (see Figure 25.1), where the balance of partnership with carers has to be considered *in each case*.

Clearly, partnership, participation and openness with a non-abusing parent, who is considering separation from the abusing partner in the children's interests, differs from the relationship a practitioner is likely to have with a family where organised abuse is suspected involving several generations. Whilst the list offers some guidance to practitioners and helps them analyse some of their grounds for decision-making in this difficult ethical field, it does highlight the shortcomings of lists of principles. Principles operate in specific contexts and require practitioners who are able to analyse their application in practice. Indeed, the document itself (DOH, 1989, page 6) refers to the principles as 'colours on the social worker painter's palette to be used in the combinations and patterns required for each picture painted/child care case handled'. The document concludes by restating this analogy:

'Principles are the colours on the social worker painter's palette. The range and quality of colour helps to produce a good painting, but it is the painter's skill which makes or mars the picture. Excessive case loads or lack of the necessary resources can be as disabling to the social worker as lack of paint to the artist, but failure to understand and apply essential principles can spoil even the best resources so that they become damaging to those they were intended to benefit.' (DOH, 1989, page 17.)

The creative and analytical practitioner is able to form good relationships with parents and children which actively take account of the power relationships between professionals, family members and children in specific contexts. Such practitioners are interested in the *process* of creating and sustaining relationships, so that the right climate is developed for working in partnership with children and their families. Adcock *et al.* (1991, pages 7–8) point to some of the attitudes necessary for partnership: respect for persons, while at the same time not colluding with carers' inappropriate

---

Children

3) Children are entitled to protection from neglect, abuse and exploitation.

Children and parents

1) Children and young people and their parents should all be considered as individuals with particular needs and potentialities.

Parents

6) Parents are individuals with needs of their own.

7) The development of a working partnership with parents is usually the most effective route to providing supplementary or substitute care for their own children.

Agency Responsibilities and 'Systems'

35) ... a balance must be struck between offering carers support (thus building confidence) and holding them accountable for the child's well-being.

DoH (1989) *The Care of Children: Principles and Practice in Regulations and Guidance*, HMSO, London.

Figure 25.1

behaviour; willingness to allow and encourage the expression of anger where a person's freedom of action may be called into question or curtailed; a sense of fairness and natural justice, so that people feel they have been asked for their views and are aware of the reasons for decisions and their rights of appeal; and finally, openness, directness and honesty, together with empathy and support (see also Petrie and James, Section III, Chapter 17).

This list of attitudes is daunting and, when considered with the earlier discussion on principles, serves to show just how resourceful practitioners have to be in the complex world of child care and child protection decision-making where, unlike the artist, the practitioner has neither the time nor the haven of his or her own studio to reflect on the relative application of principles in relation to the ever-changing canvas of a complex case.

Learning from child abuse inquiries

Child death inquiries often depict a practice canvas where the principles of practice have not been 'used in the combinations and patterns required for each picture painted/child care case handled' (DOH, 1989, page 6). While there are significant lessons to be learned from such inquiries, it is important to reflect on the dilemmas which face practitioners who seek to protect children in the current social and political context.

> 'Complete protection for children at risk in their own families is not possible unless society sanctions greater public/state scrutiny of the family. In the absence of this, an element of risk must inevitably exist in a large number of cases that come through the system. Whilst individual social workers may make mistakes in assessing degree of risk in a particular case, the existence of risk cannot be construed to be indicative of bad practice. In fact it could be argued that an acceptance of risk is necessary if the rights of parents, siblings, and "potential" victims themselves are not to be denied.' (Horne, 1990, page 101.)

This quote from Horne highlights the difficulties which face practitioners in the selection of principles in relation to specific cases, in a context in which due to very high workloads, several canvases are being painted at the same time, often in very fraught circumstances. Add to this worker stress, fear for personal safety and lack of support from professional networks, and it becomes clear why the task of protecting children is so challenging. Perception of the painting and the selection of principles become distorted. Moreover, the worker has to remain constantly alive to alternative explanations of parents' and children's behaviour in a continually evolving assessment of risk.

Reder et al. (1993a, b) provide a useful analysis of the disparity between perceived problem definitions and the behaviour of families and professionals in their study of 35 child abuse inquiry reports, published between 1973 and 1989. They identified patterns which could be grouped under three main themes: relationships within the families themselves; processes among members of the professional networks; and the interactions between professionals and families. For the purposes of this chapter, which seeks to analyse current issues in child protection training and supervision, the focus will be on the findings in relation to the professional processes and the interactions between professionals and families.

Reder et al.'s findings on professional practices are interesting: in at least one-third of cases a critical event happened at a weekend or during a public holiday, and in a further one-third of cases the person with key case responsibility was away on leave. They highlight the need for accurate, accessible information about cases whilst colleagues are absent from work. An additional point which needs to be emphasised here is the importance of teamwork and networking, with opportunities for team members to share their assessments with others.

The findings concerning inter-professional relationships (see also Corby, Section II, Chapter 11) and communication among network members identified four problematic patterns, which they termed 'closed professional system', 'polarisation', 'exaggeration of hierarchy' and 'role confusion' (Reder et al., 1933b, pages 92–93).

'In a "closed professional system", one group of workers became united by the dominant view about the case and were less sensitive to conflicting information or observations . . . in "polarisation", schisms developed between groups of workers in which their opinions about the case diverged and they shared less and less information with each other . . . in "exaggeration of hierarchy", workers presumed status relative to each other was magnified and professionals with lower perceived status deferred to the opinions of others seen as hierarchically superior.'

The authors also highlighted problems in the functioning of professional networks where events were not assessed dynamically and comprehensively. Thus, no clear overview emerged. In addition, they found that sometimes 'selective interpretations' and 'pervasive belief systems' operated.

Their findings emphasised the importance of relationships among professionals which go beyond the rudiments of so-called 'working together', where divergences of opinion and dominant views can be articulated and discussed in the interests of child protection. The relevance of the Department of Health's principles (DOH, 1989) cannot be underestimated in providing a framework for different views to be expressed.

The findings with regard to family/professional interaction indicated 'enactments of care or control conflicts' and were identified as 'dependency', 'closure', 'flight' and 'disguised compliance'.

'In "dependency", the workers tried to meet the parents' chronic dependency demands as a way of improving their ability to look after their children . . . "closure" [was a pattern] in which the family shut themselves away from the outside world . . . "Flight" was a variation of closure in which the family moved from home to home, leaving no forwarding address and failing to register with helping agents . . . "Disguised compliance" refers to apparently spontaneous co-operation by parents which defused a professional's assertive stance.' (Reder *et al.*, 1993*b*, page 95.)

Effective working relationships among different professionals, regardless of status issues, are of particular importance if 'closure' is to be determined, and potential child deaths avoided. There is also the additional problem for professionals of establishing whether co-operation is genuine or is 'disguised compliance'.

Reder *et al.* (1993*b*, page 96) described professionals as 'operating within an intricate web of relationships and their decisions were dependent on information from diverse sources'. The value of their study lies in its emphasis on the complex psychological interconnections which exist within families, between families and professional networks, and among the professionals themselves: it is the case *as a whole* which needs to be understood.

The question which now needs to be addressed is what type of education and training, supervision and consultation would best help practitioners and managers in this involved and intricate work?

Competence-based education and training

The current interest in competence-based learning originated in the United States. Rushman (1972) argues that societal demands for increased competence developed from four areas of concern which still prevail in American society: 'one, the demand of the times for increased competence; two, the demands for different sorts of competence; three, the pressure for increased opportunities to gain competence; and four, "the fear of decay" – the feeling that standards of achievement, morality and order were in decline' (cited in Ashworth and Saxton, 1990, page 4).

Some of these concerns were also felt in Britain during the 1970s. The economic crisis of the mid-1970s initiated a period of major restructuring in British industry, but more particularly in the labour force. The Manpower Services Commission was conceived and created prior to this economic crisis, and its approach was to be consensual, involving educationalists, industrialists and trade unionists (Davies and Durkin, 1991). Momentum picked up during the 1980s with a right-wing Conservative government which was 'determined once and for all to lick British industry into shape'. And following the publication in 1986 of the White Paper *Education and Training – Working Together*, the National Council for Vocational Qualifications (NCVQ) was established. Its remit was 'to implement, or secure action to implement, a system of vocational qualifications that will achieve the objectives of comprehensibility, relevance, credibility, accessibility and cost effectiveness' (cited in Ashworth and Saxton, 1990, page 5).

Jessup (1990, page 17), the NCVQ's Scientific Director, outlined the task of the NCVQ: its function was to put the emphasis on 'outputs', defined as 'standards that need to be achieved at the end of a learning programme', as distinct from 'inputs', which are 'the learning opportunities provided'. 'Standards' specify the level of performance required of a person, and are thus linked to 'statements of competence', which in turn need to incorporate the assessment of 'skills to specified standards; relevant knowledge and understanding; and the ability to use skills and to apply knowledge and understanding to the performance of relevant tasks' (cited in Ashworth and Saxton, 1990, page 5).

NCVQ statements of competence are derived from an analysis of employment requirements, which when broken down lead to an analysis of the functions employees perform. A particular focus of this analysis is the attention paid to purpose and outcome. The standards are employment-led, and the functional analysis is carried out and endorsed either by employers themselves or on their behalf. What is absolutely clear is that this shift in the 1980s has involved giving much greater control of vocational training to employers, and this point is illustrated by a quotation from the Government White Paper *Employment in the 1990s*:

> 'The system must be planned and led by employers as it is they who are best placed to judge skill needs; it must actively engage individuals of every age, background and occupation, because they have much to gain from appropriate investment in their own training and skills; it must co-operate with the education service.' (Department of Employment, 1988, page 38.)

Davies and Durkin (1991, page 7) argue that the allocations of power in this triangular relationship are unmistakable: 'In charge is the employer, with her or his needs paramount. Then, as an unavoidable necessity is the "engagement" of the individual worker, in so far as her or his interests are useful to the employer. And finally, and very much as the poor relation is the education service'. Whilst the focus of Davies and Durkin's chapter is on youth and community work and the role of further education colleges, which are now centrally funded like the universities, professional training courses within higher education ignore these changes at their peril.

Ashworth and Saxton (1990, page 4), in their seminal article, argue that there are difficulties with the whole notion of competence to which the competence movement in the United Kingdom has paid insufficient attention. Drawing on the research of Grant *et al.* (1979), they identify three key problems which still remain: 'the specification of the competence, the teaching of a competence, and the assessment of competence'. Through an examination of these three areas they argue that the competence notion, whilst superficially attractive, has been stretched too far. Their analysis questions the validity of the 'output' model as a means of setting standards for the job, and they argue that distinguishing competence from performance is difficult. Does the candidate achieving the outcome need to understand the means by which the outcome is achieved? A candidate at post-qualifying level (see social work post-qualifying award requirement 3.6(i), CCETSW 1992; page 15) may be able to work effectively in situations where they carry responsibility for those at serious risk, for example, in child abuse by following procedures alone, but they may have little appreciation of the moral and ethical context of their decision-making.

Because of the complexity of post-qualifying and advanced level training in the person-centred professions, it is important to address and be clear about the definition of competence to be used. Ashworth and Saxton (1990, page 22) argue that there are variations as to whether 'competence statements refer to the gross activity which the individual performs . . . or to the microscopic actions and skills which go to make up that gross activity'.

Competence – determining a definition

Issitt and Woodward (1992) offer an examination of how the notion of competence is being defined and put into practice in the person-centred professions. The definition of competence commonly used in relation to NVQs is, 'the ability to perform work activities to the standards required in employment' (NCVQ, 1988). However, a wider definition is given by the Training Agency:

> 'Competence is defined as the ability to perform the activities within an occupation. Competence is a wide concept which embodies the ability to transfer skills and knowledge to new situations within the occupational area. It encompasses organisation and planning of work, innovation and coping with non-routine activities. It includes those qualities of personal effectiveness that are required in the workplace to deal with co-workers, managers and customers.' (Cited in CNAA, 1991, page 12.)

Issitt and Woodward (1992) argue that the definition of competence used here is of a wider scope than the relatively simple concept outlined by the NCVQ. Role competence, transferable competence or personal competence can all be read into this definition. The way in which the Training Agency and the NCVQ suggest competencies are best specified is through the method known as functional analysis. The work of the Unit for the Development of Adult Continuing Education (UDACE) explains how this approach works:

> 'Functional analysis is concerned with the key purpose of the occupational role rather than with the process. It begins by examining the whole work role and looking for a key purpose. It then asks what has to happen, what do people have to do, for that purpose to be achieved. At this stage in the analysis, the work role need not relate to an individual: it may relate to a company or a service or a professional function. The question of what has to happen for the key purpose to be achieved begins to divide the work role into a series of activities. Continuing this division eventually yields work roles which are carried out by individuals.' (UDACE, 1989, pages 16–17.)

Drawing upon this definition, Issitt and Woodward (1992) describe how the activities relating to a key work role form 'units of competence', with each unit being subdivided into 'elements of competence'. Each element is then assessed by a set of performance criteria, which are used to determine whether the candidate can perform the activity to the required standard. This method has been used by the Accreditation of Social Services Experience and Training (ASSET) programme, which is based at Anglia Polytechnic University, to develop post-qualifying child care competences (Maisch and Winter, 1991).

It has also been used by CCETSW's Scottish Office to generate child protection competences (CCETSW, 1993c). The Scottish project goes much further in its application of a competence-based framework than the two Central Office working papers on child care at post-qualifying and advanced level (CCETSW, 1993a,b). The two approaches also demonstrate differences in how competences are defined, as indicated earlier, with the working papers following the requirements of Paper 31 (CCETSW, 1992) more closely. These requirements are written in a fairly broad way, but they do contain a much greater emphasis on process rather than purpose in the specification of their general competence statements. A further area which needs clarification is the dividing line between post-qualifying and advanced level competence.

These differences in definitions of competence need to be urgently and rigorously addressed as part of an informed debate on competence in the person-centred professions. This need will become more acute if and when competence-based multi-disciplinary training programmes in child protection emerge. The current research by Stanford *et al.* (1993) into inter-professional learning in child protection will no doubt inform this debate. This Tavistock Clinic/University of East London project has been commissioned by the English National Board (ENB) and CCETSW to establish and evaluate pilot joint courses in child protection for nurses and social workers.

Implications for Practice

Competence and practice in the person-centred professions

Some of the problems concerning definitions of competence at post-qualifying level in social work have already been raised, and these are explored more fully by Issitt and Woodward (1992). Drawing upon the experience of the ASSET programme (Maisch and Winter, 1991), they identify a key difficulty as the disaggregation of general concepts into ever-decreasing elements with even more specific performance criteria. Unified competence, as denoted by professional ability, is broken down into skill areas and then reassembled to recreate a professional competence model. Issitt and Woodward (1992, page 47) argue that:

> 'The essential problem . . . is that, at the receiving end, it is the whole interactive performance that is of significance, not bits and pieces assembled or bolted together . . . the notion of "a competent person" able subtlely and uniquely to care for others in a multitude of situational contexts seems to be lost.'

The higher the professional level, the more significant notions such as 'unified competence' and 'interactive performance' will become. Indeed, NVQ level 5 indicates the degree of sophistication required, with its emphasis on unpredictability and complexity:

> 'Competence which involves the application of a significant range of fundamental principles and complex techniques across a wide and often unpredictable variety of contexts. Very substantial personal autonomy and often significant responsibility for the work of others and for the allocation of resources feature strongly, as do personal accountabilities for analysis and diagnosis, design planning, execution and evaluation.' (NCVQ, 1991.)

As competence-based training moves across and up the person-centred professions, it is important to draw upon some of the experiences in teacher and nurse education. In teaching, similar difficulties have been identified:

> 'Many teacher educators reject the idea of competence-based teacher education on the grounds that it encourages an overemphasis on skills and technique; that it ignores vital components of teacher education as we currently understand it, that what informs performance is as important as the performance itself.' (CNAA, 1991, page 2.)

The same arguments are used by Ashworth and Morrison (1991), in which they consider the problems of competence-based nurse education. They conclude:

> 'The idea of competence as the model of teaching and assessment may be particularly attractive to those in the field of pre- and post-registration nurse education. However its claims have been overestimated. Training programmes and syllabuses should not be drawn up so as to fit the competence model. "Competence" is a technically oriented way of thinking, often inappropriate to the facilitation of the training of human beings.' (Ashworth and Morrison, 1991, page 260.)

The meaning of the last statement will now be explored in more detail. Ashworth (1992) draws a distinction between 'having NCVQ competences' and being competent, and develops some lines of criticism outlined in an earlier paper (Ashworth and Saxton, 1990). He argues, firstly, that theoretical knowledge and understanding are essential to being competent, but insufficient attention is paid to this in the specification of competences. His second criticism relates to the individualistic orientation of competence. Whilst the competence movement has rightly emphasised the importance of a candidate's ability to engage in teamwork, the focus is on personal competences. Finally, he argues that competences are based on strictly behavioural analysis, and whilst this is superficially attractive for assessment purposes, many other problems arise in its wake.

Theoretical knowledge of child abuse from a variety of sources is vital if a worker is to understand and be able to articulate the principles and psychological processes which are informing their management of a case. Knowledge used in this way can be seen as an 'interpretative resource' for the person, which enriches the account they can give of a situation, and which may be transferred to help understand similar situations. Ashworth (1992, page 11) continues the argument by concluding that '. . . competence, in the NCVQ definition, remains at the level of lived-through experience rather than reflected-on understanding'. Clearly, at both post-qualifying and advanced level there should be a clear expectation that competences must demonstrate, reflected-on understanding'.

Teamwork, both within the professional workplace and on an inter-professional basis, is crucial to child protection practice. As Reder *et al.* (1993*a*, *b*) have shown, in over a third of cases a critical event happened at a weekend or during a public holiday, and in a further third of cases the person with key responsibility was away on leave. Thus, child protection becomes a responsibility of the team as much as the individual.

A key concern of Ashworth (1992) is that the individualism of competence ignores the fact that much day-to-day work, such as child protection, is thoroughly collective. The scope for education and training in professional and inter-professional teamwork is severely restricted by separate training programmes for different professionals, and by modular training structures where individuals are exempted from certain parts of the course. Shorter modules where students dip in and out of programmes may be superficially attractive in the current financial climate, but such an approach encourages course structures which are more content-oriented, where there is less opportunity for students to share their own practice in a closed group over a period of time.

Ironically, the gradual phasing out of longer post-qualifying programmes, where students often have the opportunity to reflect critically on practice and policy away from the workplace, will give reduced opportunities for students at post-qualifying and advanced level to demonstrate some of the requirements contained in Paper 31. Similar concerns are expressed by Rushton and Martyn (1993, page 29) in their study of two away-based post-qualifying courses:

> 'In-house courses are entirely appropriate for particular types of learning but more profound and integrated learning can take place over a longer period of time within a safe and stable learning group and in a continuing learning relationship away from the pressures of the practice agency.'

The shallowness of many modular structures emphasises the training of candidates as opposed to learning. Indeed, the training structures mirror the behavioural focus of assessment in the workplace: if competences are defined in behavioural terms, then no attention is given to the mental activities underlying such activities. Whilst an emphasis on observed behaviour may hold some appeal for assessment in terms of accessibility, other difficulties emerge. Ashworth (1992, page 14) questions the supposed transferability of competences from one setting to another. Teaching and learning aimed at facilitating transferability are concerned with 'raising the awareness of the learner with respect to his/her own learning styles and potential for transfer. The act of transfer also requires skills. . . . These are usually related to the individual being able to identify her/his needs in a new situation, adjust or recognise previous learning, and assess his/her competence'.

As argued previously, such reflected-on understanding is often facilitated by away-based courses with students working in closed groups over a period of time. There is no guarantee that, simply by using the notion of competence, the depth of understanding which accompanies learning will be increased. Rather, the reason for transfer not taking place is related to the shallowness of learning. Away-based courses offer an opportunity to meet people employed in different authorities and agencies, to hear about alternative approaches, and to question commonly held assumptions within workers' organisations'.

Finally, assessment of competences and the role of the assessor require closer examination. The fact that competence statements are laid out in a comparatively clear way has persuaded some people that they are now in possession of a greatly improved, reliable and valid assessment scheme. Ashworth (1992, page 15) argues that this is a serious misunderstanding:

> 'Logically prior to any question of the reliability and validity of an assessment instrument is

the question of the human and social process of *assessing*. Assessing involves the perception of evidence about a candidate's performance by an assessor, and the formulation of a decision concerning level of performance of the person being assessed. This is a series of events in which there is enormous scope for subjectivity – especially when the competences being assessed are relatively intangible ones to do with social and personal skills, or ones in which the individual's performance is intimately connected with the context.'

Ashworth's argument is of particular significance to competence-based assessment in the person-centred professions. CCETSW's post-qualifying guidance (CCETSW, 1992) indicates that a supervisor at post-qualifying level may be the candidate's line manager. With this kind of appointment, there is likely to be considerable role confusion for the person acting as both assessor and supervisor, and this will be explored in more detail later. At advanced level, the guidance is silent on this issue, although it is doubtful if one advanced level mentor/consultant alone would be competent to assess across the extensive range of advanced level requirements.

There is also the question of funding, particularly when the level of expertise required is very high. Whoever the person appointed is likely to be and independent of cost, there will be considerable subjectivity in the assessment process. For example, a candidate's ability to promote anti-racist and anti-discriminatory practice may be seen as mere political correctness by one supervisor or consultant, but as demonstrating initiative and commitment by another. The role of supervision and consultation will be considered in more detail in the next section.

To summarise, competence-based training structures have considerable shortcomings when applied to the person-centred professions. Child protection practice is a human activity involving complex moral and ethical decision-making. It requires creative thought and understanding and if children are to be protected, it is going to involve groups of professionals debating their different views, but acting collaboratively in the interests of the child, rather than being centred on the activity of one individual.

Supervision and consultation in child protection

Morrison (1993, page 13) describes supervision as 'a process in which one worker is given responsibility to work with another worker(s) in order to meet certain organisational, professional and personal objectives'. These objectives are competent, accountable performance, continuing professional development and personal support. Consultation is distinguished from supervision because, 'whilst supervision may at times include a process of consultation, the supervisor, in contrast to the consultant, is given authority by the organisation to direct the supervisee if that is necessary in achieving the organisation's aims'.

Richards and Payne (1990, page 13) describe four principal functions of supervision, the first three of which are drawn from the work of Kadushin (1976), Pettes (1979) and Payne and Scott (1982):

'The management function: ensuring that agency policies and practices are understood and adhered to; prioritising and allocating the work; managing the workload; setting objectives and evaluating the effectiveness of what is done.

The educational function: helping staff to continue to learn and to develop professionally, so that they are able to cope with societal and organisational demands and to initiate fresh ways of approaching the work, according to changing needs.

The supportive function: enabling staff to cope with the many stresses that work entails.

The mediation function: representing staff needs to higher management, negotiating what services need to be co-ordinated, clarifying to others outside the agency the legal or resource constraints.'

Morrison (1993) provides an aims checklist under each of these headings. A closer examination reveals some of the difficulties of establishing exactly what the role of the line manager/supervisor at post-qualifying level might be. Competence-based training is often presented with a rhetoric of being individual or student-centred, but the earlier discussion on the origins of competence-based learning makes it clear that it is the employer's needs which are paramount. There may therefore be an inherent tension between ensuring the overall quality of the worker's performance (the management function), developing the professional competence of the worker (the educational function), and validating the worker both as a professional and as a person (the supportive function).

In the current political and economic climate, the assessment of competence-based learning in the workplace could become yet another tool for monitoring workers' performance, rather than improving their professional competence or providing validation. Gadsby Waters' (1992) qualitative study of the content of traditional child protection supervision sessions confirms the direction in which supervision appears to be going. The findings of her exploratory study reveal that the major focus of supervision is perceived by the majority of participants to be managerial:

'The major focus and purpose of supervision of child protection work seems to be about "behaving correctly" rather than "behaving effectively", in terms of social work practice. To "behave effectively", that is, to ensure good confident practice by social workers to best serve the needs of children suffering or at risk of abuse, the professional and supportive functions of supervision need to be far more to the fore than found in this research.' (Gadsby Waters, 1992, page 100.)

She concludes by arguing that if a worker-oriented approach cannot be incorporated within the formal supervision process, then other opportunities have to be offered to meet the professional and personal needs if workers are to practice competently and confidently. Such a conclusion would seem to point to the supervisor at post-qualifying level not being the candidate's line manager, but a consultant.

Parkinson's (1992) study of community nurse managers in Tower Hamlets who were supervising child protection cases also questions whether managers can provide both managerial and professional supervision. She begins by focusing on the supportive and professional aspects of supervision, and quotes from the Kimberley Carlile inquiry (London Borough of Greenwich, 1987, pages 192–193):

'Supervision enables practitioners to know themselves. We all have some areas of work we find more difficult than others; we all have weaknesses as well as strengths ... However experienced a worker it is possible to get stuck, confused, frightened or bored. The task of supervision is to be watchful for these signs.'

The findings of Reder et al. (1993a, b) regarding the significance of complex psychological and interpersonal processes among professionals themselves and between professionals and families support such a view of supervision, although they point out that sometimes a hierarchical or managerial relationship can impede a worker from sharing concerns and revealing vulnerability. They also emphasise the importance of an holistic understanding of cases:

> 'Since child protection work is so demanding, it is particularly necessary for practitioners to have another person with whom to discuss their work and reflect on each case *as a whole* [my emphasis]. In most instances this other person will be a supervisor but the arrangement would not work well if they disagreed about the case or, conversely shared a belief that rendered them a closed professional system. Occasionally, a managerial or hierarchical relationship inhibits the supervisee from being open about anxieties. In such circumstances, consultation with a professional from another agency can be beneficial.'

Once again, the conflict between the supportive function of supervision and the managerial function is apparent. If a supervisee is more concerned with demonstrating competence in relation to staff appraisal, they will be unlikely to raise their real feelings about particularly difficult cases, especially if these form the bulk of their workload.

Parkinson (1992) provides an example of the way in which the management function of supervision is emphasised in Department of Health guidance to senior nurses in child protection:

> '[Supervision means] to assess the workload of practitioners, both individually and as a group; to measure the quality and effectiveness of their work, to set and monitor standards of practice, and to give professional advice and monitor training.' (DHSS, 1988, page 33.)

The project she describes arose in response to a policy statement (North East Thames Regional Health Authority, 1988) which stated the nurse manager's role as: 'encompassing regular review and monitoring of all case records, case discussion, and attendance at all case conferences attended by nurses' (Parkinson, 1992, page 41). A management crisis ensued because it was felt impossible to carry out the policy without excessive management workload and/or complete exclusion of other management functions. Interestingly, Parkinson adds that the policy statement seemed to be 'one step further towards restricting and controlling community nurses rather than enabling, empowering and supporting them to take professional responsibility for their own work'.

In a climate of decreasing rather than increasing resources, devolved budgetary management and quality assurance, might a similar comment be made in relation to other person-centred professions such as social work? Indeed, might it become difficult if not impossible for such managers, themselves, to fulfil the 'empowering' and 'enabling' requirements of supervision at post-qualifying level and management at advanced level as their roles change?

Parkinson (1992) describes the project which overcame this difficulty: the management function of supervision was effectively split from its supportive, educational and mediation functions. Child protection advisers, who were experienced nursing peers, carried out the supportive and educational functions of supervision, whilst the nurse managers concentrated on management. The pilot project was evaluated by an outside researcher to ascertain attitudinal changes, including perceptions of types of advice and support, and it was reported to be a 'resounding success' by the main parties involved, that is, the nurse managers, child protection advisers and community nurses. Parkinson (1992, page 54) concludes:

> 'It is beneficial to both nurse managers and community nursing staff to separate out the professional and managerial supervisory functions since these contain elements of control

and monitoring, and elements of facilitation and enablement, which, though both essential and important, can be experienced as contradiction.'

It is argued that the supervision of child-protection social workers also faces a similar problem. The line manager who acts as a post-qualifying supervisor has to manage the contradiction between a set of managerial requirements from the employer and the 'enabling' and 'empowering' post-qualifying requirements arising from Paper 31 (CCETSW, 1992). Faced with his/her own appraisal in the current political and economical climate, a first or second tier manager is unlikely to disregard a managerial instruction which contradicts his/her 'enabling' or 'empowering' obligations to supervisees.

Summary

This chapter has sought to highlight some of the many difficulties of adopting a competence-based education and training framework for the person-centred professions. The focus has been on post-qualifying education and training of social workers who are employed in child protection, although issues have been raised in relation to other professions involved in this work.

It has been argued that the narrow and fragmented approach of competence-based education and training impedes the development of holistic, reflected-on understanding which is so important in unravelling the complex web of relationships between families and professionals. Indeed, the educational aspects of the framework and opportunities for learning are likely to decrease if competences are closely related to job purpose and away-based courses are closed down in favour of in-service training initiatives.

The desirability of a more research-minded social work profession is a valid concern of CCETSW, many academics and postgraduate students, and some employers. However, a post-qualifying framework resting on the workplace assessment of behaviourally oriented competences may seriously impede the growth of knowledge, critical analysis and intellectual rigour which are the hallmark of a research-led profession. If the implementation of the framework lacks sufficient funds, then employers will be forced to 'cut corners' to concentrate on the development of competences in the workplace, which reflect the daily demands of service delivery and are directly linked to staff appraisal. It is questionable what role research might have in such a training structure.

Such competence-based initiatives complemented by in-service modules may be attractive in the short term as a way of managing training opportunities in a harsh economic climate. However, a much fuller debate about definitions of post-qualifying and advanced level competence in the person-centred professions is now required as a matter of urgency. In this respect, we should be looking at alternative ways of defining and assessing competence. The work of Hodkinson (1992) to develop a model of competence based on a continual dialectical interaction between intellectual processes, performance and schemas, defined as mental representations of sets of related categories, may offer a way forward. The three components of competence are also intimately related to culture and context. As Hodkinson (1992, page 35) says, drawing on the work of Eraut (1994):

'To practise intelligently, role performers have to theorise, to develop their own understanding of both the situation and the role they are trying to perform. This theorising entails the integration of public theory (the accumulated wisdom of the profession, from literature or experts) and private theory (one's own personal beliefs and understanding).'

The work of Klemp (1977) on job competences for McBer and Company is cited by Elliott (1991) as offering a way forward in defining professional competence more closely. Klemp identified closely related cognitive abilities which are commonly used by above-average performers. These abilities of *synthesising parts into wholes, empathy* and *cognitive initiative*, which refers to the way people define themselves as actors in a situation rather than as victims of circumstances or events, support the view that there is an ethical dimension to competence. Elliott (1991, page 130) concludes that 'there is little evidence that the McBer approach to identifying critical abilities has been widely used by education and training agencies in the UK.' Potentially, this model might have much to offer in the identification of professional competence in child protection.

Conclusion

In conclusion, better practice in child protection cannot be derived from narrowly defined competences and a controlling managerialism. Practice in this complex field raises many moral, ethical and emotive issues, and workers are often desperate to receive personal and professional support. We surely have to look to teamwork, the educational and supportive functions of supervision, and to higher education which encourages critical reflection and the development of practitioner research: 'The more human the action, the more likely it is that the action will require creative thought and understanding, and involve a team rather than the activity of an individual alone' (Ashworth, 1992, page 16). Those employed in the education and training of child protection professionals need to collaborate now in the interests of learning, so that the holistic and collective nature of critical practice is not lost forever.

Recommendations for Further Reading

Hodkinson, P. & Issitt, M. (eds) (1995). *The Challenge of Competence: Professionalism through Vocational Education and Training.* London: Cassell.
This edited book addresses the challenges posed by the adoption of the competence approach in the person-centred professions. Several of the chapters are written by authors quoted in this chapter, and they cover such issues as: the challenge for competence in the caring professions; professionalism and competence; competence, equal opportunity and empowerment; behaviourism and competence; competence and assessment; and lessons for the future. This book is a timely contribution to the competence debate in the person-centred professions.

Jordan, B. (1991). Competencies and values. *Social Work Education 10(1):* 5–11.
This article examines a tension in CCETSW's requirements for its qualifying award, the Diploma in Social Work (CCETSW, 1989). The author argues that there are two sets of values in operation in the requirements: the radical agenda – issues of structural oppression, race, gender and class; and the traditional agenda, where the focus is on

the individual, protecting their vulnerability and rights. The second agenda, it is argued, links more clearly to the rest of the document, with its focus on the application of skills, and the acquisition of procedural and legal knowledge. Implications for social work education and training are then explored.

Kemshall, H. (1993). Assessing competence: scientific process or subjective inter-ference? Do we really see it? *Social Work Education 12(1):* 36–45.
This paper explores the role of direct evidence, such as observational data, in compe-tence-based assessment. The author offers a critique of such assessment techniques by arguing that they are subjective and affected by a predominantly white, male or-ganisational culture and power relationships between supervisors, assessors and candidates. Questions are raised as to whether competence-based assessment really does promote equal opportunities and anti-discriminatory practice in the workplace, and the author suggests changes to workplace assessment practices and procedures to make them less discriminatory.

Acknowledgments

Particular thanks to Clare Roskill, CCETSW, for sending me the unpublished drafts of the working papers on child care and for her time, to Alan Rushton for also sending me unpublished papers of his work, and to my friend and colleague Meg Bond for reading earlier drafts of this chapter.

References

Adcock, M., White, R. & Hollows, A. (1991). *Child Protection: A Training and Resource Pack for Work under the Children Act 1989.* London: National Children's Bureau.
Ashworth, P. (1992). Being competent and having competencies. *Journal of Further and Higher Education 16(3):* 8–17.
Ashworth, P. & Morrison, P. (1991). Problems of competence-based nurse education. *Nurse Education Today 11:* 256–260.
Ashworth, P. & Saxton, J. (1990). On Competence. *Journal of Further and Higher Educa-tion 14(2):* 3–25.
Central Council for Education and Training in Social Work (1989). *Diploma in Social Work: Requirements and Regulations for the Diploma in Social Work.* Paper 30. London: CCETSW.
Central Council for Education and Training in Social Work (1990). *The Requirements for Post-Qualifying Education and Training: A Framework for Continuing Professional De-velopment.* Paper 31, 1st edn. London: CCETSW.
Central Council for Education and Training in Social Work (1992). *The Requirements for Post-Qualifying Education and Training: A Framework for Continuing Professional De-velopment.* Paper 31, 2nd edn. London: CCETSW.
Central Council for Education and Training in Social Work (1993a). *Draft Working Paper on Child Care at the Post-Qualifying Level.* Unpublished paper. London: CCETSW.
Central Council for Education and Training in Social Work (1993b). *Draft Working Paper on Child Care Practice at the Advanced Award Level.* Unpublished paper. London: CCETSW.

Central Council for Education and Training in Social Work (1993c). *Competence in Child Protection: Post-Qualification*. Final Report. Edinburgh: CCETSW.

CNAA (1991). *Competence-Based Approaches to Teacher Education*. Committee for Teacher Education. London: Council for National Academic Awards.

Davies, B. & Durkin, M. (1991). 'Skill', 'competence' and 'competencies' in youth and community work. *Youth and Policy 34*: 1–11.

Department of Employment (1988). *Employment in the 1990s*. London: HMSO.

Department of Health (1989). *The Care of Children: Principles and Practice in Regulations and Guidance*. London: HMSO.

Department of Health and Social Security (1988). *Child Protection: Guidance for Senior Nurses, Health Visitors and Midwives*. London: HMSO.

Elliott, J. (1991). *Action Research for Educational Change*. Milton Keynes: Open University Press.

Eraut, M. (1994). The acquisition and use of educational theory by beginning teachers. In G. Harvard & P. Hodkinson (eds): *Action and Reflection in Teacher Education*. New Jersey: Ablex.

Gadsby Waters, J. (1992). *The Supervision of Child Protection Work*. Aldershot: Avebury.

Grant, G. *et al.* (1979). *On Competence*. San Francisco: Jossey-Bass.

Hodkinson, P. (1992). Alternative models of competence in vocational education and training. *Journal of Further and Higher Education 16(2)*: 30–39.

Horne, M. (1990). Is it social work? In The Violence Against Children Study Group: *Taking Child Abuse Seriously*. London: Unwin Hyman.

Issitt, M. & Woodward, M. (1992) Competence and contradiction. In P. Carter, T. Jeffs & M.K. Smith (eds): *Changing Social Work and Welfare*. Milton Keynes: Open University Press.

Jessup, G. (1990). National Vocational Qualifications: implications for further education. In M. Bees & M. Swords (eds): *National Vocational Qualifications and Further Education*. London: NCVQ and Kogan Page.

Kadushin, A. (1976). *Supervision in Social Work*. New York: Columbia University Press.

Klemp, G.O. (1977). *Three Factors of Success in the World of Work: Implications for Curriculum in Higher Education*. Boston: McBer and Company.

London Borough of Greenwich (1987). *A Child in Mind: Protection of Children in a Responsible Society. The Report of the Commission of Inquiry into the Circumstances Surrounding the Death of Kimberley Carlile*. London: London Borough of Greenwich.

Maisch, M. & Winter, R. (1991). *The NCVQ Functional Analysis Method as Applied to the Description of Professional Level Practice*. Paper presented to the National ASSET Conference, Chelmsford, March.

Morrison, T. (1993). *Staff Supervision in Social Care*. Harlow: Longman.

National Council for Vocational Qualifications (1988). *The NCVQ Criteria and Related Guidance*. London: NCVQ.

National Council for Vocational Qualifications (1991). *Guide to National Vocational Qualifications*. London: NCVQ.

North East Thames Regional Health Authority (1988). *Policy Statement on the Management of Child Abuse*. London: London Borough of Greenwich.

Parkinson, J. (1992). Supervision versus control: can managers provide both managerial and professional supervision? In C. Clarke & J. Naish (eds): *Key Issues in Child Protection for Health Visitors and Nurses*. Harlow: Longman.

Payne, C. & Scott, T. (1982). *Developing Supervision of Teams in Field and Residential Work*. Paper 12. London: National Institute for Social Work.

Pettes, D. (1979). *Staff and Student Supervision: A Task-Centred Approach*. London: Allen and Unwin.

Reder, P., Duncan, S. & Gray, M. (1993a). *Beyond Blame: Child Abuse Tragedies Revisited*. London: Routledge.

Reder, P., Duncan, S. & Gray, M. (1993*b*). A new look at child abuse tragedies. *Child Abuse Review 2(2): 89–100.*

Richards, M. & Payne, C. (1990). *Staff Supervision in Child Protection Work.* London: National Institute for Social Work.

Rushton, A. & Martyn, H. (1993). *Learning for Advanced Practice: A Study of Away-Based Training.* Paper 31. London: CCETSW.

Stanford, R., Loughlin, B., Talbot, M., Trowell, J. & Yelloly, M. (1993). Interprofessional learning in child protection. *Paediatric Nursing 5(3): 20–22.*

Unit for the Development of Adult Continuing Education (1989). *Understanding Competence.* Leicester: National Institute for Adult Continuing Education.

Finding a Focus in Child Protection Training

John Simmonds

Introduction

The training agenda for child protection social workers is complex. It is not my intention to discuss this in any comprehensive way, but to focus on some very specific training issues that are central to the development of competent practice. Child abuse inquiries have often highlighted the question of why social workers do not see or understand when a child is at risk, even when the evidence is presented to them. The standard answer to this seems to result in identifying the need for social workers to be trained in the signs and signals of child abuse, or to improve procedures in gathering and communicating information about children and their families. While these are necessary and important, they do not help us to understand the complex processes involved when social workers look and try to make sense of what is presented to them when undertaking an investigation or conducting an interview. The reason why this process is so difficult is due to two connected issues. Firstly, child abuse is treated as though it is something that can be seen, like a physical object, when in fact it is the outcome of a perceptual process which is highly charged with emotion. There may be physical signs and signals to be made sense of, but they always need to be placed within the context of the emotional relationship between the child and its caretakers. Secondly, it is assumed that when social workers make their observations of children and their caretakers, they do so in a way in which their emotional response to what they see is irrelevant. In my view, both these issues arise out of a difficulty in understanding the importance of the context of relationships within which child abuse in the family arises, and the context of relationship between the social worker and the family within which observations are made. The essence of relationships is that they are emotional and interactional. Observing and making sense of them is not the same as seeing and describing physical objects, and we perpetuate the confusion and difficulty for social workers by assuming in training that they are.

For instance, when a social worker undertakes a family assessment, it will be very important to understand who it is that comprises the family. In our minds, we are drawing a boundary around that family. It may often seem most obvious to draw the boundary around the people in the 'household' – within the space of the home. The family is then identified very much by the physical presence of the adults and children in that family within a particular physical space. However, there may well be import-ant features about that family that drawing the boundary in this way leaves out. For instance, the mother may well feel that she would want to include her mother within the boundary of the family because she has a close and supportive relationship with her on a daily basis, although she doesn't live actually live in the household. However, from her partner's point of view, to draw the boundary in this way may well be quite unacceptable because he regards his partner's mother as extremely interfering and undermining. How and where families draw boundaries around themselves – phys-ically, emotionally and socially – is crucial. There inevitably will be different perspec-tives about it depending on who you ask, when you ask and the point you view it from. Who controls the drawing of family boundaries, around what kinds of issues, how they are negotiated and with what effect will all be a function of the power that family members have. Where this power originates from developmentally and how it is exercised will have an important bearing on family relationships. While, therefore, the power to determine family boundaries is essential for the safety of the space within the family, it can also be a source of considerable conflict. When it is used oppressively or coercively, it can be abusive.

While physicality is the most easily identifiable aspect of the family and its bound-ary, what holds the family together, pushes it apart and determines its safety are the powerful but invisible lines of relationships and the feelings that individual family members bring to these relationships. The emotional and relationship aspects of a family are the glue which gives the space meaning, a structure and holds it together. However, while the glue may act in a similar way to something used to bond wood together, its adhesive qualities come through something that is constructed and held together in the mind by emotion – the positive and negative feelings that individuals have for one another. Again, power is what makes the glue work, but how and with what effect needs carefully scrutiny.

While, therefore, investigating, assessing and planning in child protection might focus on the immediate events around the injuries inflicted, etc., it is essential that these are placed and understood within the context of the emotional space within which the child and its caretakers interact: who has feelings for whom, what are they and most critically, is the power that drives these feelings safe? It may be necessary to focus in the first instance on the child's physical safety, but the thing that will secure the child's welfare ultimately is a secure emotional relationship with his or her caretakers where the power in the family relationships is used to facilitate growth. Making sense of this process-dominated issue requires the development of the skill to see the way in which power is used to define boundaries in relationships, a skill which has a different quality to that which is normally required in seeing physical objects.

This is powerfully demonstrated in the Bridge Child Care Consultancy Service's report on the murder of Sukina who was 5. They say:

> 'The incident began with the father asking Sukina and her sister to spell their names which they would not or could not do. When the request was repeated, both girls did not respond. The father then hit Sukina on the hand with a ruler repeatedly, asking her to spell her name. Sukina still did not do so, but her younger sister spelled her name.
> Sukina never did spell her name as her father requested and, as each demand was not

met with the response the father wanted, the attack escalated. She was beaten first with a ruler, then with a short length of rigid plastic tubing and finally with a length of kettle flex which had the kettle attachment at one end, but not the three pin plug. We do not know how long the attack lasted, but at least fifty blows were rained upon her, interspersed with repeated demands that she spelled her name.' (Bridge Child Care Consultancy Service, 1991.)

Sukina was killed as a direct result of this assault. The account is a deeply distressing reminder of the terrifying rage that adults can unleash on children when their simple, and in this case seemingly trivial, requests are ignored. Although we can only speculate about what was going through her father's mind at the time, the demand that Sukina spell her name was presumably connected with the way in which he experienced himself as needing to exercise power in relation to her. Again, it is only possible to formulate a hypothesis, but behind the power of his uncontrolled rage must lie his own experiences of being a vulnerable and terrified child. Were the caring adults in his life unresponsive to his emotional needs? Did he find himself impotent at his inability to exercise any control over the way they responded to him. The terrifying nature of the violence he perpetrated on Sukina makes it difficult to think beyond our own repulsion at the crime he committed. Yet child protection social workers are required to think about the unthinkable in their investigations and assessments as often as they find themselves intimidated into not thinking by the power of the adults that they are confronted with.

Understanding and assessing the quality of feelings and relationships within the emotional space of the family involves an active process of perception and judgement on the part of the social worker. Because of the highly charged feelings that accompany child protection work for both parties, social workers will find it difficult to remain neutral. Their sense of responsibility, their feelings for their own safety, their fears of getting it wrong, their desire to make things better or rescue the child, or their feelings of helplessness when faced with the poverty, discrimination and deprivation in a family's life may all play a part within the space of the investigation. The central dilemma that social workers have to resolve for themselves arises out of the conflict inherent in the boundaries of the investigative process. On the one hand, this boundary is marked by the power to determine whether a child has been abused and if they are in need of protection – promoting that child's welfare as a paramount consideration. On the other hand, and at the same time, this involves and requires the power of the State with all the connotations that this has with coercion. The investigative and assessment process contains within its boundary the power to do good in a very fundamental way – protect a child. It also has the power to do immense harm – to interfere with and destroy family relationships. Families also contain similar processes within their boundaries – the power to help a child grow and the power to destroy growth – physically or emotionally.

These dilemmas can result in powerful feelings, yet they are often poorly focused on. They are likely to have an important bearing on the emotional atmosphere of the investigation and assessment, because how the social worker feels about them may well influence what he or she is able to see, what he or she is able to respond to and how he or she exercises his or her power. How these dilemmas connect with the social worker's own experience of power in relationships is particularly significant. If it is too unbearable or anxiety provoking, the social worker may well block it out, not see at all and therefore not use his or her power appropriately.

Martin Ruddock, the social worker in the Kimberly Carlile case, demonstrates this issue very clearly in his written statement to the inquiry following her death:

'At the end of the session I walked with the family to the door of the building and watched as they walked across the road to where their old car was parked. I still have a clear mental picture of the way in which they all walked across the road and got into the car, parents holding children by the hand, children leaping around in the car as they got in, laughing, shouting and playing happily with one another. It was almost an archetype for a happy family scene . . . therefore could not have been more reassured by the family dynamics than I was by this overall display on this occasion.' (Blom-Cooper, 1987, page 111.)

Despite the reassuring impression left by this interview, the concern for Kimberly's 'behavioural problems' continued, although, as the inquiry reports it, within 'a policy of drift' (Blom-Cooper, 1987, page 113). A visit to the Carlile's home a month later by Martin Ruddock shows Mr Hall insisting that social services leave the family alone and the social worker unable to insist that he see Kimberly. The inquiry reports:

'Mr Hall became unyielding to the point where it was being made clear that access to Kimberly (or any of the other children) was being stubbornly and unreasonably refused. Towards the end of the visit Mr Ruddock was permitted to peep through the small glass panel at the top of the door to one of the children's bedrooms. Two children were on the floor, between the beds, with their backs to the door. All that could be seen was the back of one young head and the top of another, one smaller than another.' (Blom-Cooper, 1987, page 115.)

The fact that Kimberly was being seriously abused and in under 2 months was to be dead is a searing reminder of the problem of not seeing what there is to be seen. Much has been debated and written to try to understand what it is that happens to social workers' judgement in such situations, and to try to help them see beyond these kind of reassuring impressions. The 'rule of optimism', the assumption of a parent's 'natural' love for his or her child, and the fear of spoiling the relationship between social worker and parent by taking up difficult issues have been highlighted as particularly salient. Other approaches have been to develop procedures, schedules, checklists and instruments to help see what needs to be seen. But none of these are likely to make their desired contribution to the protection of children unless they are accompanied by the development of the capacity to use authority appropriately. However, caution needs to be exercised regarding just resorting to coercive power, although this is certainly available to social workers and is sometimes unavoidable. The risks of recreating a bullying, enraged and entrenched interaction between family and social worker are high. What gets lost is the capacity to hold in one's mind the vulnerability and risk that is shared by child, parent and social worker alike.

Training social workers to see beneath the surface of what is presented to them so that they can construct accurate and helpful pictures of a child's circumstances is a complex matter. It cannot, in my view, be adequately accomplished by traditional educational methods such as 'talk and chalk', or even necessarily by practical experience. Understanding and learning about the nature of power within emotional space is different because it involves the development of acute sensitivity to emotional process. In particular, it means drawing on the inner emotional resources and understanding of the social worker that can tolerate looking and seeing in situations of uncertainty, anxiety and risk. It means, I believe, drawing on what often feel like personal issues and developing an understanding of the relationship between personal and professional experience, and the importance of dynamic psychological processes. What follows are two examples that amplify these themes.

Andrew

The first example concerns Andrew. It focuses on the development of his capacity 'to see' that arose directly out of an understanding of the relationship between his own emotional vulnerability and one of his child clients.

Andrew is a child protection social worker in a local authority social services department. He is both well qualified and experienced. He had been off work for a week because of stress, and had arranged to talk to an independent consultant arranged through the department because he was worried that he could be on the verge of going off sick for a long time. What follows is a condensed account of the six sessions that he had with this consultant.

Andrew reported that the demands of the work were intense. He had recently been asked to complete a number of court reports and had found that they were taking much longer than normal. He felt angry at the demands being placed on him by his agency, but guilty that he was not keeping up with his work and letting his colleagues down, whom he felt were much more effective and efficient than he was. He had tried to set aside time to complete the reports by working in a separate room, but he was very aware of the pressure that this put on the team, especially when they had to cope with his allocated 'duty' periods.

It became clear as Andrew talked that he worked very hard and took his responsibilities very seriously. However, his anger and guilt about all the things that he hadn't finished, the competing demands on his time and attention, and the feeling that he was letting his colleagues down had the effect of making him feel quite overwhelmed.

Andrew said that he had discussed this problem with his line manager who was sympathetic and had offered him more time to complete the reports. Initially, this made him feel better, but he soon ended up feeling more angry and more guilty because of the increased expectations of what he should achieve.

Andrew then went on to describe an incident with a child client, Sean, who was 11. Sean had been in foster care for 6 months following a particularly difficult investigation and separation from his mother. The placement was in danger of disrupting because Sean had great difficulty in allowing his foster parents to get close to him and would often punch and hit out at them in a rage. It was almost as if Sean had drawn an impermeable boundary around himself and interpreted anybody's attempt to get close to him not as caring but as attacking and dangerous.

Andrew had been trying to work with Sean on these difficulties while awaiting a referral to a child guidance clinic. This work had not proved at all easy, as Sean was often completely uncommunicative or very destructive despite Andrew's very sensitive and creative approach. Andrew had recently discovered that Sean was very interested in computer games and had been very excited when he responded positively to a suggestion that Andrew bring along some games of his own to work on. However, when he did so, Sean reacted by destroying them in the session. Andrew was left feeling very rejected and quite furious with Sean.

Andrew went on to say that he had become very upset about this one evening after work. He had found himself quite appalled by the violent feelings that he had towards

Sean when consciously he was so keen to find a way of helping him. Finding himself wanting to hit out at Sean when he destroyed the computer games was unacceptable and distressing for him as a child protection social worker.

Andrew then described how he was the eldest of three children. When his two brothers were born, he remembered feeling very jealous and felt that he had no option but to look after himself so that his mother could look after them. However, Andrew did not feel that he was giving way to the needs of his baby brothers, but rather turning away from his mother whom he felt was abandoning him in favour of the new arrivals. This seemed to have been compounded by Andrew's description of his mother as having difficulty in being emotionally or physically demonstrative or attentive, something he had experienced as a deliberate and personal rejection of himself. His rage at his mother and his wish to hurt his baby brothers were powerful but largely hidden feelings throughout his childhood. Although they were hidden feelings, he acted as though they could easily get out of control if the circumstances were right, and he had developed an identity which largely excluded anything where he might be thought of as angry or destructive.

Andrew's subsequent development had, as he reported it, proceeded quite normally. However, at the same time he had been left with a powerful residual picture of himself as a rejected and unwanted child who had turned away from his mother in order to survive. He had a powerful fear that there was something wrong with him that made him unlovable and unable to share intimate relationships. This part of him had continued to live on despite other good developmental experiences. They had a powerful effect on the way that he was able to make and sustain intimate relationships, as each time they unconsciously confronted him with the pain of the past and the fear that it would happen again.

Andrew's exploration of this suggested that some of the issues Sean was faced with resonated with similar issues inside Andrew. Although to an outsider they couldn't have been more dissimilar – Sean was a seriously abused and very vulnerable young boy in care; Andrew, an adult professional who was well-established and educated – within the space created between them for work, they both experienced the powerful themes of rejection, abandonment, loss and the wish/fear of wanting to destroy.

In further sessions, Andrew went on to see how he had identified himself with the rejected, unwanted and isolated aspects of children in need of protection and care from neglectful and/or abusive parents. His continuing professional contact with them kept him in contact with those aspects of himself that felt damaged, and he was searching for some resolution and reparation with the past. Although Sean was only one example, he represented the very vulnerable part of Andrew that was in need of care. However, what made Andrew feel stuck were the angry and destructive feelings that were stirred up inside him when somebody appeared to want to care for him. Sean's initial excitement about the computer games and his subsequent destructive rejection of Andrew seemed to encapsulate Andrew's despair about ever breaking out of this cycle and moving forward. They also represented his fear that expressing angry and destructive feelings in relationships would always destroy them. The constant playing out of these themes through his professional work had brought Andrew to the point of breakdown – the sickness he felt inside. It had become a matter of considerable urgency that he resolve his fears about experiencing himself as destructive or being seen as destructive in both his personal and professional life.

There is nothing particularly unusual about Andrew's story. We all bring complex issues and unresolved dilemmas from our own histories into both our personal and work lives. The way in which we try to resolve these past issues through present circumstances and opportunities is a measure of the potential human beings have to reorder life events and to change them. It is also unfortunately the case that we are capable of seeing the present in terms of the past, and in doing so we perpetuate the worst aspects of it. However, while I think that there is nothing unusual about Andrew, I think professional social workers feel very uncomfortable about recognising and openly debating the interaction between the personal and the professional which this example brings up. When I have presented Andrew as an example to social workers in seminars, I have been surprised by the hostile and unsympathetic reaction towards him. Are the public likely to be reassured about the integrity and saneness of the profession by knowing that what can motivate and sustain social workers is their own personal involvement in their work? Is what I have described above only the difficulties of a particular individual who in fact should have no place in this profession as a practitioner? Or is what I have described above the potential strength of a profession that operates on the boundary of the personal and the public – where who we are as people cannot be divorced from what we do as employees?

Addressing the interaction between the personal and the professional is difficult and disturbing. It is hardly surprising that under the glare of public and media attention, particularly the child abuse inquiries and scandals about children, the elderly and people with learning difficulties in residential care, the personal has largely disappeared. The fear seems to be that if social workers become involved in their work as people, then it only has negative outcomes because they abuse, oppress or discriminate against their clients. Social work as a profession and social workers as people have become identified as dangerous. In consequence, it appears as if they need to be held in check by rules and procedures and practice and training policies that are defensive, with their emphasis on 'competency' and outcomes.

What is in danger of being lost is the rich source of insight that Andrew could develop about the nature of human development and relationships based on his own experiences and struggles. However, the issue at stake is more than the identification of the emotional impact of many practice issues. Many professions can argue that their work is emotionally taxing. It is rather that in order to undertake the work of child protection – understanding and engaging with the emotional issues with which children and their caretakers live – social workers have to draw on an understanding of their own internal emotional issues. Andrew's determination to take responsibility for himself and to understand the interaction between his own emotional conflicts and Sean's helped to develop his capacity to relate to Sean's needs, think about them and, in particular, to bear the anxiety of being rejected by him.

The next example comes from the experience of a training event for residential social workers in child care. The boundary of this event contained within it similar conflicts between growth and learning, on the one hand, and rage and destruction on the other.

Residential Care

Residential care for children and adolescents is in a crisis. The child care policies of the last decade have placed emphasis on partnership with birth parents, and fostering and adoption as preferred alternatives when this is not possible. Residential care has consequently come to be used only for children with the most challenging behaviour or special needs. Added to this are the high financial costs of residential care, the scandals of institutional abuse, the lack of investment in training and career structure for staff, and the lack of a coherent professional framework that addresses the reality of young people's needs. This has all come together to make for a service that has a poor image and reputation, and struggles to find a role for itself that is positive. If young people in residential care seem to be marginalised, alienated and damaged, then these are also words that aptly describe the image in many people's minds – lay and professional – of the residential units that care for them. There seems to be a powerful similarity between the images that we have of the residents of children's homes, the people that care for them and the homes themselves. All three are dominated by a negative image of the value that they have for society and the profession. It is an image that contrasts quite dramatically with what both need – to be valued, to be safe, to belong, to be connected, to have hope and a future. The dilemma for the social work profession and residential care is in how to promote a positive image that is open, safe, sensitive and flexible and not just defensive in order to manage those potentially negative and dangerous aspects of it.

Promoting these positive images is a very important issue at a practice level. The thoughts and feelings that any young person has about him or herself are a critical part of their psychosocial health and development. Over the course of normal develop-ment, the continuity of good enough relationships with parents or other adult carers, continued into school and other neighbourhood, community and peer relationships, provides young people with a strong enough sense of their own individual worth to provide the practical, cognitive and emotional strength to negotiate their way into an adult role. For many of the young people who are looked after in residential homes, however, the combination of abuse and disruption from ordinary family and commu-nity experiences have left them with a powerful sense of their vulnerability. In particular, they come to have a strong and pervasive set of expectations that people are unsafe and not to be trusted, and that it is better to reject before being rejected. Many of these issues are well demonstrated in the description of Sean above.

I have been particularly concerned with the demands placed on residential social workers when confronted with some of the powerful emotions that are a part of the experience of working within such settings. The feelings stirred up in residential units, those coming from the young people themselves, those coming from the residential workers and those resulting from the interaction between the two are important and powerful reminders of one of the critical dimensions of residential life – that it is highly emotive and capable of stirring up the strongest feelings. It is crucial that ways are found of helping residential workers to understand this and its impact on the residen-tial task, in order to improve the standard of care that it provides. In particular, I have been concerned with considering the conditions that promote a safe and facilitative emotional space which allows positive feelings to be expressed, but which does not hide from negative feelings.

I have conducted seminars with groups of social workers in both fieldwork and residential care to explore this. As an introduction, I ask participants to identify the kinds of feelings that have been stirred up inside them when they have worked with young people in residential care. Typically these have included positive feelings of hope, care, security, as well as negative ones such as despair, powerlessness, fear and retribution. After completing this exercise, I go on to discuss with the group what the feelings they have identified as their own tell us about what the young people might be feeling inside themselves.

I originally thought that there was nothing complex or controversial about such an exercise. Experience has taught me that this is far from the case. Some participants have never before thought very much about or identified themselves as having feelings of their own in a work setting or could see the relevance of such feelings. Others could only relate to the exercise as though I had asked them to identify the objectives of the placement or why the young person had to be admitted to residential care. For others, the feelings that were stirred up for them were just not acceptable to debate safely in a training session – the wish to physically retaliate against a child who had been violent towards you, the despair a staff member feels when a child has cut his or her wrists again, the wish to withdraw emotionally from a child who runs away, the wish to reject a child who keeps you up all night. Although it has never been explicitly identified, I wouldn't be surprised if some staff couldn't also admit to feeling sexually aroused by some young people. Although the emotive nature of residential work is easily recognisable, the language of emotions is not a safe currency in my experience. These feelings are not safe to discuss, as critical as they might be to understand. Over time, I came to see this as an important learning point in itself.

In one particular group, the beginning of the exercise proceeded as usual but was accompanied by some critical comments about the list of feelings being too negative. Some members of the group felt that negative feelings were just not acceptable in residential care because young people needed to feel cared for by staff. This seemed an understandable comment, and the group went on to identify some of the more positive feelings they had about young people being admitted to residential care. However, as I moved into discussing the nature of behaviour as communication and in particular the impact on staff of feeling pulled into interaction with a young person while at the same time being pushed away, it was clear that the reaction to the exercise – that it was too negative – was more significant than I had realised. One person forcibly commented that the feelings that I was describing staff as having – feeling anxious, upset, frightened and overwhelmed by the behaviour of the young people they care for, and sometimes feeling like responding by rejecting, emotionally with-drawing or retaliating – were nothing like she had ever experienced. She commented that if a staff member had such feelings, then she would question whether such a person should work in residential care. While the force of this comment was quite powerful and rather disabling, I felt that it was important to clarify that I was not saying that these feelings were necessarily acted upon (although I believe that there is a risk that they will be if they are not understood), but that the existence of such feelings provided a very important indicator of what the young person was feeling but unable to get help with in a way that felt safe. However, my explanation seemed to further inflame the situation, as others joined in informing me that I didn't understand anything about residential care, that if I had any experience, then it must be with very inexperienced people or in very bad establishments, and that my views were very negative. The more people said, the more personally did they express these feelings in terms of my competence, knowledge and understanding of what life was actually like for them as residential workers.

After 30 minutes of such discussion, the personal nature of the attack seemed to be unabating and I suggested that we abandon the seminar in its current form and move on to discussion of a case example I had brought. The case discussion proceeded more positively and the seminar came to an end with a subdued but more friendly feel.

This was a disturbing experience. It seemed that rather than providing a framework for understanding some of the powerful interactions that happen in residential care, the group felt that I was attacking their integrity and competence as residential workers. I had touched on the very vulnerability I was trying to address, but not in a safe way. The group experienced my interest and concern not as helpful but as attacking and persecuting.

There is a very great similarity between what I was trying to discuss as the topic of the training session itself and what happened in the interaction between myself and the group. I had started out with an assumption that I had some positive learning to offer the group that they might take away with them and use in their work. This has a parallel with the feelings that many residential workers have towards the young people in their care – that their commitment, interest and good-will provides a rich source of positive experience that the young people can use to develop and take away with them when they leave. However, what I had tapped into was the vulnerability of this group where they had experienced my positive feelings towards them and my wish to offer them something as quite the opposite – as attacking and persecuting. Over the course of the training session, I had come to experience considerable doubt about the rightness and helpfulness of my understanding, and I felt quite attacked and rejected. The person that felt vulnerable and highly anxious on that occasion was me. My desire to retaliate was not far from the surface! The training session seemed to have been taken over by the very process it was meant to clarify and understand.

The underlying assumption in any training session is that a safe enough environment exists that enables participants to relate to and take in what is being offered. In many educational experiences, this issue is hardly noticeable or explicit as the environment is familiar and based on thousands of hours in the classroom as a child, where the traditional role relationships of teacher/pupil provide the boundary that contains the anxiety associated with learning and taking in. However, in the session reported here the anxiety associated with the material under discussion had broken through and taken over. Rather than the interactional nature of behaviour being the *subject* of the session for study and reflection, the interaction between myself and the participants exemplified it. Instead of studying and learning about the feelings engendered in staff in residential care, the feelings had become enacted in our relationship.

The above example illustrates the failure of the educational structure at the time to provide a safe enough environment within which learning can take place. It does, though, still provide an opportunity for learning if the experience can be digested. This does depend on not rejecting what at the time I found to be very difficult. It would have been easy to denigrate the participants as ungrateful or stupid or unprofessional – in effect, to have rejected them and not to have seen that in the interaction between us there was some powerful material which told us a lot about what we were there to understand and from which we could all learn. While this is particularly relevant in residential care, the issue is relevant throughout child protection work, where the forces at play are immensely powerful and capable of infecting the whole process from initial investigation through decision-making to planning and intervention. The question is how we find a way of learning from these painful experiences and not just rejecting them.

Training Issues

The training issues that arise from these two examples need some exploration. As I indicated at the beginning of this chapter, understanding the nature of emotional space cannot be confined to traditional educational methods such as 'talk and chalk'. The nature of Andrew's stress is more than a difficulty in finishing court reports. It was an important key to a set of inter-related issues leading back through his work with Sean to his current struggles in personal relationships and his early family experiences. Andrew's initial presentation of his work problems was only one facet of the problem.

Helping Andrew to continue with his court reports and his work with Sean meant seeing beyond the surface of these issues to the inner space and issues they delineated. Although it was important for Andrew to understand how painful he found Sean's rejection of him, the key to his being able to continue to relate to Sean was in understanding the violent feelings stirred up when Sean destroyed the computer games and in his being able to express Sean's fear that Andrew would abandon him. Finding the emotional resilience to withstand Sean's rejection meant Andrew drawing on his inner emotional understanding of the experience of rejection and abandonment, and most particularly the defences against it.

This raises a significant question about whether all problems need to be understood in this way. Does every example of a difficulty with court reports or direct work with a child need to be approached through an understanding of inner emotional space? Is training in this area always dependent on the development of a capacity to see based on personal experience? The answer to this is a qualified 'no'! Understanding the 'cause of concern' in child protection means seeing the 'abuse' as one dimension which delineates the inner space within which the child and its caretakers relate. The kinds of issues presented to social workers in child protection investigations, assessments and planning are a combination of the application of statutory and professional frameworks, but they are always within the context of the emotional issues that have a dramatic and sometimes fatal effect on what we see, what we understand and what we do. Taking this on board does mean leaving the apparently safer, structured world of the Children Act, guidance and procedure for the messy world of people and their emotions and relationships.

The question is, what kind of processes help students to develop an understanding of the 'inner space' of feeling? Although it is possible to approach these issues theoretically or conceptually, there are real limitations to this. In the example of Andrew, the actual process of understanding and learning for him developed in three places. In the first place, in the space between Andrew and the consultant – their relationship. In the second place, in a space inside the consultant that experienced and understood the anger and fear of being rejected and abandoned. Thirdly, in a space inside Andrew that came to be able to better tolerate the fear of his rage at being abandoned in favour of his brothers. Understanding in this context is not theoretical or conceptual, although this helps. It does not come from a checklist, although there may be some key questions like, what am I feeling and what am I afraid of feeling? It is also not something you tell somebody unless it happens within a space they experience as being safe, because of the fear of being put in touch with feelings that threaten to get out of control. It is understanding that comes from the experience of links being made in the present between the personal and the professional spheres.

The framework for professional education and training of child protection social workers has not furthered the development of these issues because the issues themselves are so little on the agenda. Developments in the Diploma in Social Work and in post-qualifying training reflect developments in social work that have pushed the boundary between the personal and the professional even further into the area of bureaucracy. Yet the overwhelming evidence is that the weight of human tragedy and need that social workers are confronted with inescapably demands that this dimension has its proper place in training and development. The currency in human affairs is emotion. It is essential that in the quest for accountable, effective and efficient practice, we do not lose sight of this principal component. Failing to do so will have tragic consequences for social workers, for parents, but above all for children themselves.

References

Blom-Cooper, L. (1987). *A Child in Mind*. London Borough of Greenwich.

Bridge Child Care Consultancy (1991). *Sukina, An Evaluation Report of the Circumstances Leading to Her Death*. London: The Bridge Child Care Consultancy Service.

27

Specific Issues in Training for Child Protection Practice

Kate Wilson and Jocelyn Jones

Introduction

Earlier chapters in this book have highlighted, either explicitly or by implication, some of the issues in designing programmes for training in child protection which this chapter addresses in detail. In one sense, indeed, the very design of the book, with its inclusions and omissions, is a reflection of some of the matters of content which training programmes must attempt to resolve. Over and above issues of definition, which Harris highlights in his discussion in Section I of the somewhat arbitrary distinction between child care and child protection, and the dilemmas brought about by competency-based assessment, which Jones explores in this section, current organisational problems and developments in adult learning and modularisation also have implications for the kinds of training programmes offered.

The purpose of this chapter, then, is to review briefly both these developments and recent attempts at their resolution, before focusing on three aspects of training which offer learners the opportunity to address concerns in a way that acknowledges the complexity of the child protection task.

The first section of the chapter will therefore summarise current developments and concerns in the provision of training in child protection. Some of these, in particular the limitations of competency-based training and the need for opportunities for personal growth and exploration, have been discussed in detail in the two preceeding chapters in this section. They will therefore be touched on only briefly here, while others, such as issues concerning the incorporation of adult learning principles and the development by the Central Council for Education and Training in Social Work (CCETSW) of its post-qualifying framework for training, will be considered more fully. The design of current child protection post-qualifying programmes will then be reviewed. The final section will consider three key aspects of training, namely child observation, the teaching of anti-oppressive practice and supervision.

Current Issues in Child Protection Training

Vocational training has always been a complex matter, and perhaps nowhere has this complexity been more apparent than in the training for the personal social services. There is inevitably a tension between the need to introduce a range of theoretical and factual material, and the inculcation of personal skills involving sensitivity to the predicament of others, integrity, clarity of purpose and the ability to take difficult decisions without being judgemental. So the major changes in training which have occurred in the last 5 years may in one sense be viewed as part of a long struggle to resolve these often competing demands.

Nonetheless, those who have been involved in this teaching must also be aware of an increase in the range of issues of which trainers must take account. Nowhere is this more evident than in training for child protection. These issues involve both changes in the organisational structure of training, and in its content.

The need for improved and specialised training in child protection

The spotlight turned in the past 5 years on social work training has been noticeable particularly in the field of child care, where a number of well-publicised inquiries highlighted what were held to be the inadequacies of training. Social workers were criticised, *inter alia*, for their lack of knowledge of the relevant law, their failure to follow procedures and their lack of professional skill in working with abusing families. These criticisms culminated in the recommendations by the Butler-Sloss inquiry (1988) which emphasised the need for improved and specialised training. Recent years have thus seen: a) an acceptance that qualifying programmes for social workers need to provide opportunities for students to specialise, and that the old form of generalist training is no longer able to address the increased complexity of the task; and b) that there is a need for continuing post-qualifying training, which would focus on those special demands and tasks which practitioners experience as particularly difficult and complex.

The inquiry also highlighted deficiencies in the child protection training of other professional groups, who, although they may be less centrally involved than social workers, nonetheless have a critical role in the recognition and early stages of intervention. Changes in the content of qualifying courses and an extensive programme of in-service training have been introduced, and joint initiatives between the CCETSW and the English National Board for Nursing, Midwifery and Health Visiting (ENB) have been undertaken to try and ensure some compatability in training, particularly in relation to inter-professional working (ENB, 1994.)

Modularisation, credit accumulation and transfer

Partly as a result of government policies, the university sector has had to implement major organisational changes to take account of a rapidly growing and changing student population. Modular provision with credit accumulation is being widely introduced, in part because it permits greater flexibility in the timing and structures of the programmes offered (CNAA, 1989).

Both the advantages and disadvantages of modular teaching need to be acknowledged. From the point of view of the practitioner/learner, modular provision, in theory at least, should allow the possibility of flexible timing, with the opportunity to undertake short blocks of training at times which can be adapted to suit the demands of a professional workload. It should also be possible for individuals to put together their own training packages adapted to suit their particular interests and needs, by taking modules offered by different training settings. Equally, the establishments themselves should be in a position to develop areas of particular strength, thereby obviating the need to provide a comprehensive programme of training. Thus, a setting with a depth of teaching and practice experience in therapeutic work could provide this as a particular specialism, leaving others to provide specialist modules in, say, management or out-of-home care.

The disadvantages of these structures, both to the consumers and also to the providers, must also be recognised. It is acknowledged (CNAA, 1989) that modular provision may make it harder to develop opportunities for sharing, trust and learning from peers through membership of a stable group which adult learners particularly value (Wilson and Bradley, 1994), and which are arguably central to the learning needs of the advanced practitioner.

In practical terms, too, for the programme providers, flexibility may lead to increased difficulty in terms of planning, in that it becomes harder to develop long-term plans if the numbers of those opting for specific modules become increasingly unpredictable. The universities also have some way to go in adapting the pattern of the provision of higher degrees to credit accumulation and transfer.

Adult learning theories

Ideas about how people learn and knowledge about the characteristics of adult learners have also begun to have an impact on programme design and content. Although the theories themselves have been around for some time (Knowles, 1978), their implications have only recently received significant recognition in higher education settings. The greater emphasis on market forces and consumer opinion has undoubtedly accelerated this process.

It has long been received wisdom that learning new material does not come easily to adults. William James, writing in 1890, in a much quoted passage argues that, 'The ideas gained by men before they are 25 are practically the only ideas they shall have in their lives. They cannot get anything new.'

This conclusion was based on experimental studies which consistently reported that a decline in learning performance was evident as people grew older. This has, however, been shown to be not the result of a lessening ability to learn, but of other factors associated with the style of adult learning. When these are properly taken into account, adult learners show no relative decrement in learning outcomes. Theories of adult learning have stressed the fact that adults have accumulated experiences which can be a rich resource for learning; that in adults a readiness to learn is (usually) a function of the need to perform social roles; and that adults tend to have a predominantly problem-centred orientation to learning. 'Andragogy' (the theory of adult learning) therefore suggests the following factors to be most significant in facilitating effective learning by adults:

1. *The meaningfulness of the material to be learned*. The closer it appears to be to the adults' aspirations, the better the learning. This is particularly important in relation

to the memory strategies typically employed by adults, and they are helped by being involved in the process of identifying what they need to learn.

2. *Rapid implementation of knowledge.* Adults show relatively better recall when they are required to apply knowledge and skills at or soon after the first time of learning.

3. *Anxiety about performance.* This has a greater effect on adult self-esteem and self-confidence and hence on learning, than it does on children.

4. *Speed of performance.* Adults achieve better performance when they are able to operate at their own speed.

To some extent, post-qualifying training fits well within the framework of adult learning suggested by the above (for example, in relation to the perceived relevance of the material), but there are tensions. In particular, the thrust induced by market-oriented education towards expansion of numbers is potentially at odds with the emphasis in adult learning on utilising the previous knowledge and experience of the individual, with its commensurate need to individualise both course content and the processes by which new knowledge is acquired.

The post-qualifying framework for social work training

CCETSW has introduced a new framework for post-qualifying education, with two levels of achievement: the post-qualifying level and the advanced level. The advanced award is conferred when both levels have been satisfactorily completed, each level requiring 120 credits for completion. CCETSW defines the post-qualifying level as equivalent to the academic level of the final year of an undergraduate degree, and the advanced level as equivalent to the academic level of a master's degree (CCETSW, 1992). The whole framework is based on a system of credit accumulation and transfer, of which modularisation is an essential part, enabling students to collect credits from different courses of training.

The management of post-qualifying training has been devolved to a complex structure of local consortia, based on partnerships between local authorities and training establishments. These partnerships themselves reflect CCETSW policy, developed in an attempt to meet employers' demands for training better adapted to the requirements of the workplace, of requiring that training programmes at qualifying level should be based on active collaboration between educational institutions and social services agencies (CCETSW, 1991). The consortia will have responsibility for validating training programmes at the two post-qualifying levels and providing funding for those wishing to undertake them, and thus will encourage and support individually developed packages of training. The regional consortia are responsible for devising credit-rating schemes which can be applied to programmes within their locality. CCETSW defines a credit as, 'a unit for recognising the professional competence acquired by a worker' (CCETSW, 1992, 2.2.2), and the competences required at both post-qualifying and advanced level are very broadly outlined in Paper 31 (CCETSW, 1992, 3.5, 3.6 and 4.4.3).

The relationship between credits and competences, together with the need to tie credit rating in with the systems used by other professional validating bodies has bedevilled the post-qualifying system and has hindered the development of the regional consortia. Of eight post-qualifying child care programmes informally surveyed (August 1994), none had yet been given a credit rating under the new system.

As with funding changes in the health service, where the money is intended to go to the patient, so here, funding will directly support the individual rather than being allocated to particular training programmes as it was in the past. (Under the old system, for example, a training programme, once validated, would be supported by a centrally administered, set number of bursaries.) This is consistent with the development of individually tailored training packages supported by credit accumulation and transfer described above.

However, it remains to be seen whether or not the framework is sufficiently well resourced to be able to support such a complicated and time-consuming system, and whether the gains from what appears to be a more sophisticated and intellectually sound approach justify abandoning a system that was administratively clear and efficient. It makes long-term planning potentially difficult for away-based programmes, and it may in practice decrease flexibility for consumers. Consortia may prefer to support individuals wishing to attend programmes offered by those within the consortium, rather than provide funding for programmes outside the particular consortium. Over and above this, the modest level of expenditure (6.6% of the training support grant in the year 1992–93, Social Services Inspectorate (SSI), 1994) on post-qualifying training suggests that there are considerable problems in releasing resources for training at this level which need to be addressed.

Structure and locus of training

An issue closely connected with the development of consortia is that involving the place and organisation of training, traditionally differentiated as 'in-house' or 'away-based'. In away-based programmes, a significant amount of time is spent in an educational setting removed from the workplace and its intrusions, and participants are usually drawn from different employing agencies. In-house programmes, by contrast, are organised and supported by the agency, and course participants are usually colleagues from the same agency. However, there is, as Rushton and Martyn (1993) point out, 'often a good deal of interchange in the two models', at least at the level of teaching, in that 'practitioners will frequently be engaged to teach in educational settings, and college and university lecturers will teach on "in-house" courses where some of the training may be located in educational settings.' (Rushton and Martyn, 1993, page 27.)

Again, there are advantages and disadvantages for both models. There is a risk that agency-based programmes develop a narrow curriculum, perpetuating an uncritical acceptance of existing policies and limited awareness of alternative approaches. This, however, has to be balanced against the possibility that educational settings become remote from the pressures and demands of the workplace, and that those on away-based courses experience difficulties in integrating their knowledge with the demands of practice. As the study quoted above observes, 'too many course members . . . on return to work, were anxious about losing their educational gains.' However, the authors of this study express their concern lest the 'away-based' model becomes lost in the new structure. They conclude that their findings go some way towards validating year-long specialist courses offered away from the site of practice, and they point out that course participants in their study expressed an overwhelming preference for away-based training courses. Although it is vital that the interplay between the immediacies of the practice environment and more formal theoretical material is kept to the fore, they suggest that this can be achieved both through management commit-tees and through maintaining a focus in teaching on the learners' currently held cases (Rushton and Martyn, 1993).

Anecdotal evidence suggests that employers have a preference not only for the kinds of modular provision outlined above, but also for 'in-house', agency-commissioned training. Despite this, it seems important to retain a diversity of provision, and it would be unfortunate if consortia become so employer-led that support for away-based provision diminishes.

Joint professional training

A further issue for trainers from all the professions involved in child protection is the extent to which training should be multi-disciplinary or should be offered to single professions. The experience of running a multi-disciplinary programme at the Univer-sity of Hull[1] (designed for a range of professionals, but which in practice only recruited social workers, nurses and health visitors) suggests, perhaps predictably, that this approach has both advantages and limitations. Social work and health professionals undoubtedly found the experience of a sustained period of shared training enriching, in that it heightened knowledge of the others' tasks, and the different disciplines provided additional learning. Nonetheless, the stresses arising from the differences in the child protection role also needed to be managed, and the difficulty of establishing an acceptable homogeneity in learning objectives for the group was recognised. It was clearly valuable for health visitors to 'know about' planning in child care, for example, or about issues in out-of-home care, but the fact that their involvement in this from the point of view of direct practice was so much more limited inevitably created tensions for the programme.

Other difficulties experienced on the Hull programme, which are also highlighted in a study of child protection courses for health and social services professionals (ENB, 1994), were the differences of educational background and perspective, which some-times lead to problems between those with a process orientation to learning and those used to a more didactic and prescriptive approach. It was also important, but not always easy, to maintain a balance between health and social services participation in course planning and leadership, teaching and assessment. Health service profession-als, for example, rarely formed more than 25% of the student cohort, so that ensuring that their learning needs were kept consistently to the fore sometimes proved prob-lematic. Efforts to recruit from other professions, in particular teachers, were unsuc-cessful, largely it seemed because the day-release structure of the programme did not offer a good fit with the demands of teachers' working environment.

In practice, it seems likely that the modular approach to training will provide a solution to at least some of these tensions, with certain core modules being offered on a multi-disciplinary basis, and others catering for the specialist roles of the different professionals.

Issues of content

Decisions concerning course content are partly those which arise in all vocational training – for example, the extent to which training programmes reflect agency

[1]This programme is no longer offered

requirements or are critical of them – and are partly unique to child care training.

A particular dilemma concerns the appropriate boundary to be set around the subject. Harris (Section I, Chapter 2) draws attention to the somewhat arbitrary nature of the focus of concern in child protection. Not only is our remit, as Harris argues, narrowly limited in terms of our own culture, but also many policies which might be regarded as the legitimate concern of child protection workers are excluded from it. Thus, as Parton (1991) makes clear, the virtual removal of 16–18-year-olds from the social security safety net, with all its implications of harm to this vulnerable group of young people, was not discussed by Parliament in the major revision of child care policy in the late 1980s. The distinction between other forms of child care and child protection is also a fairly arbitrary one. Training programmes for child protection have therefore to decide the extent to which they focus narrowly on those services which concern intervention under Part VI of the Children Act 1989 and on others directed more broadly at children in need.

Related to this are issues which reflect the changing role of child protection workers based in social services departments and health authorities. Changes in the organisation of the provision of services which are embodied principally in the National Health and Community Care Act 1990 and the Children Act 1989 suggest a clear demarcation between the purchaser of services (normally the local authority) and the provider of services (usually those in the voluntary or 'not-for-profit' sector). Traditionally, much therapeutic work was undertaken by social workers (and, indeed, major therapeutic innovations have derived from social work practice). However, the role of the practitioner in a statutory setting is becoming more that of case manager, acting as a broker in setting up care packages for children and families and purchasing services, such as risk assessments or psychosocial help from others on behalf of children, their parents and the agency. This creates dilemmas in designing a programme which reflects the current child protection task, while nonetheless retaining enough of a focus on training for such things as direct work with children and families. Without some knowledge and skill in this area, for example, it is arguable whether the worker would be able successfully to carry out the central tasks of the child protection role.

The content of training at qualifying and post-qualifying levels for the different professions

Trainers need to distinguish between syllabus content at qualifying and post-qualifying levels. The CCETSW guidance on training in child care at qualifying diploma level, for example (1991), sets out the basic knowledge and skills which might be appropriate for qualified workers whose particular area of practice is in child care. But because the possibility of obtaining practice experience in statutory work at this level may be limited to undertaking joint work with experienced practitioners, the authors of this document argue that the component which focuses on child protection should be limited in scope. Further training in this area should instead be undertaken in the first year post-qualification, and thereafter. A further issue to be considered when designing training programmes is that which arises from the differences between the various professional groups in the frequency with which they encounter child abuse, and the extent of their involvement in the child protection process. Stevenson (Chapter 12), writing about the complexities of inter-professional working, distinguishes between those agencies and professionals on the 'outer circle', where child abuse is not centre stage, such as GPs, nurses, probation officers, some social workers and teachers, and those for whom it is a top priority. Within the outer circle professionals, this may lead to problems such as the atrophying of knowledge – it is hard to remember what you have learned if this knowledge is used only occasionally – and problems in setting up working arrangements which ensure an appropriate response. And between those in the inner and outer circles, different priorities may lead to problems of communication and engagement, so that it is easy for the 'outer circle' to be marginalised and even to encourage this process.

These differences need to be reflected in training, with a training continuum from those components required on a basic level at the outer circle, through to an inner circle where involvement in child abuse issues is central. Thus, training for those for whom child abuse is not centre stage should be structured in a way which recognises the need for periodic reinforcement and should at a minimum ensure that trainees can demonstrate:

- knowledge of aetiology, patterns and prevalence of child abuse;
- the ability to recognise signs and symptoms;
- skill at listening and responding sensitively to children;
- knowledge of own agency procedures and those of other relevant agencies;
- some knowledge of the legal framework in which these agencies operate.

This minimum training would not, of course, take account of the specialist knowledge required by the particular professional role, such as the kind of monitoring undertaken by teachers which Peake describes in Chapter 13. Nor would it take account of the needs of those practitioners appointed to a specialist role within their agency, such as a designated teacher or police officer undertaking investigations. For these specialists, training might include much, although not all, of what would be appropriate for those involved at the 'inner circle' of child protection work. Here, it might be expected that at the end of a period of post-qualifying training practitioners should be able to demonstrate:

- knowledge of the content of their basic training, but in a more detailed way;
- self-knowledge and the ability to acknowledge personal responses;
- skills in assessing risk and evaluating outcomes;
- knowledge of current research and the ability to evaluate complex findings;
- knowledge of attachment theory and theories of grief and loss;
- skills in child observation and assessment;
- the ability to undertake diagnostic and validation interviews;
- detailed knowledge of child care policy and child care law;
- the ability to engage and work in partnership with parents and family members;
- the ability to prepare and present evidence in an appropriate way to courts/case conferences.

Such lists can at best only be signposts to the direction training should take. A number of writers (for example, Trowell, 1991a) have made detailed suggestions concerning what should be included in the curriculum, particularly in relation to child sexual abuse. However, a more useful approach at the advanced level may be to consider the complex processes involved in the role of child protection, and the kinds of knowledge and structures needed to address these. For example, in an article about the task of engaging in child protection work, based on a series of discussions with a group of experienced and competent specialist child protection practitioners, Archer and Whitaker (1992) set out the basis of a systematic approach to learning which focuses on those special demands and tasks which are experienced as both crucial to the work and particularly difficult, namely the need:

- to take action quickly, in the face of incomplete or contradictory information and without adequate time to reflect;
- to make the welfare of the child the prime consideration, but to help the family as well;
- to work effectively with other professionals when roles and locus of decision-making power are not clear or are differently understood;
- to do the best for the child, sometimes in the face of inadequate resources;
- to judge ahead of time the possibility of 'secondary abuse' and to take this into account when planning;
- to function effectively in court;
- to manage case conferences, and manage oneself in case conferences, often in an atmosphere of emergency, tension and powerful feelings; and
- to manage the feelings stirred up by the work.

Others might wish to modify this list, since in this rapidly changing area of practice concerns fluctuate, and it is important to be responsive to current preoccupations. At the time of writing, for example, other aspects of the child protection process such as conducting investigations are likely to stir up anxieties equal to those involved in participating in case conferences. However, what seems clear from this is that any training programme at post-qualifying level needs to take account not only of the core tasks of child protection – what Archer and Whitaker (1992, page 74) call the 'easily nameable and generally acknowledged parts of the task' – but also the less easily identified *processes* involved in undertaking these. These might include, in addition to those suggested above, the need to avoid mistakes, the need to recognise bias or learning disablement, and the need to avoid attracting adverse criticism from the media. In all this, the importance of developing a firm knowledge base, particularly through the recognition of the contributions from research, while at the same time encouraging the ability to undertake internal work in reflecting and in learning to manage stressful events, needs to be recognised.

To conclude this part of the chapter, it seems right and proper that training programmes should take many forms, in order to cater for the diverse needs of practitioners. Differences in the training needs of the professional groups, whose role and involvement in child protection will vary, need to be recognised. While short, in-house training, offered on a single or multi-professional basis, will be the appropriate forum in which to address some topics, there is also the need to provide sustained 'away-based' forms of training, so that practitioners can have the opportunity for the kinds of reflective work and sharing of concerns which the complexity of their task requires.

The Curriculum and Structure of Current 'Away-Based' Programmes: A Brief Review

The existing cohort of sustained, usually award-bearing programmes suggests a diversity of responses to the above dilemmas. Many, although not all, of the programmes currently provided have adopted a modular structure, with in many cases short, free-standing modules which can either be taken as discreet components or as part of a sustained programme leading to a formal qualification. Although some programmes, such as the post-qualifying diploma at Leicester University (the Msc/Diploma in Child Protection Studies), judging from their titles and content, maintain a child protection focus, others, such as that offered by the Tavistock Clinic, offer a programme in child care practice, policy and research. Another new programme, that at Bristol University, is described as an MSc in Child Welfare, and while covering many of the subject areas traditionally associated with child protection (such as direct work with children, inter-professional working, and new knowledge and research in child protection), it offers a module in early childhood services and accepts as credits units from the MSc in Gender and Social Policy and Education. Entry to the majority of the away-based programmes is restricted to those with a social work qualification, but a few, such as that at Bristol University, are open to other qualified practitioners.

A programme which aims to offer students the advanced award will have to demonstrate, to the satisfaction of the local consortium, how the different elements of the programme contribute to the attainment of the required competences listed in Paper 31 (CCETSW, 1992). It should be noted that a number of these competences make reference to particular areas of practice, and those designing programmes need to look carefully at the relationship between practice and academic learning in their programmes.

The extent to which programmes involve a practice component, and the ways in which this is assessed and supervised, also varies considerably. Current thinking (for example, by the East Pennine Consortium) suggests that practice need not form an integral element of a Masters programme. However, programme providers must demonstrate how taught elements and assessment are integrated with past, current or future practice. Of the nine post-qualifying child protection programmes looked at in a recent (unpublished) survey, one programme had no practice component. In two courses, up to 50% of the time is spent in practice. Other courses require students to accumulate the practice experience necessary to complete the course assignments.

To take one example, in the programme offered by Huddersfield University, a postgraduate certificate is awarded on successful completion of four core modules (policy and organisational contexts of child protection, the legal framework, assessment and planning, and interventions), all offered in the first two semesters. The diploma is awarded on successful completion of the certificate modules, plus either a practice module or a module involving an analysis of decision-making processes or social research and evaluation. The practice component is undertaken in a combination of the students' own work setting, a setting similar to their own, and a work setting different to their own. They are supported in their practice by a mentor, and assessment is by means of a portfolio, which includes one piece of 'live' evidence and examples of the students' work in different aspects of child protection.

One feature common to a number of child protection programmes is the use of practice consultants or supervisors to oversee the practice components of the course and, in some cases, to produce a report on the student's practice. The CCETSW requires the local consortia to provide a mentor or consultant whose primary task is to guide a candidate on their route through the post-qualifying system (CCETSW, 1992, 4.6.1). Mentors will also advise candidates on the compilation of the portfolio, which has to be presented when the necessary 120 credits have been accumulated. It is not clear whether a mentor's role could also extend to supervising the practice element of a programme, or indeed where the numbers of mentors necessary will come from, given that there is to date no established scheme for training them.

Specific Dimensions of Training

I have argued thus far that training in child protection at post-qualifying level must not only provide opportunities for updating and amplifying knowledge, and the development of a range of skills, but must also allow opportunities for what Jones in her earlier chapter calls reflected-on understanding, i.e. theoretical knowledge *and* the ability to articulate the principles and psychological processes which are informing the practitioner's management of a case. In meeting these diverse training needs, a variety of structures is required. Programmes cannot attempt to address the whole range of knowledge required for training, and some specialisation is not only inevitable but appropriate. However, the argument for some training which emphasises the necessity for the development of internal skills and reflection on judgements and attitudes, made in the two earlier chapters in this section as well as here, seems overwhelming. In the second part of this chapter, therefore, three components of training which may be fruitful in encouraging this are considered in more detail. While recognising that not all programmes can or should provide these, we include them as exemplars of the kind of advanced level training that we have in mind.

Child observation

The inclusion of periods of observing infants and young children in training courses for many of the helping professions is not unusual. Many training courses include brief observation and the study of an individual child as part of the curriculum, and more recently CCETSW has supported initiatives designed to encourage the inclusion of a period of child observation in training programmes for social workers.

Such observation may be undertaken for different reasons, and hence require different structures to achieve these objectives. Tough (1978), for example, discusses the kinds of observations which trainee psychologists make in order to develop skills in conducting cognitive tests, and her model, which involves observing a particular child on one or two occasions, may have some relevance to social workers and other care workers. The requirement, for example, to apply the Sheridan developmental checklist (Department of Health, 1988) to a child, or to conduct a simple cognitive test, may be useful in reinforcing students' knowledge of child development and their ability to interpret information and assessments made by other professionals.

However, a number of post-qualifying courses have introduced a sustained period of observation as a component, seeing this as a means of helping students to address some of the more elusive concerns over their role in relation to working with complex and often painful material, which earlier chapters in this section have highlighted. The model adopted is derived from that developed at the Tavistock Clinic, where infant observation was introduced initially in training courses for child psychotherapists. The model has subsequently been modified to take account of the different training needs and availability of other professionals. Students are asked to observe an infant or young child in interaction with his or her carer(s) over a period of some weeks, and to present their observations for discussion at a weekly seminar group. (A detailed discussion of the format of the model is given in Wilson, 1992, and Trowell and Miles, 1991, to which the reader is referred.) Unlike those described, for example, by Tough (1978), the observations are relatively unstructured and emphasise the interplay between what is being observed and the observer's reactions to it.

Although Trowell suggests that infant observation (i.e. of a child under 12 months) provides a more intense experience and a greater opportunity to develop the capacity to observe and record, she notes that the alternative young child observation may be 'more manageable and less disturbing to the observer.' (1991*b*, page 99.)

The hour-long observations are recorded from memory afterwards, experience so far suggesting that the effort involved in recalling and trying to put into words feelings and communications is an important part of developing the skill of observing. Students are encouraged to be literal and factual in their accounts, recording in as much detail as possible the child's activities, verbal and non-verbal exchanges between the child and other people present, and the feelings of the observer, so that the seminar group is able to consider the evidence from the observation before it is interpreted in more abstract, theoretical terms.

What can be learnt from such observation? First, those skills relating to 'stance', which I take to be an issue in all assessment and therapeutic work. By this I mean the ability to become involved and engaged in what the other person is feeling and experiencing sufficiently to be able to recognise those feelings, while at the same time retaining enough detachment to reflect on what one is observing. The capacity to be able to recognise the emotional interactions of those one is observing, to be aware of one's own emotions and to differentiate between the two is crucial here. Being aware of one's own responses as an invaluable source of data, and learning to recognise what comes from oneself and what comes from the observed person is a crucial part of any assessment. Observation can help develop the capacity to integrate these and reflect on feelings and observations before making judgements and decisions. Rustin (1989), discussing the rationale for devoting so much training time to the activity of observation, underlines the learning which takes place from recognising one's own personal response to the observation:

> 'In this latter category are the issues of how one finds a place for oneself in the family during visits, one's identification with different members of the family, one's response to anxiety and uncertainty and a large measure of helplessness, and one's exposure to some of one's own personal problems as a consequence of the impact of the observations.' (Rustin, 1989, page 8).

This point, concerning the opportunity offered by observation to learn to handle personal feelings which may be aroused by having to work with acutely painful situations is elaborated by Trowell and Miles (1991), who discuss the sometimes difficult experiences generated by the observations:

> 'It is extremely difficult to bear such pain or the associated feelings that might be stirred by what is seen from the worker's own past experience. Action can so easily take over as a way of avoiding the impact of what is seen, if it can be seen at all. Observation training, with its supporting seminars, gives the opportunity to reflect on the experience, and to understand and tolerate the emotional impact.' (1991, page 53.)

Second, and related to this, observation provides the opportunity to practise the skill of observing the child, while at the same time sustaining contact with the child's carers or other adults present. Learning to be appropriately responsive, yet avoiding being drawn into giving advice or acting, is one means of developing the ability to maintain a focus on the child, while being alert to the interaction between the child and family members.

Third, it provides an opportunity to sharpen observation skills. This includes learning to differentiate between observation, hypothesis and assessment; the importance of not prejudging situations; and the readiness to modify first impressions. Freed, in systematic observation, from the pressure to make decisions, the observer can be given time to see what is happening, to experience the interaction between the child and care giver, and to revise first impressions in the light of new information. The expectation is, and it is one on which much training in the personal social services is based, that learning derived from work undertaken in protected 'laboratory' conditions may be generalised to more typical working situations.

Observation, then, can provide the opportunity to address many of the concerns outlined in earlier chapters, i.e. the capacity to be integrative and reflective, to register non-verbal as well as verbal communications, to learn to participate as well as observe, and to be aware of one's own personal responses and projections. Although these may be regarded as key learning points, there are in addition a range of subsidiary issues which may be drawn out in discussing and analysing the observations within the seminar group. Thus, the students' knowledge of attachment theory and behaviour; systems perspectives; child development; psychodynamic and cognitive perspectives; and issues of gender, race and culture can be developed through the pooling of different observation experiences within the group. This kind of inductive learning is useful, in that it involves the application to practice of theoretical knowledge. Its effectiveness does, of course, depend on the competence of the seminar leader, whose knowledge and skill in attending to the different levels of learning in the group, which observation training requires, are crucial to its success.

Partnership

The notion of partnership is central to the Children Act 1989, and the intention is that it should permeate all aspects of practice. All training programmes aimed at promoting ways of working in partnership with families need to take account of the power relationships within families, between professionals and family members, and amongst members of the multi-disciplinary professional group. These relationships can be analysed at both a structural and interpersonal level. This section seeks to offer a framework for analysing the process of partnership, and is based on an earlier paper on partnership with parents (Jones, 1994).

The accompanying guidance on the Children Act 1989 acknowledges the structural factors which impinge on the lives of children and families, and links partnership with anti-racist and anti-discriminatory practice (Department of Health, 1989). However, Phillipson (1992) argues that the concept of oppression, rather than discrimination, is more helpful when it comes to analysing structural and interpersonal power relationships. Seeking to combat oppression requires a fundamental revision of a person's values, their personal and professional relationships, and the nature of institutions, whilst anti-discriminatory practice is characterised by a more reformist practice of challenging unfairness and injustice.

To 'oppress' means 'to overwhelm with superior weight or numbers or irresistible power; lie heavy on, weigh down . . . [with reference to the spirits or imagination of a person]; govern tyrannically, keep under by coercion, subject to continual cruelty or injustice' (*The Concise Oxford English Dictionary*, page 50). Concepts such as domination and subordination become important tools when the different dimensions of oppression affecting individual's lives are analysed. As Collins (1990), an African-American feminist, says:

> 'Although most individuals have little difficulty identifying their own victimisation within some major system of oppression . . . they typically fail to see how their thoughts and actions uphold somebody else's subordination . . . Each individual derives varying amounts of penalty and privilege from the multiple systems of oppression which frame everybody's lives.' (Collins, 1990, page 229.)

Thus, it is important to understand how these 'multiple systems of oppression' affect individuals. A framework which addresses the interlocking nature of oppression helps remind us of the experience of 'the other', and the ways in which we might share some dimensions of oppression, but differ in others. Each individual's experience of the interlocking nature of oppression is unique, and an understanding of one type of oppression cannot be substituted for another. Oppression may be experienced along a number of dimensions, and characteristics of those in the dominant and subordinate groups in British society are shown in Table 27.1.

Professionals working in the field of child care and child protection need to acquire an understanding of their own 'matrix of domination' (Collins, 1990, page 229) using a framework such as that outlined in Table 27.1. In this way, they can begin to understand their own unique configuration of the different dimensions of oppression,

Table 27.1 *Dominant and subordinate groups in British society.*

Division	Dominant group	Subordinate group
Race	white	non-white and divisions within
Language	'Queen's English'	non-English regional
Religion	Christianity	non-Christian or fringe Christian and strongly held religious beliefs
Class	social classes 1–3 ownership of wealth	social classes 4–5 lack of wealth
Employment status	professional/managerial	unskilled workers unwaged and unemployed people children
Sexual orientation	heterosexual	homosexual bi-sexual
Age	25–35 years	children and young adults people aged 40 + years
Gender	men	women
Ability/health	able-bodied fit, slim intellect those with access to better education	people with disabilities and learning difficulties people with mental illness those without access to better education

their capacity to dominate and to be victimised depending upon their relationships with others, be they parents, children or other professionals.

Using such a framework as a way of analysing different 'matrices of domination' is an essential first step in power-sharing. If professionals understand their position, they can use their power to empower rather than disempower parents and children; to help understand the powerlessness of vulnerable young children in families where a patriarchal head silences them and their mother; and to recognise those situations where they may need support from other professionals, for example, at a case conference, where there are differences amongst those involved. The status of the supporting professionals is important here.

An intellectual and emotional understanding of the structural and interpersonal dimensions of oppression is essential for any practitioner who is serious about working in partnership with children, parents and other professionals. Through such a framework, practitioners become attuned to the process of partnership, where seemingly minute but informed choices given to service users can begin to equalise the power differentials between people with very different 'matrices of domination'. At the same time, the dangers of collusive, as distinct from anti-oppressive practice, can be addressed where, for example, a worker attempting to practise in an anti-oppressive way over-identifies with a service user because they are of the same gender or ethnic origin, or because they fear being labelled as 'racist', 'sexist' or 'heterosexist' if they remove an abused and neglected child from a parent who is unable to look after their child.

Partnership and anti-oppressive practice are the foundation of good child care and child protection practice. Training programmes need to address these principles at the outset, after group ground rules have been discussed and agreed. Opportunities to analyse power relationships in practice can be created in a variety of ways, for example, by analysing case conference dynamics from part of a videotape (Roberts and Will, 1989) or from an inquiry, such as the first case conference held on Jasmine Beckford in 1981 (London Borough of Brent, 1985). Students' own case material frequently provides excellent examples of power relationships amongst professionals, and between them and family members. Videotaped, small group role-plays of critical incidents can be analysed by the whole group in a plenary session. Finally, locally produced practice guides, such as the account of an investigation into organised abuse written by the Poplar Project team (London Borough of Tower Hamlets, 1991) or the Castle Hill School investigation (Brannan et al., 1993; Jones, 1993), provide valuable material for discussion on oppression, disempowerment and strategies for empowerment.

By developing opportunities to analyse dimensions of oppression, and by recognising their own capacity for domination and victimisation, lecturers and students, trainers and participants, can begin to appreciate the dual processes of partnership in education and training, and in practice. The education and training climate needs to offer support and informed choice to rejuvenate and empower those who are faced with the day-to-day practical and emotional demands of supporting parents and protecting children in situations which are frequently characterised by poverty, limited resources and a lack of preventive services.

Supervision

There is a large and developing literature on supervision in the helping professions, and it is beyond the scope of this chapter to do justice to the myriad issues raised in it, not least because many of these concern the different internal organisational and assessment structures in training in the different professions. In many respects, however, the practice component may form the key to what the student gains from the training programme, in that it can be the point at which he or she is helped as an individual to integrate and to put into practice what has been learned, and to identify areas in his or her practice which still need to be developed. It is therefore clearly essential that programmes give some thought to what they are trying to achieve in the practice component, to the role of supervision within this, to the structures that are most likely to achieve these goals, and that they anticipate some of the dilemmas that may arise in the process.

Kadushin (1976), writing some years ago about supervision in social work, suggested that supervision can be seen, broadly speaking, as having three functions: namely, educative, supportive and managerial. The educative function is principally concerned with developing the knowledge, understanding and skill of the student in relation to his or her intervention with clients. The supportive function is, as Hawkins and Shohet (1992) suggest, a way

> 'of responding to how any workers who are engaged in intimate therapeutic work with clients are necessarily allowing themselves to be affected by the distress, pain and fragmentation of the client'

and providing them with necessary time 'to become aware of how this has affected them and to deal with any emotions . . . which may have been produced through empathy with the client or restimulated by the client, or by a reaction to the client.' (Hawkins and Shohet, 1992, page 42.)

And thirdly, the managerial function is concerned to ensure that policies and procedures are adhered to, appropriate planning decisions are made, resources utilised and overall a proper standard of work is achieved on the agency's behalf. Under these broad headings, a range of specific tasks for the supervision session may be identified.

There is clearly a considerable overlap between these different functions, and the extent to which they are given prominence in a supervisory context will vary. Supervision in a setting which provides counselling for adult survivors of abuse, for example, will largely have an educative and supportive focus. Here, the relationship between agency, supervisee and the programme may be a relatively straightforward one. Nonetheless, problems of ensuring adequate standards in supervision are considerable. In social work, nurse and teacher training, considerable effort has gone into developing supervisory (or practice teaching) skills at qualifying level, but, particularly in social work, the problem of finding appropriate supervised placements is endemic. The difficulties in finding placements at post-qualifying level have barely begun to be addressed, and it is partly for this reason that some programmes have adopted systems which attempt to circumvent problems of the availability and suitability of supervisors (see below). A further problem, particularly in conducting multi-disciplinary training, lies in the very different traditions of supervision among the different professions. Health visitor students on the programme, for example, at the University of Hull reported that they rarely received any form of managerial supervision, let alone supervision with the kind of educative and supportive focus suggested here.

Experience on this post-qualifying, multi-disciplinary programme in child protection suggests, however, that it is the second, supportive function which constitutes the greatest unmet need among practitioners. Partly because of the problems suggested above, meeting this need is not always straightforward. In addition, as in all supervision, there is a boundary to be maintained, in matters concerning the emotional impact of the job, between supervision and counselling/therapy. It is important in supervision to remain focused on work issues, and to consider personal matters only when they are having a direct impact on the work discussed or are affecting the supervisory relationship. Where it appears that the issues are more than can be appropriately dealt with in supervision, the supervisor may encourage the practitioner to seek some form of counselling or therapeutic help.

Most training programmes for therapists and counsellors stipulate that trainees undertake some form of personal supervision as a requirement of the course. As Aveline (1993) suggests,

> 'It brings together theoretical learning and psychotherapy practice in an experience that makes personal sense of the two . . . [and] provides a means through which sufficient self-understanding can be gained for therapists to recognise how their personality and life experience affect their ability to be objective and to reduce their tendency to impose their own solutions on the life problems of their patients'. (Aveline, 1993, page 334.)

Training programmes do, however, need to give some thought to issues of confidentiality between programme, supervisor and trainee, since it is possible that serious doubts may arise as to the trainee's suitability for the profession. It may be appropriate, for example, for the programme as a requirement of the course to seek confirmation from the supervisor at the end of counselling that nothing has emerged in therapy which gives grounds for doubting the trainee's safety in undertaking a child protection role.

In contrast to training for counselling and therapy, child protection programmes rarely, if ever, stipulate that students should undergo a period of personal counselling. This presumably reflects a split which is developing between the statutory child protection work undertaken by social workers and to some extent health workers, and therapeutic work undertaken by practitioners in such settings as family centres, who may have undergone a variety of forms of initial training. (The case against this apparent erosion of the traditional involvement by social workers in practice of a therapeutic or counselling nature has been set out elsewhere; Cigno and Wilson, 1994.) Nonetheless, the arguments for a requirement by child protection programmes that participants should undergo some form of personal counselling seem as compelling as those put forward for trainee therapists.

The managerial function of supervision in child protection programmes is also complex. In child protection settings, there will always be an issue about who has managerial responsibility for the student's workload, and insofar as any supervision inevitably involves some element of quality control, how these shared responsibilities are worked out. The experience on one programme suggests that in order for the educative and supportive functions to be given sufficient prominence in supervision, it is important for the formal management role and the supportive/educative role to be split. It was therefore stipulated that the student's line manager should not also act as the student's practice supervisor on the programme. Although this division did usually ensure that supervision gave proper emphasis to the student's overall professional development and learning, problems occasionally arose when the views of manager and supervisor over the conduct of a case diverged. Such difficulties could be compounded in the transactions between student, manager, supervisor and programme, as the following example of problems to be negotiated illustrates.

> A qualified and experienced child protection worker, based in a busy urban social services department, was supervised for the practice component of the child protection programme by a senior practitioner from another social work agency. The student presented as part of her portfolio to the assessment board a complex case in which two children, who had experienced a number of incidents of maltreatment and neglect and whose younger sibling had died in unexplained circumstances, continued to remain with their mentally ill mother, despite the latter's unwillingness or inability to co-operate in any treatment programme. The student's line manager had assessed the case and decided that there were insufficient grounds for removing the children, and that they should remain with their mother under a voluntary agreement, with the student continuing to act as key worker and to offer support. The student's supervisor had expressed disquiet at the care plan, but had felt she did not have the authority to go further. The assessment board did not consider that sufficient recognition had been given to the serious risks to the children which seemed apparent in the case presentation and thought that the student had, at the very least, failed to document and bring to the line manager's attention the continuing concerns that she felt about the children's welfare. Although the board was mindful of the fact that managerial responsibility for the case did not lie with the student, it nonetheless felt unable to pass her on the evidence offered.

Models of supervision

From an informal review of current post-qualifying programmes, it is clear that there are a variety of models through which programmes address the development of the student's practice learning. At one end of the continuum, a programme may exclude any formal component of assessed practice and rely on case discussion within the educational setting as the means of helping the student to develop his or her practice. Another model is one where the student, usually working with the help of a mentor who offers advice and a varying degree of supervision of practice, develops a portfolio of work which is presented for assessment by the programme providers as part of the requirement for the award. Examples of practice may be stipulated, may be presented in written or recorded form, and may include such things as an account of an investigation, a court report, a risk assessment or a piece of direct work with a child. Alternatively, the model more traditionally associated with social work qualifying programmes may be adopted, with a supervisor who completes an assessment of the student's practice for the programme, and the student practitioner undertaking part of the practice component in an agency other than his or her own.

Finally, the model at the University of Hull was one in which part of the practice component was supervised directly by staff engaged by the programme expressly for the purpose. Students could opt to undertake a piece of direct practice involving one of three approaches: non-directive play therapy, family therapy and behavioural work, and were offered a specified number of supervision sessions on this. The model has considerable advantages, in that it provides supervision of a consistent quality by practitioners who are expert in the approach, and it provides the students with the experience, unusual to the majority of them, of detailed, systematic discussion of their practice. Particularly in the supervision of play therapy, core aspects of the student's personal style and approach (for example, a difficulty in setting limits, an inability to 'stay with' a child's emotional stress) emerged rapidly and could, where appropriate, be worked on elsewhere. The model has certain disadvantages, in being more complex and expensive administratively than other 'arm's length' styles of supervision.

Conclusion

This chapter has provided an overview of some of the main issues which need to be addressed in designing training for child protection work, particularly at post-qualifying level. Although it has focused in detail on the framework currently being devised for the social work profession, many of the concerns arising from changes in the provision of training in higher education and post-qualifying training have implications for all the helping professions, and the discussion reflects this. This chapter has emphasised, as earlier chapters in this section of the *Handbook* have done, the need for training which does more than deal with the easily identifiable components of the child protection role, and which allows for opportunities to address some of the complex and sensitive issues which arise for the practitioner in this difficult and often painful work.

Substantial regroupings in the delivery of services by the helping professions are underway, which means that the traditional links between professional qualification and task no longer pertain, and that the appropriateness of the basic social work qualification for many of those activities hitherto undertaken by professional social workers is being questioned. Changes in professional training to reflect these shifts are also inevitable, and a chapter such as this can only provide a snapshot of the field as it appears at a particular time. Whoever undertakes it, however, the core task of providing a sensitive and non-judgemental service to children and families in distress remains. So, therefore, does the need for the effective training of those providing the service.

Acknowledgements

Particular thanks to the students on the 1993–94 Leicester University Diploma in Child Protection Studies programme who developed Table 27.1 as part of their coursework.

Further Reading

CCETSW has published a range of papers which consider the training requirements for all social workers, and for those whose area of particular practice is child care. Paper 30 (1989), which set out the regulations for the new diploma in social work, is currently being revised. Paper 31 (1992) sets out the framework for the post-qualifying and advanced qualification. Of the remainder, probably the most useful include:

Central Council for Education and Training in Social Work (1991). *The Teaching of Child Care in the Diploma in Social Work: Guidance Notes for Programme Planners*. London: CCETSW.
This delineates the course content and competencies which might be expected at qualifying level for social workers, but it stresses that much further work is needed after qualification in order to perform adequately in child care. There are additional commissioned papers, including a useful one by Rushton and Berelowitz on the teaching of child development to diploma students, which also provides helpful suggestions for further reading.

Pietroni, M. (ed.) (1991). *Right or Privilege*. London: CCETSW.
This is a collection of papers produced by a working group drawn from a range of professions, set up to consider post-qualifying training. It considers models of post-qualifying training for the different professions, and a number of papers make detailed suggestions for the design of individual components of a training programme, including race training, training in the use of law, and inter-professional and inter-agency work.

Few, if any, of the major texts on child abuse cover issues of training in much detail. Training for therapeutic work receives more attention, and discussion on this includes:

Dryden, W. & Feltham, C. (1994). *Developing Counsellor Training*. London: Sage.
This provides guidelines for those involved in the planning, implementation and evaluation of counsellor training programmes.

There are a number of books on supervision, including the following, which addresses supervision both from the point of view of supervisor and supervisee, at a level which is useful for those in a range of helping professions:

Hawkins, P. & Shonet, R. (1992). *Supervision in the Helping Professions*. Milton Keynes: Open University Press.

Although the following was written to address issues of gender oppression for social work students, its contribution to the wider debate around the concepts of discrimination and oppression is invaluable. It is essential reading for trainers who want to understand the meaning of anti-oppressive practice, and how to integrate it throughout their training. A particular strength is the author's references to black writings and literature:

Phillipson, J. (1992). *Practising Equality: Women, Men and Social Work*. London: Central Council for Education and Training in Social Work.

References

Archer, L. & Whitaker, D. (1992). Decisions, tasks and uncertainties in child protection work. *Journal of Social Work Practice 6(1): 63–76*.

Aveline, M. (1993). The training and supervision of individual therapists. In W. Dryden (ed.): *Individual Therapy*, pages 313–339. Milton Keynes: Open University Press.

Brannan, C., Jones, J. & Murch, M. (1993). *Castle Hill Report: Practice Guide*. Shrewsbury: Shrewsbury County Council.

Butler-Sloss, Lord Justice (1988). *Report of the Inquiry into Child Abuse in Cleveland, 1987*. Cm. 412. London: HMSO.

Central Council for Education and Training in Social Work (1991). *The Teaching of Child Care in the Diploma in Social Work: Guidance Notes for Programme Planners*. London: CCETSW.

CCETSW (1991b) *Rules and Requirements for the Diploma in Social Work (Paper 30)*. Second Edition. London: CCETSW.

Central Council for Education and Training in Social Work (1992). *The Requirements for Post-Qualifying Education and Training in the Personal Social Services*, 2nd edn. Paper 31. London: CCETSW.

Cigno, K. & Wilson, K. (1994). Effective strategies for working with children and families: issues in the provision of therapeutic help. *Practice 6(4): 285–298*.

CNAA (1989). *Going Modular: Information Services Discussion*. Paper 2. London: Council for National Academic Awards.

Collins, P. (1990). *Black Feminist Thought: Knowledge, Consciousness and the Politics of Empowerment*. New York and London: Routledge.

Department of Health (1988). *Protecting Children: A Guide for Social Workers Undertaking a Comprehensive Assessment*. London: HMSO.

Department of Health (1989). *The Care of Children: Principles and Practice in Regulations and Guidance*. London: HMSO.

English National Board for Nursing, Midwifery and Health Visiting (1994). *Training and Evaluation Initiative: To Develop a Model of Shared Teaching and Learning within Child Protection Courses*. Research highlights. London: ENB.

Hawkins, P. & Shohet, R. (1992). *Supervision in the Helping Professions*. Milton Keynes: Open University Press.

Jones, J. (1993). Child abuse: developing a framework for understanding power relationships in practice. In H. Ferguson, R. Gilligan & R. Torode (eds): *Surviving Childhood Adversity: Issues for Policy and Practice*. Dublin: Social Studies Press.

Jones, J. (1994). Child protection and anti-oppressive practice: the dynamics of partnership with parents explored. *Early Child Development and Care 102: 101–113*.

Kadushin, A. (1976). *Supervision in Social Work*. New York: Columbia University Press.

Knowles, M. (1978). *The Adult Learner: A Neglected Species*, 2nd edn. London: Gulf Publishing.

London Borough of Brent (1985). *A Child in Trust: The Report of the Panel of Inquiry into the Circumstances Surrounding the Death of Jasmine Beckford*. London: London Borough of Brent.

London Borough of Tower Hamlets (1991). *Poplar Project: A Social Work Team's Account of its Work with a Group of Sexually Abused Young People*. London: London Borough of Tower Hamlets.

Parton, N. (1991). *Governing the Family: Child Care, Child Protection and the State*. London: Macmillan.

Phillipson, J. (1992). *Practising Equality: Women, Men and Social Work*. London: Central Council for Education and Training in Social Work.

Roberts, J. & Will, D. (1989). *Case Conference Dynamics*. Edinburgh: MacMed Videos.

Rushton, A. & Martyn, H. (1993). *Learning for Advanced Practice: A Study of Away-Based Training*. Paper 31. London: CCETSW.

Rustin, M. (1989). Encountering primitive anxieties. In L. Miller, M. Rustin, M. Rustin & J. Shuttleworth (eds): *Closely Observed Infants*. London: Duckworth.

Social Services Inspectorate (1994). *Training Spending under the Training Support Act: A Report on Targets and Achievements, 1992/3*. London: Social Services Inspectorate.

Stevenson, O. (1988). Multi-disciplinary work – where next? *Child Abuse Review 2(1): 5–9*.

Tough, J. (1978). *Listening to Children Talking*. London: Warde Locke.

Trowell, J. (1991a). Teaching about child sexual abuse. In M. Pietroni (ed.): *Right or Privilege*. London: CCETSW.

Trowell, J. (1991*b*). Use of observational skills in social work training. In M. Pietroni (ed.): *Right or Privilege*. London: CCETSW.

Trowell, J. & Miles, G. (1991). The contribution of observation training to professional development. *Journal of Social Work Practice 5(1):* 51–60.

Wilson, K. (1992). The place of observation in social work training. *Journal of Social Work Practice 6(1):* 37–48.

Wilson, K. & Bradley, G. (1994). New challenges in social work education. *Social Work Education 13(2):* 5–24.

28

Taking Stock: Past Developments and Future Directions in Child Protection

Christine Hallett

Knowledge of Child Abuse

This volume is a reflection of the increase in knowledge concerning child abuse which has characterised the three decades following the 'rediscovery' of the problem associated with Kempe's influential article (1962). As Harris notes in Chapter 2, definitions of child abuse are historically and culturally specific, and recent years have witnessed a widening of the term from physical injury to encompass emotional abuse, neglect, sexual abuse and, more recently, organised and ritualistic abuse. While there has also been a concern with both the secondary victimisation of children in forms of substitute care and abuse by strangers, the main focus has been upon intrafamilial abuse.

Broader definitions of the kind offered by Gil that,

> 'abuse of children is human-originated acts of commission or omission and human-created or tolerated conditions that inhibit or preclude unfolding and developing of the inherent potential of children' (Gil, 1981, page 295.)

are rejected in public policy and professional practice. The wide-ranging radical agenda of social reform inherent in such a definition is eschewed in favour of a focus mainly on intrafamilial behaviour.

Incidence and Prevalence

Acknowledging the formidable methodological difficulties posed, *inter alia*, by changing definitions and non-comparable samples, Creighton reviews, in Chapter 1, data concerning the incidence and prevalence of different forms of child abuse. The registration data, derived from National Society for the Prevention of Cruelty to Children (NSPCC) studies and the statistics collected and published by the Department of Health (DOH), yield useful information about matters such as the types of abuse suffered by children, and the gender and age of victims, at least in respect of those cases which come to the knowledge of official agencies and meet the criteria for registration.

Remaining Uncertainties

Despite some advances in knowledge, much remains to be done in furthering an understanding of the causes, manifestations and consequences of child abuse. Particularly important is an exploration of the interplay between the structural and the personal. There is a need for better understanding of the link between social conditions, for example, poverty and stress or patterns of male socialisation experienced by many, which may engender child abuse, and the specific factors of circumstance or personality which lead some people to abuse children and, just as important, which prevent others, similarly placed, from so doing.

Frosh, in Chapter 4, explores these issues with specific reference to child sex abusers, noting the limitations in current knowledge and the heterogeneity amongst abusers. He concludes that there are no simple typologies for classifying sex abusers. The conclusions presented are appropriately tentative and equivocal.

The need for caution and specificity which Frosh displays with respect to sex abusers can usefully be extended to child abuse generally. The term, as it is currently used in societies such as ours, encompasses varied behaviours with differing degrees of severity and varied outcomes in the short and long term for those who are abused. Since child abuse is not a tightly delineated medical syndrome (Richards, 1975), it should not be expected that the causes of abuse or the characteristics of abusers can be universally and clearly discerned. There is an urgent need for disaggregation of the term 'child abuse' and for more limited, specific studies of the nature, cause and consequences and the many differentiated behaviours encompassed by the term 'child abuse'.

Developments in Child Protection Policy

In the United Kingdom, the last 20 years have seen the development and implementation of inter-agency policy machinery for the management of child abuse. Although it built upon existing local initiatives and a previous circular (Department of Health and Social Security (DHSS), 1972) which recommended the establishment of multi-agency committees (Area Review Committees), an important circular entitled *Non-Accidental Injury to Children* was issued in 1974 (DHSS, 1974a) following the Maria Colwell inquiry (DHSS, 1974b). This outlined more fully the role and functions of Area Review Committees and recommended the setting up of local registers of abused children and the holding of multi-disciplinary case conferences for all cases of child abuse. Since then, the vocabulary has developed and changed, as have some aspects of policy, notably in response to child sexual abuse, but there has been a marked degree of policy continuity in the machinery of child protection with the perpetuation of local procedural guidelines, child protection registers, area child protection committees and child protection conferences.

Aspects of the child protection process are explored in this volume, for example, assessment (Adcock, Chapter 10), inter-professional co-operation (Corby, Chapter 11), child protection conferences (Stevenson, Chapter 12) and the role of the courts (Lane and Walsh, Chapter 14) and of the guardian *ad litem* (Head, Chapter 15). Other studies, particularly some of those sponsored by the Department of Health programme of research into child abuse, have also shed considerable light on the child protection process, notably studies of referral and registration (Gibbons *et al.*, 1995), family involvement (Thoburn *et al.*, 1995), decision-making and outcome (Farmer and Owen, 1995) and inter-agency co-ordination (Birchall, 1995; Hallett and Birchall, 1992; Hallett, 1995).

The policies and procedures have institutionalised a relatively clear division of labour in child protection and established mechanisms for inter-agency referral, investigation, registration, the exchange and appraisal of information in child protection conferences, assessment and (albeit with some difficulty) parental participation. There is a widespread recognition of the need for a multi-disciplinary response to child abuse which aggregates the skills and knowledge of a variety of different professions. While aspects of this system are criticised in this volume and elsewhere, Farmer and Owen (1995) found that a high proportion (70%) of the children in their study were protected.

Children's Rights

There have also been important developments in respect of the rights of children. All systems of child protection involve striking a balance between the rights, duties and responsibilities of parents, the rights, needs and wishes of children, and the role of the State in mediating and intervening between these. The balance between these shifts over time and, as Harris suggests in Chapter 2, there are no final resolutions of the potential and actual conflicts. In British child care policy in recent years the pendulum has swung between a child rescue orientation associated with planning for permanence described by Fox Harding (1991) as 'state paternalism and child protection' (exemplified in the 1975 Children Act), and a greater emphasis on voluntarism and the support of parents enshrined in the Children Act 1989.

Alongside these pendulum shifts, there has been a growing concern with children's rights. This is part of a process of the disaggregation of the family unit in which women, and subsequently children, have come to be viewed as having some rights as individuals in contrast to their previous patriarchal subordination to the interests of the 'paterfamilias'.

One variant of this is the child liberation movement, which is summarised well by Fox Harding (1991). Essentially, according to authors such as Holt (1975) this postulates that adults and the State adopt a patronising and authoritarian approach to children which fundamentally undermines the civil rights and freedom of children and underestimates their capacity for self-direction and responsibility. British child protection practice has not endorsed such views. However, varied developments, including the United Nations Charter of Children's Rights and the observations of the Cleveland report (Cm 412, 1988) that the child is a person and not the object of concern, have contributed to a reappraisal of the position of the child in child protection policy and practice. This is reflected in the Children Act 1989, with its emphasis on ascertaining and taking account of the wishes and feelings of the child. The issue is explored in this volume, for example, in relation to assessment, individual work with children and out-of-home placements.

Developments in Knowledge for Practice

This volume testifies to the significant advances in knowledge for practice available to practitioners in child protection. As Thoburn convincingly argues in Chapter 24 with reference to out-of-home care for the abused or neglected child, there is a need to avoid dogmatism and the over-simplification of research findings, which must be appraised with care in respect of each unique child's needs and circumstances. Nonetheless, there is a body of knowledge to underpin child protection practice. Some, as Thoburn (Chapter 24) and Crompton (Chapter 18) suggest, is not new but is a restatement of fundamental principles of working imaginatively and sensitively with individual children. In addition, there is a growing practice literature of specific relevance to child protection, particularly for the early phases of the construction of a case of child abuse. It is exemplified in this volume in accounts of assessment (Adcock, Chapter 10), inter-professional work (Corby, Chapter 11) and initial child protection conferences (Stevenson, Chapter 12). It provides a stark contrast with the level of knowledge, not only of practice but also of child abuse, available at the time of the Maria Colwell inquiry in 1973. Considerable progress has been made. For the practitioner, the knowledge explosion is both a support and a snare; a support in that there are principles and practices to guide work in child protection, and a snare in that social workers can reasonably be expected to be familiar with such knowledge. Yet, as a profession, social work is not marked by the production or consumption of research by practitioners, nor by well-developed schemes of post-qualifying training and professional updating. The difficulties of acquiring such knowledge in a 2-year training, which is still largely generic, have long been pointed out, in vain, not only by social work educators and the CCETSW but also by inquiries into child protection cases, notably that of Kimberly Carlile (London Borough of Greenwich, 1987) and the Clyde report into events in Orkney (Clyde, 1992).

Future Directions

Thus far, this chapter has suggested that there have been significant developments in knowledge, policy and practice concerning child abuse. These have occurred over a relatively short space of time and have transformed child welfare in the United Kingdom and elsewhere. One important future direction was signalled at the beginning of the chapter: namely, the need for the disaggregation of the term 'child abuse' and, in a post-modern context, the need for the abandonment of the search for grand causes in favour of more modest and specific endeavours.

Three other future directions seem particularly important. The first centres on the future role of the police, which is itself part of the wider issue of the dominance of socio-medical or legal discourse in child protection. One of the most significant developments in child protection practice in recent years, associated particularly with increased public and professional recognition of the problem of child sexual abuse, has been a shift, characterised by Parton (1991), from a socio-medical to a socio-legal discourse. The police are now inscribed at the heart of the process by which cases come to be labelled as child abuse cases. As Harris notes in Chapter 2, the changed responses of the police to the problem have fundamentally altered the relationship between the police and social workers, exemplified by their collaboration in the initial investigation which Harris describes as 'that truly remarkable activity, the "joint investigation" '.

This is a profound transformation from the position existing in the 1970s. The shift is evident from a comparison of the current policy concerning the role of the police as set out in *Working Together* (Home Office *et al.*, 1991) with the guidance contained in the 1974 circular of guidance (DHSS, 1974*a*). This latter listed professions and agencies which 'a case conference should normally include' as follows:

a. persons having statutory responsibilities for the continuing care of the child, e.g. the appropriate senior member of the social services department, the consultant in charge of the patient's medical care;
b. persons concerned with the provision of services likely to be relevant to the case, e.g. area social worker, voluntary agency representatives, family doctor and health visitor, psychiatrist treating child or parents, day nursery matron;
c. persons with information regarding the child and his/her family, e.g. family doctor and health visitor (if not included under b., social workers including probation officers in previous and present contact, paediatrician and members of medical and nursing staff. (DHSS, 1974*a*, page 4.)

The dominance of health and social services staff is evident. The police were then included in the category of 'others who may also be invited when appropriate'. By contrast, a senior manager in social services, interviewed in my study (Hallett, 1995), summarised the current position as follows:

> 'I think, in many ways, our closest colleagues are the coppers. They are in it up to their necks as we are.' (Hallett, 1995.)

Despite extensive police involvement in investigations, studies suggest that successful prosecutions are relatively rare. For example, Moran-Ellis *et al.* (1991), in a study of outcomes of investigations of sexual abuse cases only in 1989 and 1990, found prosecution rates of 12% at one research site and 7% in another. Creighton's (1992) study reported that criminal proceedings occurred in 17% of registered sexual abuse cases in the sample of 1732, and in 9% of the sample of 2786 physical abuse cases in 1988–90.

Several commentators here and elsewhere in Europe have questioned the central role of the police in British child protection services and the consequences of emphasising child abuse as a crime, rather than as a symptom of individual or family malfunctioning. Lampo and Marneffe (1993) summarise the key differences between a judicial and a medico-social approach as follows:

Table 28.1 *Models of child protection services (from Lampo and Marneffe, 1993).*

Judicial model	Medico-social model
Child abuse and neglect are criminal offences	Child abuse and neglect are the result of family dysfunction
The initial response is investigation	The initial response is diagnosis
Protection of the child is sought through penalising or punishing parents	Protection of the child is sought through therapy and family support
Therapy or guidance is mandatory	Parental consent is given to follow therapy or accept guidance

By contrast, many would point to the dangers of *de facto* decriminalisation, not least because failure to enforce the law suggests that child abuse is not regarded seriously by society, thus colluding with abusers and failing to deter future offenders. Prosecution can be important to survivors in demonstrating that their abuse has been taken seriously, and that the blame and responsibility has properly been placed on the abuser. It is also important for the future protection of children to have abusers clearly identified, following conviction, as Schedule 1 offenders. These are complex and contentious matters, but it is likely that the respective roles of police and social workers and prosecution policies and practices will be reappraised in the future.

Developing Intervention and Evaluating its Effectiveness

A second future direction concerns intervention following referral, investigation and registration. Central government guidance identifies six phases of work in individual cases of child abuse, namely:

- referral and recognition;
- immediate protection and planning the investigation;
- investigation and initial reassessment;
- child protection conference and decision-making about the need for registration;
- comprehensive assessment and planning;
- implementation, review and, where appropriate, deregistration. (Home Office et al., 1991, page 27.)

Several chapters in this volume focus on the early stages, and it is clear from several research studies (e.g. Farmer and Owen, 1993; Gibbons et al., 1993; Hallett, 1993) that significant resources and most major multi-disciplinary efforts are focused on the early stages. Farmer and Owen's study testifies to the relatively small proportion of time (on average only 9 minutes) devoted to the child protection plan in initial child protection conferences. Hallett (1993) points to the dominance of only one agency, the social services department, in ongoing intervention and Stevenson, in Chapter 12, alludes to the relative neglect of review conferences in studies of the functioning of child protection conferences. Lynch (1992) has trenchantly questioned the wisdom and morality of a system which devotes significant resources to case identification and the determination of case status without offering significant and effective help.

There are two urgent priorities here. The first is the development of a range of interventions to help abused children, their families and abusers, following identification. This requires creativity, imagination and resources. The second is the evaluation of the effectiveness of such interventions.

The Relationship Between Child Protection and Child Welfare

The final future direction selected for brief consideration here is the need to re-examine the relationship between child protection and broader child care policy and practice. As is suggested above, the emphasis on identification and the correct determination of case status characterises much British child protection practice. This is unsurprising in view of the need for the avoidance of tragedy in the context of a succession of highly publicised inquiries into the handling of cases of child abuse. However, as several authors in this volume suggest, it is important to focus not only on the protection of children but also on meeting their needs. The Children Act 1989 legitimises this activity with its emphasis on support services for children in need. It is not clear, however, that the policies, practices or resources are in place (DOH, 1993) to move from a focus on the identification and management of child protection cases to the provision of accessible, supportive, available services to meet the wider needs of children and their families.

References

Birchall, G. (1995). *Working Together in Child Protection: Report of Phase Two, a survey of the experience & perceptions of six key professions* London: HMSO.

Clyde, J. (1992). *The Report of the Inquiry into the Removal of Children from Orkney in February 1991*. Edinburgh: HMSO.

Cm 412 (1988). *Report of the Inquiry into Child Abuse in Cleveland, 1987*. London: HMSO.

Creighton, S. (1992). *Child Abuse Trends in England and Wales 1988–90*. London: NSPCC.

Department of Health (1993). *Children Act Report 1992*. London: HMSO

Department of Health and Social Security (1972). Battered Babies. Letter LASSL (26)12.

Department of Health and Social Security (1974a). *Non-Accidental Injury to Children.* LASSL (74)13.

Department of Health and Social Security (1974b). *Report of the Committee of Inquiry into the Care and Supervision Provided in Relation to Maria Colwell.* London: HMSO.

Farmer, E. & Owen, M. (1995). *Child Protection Practise: Private risks and public remedies.* London: HMSO

Fox Harding, L. (1991). *Perspectives in Child Care Policy*. London: HMSO.

Gibbons, J., Conroy, S. & Bell, C. (1995). *Operating the Child Protection System*. London: HMSO.

Gil, D. (1981). The United States versus child abuse. In L. Pelton (ed.): *The Social Context of Child Abuse and Neglect*. New York: Free Press.

Hallett, C. (1995). *Inter-agency Coordination in Child Protection*. London: HMSO.

Hallett, C. & Birchall, E. (1992). *Co-ordination and Child Protection: A Review of the Literature*. London: HMSO.

Holt, J. (1975). *Escape from Childhood. The Needs and Rights of Children*. Harmondsworth: Penguin.

Home Office, Department of Health, Department of Education and Science, Welsh Office (1991). *Working Together*. London: HMSO.

Kempe, C.H., Silverman, F.N., Steele, B.F., Droegemueller, W. & Silver, H.K. (1962). The battered child syndrome. *Journal of the American Medical Association 181(1)*: 17–24.

Lampo, A. & Marneffe, C. (1993). *Prevention of Child Abuse and Neglect: Child Protection or Mere Registration*. 4th European Conference on Child Abuse and Neglect, Padua, Italy.

London Borough of Greenwich (1987). *A Child in Mind: The Protection of Children in a Responsible Society*. London: Borough of Greenwich.

Lynch, M. (1992) Child protection: Have we lost our way? *Adoption and Fostering 16,4*, 15–22.

Moran-Ellis, J., Conroy, S., Fielding, N. & Tunstill, J. (1991). *Investigation of Child Sexual Abuse: an Executive Summary*. Surrey: University of Surrey.

Parton, N. (1991). *Governing the Family: Child Care, Child Protection and the State*. Basingstoke: Macmillan.

Richards, M. (1975). Non-accidental injury to children in an ecological perspective. In DHSS: *Non-Accidental Injury to Children: Proceedings of a Conference*. London: HMSO.

Thoburn, J., Lewis, A. & Shemmings, D. (1995). *Paternalism or Partnership? Family involvement in the child protection process*. London: HMSO.

Index